U0940384

世界贸易组织

政府采购协定

Agreement on Government Procurement

（中英文对照）

商务部世界贸易组织司　编译

中国财政经济出版社

图书在版编目（CIP）数据

政府采购协定：汉英对照/商务部世界贸易组织司编；索必成，王琛，张笑寒译. —北京：中国财政经济出版社，2009. 9

书名原文：Agreement on Government Procurement

ISBN 978 - 7 - 5095 - 1793 - 2

Ⅰ. 政… Ⅱ. ①商…②索…③王…④张… Ⅲ. 政府采购 - 国际贸易 - 贸易协定 - 汉、英 Ⅳ. D996. 2

中国版本图书馆 CIP 数据核字(2009)第 163045 号

责任编辑：吴　敏　　　　责任校对：范　爽

封面设计：北平面　　　　版式设计：李香杰

译者：索必成、王琛、张笑寒

中国财政经济出版社出版

URL：http：//www. cfeph. cn

E - mail：cfeph @ cfeph. cn

社址：北京市海淀区阜成路甲 28 号　邮政编码：100142

发行处电话：88190406　财经书店电话：64033436

涿州市新华印刷有限公司印刷　各地新华书店经销

787 × 1092 毫米　16 开　58. 5 印张　1 200 000 字

2009 年 9 月第 1 版　2009 年 9 月涿州第 1 次印刷

印数：1—2 060　定价：160. 00 元

ISBN 978 - 7 - 5095 - 1793 - 2/F · 1515

（图书出现印装问题，本社负责调换）

本社质量投诉电话：010 - 88190744

译者序

本书收录了世界贸易组织(WTO)《1994 年政府采购协定》文本及各附录的原文和中文译文，还收录了《1994 年政府采购协定》修改本的英文原文和中译文，附在本书最后。

《政府采购协定》的作准语文为英文本、法文本或西班牙文本，中文译文仅供参考，不具法律效力，特别是对于各参加方具体承诺中包含的各实体名称和刊物名称等，中译文并非固定译法，仅为例示性质，应以作准语文为准。

协定文本、各附录和各附件原文的页码均独立编排，本书在编辑时在保留原页码的同时，另对全书页码统一编排，并据此编制了目录，以方便读者阅读。

本书在翻译过程中，得到了商务部有关司局和驻外机构的协助，在此表示感谢。

《政府采购协定》历史沿革

1947年	政府采购排除在GATT管辖范围之外 (GATT 第3条第8款和第17条第2款)
1979年4月	《1979年政府采购协定》签署
1981年1月	《1979年政府采购协定》生效
1983年11月	根据《1979年政府采购协定》第9条第6款(b)项 开始谈判
1986年11月	达成对《1979年政府采购协定》第1、2、4、5及6 条进行修正的议定书
1988年1月	《1979年政府采购协定》修正本生效
1994年4月	《1994年政府采购协定》签署
1996年1月	《1994年政府采购协定》生效
1997年2月至今	根据《1994年政府采购协定》第24条第7款 开始谈判
2006年12月	《1994年政府采购协定》修改本临时议定文本

《1994年政府采购协定》参加方

参加方	生效日期/加入日期
加拿大	1996年1月1日
欧洲共同体[1] **及其27个成员国：**	
奥地利、比利时、丹麦、芬兰、法国、德国、希腊、爱尔兰、意大利、卢森堡、荷兰、葡萄牙、西班牙、瑞典、英国	1996年1月1日
塞浦路斯、捷克、爱沙尼亚、匈牙利、拉脱维亚、立陶宛、马耳他、波兰、斯洛伐克、斯洛文尼亚	2004年5月1日
保加利亚、罗马尼亚	2007年1月1日
中国香港	1997年6月19日
冰岛	2001年4月28日
以色列	1996年1月1日
日本	1996年1月1日
韩国	1997年1月1日
列支敦士登	1997年9月18日
荷属阿鲁巴	1996年10月25日
挪威	1996年1月1日
新加坡	1997年10月20日
瑞士	1996年1月1日
中国台北[2]	2009年7月15日
美国	1996年1月1日

注：

1. 由于法律原因，欧洲联盟在WTO事务中正式称为“欧洲共同体(European Communities)”。欧盟是具有自身权利的WTO成员，其27个成员国也均为具有自身权利的WTO成员，欧盟及其成员国合计为28个WTO成员。
2. 即台湾、澎湖、金门、马祖单独关税区，在WTO中简称“Chinese Taipei(中国台北)”。根据WTO政府采购委员会的决定，中国台北的《政府采购协定》涵盖范围中所使用的称谓和术语仅用于澄清其涵盖范围，并不具有主权含义。

目录

页码

TABLE OF CONTENTS

图例

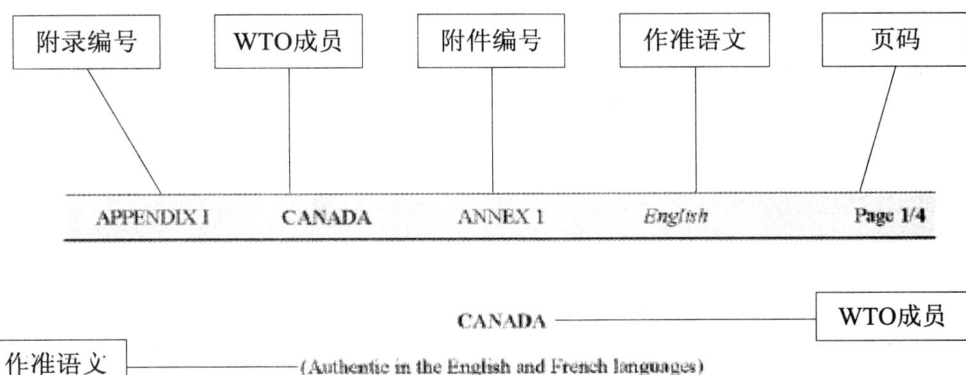

CANADA — WTO成员

作准语文 — (Authentic in the English and French languages)

ANNEX 1

Federal Government Entities

Thresholds:	130,000 SDRs	-	***Goods***
	130,000 SDRs	-	***Services*** covered in Annex 4
	5,000,000 SDRs	-	***Construction*** covered in Annex 5

List of entities:

1. Department of Agriculture and Agri-Food
2. Canadian Food Inspection Agency (Not including procurements respecting FSCs 36, 70 and 74 in respect of the administration and enforcement of the *Fish Inspection Act*.)
3. Department of Canadian Heritage (Not including procurements respecting FSCs 36, 70 and 74 in respect of those functions that were formerly the responsibility of the Department of Communications.)
4. Office of the Coordinator, Status of Women
5. Parks Canada Agency
6. Department of Citizenship and Immigration
7. Immigration and Refugee Board
8. Department of the Environment
9. Department of Foreign Affairs and International Trade
10. Canadian International Development Agency (on its own account)
11. Department of Finance
12. Canadian International Trade Tribunal
13. Municipal Development and Loan Board
14. Office of the Superintendent of Financial Institutions
15. Department of Fisheries and Oceans (Not including procurements respecting FSCs 36, 70 and 74.) (For purposes of Article XXIII, the national security considerations applicable to the Department of National Defence are equally applicable to the Canadian Coast Guard other than the functions of the Canadian Coast Guard retained by the Department of Transport pursuant to Order under the *Public Service Rearrangement and Transfer of Duties Act* published in the Canada Gazette, Part II, as SI/95-46, namely the Harbours and Ports Directorate, the regional Harbours and Ports Branches, the Marine Regulatory Directorate, the Ship Inspection Directorate and the regional Ship Inspection Branches of the Canadian Coast Guard.)
16. Department of Health
17. Medical Research Council
18. Department of Human Resources Development
19. Canada Employment Insurance Commission
20. Canada Labour Relations Board

法律文件编号

9 December 2003 (WT/Let/454)

法律文件生效日期

AGREEMENT ON GOVERNMENT PROCUREMENT

1994 年政府采购协定

AGREEMENT ON GOVERNMENT PROCUREMENT

Parties to this Agreement (hereinafter referred to as "Parties"),

Recognizing the need for an effective multilateral framework of rights and obligations with respect to laws, regulations, procedures and practices regarding government procurement with a view to achieving greater liberalization and expansion of world trade and improving the international framework for the conduct of world trade;

Recognizing that laws, regulations, procedures and practices regarding government procurement should not be prepared, adopted or applied to foreign or domestic products and services and to foreign or domestic suppliers so as to afford protection to domestic products or services or domestic suppliers and should not discriminate among foreign products or services or among foreign suppliers;

Recognizing that it is desirable to provide transparency of laws, regulations, procedures and practices regarding government procurement;

Recognizing the need to establish international procedures on notification, consultation, surveillance and dispute settlement with a view to ensuring a fair, prompt and effective enforcement of the international provisions on government procurement and to maintain the balance of rights and obligations at the highest possible level;

Recognizing the need to take into account the development, financial and trade needs of developing countries, in particular the least-developed countries;

Desiring, in accordance with paragraph 6(b) of Article IX of the Agreement on Government Procurement done on 12 April 1979, as amended on 2 February 1987, to broaden and improve the Agreement on the basis of mutual reciprocity and to expand the coverage of the Agreement to include service contracts;

Desiring to encourage acceptance of and accession to this Agreement by governments not party to it;

Having undertaken further negotiations in pursuance of these objectives;

Hereby *agree* as follows:

政府采购协定

本协定各参加方(以下简称“各参加方”)，

认识到需要就有关政府采购的法律、法规、程序和做法建立一个有效的权利和义务的多边体制，以期实现世界贸易更大程度的自由化和扩大、改善进行世界贸易的国际框架；

认识到有关政府采购的法律、法规、程序和做法的制定、采用或对国外或国内产品和服务及对国外或国内供应商的适用不应对国内产品或服务或国内供应商提供保护，也不应在国外产品或服务或国外供应商之间造成歧视；

认识到有关政府采购的法律、法规、程序和做法宜具有透明度；

认识到需要建立关于通知、磋商、监督和争端解决的国际程序，以期保证有关政府采购的国际规定得到公平、迅速和有效的实施，并维持权利与义务的最大可能的平衡；

认识到需要考虑发展中国家、特别是最不发达国家的发展、财政和贸易需要；

期望依照 1979 年 4 月 12 日订立并于 1987 年 2 月 2 日修正的《政府采购协定》第 9 条第 6 款(b)项的规定，在互惠的基础上扩展和改善该协定，并扩大该协定的适用范围以包括服务合同；

期望鼓励未参加本协定的政府接受和加入本协定；

为追求这些目标而承诺进行进一步谈判；

特此协议如下；

Article I

Scope and Coverage

1. This Agreement applies to any law, regulation, procedure or practice regarding any procurement by entities covered by this Agreement, as specified in Appendix I.[1]

2. This Agreement applies to procurement by any contractual means, including through such methods as purchase or as lease, rental or hire purchase, with or without an option to buy, including any combination of products and services.

3. Where entities, in the context of procurement covered under this Agreement, require enterprises not included in Appendix I to award contracts in accordance with particular requirements, Article III shall apply *mutatis mutandis* to such requirements.

4. This Agreement applies to any procurement contract of a value of not less than the relevant threshold specified in Appendix I.

Article II

Valuation of Contracts

1. The following provisions shall apply in determining the value of contracts[2] for purposes of implementing this Agreement.

2. Valuation shall take into account all forms of remuneration, including any premiums, fees, commissions and interest receivable.

3. The selection of the valuation method by the entity shall not be used, nor shall any procurement requirement be divided, with the intention of avoiding the application of this Agreement.

4. If an individual requirement for a procurement results in the award of more than one contract, or in contracts being awarded in separate parts, the basis for valuation shall be either:

    (a) the actual value of similar recurring contracts concluded over the previous fiscal year or 12 months adjusted, where possible, for anticipated changes in quantity and value over the subsequent 12 months; or

    (b) the estimated value of recurring contracts in the fiscal year or 12 months subsequent to the initial contract.

5. In cases of contracts for the lease, rental or hire purchase of products or services, or in the case of contracts which do not specify a total price, the basis for valuation shall be:

    (a) in the case of fixed-term contracts, where their term is 12 months or less, the total contract value for their duration, or, where their term exceeds 12 months, their total value including the estimated residual value;

    (b) in the case of contracts for an indefinite period, the monthly instalment multiplied by 48.

If there is any doubt, the second basis for valuation, namely (b), is to be used.

---

[1] For each Party, Appendix I is divided into five Annexes:

- Annex 1 contains central government entities.
- Annex 2 contains sub-central government entities.
- Annex 3 contains all other entities that procure in accordance with the provisions of this Agreement.
- Annex 4 specifies services, whether listed positively or negatively, covered by this Agreement.
- Annex 5 specifies covered construction services.

Relevant thresholds are specified in each Party's Annexes.

[2] This Agreement shall apply to any procurement contract for which the contract value is estimated to equal or exceed the threshold at the time of publication of the notice in accordance with Article IX.

第1条
范围

1. 本协定适用于有关本协定涵盖实体所从事的任何采购的任何法律、法规、程序或做法，本协定所涵盖实体在附录1[1]中列明。

2. 本协定适用于通过任何契约方式进行的采购，包括通过购买、租赁、租购等方法，无论有无购买选择权，包括产品和服务的任何组合。

3. 如实体在从事本协定涵盖的采购时，要求未列入附录1的企业依照特殊要求授予合同，则第3条在细节上作必要修改后应适用于此类要求。

4. 本协定适用于价值不低于附录1所列有关最低限额的任何采购合同。

第2条
合同估价

1. 下列规定应适用于为实施本协定的目的而进行的对合同价值[2]的确定。

2. 估价应考虑所有形式的报酬，包括任何奖金、酬金、佣金和应收利息。

3. 实体对估价方法的选择不得用于避免本协定的适用，也不得为此目的而分割任何采购要求。

4. 如一单项采购要求授予一个以上的合同，或使合同分几部分授予，则估价基础应为：

(a) 前一财政年度或12个月中订立的类似续生合同的实际价值，如可能，根据在其后12个月中数量和金额的预期变化进行调整；或

(b) 在本财政年度或最初合同订立后的12个月中订立的续生合同的估计价值。

5. 对于产品或服务的租赁、租购合同或对于未列明总价的合同，估价基础应为：

(a) 对于定期合同，如其期限等于或少于12个月，则估价基础应为合同有效期内的合同总价值，或如果其期限超过12个月，则估价基础应为包括估计的剩余价值在内的合同总价值。

(b) 对于期限不确定的合同，估价基础应为月摊付额与48的乘积。

如有任何疑问，则使用第二种估价基础，即(b)项。

---

[1] 对于每一参加方，附录1分为5个附件：
- 附件1包含中央政府实体。
- 附件2包含地方政府实体。
- 附件3包含依照本协定规定进行采购的所有其他实体。
- 附件4列明本协定涵盖的服务，无论以肯定列表形式还是以否定列表形式。
- 附件5列明所涵盖的建筑服务。

有关最低限额列在每一参加方的附件中。

[2] 本协定应适用于估计合同价值等于或超过依照第9条公布有关通知时的最低限额的任何采购合同。

6. In cases where an intended procurement specifies the need for option clauses, the basis for valuation shall be the total value of the maximum permissible procurement, inclusive of optional purchases.

Article III

National Treatment and Non-discrimination

1. With respect to all laws, regulations, procedures and practices regarding government procurement covered by this Agreement, each Party shall provide immediately and unconditionally to the products, services and suppliers of other Parties offering products or services of the Parties, treatment no less favourable than:

(a) that accorded to domestic products, services and suppliers; and

(b) that accorded to products, services and suppliers of any other Party.

2. With respect to all laws, regulations, procedures and practices regarding government procurement covered by this Agreement, each Party shall ensure:

(a) that its entities shall not treat a locally-established supplier less favourably than another locally-established supplier on the basis of degree of foreign affiliation or ownership; and

(b) that its entities shall not discriminate against locally-established suppliers on the basis of the country of production of the good or service being supplied, provided that the country of production is a Party to the Agreement in accordance with the provisions of Article IV.

3. The provisions of paragraphs 1 and 2 shall not apply to customs duties and charges of any kind imposed on or in connection with importation, the method of levying such duties and charges, other import regulations and formalities, and measures affecting trade in services other than laws, regulations, procedures and practices regarding government procurement covered by this Agreement.

Article IV

Rules of Origin

1. A Party shall not apply rules of origin to products or services imported or supplied for purposes of government procurement covered by this Agreement from other Parties, which are different from the rules of origin applied in the normal course of trade and at the time of the transaction in question to imports or supplies of the same products or services from the same Parties.

2. Following the conclusion of the work programme for the harmonization of rules of origin for goods to be undertaken under the Agreement on Rules of Origin in Annex 1A of the Agreement Establishing the World Trade Organization (hereinafter referred to as "WTO Agreement") and negotiations regarding trade in services, Parties shall take the results of that work programme and those negotiations into account in amending paragraph 1 as appropriate.

6． 如一预定采购列明需要选择性条款，则估价基础应为允许进行的最大限度采购的总价值，包括选择性购买。

第 3 条
国民待遇和非歧视

1． 对于本协定涵盖的有关政府采购的所有法律、法规、程序和做法，每一参加方应立即无条件地对其他参加方的产品、服务或提供产品或服务的其他参加方的供应商提供不低于下列水平的待遇：

(a) 给予国内产品、服务和供应商的待遇；及

(b) 给予任何其他参加方的产品、服务和供应商的待遇。

2． 对于本协定涵盖的有关政府采购的所有法律、法规、程序和做法，每一参加方应保证：

(a) 其实体不得依据外国联营或所有权的程度而给予一当地设立的供应商的待遇低于给予另一当地设立的供应商的待遇；

(b) 其实体不得依据供应产品或服务的生产国而歧视当地设立的供应商，只要该生产国依照第 4 条的规定属本协定的参加方。

3． 第 1 款和第 2 款的规定不得适用于对进口征收或与进口有关的关税和任何种类的费用，征收此类税费的方法、其他进口法规和手续以及本协定涵盖的、除有关政府采购的法律、法规、程序和做法外的影响服务贸易的措施。

第 4 条
原产地规则

1． 一参加方为本协定涵盖的政府采购目的而对自其他参加方进口的产品或服务实行的原产地规则不得区别于在正常贸易过程中和在所涉交易时对相同参加方的相同产品或服务的进口或供应所实行的原产地规则。

2． 在根据《建立世界贸易组织协定》(下称"《WTO 协定》")附件 1A 所列《原产地规则协定》进行的有关协调货物原产地规则的工作计划及关于服务贸易的谈判结束后，各参加方在修正第 1 款时应酌情考虑该工作计划和这些谈判的结果。

Article V

Special and Differential Treatment for Developing Countries

Objectives

1. Parties shall, in the implementation and administration of this Agreement, through the provisions set out in this Article, duly take into account the development, financial and trade needs of developing countries, in particular least-developed countries, in their need to:

(a) safeguard their balance-of-payments position and ensure a level of reserves adequate for the implementation of programmes of economic development;

(b) promote the establishment or development of domestic industries including the development of small-scale and cottage industries in rural or backward areas; and economic development of other sectors of the economy;

(c) support industrial units so long as they are wholly or substantially dependent on government procurement; and

(d) encourage their economic development through regional or global arrangements among developing countries presented to the Ministerial Conference of the World Trade Organization (hereinafter referred to as the "WTO") and not disapproved by it.

2. Consistently with the provisions of this Agreement, each Party shall, in the preparation and application of laws, regulations and procedures affecting government procurement, facilitate increased imports from developing countries, bearing in mind the special problems of least-developed countries and of those countries at low stages of economic development.

Coverage

3. With a view to ensuring that developing countries are able to adhere to this Agreement on terms consistent with their development, financial and trade needs, the objectives listed in paragraph 1 shall be duly taken into account in the course of negotiations with respect to the procurement of developing countries to be covered by the provisions of this Agreement. Developed countries, in the preparation of their coverage lists under the provisions of this Agreement, shall endeavour to include entities procuring products and services of export interest to developing countries.

Agreed Exclusions

4. A developing country may negotiate with other participants in negotiations under this Agreement mutually acceptable exclusions from the rules on national treatment with respect to certain entities, products or services that are included in its coverage lists, having regard to the particular circumstances of each case. In such negotiations, the considerations mentioned in subparagraphs 1(a) through 1(c) shall be duly taken into account. A developing country participating in regional or global arrangements among developing countries referred to in subparagraph 1(d) may also negotiate exclusions to its lists, having regard to the particular circumstances of each case, taking into account, *inter alia*, the provisions on government procurement provided for in the regional or global arrangements concerned and, in particular, products or services which may be subject to common industrial development programmes.

第 5 条
发展中国家的特殊和差别待遇

目标

1. 各参加方在实施和管理本协定时，应通过本条所列规定，适当考虑发展中国家、特别是最不发达国家的发展、财政和贸易需要，以满足它们的下列需要：

(a) 保障其国际收支地位，并保证足以实施经济发展计划的储备水平；

(b) 促进国内产业的建立或发展，包括农村或落后地区小型工业和家庭手工业的发展；以及其他经济部门的发展；

(c) 支持完全或实质上依赖政府采购的工业单位；以及

(d) 通过向世界贸易组织(下称"WTO")部长级会议提交且该会议对此不持异议的发展中国家间的区域或全球安排，鼓励其经济发展。

2. 在符合本协定规定的前提下，每一参加方在制定和实施影响政府采购的法律、法规和程序时，应便利来自发展中国家的进口的增长，同时记住最不发达国家和经济发展处于较低阶段国家的特殊问题。

范围

3. 为保证发展中国家在符合其发展、财政和贸易需要的条件下能够遵守本协定，在关于本协定规定将涵盖的发展中国家采购的谈判过程中，应适当考虑第 1 款所列目标。发达国家在根据本协定的规定制定范围清单时，应努力列入购买对发展中国家有出口利益的产品和服务的实体。

议定的例外

4. 一发展中国家可与根据本协定所进行谈判的其他参加方谈判双方接受的、该发展中国家范围清单所含部分实体、产品或服务对国民待遇规则的例外，同时考虑每种情况的特殊性。在此类谈判中，应适当考虑第 1 款(a)项至(c)项所指的因素。参加第 1 款(d)项所指的发展中国家间区域或全球安排的一发展中国家也可谈判对其清单的例外，同时特别每种情况的特殊性，并应特别考虑有关区域或全球安排中规定的政府采购规定，特别是可能受共同产业发展计划约束的产品或服务。

5. After entry into force of this Agreement, a developing country Party may modify its coverage lists in accordance with the provisions for modification of such lists contained in paragraph 6 of Article XXIV, having regard to its development, financial and trade needs, or may request the Committee on Government Procurement (hereinafter referred to as "the Committee") to grant exclusions from the rules on national treatment for certain entities, products or services that are included in its coverage lists, having regard to the particular circumstances of each case and taking duly into account the provisions of subparagraphs 1(a) through 1(c). After entry into force of this Agreement, a developing country Party may also request the Committee to grant exclusions for certain entities, products or services that are included in its coverage lists in the light of its participation in regional or global arrangements among developing countries, having regard to the particular circumstances of each case and taking duly into account the provisions of subparagraph 1(d). Each request to the Committee by a developing country Party relating to modification of a list shall be accompanied by documentation relevant to the request or by such information as may be necessary for consideration of the matter.

6. Paragraphs 4 and 5 shall apply *mutatis mutandis* to developing countries acceding to this Agreement after its entry into force.

7. Such agreed exclusions as mentioned in paragraphs 4, 5 and 6 shall be subject to review in accordance with the provisions of paragraph 14 below.

Technical Assistance for Developing Country Parties

8. Each developed country Party shall, upon request, provide all technical assistance which it may deem appropriate to developing country Parties in resolving their problems in the field of government procurement.

9. This assistance, which shall be provided on the basis of non-discrimination among developing country Parties, shall relate, *inter alia*, to:

- the solution of particular technical problems relating to the award of a specific contract; and
- any other problem which the Party making the request and another Party agree to deal with in the context of this assistance.

10. Technical assistance referred to in paragraphs 8 and 9 would include translation of qualification documentation and tenders made by suppliers of developing country Parties into an official language of the WTO designated by the entity, unless developed country Parties deem translation to be burdensome, and in that case explanation shall be given to developing country Parties upon their request addressed either to the developed country Parties or to their entities.

Information Centres

11. Developed country Parties shall establish, individually or jointly, information centres to respond to reasonable requests from developing country Parties for information relating to, *inter alia*, laws, regulations, procedures and practices regarding government procurement, notices about intended procurements which have been published, addresses of the entities covered by this Agreement, and the nature and volume of products or services procured or to be procured, including available information about future tenders. The Committee may also set up an information centre.

5. 本协定生效后，一发展中国家参加方可依照本协定第 24 条第 6 款包含的关于修改范围清单的规定修改其清单，同时注意其发展、财政和贸易需要，或可请求政府采购委员会(下称“委员会”)对其范围清单中包含的部分实体、产品或服务给予国民待遇规则的例外，同时注意每种情况的特殊性，并适当考虑第 1 款(a)项至(c)项的规定。在本协定生效后，一发展中国家参加方还可请求委员会按照其参与发展中国家间区域或全球安排的情况，对其范围清单中部分实体、产品或服务给予例外，同时注意每种情况的特殊性，并适当考虑第 1 款(d)项的规定。一发展中国家向委员会提出的有关修改其清单的每一请求均应附与请求有关的文件或附考虑此事项所必需的信息。

6. 第 4 款和第 5 款在细节上作必要修改后应适用于本协定生效后加入本协定的发展中国家。

7. 第 4 款、第 5 款和第 6 款所提及的此类议定的例外应依照以下第 14 款的规定进行审议。

对发展中国家参加方的技术援助

8. 应请求，每一发达国家参加方应向发展中国家参加方提供其认为解决这些国家在政府采购领域的问题适当的所有技术援助。

9. 这一在发展中国家参加方之间非歧视基础上提供的技术援助应特别涉及：

- 解决与授予一特定合同有关的特殊技术问题；及
- 提出请求的参加方与另一参加方同意在此援助中处理的任何其他问题。

10. 第 8 款和第 9 款所指的技术援助可包括将发展中国家参加方的供应商提交的资格文件和投标译为有关实体指定的 WTO 一正式语文，除非有关发达国家参加方认为翻译难以负担，在此种情况下，应请求，该发达国家参加方或其实体应向发展中国家参加方进行说明。

信息中心

11. 发达国家参加方应单独或联合建立信息中心，以答复发展中国家参加方提出的关于提供特别与如下内容有关的信息：与有关政府采购的法律、法规、程序和做法、已公布的预定采购的通知、本协定涵盖实体的地址以及已购或拟购产品或服务的性质和数量，包括可获得的关于未来投标的信息。委员会也可建立一信息中心。

Special Treatment for Least-Developed Countries

12. Having regard to paragraph 6 of the Decision of the CONTRACTING PARTIES to GATT 1947 of 28 November 1979 on Differential and More Favourable Treatment, Reciprocity and Fuller Participation of Developing Countries (BISD 26S/203-205), special treatment shall be granted to least-developed country Parties and to the suppliers in those Parties with respect to products or services originating in those Parties, in the context of any general or specific measures in favour of developing country Parties. A Party may also grant the benefits of this Agreement to suppliers in least-developed countries which are not Parties, with respect to products or services originating in those countries.

13. Each developed country Party shall, upon request, provide assistance which it may deem appropriate to potential tenderers in least-developed countries in submitting their tenders and selecting the products or services which are likely to be of interest to its entities as well as to suppliers in least-developed countries, and likewise assist them to comply with technical regulations and standards relating to products or services which are the subject of the intended procurement.

Review

14. The Committee shall review annually the operation and effectiveness of this Article and, after each three years of its operation on the basis of reports to be submitted by Parties, shall carry out a major review in order to evaluate its effects. As part of the three-yearly reviews and with a view to achieving the maximum implementation of the provisions of this Agreement, including in particular Article III, and having regard to the development, financial and trade situation of the developing countries concerned, the Committee shall examine whether exclusions provided for in accordance with the provisions of paragraphs 4 through 6 of this Article shall be modified or extended.

15. In the course of further rounds of negotiations in accordance with the provisions of paragraph 7 of Article XXIV, each developing country Party shall give consideration to the possibility of enlarging its coverage lists, having regard to its economic, financial and trade situation.

Article VI
Technical Specifications

1. Technical specifications laying down the characteristics of the products or services to be procured, such as quality, performance, safety and dimensions, symbols, terminology, packaging, marking and labelling, or the processes and methods for their production and requirements relating to conformity assessment procedures prescribed by procuring entities, shall not be prepared, adopted or applied with a view to, or with the effect of, creating unnecessary obstacles to international trade.

2. Technical specifications prescribed by procuring entities shall, where appropriate:

   (a) be in terms of performance rather than design or descriptive characteristics; and

最不发达国家的特殊待遇

12. 注意到 GATT 1947 缔约方全体于 1979 年 11 月 28 日通过的《关于发展中国家差别和更优惠待遇、互惠和更充分参与的决定》(BISD 26 册 203 至 205 页) 第 6 段规定，在优惠发展中国家的任何一般或具体措施的范围内，应对最不发达国家参加方和这些参加方中供应原产于这些参加方的产品或服务的供应商给予特殊待遇。一参加方还可对非本协定参加方的最不发达国家中的供应商在原产于这些国家的产品或服务方面给予本协定的利益。

13. 应请求，每一发达国家参加方应向最不发达国家参加方中潜在的投标人在提交投标书和选择可能对其实体有利益的产品或服务时提供其认为适当的援助，以及向最不发达国家中的供应商提供此类援助，并以同样方式帮助它们遵守与属预定采购标的产品或服务有关的技术法规和标准。

审议

14. 委员会应每年对本条的运用情况和有效性进行审议，并依据各参加方提供的报告在实施期内每三年进行一次主要审议，以评估其效果。作为三年期审议的一部分并为使本协定的规定得到最大程度的实施，特别包括第 3 条的规定，同时注意有关发展中国家的发展、财政和贸易情况，委员会应审查是否应修改或延长依照本条第 4 款至第 6 款的规定所规定的例外。

15. 在依照第 24 条第 7 款的规定进行的未来回合的谈判过程中，每一发展中国家参加方应考虑扩大其范围清单的可能性，同时注意其经济、财政和贸易情况。

第 6 条
技术规格

1. 技术规格规定拟购产品或服务的特征，如质量、性能、安全和体积、符号、术语、包装、标志和标签，或生产工艺和方法以及与采购实体规定的合格评定程序有关的要求，其制定、采用或实施不得以对国际贸易造成不必要的障碍为目的，也不得产生此种效果。

2. 采购实体规定的技术规格，在适当时：

   (a) 应依据性能而非设计或描述特征；及

(b) be based on international standards, where such exist; otherwise, on national technical regulations[3], recognized national standards[4], or building codes.

3. There shall be no requirement or reference to a particular trademark or trade name, patent, design or type, specific origin, producer or supplier, unless there is no sufficiently precise or intelligible way of describing the procurement requirements and provided that words such as "or equivalent" are included in the tender documentation.

4. Entities shall not seek or accept, in a manner which would have the effect of precluding competition, advice which may be used in the preparation of specifications for a specific procurement from a firm that may have a commercial interest in the procurement.

Article VII

Tendering Procedures

1. Each Party shall ensure that the tendering procedures of its entities are applied in a non-discriminatory manner and are consistent with the provisions contained in Articles VII through XVI.

2. Entities shall not provide to any supplier information with regard to a specific procurement in a manner which would have the effect of precluding competition.

3. For the purposes of this Agreement:

(a) Open tendering procedures are those procedures under which all interested suppliers may submit a tender.

(b) Selective tendering procedures are those procedures under which, consistent with paragraph 3 of Article X and other relevant provisions of this Agreement, those suppliers invited to do so by the entity may submit a tender.

(c) Limited tendering procedures are those procedures where the entity contacts suppliers individually, only under the conditions specified in Article XV.

Article VIII

Qualification of Suppliers

In the process of qualifying suppliers, entities shall not discriminate among suppliers of other Parties or between domestic suppliers and suppliers of other Parties. Qualification procedures shall be consistent with the following:

(a) any conditions for participation in tendering procedures shall be published in adequate time to enable interested suppliers to initiate and, to the extent that it is compatible with efficient operation of the procurement process, complete the qualification procedures;

---

[3] For the purpose of this Agreement, a technical regulation is a document which lays down characteristics of a product or a service or their related processes and production methods, including the applicable administrative provisions, with which compliance is mandatory. It may also include or deal exclusively with terminology, symbols, packaging, marking or labelling requirements as they apply to a product, service, process or production method.

[4] For the purpose of this Agreement, a standard is a document approved by a recognized body, that provides, for common and repeated use, rules, guidelines or characteristics for products or services or related processes and production methods, with which compliance is not mandatory. It may also include or deal exclusively with terminology, symbols, packaging, marking or labelling requirements as they apply to a product, service, process or production method.

(b) 如存在国际标准，则应依据国际标准；如无国际标准，则应根据国家技术法规[3]、公认的国家标准[4]或建筑规格。

3. 不得要求或提及一特定商标或商号、专利、设计或型号、具体原产地、生产商或供应商，除非无足够准确或易懂的方法描述采购要求，且需在招标文件中包括如"或相当于"等措辞。

4. 各实体不得以具有妨碍竞争效果的方式，寻求或接受在制定一具体采购规格时可采用的、与该采购有商业利益的公司提出的建议。

第7条
招标程序

1. 每一参加方应保证其实体的招标程序以非歧视的方式实施，并与第 7 条至第 16 条的规定相一致。

2. 各实体不得以具有妨碍竞争效果的方式，向任何供应商提供有关特定采购的信息。

3. 就本协定而言：

(a) 公开招标程序指所有感兴趣的供应商均可据此提交投标书的程序。

(b) 选择性招标程序指与第 10 条第 3 款和本协定其他有关规定相一致的程序，有关实体邀请的供应商可据此进行投标。

(c) 有限招标程序指仅根据第 15 条列明条件的程序，有关实体据此与供应商进行单独接触。

第8条
供应商资格

各实体在审查供应商资格时，不得在其他参加方的供应商之间或在本国供应商与其他参加方的供应商之间造成歧视。资格审查程序应与下列规定相一致：

(a) 参加招标程序的任何条件应充分提前公布，以使感兴趣的供应商开始资格审查程序，并在与采购过程的有效实施相符的限度内，完成资格审查程序；

[3] 就本协定而言，技术法规指规定强制执行的产品特性或其相关工艺和生产方法、包括适用的管理规定在内的文件。该文件还可包括或专门关于适用于产品、工艺或生产方法的专门术语、符号、包装、标志或标签要求。

[4] 就本协定而言，标准经公认机构批准的、规定非强制执行的、供通用或重复使用的产品或相关工艺或生产方法的规则、指南或特性的文件。该文件还可包括或专门关于适用于产品、工艺或生产方法的专门术语、符号、包装、标志或标签要求。

(b) any conditions for participation in tendering procedures shall be limited to those which are essential to ensure the firm's capability to fulfil the contract in question. Any conditions for participation required from suppliers, including financial guarantees, technical qualifications and information necessary for establishing the financial, commercial and technical capacity of suppliers, as well as the verification of qualifications, shall be no less favourable to suppliers of other Parties than to domestic suppliers and shall not discriminate among suppliers of other Parties. The financial, commercial and technical capacity of a supplier shall be judged on the basis both of that supplier's global business activity as well as of its activity in the territory of the procuring entity, taking due account of the legal relationship between the supply organizations;

(c) the process of, and the time required for, qualifying suppliers shall not be used in order to keep suppliers of other Parties off a suppliers' list or from being considered for a particular intended procurement. Entities shall recognize as qualified suppliers such domestic suppliers or suppliers of other Parties who meet the conditions for participation in a particular intended procurement. Suppliers requesting to participate in a particular intended procurement who may not yet be qualified shall also be considered, provided there is sufficient time to complete the qualification procedure;

(d) entities maintaining permanent lists of qualified suppliers shall ensure that suppliers may apply for qualification at any time; and that all qualified suppliers so requesting are included in the lists within a reasonably short time;

(e) if, after publication of the notice under paragraph 1 of Article IX, a supplier not yet qualified requests to participate in an intended procurement, the entity shall promptly start procedures for qualification;

(f) any supplier having requested to become a qualified supplier shall be advised by the entities concerned of the decision in this regard. Qualified suppliers included on permanent lists by entities shall also be notified of the termination of any such lists or of their removal from them;

(g) each Party shall ensure that:

(i) each entity and its constituent parts follow a single qualification procedure, except in cases of duly substantiated need for a different procedure; and

(ii) efforts be made to minimize differences in qualification procedures between entities.

(h) nothing in subparagraphs (a) through (g) shall preclude the exclusion of any supplier on grounds such as bankruptcy or false declarations, provided that such an action is consistent with the national treatment and non-discrimination provisions of this Agreement.

Article IX

Invitation to Participate Regarding Intended Procurement

1. In accordance with paragraphs 2 and 3, entities shall publish an invitation to participate for all cases of intended procurement, except as otherwise provided for in Article XV (limited tendering). The notice shall be published in the appropriate publication listed in Appendix II.

2. The invitation to participate may take the form of a notice of proposed procurement, as provided for in paragraph 6.

(b) 参加招标程序的任何条件应限于对保证公司履行所涉合同的能力所必需的条件。对供应商参加招标所要求的任何条件，包括财政担保、技术资格及确定供应商的财政、商业和技术能力所必需的信息，以及对资格的核实，与本国供应商相比，不得不利于其他参加方的供应商，也不得在其他参加方的供应商之间造成歧视。供应商的财政、商业和技术能力应根据该供应商的全球商业活动及其在采购实体所在地的商业活动进行判断，同时适当考虑供应机构之间的法律关系；

(c) 供应商资格审查的过程和所需时间不得用以阻止其他参加方的供应商列入供应商名单，或阻止其成为一特定预定采购所考虑的对象。各实体应承认符合参加一特定预定采购条件的国内供应商或其他参加方的供应商均为合格供应商。要求参加一特定预定采购、但未合格的供应商也应予以考虑，只要有足够的时间完成资格审查程序。

(d) 保存合格供应商常设名单的实体应保证供应商可随时提出资格申请；并保证提出请求的所有合格供应商均在合理的较短时间被列入该名单；

(e) 如在根据第 9 条第 1 款公布通知后，一尚未合格的供应商请求参加一预定采购，则有关实体应迅速开始资格审查程序；

(f) 对于提出成为合格供应商请求的任何供应商，有关实体应将与此有关的决定通知该供应商。对于有关实体列入常设名单的合格供应商，有关实体应将任何此类名单的废止或供应商名址自名单中去除的情况通知该供应商；

(g) 每一参加方应保证;

  (i) 每一实体及其组成部分遵循单一的资格审查程序，除非能够适当证明有必要采用不同的程序；及

  (ii) 努力缩小各实体之间资格审查程序的差异。

(h) (a)项至(g)项的任何规定不得妨碍因破产或虚报等原因而排除任何供应商，只要此类行动与本协定的国民待遇和非歧视规定相一致。

第 9 条
关于预定采购的邀请

1． 依照第 2 款和第 3 款，各实体应公布邀请参加各种预定采购的通知，除第 15 条(有限招标程序)另有规定外。该通知应在附录 2 所列有关出版物中公布。

2． 参加采购的邀请可按第 6 款的规定采取拟议采购通知的形式。

3. Entities in Annexes 2 and 3 may use a notice of planned procurement, as provided for in paragraph 7, or a notice regarding a qualification system, as provided for in paragraph 9, as an invitation to participate.

4. Entities which use a notice of planned procurement as an invitation to participate shall subsequently invite all suppliers who have expressed an interest to confirm their interest on the basis of information which shall include at least the information referred to in paragraph 6.

5. Entities which use a notice regarding a qualification system as an invitation to participate shall provide, subject to the considerations referred to in paragraph 4 of Article XVIII and in a timely manner, information which allows all those who have expressed an interest to have a meaningful opportunity to assess their interest in participating in the procurement. This information shall include the information contained in the notices referred to in paragraphs 6 and 8, to the extent such information is available. Information provided to one interested supplier shall be provided in a non-discriminatory manner to the other interested suppliers.

6. Each notice of proposed procurement, referred to in paragraph 2, shall contain the following information:

(a) the nature and quantity, including any options for further procurement and, if possible, an estimate of the timing when such options may be exercised; in the case of recurring contracts the nature and quantity and, if possible, an estimate of the timing of the subsequent tender notices for the products or services to be procured;

(b) whether the procedure is open or selective or will involve negotiation;

(c) any date for starting delivery or completion of delivery of goods or services;

(d) the address and final date for submitting an application to be invited to tender or for qualifying for the suppliers' lists, or for receiving tenders, as well as the language or languages in which they must be submitted;

(e) the address of the entity awarding the contract and providing any information necessary for obtaining specifications and other documents;

(f) any economic and technical requirements, financial guarantees and information required from suppliers;

(g) the amount and terms of payment of any sum payable for the tender documentation; and

(h) whether the entity is inviting offers for purchase, lease, rental or hire purchase, or more than one of these methods.

7. Each notice of planned procurement referred to in paragraph 3 shall contain as much of the information referred to in paragraph 6 as is available. It shall in any case include the information referred to in paragraph 8 and:

(a) a statement that interested suppliers should express their interest in the procurement to the entity;

(b) a contact point with the entity from which further information may be obtained.

8. For each case of intended procurement, the entity shall publish a summary notice in one of the official languages of the WTO. The notice shall contain at least the following information:

(a) the subject matter of the contract;

(b) the time-limits set for the submission of tenders or an application to be invited to tender; and

(c) the addresses from which documents relating to the contracts may be requested.

3. 附件 2 和附件 3 中的实体可按第 7 款的规定使用计划采购通知，或按第 9 款的规定，使用关于资格审查制度的通知，作为参加采购的邀请。

4. 使用计划采购通知作为参加采购邀请的实体，应随后邀请所有表示兴趣的供应商，根据至少包括第 6 款所指信息的信息确认其利益。

5. 使用关于资格审查制度通知作为参加采购邀请的实体，在遵守第 18 条第 4 款规定的前提下，应及时提供信息，使所有表示兴趣的供应商有机会评估其参加该项采购的利益。此信息应包括第 6 款和第 8 款所指的通知中包含的信息，只要此类信息可获得。对一感兴趣的供应商提供的信息应以非歧视的方式向其他感兴趣的供应商提供。

6. 第 2 款所指的每一份拟议采购的通知应包括下列信息：

(a) 性质和数量，包括进一步采购的任何选择权，如可能，包括对行使此类选择权时间的估计；对于续生合同，包括性质和数量，如可能，包括对拟购产品或服务的招标随后作出通知时间的估计；

(b) 程序是否是公开的还是选择性的，或是否涉及谈判；

(c) 开始或完成产品或服务交货的任何日期；

(d) 提交要求被邀请参加招标的申请、供应商名单资格审查或接收投标书的地址和最后期限，以及必须使用的一种或多种语文；

(e) 授予合同和提供获得规格和其他文件所必需的任何信息的实体的地址；

(f) 要求供应商提供的任何经济和技术要求、财政担保和信息；

(g) 对招标文件应付的任何数量款项的金额和支付条件；以及

(h) 该实体是否正在邀请对购买、租赁、租购或一种以上的此类方法进行报盘。

7. 第 3 款所指计划采购的每一份通知应尽可能多地包括第 6 款所指的、可获得的信息。此类通知无论如何应包括第 8 款所指的信息及：

(a) 感兴趣的供应商向有关实体表明其对此项采购感兴趣的说明；

(b) 可获得进一步信息的有关实体的联络点。

8. 对于每一项预定采购，有关实体应使用 WTO 一种官方语文公布简要通知。该通知应至少包括下列信息：

(a) 合同标的物；

(b) 所订立的提交投标书和投标申请的时限；

(c) 可请求得到与合同有关文件的地址。

9. In the case of selective tendering procedures, entities maintaining permanent lists of qualified suppliers shall publish annually in one of the publications listed in Appendix III a notice of the following:

(a) the enumeration of the lists maintained, including their headings, in relation to the products or services or categories of products or services to be procured through the lists;

(b) the conditions to be fulfilled by suppliers with a view to their inscription on those lists and the methods according to which each of those conditions will be verified by the entity concerned; and

(c) the period of validity of the lists, and the formalities for their renewal.

When such a notice is used as an invitation to participate in accordance with paragraph 3, the notice shall, in addition, include the following information:

(d) the nature of the products or services concerned;

(e) a statement that the notice constitutes an invitation to participate.

However, when the duration of the qualification system is three years or less, and if the duration of the system is made clear in the notice and it is also made clear that further notices will not be published, it shall be sufficient to publish the notice once only, at the beginning of the system. Such a system shall not be used in a manner which circumvents the provisions of this Agreement.

10. If, after publication of an invitation to participate in any case of intended procurement, but before the time set for opening or receipt of tenders as specified in the notices or the tender documentation, it becomes necessary to amend or re-issue the notice, the amendment or the re-issued notice shall be given the same circulation as the original documents upon which the amendment is based. Any significant information given to one supplier with respect to a particular intended procurement shall be given simultaneously to all other suppliers concerned in adequate time to permit the suppliers to consider such information and to respond to it.

11. Entities shall make clear, in the notices referred to in this Article or in the publication in which the notices appear, that the procurement is covered by the Agreement.

Article X

Selection Procedures

1. To ensure optimum effective international competition under selective tendering procedures, entities shall, for each intended procurement, invite tenders from the maximum number of domestic suppliers and suppliers of other Parties, consistent with the efficient operation of the procurement system. They shall select the suppliers to participate in the procedure in a fair and non-discriminatory manner.

2. Entities maintaining permanent lists of qualified suppliers may select suppliers to be invited to tender from among those listed. Any selection shall allow for equitable opportunities for suppliers on the lists.

3. Suppliers requesting to participate in a particular intended procurement shall be permitted to submit a tender and be considered, provided, in the case of those not yet qualified, there is sufficient time to complete the qualification procedure under Articles VIII and IX. The number of additional suppliers permitted to participate shall be limited only by the efficient operation of the procurement system.

4. Requests to participate in selective tendering procedures may be submitted by telex, telegram or facsimile.

9. 对于选择性招标程序，保存合格供应商常设名单的实体应每年在附录 3 所列出版物上公布关于下列内容的通知：

(a) 所保存名单的细目，包括与通过名单购买的产品或服务，或产品或服务类别有关的标题；

(b) 供应商为被列入这些名单而应满足的条件及有关实体核实每一项条件的方法；

(c) 名单的有效期和展期手续。

如此种通知依照第 3 款用作参加采购的邀请，则该通知还应包括下列信息：

(d) 有关产品或服务的性质；

(e) 关于该通知可构成参加采购邀请的说明。

但是，如资格审查制度的有效期为 3 年或不足 3 年，且如果该制度的有效期在通知中明确说明，而通知明确说明不再公布其他通知，则只需在该制度开始实施时只公布一次通知。此种制度不得以规避本协定规定的方式使用。

10. 在公布关于任何形式预定采购的邀请后至有关通知或招标文件列明的开启或接收投标书的日期之前，如有必要修正或重新发布通知，则经修正或重新发布的通知的发行量应与据以作出修正的原文件的发行量相同。给予一供应商的关于一特定预定采购的任何重要信息应同时给予所有其他供应商，以使供应商有充分的时间考虑此类信息，并就此作出反应。

11. 各实体应在本条所指的通知中或刊载通知的出版物上明确说明该项采购为本协定所涵盖。

第 10 条
选择程序

1. 为保证选择性招标程序下的国际竞争最佳有效，对于每一项预定采购，各实体应在与采购制度有效运转相一致的情况下，邀请最大数量的国内供应商和其他参加方的供应商进行招标。它们应以公平和非歧视的方式选择供应商参加有关程序。

2. 保存合格供应商常设名单的实体可自被列入名单者中选择将被邀请参加招标的供应商。任何选择应允许名单中的供应商获得公平的机会。

3. 应允许请求参加特定预定采购的供应商提交投标书并予以考虑，对于未经资格审查的供应商，只要有足够的时间完成第 8 条和第 9 条下的资格审查程序。准予参加招标的额外供应商的数量应仅以采购制度的有效运转为限。

4. 参加选择性招标程序的请求可通过电传、电报或传真提交。

Article XI

Time-limits for Tendering and Delivery

General

1. (a) Any prescribed time-limit shall be adequate to allow suppliers of other Parties as well as domestic suppliers to prepare and submit tenders before the closing of the tendering procedures. In determining any such time-limit, entities shall, consistent with their own reasonable needs, take into account such factors as the complexity of the intended procurement, the extent of subcontracting anticipated and the normal time for transmitting tenders by mail from foreign as well as domestic points.

(b) Each Party shall ensure that its entities shall take due account of publication delays when setting the final date for receipt of tenders or of applications to be invited to tender.

Deadlines

2. Except in so far as provided in paragraph 3,

(a) in open procedures, the period for the receipt of tenders shall not be less than 40 days from the date of publication referred to in paragraph 1 of Article IX;

(b) in selective procedures not involving the use of a permanent list of qualified suppliers, the period for submitting an application to be invited to tender shall not be less than 25 days from the date of publication referred to in paragraph 1 of Article IX; the period for receipt of tenders shall in no case be less than 40 days from the date of issuance of the invitation to tender;

(c) in selective procedures involving the use of a permanent list of qualified suppliers, the period for receipt of tenders shall not be less than 40 days from the date of the initial issuance of invitations to tender, whether or not the date of initial issuance of invitations to tender coincides with the date of the publication referred to in paragraph 1 of Article IX.

3. The periods referred to in paragraph 2 may be reduced in the circumstances set out below:

(a) if a separate notice has been published 40 days and not more than 12 months in advance and the notice contains at least:

(i) as much of the information referred to in paragraph 6 of Article IX as is available;

(ii) the information referred to in paragraph 8 of Article IX;

(iii) a statement that interested suppliers should express their interest in the procurement to the entity; and

(iv) a contact point with the entity from which further information may be obtained,

the 40-day limit for receipt of tenders may be replaced by a period sufficiently long to enable responsive tendering, which, as a general rule, shall not be less than 24 days, but in any case not less than 10 days;

(b) in the case of the second or subsequent publications dealing with contracts of a recurring nature within the meaning of paragraph 6 of Article IX, the 40-day limit for receipt of tenders may be reduced to not less than 24 days;

(c) where a state of urgency duly substantiated by the entity renders impracticable the periods in question, the periods specified in paragraph 2 may be reduced but shall in no case be less than 10 days from the date of the publication referred to in paragraph 1 of Article IX; or

第 11 条
投标和交货期限

总则

1. (a) 任何规定的时限应充分，以允许其他参加方的供应商以及国内供应商在招标程序截止之前准备和提交投标书。在确定任何此类时限时，各实体应在与其各自合理需要一致的情况下，考虑如特定采购的复杂性、预期分包的程度以及自国外和国内各地邮寄投标书所需的正常时间。

   (b) 每一参加方应保证其实体在确定有关接收投标书或申请的最后日期时适当考虑公布迟误的因素。

截止期限

2. 除第 3 款规定外，

   (a) 在公开程序中，接收投标的期限自第 9 条第 1 款所指的公布日期起计算不得少于 40 天；

   (b) 在不涉及使用合格供应商常设名单的选择性招标程序中，提交要求被邀请参加投标的申请的期限自第 9 条第 1 款所指的公布日期起计算不得少于 25 天；接收投标书的期限自发布招标邀请之日起无论如何不得少于 40 天；

   (c) 在涉及使用合格供应商常设名单的选择性招标程序中，接收投标书的期限自首次发布招标邀请之日起不得少于 40 天，无论首次发布招标邀请的日期是否与第 9 条第 1 款所指的公布日期相同。

3. 本条第 2 款所指的期限可在下列情况下予以缩短：

   (a) 如一单独通知已预先公布 40 天但不超过 12 个月，且该通知至少包括：

      (i) 可获得的尽可能多的第 9 条第 6 款所指的信息；

      (ii) 第 9 条第 8 款所指的信息；

      (iii) 关于感兴趣的供应商应向有关实体表明对此项采购感兴趣的说明；以及

      (iv) 可获得进一步信息的有关实体的联络点。

   则接收投标的 40 天时限可由一能够提出符合要求的投标的足够长的期限所代替，该期限通常不得少于 24 天，但无论如何不得少于 10 天；

   (b) 在处理属第 9 条第 6 款范围内的续生合同的第二次或随后公布的情况下，接收投标书的 40 天时限可缩短为不少于 24 天；

   (c) 如有关实体充分证明出现紧急情况使所涉期限不可行，则本条第 2 款列明的期限可缩短，但自第 9 条第 1 款所指的公布日期起计算无论如何不得少于 10 天；或

(d) the period referred to in paragraph 2(c) may, for procurements by entities listed in Annexes 2 and 3, be fixed by mutual agreement between the entity and the selected suppliers. In the absence of agreement, the entity may fix periods which shall be sufficiently long to enable responsive tendering and shall in any case not be less than 10 days.

4. Consistent with the entity's own reasonable needs, any delivery date shall take into account such factors as the complexity of the intended procurement, the extent of subcontracting anticipated and the realistic time required for production, de-stocking and transport of goods from the points of supply or for supply of services.

Article XII

Tender Documentation

1. If, in tendering procedures, an entity allows tenders to be submitted in several languages, one of those languages shall be one of the official languages of the WTO.

2. Tender documentation provided to suppliers shall contain all information necessary to permit them to submit responsive tenders, including information required to be published in the notice of intended procurement, except for paragraph 6(g) of Article IX, and the following:

(a) the address of the entity to which tenders should be sent;

(b) the address where requests for supplementary information should be sent;

(c) the language or languages in which tenders and tendering documents must be submitted;

(d) the closing date and time for receipt of tenders and the length of time during which any tender should be open for acceptance;

(e) the persons authorized to be present at the opening of tenders and the date, time and place of this opening;

(f) any economic and technical requirement, financial guarantees and information or documents required from suppliers;

(g) a complete description of the products or services required or of any requirements including technical specifications, conformity certification to be fulfilled, necessary plans, drawings and instructional materials;

(h) the criteria for awarding the contract, including any factors other than price that are to be considered in the evaluation of tenders and the cost elements to be included in evaluating tender prices, such as transport, insurance and inspection costs, and in the case of products or services of other Parties, customs duties and other import charges, taxes and currency of payment;

(i) the terms of payment;

(j) any other terms or conditions;

(k) in accordance with Article XVII the terms and conditions, if any, under which tenders from countries not Parties to this Agreement, but which apply the procedures of that Article, will be entertained.

Forwarding of Tender Documentation by the Entities

3. (a) In open procedures, entities shall forward the tender documentation at the request of any supplier participating in the procedure, and shall reply promptly to any reasonable request for explanations relating thereto.

(d) 对于附件2和附件3所列实体进行的采购，第2款(c)项所指的期限可通过在有关实体与被选供应商之间达成的协议确定。如未达成协议，有关实体可确定足够长的期限，以便使投标符合要求，且无论如何不得少于10天。

4. 在与有关实体合理需要相一致的情况下，任何交货日期应考虑到预定采购的复杂性、预期分包的程度以及生产、缩减储量和自供货点运输货物或提供服务所需的实际时间。

第12条
招标文件

1. 如在招标程序中，一实体允许以几种语文提交投标书，则其中一种语文应为WTO的一种正式语文。

2. 向供应商提供的招标文件应包含允许其提交符合要求的投标书的所有信息，包括在特定采购通知中要求公布的信息，但第9条第6款(g)项的规定除外，以及下列信息：

(a) 递送投标书的有关实体的地址；

(b) 递送关于获得补充信息的请求的地址；

(c) 投标书和招标文件必须使用的一种或几种语文；

(d) 接收投标书的截止日期和时间以及投标书开放供接受的任何持续时间；

(e) 开标时获准在场的人员及开标的日期、时间和地点；

(f) 要求供应商提供的任何经济和技术要求、财政担保以及信息或文件；

(g) 对所需产品或服务的完整描述及对任何要求的完整描述，包括技术规格、需满足的合格认证、必需的设计图、图纸和说明材料；

(h) 授予合同的标准，包括评审投标书时需考虑的除价格以外的任何因素以及在评审投标价格时需包括的费用因素，如运输、保险和检查费用，对于其他参加方的产品或服务，还包括关税和其他进口费用、国内税和支付货币；

(i) 支付条件；

(j) 任何其他条款或条件；

(k) 依照第17条的条款和条件(若有的话)，据此来自非本协定参加方国家的投标书可予以接受，但适用该条的程序。

有关实体转交招标文件

3. (a) 在公开程序中，在参加该程序的任何供应商请求下，各实体应转交招标文件，并迅速答复有关对招标文件进行说明的合理请求。

(b) In selective procedures, entities shall forward the tender documentation at the request of any supplier requesting to participate, and shall reply promptly to any reasonable request for explanations relating thereto.

(c) Entities shall reply promptly to any reasonable request for relevant information submitted by a supplier participating in the tendering procedure, on condition that such information does not give that supplier an advantage over its competitors in the procedure for the award of the contract.

Article XIII

Submission, Receipt and Opening of Tenders and Awarding of Contracts

1. The submission, receipt and opening of tenders and awarding of contracts shall be consistent with the following:

(a) tenders shall normally be submitted in writing directly or by mail. If tenders by telex, telegram or facsimile are permitted, the tender made thereby must include all the information necessary for the evaluation of the tender, in particular the definitive price proposed by the tenderer and a statement that the tenderer agrees to all the terms, conditions and provisions of the invitation to tender. The tender must be confirmed promptly by letter or by the despatch of a signed copy of the telex, telegram or facsimile. Tenders presented by telephone shall not be permitted. The content of the telex, telegram or facsimile shall prevail where there is a difference or conflict between that content and any documentation received after the time-limit; and

(b) the opportunities that may be given to tenderers to correct unintentional errors of form between the opening of tenders and the awarding of the contract shall not be permitted to give rise to any discriminatory practice.

Receipt of Tenders

2. A supplier shall not be penalized if a tender is received in the office designated in the tender documentation after the time specified because of delay due solely to mishandling on the part of the entity. Tenders may also be considered in other exceptional circumstances if the procedures of the entity concerned so provide.

Opening of Tenders

3. All tenders solicited under open or selective procedures by entities shall be received and opened under procedures and conditions guaranteeing the regularity of the openings. The receipt and opening of tenders shall also be consistent with the national treatment and non-discrimination provisions of this Agreement. Information on the opening of tenders shall remain with the entity concerned at the disposal of the government authorities responsible for the entity in order that it may be used if required under the procedures of Articles XVIII, XIX, XX and XXII.

(b) 在选择性程序中，在请求参加的任何供应商请求下，各实体应转交招标文件，并迅速答复有关对招标文件进行说明的合理请求。

(c) 各实体应迅速答复参加招标程序的供应商关于提供有关信息的任何合理请求，条件是此类信息不使该供应商在授予合同的过程中获得优于其竞争者的有利条件。

第13条

投标书的提交、接收和开启及合同的授予

1. 投标书的提交、接收和开启及合同的授予应与下列规定相一致：

(a) 投标书通常应以书面形式直接或通过邮寄提交。如允许使用电传、电报或传真提交投标书，则投标书必须包括评审投标书所必需的所有信息，特别是投标人所提的最终价格及投标人关于同意投标邀请中的所有条款、条件和规定的说明。投标书必须迅速通过信函或发出电传、电报或传真的签字副本予以确认。不得允许通过电话提交投标书。如电传、电报或传真的内容与逾期收到的任何文件存在差别或相抵触，则应以电传、电报或传真的内容为准；以及

(b) 可给予投标人的在开标和授予合同之间更正表格中非故意错误的机会不得造成任何歧视性做法；

投标书的接收

2. 如仅由于实体处理不当而造成迟延，而致使投标文件中指定的办事机构逾期收到投标书，则该供应商不得因此而受到处罚。如有关实体的程序如此作出规定，则在其他例外情况下，投标书也可予以考虑。

投标书的开启

3. 由实体根据公开或选择性招标程序征得的所有投标书，应根据保证开标的规律性而制定的程序和条件予以接收和开启。投标书的接收和开启还应与本协定的国民待遇和非歧视规定相一致。有关开标的信息应由有关实体保存，供负责该实体的政府主管机关处理，以便在第18条、第19条、第20条和第22条中的程序要求时使用。

Award of Contracts

4. (a) To be considered for award, a tender must, at the time of opening, conform to the essential requirements of the notices or tender documentation and be from a supplier which complies with the conditions for participation. If an entity has received a tender abnormally lower than other tenders submitted, it may enquire with the tenderer to ensure that it can comply with the conditions of participation and be capable of fulfilling the terms of the contract.

(b) Unless in the public interest an entity decides not to issue the contract, the entity shall make the award to the tenderer who has been determined to be fully capable of undertaking the contract and whose tender, whether for domestic products or services, or products or services of other Parties, is either the lowest tender or the tender which in terms of the specific evaluation criteria set forth in the notices or tender documentation is determined to be the most advantageous.

(c) Awards shall be made in accordance with the criteria and essential requirements specified in the tender documentation.

Option Clauses

5. Option clauses shall not be used in a manner which circumvents the provisions of the Agreement.

Article XIV
Negotiation

1. A Party may provide for entities to conduct negotiations:

(a) in the context of procurements in which they have indicated such intent, namely in the notice referred to in paragraph 2 of Article IX (the invitation to suppliers to participate in the procedure for the proposed procurement); or

(b) when it appears from evaluation that no one tender is obviously the most advantageous in terms of the specific evaluation criteria set forth in the notices or tender documentation.

2. Negotiations shall primarily be used to identify the strengths and weaknesses in tenders.

3. Entities shall treat tenders in confidence. In particular, they shall not provide information intended to assist particular participants to bring their tenders up to the level of other participants.

4. Entities shall not, in the course of negotiations, discriminate between different suppliers. In particular, they shall ensure that:

(a) any elimination of participants is carried out in accordance with the criteria set forth in the notices and tender documentation;

(b) all modifications to the criteria and to the technical requirements are transmitted in writing to all remaining participants in the negotiations;

(c) all remaining participants are afforded an opportunity to submit new or amended submissions on the basis of the revised requirements; and

(d) when negotiations are concluded, all participants remaining in the negotiations shall be permitted to submit final tenders in accordance with a common deadline.

合同的授予

4. (a) 投标书只有在开启时符合通知或招标文件中的基本要求，并由符合参加条件的供应商提出，方可被考虑授予合同。如一实体收到一项比所提交的其他投标书条件异常低的投标书，则该实体可询问该投标人，以保证该投标人能够遵守参加的条件并能够履行合同条款。

(b) 除非一实体为了公众利益而决定不签发合同，否则该实体应将合同授予已被确定完全有能力执行合同的投标人，且其投标书无论对于国内产品或服务，还是对于其他参加方的产品或服务，均为价格最低的投标书，或为根据通知或招标文件中所列具体评审标准被确定为最具优势的投标书。

(c) 应依照招标文件列明的标准和基本要求授予合同。

选择权条款

5. 选择权条款不得以规避本协定规定的方式使用。

第 14 条
谈判

1. 一参加方在下列情况下可规定各实体进行谈判：

(a) 在各实体已表明此种意向的采购中，即在第 9 条第 2 款所指的通知中(邀请供应商参加拟议采购的程序)；或

(b) 如评审显示，就通知或招标文件中所列具体评审标准而言，任何投标书都不具明显优势。

2. 谈判应主要用于确定投标书的优势和劣势。

3. 各实体应将投标书视为机密。特别是，它们不得提供旨在帮助某些参加者将其投标书提高至与其他参加者相同水平的信息。

4. 在谈判过程中，各实体不得在不同供应商之间造成歧视。它们特别应保证：

(a) 参加者的排除应依照通知和招标文件中所列标准进行；

(b) 对标准和技术要求的所有修改应以书面形式传送至参加谈判的所有其他供应商；

(c) 向所有其他参加方提供机会，以便根据修改后的要求提出新的或修正的投标书；以及

(d) 在谈判结束时，应允许谈判中所有其他参加者依照一共同的截止日期提交最后投标书。

Article XV

Limited Tendering

1. The provisions of Articles VII through XIV governing open and selective tendering procedures need not apply in the following conditions, provided that limited tendering is not used with a view to avoiding maximum possible competition or in a manner which would constitute a means of discrimination among suppliers of other Parties or protection to domestic producers or suppliers:

(a) in the absence of tenders in response to an open or selective tender, or when the tenders submitted have been collusive, or not in conformity with the essential requirements in the tender, or from suppliers who do not comply with the conditions for participation provided for in accordance with this Agreement, on condition, however, that the requirements of the initial tender are not substantially modified in the contract as awarded;

(b) when, for works of art or for reasons connected with protection of exclusive rights, such as patents or copyrights, or in the absence of competition for technical reasons, the products or services can be supplied only by a particular supplier and no reasonable alternative or substitute exists;

(c) in so far as is strictly necessary when, for reasons of extreme urgency brought about by events unforeseeable by the entity, the products or services could not be obtained in time by means of open or selective tendering procedures;

(d) for additional deliveries by the original supplier which are intended either as parts replacement for existing supplies, or installations, or as the extension of existing supplies, services, or installations where a change of supplier would compel the entity to procure equipment or services not meeting requirements of interchangeability with already existing equipment or services[5];

(e) when an entity procures prototypes or a first product or service which are developed at its request in the course of, and for, a particular contract for research, experiment, study or original development. When such contracts have been fulfilled, subsequent procurements of products or services shall be subject to Articles VII through XIV[6];

(f) when additional construction services which were not included in the initial contract but which were within the objectives of the original tender documentation have, through unforeseeable circumstances, become necessary to complete the construction services described therein, and the entity needs to award contracts for the additional construction services to the contractor carrying out the construction services concerned since the separation of the additional construction services from the initial contract would be difficult for technical or economic reasons and cause significant inconvenience to the entity. However, the total value of contracts awarded for the additional construction services may not exceed 50 per cent of the amount of the main contract;

---

[5] It is the understanding that "existing equipment" includes software to the extent that the initial procurement of the software was covered by the Agreement.

[6] Original development of a first product or service may include limited production or supply in order to incorporate the results of field testing and to demonstrate that the product or service is suitable for production or supply in quantity to acceptable quality standards. It does not extend to quantity production or supply to establish commercial viability or to recover research and development costs.

第 15 条
有限招标

1． 第 7 条至第 14 条适用于公开和选择性招标程序的规定不需在下列条件下适用，只要有限招标不用以避免最大可能的竞争或构成在其他参加方的供应商之间造成歧视或保护国内生产者或供应商的手段：

(a) 如公开或选择性招标无投标书，或如果提交的投标书是串通的，或不符合招标的基本要求，或来自不符合依照本协定规定的参加条件的供应商，但条件是在授予的合同中未对最初招标的要求进行实质性修改；

(b) 如对于艺术作品或因保护专利或版权等专有权利有关的原因，或由于技术原因而无竞争，产品或服务只能由一特定供应商供应，且不存在合理的选择或替代；

(c) 在绝对必要的情况下，如由于有关实体未能预见的事件所造成的极为紧急的情况，产品或服务不能通过公开或选择性招标程序迅速供应；

(d) 对于原供应商的额外交货，目的在于为现有供应或装置更换部件，或扩大现有供应、服务或装置，而如果更换供应商将迫使有关实体采购的设备或服务不能满足与现有设备或服务[5]的互换性要求；

(e) 一实体采购应其请求在关于研究、实验、考察或原始开发的特定合同执行过程中开发的原型或第一个产品或服务。如此类合同得以履行，则随后进行的产品或服务的采购应遵守第 7 条至第 14 条[6]的规定；

(f) 未包括在最初合同中的、但属原始招标文件目标范围内的额外建筑服务，由于无法预见的情况，成为完成合同所述建筑服务的必要内容，而因技术或经济原因，将额外建筑服务与最初合同进行分离难以做到，且会给有关实体造成严重不便，有关实体需要将额外建筑服务的合同授予实施有关建筑服务的承包商。但是，所授予的额外建筑服务合同的总价值不得超过主合同数额的 50%；

[5] 各方理解，“现有设备”包括软件，只要软件的最初采购在本协定涵盖范围内。

[6] 第一个产品或服务的原始开发可包括有限的生产或供应，以便包含实地实验的结果，并证明该产品或服务适宜大量生产或供应，达到可接受的质量标准。此概念并不延伸至为形成商业活力或收回科研与开发成本而进行的大量生产或供应。

(g) for new construction services consisting of the repetition of similar construction services which conform to a basic project for which an initial contract was awarded in accordance with Articles VII through XIV and for which the entity has indicated in the notice of intended procurement concerning the initial construction service, that limited tendering procedures might be used in awarding contracts for such new construction services;

(h) for products purchased on a commodity market;

(i) for purchases made under exceptionally advantageous conditions which only arise in the very short term. This provision is intended to cover unusual disposals by firms which are not normally suppliers, or disposal of assets of businesses in liquidation or receivership. It is not intended to cover routine purchases from regular suppliers;

(j) in the case of contracts awarded to the winner of a design contest provided that the contest has been organized in a manner which is consistent with the principles of this Agreement, notably as regards the publication, in the sense of Article IX, of an invitation to suitably qualified suppliers, to participate in such a contest which shall be judged by an independent jury with a view to design contracts being awarded to the winners.

2. Entities shall prepare a report in writing on each contract awarded under the provisions of paragraph 1. Each report shall contain the name of the procuring entity, value and kind of goods or services procured, country of origin, and a statement of the conditions in this Article which prevailed. This report shall remain with the entities concerned at the disposal of the government authorities responsible for the entity in order that it may be used if required under the procedures of Articles XVIII, XIX, XX and XXII.

Article XVI
Offsets

1. Entities shall not, in the qualification and selection of suppliers, products or services, or in the evaluation of tenders and award of contracts, impose, seek or consider offsets.[7]

2. Nevertheless, having regard to general policy considerations, including those relating to development, a developing country may at the time of accession negotiate conditions for the use of offsets, such as requirements for the incorporation of domestic content. Such requirements shall be used only for qualification to participate in the procurement process and not as criteria for awarding contracts. Conditions shall be objective, clearly defined and non-discriminatory. They shall be set forth in the country's Appendix I and may include precise limitations on the imposition of offsets in any contract subject to this Agreement. The existence of such conditions shall be notified to the Committee and included in the notice of intended procurement and other documentation.

[7] Offsets in government procurement are measures used to encourage local development or improve the balance-of-payments accounts by means of domestic content, licensing of technology, investment requirements, counter-trade or similar requirements.

(g) 由重复提供类似建筑服务所组成的新建筑服务，该项服务符合依照第 7 条至第 14 条授予的最初合同中的基本工程项目，且有关实体在关于该最初建筑服务的预定采购通知中已表明，在授予此类新建筑服务合同时可能使用有限招标程序；

(h) 在商品市场上采购的产品；

(i) 对于在非常短的时间内出现的特别有利的条件下进行的采购。本规定旨在涵盖不属供应商的公司所进行的非正常处理，或对进行财产清算或财务清算的企业资产的处理。本规定无意涵盖正常供应商进行的例行采购；

(j) 对于将合同授予设计比赛获胜者的情况，只要比赛是按与本协定一致的原则组织的，特别是关于向符合资格的供应商作出属第 9 条意义上的邀请参加此种比赛公告的规定，此种比赛应由独立评判委员会进行评判，以期将设计合同授予比赛获胜者。

2. 各实体应就根据本条第 1 款规定授予的每份合同准备书面报告。每份报告均应包含采购实体的名称、所购货物或服务的价值和种类、原产国以及对所适用的木条中条件的说明。该报告应由有关实体保留，供负责该实体的政府主管机关处理，以便在第 18 条、第 19 条、第 20 条和第 22 条中的程序要求时使用。

第 16 条

补偿

1. 各实体在对供应商、产品或服务进行资格审查和选择时，或在评审投标书和授予合同时，不得强加、寻求和考虑补偿。[7]

2. 尽管如此，注意到一般政策因素，包括与发展有关的因素，一发展中国家在加入本协定时可就使用补偿问题进行谈判，如包含当地含量的要求等。此类要求只用于参加采购程序的资格审查，而不用作授予合同的标准。条件应客观、明确规定和非歧视，并应列入该国的附录 1 中，可包括对属本协定管辖范围的任何合同强加补偿的明确限制。此类条件的存在应通知委员会，并包括在预定采购通知和其他招标文件。

[7] 政府采购中的“补偿”指通过当地含量、技术许可、投资要求、反向贸易或类似要求等手段用以鼓励当地发展或改善国际收支账户的措施。

Article XVII

Transparency

1. Each Party shall encourage entities to indicate the terms and conditions, including any deviations from competitive tendering procedures or access to challenge procedures, under which tenders will be entertained from suppliers situated in countries not Parties to this Agreement but which, with a view to creating transparency in their own contract awards, nevertheless:

(a) specify their contracts in accordance with Article VI (technical specifications);

(b) publish the procurement notices referred to in Article IX, including, in the version of the notice referred to in paragraph 8 of Article IX (summary of the notice of intended procurement) which is published in an official language of the WTO, an indication of the terms and conditions under which tenders shall be entertained from suppliers situated in countries Parties to this Agreement;

(c) are willing to ensure that their procurement regulations shall not normally change during a procurement and, in the event that such change proves unavoidable, to ensure the availability of a satisfactory means of redress.

2. Governments not Parties to the Agreement which comply with the conditions specified in paragraphs 1(a) through 1(c), shall be entitled if they so inform the Parties to participate in the Committee as observers.

Article XVIII

Information and Review as Regards Obligations of Entities

1. Entities shall publish a notice in the appropriate publication listed in Appendix II not later than 72 days after the award of each contract under Articles XIII through XV. These notices shall contain:

(a) the nature and quantity of products or services in the contract award;

(b) the name and address of the entity awarding the contract;

(c) the date of award;

(d) the name and address of winning tenderer;

(e) the value of the winning award or the highest and lowest offer taken into account in the award of the contract;

(f) where appropriate, means of identifying the notice issued under paragraph 1 of Article IX or justification according to Article XV for the use of such procedure; and

(g) the type of procedure used.

2. Each entity shall, on request from a supplier of a Party, promptly provide:

(a) an explanation of its procurement practices and procedures;

(b) pertinent information concerning the reasons why the supplier's application to qualify was rejected, why its existing qualification was brought to an end and why it was not selected; and

(c) to an unsuccessful tenderer, pertinent information concerning the reasons why its tender was not selected and on the characteristics and relative advantages of the tender selected as well as the name of the winning tenderer.

3. Entities shall promptly inform participating suppliers of decisions on contract awards and, upon request, in writing.

第 17 条
透明度

1．　每一参加方应鼓励各实体表明其据以接受来自非本协定参加方的供应商投标书的条款和条件，包括对竞争性招标程序的任何背离或对质疑程序的使用，以期使其合同的授予具有透明度，尽管这些条款和条件：

(a)　依照第 6 条(技术规格)规定其合同内容；

(b)　公布第 9 条所指的采购通知，包括在以 WTO 一官方语文公布的第 9 条第 8 款所指的通知中(预定采购的通知摘要)，表明据以接受来自本协定参加方供应商的投标书的条款和条件；

(c)　愿意保证其采购法规在一项采购中通常不发生变更，如此类变更被证明不可避免，则保证可获得满意的补救方法。

2．　遵守第 1 款(a)项至(c)项所列条件的非本协定参加方的政府有权在告知各参加方的情况下，作为观察员参加委员会。

第 18 条
关于实体义务的信息和审议

1．　各实体应不迟于根据第 13 条至第 15 条授予合同后的 72 天，在附录 2 所列有关出版物上公布通知。这些通知应包括：

(a)　授予合同中产品或服务的性质和数量；

(b)　授予合同的实体的名称和地址；

(c)　授予日期；

(d)　中标投标人的名称和地址；

(e)　获胜决标的价值或在授予合同过程中予以考虑的最高和最低报盘；

(f)　在适当时，用以确定根据第 9 条第 1 款发布通知的方法或根据第 15 条提出的使用此类程序的理由；以及

(g)　使用的程序类型。

2．　应一参加方的供应商的请求，每一实体应迅速提供：

(a)　关于其采购做法和程序的说明；

(b)　关于该供应商的资格申请为什么被拒绝、其现有资格为什么被取消以及为什么未被选中原因的有关信息；

(c)　对于未中标投标人，有关其投标书未被选中的原因及有关被选中投标书的特点和相对优势以及中标投标人的名称。

3．　各实体应迅速告知参加投标的供应商有关合同授予的决定，应请求，应以书面形式告知。

4. However, entities may decide that certain information on the contract award, contained in paragraphs 1 and 2(c), be withheld where release of such information would impede law enforcement or otherwise be contrary to the public interest or would prejudice the legitimate commercial interest of particular enterprises, public or private, or might prejudice fair competition between suppliers.

Article XIX

Information and Review as Regards Obligations of Parties

1. Each Party shall promptly publish any law, regulation, judicial decision, administrative ruling of general application, and any procedure (including standard contract clauses) regarding government procurement covered by this Agreement, in the appropriate publications listed in Appendix IV and in such a manner as to enable other Parties and suppliers to become acquainted with them. Each Party shall be prepared, upon request, to explain to any other Party its government procurement procedures.

2. The government of an unsuccessful tenderer which is a Party to this Agreement may seek, without prejudice to the provisions under Article XXII, such additional information on the contract award as may be necessary to ensure that the procurement was made fairly and impartially. To this end, the procuring government shall provide information on both the characteristics and relative advantages of the winning tender and the contract price. Normally this latter information may be disclosed by the government of the unsuccessful tenderer provided it exercises this right with discretion. In cases where release of this information would prejudice competition in future tenders, this information shall not be disclosed except after consultation with and agreement of the Party which gave the information to the government of the unsuccessful tenderer.

3. Available information concerning procurement by covered entities and their individual contract awards shall be provided, upon request, to any other Party.

4. Confidential information provided to any Party which would impede law enforcement or otherwise be contrary to the public interest or would prejudice the legitimate commercial interest of particular enterprises, public or private, or might prejudice fair competition between suppliers shall not be revealed without formal authorization from the party providing the information.

5. Each Party shall collect and provide to the Committee on an annual basis statistics on its procurements covered by this Agreement. Such reports shall contain the following information with respect to contracts awarded by all procurement entities covered under this Agreement:

(a) for entities in Annex 1, statistics on the estimated value of contracts awarded, both above and below the threshold value, on a global basis and broken down by entities; for entities in Annexes 2 and 3, statistics on the estimated value of contracts awarded above the threshold value on a global basis and broken down by categories of entities;

(b) for entities in Annex 1, statistics on the number and total value of contracts awarded above the threshold value, broken down by entities and categories of products and services according to uniform classification systems; for entities in Annexes 2 and 3, statistics on the estimated value of contracts awarded above the threshold value broken down by categories of entities and categories of products and services;

(c) for entities in Annex 1, statistics, broken down by entity and by categories of products and services, on the number and total value of contracts awarded under each of the cases of Article XV; for categories of entities in Annexes 2 and 3, statistics on the total value of contracts awarded above the threshold value under each of the cases of Article XV; and

4.　　但是，各参加方可决定保留第 1 款和第 2 款(c)项包含的有关合同授予的某些信息，如发布此类信息则会妨碍执法或违背公众利益或损害特定公私企业的合法商业利益，或可能损害供应商之间的公平竞争。

第 19 条
关于各参加方义务的信息和审议

1.　　每一实体应在附录 4 所列有关出版物上，以使其他参加方和供应商知晓的方式，迅速公布有关本协定所涵盖的有关政府采购的、普遍适用的任何法律、法规、司法判决、行政裁决和任何程序(包括标准合同条款)。应请求，每一参加方应准备向任何其他参加方就其政府采购程序作出说明。

2.　　属本协定参加方的未中标投标人的政府，在不损害第 22 条规定的情况下，可寻求保证该项采购以公平和公正的方式进行所必需的、关于合同授予的额外信息。为此，进行采购的政府应提供关于中标投标书的特点和相对优势以及合同价格的信息。通常后面的信息可由未中标投标人的政府披露，只要该政府谨慎地行使此权利。在发布此信息会损害未来投标中竞争的情况下，除非与给予未中标投标人政府该信息的参加方进行磋商并达成协议，否则此信息不得披露。

3.　　应请求，应向任何其他参加方提供关于本协定所涵盖实体进行的采购及其所授予的各合同的信息。

4.　　向任何参加方提供的机密信息，如这些信息发布将妨碍执法或违背公众利益或损害特定公私企业的合法商业利益，或可能损害供应商之间的公平竞争，则未经提供该信息的参加方正式授权，不得披露。

5.　　每一参加方应每年收集并向委员会提供其属本协定涵盖范围的采购的统计数字。此类报告应包含关于本协定项下涵盖的所有采购实体所授予合同的下列信息：

(a)　对于附件 1 中实体，关于在全球范围内并按实体分解的、高于或低于最低限额的所授予合同的估计价值的统计数字；对于附件 2 和附件 3 中实体，关于在全球范围内并按实体类别分解的、高于最低限额的所授予合同的估计价值的统计数字；

(b)　对于附件 1 中实体，关于按实体及按统一分类制度的产品或服务类别分解的、高于最低限额的所授予合同的数量和总价值的统计数字；对于附件 2 和附件 3 中实体，关于按实体类别及产品或服务类别分解的、高于最低限额的所授予合同的估计价值的统计数字；

(c)　对于附件 1 中实体，关于按实体及产品或服务类别分解的、根据第 15 条的每一种情况所授予合同的数量和总价值的统计数字；对于附件 2 和附件 3 中实体，关于高于最低限额的、根据第 15 条的每一种情况所授予合同的总价值的统计数字；

(d) for entities in Annex 1, statistics, broken down by entities, on the number and total value of contracts awarded under derogations to the Agreement contained in the relevant Annexes; for categories of entities in Annexes 2 and 3, statistics on the total value of contracts awarded under derogations to the Agreement contained in the relevant Annexes.

To the extent that such information is available, each Party shall provide statistics on the country of origin of products and services purchased by its entities. With a view to ensuring that such statistics are comparable, the Committee shall provide guidance on methods to be used. With a view to ensuring effective monitoring of procurement covered by this Agreement, the Committee may decide unanimously to modify the requirements of subparagraphs (a) through (d) as regards the nature and the extent of statistical information to be provided and the breakdowns and classifications to be used.

Article XX

Challenge Procedures

Consultations

1. In the event of a complaint by a supplier that there has been a breach of this Agreement in the context of a procurement, each Party shall encourage the supplier to seek resolution of its complaint in consultation with the procuring entity. In such instances the procuring entity shall accord impartial and timely consideration to any such complaint, in a manner that is not prejudicial to obtaining corrective measures under the challenge system.

Challenge

2. Each Party shall provide non-discriminatory, timely, transparent and effective procedures enabling suppliers to challenge alleged breaches of the Agreement arising in the context of procurements in which they have, or have had, an interest.

3. Each Party shall provide its challenge procedures in writing and make them generally available.

4. Each Party shall ensure that documentation relating to all aspects of the process concerning procurements covered by this Agreement shall be retained for three years.

5. The interested supplier may be required to initiate a challenge procedure and notify the procuring entity within specified time-limits from the time when the basis of the complaint is known or reasonably should have been known, but in no case within a period of less than 10 days.

6. Challenges shall be heard by a court or by an impartial and independent review body with no interest in the outcome of the procurement and the members of which are secure from external influence during the term of appointment. A review body which is not a court shall either be subject to judicial review or shall have procedures which provide that:

(a) participants can be heard before an opinion is given or a decision is reached;

(b) participants can be represented and accompanied;

(c) participants shall have access to all proceedings;

(d) proceedings can take place in public;

(e) opinions or decisions are given in writing with a statement describing the basis for the opinions or decisions;

(f) witnesses can be presented;

(g) documents are disclosed to the review body.

(d) 对于附件 1 中实体，关于按实体分解的、根据本协定有关附件中的背离规定所授予合同的数量和总价值的统计数字；对于附件 2 和附件 3 中实体，关于根据本协定有关附件中的背离规定所授予合同的数量和总价值的统计数字。

在可获得此类信息的限度内，每一参加方应提供关于其实体所购产品和服务原产国的统计数字。为保证此类统计数字的可比性，委员会应就使用的方法提供指导。为保证对本协定涵盖的采购进行有效监督，委员会可经全体一致决定可修改(a)项至(d)项有关拟提供的统计数字的性质和程度及所使用的分解和分类的要求。

第 20 条
质疑程序

磋商

1. 如一供应商就在一项采购过程中存在违反本协定情况提出申诉，则每一参加方应鼓励该供应商与采购实体进行磋商以寻求解决其申诉。在此类情况下，采购实体应对任何此类申诉给予公正和及时的考虑，且以不损害在质疑制度下获得纠正措施的方式进行。

质疑

2. 每一参加方应规定非歧视、及时、透明和有效的程序，以使各供应商对其拥有或曾经拥有利益的采购的过程中产生的被指控的违反本协定的情况提出质疑。

3. 每一参加方应书面形式规定其质疑程序并使其可普遍获得。

4. 每一参加方应保证与本协定所涵盖采购过程的所有方面有关的文件应保留 3 年。

5. 可要求感兴趣的供应商在规定的时限内开始质疑程序并通知采购实体。该时限自已知或理应知道申诉依据时开始，但无论如何不得少于 10 天。

6. 质疑应由一法院或对采购结果无利害关系的公正独立的审查机构进行审理，其机构成员在任职期间应不受外部影响。如一审查机构不是法院，则该机构应接受司法审查，或应有规定下列内容的程序：

(a) 可在提出意见或作出决定前对听取参加人的意见；

(b) 参加人可被代表和陪同；

(c) 参加人应可参加所有程序；

(d) 诉讼程序可公开进行；

(e) 意见或决定可以书面形式提出，并附关于描述提出意见或作出决定依据的说明；

(f) 证人可出席；

(g) 文件可向审查机构披露。

7. Challenge procedures shall provide for:

(a) rapid interim measures to correct breaches of the Agreement and to preserve commercial opportunities. Such action may result in suspension of the procurement process. However, procedures may provide that overriding adverse consequences for the interests concerned, including the public interest, may be taken into account in deciding whether such measures should be applied. In such circumstances, just cause for not acting shall be provided in writing;

(b) an assessment and a possibility for a decision on the justification of the challenge;

(c) correction of the breach of the Agreement or compensation for the loss or damages suffered, which may be limited to costs for tender preparation or protest.

8. With a view to the preservation of the commercial and other interests involved, the challenge procedure shall normally be completed in a timely fashion.

Article XXI

Institutions

1. A Committee on Government Procurement composed of representatives from each of the Parties shall be established. This Committee shall elect its own Chairman and Vice-Chairman and shall meet as necessary but not less than once a year for the purpose of affording Parties the opportunity to consult on any matters relating to the operation of this Agreement or the furtherance of its objectives, and to carry out such other responsibilities as may be assigned to it by the Parties.

2. The Committee may establish working parties or other subsidiary bodies which shall carry out such functions as may be given to them by the Committee.

Article XXII

Consultations and Dispute Settlement

1. The provisions of the Understanding on Rules and Procedures Governing the Settlement of Disputes under the WTO Agreement (hereinafter referred to as the "Dispute Settlement Understanding") shall be applicable except as otherwise specifically provided below.

2. If any Party considers that any benefit accruing to it, directly or indirectly, under this Agreement is being nullified or impaired, or that the attainment of any objective of this Agreement is being impeded as the result of the failure of another Party or Parties to carry out its obligations under this Agreement, or the application by another Party or Parties of any measure, whether or not it conflicts with the provisions of this Agreement, it may with a view to reaching a mutually satisfactory resolution of the matter, make written representations or proposals to the other Party or Parties which it considers to be concerned. Such action shall be promptly notified to the Dispute Settlement Body established under the Dispute Settlement Understanding (hereinafter referred to as "DSB"), as specified below. Any Party thus approached shall give sympathetic consideration to the representations or proposals made to it.

3. The DSB shall have the authority to establish panels, adopt panel and Appellate Body reports, make recommendations or give rulings on the matter, maintain surveillance of implementation of rulings and recommendations, and authorize suspension of concessions and other obligations under this Agreement or consultations regarding remedies when withdrawal of measures found to be in contravention of the Agreement is not possible, provided that only Members of the WTO Party to this Agreement shall participate in decisions or actions taken by the DSB with respect to disputes under this Agreement.

7. 质疑程序应规定：

(a) 快速的临时措施，以纠正违反本协定的行为和保持商业机会。此种行动可能造成该采购过程的中止。但是，质疑程序可规定在决定是否应采取此类措施时，可考虑到对有关利益包括公众利益所造成的重大不利后果。在此种情况下，应以书面形式提供不采取行动的合法理由；

(b) 对质疑的理由进行评价和作出有关决定的可能性；

(c) 对违反本协定行为的纠正或对所受损失或损害的赔偿，此类赔偿可限于为准备投标书或抗诉所需的费用。

8. 为保护商业利益和所涉及的其他利益，质疑程序通常应及时完成。

第21条
机构

1. 应设立由每一参加方代表组成的政府采购委员会。委员会应选举自己的主席和副主席，并在必要时召开会议，但每年不得少于一次，目的在于向各参加方提供机会，就有关本协定运用或促进本协定目标实现的任何事项进行磋商，并履行各参加方可能指定的其他职责。

2. 委员会可设立工作组或其他附属机构，以执行委员可能给予的职能。

第22条
磋商和争端解决

1. 应适用《WTO 协定》项下的《关于争端解决规则与程序的谅解》(下称"《争端解决谅解》")的规定，除非以下另有具体规定。

2. 如任何参加方认为由于另一个或多个参加方未能履行其在本协定项下的义务，或由于另一个或多个参加方实施无论是否违背本协定规定的任何措施，而使其在本协定项下直接或间接获得的利益丧失或减损，或阻碍本协定任何目标的实现，则该参加方为达成关于该事项的双方满意的解决办法，可向其认为有关的另一个或多个参加方提出书面交涉或建议。此种行动应迅速通知根据《争端解决谅解》设立的争端解决机构(下称"DSB")，如下所述。任何被如此接洽的参加方应积极考虑向其提出的交涉和建议。

3. DSB 有权设立专家组，通过专家组和上诉机构报告，就有关事项提出建议或作出裁决，监督裁决和建议的执行，并授权中止本协定项下的减让和其他义务，或在不可能撤销被认为不符合本协定的措施时，授权就补救问题进行磋商，但是只有属WTO成员的本协定参加方方可参加DSB就本协定项下的争端所作出的决定或采取的行动。

4. Panels shall have the following terms of reference unless the parties to the dispute agree otherwise within 20 days of the establishment of the panel:

> "To examine, in the light of the relevant provisions of this Agreement and of (name of any other covered Agreement cited by the parties to the dispute), the matter referred to the DSB by (name of party) in document ... and to make such findings as will assist the DSB in making the recommendations or in giving the rulings provided for in this Agreement."

In the case of a dispute in which provisions both of this Agreement and of one or more other Agreements listed in Appendix 1 of the Dispute Settlement Understanding are invoked by one of the parties to the dispute, paragraph 3 shall apply only to those parts of the panel report concerning the interpretation and application of this Agreement.

5. Panels established by the DSB to examine disputes under this Agreement shall include persons qualified in the area of government procurement.

6. Every effort shall be made to accelerate the proceedings to the greatest extent possible. Notwithstanding the provisions of paragraphs 8 and 9 of Article 12 of the Dispute Settlement Understanding, the panel shall attempt to provide its final report to the parties to the dispute not later than four months, and in case of delay not later than seven months, after the date on which the composition and terms of reference of the panel are agreed. Consequently, every effort shall be made to reduce also the periods foreseen in paragraph 1 of Article 20 and paragraph 4 of Article 21 of the Dispute Settlement Understanding by two months. Moreover, notwithstanding the provisions of paragraph 5 of Article 21 of the Dispute Settlement Understanding, the panel shall attempt to issue its decision, in case of a disagreement as to the existence or consistency with a covered Agreement of measures taken to comply with the recommendations and rulings, within 60 days.

7. Notwithstanding paragraph 2 of Article 22 of the Dispute Settlement Understanding, any dispute arising under any Agreement listed in Appendix 1 to the Dispute Settlement Understanding other than this Agreement shall not result in the suspension of concessions or other obligations under this Agreement, and any dispute arising under this Agreement shall not result in the suspension of concessions or other obligations under any other Agreement listed in the said Appendix 1.

Article XXIII

Exceptions to the Agreement

1. Nothing in this Agreement shall be construed to prevent any Party from taking any action or not disclosing any information which it considers necessary for the protection of its essential security interests relating to the procurement of arms, ammunition or war materials, or to procurement indispensable for national security or for national defence purposes.

2. Subject to the requirement that such measures are not applied in a manner which would constitute a means of arbitrary or unjustifiable discrimination between countries where the same conditions prevail or a disguised restriction on international trade, nothing in this Agreement shall be construed to prevent any Party from imposing or enforcing measures: necessary to protect public morals, order or safety, human, animal or plant life or health or intellectual property; or relating to the products or services of handicapped persons, of philanthropic institutions or of prison labour.

4. 专家组应具有下列职权范围，除非争端各方在专家组设立后20天内另有议定：“按照本协定的有关规定和(争端各方引用的任何其他适用协定名称)的有关规定，审查(争端方名称)在……文件中提交DSB的事项，并提出调查结果以协助DSB提出建议或作出该协定规定的裁决。”

在一争端方援引本协定的规定和《争端解决谅解》附录1所列一个或多个协定规定的情况下，第3款应只适用于专家组报告中有关解释和适用本协定的部分。

5. DSB设立审查本协定项下争端的专家组应包括政府采购领域的合格人士。

6. 应尽一切努力尽最大可能加快争端解决程序。尽管有《争端解决谅解》第12条第8款和第9款的规定，但是专家组仍应尝试在专家组组成和职权范围议定后不迟于4个月向争端各方提交最后报告，如有迟延，则不迟于7个月提交最后报告。因此，还应尽一切努力将《争端解决谅解》第20条第1款和第21条第4款中设想的期限缩短2个月。此外，尽管有《争端解决谅解》第21条第5款的规定，但是在不能就为符合建议和裁决而采取的措施是否存在或是否与一适用协定相一致的问题达成协议的情况下，专家组仍应尝试在60天内作出决定。

7. 尽管有《争端解决谅解》第22条第2款的规定，但是在《争端解决谅解》附录1所列除本协定外的任何协定项下产生的任何争端，均不得造成本协定项下减让或其他义务的中止，且本协定项下产生的任何争端不得造成上述附录1所列任何其他协定项下减让或其他义务的中止。

第23条
本协定的例外

1. 本协定的任何规定不得解释为妨碍任何参加方在与武器、弹药或军事物资的采购有关或与国家安全或国防目的所必需的采购有关的基本安全利益方面，采取其认为必需的任何行动或不披露任何信息。

2. 在遵守关于此类措施的实施方式不构成对条件相同的国家造成任意或不合理歧视的手段或不构成对国际贸易的变相限制要求的前提下，本协定的任何规定不得解释为妨碍任何参加方采取或实施下列措施：为保护公共道德、秩序或安全、人类和动植物的生命和健康或知识产权所必需的措施；或与残疾人、慈善机构或监狱囚犯产品或服务有关的措施。

Article XXIV

Final Provisions

1. *Acceptance and Entry into Force*

This Agreement shall enter into force on 1 January 1996 for those governments[8] whose agreed coverage is contained in Annexes 1 through 5 of Appendix I of this Agreement and which have, by signature, accepted the Agreement on 15 April 1994 or have, by that date, signed the Agreement subject to ratification and subsequently ratified the Agreement before 1 January 1996.

2. *Accession*

Any government which is a Member of the WTO, or prior to the date of entry into force of the WTO Agreement which is a contracting party to GATT 1947, and which is not a Party to this Agreement may accede to this Agreement on terms to be agreed between that government and the Parties. Accession shall take place by deposit with the Director-General of the WTO of an instrument of accession which states the terms so agreed. The Agreement shall enter into force for an acceding government on the 30th day following the date of its accession to the Agreement.

3. *Transitional Arrangements*

(a) Hong Kong and Korea may delay application of the provisions of this Agreement, except Articles XXI and XXII, to a date not later than 1 January 1997. The commencement date of their application of the provisions, if prior to 1 January 1997, shall be notified to the Director-General of the WTO 30 days in advance.

(b) During the period between the date of entry into force of this Agreement and the date of its application by Hong Kong, the rights and obligations between Hong Kong and all other Parties to this Agreement which were on 15 April 1994 Parties to the Agreement on Government Procurement done at Geneva on 12 April 1979 as amended on 2 February 1987 (the "1988 Agreement") shall be governed by the substantive[9] provisions of the 1988 Agreement, including its Annexes as modified or rectified, which provisions are incorporated herein by reference for that purpose and shall remain in force until 31 December 1996.

(c) Between Parties to this Agreement which are also Parties to the 1988 Agreement, the rights and obligations of this Agreement shall supersede those under the 1988 Agreement.

(d) Article XXII shall not enter into force until the date of entry into force of the WTO Agreement. Until such time, the provisions of Article VII of the 1988 Agreement shall apply to consultations and dispute settlement under this Agreement, which provisions are hereby incorporated in the Agreement by reference for that purpose. These provisions shall be applied under the auspices of the Committee under this Agreement.

(e) Prior to the date of entry into force of the WTO Agreement, references to WTO bodies shall be construed as referring to the corresponding GATT body and references to the Director-General of the WTO and to the WTO Secretariat shall be construed as references to, respectively, the Director-General to the CONTRACTING PARTIES to GATT 1947 and to the GATT Secretariat.

4. *Reservations*

---

[8] For the purpose of this Agreement, the term "government" is deemed to include the competent authorities of the European Communities.

[9] All provisions of the 1988 Agreement except the Preamble, Article VII and Article IX other than paragraphs 5(a) and (b) and paragraph 10.

第24条
最后条款

1．　**接受和生效**

本协定应于1996年1月1日对议定范围已包含在本协定附录1的附件1至附件5中、并于1994年4月15日通过签字接受本协定的政府生效，或对截至该日期虽已签署本协定但尚需核准、且随后于1996年1月1日之前已核准本协定的政府[8]生效。

2．　**加入**

任何属WTO成员的政府，或在《WTO协定》生效之日前已成为GATT 1947缔约方、但非本协定参加方的政府，可根据其与各参加方议定的条件加入本协定。加入在将说明议定加入条件的加入书交存WTO总干事后生效。本协定在申请加入的政府加入本协定后第30天对该政府生效。

3．　**过渡安排**

(a) 香港和韩国可推迟至不迟于1997年1月1日的一日期实施本协定除第21条和第22条外的条款。如其实施有关规定的日期早于1997年1月1日，则应提前30天向WTO总干事作出通知。

(b) 在本协定生效之日至香港实施本协定之日之间，香港与在1994年4月15日已成为1979年4月12日订于日内瓦、并于1987年2月2日修正的《政府采购协定》（"1988年协定"）的本协定参加方之间的权利和义务应适用1988年协定的实质性[9]条款，包括该协定经修改或更正的附件，这些条款为此目的通过引用已并入本协定并在1996年12月31日之前保持有效。

(c) 在既属本协定参加方又属1988年协定参加方之间，本协定的权利和义务应取代1988年协定项下的权利和义务。

(d) 本协定第22条在《WTO协定》生效之日前不得生效。在此之前，1988年协定的第7条的规定应适用于本协定项下的争端解决和磋商，这些规定为此目的通过引用特此并入本协定。这些规定应在本协定项下的委员会主持下实施。

(e) 在《WTO协定》生效之日前，所指的WTO各机构应理解为指相应的GATT机构，所指的WTO总干事和WTO秘书处应分别理解为指GATT 1947缔约方全体的总干事和GATT秘书处。

4．　**保留**

---

[8] 就本协定方而言，"政府"一词被视为包括欧共体的主管机关。

[9] 即1988年协定中除序言、第7条和第9条以外的所有条款，第9条第5款(a)项和(b)项及第10款除外。

Reservations may not be entered in respect of any of the provisions of this Agreement.

5. *National Legislation*

(a) Each government accepting or acceding to this Agreement shall ensure, not later than the date of entry into force of this Agreement for it, the conformity of its laws, regulations and administrative procedures, and the rules, procedures and practices applied by the entities contained in its lists annexed hereto, with the provisions of this Agreement.

(b) Each Party shall inform the Committee of any changes in its laws and regulations relevant to this Agreement and in the administration of such laws and regulations.

6. *Rectifications or Modifications*

(a) Rectifications, transfers of an entity from one Annex to another or, in exceptional cases, other modifications relating to Appendices I through IV shall be notified to the Committee, along with information as to the likely consequences of the change for the mutually agreed coverage provided in this Agreement. If the rectifications, transfers or other modifications are of a purely formal or minor nature, they shall become effective provided there is no objection within 30 days. In other cases, the Chairman of the Committee shall promptly convene a meeting of the Committee. The Committee shall consider the proposal and any claim for compensatory adjustments, with a view to maintaining a balance of rights and obligations and a comparable level of mutually agreed coverage provided in this Agreement prior to such notification. In the event of agreement not being reached, the matter may be pursued in accordance with the provisions contained in Article XXII.

(b) Where a Party wishes, in exercise of its rights, to withdraw an entity from Appendix I on the grounds that government control or influence over it has been effectively eliminated, that Party shall notify the Committee. Such modification shall become effective the day after the end of the following meeting of the Committee, provided that the meeting is no sooner than 30 days from the date of notification and no objection has been made. In the event of an objection, the matter may be pursued in accordance with the procedures on consultations and dispute settlement contained in Article XXII. In considering the proposed modification to Appendix I and any consequential compensatory adjustment, allowance shall be made for the market-opening effects of the removal of government control or influence.

7. *Reviews, Negotiations and Future Work*

(a) The Committee shall review annually the implementation and operation of this Agreement taking into account the objectives thereof. The Committee shall annually inform the General Council of the WTO of developments during the periods covered by such reviews.

(b) Not later than the end of the third year from the date of entry into force of this Agreement and periodically thereafter, the Parties thereto shall undertake further negotiations, with a view to improving this Agreement and achieving the greatest possible extension of its coverage among all Parties on the basis of mutual reciprocity, having regard to the provisions of Article V relating to developing countries.

(c) Parties shall seek to avoid introducing or prolonging discriminatory measures and practices which distort open procurement and shall, in the context of negotiations under subparagraph (b), seek to eliminate those which remain on the date of entry into force of this Agreement.

对本协定的任何规定均不得提出保留。

5. **国内立法**

(a) 接受或加入本协定的每一政府应保证在不迟于本协定对其生效之日，使其法律、法规、管理程序及其附件中实体实施的规则、程序和做法符合本协定的规定。

(b) 每一参加方应将其与本协定有关的法律和法规的任何变更及此类法律和法规的管理方面的任何变更通知委员会。

6. **更正或修改**

(a) 任何更正、将一实体从一附件转入另一附件、或在特殊情况下与附录 1 至附录 4 有关的其他修改，应向委员会作出通知，同时附关于变更对本协定中议定适用范围可能产生的结果的信息。如更正、转入或其他修改仅属形式上的或微小的性质，则只要在 30 天内无异议即可生效。在其他情况下，委员会主席应迅速召开委员会会议。委员会应审议有关建议和关于补偿性调整的任何主张，以期在作出此类通知前维持权利与义务的平衡和本协定所规定的双方同意的适用范围的可比水平。如未达成协议，则该事项可依照第 22 条包含的规定进行起诉。

(b) 如一参加方在行使其权利时，以政府对一实体的控制或影响已有效消除为由希望将该实体从附录 1 中去除，则该参加方应通知委员会。该项修改应在随后召开的委员会会议结束后次日生效，只要该会议不在自作出通知之日起早于 30 天内召开且对此未提出异议。如提出异议，则该事项可依照第 22 条包含的磋商和争端解决程序进行起诉。在考虑对附录 1 的拟议修改和任何由此引起的补偿性调整时，应考虑取消政府控制或影响所产生的市场开放效果。

7. **审议、谈判和未来的工作**

(a) 委员会应每年审议本协定的实施和运用情况，同时考虑本协定的目标。委员会应每年就此类审议所涉及期间的进展情况向 WTO 总理事会作出通知。

(b) 在不迟于本协定生效之日起第三年年款及此后定期，参加方应进行进一步谈判，以期在互惠基础上改进本协定，并尽最大可能在所有参加方之间实现本协定适用范围的扩大，同时注意到第 5 条与发展中国家有关的规定。

(c) 各参加方应寻求避免采用或延长扭曲公开采购的歧视性措施和做法，并应在(b)项规定的谈判过程中寻求取消在本协定生效之日保留的措施和做法。

8. *Information Technology*

With a view to ensuring that the Agreement does not constitute an unnecessary obstacle to technical progress, Parties shall consult regularly in the Committee regarding developments in the use of information technology in government procurement and shall, if necessary, negotiate modifications to the Agreement. These consultations shall in particular aim to ensure that the use of information technology promotes the aims of open, non-discriminatory and efficient government procurement through transparent procedures, that contracts covered under the Agreement are clearly identified and that all available information relating to a particular contract can be identified. When a Party intends to innovate, it shall endeavour to take into account the views expressed by other Parties regarding any potential problems.

9. *Amendments*

Parties may amend this Agreement having regard, *inter alia*, to the experience gained in its implementation. Such an amendment, once the Parties have concurred in accordance with the procedures established by the Committee, shall not enter into force for any Party until it has been accepted by such Party.

10. *Withdrawal*

(a) Any Party may withdraw from this Agreement. The withdrawal shall take effect upon the expiration of 60 days from the date on which written notice of withdrawal is received by the Director-General of the WTO. Any Party may upon such notification request an immediate meeting of the Committee.

(b) If a Party to this Agreement does not become a Member of the WTO within one year of the date of entry into force of the WTO Agreement or ceases to be a Member of the WTO, it shall cease to be a Party to this Agreement with effect from the same date.

11. *Non-application of this Agreement between Particular Parties*

This Agreement shall not apply as between any two Parties if either of the Parties, at the time either accepts or accedes to this Agreement, does not consent to such application.

12. *Notes, Appendices and Annexes*

The Notes, Appendices and Annexes to this Agreement constitute an integral part thereof.

13. *Secretariat*

This Agreement shall be serviced by the WTO Secretariat.

14. *Deposit*

This Agreement shall be deposited with the Director-General of the WTO, who shall promptly furnish to each Party a certified true copy of this Agreement, of each rectification or modification thereto pursuant to paragraph 6 and of each amendment thereto pursuant to paragraph 9, and a notification of each acceptance thereof or accession thereto pursuant to paragraphs 1 and 2 and of each withdrawal therefrom pursuant to paragraph 10 of this Article.

15. *Registration*

This Agreement shall be registered in accordance with the provisions of Article 102 of the Charter of the United Nations.

Done at Marrakesh this fifteenth day of April one thousand nine hundred and ninety-four in a single copy, in the English, French and Spanish languages, each text being authentic, except as otherwise specified with respect to the Appendices hereto.

8. **信息技术**

为保证本协定不对技术进步构成不必要的障碍，各参加方应经常在委员会中就在政府采购中使用信息技术的进展情况进行磋商，如必要还应谈判修改本协定。这些磋商的目的特别在于保证信息技术的使用通过透明的程序促进公开、非歧视和有效的政府采购，并保证本协定项下涵盖的合同可以明确确定且与一合同有关的所有可获得的信息可以明确确定。如一方拟进行革新，则应努力考虑其他参加方就任何潜在问题表明的意见。

9. **修正**

各参加方可修正本协定，应特别注意在本协定实施过程中获得的经验。一旦本协定参加方依照委员会制定的程序同意此种修正，即应只对已接受修正的参加方生效。

10. **退出**

(a) 任何参加方均可退出本协定。该退出应在 WTO 总干事收到书面退出通知之日起 60 天期满后生效。任何参加方在收到此类通知后，可请求立即召开委员会会议。

(b) 如本协定一参加方在《WTO 协定》生效之日起 1 年内未能成为 WTO 成员或不再为 WTO 成员，则该参加方应自同日起不再为本协定的参加方。

11. **本协定在特定参加方之间的不适用**

任何参加方，如在自己成为参加方或在另一参加方成为参加方时，不同意在彼此之间适用本协定，则本协定不在该两参加方之间适用。

12. **注释、附录和附件**

本协定的注释、附录和附件为本协定的组成部分。

13. **秘书处**

本协定由 WTO 秘书处提供服务。

14. **交存**

本协定应交存 WTO 总干事。总干事应迅速向每一参加方提供一份本协定经核证的副本、根据本条第 6 款进行每一项更正或修改的副本、本条第 9 款下每一项修正的副本，以及关于本条第 1 款和第 2 款所述接受或加入、本条第 10 款所述的退出通知。

15. **登记**

本协定应依照《联合国宪章》第 102 条的规定予以登记。

1994 年 4 月 15 日订于马拉喀什，正本一份用英文、法文和西班牙文写成，三种文本具有同等效力，除非本协定附录另有规定。

NOTES

The terms "country" or "countries" as used in this Agreement, including the Appendices, are to be understood to include any separate customs territory Party to this Agreement.

In the case of a separate customs territory Party to this Agreement, where an expression in this Agreement is qualified by the term "national", such expression shall be read as pertaining to that customs territory, unless otherwise specified.

Article 1, paragraph 1

Having regard to general policy considerations relating to tied aid, including the objective of developing countries with respect to the untying of such aid, this Agreement does not apply to procurement made in furtherance of tied aid to developing countries so long as it is practised by Parties.

注释

本协定包括其附录中使用“国家”一词应理解为包括属本协定参加方的任何单独关税区。

对于本协定的单独关税区参加方，如本协定的措辞被冠以“国家(的)”一词，则此措辞应被理解为与该单独关税区有关，除非另有规定。

第 1 条第 1 款

注意到有关限制性援助的一般政策因素，包括发展中国家有关去除此种援助的限制性条件的目标，只要各参加方实行这种做法，本协定即不适用于为促进对发展中国家给予的限制性援助而进行的采购。

APPENDIX I
附录 1

APPENDIX I

Annexes 1 through 5 setting out the scope of this Agreement:

Annex 1	Central Government Entities
Annex 2	Sub-Central Government Entities
Annex 3	All Other Entities that Procure in Accordance with the Provisions of this Agreement
Annex 4	Services
Annex 5	Construction Services

APPENDICE I

Annexes 1 à 5 définissant la portée du présent accord:

Annexe 1	Entités du gouvernement central
Annexe 2	Entités des gouvernements sous-centraux
Annexe 3	Toutes les autres entités qui passent des marchés conformément aux dispositions du présent accord
Annexe 4	Services
Annexe 5	Services de construction

APÉNDICE I

Anexos 1 a 5, en los que se establece el alcance del presente Acuerdo:

Anexo 1	Entidades de los gobiernos centrales
Anexo 2	Entidades de los gobiernos subcentrales
Anexo 3	Demás entidades que se rigen en sus contratos por las disposiciones del presente Acuerdo
Anexo 4	Servicios
Anexo 5	Servicios de construcción

1 March 2000 (WT/Let/330)

附录 1

附件 1 至 5 列出本协定的范围：

附件 1	中央政府实体
附件 2	次中央政府实体
附件 3	依照本协定条款进行采购的所有其他实体
附件 4	服务
附件 5	建筑服务

2000 年 3 月 1 日 (WT/Let/330)

CANADA
加拿大

CANADA

(Authentic in the English and French languages)

ANNEX 1

Federal Government Entities

Thresholds:	130,000 SDRs	-	***Goods***
	130,000 SDRs	-	***Services*** covered in Annex 4
	5,000,000 SDRs	-	***Construction*** covered in Annex 5

List of entities:

1. Department of Agriculture and Agri-Food
2. Canadian Food Inspection Agency (Not including procurements respecting FSCs 36, 70 and 74 in respect of the administration and enforcement of the *Fish Inspection Act.*)
3. Department of Canadian Heritage (Not including procurements respecting FSCs 36, 70 and 74 in respect of those functions that were formerly the responsibility of the Department of Communications.)
4. Office of the Coordinator, Status of Women
5. Parks Canada Agency
6. Department of Citizenship and Immigration
7. Immigration and Refugee Board
8. Department of the Environment
9. Department of Foreign Affairs and International Trade
10. Canadian International Development Agency (on its own account)
11. Department of Finance
12. Canadian International Trade Tribunal
13. Municipal Development and Loan Board
14. Office of the Superintendent of Financial Institutions
15. Department of Fisheries and Oceans (Not including procurements respecting FSCs 36, 70 and 74.) (For purposes of Article XXIII, the national security considerations applicable to the Department of National Defence are equally applicable to the Canadian Coast Guard other than the functions of the Canadian Coast Guard retained by the Department of Transport pursuant to Order under the *Public Service Rearrangement and Transfer of Duties Act* published in the Canada Gazette, Part II, as SI/95-46, namely the Harbours and Ports Directorate, the regional Harbours and Ports Branches, the Marine Regulatory Directorate, the Ship Inspection Directorate and the regional Ship Inspection Branches of the Canadian Coast Guard.)
16. Department of Health
17. Medical Research Council
18. Department of Human Resources Development
19. Canada Employment Insurance Commission
20. Canada Labour Relations Board

9 December 2003 (WT/Let/454)

加拿大

(以英文和法文为准)

附件 1

联邦政府实体

门槛金额:	130,000 特别提款权	-	***货物***
	130,000 特别提款权	-	*附件 4 所涵盖的**服务***
	5,000,000 特别提款权	-	*附件 5 所涵盖的**建筑***

实体清单:

1. 农业部
2. 加拿大食品检验局 (不包括在管理和执行《鱼类检查法》方面关于 FSC 36、70 和 74 的采购)
3. 加拿大遗产部 (不包括在原属交通部职责的职能方面关于 FSC 36、70 和 74 的采购)
4. 妇女地位协调办公室
5. 加拿大公园管理局
6. 公民和移民部
7. 移民和难民局
8. 环境部
9. 外交和国际贸易部
10. 加拿大国际开发署 (自有预算采购)
11. 财政部
12. 加拿大国际贸易法庭
13. 城市发展和贷款局
14. 金融机构监理局
15. 渔业和海洋部 (不包括关于 FSC 36、70 和 74 的采购。) (就第 23 条而言，适用于国防部的国家安全考虑同等适用于加拿大海岸警卫队，但运输部根据《加拿大公告》第 SI/95-46 号第 2 部分所载《公共服务重新安排及职责移交法》所发指令保留的加拿大海岸警卫队的职能除外，即加拿大海岸警卫队所属港务局、地区港务管理机构、海事局、船舶检验局及地区船舶检验机构。)
16. 卫生部
17. 医学研究理事会
18. 人力资源发展部
19. 加拿失业保险委员会
20. 加拿大劳工关系局

2003 年 12 月 9 日 (WT/Let/454)

21. Department of Indian Affairs and Northern Development
22. Department of Industry (Not including procurements respecting FSCs 36, 70 and 74 in respect of telecommunications, except in relation to (a) planning and coordination of telecommunication services for departments, boards and agencies of the Government of Canada, and (b) broadcasting, other than in relation to spectrum management and the technical aspects of broadcasting.)
23. National Research Council of Canada
24. Natural Sciences and Engineering Research Council of Canada
25. Social Sciences and Humanities Research Council
26. Department of Justice
27. Canadian Human Rights Commission
28. Statute Revision Commission
29. Supreme Court of Canada
30. Canada Customs and Revenue Agency
31. Department of Natural Resources
32. Canadian Nuclear Safety Commission
33. National Energy Board (on its own account)
34. Department of Public Works and Government Services (on its own account) (Not including procurements respecting FSCs 36, 70 and 74 in respect of the Government Telecommunications Agency.)
35. Public Service Commission
36. Department of the Solicitor General
37. Correctional Service of Canada
38. National Parole Board
39. Department of Transport (Not including procurements respecting FSCs 36, 70 and 74.) (For purposes of Article XXIII, the national security considerations applicable to the Department of National Defence are equally applicable to the functions of the Canadian Coast Guard retained by the Department of Transport pursuant to Order under the *Public Service Rearrangement and Transfer of Duties Act* published in the Canada Gazette, Part II, as SI/95-46, namely the Harbours and Ports Directorate, the regional Harbours and Ports Branches, the Marine Regulatory Directorate, the Ship Inspection Directorate and the regional Ship Inspection Branches of the Canadian Coast Guard.)
40. Treasury Board Secretariat
41. Department of Veterans Affairs
42. Department of Western Economic Diversification (on its own account)
43. Atlantic Canada Opportunities Agency (on its own account)
44. Office of the Auditor General
45. Canada Economic Development for the Regions of Quebec
46. Canadian Centre for Management Development
47. Canadian Radio-television and Telecommunications Commission (on its own account)
48. Civil Aviation Tribunal
49. Commissioner for Federal Judicial Affairs
50. Registry of the Competition Tribunal
51. Copyright Board
52. Registry of the Federal Court of Canada
53. Office of the Grain Transportation Agency Administrator (on its own account)
54. Hazardous Materials Information Review Commission
55. Offices of the Information and Privacy Commissioners of Canada
56. The National Archives of Canada

9 December 2003 (WT/Let/454)

21. 印第安事务和北部发展部
22. 工业部 (不包括电信方面关于 FSC 36、70 和 74 的采购，但以下情况除外：(a)提供加拿大政府各部、局和署的电信服务的规划和协调，及(b)广播，但光谱管理和广播技术方面除外。)
23. 加拿大国家研究理事会
24. 加拿大自然科学和工程研究理事会
25. 社会科学和人文学研究理事会
26. 司法部
27. 加拿大人权委员会
28. 法令修改委员会
29. 加拿大最高法院
30. 加拿大海关和税务署
31. 自然资源部
32. 加拿大核安全委员会
33. 国家能源局(自有预算采购)
34. 公共工程和政府服务部 (自有预算采购)(不包括政府通信署关于 FSC 36、70 和 74 的采购。)
35. 公共服务委员会
36. 副检察长署
37. 加拿大惩教局
38. 国家假释委员会
39. 运输部 (不包括关于 FSC 36、70 和 74 的采购。) (就第 23 条而言，适用于国防部的国家安全考虑同等适用于运输部根据《加拿大公告》第 SI/95-46 号第 2 部分所载《公共服务重新安排及职责移交法》所发指令保留的加拿大海岸警卫队的职能，即加拿大海岸警卫队所属港务局、地区港务管理机构、海事局、船舶检验局及地区船舶检验机构)。
40. 国库部
41. 退伍军人事务部
42. 西部经济多元化部(自有预算采购)
43. 大西洋加拿大机会署(自有预算采购)
44. 审计长办公室
45. 加拿大魁北克地区经济发展署
46. 加拿大管理发展中心
47. 加拿大广播电视和通信委员会(自有预算采购)
48. 民用航空法庭
49. 联邦司法事务专署
50. 竞争局
51. 版权局
52. 加拿大联邦法院登记处
53. 粮食运输机构署长办公室 (自有预算采购)
54. 危险物质信息审查委员会
55. 加拿大信息和隐私专员办公室
56. 加拿大国家档案馆

57. National Farm Products Council
58. The National Library
59. Canada Transportation Agency (on its own account)
60. Northern Pipeline Agency (on its own account)
61. Patented Medicine Prices Review Board
62. Petroleum Monitoring Agency
63. Privy Council Office
64. Canadian Intergovernmental Conference Secretariat
65. Office of the Commissioner of Official Languages
66. Public Service Staff Relations Board
67. Office of the Governor General's Secretary
68. Office of the Chief Electoral Officer
69. Federal-Provincial Relations Office
70. Statistics Canada
71. Registry of the Tax Court of Canada
72. Canadian Centre for Occupational Health and Safety
73. Canadian Transportation Accident Investigation and Safety Board
74. Director of Soldier Settlement
75. Director, The Veterans' Land Act
76. Fisheries Prices Support Board
77. National Battlefields Commission
78. Royal Canadian Mounted Police
79. Royal Canadian Mounted Police External Review Committee
80. Royal Canadian Mounted Police Public Complaints Commission
81. Department of National Defence
82. Public Health Agency of Canada

THE FOLLOWING PRODUCTS PURCHASED BY THE DEPARTMENT OF NATIONAL DEFENCE, COAST GUARD AND THE RCMP ARE INCLUDED IN THE COVERAGE OF THIS AGREEMENT SUBJECT TO THE PROVISIONS OF ARTICLE XXIII. (NUMBERS REFER TO THE FEDERAL SUPPLY CLASSIFICATION CODE)

22. Railway Equipment
23. Motor vehicles, trailers and cycles (except buses in 2310, military trucks and trailers in 2320 and 2330 and tracked combat, assault and tactical vehicles in 2350)
24. Tractors
25. Vehicular equipment components
26. Tires and tubes
29. Engine accessories
30. Mechanical power transmission equipment
32. Woodworking machinery and equipment
34. Metal working equipment
35. Service and trade equipment
36. Special industry machinery
37. Agricultural machinery and equipment
38. Construction, mining, excavating and highway maintenance equipment
39. Materials handling equipment
40. Rope, cable, chain and fittings
41. Refrigeration and air conditioning equipment

22 July 2007 (WT/Let/581)

57. 国家农产品理事会
58. 国家图书馆
59. 加拿大运输署 (自有预算采购)
60. 北方管道署 (自有预算采购)
61. 专利药品价格审查局
62. 石油监管署
63. 加拿大枢密院
64. 加拿大政府间会议秘书处
65. 官方语言专员办公室
66. 公共服务人员关系局
67. 总督办公室
68. 首席选举官办公室
69. 联邦-省关系办公室
70. 加拿大统计署
71. 加拿大税务法庭登记局
72. 加拿大职业健康和安全中心
73. 加拿大运输事故调查和安全局
74. 士兵安置署
75. 《退伍军人土地法》署
76. 渔业价格支持局
77. 国家战场委员会
78. 加拿大皇家骑警
79. 加拿大皇家骑警外部审查委员会
80. 加拿大皇家骑警公共投诉委员会
81. 国防部
82. 加拿大公共卫生署

国防部、海岸警卫队和加拿大皇家骑警采购的下列产品包含在本协定涵盖范围之内，取决于第 23 条的规定。(数字指联邦供应分类编码)

22. 铁路设备
23. 地面效应车、机动车辆、拖车和自行车(2310 中的公共汽车、2320 和 2330 中的军用卡车和拖车及 2350 中的履带式战斗、攻击和战术车辆除外)
24. 拖拉机
25. 机动车部件
26. 轮胎和内胎
29. 发动机配件
30. 机械动力传输设备
32. 木工机器和设备
34. 金属加工设备
35. 服务和销售设备
36. 特殊工业机器
37. 农业机器和设备
38. 建筑、采矿、开凿和公路维护设备
39. 材料处理设备
40. 粗绳、电缆、链条和配件
41. 冷却、空调和空气循环装备

2007 年 7 月 22 日 (WT/Let/581)

42. Fire fighting, rescue and safety equipment (except 4220 Marine Life-saving and diving equipment, 4230 Decontaminating and impregnating equipment)
43. Pumps and compressors
44. Furnace, steam plant, drying equipment and nuclear reactors
45. Plumbing, heating and sanitation equipment
46. Water purification and sewage treatment equipment
47. Pipe, tubing, hose and fittings
48. Valves
49. Maintenance and repair shop equipment
52. Measuring tools
53. Hardware and abrasives
54. Prefabricated structures and scaffolding
55. Lumber, millwork, plywood and veneer
56. Construction and building materials
61. Electric wire and power and distribution equipment
62. Lighting fixtures and lamps
63. Alarm and signal systems
65. Medical, dental and veterinary equipment and supplies
66. Instruments and laboratory equipment (except 6615: Automatic pilot mechanisms and airborne Gyro components 6665: Hazard-detecting instruments and apparatus)
67. Photographic equipment
68. Chemicals and chemical products
69. Training aids and devices
70. General purpose automatic data processing equipment, software, supplies and support equipment (except 7010 ADPE configurations)
71. Furniture
72. Household and commercial furnishings and appliances
73. Food preparation and serving equipment
74. Office machines, visible record equipment and automatic data processing equipment
75. Office supplies and devices
76. Books, maps and other publications (except 7650 drawings and specifications)
77. Musical instruments, phonographs and home-type radios
78. Recreational and athletic equipment
79. Cleaning equipment and supplies
80. Brushes, paints, sealers and adhesives
81. Containers, packaging and packing supplies
85. Toiletries
87. Agricultural supplies
88. Live animals
91. Fuels, lubricants, oils and waxes
93. Non-metallic fabricated materials
94. Non-metallic crude materials
96. Ores, minerals and their primary products
99. Miscellaneous

Note to Annex 1

The General Notes apply to this Annex.

42. 消防、援救和安全设备(4220 船用救生和潜水设备、4230 净化和浸渍设备除外)
43. 泵和压缩机
44. 火炉、蒸气设备、烘干设备和核反应堆
45. 管道、加热和卫生设备
46. 水净化和污水处理设备
47. 管和配件
48. 阀
49. 维护和修理商店设备
52. 测量工具
53. 硬件和研磨剂
54. 预制件和脚手架
55. 木材、木制品、胶合板和饰面板
56. 建筑材料
61. 电线及电力传输设备
62. 照明器材和灯
63. 警报、信号和探测系统
65. 内科、牙科和兽医设备和耗材
66. 仪器和实验室设备(6615: 自动驾驶装置机载陀螺组件 6665: 危险检测仪器和装置除外)
67. 摄影设备
68. 化学药品和化工品
69. 教具和训练器材
70. 自动化处理设备软件、耗材和配套设备(7010 自动化处理系统结构除外)
71. 家具
72. 家用和商业家具和器械
73. 食品加工和供餐设备
74. 办公设备
75. 办公用品和装置
76. 书、地图和其他出版物 (7650 幅图画和说明书除外)
77. 乐器、留声机和家用收音机
78. 娱乐和运动器材
79. 清洁设备和耗材
80. 刷子、油漆、封条和粘合剂
81. 容器、包装材料和包装用品
85. 盥洗用品
87. 农业供给
88. 活动物
91. 燃料、润滑剂、油和蜡
93. 非金属制品
94. 非金属原料
96. 矿石、矿物及其初级产品
99. 杂项制品

附件 1 注释

总注释适用于本附件。

2003 年 12 月 9 日 (WT/Let/454)

ANNEX 2

Sub-Central Government Entities

Thresholds:	355,000 SDRs	-	***Goods***
	355,000 SDRs	-	***Services*** to be specified initially on or before 15 April 1994 with the final list to be provided within eighteen months after the conclusion of the new Government Procurement Agreement.
	5,000,000 SDRs	-	***Construction Services*** to be specified initially on or before 15 April 1994 with the final list to be provided within eighteen months after the conclusion of the new Government Procurement Agreement.

List of Entities:

The Canadian Government offers to cover entities in all ten provinces on the basis of commitments obtained from provincial governments. The initial provincial entities list will be specified on or before 15 April 1994 with the final list to be provided within eighteen months after the conclusion of the new Government Procurement Agreement.

Notes to Annex 2

1. Exceptions for all Provinces: steel, motor vehicles and coal

Province-specific exceptions: in addition, a limited number of individual provincial exceptions may be specified at a later date in accordance with commitments received from such provinces.

2. Nothing in this offer shall be construed to prevent any provincial entity from applying restrictions that promote the general environmental quality in that province, as long as such restrictions are not disguised barriers to international trade.

3. This offer shall not apply to any procurement made by a covered entity on behalf of a non-covered entity.

4. The General Notes apply to this Annex.

1 March 2000 (WT/Let/330)

附件 2

次中央实体

门槛金额:	355,000 特别提款权	-	***货物***
	355,000 特别提款权	-	***服务***，1994 年 4 月 15 日或之前初步列明，最终清单将在新的《政府采购协定》达成后 18 个月内提供。
	5,000,000 特别提款权	-	***建筑服务***，1994 年 4 月 15 日或之前初步列明，最终清单将在新的《政府采购协定》达成后 18 个月内提供。

实体清单:

在获得省级政府承诺的基础上，加拿大愿意涵盖全部 10 个省的实体。省级实体的初步清单将于 1994 年 4 月 15 日或之前列明，最终清单将在新的《政府采购协定》达成后 18 个月内提供。

附件 2 注释

1.　所有省份例外：钢、机动车辆和煤。

特定省份例外：此外，有限数量的个别省份例外可能依照自此类省份收到的承诺在稍后列明。

2.　本出价任何内容不得解释为阻止任何省级实体实施促进该省总体环境质量的限制措施，只要此类措施不是对国际贸易的变相壁垒。

3.　本出价不适用于涵盖实体代表非涵盖实体所进行的任何采购。

4.　总注释适用于本附件。

ANNEX 3

Government Enterprises

Thresholds:	355,000 SDRs	-	***Goods***
	355,000 SDRs	-	***Services*** covered in Annex 4
	5,000,000 SDRs	-	***Construction*** covered in Annex 5

Federal Enterprises

1. Canada Post Corporation
2. National Capital Commission
3. St. Lawrence Seaway Authority (For greater certainty, Article XIX:4 applies to procurements by St. Lawrence Seaway Authority respecting the protection of the commercial confidentiality of information provided.)
4. Royal Canadian Mint (not including procurement by or on behalf of the Royal Canadian Mint of direct inputs for use in minting anything other than Canadian legal tender. For greater certainty, Article XIX:4 applies to procurements by the Royal Canadian Mint respecting the protection of the commercial confidentiality of information provided.)
5. Canadian Museum of Civilization
6. Canadian Museum of Nature
7. National Gallery of Canada
8. National Museum of Science and Technology
9. Defence Construction (1951) Ltd.

Sub-central Enterprises

Coverage of Sub-central Enterprises for Goods, Services and Construction Services is to be specified initially on or before 15 April 1994 with the final list to be provided within eighteen months after the conclusion of the new Government Procurement Agreement.

Note to Annex 3

The General Notes apply to this Annex.

附件 3

政府企业

门槛金额:	355,000 特别提款权	-	**货物**
	355,000 特别提款权	-	附件 4 所涵盖的**服务**
	5,000,000 特别提款权	-	附件 5 所涵盖的**建筑**

联邦企业

1. 加拿大邮政公司
2. 首都委员会
3. 圣劳伦斯航道管理局(为更加明确，第 19 条第 4 款适用于圣劳伦斯航道管理局关于保护所提供信息的商业机密的采购。)
4. 加拿大皇家铸币厂(不包括加拿大皇家造币厂进行的或代表其进行的在除加拿大法定货币之外的任何铸造过程中使用的直接投入物的采购。为更加明确，第 19 条第 4 款适用于加拿大皇家铸币厂关于保护所提供信息的商业机密的采购。)
5. 加拿大文明博物馆
6. 加拿大自然博物馆
7. 国家美术馆
8. 国家科学技术博物馆
9. 国防建设 (1951) 有限公司

次中央企业

次中央企业的货物、服务以及建筑服务的涵盖范围将在 1994 年 4 月 15 日或之前初步列明，最终清单将在新的《政府采购协定》达成后 18 个月内提供。

附件 3 注释

总注释适用于本附件。

2000 年 3 月 1 日 (WT/Let/330)

ANNEX 4

Services

Canada offers to include in this "Services" Annex Federal entities listed under Annex 1 and Federal enterprises listed under Annex 3. The inclusion of "Services" for sub-central entities under Annex 2 and sub-central enterprises under Annex 3 are to be specified initially on or before 15 April 1994 with the final list to be provided within eighteen months after the conclusion of the new Government Procurement Agreement. With respect to the terms of this Agreement, those services to be included are as identified within the document MTN.GNS/W/120. Domestically, Canada will be utilizing the "Common Classification System" for purposes of implementing this Agreement. This list of services may be revised following further technical work among the Parties and adjustments, as appropriate, to establish equitable coverage.

Canada offers to cover the following services with respect to the CPC services classification system:

861	Legal Services (advisory services on foreign and international law only)
862	Accounting, auditing and book-keeping services
863	Taxation Services (excluding legal services)
8671	Architectural services
8672	Engineering services
8673	Integrated engineering services (excluding 86731 Integrated engineering services for transportation infrastructure turnkey projects)
8674	Urban planning and landscape architectural services
841	Consultancy services related to the installation of computer hardware
842	Software implementation services, including systems and software consulting services, systems analysis, design, programming and maintenance services
843	Data processing services, including processing, tabulation and facilities management services
844	Data base services
845	Maintenance and repair services of office machinery and equipment including computers
849	Other computer services
821	Real estate services involving own or leased property
822	Real estate services on a fee or contract basis

附件 4

服务

加拿大的出价包括将附件 1 中所列联邦实体和附件 3 中所列联邦企业包含在“服务”附件中。附件 2 中次中央实体和附件 3 中次中央企业“服务”的纳入将在 1994 年 4 月 15 日或之前初步列明，最终清单将在新的《政府采购协定》达成后 18 个月内提供。对于本协定中的术语，所包含的服务为 MTN.GNS/W/120 号文件所确定的服务。在国内，加拿大将采用“共同分类系统”以实施本协定。本服务清单可在各参加方之间的进一步技术工作和调整后酌情修改，以形成公平的涵盖范围。

加拿大愿意涵盖按照 CPC 服务分类系统分类的下列服务：

861	法律服务 (仅限于关于外国法和国际法的咨询服务)
862	会计、审计和簿记服务
863	税收服务 (不包括法律服务)
8671	建筑设计服务
8672	工程服务
8673	综合工程服务(不包括 86731 运输基础设施启钥集中工程服务)
8674	城市规划和园林景观工程
841	与计算机硬件安装有关的咨询服务
842	软件执行服务，包括系统和软件咨询服务、系统分析、设计、程序编制和维护服务
843	数据处理服务，包括处理、制表和设备管理服务
844	数据库服务
845	办公用机械和设备，包括计算机的维修服务
849	其他计算机服务
821	涉及自有或租赁房地产服务
822	基于收费或合同的房地产服务

83106 to 83109 only	Leasing or rental services concerning machinery and equipment without operator
83203 to 83209 only	Leasing or rental services concerning personal and household goods
86501	General management consulting services
86503	Marketing management consulting services
86504	Human resources management consulting services
86505	Production management consulting services
8660	Services related to management consulting (except 86602 Arbitration and conciliation services)
8676	Technical testing and analysis services including quality control and inspection (except with reference to FSC 58 and transportation equipment)
8814	Services incidental to forestry and logging, including forest management
883	Services incidental to mining, including drilling and field services
633	Repair services of personal and household goods
8861 to 8864, and 8866	Repair services incidental to metal products, machinery and equipment
874	Building-cleaning services
876	Packaging services
7512	Commercial courier services (including multi-modal)
7523	Electronic mail
7523	Voice mail
7523	On-line information and data base retrieval
7523	Electronic data interchange (EDI)
7523	Enhanced/value-added facsimile services, including store and forward, store and retrieve

1 March 2000 (WT/Let/330)

83106 至 83109 仅限	不配备技师的机械和设备租赁或出租服务
83203 至 83209 仅限	涉及个人和家庭物品的租赁或出租服务
86501	一般管理咨询服务
86503	市场管理咨询服务
86504	人力资源管理咨询服务
86505	生产管理咨询服务
8660	与管理咨询有关的服务(86602 仲裁和调解服务除外)
8676	技术测试和分析服务，包括质量控制和检验(FSC 58 和运输设备除外)
8814	从属林业和伐木业的服务，包括森林管理
883	从属采矿业的服务，包括钻探和矿田服务
633	个人和家用物品的修理服务
8861 至 8864 及 8866	从属金属产品、机械和设备的修理服务
874	建筑物清洁服务
876	包装服务
7512	商业递服务(包括多种模式)
7523	电子邮件
7523	语音邮件
7523	在线信息与数据库回收
7523	电子数据交换 (EDI)
7523	增值传真服务，包括保存并转发，保存并恢复密码和协议转换

	Code and protocol conversion
843	On-line information and/or data processing (including transaction processing)
940	Sewage and refuse disposal, sanitation and similar services
641	Hotel and similar accommodation services
642/3	Food and beverage serving services
7471	Travel agency and tour operator services

Notes to Annex 4

1. The General Notes apply to this Annex.

2. This offer is subject to the terms and conditions set out in the Canadian offer on trade in services.

3. Canada's offer in telecommunications is limited to enhanced or value added services for the supply of which the underlying telecommunications facilities are leased from providers of public telecommunications transport networks.

4. The Canadian offer does **not** include the following:

* management and operation contracts of certain government or privately-owned facilities used for government purposes, including federally-funded research and development;
* coin minting;
* public utilities;
* architectural and engineering related to airfield, communications and missile facilities;
* shipbuilding and repair and related architectural and engineering services;
* all services, with reference to those goods purchased by the Department of National Defence, the Royal Canadian Mounted Police and the Canadian Coast Guard which are not identified as subject to coverage by this agreement;
* services procured in support of military forces located overseas;
* printing and publishing services; and,
* procurement of transportation services that form a part of, or are incidental to, a procurement contract.

1 March 2000 (WT/Let/330)

843 在线信息和/或数据处理(包括交易处理)

940 污水和垃圾处理、卫生及类似服务

641 旅馆及类似住宿服务

642/3 食品和饮料供应服务

7471 旅行社和旅游经营者服务

附件 4 注释

1. 总注释适用于本附件。

2. 本出价应受加拿大关于服务贸易的出价中所规定的条款和条件管辖。

3. 加拿大电信出价仅限于自公共电信传输网络供应商处租赁基本通信设施而提供的增强型或增值服务。

4. 加拿大出价不含下列内容：

* 某些政府设施或用于政府目的私有设施的管理和运营合同，包括联邦资助的研究和开发；
* 铸币；
* 公用事业；
* 与机场、交通及导弹设施有关的建筑设计和工程；
* 造船和修船及相关建筑设计和工程服务；
* 与国防部、加拿大皇家骑警及加拿大海岸警卫队购买的、未确定受本协定涵盖的货物有关的所有服务；
* 为支持海外驻军而购买的服务；
* 印刷和出版服务；以及
* 构成一采购合同一部分的运输服务或一采购合同所附带的运输服务的采购。

2000 年 3 月 1 日 (WT/Let/330)

ANNEX 5

Construction Services

Canada offers to include in this "Construction Services" Annex, Federal entities listed under Annex 1 and Federal enterprises listed under Annex 3. The inclusion of "Construction Services" for sub-central entities under Annex 2 and sub-central enterprises under Annex 3 are to be specified initially on or before 15 April 1994 with the final list to be provided within eighteen months after the conclusion of the new government procurement agreement.

Definition:

A construction services contract is a contract which has as its objective the realization by whatever means of civil or building works, in the sense of Division 51 of the Central Product Classification.

List of Division 51, CPC:

All services contained in Division 51 CPC.

Notes to Annex 5

1. Notwithstanding anything in this Agreement, this Agreement does not apply to procurements in respect of:

   (a) Dredging; and

   (b) Construction contracts tendered on behalf of the Departments of Transport.

2. The General Notes apply to this Annex.

附件 5

建筑服务

加拿大的出价包括在本"建筑服务"附件中纳入附件 1 中所列联邦实体和附件 3 中所列联邦企业。附件 2 中次中央实体和附件 3 中的次中央企业"建筑服务"的纳入情况将在 1994 年 4 月 15 日或之前初步列明，最终清单将在新的《政府采购协定》达成后 18 个月内提供。

定义：

建筑服务合同是指根据《中央产品分类》第 51 类，以通过任何土木或建筑工程手段实现目的的合同。

CPC 第 51 类清单：

CPC 51 类包含的所有服务。

附件 5 注释

1. 尽管本协定有任何规定，但是本协定不适用于有关下列内容的采购：

   (a) 疏浚；及

   (b) 代表运输部招标的建筑合同。

2. 总注释适用于本附件。

2000 年 3 月 1 日 (WT/Let/330)

GENERAL NOTES

1. Notwithstanding anything in these Annexes, the Agreement does not apply to procurements in respect of:

   (a) shipbuilding and repair;

   (b) urban rail and urban transportation equipment, systems, components and materials incorporated therein as well as all project related materials of iron or steel;

   (c) contracts respecting FSC 58 (communications, detection and coherent radiation equipment);

   (d) set-asides for small and minority businesses;

   (e) agricultural products made in furtherance of agricultural support programs or human feeding programs;

   (f) national security exemptions include oil purchases related to any strategic reserve requirements; and,

   (g) national security exceptions including procurements made in support of safeguarding nuclear materials or technology.

2. Procurement in terms of Canadian coverage is defined as contractual transactions to acquire property or services for the direct benefit or use of the government. The procurement process is the process that begins after an entity has decided on its requirement and continues through to and including contract award. It does not include non-contractual agreements or any form of government assistance, including but not limited to, cooperative agreements, grants, loans, equity infusions, guarantees, fiscal incentives, and government provision of goods and services, given to individuals, firms, private institutions, and sub-central governments. It does not include procurements made with a view to commercial resale or made by one entity or enterprise from another entity or enterprise of Canada.

3. Any exclusion that is related either specifically or generally to Federal or sub-central entities or enterprises in Annex 1, Annex 2 or Annex 3 will also apply to any successor entity or entities, enterprise or enterprises, in such a manner as to maintain the value of this offer.

4. Until such time as there is a mutually agreed list of services to be covered by all Parties, a service listed in Annex 4 is covered with respect to a particular Party only to the extent that such Party has provided reciprocal access to that service.

5. Where a contract to be awarded by an entity is not covered by this Agreement, this Agreement shall not be construed to cover any good or service component of that contract.

6. The offer by Canada, with respect to goods and services (including construction) in Annexes 2 and 3, is subject to negotiation of mutually acceptable commitments (including thresholds) with other Parties, with initial commitments to be specified on or before

总注释

1. 尽管各附件的任何规定，但是本协定不适用于关于下列内容的采购：

   (a) 造船和修船；

   (b) 城市铁路和城市交通运输设备、系统、组件及所含材料以及所有与项目有关的钢铁材料；

   (c) 有关 FSC 58 的合同(通信、探测和相干辐射设备)；

   (d) 给予小企业和少数族裔企业的合同；

   (e) 为促进农业支持计划或人类供给计划而制造的农产品；

   (f) 国家安全豁免，包括与任何战略储备要求相关的石油采购；以及

   (g) 国家安全例外，包括为支持保护核物质或技术而进行的采购。

2. 就加拿大涵盖范围而言，采购定义为为政府直接利益或使用而获得资产或服务的合同交易。采购过程为一实体已就其要求作出决定后开始并持续至、且包含合同授予的过程。不包括非契约性协议或任何形式的政府援助，包括但不仅限于给予个人、公司、私人机构和次中央政府的合作协议、赠款、贷款、投股、担保、财政激励及政府提供货物和服务。不包括旨在进行商业转售而进行的采购或一实体或企业从另一加拿大实体或企业进行的采购。

3. 任何具体或普遍涉及附件 1、附件 2 或附件 3 中联邦或次中央实体或企业的排除，将以保持本出价价值的方式，同样适用于一个或多个任何继承实体或企业。

4. 在形成一份所有参加方均涵盖的共同议定的服务清单之前，对于附件 4 中所列一服务，仅在一特定参加方已对该服务提供对等准入时，方针对该参加方而涵盖其中。

5. 如一合同由本协定未涵盖的实体授予，则本协定不得解释为涵盖该合同的任何货物或服务组成部分。

6. 加拿大关于附件 2 和 3 中货物和服务（包括建筑）的出价取决于与其他参加方就共同接受的承诺（包括门槛金额）所进行的谈判，初步承诺将在 1994 年 4 月 15 日或之前列明，具

15 April 1994 and specific commitments to be confirmed within eighteen months after the conclusion of the new Government Procurement Agreement.

7. The Agreement shall not apply to contracts under an international agreement and intended for the joint implementation or exploitation of a project.

8. For the European Union, Canada's offer excludes procurements of FSC 70, 74 and 36 until such time as reciprocal access is provided.

9. For the European Union, this Agreement shall not apply to contracts awarded by entities in Annexes 1 and 2 in connection with activities in the field of drinking water, energy, transport or telecommunications.

1 March 2000 (WT/Let/330)

体承诺将在新的《政府采购协定》达成后 18 个月内确认。

7. 本协定不适用于根据国际协定旨在联合实施或开发一项目的合同。

8. 对于欧洲联盟，加拿大的出价不包括 FSC 70、74 和 36 的采购，直至获得对等准入时止。

9. 对于欧洲联盟，本协定不适于附件 1 和 2 中实体授予的与饮用水、能源、运输或电信领域活动有关的合同。

2000 年 3 月 1 日 (WT/Let/330)

CANADA

(Les versions française et anglaise font foi)

ANNEXE 1

Entités du gouvernement fédéral

Valeurs de seuil:	130 000 DTS	-	***Produits***
	130 000 DTS	-	***Services*** visés à l'Annexe 4
	5 000 000 DTS	-	***Travaux*** visés à l'Annexe 5

Liste des entités:

1. Ministère de l'Agriculture et de l'Agroalimentaire
2. Agence canadienne d'inspection des aliments (à l'exclusion des marchés portant sur les produits repris aux n os 36, 70 et 74 de la Classification fédérale des approvisionnements (FSC) et de l'application de la *Loi sur l'inspection du poisson*)
3. Ministère du Patrimoine canadien (à l'exclusion des marchés portant sur les produits repris aux n os 36, 70 et 74 de la Classification fédérale des approvisionnements (FSC) concernant les fonctions qui relevaient auparavant du ministère des Communications.)
4. Bureau de la coordonnatrice, Situation de la femme
5. Agence Parcs Canada
6. Ministère de la Citoyenneté et de l'Immigration
7. Commission de l'Immigration et du statut de réfugié
8. Ministère de l'Environnement
9. Ministère des Affaires étrangères et du Commerce international
10. Agence canadienne de développement international (pour son propre compte)
11. Ministère des Finances
12. Tribunal canadien du commerce extérieur
13. Office du développement municipal et des prêts aux municipalités
14. Bureau du surintendant des institutions financières
15. Ministère des Pêches et des Océans (à l'exclusion des marchés portant sur les produits repris aux nos 36, 70 et 74 de la Classification fédérale des approvisionnements (FSC)) (Aux fins de l'article XXIII, les considérations de sécurité nationale qui valent pour le ministère de la Défense nationale s'appliquent également à la Garde côtière canadienne sauf pour les fonctions de la Garde côtière canadienne conservées par le ministère des Transports conformément à l'arrêté pris en vertu de la *Loi sur les restructurations et les transferts d'attributions dans l'administration publique* publié dans la Gazette du Canada, Partie I, sous la référence SI/95-46, soit celles de la Direction des havres et des ports et des divisions régionales des havres et des ports, de la Direction de la réglementation maritime, de la Direction des inspections de navires et les divisions régionales des inspections des navires de la Garde côtière canadienne.)
16. Ministère de la Santé
17. Conseil de recherches médicales
18. Ministère du Développement des ressources humaines
19. Commission de l'assurance-emploi du Canada

9 December 2003 (WT/Let/454)

20. Conseil canadien des relations du travail
21. Ministère des Affaires indiennes et du Nord canadien
22. Ministère de l'Industrie (à l'exclusion des marchés portant sur les produits repris aux n°s 36, 70 et 74 de la Classification fédérale des approvisionnements (FSC) en matière de télécommunications, sauf en ce qui concerne a) la planification et la coordination des services de télécommunications pour les ministères, les conseils et les organismes du gouvernement du Canada, et b) la radiodiffusion, sauf en ce qui concerne la gestion du spectre et les volets techniques de la radiodiffusion.)
23. Conseil national de recherches du Canada
24. Conseil de recherches en sciences naturelles et en génie du Canada
25. Conseil de recherches en sciences humaines
26. Ministère de la Justice
27. Commission canadienne des droits de la personne
28. Commission de révision des lois
29. Cour suprême du Canada
30. Agence des douanes et du revenu du Canada
31. Ministère des Ressources naturelles
32. Commission canadienne de sûreté nucléaire
33. Office national de l'énergie (pour son propre compte)
34. Ministère des Travaux publics et des Services gouvernementaux (pour son propre compte) (à l'exclusion des marchés portant sur les produits repris aux n°s 36, 70 et 74 de la Classification fédérale des approvisionnements (FSC) concernant l'Agence des télécommunications gouvernementales.)
35. Commission de la fonction publique
36. Ministère du Solliciteur général
37. Service correctionnel du Canada
38. Commission nationale des libérations conditionnelles
39. Ministère des Transports (à l'exclusion des marchés portant sur les produits repris aux n°s 36, 70 et 74 de la Classification fédérale des approvisionnements (FSC)) (Aux fins de l'article XXIII, les considérations de sécurité nationale qui valent pour le ministère de la Défense nationale s'appliquent également à la Garde côtière canadienne conservées par le ministère des Transports conform ément à l'arrêté pris en vertu de la *Loi sur les restructurations et les transferts d'attributions dans l'administration publique* publié dans la Gazette du Canada, Partie I, sous la référence SI/95-46, soit celles de la Direction des havres et des ports et des divisions régionales des havres et des ports, de la Direction de la réglementation maritime, de la Direction des inspections de navires et les divisions régionales des inspections des navires de la Garde côtière canadienne.)
40. Secrétariat du Conseil du Trésor
41. Ministère des Anciens combattants
42. Ministère de la Diversification de l'économie de l'Ouest (pour son propre compte)
43. Agence de promotion économique du Canada atlantique (pour son propre compte)
44. Bureau du vérificateur général
45. Développement économique Canada pour les régions du Québec
46. Centre canadien de gestion
47. Conseil de la radiodiffusion et des télécommunications canadiennes (pour son propre compte)
48. Tribunal de l'aviation civile
49. Commissaire à la magistrature fédérale
50. Greffe du Tribunal de la concurrence
51. Commission du droit d'auteur

52. Greffe de la Cour fédérale du Canada
53. Bureau de l'Administrateur de l'Office du transport du grain (pour son propre compte)
54. Conseil de contrôle des renseignements relatifs aux matières dangereuses
55. Bureaux des commissaires du Canada à l'information et à la protection de la vie privée
56. Archives nationales du Canada
57. Conseil national des produits agricoles
58. Bibliothèque nationale
59. Office des transports du Canada (pour son propre compte)
60. Administration du pipeline du Nord (pour son propre compte)
61. Conseil d'examen du prix des médicaments brevetés
62. Agence de surveillance du secteur pétrolier
63. Bureau du Conseil privé
64. Secrétariat des conférences intergouvernementales canadiennes
65. Commissariat aux langues officielles
66. Commission des relations de travail dans la fonction publique
67. Bureau du chef de Cabinet du Gouverneur général
68. Bureau du Directeur général des élections
69. Secrétariat des relations fédérales-provinciales
70. Statistique Canada
71. Greffe de la Cour canadienne de l'impôt
72. Centre canadien d'hygiène et de sécurité au travail
73. Bureau canadien d'enquête sur les accidents de transport et de la sécurité des transports
74. Directeur de l'établissement des soldats
75. Directeur, Loi sur les terres destinées aux anciens combattants
76. Commission de soutien des prix des produits de la pêche
77. Commission des champs de bataille nationaux
78. Gendarmerie royale du Canada
79. Comité externe d'examen de la Gendarmerie royale du Canada
80. Commission des plaintes du public contre la Gendarmerie royale du Canada
81. Ministère de la Défense nationale
82. Agence de la santé publique du Canada

LES PRODUITS SUIVANTS ACHETÉS PAR LE MINISTÈRE DE LA DÉFENSE NATIONALE, LA GARDE CÔTIÈRE ET LA GENDARMERIE ROYALE DU CANADA FONT PARTIE DU CHAMP D'APPLICATION DU PRÉSENT ACCORD, SOUS RÉSERVE DES DISPOSITIONS DE L'ARTICLE XXIII. (LES NUMÉROS SONT CEUX DE LA CLASSIFICATION FÉDÉRALE DES APPROVISIONNEMENTS.)

22. Matériel ferroviaire
23. Véhicules automobiles, remorques et cycles (sauf les autobus compris dans 2310, les camions et remorques militaires compris dans 2320 et 2330, et les véhicules chenillés de combat, d'attaque et de tactique compris dans 2350)
24. Tracteurs
25. Pièces de véhicules
26. Enveloppes et chambres à air
29. Accessoires de moteurs
30. Matériel de transmission de l'énergie mécanique
32. Machines et matériel pour le travail du bois

34. Machines pour le travail des métaux
35. Matériel de service et de commerce
36. Machines industrielles spéciales
37. Machines et matériel agricoles
38. Matériel de construction, d'extraction, d'excavation et d'entretien routier
39. Matériel de manutention des matériaux
40. Cordages, câbles, chaînes et accessoires
41. Matériel de réfrigération et de climatisation
42. Matériel de lutte contre l'incendie, de sauvetage et de sécurité (sauf 4220 : Équipement de plongée et de sauvetage en mer, 4230 : Équipement d'imprégnation et de décontamination)
43. Pompes et compresseurs
44. Matériel de fours, de générateurs de vapeur, de séchage, et réacteurs nucléaires
45. Matériel de plomberie, de chauffage et sanitaire
46. Matériel d'épuration de l'eau et de traitement des eaux usées
47. Éléments de canalisation, tuyaux et accessoires
48. Robinets-vannes
49. Matériel d'ateliers d'entretien et de réparation
52. Instruments de mesure
53. Articles de quincaillerie et abrasifs
54. Éléments de construction préfabriqués et éléments d'échafaudages
55. Bois de construction, sciages, contreplaqués et bois de placage
56. Matériaux de construction
61. Fils électriques, matériel de production et de distribution d'énergie
62. Lampes et accessoires d'éclairage
63. Systèmes d'alarme et de signalisation
65. Fournitures et matériel médicaux, dentaires et vétérinaires
66. Instruments, matériel de laboratoire (sauf 6615 : Mécanismes de pilotage automatique et éléments de gyroscopes d'aéronefs, 6665 : Instruments et appareils de détection des dangers)
67. Matériel photographique
68. Substances et produits chimiques
69. Matériels et appareils d'enseignement
70. Matériel d'informatique général, logiciel, fournitures et matériel auxiliaire (sauf 7010 : Configurations d' équipement de traitement automatique des données)
71. Meubles
72. Articles et appareils pour l'équipement des ménages et des lieux publics
73. Matériel de cuisine et de table
74. Machines de bureau, matériel de bureaumatique et d'informatique de bureau
75. Fournitures et appareils de bureau
76. Livres, cartes et publications diverses (sauf 7650 : Plans et spécifications)
77. Instruments de musique, phonographes et récepteurs radiophoniques domestiques
78. Matériel de plaisance et d'athlétisme
79. Matériel et fournitures de nettoyage
80. Pinceaux, peinture, produits d'obturation et adhésifs
81. Conteneurs, matériaux et fournitures d'emballage
85. Articles de toilette
87. Fournitures pour l'agriculture
88. Animaux vivants
91. Combustibles, lubrifiants, huiles et cires
93. Fabrications non métalliques

94. Matières brutes non métalliques
96. Minerais, minéraux et leurs dérivés primaires
99. Divers

Note relative à l'Annexe 1

Les Notes générales s'appliquent à la présente annexe.

ANNEXE 2

Entités des gouvernements sous-centraux

Valeurs de seuil:	355 000 DTS	-	***Produits***
	355 000 DTS	-	***Services*** dont la liste initiale sera établie au plus tard pour le 15 avril 1994, la liste définitive devant être communiquée dans un délai de 18 mois après la conclusion du nouvel accord sur les marchés publics.
	5 000 000 DTS	-	***Services de construction*** dont la liste initiale sera établie au plus tard pour le 15 avril 1994, la liste définitive devant être communiquée dans un délai de 18 mois après la conclusion du nouvel accord sur les marchés publics.

Liste des entités:

Le gouvernement canadien offre d'inclure des entités des dix provinces sur la base des engagements obtenus des gouvernements provinciaux. La liste initiale des entités provinciales sera établie au plus tard pour le 15 avril 1994, la liste définitive devant être communiquée dans un délai de 18 mois après la conclusion du nouvel Accord sur les marchés publics.

Notes relatives à l'Annexe 2

1. Exceptions valables pour toutes les provinces: acier, véhicules automobiles et charbon.

   Exceptions propres à certaines provinces: en outre, un nombre limité d'exceptions concernant les différentes provinces pourront être spécifiées à une date ultérieure, conformément aux engagements reçus des provinces.

2. Rien dans la présente offre ne sera interprété comme empêchant une entité d'une province d'appliquer des restrictions visant à promouvoir la qualité générale de l'environnement dans cette province, pour autant que ces restrictions ne constituent pas des obstacles déguisés au commerce international.

3. La présente offre ne s'applique pas aux marchés passés par une entité visée pour le compte d'une entité non visé e.

4. Les Notes générales s'appliquent à la présente annexe.

1 March 2000 (WT/Let/330)

ANNEXE 3

Entreprises publiques

Valeurs de seuil:	355 000 DTS	-	***Produits***
	355 000 DTS	-	***Services*** visés à l'Annexe 4
	5 000 000 DTS	-	***Travaux*** visés à l'Annexe 5

Entreprises fédérales

1. Société canadienne des postes
2. Commission de la capitale nationale
3. Administration de la voie maritime du Saint-Laurent. (Pour plus de précision, les dispositions du paragraphe 4 de l'article XIX s'appliquent aux marchés passés par l'Administration de la voie maritime du Saint-Laurent, aux fins de la protection des renseignements commerciaux communiqués à titre confidentiel.)
4. Monnaie royale canadienne (à l'exclusion des marchés passés par la Monnaie royale canadienne, ou en son nom, pour l'achat de matières premières destinées à être utilisées directement pour frapper de la monnaie n'ayant pas cours légal au Canada. Pour plus de précision, les dispositions du paragraphe 4 de l'article XIX s'appliquent aux marchés passés par la Monnaie royale canadienne aux fins de la protection des renseignements commerciaux communiqués à titre confidentiel).
5. Musée canadien des civilisations
6. Musée canadien de la nature
7. Musée des beaux-arts du Canada
8. Musée national des sciences et de la technologie
9. Construction de Défense (1951) Limitée.

Entreprises sous-centrales

La liste initiale des entreprises sous-centrales qui entrent dans le champ d'application de l'accord pour ce qui est des produits, des services et des services de construction sera établie au plus tard pour le 15 avril 1994, la liste définitive devant être communiquée dans un délai de 18 mois après la conclusion du nouvel Accord sur les marchés publics.

Note relative à l'Annexe 3

Les Notes générales s'appliquent à la présente annexe.

ANNEXE 4

Services

Le Canada offre d'inclure dans la présente annexe relative aux "Services" les entités fédérales énumérées à l'Annexe 1 et les entreprises fédérales énumérées à l'Annexe 3. Pour ce qui est des entités sous-centrales visées à l'Annexe 2 et des entreprises sous-centrales visées à l'Annexe 3, la liste initiale des services entrant dans le champ d'application de l'accord sera établie au plus tard pour le 15 avril 1994, la liste définitive devant être communiquée dans un délai de 18 mois après la conclusion du nouvel Accord sur les marchés publics. S'agissant des termes du présent accord, les services qui seront inclus sont ceux qui sont indiqués dans le document MTN.GNS/W/120. Sur le plan intérieur, le Canada utilisera le "Système commun de classification" aux fins de la mise en oeuvre du présent accord. La présente liste de services pourra être révisée à la suite d'autres travaux techniques entre les Parties et des ajustements pourront y être apportés, selon qu'il sera approprié, afin que le contenu en soit équitable.

Le Canada offre d'inclure les services suivants classés selon le système de classification des services de la CPC:

861	Services juridiques (conseils juridiques en matière de droit international et de droit étranger uniquement)
862	Services comptables, d'audit et de tenue de livres
863	Services de conseil fiscal (à l'exclusion des services juridiques)
8671	Services d'architecture
8672	Services d'ingénierie
8673	Services intégrés d'ingénierie (sauf 86731: Services intégrés d'ingénierie pour les projets de construction clés en main d'infrastructures de transport)
8674	Services d'aménagement urbain et d'architecture paysagère
841	Services de consultations en matière d'installation des matériels informatiques
842	Services de réalisation de logiciels, y compris les services de consultations en matière de systèmes et de logiciels, ainsi que les services d'analyse de systèmes, de conception, de programmation et de maintenance
843	Services de traitement de données, y compris les services de traitement, de tabulation et de gestion des installations
844	Services de base de données
845	Services d'entretien et de réparation de machines et de matériel de bureau, y compris les ordinateurs

849	Autres services informatiques
821	Services immobiliers se rapportant à des biens propres ou loués
822	Services immobiliers à forfait ou sous contrat
83106 à 83109 uniquement	Services de location simple ou en crédit-bail de machines et de matériel, sans opérateurs
83203 à 83209 uniquement	Services de location simple ou en crédit-bail d'articles personnels et domestiques
86501	Services de consultations en matière de gestion générale
86503	Services de consultations en matière de gestion de la commercialisation
86504	Services de consultations en matière de gestion des ressources humaines
86505	Services de consultations en matière de gestion de la production
8660	Services connexes aux services de consultations en matière de gestion (sauf 86602: Services d'arbitrage et de conciliation)
8676	Services d'essais et d'analyses techniques, y compris d'inspection et de contrôle de la qualité (à l'exclusion du matériel de transport et du numéro 58 de la FSC)
8814	Services annexes à la sylviculture et à l'exploitation forestière, y compris la gestion des forêts
883	Services annexes aux industries extractives, y compris les services d'exploration et de forage
633	Services de réparation d'articles personnels et domestiques
8861 à 8864 et 8866	Services de réparation annexes à la fabrication de produits en métaux, de machines et de matériel
874	Services de nettoyage de bâtiments
876	Services de conditionnement
7512	Services commerciaux de courrier (y compris les services de courrier multimodaux)
7523	Services de courrier électronique
7523	Services d'audiomessagerie téléphonique

7523	Services directs de recherche d'informations permanente et de serveur de base de données
7523	Services d'échange électronique de données
7523	Services améliorés/à valeur ajoutée de télécopie, y compris enregistrements et retransmission et enregistrement et recherche
	Services de conversion de codes et de protocoles
843	Services de traitement en direct de l'information et/ou de données (y compris traitement de transactions)
940	Services d'assainissement et d'enlèvement des ordures, services de voirie et services analogues
641	Services d'hôtellerie et services d'hébergement analogues
642-643	Services de restauration et de vente de boissons
7471	Services d'agences de voyages et d'organisateurs touristiques

Notes relatives à l'Annexe 4

1. Les Notes générales s'appliquent à la présente annexe.

2. La présente offre est faite sous réserve des conditions énoncées dans l'offre du Canada relative au commerce des services.

3. Dans le domaine des télécommunications, l'offre du Canada se limite aux services améliorés ou à valeur ajoutée qui sont fournis au moyen d'installations de télécommunications de base louées à des fournisseurs de réseaux publics de transport des télécommunications.

4. L'offre du Canada ne comprend **pas** ce qui suit:

   * les contrats de gestion et d'exploitation de certaines installations publiques ou privées utilisées à des fins publiques, y compris la recherche-développement financée par le gouvernement fédéral;

   * la frappe de la monnaie;

   * les services d'utilité publique;

   * les services d'architecture et d'ingénierie se rapportant à des aérodromes ainsi qu'à des installations de communications ou de missiles;

   * la construction navale et la réparation de navires ainsi que les services d'architecture et d'ingénierie s'y rapportant;

* s'agissant des produits achetés par le Ministère de la défense nationale, la Gendarmerie royale du Canada et la Garde côtière canadienne, tous les services qui ne sont pas indiqués comme entrant dans le champ d'application du présent accord;

* les services achetés pour appuyer les forces militaires se trouvant à l'étranger;

* les services d'imprimerie et d'édition; et

* les marchés de services de transport qui font partie d'un marché ou qui y sont accessoires.

ANNEXE 5

Services de construction

Le Canada offre d'inclure dans la présente annexe relative aux "Services de construction" les entités fédérales énumérées à l'Annexe 1 et les entreprises fédérales énumérées à l'Annexe 3. Pour ce qui est des entit és sous-centrales visées à l'Annexe 2 et des entreprises sous-centrales visées à l'Annexe 3, la liste initiale des services de construction entrant dans le champ d'application de l'accord sera établie au plus tard pour le 15 avril 1994, la liste définitive devant être communiquée dans un délai de 18 mois après la conclusion du nouvel Accord sur les marchés publics.

Définition:

Un contrat de services de construction est un contrat qui a pour objectif la réalisation, par quelque moyen que ce soit, de travaux de construction d'ouvrages de génie civil ou de bâtiments, au sens de la division 51 de la Classification centrale de produits (CPC).

Liste de services relevant de la division 51 de la CPC:

Tous les services énumérés dans la division 51 de la CPC.

Notes relatives à l'Annexe 5

1. Nonobstant les dispositions du présent accord, celui-ci ne s'applique pas:

   a) aux marchés portant sur des travaux de dragage; ni

   b) aux marchés de travaux passés pour le compte des ministères des transports.

2. Les Notes générales s'appliquent à la présente annexe.

1 March 2000 (WT/Let/330)

NOTES GENERALES

1. Nonobstant les présentes annexes, l'accord n'est pas applicable dans les cas suivants:

a) construction navale et réparation de navires;

b) chemins de fer urbains et matériel de transport urbain, systèmes, composants et matériaux entrant dans leur fabrication, ainsi que tout le matériel en fer ou en acier destiné à des ouvrages;

c) marchés portant sur les produits relevant du n° 58 de la Classification fédérale des approvisionnements (matériel de communication, matériel de détection des radiations et d'émission de rayonnement cohérent);

d) marchés réservés aux petites entreprises et aux entreprises détenues par des minorités;

e) marchés de produits agricoles passés en application de programmes de soutien à l'agriculture ou de programmes d'aide alimentaire;

f) exemptions pour des raisons de sécurité nationale, visant notamment les achats de pétrole nécessaires au maintien de réserves stratégiques;

g) exceptions pour des raisons de sécurité nationale, visant notamment les marchés passés aux fins du contrôle des matières ou des technologies nucléaires.

2. Pour le Canada, les marchés entrant dans le champ d'application s'entendent de transactions contractuelles visant l'acquisition de biens ou de services devant bénéficier directement au gouvernement ou être utilisés directement par celui-ci. Le processus de passation d'un marché débute après qu'une entité a défini ses besoins et se poursuit jusque et y compris l'adjudication. Ne sont pas compris les accords non contractuels et toute forme d'aide publique, y compris, mais pas uniquement, les accords de coopération, les subventions, les prêts, les apports en capital, les garanties, les incitations fiscales et la fourniture par le gouvernement fédéral de produits et de services à des particuliers, des entreprises, des institutions privées et des gouvernements sous-centraux. Ne sont pas compris non plus les achats réalisés à des fins de revente commerciale ou effectués par une entité ou une entreprise auprès d'une autre entité ou d'une autre entreprise du Canada.

3. Toute exclusion liée expressément ou d'une manière générale à des entités ou à des entreprises fédérales ou sous-centrales énumérées à l'Annexe 1, à l'Annexe 2 ou à l'Annexe 3 s'appliquera également à toute entité ou entreprise qui pourrait leur succéder, afin de maintenir la valeur de la présente offre.

4. Tant que toutes les Parties ne seront pas convenues d'un commun accord d'une liste des services entrant dans le champ d'application, un service énuméré à l'Annexe 4 ne sera visé pour ce qui concerne une Partie donnée que dans la mesure où cette Partie aura accordé un accès réciproque au service considéré.

5. Dans le cas où une entité adjugera un marché qui n'est pas visé par le présent accord, celui-ci ne sera pas interprété comme s'appliquant à tout produit ou service entrant dans ce marché.

1 March 2000 (WT/Let/330)

6. S'agissant des produits et des services (y compris les travaux) énumérés aux Annexes 2 et 3, l'offre du Canada est subordonnée à la négociation avec les autres Parties d'engagements mutuellement acceptables (y compris de seuils), les engagements initiaux devant être spécifié s au plus tard pour le 15 avril 1994 et les engagements spécifiques confirmés dans un délai de 18 mois après la conclusion du nouvel Accord sur les marchés publics.

7. L'accord ne s'applique pas aux marchés passés en vertu d'un accord international et portant sur la réalisation ou l'exploitation en commun d'un ouvrage.

8. En ce qui concerne l'Union européenne, le Canada exclut de son offre les marchés portant sur les produits relevant des n° 70, 74 et 36 de la FSC tant qu'un accès réciproque ne lui aura pas été accordé.

9. En ce qui concerne l'Union européenne, le présent accord ne s'applique pas aux marchés passés par les entités visées aux Annexes 1 et 2 et portant sur des activités dans les secteurs de l'eau potable, de l'énergie, des transports et des télécommunications.

EUROPEAN COMMUNITIES
欧洲共同体

EUROPEAN COMMUNITIES
COMMUNAUTES EUROPEENNES
COMUNIDADES EUROPEAS

ANNEX 1- ANNEXE 1 - ANEXO 1

Entities which Procure in Accordance with the Provisions of this Agreement
Entités qui passent des marchés conformément aux dispositions du présent accord
Entidades que se rigen en sus contratos por las disposiciones del presente acuerdo

SUPPLIES / FOURNITURES / SUMINISTROS

Thresholds:	SDR 130,000
Valeurs de seuil:	DTS 130 000
Valores de umbral:	DEG 130.000

SERVICES / SERVICES / SERVICIOS
specified in Annex 4 / spécifiés dans l'Annexe 4 / detallados en el Anexo 4

Thresholds:	SDR 130,000
Valeurs de seuil:	DTS 130 000
Valores de umbral:	DEG 130.000

WORKS / TRAVAUX / OBRAS
specified in Annex 5 / spécifiés dans l'Annexe 5 / detalladas en el Anexo 5

Thresholds:	SDR 5,000,000
Valeurs de seuil:	DTS 5 000 000
Valores de umbral:	DEG 5.000.000

***LIST OF ENTITIES / LISTE DES ENTITES / LISTA DE LAS ENTIDADES*:**

1. EUROPEAN COMMUNITIES ENTITIES
ENTITES DE LA COMMUNAUTE EUROPEENNE
ENTIDADES DE LA COMUNIDAD EUROPEA:

1. THE COUNCIL OF THE EUROPEAN UNION / LE CONSEIL DE L'UNION EUROPÉENNE / EL CONSEJO DE LA UNIÓN EUROPEA.

2. THE EUROPEAN COMMISSION / LA COMMISSION EUROPÉENNE / LA COMISIÓN EUROPEA.

2. THE FOLLOWING CONTRACTING AUTHORITIES OF THE STATE
LES POUVOIRS ADJUDICATEURS DE L'ÉTAT QUI SUIVENT
LOS SIGUIENTES PODERES ADJUDICADORES DEL ESTADO:

欧洲共同体

附件 1

依照本协定条款进行采购的实体

供应品

门槛金额: 130,000 特别提款权

服务
附件 4 列出

门槛金额: 130,000 特别提款权

工程
附件 5 列出

门槛金额: 5,000,000 特别提款权

实体清单:

1.	**欧洲共同体**:

1. 欧洲联盟理事会

2. 欧洲联盟委员会

2.	**下列各国缔约机构**:

2007 年 1 月 1 日 (WT/Let/556)

BELGIUM - BELGIQUE - BÉLGICA

(La version française fait foi)

(A) L'État fédéral:

1. Services du Premier Ministre
2. Ministère des Affaires économiques
3. Ministère des Affaires étrangères, du Commerce extérieur et de la Coopération au développement
4. Ministère des Affaires sociales, de la Santé publique et de l'Environnement
5. Ministère des Classes moyennes et de l'Agriculture
6. Ministère des Communications et de l'Infrastructure
7. Ministère de la Défense nationale[1]
8. Ministère de l'Emploi et du Travail
9. Ministère des Finances
10. Ministère de la Fonction publique
11. Ministère de l'Intérieur
12. Ministère de la Justice

(B) Autres:

1. la Poste[2]
2. la Régie des Bâtiments
3. L'Office national de Sécurité Sociale
4. L'Institut national d'Assurances sociales pour Travailleurs indépendants
5. L'Institut national d'Assurance Maladie-Invalidité
6. L'Office national des Pensions
7. La Caisse auxiliaire d'Assurance Maladie-Invalidité
8. Le Fonds des Maladies professionnelles
9. L'Office national de l'Emploi

---

[1] Matériel non militaire figurant dans la partie (3) de la présente annexe.
[2] Activités postales visées par la loi du 24 décembre 1993.

比利时

(仅以法文为准)

(A) 联邦机构：

1. 首相府
2. 经济事务部
3. 外交、外贸和发展合作部
4. 社会事务、公共卫生和环境部
5. 中产阶级农业部
6. 通信基础设施部
7. 国防部 [1]
8. 就业和劳动部
9. 财政部
10. 国家职能部
11. 内政部
12. 司法部

(B) 其他：

1. 邮政局 [2]
2. 建筑管理局
3. 国家社会安全办公室
4. 国家自由职业者社会保险局
5. 国家病残保险局
6. 国家养老保险办公室
7. 病残保险辅助基金
8. 职业病基金
9. 国家就业办公室

[1] 非军事物资包含在本附件第 3 部分。
[2] 《邮政法》自 1993 年 12 月 3 日起生效。

BULGARIA – BULGARIE - BULGARIA

(Authentic in the English language only)

1. Администрация на Народното събрание (Administration of the National Assembly)
2. Администрация на Президента (Administration of the President)
3. Администрация на Министерския съвет (Administration of the Council of Ministers)
4. Конституционен съд (Constitutional Court)
5. Българска народна банка (Bulgarian National Bank)
6. Министерство на външните работи (Ministry of Foreign Affairs)
7. Министерство на вътрешните работи (Ministry of the Interior)
8. Министерство на държавната администрация и административната реформа (Ministry of State Administration and Administrative Reform)
9. Министерство на държавната политика при бедствия и аварии (Ministry of State Policy for Disasters and Accidents)
10. Министерство на земеделието и горите (Ministry of Agriculture and Forestry)
11. Министерство на здравеопазването (Ministry of Health)
12. Министерство на икономиката и енергетиката (Ministry of Economy and Energy)
13. Министерство на културата (Ministry of Culture)
14. Министерство на образованието и науката (Ministry of Education and Science)
15. Министерство на околната среда и водите (Ministry of Environment and Water)
16. Министерство на отбраната (Ministry of Defence[3])
17. Министерство на правосъдието (Ministry of Justice)
18. Министерство на регионалното развитие и благоустройството (Ministry of Regional Development and Public Works)
19. Министерство на транспорта (Ministry of Transport)
20. Министерство на труда и социалната политика (Ministry of Labour and Social Policy)
21. Министерство на финансите (Ministry of Finance)

[3] Non-warlike materials contained in Part (3) of this Annex.

保加利亚

(仅以英文为准)

1. 国民议会
2. 总统府
3. 部长会议
4. 宪法法院
5. 保加利亚国家银行
6. 外交部
7. 内政部
8. 国家行政管理和行政改革部
9. 灾害和事故国家政策部
10. 农业和林业部
11. 卫生部
12. 经济和能源部
13. 文化部
14. 教育和科学部
15. 环境和水资源部
16. 国防部 [3]
17. 司法部
18. 地区发展和公共工程部
19. 运输部
20. 劳动和社会政策部
21. 财政部

[3]非军事物资包含在本附件第 3 部分。

22. държавни агенции, държавни комисии, изпълнителни агенции и други държавни институции, създадени със закон или с постановление на Министерския съвет, които имат функции във връзка с осъществяването на изпълнителната власт (state agencies, state commissions, executive agencies and other state authorities established by law or by Council of Ministers' decree having a function relating to the exercise of executive power):

(1) Агенция за ядрено регулиране (Nuclear Regulatory Agency)

(2) Държавна комисия за енергийно и водно регулиране (Energy and Water State Regulatory Commission)

(3) Държавна комисия по сигурността на информацията (State Commission on Information Security)

(4) Комисия за защита на конкуренцията (Commission for Protection of Competition)

(5) Комисия за защита на личните данни (Commission for Personal Data Protection)

(6) Комисия за защита от дискриминация (Commission for Protection Against Discrimination)

(7) Комисия за регулиране на съобщенията (Communications Regulation Commission)

(8) Комисия за финансов надзор (Financial Supervision Commission)

(9) Патентно ведомство на Република България (Patent Office of the Republic of Bulgaria)

(10) Сметна палата на Република България (National Audit Office of the Republic of Bulgaria)

(11) Агенция за приватизация (Privatization Agency)

(12) Агенция за следприватизационен контрол (Agency for Post-privatization Control)

(13) Български институт по метрология (Bulgarian Institute for Metrology)

(14) Главно управление на архивите (General Department of Archives)

(15) Държавна агенция "Държавен резерв и военновременни запаси" (State Agency "State Reserve and War-Time Stocks")

(16) Държавна агенция за бежанците (State Agency for Refugees)

22. 根据法律或部长理事会命令设立的具有与行使行政权力有关的职能的国家局、国家委员会、行政机构和其他国家机构：

(1) 原子能管理局

(2) 国家能源和水资源管理委员会

(3) 国家信息安全委员会

(4) 保护竞争委员会

(5) 个人信息保护委员会

(6) 反歧视委员会

(7) 通信管理委员会

(8) 金融监管委员会

(9) 保加利亚共和国专利办公室

(10) 保加利亚共和国国家审计办公室

(11) 私有化局

(12) 后私有化控制局

(13) 保加利亚气象研究所

(14) 档案总局

(15) 国家"国家储备和战时储备"局

(16) 国家难民局

(17) Държавна агенция за българите в чужбина (State Agency for Bulgarians Abroad)

(18) Държавна агенция за закрила на детето (State Agency for Child Protection)

(19) Държавна агенция за информационни технологии и съобщения (State Agency for Information Technology and Communications)

(20) Държавна агенция за метрологичен и технически надзор (State Agency for Metrological and Technical Surveillance)

(21) Държавна агенция за младежта и спорта (State Agency for Youth and Sports)

(22) Държавна агенция по туризма (State Agency for Tourism)

(23) Държавна комисия по стоковите борси и тържища (State Commission on Commodity Exchanges and Market-places)

(24) Институт по публична администрация и европейска интеграция (Institute of Public Administration and European Integration)

(25) Национален статистически институт (National Statistical Institute)

(26) Агенция "Митници" (Customs Agency)

(27) Агенция за държавна и финансова инспекция (Public Financial Inspection Agency)

(28) Агенция за държавни вземания (State Receivables Collection Agency)

(29) Агенция за социално подпомагане (Social Assistance Agency)

(30) Агенция за финансово разузнаване (Financial Intelligence Agency)

(31) Агенция за хората с увреждания (Agency for Persons with Disabilities)

(32) Агенция по вписванията (Registry Agency)

(33) Агенция по енергийна ефективност (Energy Efficiency Agency)

(34) Агенция по заетостта (Employment Agency)

(35) Агенция по кадастъра (Cadastre Agency)

(36) Агенция по обществени поръчки (Public Procurement Agency)

(37) Българска агенция за инвестиции (Bulgarian Investment Agency)

(38) Главна дирекция "Гражданска въздухоплавателна администрация" (General Directorate "Civil Aviation Administration")

(17) 国家海外保加利亚人事务局

(18) 国家儿童保护局

(19) 国家信息技术和通信局

(20) 国家计量和技术监督局

(21) 国家青年和运动局

(22) 国家旅游局

(23) 国家商品交换和市场局

(24) 公共管理和欧洲一体化研究所

(25) 国家统计研究所

(26) 海关局

(27) 公共财政监督局

(28) 国家债务收缴局

(29) 社会援助局

(30) 金融情报局

(31) 残疾人事务局

(32) 注册局

(33) 能源效率局

(34) 就业局

(35) 不动产局

(36) 公共采购局

(37) 保加利亚投资局

(38) 民用航空管理总局

(39) Дирекция за национален строителен контрол (Directorate for National Construction Supervision)

(40) Държавна комисия по хазарта (State Commission on Gambling)

(41) Изпълнителна агенция "Автомобилна администрация" (Executive Agency "Automobile Administration")

(42) Изпълнителна агенция "Борба с градушките" (Executive Agency "Hail Suppression")

(43) Изпълнителна агенция "Българска служба за акредитация" (Executive Agency "Bulgarian Accreditation Service")

(44) Изпълнителна агенция "Главна инспекция по труда" (Executive Agency "General Labour Inspectorate")

(45) Изпълнителна агенция "Железопътна администрация" (Executive Agency "Railway Administration")

(46) Изпълнителна агенция "Морска администрация" (Executive Agency "Maritime Administration")

(47) Изпълнителна агенция "Национален филмов център" (Executive Agency "National Film Centre")

(48) Изпълнителна агенция "Пристанищна администрация" (Executive Agency "Port Administration")

(49) Изпълнителна агенция "Проучване и поддържане на река Дунав" (Executive Agency "Exploration and Maintenance of the Danube River")

(50) Изпълнителна агенция "Пътища" (Roads Executive Agency)

(51) Изпълнителна агенция за икономически анализи и прогнози (Executive Agency for Economic Analysis and Forecasting)

(52) Изпълнителна агенция за насърчаване на малките и средни предприятия (Executive Agency for Promotion of Small and Medium Enterprises)

(53) Изпълнителна агенция по лекарствата (Executive Agency on Medicines)

(54) Изпълнителна агенция по лозата и виното (Executive Agency on Vine and Wine)

(55) Изпълнителна агенция по околна среда (Executive Environment Agency)

(56) Изпълнителна агенция по почвените ресурси (Executive Agency on Soil Resources)

(39) 国家建设监督局

(40) 国家赌博委员会

(41) “汽车管理”执行局

(42) “防雹”执行局

(43) “保加利亚认证服务”执行局

(44) “劳动总监察”执行局

(45) “铁路管理”执行局

(46) “海事管理”执行局

(47) “国家电影中心”执行局

(48) “港口管理”执行局

(49) “多瑙河开发和养护” 执行局

(50) 道路执行局

(51) 经济分析和预测执行局

(52) 中小企业促进执行理局

(53) 药品执行局

(54) 葡萄和葡萄酒执行局

(55) 环境执行局

(56) 土地资源执行局

(57) Изпълнителна агенция по рибарство и аквакултури (Executive Agency on Fisheries and Aquaculture)

(58) Изпълнителна агенция по селекция и репродукция в животновъдството (Executive Agency for Selection and Reproduction in Animal Husbandry)

(59) Изпълнителна агенция по сортоизпитване, апробация и семеконтрол (Executive Agency for Plant Variety Testing, Field Inspection and Seed Control)

(60) Изпълнителна агенция по трансплантация (Transplantation Executive Agency)

(61) Изпълнителна агенция по хидромелиорации (Executive Agency on Hydromelioration)

(62) Комисията за защита на потребителите (Commission for Consumer Protection)

(63) Контролно-техническата инспекция (Control Technical Inspectorate)

(64) Национална агенция за приходите (National Revenue Agency)

(65) Национална ветеринарномедицинска служба (National Veterinary Service)

(66) Национална служба за растителна защита (National Service for Plant Protection)

(67) Национална служба по зърното и фуражите (National Grain and Feed Service)

(68) Национално управление по горите (National Forestry Board)

(57) 渔业和水产执行局

(58) 动物繁殖选择和繁育执行局

(59) 植物种类测试、现场检验和种子检验执行局

(60) 移植器官执行局

(61) 水利土壤改良执行局

(62) 消费者保护委员会

(63) 控制技术监察局

(64) 国家税务局

(65) 国家兽医局

(66) 国家植物保护局

(67) 国家粮食和饲料局

(68) 国家林业局

CZECH REPUBLIC – REPUBLIQUE TCHEQUE – REPÚBLICA CHECA

(Authentic in the English language only)

Contracting authorities are the following (non-exhaustive list):

Ministerstvo dopravy (Ministry of Transport)
Ministerstvo informatiky (Ministry of Informatics)
Ministerstvo financí (Ministry of Finance)
Ministerstvo kultury (Ministry of Culture)
Ministerstvo obrany (Ministry of Defence)[4]
Ministerstvo pro místní rozvoj (Ministry for Regional Development)
Ministerstvo práce a sociálních věcí (Ministry of Labour and Social Affairs)
Ministerstvo průmyslu a obchodu (Ministry of Industry and Trade)
Ministerstvo spravedlnosti (Ministry of Justice)
Ministerstvo školství, mládeže a tělovýchovy (Ministry of Education, Youth and Sports)
Ministerstvo vnitra (Ministry of the Interior)
Ministerstvo zahraničních věcí (Ministry of Foreign Affairs)
Ministerstvo zdravotnictví (Ministry of Health)
Ministerstvo zemědělství (Ministry of Agriculture)
Ministerstvo životního prostředí (Ministry of the Environment)
Poslanecká sněmovna PČR (Chamber of Deputies of the Parliament of the Czech Republic)
Senát PČR (Senate of the Parliament of the Czech Republic)
Kancelář prezidenta (Office of the President)
Český statistický úřad (Czech Statistical Office)
Český úřad zeměměřičský a katastrální (Czech Office for Surveying, Mapping and Cadastre)
Úřad průmyslového vlastnictví (Industrial Property Office)
Úřad pro ochranu osobních údajů (Office for Personal Data Protection)
Bezpečnostní informační služba (Security Information Service)
Národní bezpečnostní úřad (National Security Authority)
Česká akademie věd (Academy of Sciences of the Czech Republic)

[4] Non-warlike materials contained in Part (3) of this Annex.

捷克

(仅以英文为准)

缔约机关如下 (非详尽清单):

运输部
信息部
财政部
文化部
国防部[4]
地区发展部
劳动和社会事务部
工业和贸易部
司法部
教育、青年和体育部
内务部
外交部
卫生部
农业部
环境部
捷克共和国议会众议院
捷克共和国议会参议院
总统办公室
捷克统计局
捷克勘测、测绘和地籍管理局
工业产权办公室
个人资料保护办公室
安全情报局
国家安全局
捷克共和国科学院

[4]非军事物资包含在本附件第 3 部分。

Vězeňská služba (Prison Service)

Český báňský úřad (Czech Mining Authority)

Úřad pro ochranu hospodářské soutěže (Office for the Protection of Competition)

Správa státních hmotných rezerv (Administration of the State Material Reserves)

Státní úřad pro jadernou bezpečnost (State Office for Nuclear Safety)

Komise pro cenné papíry (Czech Securities Commission)

Energetický regulační úřad (Energy Regulatory Office)

Úřad vlády České republiky (Office of the Government of the Czech Republic)

Ústavní soud (Constitutional Court)

Nejvyšší soud (Supreme Court)

Nejvyšší správní soud (Supreme Administrative Court)

Nejvyšší státní zastupitelství (Supreme Public Prosecutor's Office)

Nejvyšší kontrolní úřad (Supreme Audit Office)

Kancelář Veřejného ochránce práv (Office of the Public Defender of Rights)

Grantová agentura České republiky (Grant Agency of the Czech Republic)

Český úřad bezpečnosti práce (Czech Authority of Safety Work)

Český telekomunikační úřad (Czech Telecommunication Office)

监狱管理局
捷克矿业局
竞争保护办公室
国家物资储备管理局
国家核安全办公室
捷克证券委员会
能源管理办公室
捷克共和国政府办公厅
宪法法院
最高法院
最高行政法院
最高检察官公署
最高审计署
公权维护官公署
捷克共和国科学基金会
捷克安全生产局
捷克电信办公室

DENMARK - DANEMARK - DINAMARCA

(Authentic in the English language only)

1.	(Parliament) - (Auditor General of Denmark)		Folketinget - Rigsrevisionen
2.	Prime Minister's Office		
3.	Ministry of Foreign Affairs	-	2 departments
4.	Ministry of Labour	-	5 agencies and institutions
5.	Ministry of Housing and Urban Affairs	-	7 agencies and institutions
6.	Ministry of Industry and Trade	-	7 agencies and institutions
7.	Ministry of Finance	-	3 agencies and institutions
8.	Ministry of Research	-	1 agency
9.	Ministry of Defence[5] (1)	-	Several institutions
10.	Ministry of the Interior	-	2 agencies
11.	Ministry of Justice	-	2 directorates and several police offices and courts
12.	Ministry of Ecclesiastical Affairs	-	10 diocesan authorities
13.	Ministry of Cultural Affairs	-	3 institutions and several state-owned museums and higher education institutions
14.	Ministry of Agriculture and Fisheries	-	23 directorates and institutions
15.	Ministry of Environment and Energy	-	6 agencies and research establishment "Risø"
16.	Ministry of Taxes and Duties	-	1 agency
17.	Ministry of Social Affairs	-	4 agencies and institutions
18.	Ministry of Health	-	Several institutions including the State Serum Institute
19.	Ministry of Education	-	6 directorates and 12 universities and other higher education institutions
20.	Ministry of Economic Affairs	-	Statistical bureau (Statistics Denmark)
21.	Ministry of Transport		

[5] Non-warlike materials contained in Part (3) of this Annex.

丹麦

(仅以英文为准)

1.	(丹麦议会) –丹麦总审计署		
2.	首相府		
3.	外交部	-	2 个司局
4.	劳工部	-	5 个机构
5.	住房和城市事务部	-	7 个机构
6.	工业和贸易部	-	7 个机构
7.	财政部	-	3 个机构
8.	研究部	-	1 个机构
9.	国防部[5] (1)	-	若干机构
10.	内政部	-	2 个机构
11.	司法部	-	2 个司和若干警察局和法院
12.	宗教事务部	-	10 个 教区管理机构
13.	文化事务部	-	3 个机构和若干国家博物馆和高等教育机构
14.	农业和渔业部	-	23 个司和机构
15.	环境和能源部	-	6 个机构和“瑞索”实验室
16.	税务部	-	1 个机构
17.	社会事务部	-	4 个机构
18.	卫生部	-	若干机构，包括国家血清研究所
19.	教育部	-	6 个司和 12 所大学及其他高等教育机构
20.	经济事务部	-	统计局 (丹麦统计局)
21.	运输部		

[5] 非军事物资包含在本附件第 3 部分。

GERMANY - ALLEMAGNE - ALEMANIA

(Authentic in the English language only)

1.	Federal Foreign Office	Auswärtiges Amt
2.	Federal Chancellery	Bundeskanzleramt
3.	Federal Ministry of Labour and Social Affairs	Bundesministerium für Arbeit und Sozialordnung
4.	Federal Ministry of Education, Science, Research and Technology	Bundesministerium für Bildung, Wissenschaft, Forschung und Technologie
5.	Federal Ministry for Food, Agriculture and Forestry	Bundesministerium für Ernährung, Landwirtschaft und Forsten
6.	Federal Ministry of Finance	Bundesministerium der Finanzen
7.	Federal Ministry of the Interior (civil goods only)	Bundesministerium des Innern
8.	Federal Ministry of Health	Bundesministerium für Gesundheit
9.	Federal Ministry for Family Affairs, Senior Citizens, Women and Youth	Bundesministerium für Familie, Senioren, Frauen und Jugend
10.	Federal Ministry of Justice	Bundesministerium der Justiz
11.	Federal Ministry for Regional Planning, Building and Urban Development	Bundesministerium für Raumordnung, Bauwesen und Städtebau
12.	Federal Ministry of Post and Telecommunications[6]	Bundesministerium für Post- und Telekommunikation
13	Federal Ministry of Transport	Bundesministerium für Verkehr
14.	Federal Ministry of Economic Affairs	Bundesministerium für Wirtschaft
15.	Federal Ministry for Economic Co-operation	Bundesministerium für wirtschaftliche Zusammenarbeit
16.	Federal Ministry of Defence[7]	Bundesministerium der Verteidigung
17.	Federal Ministry of Environment, Nature Conservation and Reactor Safety	Bundesministerium für Umwelt, Naturschutz und Reaktorsicherheit

Note

According to existing national obligations, the entities contained in this list must, in conformity with special procedures, award contracts to certain groups in order to remove difficulties caused by the last war.

[6] Except telecommunication equipment.
[7] Non-warlike materials contained in Part (3) of this Annex.

德国

(仅以英文为准)

1. 联邦外交部
2. 联邦总理府
3. 联邦劳动和社会事务部
4. 联邦教育、科学、研究和技术部
5. 联邦食品、农业和林业部
6. 联邦财政部
7. 联邦内政部(仅限民用货物)
8. 联邦卫生部
9. 联邦家庭、老人、妇女和青年部
10. 联邦司法部
11. 联邦地区规划、建设和城市发展部
12. 联邦邮政和电信部[6]
13 联邦运输部
14. 联邦经济事务部
15. 联邦经济合作部
16. 联邦国防部[7]
17. 联邦环境、自然保护和核安全部

注释

根据现行国家义务，本清单所含实体在符合特殊程序的情况下，必须将合同授予某些团体以消除上一次战争所带来的困难。

[6]电信设备除外。

[7]非军事物资包含在本附件第 3 部分。

<u>2007 年 1 月 1 日 (WT/Let/556)</u>

ESTONIA – ESTONIE - ESTONIA

(Authentic in the English language only)

1. Vabariigi Presidendi Kantselei (Office of the President of the Republic of Estonia)
2. Eesti Vabariigi Riigikogu (Parliament of the Republic of Estonia)
3. Eesti Vabariigi Riigikohus (Supreme Court of the Republic of Estonia)
4. Riigikontroll (The State Audit Office of the Republic of Estonia)
5. Õiguskantsler (Legal Chancellor)
6. Riigikantselei (The State Chancellery)
7. Rahvusarhiiv (The National Archives of Estonia)
8. Haridus- ja Teadusministeerium (Ministry of Education and Research)
9. Justiitsministeerium (Ministry of Justice)
10. Kaitseministeerium (Ministry of Defence)[8]
11. Keskkonnaministeerium (Ministry of Environment)
12. Kultuuriministeerium (Ministry of Culture)
13. Majandus- ja Kommunikatsiooniministeerium (Ministry for Economy and Communication)
14. Põllumajandusministeerium (Ministry of Agriculture)
15. Rahandusministeerium (Ministry of Finance)
16. Siseministeerium (Ministry of Internal Affairs)
17. Sotsiaalministeerium (Ministry of Social Affairs)
18. Välisministeerium (Ministry of Foreign Affairs)
19. Keeleinspektsioon (The Language Inspectorate)
20. Riigiprokuratuur (Prosecutor's Office)
21. Teabeamet (The Information Board)
22. Maa-amet (Land Board)
23. Keskkonnainspektsioon (Environmental Inspectorate)
24. Metsakaitse- ja Metsauuenduskeskus (Centre of Forest Protection and Silviculture)
25. Muinsuskaitseamet (The Heritage Conservation Inspectorate)
26. Patendiamet (Patent Office)
27. Tehnilise Järelevalve Inspektsioon (The Technical Inspectorate)

[8] Non-warlike materials contained in Part (3) of this Annex.

爱沙尼亚

(仅以英文为准)

1. 爱沙尼亚共和国总统办公室
2. 爱沙尼亚共和国议会
3. 爱沙尼亚共和国最高法院
4. 爱沙尼亚共和国国家审计办公室
5. 大法官
6. 国家大法官法庭
7. 爱沙尼亚国家档案馆
8. 教育研究部
9. 司法部
10. 国防部[8]
11. 环境部
12. 文化部
13. 经济和交通部
14. 农业部
15. 财政部
16. 内政部
17. 社会事务部
18. 外交部
19. 语言监察局
20. 检察官办公室
21. 信息局
22. 土地局
23. 环境监察局
24. 森林保护和造林中心
25. 传统保护监察局
26. 专利办公室
27. 技术监察局

[8]非军事物资包含在本附件第 3 部分。

28. Energiaturu Inspektsioon (The Energy Market Inspectorate)
29. Tarbijakaitseamet (The Consumer Protection Board)
30. Riigihangete Amet (Public Procurement Office)
31. Eesti Patendiraamatukogu (Estonian Patent Library)
32. Taimetoodangu Inspektsioon (The Plant Production Inspectorate)
33. Põllumajanduse Registrite ja Informatsiooni Amet (Agricultural Registers and Information Board)
34. Veterinaar- ja Toiduamet (The Veterinary and Food Board)
35. Konkurentsiamet (The Competition Board)
36 Maksu –ja Tolliamet (Tax and Customs Board)
37. Statistikaamet (Statistical Office)
38. Kaitsepolitseiamet (The Security Police Board)
39. Proovikoda (Assay Office)
40. Kodakondsus- ja Migratsiooniamet (Citizenship and Migration Board)
41. Piirivalveamet (The Border Guard Administration)
42. Politseiamet (The Police Board)
43. Kohtuekspertiisi ja Kriminalistika Keskus (Centre of Forensic and Criminalistic Science)
44. Keskkriminaalpolitsei (Central Criminal Police)
45. Päästeamet (The Rescue Board)
46. Andmekaitse Inspektsioon (The Data Protection Inspectorate)
47. Ravimiamet (Agency of Medicines)
48. Sotsiaalkindlustusamet (Social Insurance Board)
49. Tööturuamet (Labour Market Board)
50. Tervishoiuamet (Health Care Board)
51. Tervisekaitseinspektsioon (Health Protection Inspectorate)
52. Tööinspektsioon (Labour Inspectorate)
53. Lennuamet (Civil Aviation Administration)
54. Maanteeamet (Road Administration)
55. Sideamet (Communications Board)
56. Veeteede Amet (Maritime Administration)
57. Raudteeamet (Estonian Railway Administration)

28. 能源市场监察局
29. 消费者保护局
30. 公共采购办公室
31. 爱沙尼亚专利图书馆
32. 工厂生产监察局
33. 农业注册和信息局
34. 兽医和食品局
35. 竞争局
36. 税务和关税局
37. 统计办公室
38. 秘密警察局
39. 检验办公室
40. 公民和移民局
41. 边境警卫管理局
42. 警察局
43. 法医和刑事科学中心
44. 中央刑事警察局
45. 救援局
46. 数据保护监察局
47. 药品局
48. 社会保险局
49. 劳动力市场局
50. 卫生保健局
51. 卫生防护局
52. 劳动监察局
53. 民用航空管理局
54. 道路管理局
55. 通信局
56. 海事管理局
57. 爱沙尼亚铁路管理局

GREECE - GRÈCE - GRECIA

(Authentic in the English language only)

List of entities

1. Ministry of the Interior, Public Administration and Decentralization
2. Ministry of Foreign Affairs
3. Ministry of National Economy
4. Ministry of Finance
5. Ministry of Development
6. Ministry of Environment, Planning and Public Works
7. Ministry of Education and Religion
8. Ministry of Agriculture
9. Ministry of Labour and Social security
10. Ministry of Health and Social Selfare
11. Ministry of Justice
12. Ministry of Culture
13. Ministry of Merchant Marine
14. Ministry of Macedonia and Thrace
15. Ministry of the Aegean
16. Ministry of Transport and Communications
17. Ministry for Press and Media
18. Ministry to the Prime Minister
19. Army General Staff
20. Navy General Staff
21. Airforce General Staff
22. General Secretariat for Equality
23. General Secretariat for Greeks Living Abroad
24. General Secretariat for Commerce
25. General Secretariat for Research and Technology
26. General Secretariat for Industry
27. General Secretariat for Public Works
28. General Secretariat for Youth

1 January 2007 (WT/Let/556)

希腊

(仅以英文为准)

实体清单

1. 内政、公共管理和权力下放部
2. 外交部
3. 国民经济部
4. 财政部
5. 发展部
6. 环境、计划和公共工程部
7. 教育和宗教事务部
8. 农业部
9. 劳动和社会保障部
10. 卫生和社会福利部
11. 司法部
12. 文化部
13. 海运部
14. 马其顿和色雷斯部
15. 爱琴海部
16. 交通和通信部
17. 新闻和媒体部
18. 总理办事机构
19. 陆军总参谋部
20. 海军总参谋部
21. 空军总参谋部
22. 男女平等总秘书处
23. 海外希腊人总秘书处
24. 商业总秘书处
25. 研究和技术总秘书处
26. 产业总秘书处
27. 公共工程总秘书处
28. 青年工作总秘书处

29. General Secretariat for Further Education
30. General Secretariat for Social Security
31. General Secretariat for Sports
32. General State Laboratory
33. National Centre of Public Administration
34. National Printing Office
35. National Statistical Service
36. National Welfare Organisation
37. University of Athens
38. University of Thessaloniki
39. University of Patras
40. University of Ioannina
41. University of Thrace
42. University of Macedonia
43. University of the Aegean
44. Polytechnic School of Crete
45. Sivitanidios Technical School
46. Eginitio Hospital
47. Areteio Hospital
48. Greek Atomic Energy Commission
49. Greek Highway Fund
50. Hellenic Post (EL. TA.)
51. Workers' Housing Organisation
52. Farmers' Insurance Organisation
53. Public Material Management Organisation
54. School Building Organisation

29. 继续教育总秘书处
30. 社会保障总秘书处
31. 体育工作总秘书处
32. 国家总实验室
33. 国家公共行政管理中心
34. 国家印刷办公室
35. 国家统计局
36. 国家福利组织
37. 雅典大学
38. 萨洛尼卡大学
39. 佩特雷大学
40. 爱奥尼亚大学
41. 色雷斯大学
42. 马其顿大学
43. 爱琴海大学
44. 克利特理工学院
45. 斯维坦尼迪奥斯工业学校
46. 埃基尼迪奥医院
47. 阿热泰伊奥医院
48. 希腊原子能委员会
49. 希腊公路基金
50. 希腊邮政
51. 工人住房组织
52. 农民保险组织
53. 公共物资管理组织
54. 学校建筑组织

SPAIN - ESPAGNE - ESPAÑA

(Esta lista es auténtica en la versión española)

1. Ministerio de Asuntos Exteriores
2. Ministerio de Justicia
3. Ministerio de Defensa[9]
4. Ministerio de Economía y Hacienda
5. Ministerio del Interior
6. Ministerio de Fomento
7. Ministerio de Educación y Cultura
8. Ministerio de Trabajo y Asuntos Sociales
9. Ministerio de Industria y Energía
10. Ministerio de Agricultura, Pesca y Alimentación
11. Ministerio de la Presidencia
12. Ministerio para las Administraciones Públicas
13. Ministerio de Sanidad y Consumo
14. Ministerio de Medio Ambiente

[9] Material no militar incluído en la parte (3) de este Annexo.

西班牙

(仅以西班牙文为准)

1. 外交部
2. 司法部
3. 国防部[9]
4. 经济财政部
5. 内政部
6. 发展部
7. 教育文化部
8. 劳动和社会事务部
9. 工业能源部
10. 农业、渔业和食品部
11. 首相府部
12. 公共行政管理部
13. 卫生和消费部
14. 环境部

[9]非军事物资包含在本附件第 3 部分。

FRANCE - FRANCE - FRANCIA

(La version française fait foi)

(A) Principales entités acheteuses

(a) *Budget général*

1. Services du Premier Ministre
2. Ministère des Affaires Sociales, de la Santé et de la Ville
3. Ministère de l'Intérieur et de l'Aménagement du Territoire
4. Ministère de la Justice
5. Ministère de la Défense
6. Ministère des Affaires Etrangères
7. Ministère de l'Education Nationale
8. Ministère de l'Economie
9. Ministère de l'Industrie, des Postes et Télécommunications et du Commerce Extérieur
10. Minitère de l'Equipement, des Transports et du Tourisme
11. Ministère des Entreprises et du Développement Economique, chargé des Petites et Moyennes Entreprises et du Commerce et de l'Artisanat
12. Ministère du Travail, de l'Emploi et de la Formation Professionnelle
13. Ministère de la Culture et de la Francophonie
14. Ministère du Budget
15. Ministère de l'Agriculture et de la Pêche
16. Ministère de l'Enseignement Supérieur et de la Recherche
17. Ministère de l'Environnement
18. Ministère de la Fonction Publique
19. Ministère du Logement
20. Ministère de la Coopération
21. Ministère des Départements et Territoires d'Outre-Mer
22. Ministère de la Jeunesse et des Sports
23. Ministère de la Communication
24. Ministère des anciens Combattants et Victimes de Guerre

法国

(仅以法文为准)

(A) 主要采购实体

(a) *一般预算*

1. 总理府
2. 社会事务、健康和城市部
3. 内政和领土整治部
4. 司法部
5. 国防部
6. 外交部
7. 国民教育部
8. 经济部
9. 工业、邮政电信和外贸部
10. 设备、运输和旅游部
11. 企业和经济发展部，负责中小企业、商业和手工业
12. 劳动、就业和职业培训部
13. 文化和法语推广部
14. 预算部
15. 农业和渔业部
16. 高等教育和研究部
17. 环境部
18. 公共职能部
19. 住房部
20. 合作部
21. 海外省和海外领地部
22. 青年事务和体育部
23. 通信部
24. 老兵和战争受害者福利部

(b) *Budget annexe*

On peut notamment signaler:

1. Imprimerie Nationale

(c) *Comptes spéciaux du Trésor*

On peut notamment signaler:

1. Fonds forestiers national;
2. Soutien financier de l'industrie cinématographique et de l'industrie des programmes audio-visuels;
3. Fonds national d'aménagement foncier et d'urbanisme;
4. Caisse autonome de la reconstruction.

(B) Etablissements publics nationaux à caractère administratif

1. Académie de France à Rome;
2. Académie de Marine;
3. Académie des Sciences d'Outre-Mer;
4. Agence Centrale des Organismes de Sécurité Sociale (A.C.O.S.S.);
5. Agences Financières de Bassins;
6. Agence Nationale pour l'Amélioration des Conditions de Travail (A.N.A.C.T.);
7. Agence Nationale pour l'Amélioration de l'Habitat (A.N.A.H.);
8. Agence Nationale pour l'Emploi (A.N.P.E.);
9. Agence Nationale pour l'Indemnisation des Français d'Outre-Mer (A.N.I.F.O.M.);
10. Assemblée Permanente des Chambres d'Agriculture (A.P.C.A.);
11. Bibliothèque Nationale;
12. Bibliothèque Nationale et Universitaire de Strasbourg;
13. Bureau d'Etudes des Postes et Télécommunications d'Outre-Mer (B.E.P.T.O.M.);
14. Caisse des Dépôts et Consignations;
15. Caisse Nationale des Allocations Familiales (C.N.A.F.);
16. Caisse Nationale d'Assurance Maladie des Travailleurs Salariés (C.N.A.M.);
17. Caisse Nationale d'Assurance-Vieillesse des Travailleurs Salariés (C.N.A.V.T.S.);
18. Caisse Nationale des Autoroutes (C.N.A.)
19. Caisse Nationale Militaire de Sécurité Sociale (C.N.M.S.S.);

(b) *附加预算*

特别注意：

1. 国家印刷局

(c) *国库司专门账号*

特别注意：

1. 国家森林基金
2. 电影产业和视听节目产业财政支持
3. 土地整治和城市化国家基金
4. 重建自治银行

(B) 国家公共管理机构

1. 驻罗马法兰西学院
2. 海军学院
3. 海外科学学院
4. 社会保障机构中央管理署
5. 流域地区金融署
6. 国家改善劳动条件署
7. 国家改善居住条件署
8. 国家就业署
9. 国家海外法国人补偿署
10. 农业公会常务委员会
11. 国家图书馆
12. 斯特拉斯堡国家和大学教育图书馆
13. 海外邮政通信研究部
14. 储蓄信托局
15. 国家家庭补助金管理局
16. 国家工薪职工疾病保险管理局
17. 国家工薪职工养老保险管理局
18. 国家高速公路经费管理局
19. 国家军人社会保障金管理局

20. Caisse Nationale des Monuments Historiques et des Sites;
21. Caisse Nationale des Télécommunications[10];
22. Caisse de Garantie du Logement Social;
23. Casa de Velasquez;
24. Centre d'Enseignement Zootechnique de Rambouillet;
25. Centre d'Etudes du Milieu et de Pédagogie Appliquée du Ministère de l'Agriculture;
26. Centre d'Etudes Supérieures de Sécurité Sociale;
27. Centres de Formation Professionnelle Agricole;
28. Centre National d'Art et de Culture Georges Pompidou;
29. Centre National de la Cinématographie Française;
30. Centre National d'Etudes et de Formation pour l'Enfance Inadaptée;
31. Centre National d'Etudes et d'Expérimentation du Machinisme Agricole, du Génie Rural, des Eaux et des Forêts;
32. Centre National de Formation pour l'Adaptation Scolaire et l'Education Spécialisée (C.N.E.F.A.S.E.S.);
33. Centre National de Formation et de Perfectionnement des Professeurs d'Enseignement Ménager Agricole;
34. Centre National des Lettres;
35. Centre National de Documentation Pédagogique;
36. Centre National des Oeuvres Universitaires et Scolaires (C.N.O.U.S.);
37. Centre National d'Opthalmologie des Quinze-Vingts;
38. Centre National de Préparation au Professorat de Travaux Manuels Éducatifs et d'Enseignement Ménager;
39. Centre National de Promotion Rurale de Marmilhat;
40. Centre National de la Recherche Scientifique (C.N.R.S.);
41. Centre Régional d'Education Populaire d'Ile de France;
42. Centres d'Education Populaire et de Sport (C.R.E.P.S.);
43. Centres Régionaux des Oeuvres Universitaires (C.R.O.U.S.);
44. Centres Régionaux de la Propriété Forestière;
45. Centre de Sécurité Sociale des Travailleurs Migrants;
46. Chancelleries des Universités;
47. Collège de France

[10] Postes seulement.

20. 国家文物古迹经费管理局
21. 国家通信经费管理局[10]
22. 社会租房保障金管理局
23. 委拉兹盖斯学院
24. 朗布耶畜牧学教育中心
25. 农业部应用教学研究中心
26. 社会保障高级研究中心
27. 农业专业人才培训中心
28. 乔治蓬皮杜国家艺术文化中心
29. 国家法语电影中心
30. 智力和心理残障儿童国家研究和培训中心
31. 农业机械化、农村工程、水利和森林国家研究和实验中心
32. 教学适应和特殊教育国家培训中心
33. 国家农务教育专家培训进修中心
34. 国家文学中心
35. 国家教材中心
36. 国家大学和学校事务中心
37. 国家甘兹万特眼科中心
38. 国家手工劳务教学师资预备中心
39. 国家玛秘拉农业促进中心
40. 国家科研中心
41. 巴黎大区大众教育中心
42. 大众教育和体育中心
43. 大区大学事务管理中心
44. 大区森林产权管理中心
45. 移民劳工社会保障中心
46. 大学事务总署
47. 法兰西学院

[10] 仅限邮政。

48. Commission des Opérations de Bourse;
49. Conseil Supérieur de la Pêche;
50. Conservatoire de l'Espace Littoral et des Rivages Lacustres;
51. Conservatoire National des Arts et Métiers;
52. Conservatoire National Supérieur de Musique;
53. Conservatoire National Supérieur d'Art Dramatique;
54. Domaine de Pompadour;
55. Ecole Centrale - Lyon;
56. Ecole Centrale des Arts et Manufactures;
57. Ecole Française d'Archéologie d'Athènes;
58. Ecole Française d'Extrême-Orient;
59. Ecole Française de Rome;
60. Ecole des Hautes Études en Sciences Sociales;
61. Ecole Nationale d'Administration;
62. Ecole Nationale de l'Aviation Civile (E.N.A.C.);
63. Ecole Nationale des Chartes;
64. Ecole Nationale d'Equitation;
65. Ecole Nationale du Génie Rural des Eaux et des Forêts (E.N.G.R.E.F.);
66. Ecoles Nationales d'Ingénieurs;
67. Ecole Nationale d'Ingénieurs des Industries des Techniques Agricoles et Alimentaires;
68. Ecoles Nationales d'Ingénieurs des Travaux Agricoles;
69. Ecole Nationale des Ingénieurs des Travaux Ruraux et des Techniques Sanitaires;
70. Ecole Nationale des Ingénieurs des Travaux des Eaux et Forêts (E.N.I.T.E.F.);
71. Ecole Nationale de la Magistrature;
72. Ecoles Nationales de la Marine Marchande;
73. Ecole Nationale de la Santé Publique (E.N.S.P.);
74. Ecole Nationale de Ski et d'Alpinisme;
75. Ecole Nationale Supérieure Agronomique - Montpellier;
76. Ecole Nationale Supérieure Agronomique - Rennes;
77. Ecole Nationale Supérieure des Arts Décoratifs;
78. Ecole Nationale Supérieure des Arts et Industries - Strasbourg;
79. Ecole Nationale Supérieure des Arts et Industries Textiles - Roubaix;
80. Ecoles Nationales Supérieures d'Arts et Métiers;

48. 股票市场交易委员会
49. 渔业高级委员会
50. 滨海湖泊管理局
51. 国家艺术和手工艺学院
52. 国家高等音乐学院
53. 国家高等戏剧艺术学院
54. 庞芭杜庄园
55. 里昂中央理工大学
56. 技术和制造业中央学院
57. 法国雅典考古学学院
58. 法国远东学院
59. 法国罗马学院
60. 高等社会科学学院
61. 国立行政学院
62. 国家民用航空学院
63. 国家夏尔特学院
64. 国家马术学校
65. 国家水利和森林农业工程学院
66. 国家工程师学院
67. 国家农业和食品技术工业工程师学院
68. 国家农业工程工程师学院
69. 国家农业工程和卫生技术工程师学院
70. 国家水利和森林工程工程师学院
71. 国家法官学院
72. 国家商船学院
73. 国家公共健康学院
74. 国家滑雪和登山学院
75. 国家高等农艺学学院—蒙彼利埃
76. 国家高等农艺学学院—雷恩
77. 国家高等装饰艺术学院
78. 国家高等艺术和工业学校—斯特拉斯堡
79. 国家高等纺织工艺学校—卢贝
80. 国家高等艺术和工艺学校

81. Ecole Nationale Supérieure des Beaux-Arts;
82. Ecole Nationale Supérieure des Bibliothécaires;
83. Ecole Nationale Supérieure de Céramique Industrielle;
84. Ecole Nationale Supérieure de l'Electronique et de ses Applications (E.N.S.E.A.);
85. Ecole Nationale Supérieure d'Horticulture;
86. Ecole Nationale Supérieure des Industries Agricoles Alimentaires;
87. Ecole Nationale Supérieure du Paysage (Rattachée à l'Ecole Nationale Supérieure d'Horticulture);
88. Ecole Nationale Supérieure des Sciences Agronomiques Appliquées (E.N.S.S.A.);
89. Ecoles Nationales Vétérinaires;
90. Ecole Nationale de Voile;
91. Ecoles Normales d'Instituteurs et d'Institutrices;
92. Ecoles Normales Nationales d'Apprentissage;
93. Ecoles Normales Supérieures;
94. Ecole Polytechnique;
95. Ecole Technique Professionelle Agricole et Forestière de Meymac (Corrèze)
96. Ecole de Sylviculture - Crogny (Aube);
97. Ecole de Viticulture et d'Oenologie de la Tour Blanche (Gironde);
98. Ecole de Viticulture - Avize (Marne);
99. Etablissement National de Convalescents de Saint-Maurice;
100. Etablissement National des Invalides de la Marine (E.N.I.M.);
101. Etablissement National de Bienfaisance Koenigs-Wazter;
102. Fondation Carnegie;
103. Fondation Singer-Polignac;
104. Fonds d'Action Sociale pour les Travailleurs Immigrés et leurs Familles;
105. Hôpital-Hospice National Dufresne-Sommeiller;
106. Institut de l'Elevage et de Médicine Vérérinaire des Pays Tropicaux (I.E.M.V.P.T.)
107. Institut Français d'Archéologie Orientale du Caire;
108. Institut Géographique National;
109. Institut Industriel du Nord;
110. Institut International d'Administration Publique (I.I.A.P.);
111. Institut National Agronomique de Paris-Grignon;
112. Institut National des Appellations d'Origine des Vins et Eux-de-Vie (I.N.A.O.V.E.V.);

81. 国家高等美术学校
82. 国家高等图书员管理员学校
83. 国家高等工业陶瓷学校
84. 国家高等电子和电子应用学院
85. 国家高等园艺学校
86. 国家高等农副食品工业学校
87. 国家高等景观学校(附属于国家高等园艺学校)
88. 国家高等应用农艺学校
89. 国家兽医学校
90. 国立帆船学校
91. 小学教师师范学校
92. 国立学徒师范学校
93. 高等师范学校
94. 巴黎理工学校
95. 美马柯农林职业技术学校(科雷兹)
96. 克洛尼林业学校(奥贝)
97. 杜布兰奇葡萄栽培和酿酒工艺学校(吉龙德)
98. 阿维兹葡萄栽培学校(马恩)
99. 圣-莫里斯国家康复中心
100. 国家海军伤残士兵机构
101. 凯尼格斯-沃则塔国家慈善机构
102. 卡内吉基金会
103. 辛格-波利纳克基金会
104. 移民劳工和其家庭社会保障基金
105. 国家杜夫伦-索迈耶医院—养老院
106. 热带国家畜牧和兽医药研究所
107. 法国东方考古开罗研究所
108. 国家地理研究所
109. 北方工业研究所
110. 国际公共管理研究所
111. 巴黎-格里尼翁国立农艺研究所
112. 国家葡萄酒、烈性酒产地命名研究所

113. Institut National d'Astronomie et de Géophysique (I.N.A.G.);
114. Institut National de la Consommation (I.N.C.);
115. Institut National d'Education Populaire (I.N.E.P.);
116. Institut National d'Etudes Démographiques (I.N.E.D.);
117. Institut National des Jeunes Aveugles - Paris;
118. Institut National des Jeunes Sourdes - Bordeaux;
119. Institut National des Jeunes Sourds - Chambéry;
120. Institut National des Jeunes Sourds - Metz;
121. Institut National des Jeunes Sourds - Paris;
122. Institut National de Physique Nucléaire et de Physique des Particules (I.N.P.N.P.P);
123. Institut National de Promotion Supérieure Agricole;
124. Institut National de la Propriété Industrielle;
125. Institut National de la Recherche Agronomique (I.N.R.A.);
126. Institut National de Recherche Pédagogique (I.N.R.P.);
127. Institut National de la Santé et de la Recherche Médicale (I.N.S.E.R.M.);
128. Institut National des Sports;
129. Instituts Nationaux Polytechniques;
130. Instituts Nationaux des Sciences Appliquées;
131. Instituts National Supérieur de Chimie Industrielle de Rouen;
132. Institut National de Recherche en Informatique et en Automatique (I.N.R.I.A.);
133. Institut National de Recherche sur les Transports et leur Sécurité (I.N.R.T.S.);
134. Instituts Régionaux d'Administration;
135. Institut Supérieur des Matériaux et de la Construction Mécanique de Saint-Ouen
136. Musée de l'Armée;
137. Musée Gustave Moreau;
138. Musée de la Marine;
139. Musée National J.J. Henner;
140. Musée National de la Légion d'Honneur;
141. Musée de la Poste;
142. Muséum National d'Histoire Naturelle;
143. Musée Augustre Rodin;
144. Observatoire de Paris;
145. Office de Coopération et d'Accueil Universitaire;

113. 国家天文学和地球物理学研究所
114. 国家消费研究所
115. 国家大众教育研究所
116. 国家人口研究所
117. 失明青年国家学校–巴黎分校
118. 失聪青年国家学校—波尔多分校
119. 失聪青年国家学校—尚贝利分校
120. 失聪青年国家学校—梅斯分校
121. 失聪青年国家学校—巴黎分校
122. 国家核物理和粒子物理研究所
123. 国家农业高级推广研究所
124. 国家工业产权局
125. 国家农艺研究所
126. 国家教育科研所
127. 国家健康和医学研究院
128. 国家体育学院
129. 国家理工学院
130. 国家应用科学学院
131. 鲁昂国家高等工业化学学院
132. 国家信息科学和自动化控制研究所
133. 国家交通运输安全研究所
134. 地区行政学院
135. 圣·图安材料和机械制造高等学院
136. 军事博物馆
137. 居斯塔夫·莫罗美术馆
138. 海军博物馆
139. 亨纳尔国家博物馆
140. 国家荣誉勋章博物馆
141. 邮政博物馆
142. 国家自然历史博物馆
143. 奥古斯特·罗丹博物馆
144. 巴黎天文台
145. 大学合作和接待署

146. Office Français de Protection des Réfugiés et Apatrides;

147. Office National des Anciens Combattants;

148. Office National de la Chasse;

149. Office National d'Information sur les Enseignements et les Professions (O.N.I.E.P.);

150. Office National d'Immigration (O.N.I.);

151. O.R.S.T.O.M. – Institut Français de Recherche Scientifique pour le Développement en Coopération;

152. Office Universitaire et Culturel Français pour l'Algérie;

153. Palais de la Découverte;

154. Parcs Nationaux;

155. Réunion des Musées Nationaux;

156. Syndicat des Transports Parisiens;

157. Thermes Nationaux - Aix-les-Bains;

158. Universités.

(C) Autre organisme public national

1. Union des Groupements d'Achats Publics (U.G.A.P.).

146. 国家难民和无国籍人士保护署
147. 国家退伍军人署
148. 国家狩猎办公室
149. 国家教育和职业信息办公室
150. 国家移民局
151. 法国合作发展科研所
152. 阿尔及利亚法国大学和文化事务署
153. 发现馆
154. 国家公园
155. 国家博物馆联合会
156. 巴黎运输业联合会
157. 艾克斯-雷-百恩国家温泉浴场
158. 各大学

(C) 其他国家公共机构

1. 公共采购集团联合会

IRELAND - IRLANDE - IRLANDA

(Authentic in the English language only)

(A) Main purchasing entities

1. Office of Public Works

(B) Other Departments

1. President's Establishment;
2. Houses of the Oireachtas (Parliament);
3. Department of the Taoiseach (Prime Minister);
4. Office of the Tánaiste (Deputy Prime Minister);
5. Central Statistics Office;
6. Department of Arts, Culture and the Gaeltacht;
7. National Gallery of Ireland;
8. Department of Finance;
9. State Laboratory;
10. Office of the Comptroller and Auditor General;
11. Office of the Attorney General;
12. Office of the Director of Public Prosecutions;
13. Valuation Office;
14. Civil Service Commission;
15. Office of the Ombudsman;
16. Office of the Revenue Commissioners;
17. Department of Justice;
18. Commissioners of Charitable Donations and Bequests for Ireland;

爱尔兰

(仅以英文为准)

(A) 主要采购实体

1. 公共工程办公室

(B) 其他部门

1. 总统府；
2. 议会；
3. 首相府；
4. 副首相府办公室；
5. 中央统计办公室；
6. 艺术、文化和爱尔兰语区部；
7. 爱尔兰国家美术馆；
8. 财政部；
9. 国家实验室；
10. 审计官和总审计长办公室；
11. 首席检察官办公室；
12. 检察长办公室；
13. 估价办公室；
14. 行政事务委员会；
15. 巡视官办公室；
16. 税收专员办公室；
17. 司法部；
18. 爱尔兰慈善捐赠和遗产专员办公室；

2007 年 1 月 1 日 (WT/Let/556)

19. Department of the Environment;
20. Department of Education;
21. Department of the Marine;
22. Department of Agriculture, Food and Forestry;
23. Department of Enterprise and Employment
24. Department of Tourism and Trade
25. Department of Defence[11];
26. Department of Foreign Affairs;
27. Department of Social Welfare;
28. Department of Health;
29. Department of Transport, Energy and Communications

[11] Non-warlike materials contained in Part (3) of this Annex.

19.　环境部；

20.　教育部；

21.　海事部；

22.　农业、食品和林业部；

23.　企业和就业部；

24.　旅游和贸易部；

25.　国防部[11]；

26.　外交部；

27.　社会福利部；

28.　卫生部；

29.　交通、能源和通信部

[11]非军事物资包含在本附件第 3 部分。

ITALY - ITALIE – ITALIA

(Authentic in the English language only)

Purchasing Entities

1.	Presidency of the Council of Ministers with Ministry of Cultural Affairs	Presidenza del Consiglio dei Ministri con il Ministero del Beni Culturali
2.	Ministry of Foreign Affairs	Ministero degli affari esteri
3.	Ministry of the Interior	Ministero dell'Interno
4.	Ministry of Justice	Ministero di Grazia e Giustizia
5.	Ministry of the Treasury[12]	Ministero del Tesoro
6.	Ministry of Finance[13]	Ministero delle Finanze
7.	Ministry of Defence[14]	Ministero della Difesa
8.	Ministry of Industry, Trade, Handicraft and Tourism	Ministero dell'Industria, del Commercio e Dell'artigianato
9.	Ministry of Public Works	Ministero del Lavori Pubblici
10.	Ministry of Transports	Ministero del Trasporti
11.	Ministry of Posts and Telecommunications[15]	Ministero delle Poste e Telecommunicazioni
12.	Ministry of Health	Ministero della Sanità
13.	Ministry of Education, University, Scientifical and Technological Research	Ministero della Pubblica Istruzione, dell'Università e della ricerca scientifica e tecnologica
14.	Ministry of Employment and Social Security	Ministero del Lavoro e della Previdenza Sociale
15.	Ministry of Environment	Ministero dell'Ambiente
16.	Ministry of Foreign Trade	Ministero del Commercio con l'Estero
17.	Ministry of Agriculture resources	Ministero delle Risorce Agricole, Alimentari e Forestali

[12] Acting as the central purchasing entity for most of the other Ministries or entities.
[13] Not including purchases made by the tobacco and salt monopolies.
[14] Non-warlike materials contained in Part (3) of this Annex.
[15] Postal business only.

意大利

(仅以英文为准)

采购实体

1. 内阁及文化事务部
2. 外交部
3. 内政部
4. 司法部
5. 国库部[12]
6. 财政部[13]
7. 国防部[14]
8. 工业、贸易、手工业和旅游部
9. 公共工程部
10. 交通部
11. 邮政和电信部[15]
12. 卫生部
13. 教育、大学和科技研究部
14. 就业和社会保障部
15. 环境部
16. 对外贸易部
17. 农业资源部

[12] 作为其他大部分部或实体的集中采购实体。
[13] 不包括烟草和盐专卖商进行的采购。
[14] 非军事物资包含在本附件第 3 部分。
[15] 仅限邮政。

CYPRUS – CHYPRE - CHIPRE

(Authentic in the English language only)

1. (a) Προεδρία και Προεδρικό Μέγαρο (Presidency and Presidential Palace)
   (b) Γραφείο Συντονιστή Εναρμόνισης (Office of the Coordinator for Harmonisation)
2. Υπουργικό Συμβούλιο (Council of Ministers)
3. Βουλή των Αντιπροσώπων (House of Representatives)
4. Δικαστική Υπηρεσία (Judicial Service)
5. Νομική Υπηρεσία της Δημοκρατίας (Law Office of the Republic)
6. Ελεγκτική Υπηρεσία της Δημοκρατίας (Audit Office of the Republic)
7. Επιτροπή Δημόσιας Υπηρεσίας (Public Service Commission)
8. Επιτροπή Εκπαιδευτικής Υπηρεσίας (Educational Service Commission)
9. Γραφείο Επιτρόπου Διοικήσεως (Office of the Commissioner for Administration (Ombudsman))
10. Επιτροπή Προστασίας Ανταγωνισμού (Commission for the Protection of Competition)
11. Υπηρεσία Εσωτερικού Ελέγχου (Internal Audit Service)
12. Γραφείο Προγραμματισμού (Planning Bureau)
13. Γενικό Λογιστήριο της Δημοκρατίας (Treasury of the Republic)
14. Γραφείο Επιτρόπου Προστασίας Δεδομένων Προσωπικού Χαρακτήρα (Office of the Personal Character Data Protection Commissioner)
15. Γραφείο Επιτρόπου Νομοθεσίας (Law Commissioner Office)
16. Γραφείο Εφόρου Δημοσίων Ενισχύσεων (Office of the Commissioner for the Public Aid)
17. Υπουργείο Άμυνας (Ministry of Defence)[16]
18. (a) Υπουργείο Γεωργίας, Φυσικών Πόρων και Περιβάλλοντος (Ministry of Agriculture, Natural Resources and Environment)
    (b) Τμήμα Γεωργίας (Department of Agriculture)

[16] Non-warlike materials contained in Part (3) of this Annex.

塞浦路斯

(仅以英文为准)

1. (a) 总统和总统府

   (b) 和平协调官办公室

2. 内阁

3. 众议院

4. 司法部

5. 共和国法律办公室

6. 共和国审计办公室

7. 公共服务委员会

8. 教育服务委员会

9. 行政管理专员办公室(巡视官)

10. 保护竞争委员会

11. 内部审计局

12. 规划局

13. 共和国国库

14. 个人信息保护专员办公室

15. 法律专员办公室

16. 公共援助专员办公室

17. 国防部[16]

18. (a) 农业、自然资源和环境部

    (b) 农业司

[16]非军事物资包含在本附件第 3 部分。

(c) Κτηνιατρικές Υπηρεσίες (Veterinary Services)

(d) Τμήμα Δασών (Forest Department)

(e) Τμήμα Αναπτύξεως Υδάτων (Water Development Department)

(f) Τμήμα Γεωλογικής Επισκόπησης (Geological Survey Department)

(g) Μετεωρολογική Υπηρεσία (Meteorological Service)

(h) Τμήμα Αναδασμού (Land Consolidation Department)

(i) Υπηρεσία Μεταλλείων (Mines Service)

(j) Ινστιτούτο Γεωργικών Ερευνών (Agricultural Research Institute)

(k) Τμήμα Αλιείας και Θαλάσσιων Ερευνών (Department of Fisheries and Marine Research)

19. (a) Υπουργείο Δικαιοσύνης και Δημοσίας Τάξεως (Ministry of Justice and Public Order)

(b) Αστυνομία (Police)

(c) Πυροσβεστική Υπηρεσία Κύπρου (Cyprus Fire Service)

(d) Τμήμα Φυλακών (Prison Department)

(e) Κεντρική Υπηρεσία Πληροφοριών (Central Information Service)

20. (α) Υπουργείο Εμπορίου, Βιομηχανίας και Τουρισμού (Ministry of Commerce, Industry and Tourism)

(b) Υπηρεσία Εποπτείας και Ανάπτυξης Συνεργατικών Εταιρειών (Cooperative Societies΄ Supervision and Development Authority)

(c) Τμήμα Εφόρου Εταιρειών και Επίσημου Παραλήπτη (Department of Registrar of Companies and Official Receiver)

21. (a) Υπουργείο Εργασίας και Κοινωνικών Ασφαλίσεων (Ministry of Labour and Social Insurance)

(b) Τμήμα Εργασίας (Department of Labour)

(c) Τμήμα Κοινωνικών Ασφαλίσεων (Department of Social Insurance)

(d) Τμήμα Υπηρεσιών Κοινωνικής Ευημερίας (Department of Social Welfare Services)

(e) Κέντρο Παραγωγικότητας Κύπρου (Productivity Centre Cyprus)

(f) Ανώτερο Ξενοδοχειακό Ινστιτούτο Κύπρου (Higher Hotel Institute Cyprus)

(g) Ανώτερο Τεχνολογικό Ινστιτούτο (Higher Technical Institute)

(c) 兽医服务局

(d) 森林司

(e) 水利开发司

(f) 地质勘测司

(g) 气象服务司

(h) 土地集约司

(i) 采矿局

(j) 农业研究所

(k) 渔业和海洋研究局

19. (a) 司法和社会治安部

(b) 警察

(c) 塞浦路斯消防局

(d) 监狱司

(e) 中央信息局

20. (a) 商业、工业和旅游部

(b) 合作社监督和发展局

(c) 企业注册和破产管理司

21. (a) 劳动和社会保险部

(b) 劳动司

(c) 社会保险司

(d) 社会福利服务司

(e) 塞浦路斯生产力促进中心

(f) 塞浦路斯高级酒店协会

(g) 高等技术协会

(h) Τμήμα Επιθεώρησης Εργασίας (Department of Labour Inspection)

(i) Υπηρεσία Βιομηχανικών Σχέσεων (Industrial Relations Service)

22. (a) Υπουργείο Εσωτερικών (Ministry of the Interior)

(b) Επαρχιακές Διοικήσεις (District Administrations)

(c) Τμήμα Πολεοδομίας και Οικήσεως (Town Planning and Housing Department)

(d) Τμήμα Αρχείου Πληθυσμού και Μεταναστεύσεως (Civil Registry and Migration Department)

(e) Τμήμα Κτηματολογίου και Χωρομετρίας (Department of Lands and Surveys)

(f) Γραφείο Τύπου και Πληροφοριών (Press and Information Office)

(g) Πολιτική Άμυνα (Civil Defence)

(h) Κυπριακό Πρακτορείο Ειδήσεων (Cyprus News Agency)

(i) Ταμείο Θήρας (Game Fund)

(j) Υπηρεσία Μέριμνας και Αποκαταστάσεων Εκτοπισθέντων (Service for the care and rehabilitation of displaced persons)

23. Υπουργείο Εξωτερικών (Ministry of Foreign Affairs)

24. (a) Υπουργείο Οικονομικών (Ministry of Finance)

(b) Τελωνεία (Customs and Excise)

(c) Τμήμα Εσωτερικών Προσόδων (Department of Inland Revenue)

(d) Στατιστική Υπηρεσία (Statistical Service)

(e) Τμήμα Κρατικών Αγορών και Προμηθειών (Department of Government Purchasing and Supply)

(f) Τμήμα Δημόσιας Διοίκησης και Προσωπικού (Public Administration and Personnel Department)

(g) Κυβερνητικό Τυπογραφείο (Government Printing Office)

(h) Τμήμα Υπηρεσιών Πληροφορικής (Department of Information Technology Services)

25. Υπουργείο Παιδείας και Πολιτισμού (Ministry of Education and Culture)

26. (a) Υπουργείο Συγκοινωνιών και Έργων (Ministry of Communications and Works)

(b) Τμήμα Δημοσίων Έργων (Department of Public Works)

(h) 劳动监察司

(i) 劳资关系服务司

22. (a) 内政部

(b) 行政区域管理司

(c) 城镇规划和住房司

(d) 国民登记和移民司

(e) 国土和勘测司

(f) 新闻和信息办公室

(g) 民防

(h) 塞浦路斯通讯社

(i) 竞赛基金

(j) 难民关怀和安置司

23. 外交部

24. (a) 财政部

(b) 税务司

(c) 国内税收司

(d) 统计局

(e) 政府采购和供应司

(f) 公共管理和人事司

(g) 政府印刷办公室

(h) 信息技术服务司

25. 教育和文化部

26. (a) 通信和工程部

(b) 公共工程司

(c) Τμήμα Αρχαιοτήτων (Department of Antiquities)

(d) Τμήμα Πολιτικής Αεροπορίας (Department of Civil Aviation)

(e) Τμήμα Εμπορικής Ναυτιλίας (Department of Merchant Shipping)

(f) Τμήμα Ταχυδρομικών Υπηρεσιών (Postal Services Department)

(g) Τμήμα Οδικών Μεταφορών (Department of Road Transport)

(h) Τμήμα Ηλεκτρομηχανολογικών Υπηρεσιών (Department of Electrical and Mechanical Services)

(i) Τμήμα Ηλεκτρονικών Επικοινωνιών (Department of Electronic Telecommunications)

27. (a) Υπουργείο Υγείας (Ministry of Health)

(b) Φαρμακευτικές Υπηρεσίες (Pharmaceutical Services)

(c) Γενικό Χημείο (General Laboratory)

(d) Ιατρικές Υπηρεσίες και Υπηρεσίες Δημόσιας Υγείας (Medical and Public Health Services)

(e) Οδοντιατρικές Υπηρεσίες (Dental Services)

(f) Υπηρεσίες Ψυχικής Υγείας (Mental Health Services)

(c) 古迹司

(d) 民用航空司

(e) 商船运输司

(f) 邮政服务司

(g) 道路运输司

(h) 机电服务司

(i) 电子通信司

27. (a) 卫生部

(b) 医药局

(c) 总实验室

(d) 医疗和公共健康局

(e) 牙科局

(f) 心理健康局

LATVIA – LETTONIE - LETONIA

(Authentic in the English language only)

1. Valsts prezidenta kanceleja (Chancellery of the State President)
2. Saeimas kanceleja (Chancellery of the Parliament)
3. Aizsardzības ministrija un tās pakļautībā un pārraudzībā esošās iestādes (Ministry of Defence and institutions subordinate to it and under its supervision)[17]
4. Ārlietu ministrija un tās pakļautībā un pārraudzībā esošās iestādes (Ministry of Foreign Affairs and institutions subordinate to it and under its supervision)
5. Ekonomikas ministrija un tās pakļautībā un pārraudzībā esošās iestādes (Ministry of Economics and institutions subordinate to it and under its supervision)
6. Finanšu ministrija un tās pakļautībā un pārraudzībā esošās iestādes (Ministry of Finance and institutions subordinate to it and under its supervision)
7. Iekšlietu ministrija un tās pakļautībā un pārraudzībā esošās iestādes (Ministry of the Interior and institutions subordinate to it and under its supervision)
8. Izglītības un zinātnes ministrija un tās pakļautībā un pārraudzībā esošās iestādes (Ministry of Education and Science and institutions subordinate to it and under its supervision)
9. Kultūras ministrija un tās pakļautībā un pārraudzībā esošās iestādes (Ministry of Culture and institutions subordinate to it and under its supervision)
10. Labklājības ministrija un tās pakļautībā un pārraudzībā esošās iestādes (Ministry of Welfare and institutions subordinate to it and under its supervision)
11. Reģionālās attīstības un pašvaldību lietu ministrija un tās pakļautībā un pārraudzībā esošās iestādes (Ministry of Regional Development and local governments and institutions subordinate to it and under its supervision)
12. Satiksmes ministrija un tās pakļautībā un pārraudzībā esošās iestādes (Ministry of Transport and institutions subordinate to it and under its supervision)
13. Tieslietu ministrija un tās pakļautībā un pārraudzībā esošās iestādes (Ministry of Justice and institutions subordinate to it and under its supervision)
14. Veselības ministrija un tās pakļautībā un pārraudzībā esošās iestādes (Ministry of Health and institutions subordinate to it and under its supervision)

[17] Non-warlike materials contained in Part (3) of this Annex.

拉脱维亚

(仅以英文为准)

1. 国家总统官邸
2. 国会
3. 国防部及其附属和管理机构[17]
4. 外交部及其附属和管理机构
5. 经济部及其附属和管理机构
6. 财政部及其附属和管理机构
7. 内政部及其附属和管理机构
8. 教育和科学部及其附属和管理机构
9. 文化部及其附属和管理机构
10. 福利部及其附属和管理机构
11. 地区发展和地方政府部及其附属和管理机构
12. 运输部及其附属和管理机构
13. 司法部及其附属和管理机构
14. 卫生部及其附属和管理机构

[17]非军事物资包含在本附件第 3 部分。

15. Vides ministrija un tās pakļautībā un pārraudzībā esošās iestādes (Ministry of Environment and institutions subordinate to it and under its supervision)
16. Zemkopības ministrija un tās pārraudzībā esošās iestādes (Ministry of Agriculture and institutions under its supervision)
17. Īpašu uzdevumu ministrs bērnu un ģimenes lietās un tā pakļautībā un pārraudzībā esošās iestādes (Minister for Special Assignments for Children and Family Affairs and institutions subordinate to it and under its supervision)
18. Īpašu uzdevumu ministrs sabiedrības integrācijas lietās un tā pakļautībā un pārraudzībā esošās iestādes (Minister for Special Assignments for Integration Affairs and institutions subordinate to it and under its supervision)
19. Augstākās izglītības padome (Council of Higher Education)
20. Eiropas lietu birojs (European Affairs Bureau)
21. Valsts kanceleja un tās pakļautībā un pārraudzībā esošās iestādes (State Chancellery and institutions subordinate to it and under its supervision)
22. Centrālā vēlēšanu komisija (Central Election Commission)
23. Finansu un kapitāla tirgus komisija (Financial and Capital Market Commission)
24. Latvijas Banka (Bank of Latvia)
25. Nacionālie bruņotie spēki (National Armed Forces)
26. Nacionālā radio un televīzijas padome (National Broadcasting Council)
27. Sabiedrisko pakalpojumu regulēšanas komisija (Public Utilities Commission)
28. Satversmes aizsardzības birojs (Constitution Defence Bureau)
29. Valsts cilvēktiesību birojs (State Human Rights Bureau)
30. Valsts kontrole (State Audit Office)
31. Satversmes tiesa (Constitutional Court)
32. Augstākā tiesa (Supreme Court)
33. Prokuratūra un tās pārraudzībā esošās iestādes (Prosecutor's Office and institutions under its supervision)

15. 环境部及其附属和管理机构

16. 农业部及其管理机构

17. 儿童和家庭事务特别任务部及其附属和管理机构

18. 一体化事务特别任务部及其附属和管理机构

19. 高等教育理事会

20. 欧洲事务局

21. 内阁及其附属和管理机构

22. 中央选举委员会

23. 金融和资本市场委员会

24. 拉脱维亚银行

25. 国家武装部队

26. 国家广播委员会

27. 公用事业委员会

28. 宪法维护局

29. 国家人权局

30. 国家审计办公室

31. 宪法法院

32. 最高法院

33. 检察官办公室及其管理机构

LITHUANIA – LITUANIE - LITUANIA

(Authentic in the English language only)

1. Prezidento kanceliarija (Chancellery of the Office of the President)
2. Seimo kanceliarija (Chancellery of the Seimas (Parliament))
3. Konstitucinis Teismas (The Constitutional Court)
4. Vyriausybės kanceliarija (Chancellery of the Government)
5. Aplinkos ministerija ir įstaigos prie ministerijos (Ministry of Environment and institutions under the Ministry)
6. Finansų ministerija ir įstaigos prie ministerijos (Ministry of Finance and institutions under the Ministry)
7. Krašto apsaugos ministerija ir įstaigos prie ministerijos (Ministry of National Defence and institutions under the Ministry)[18]
8. Kultūros ministerija ir įstaigos prie ministerijos (Ministry of Culture and institutions under the Ministry)
9. Socialinės apsaugos ir darbo ministerija ir įstaigos prie ministerijos (Ministry of Social Security and Labour and institutions under the Ministry)
10. Susisiekimo ministerija ir įstaigos prie ministerijos (Ministry of Transport and Communications and institutions under the Ministry)
11. Sveikatos apsaugos ministerija ir įstaigos prie ministerijos (Ministry of Health and institutions under the Ministry)
12. Švietimo ir mokslo ministerija ir įstaigos prie ministerijos (Ministry of Education and Science and institutions under the Ministry)
13. Teisingumo ministerija ir įstaigos prie ministerijos (Ministry of Justice and institutions under the Ministry)
14. Ūkio ministerija ir įstaigos prie ministerijos (Ministry of Economy and institutions under the Ministry)
15. Užsienio reikalų ministerija ir įstaigos prie ministerijos (Ministry of Foreign Affairs and institutions under the Ministry)
16. Vidaus reikalų ministerija ir įstaigos prie ministerijos (Ministry of Internal Affairs and institutions under the Ministry)
17. Žemės ūkio ministerija ir įstaigos prie ministerijos (Ministry of Agriculture and institutions under the Ministry)
18. Nacionalinė teismų administracija (National Courts Administration)

[18] Non-warlike materials contained in Part (3) of this Annex.

立陶宛

(仅以英文为准)

1. 总统府
2. 国会赛玛斯
3. 宪法法院
4. 总理府
5. 环境部及其下属机构
6. 财政部及其下属机构
7. 国防部及其下属机构[18]
8. 文化部及其下司机构
9. 社会保障和劳动部及其下属机构
10. 运输和通信部及其下属机构
11. 卫生部及其下属机构
12. 教育和科学部及其下属机构
13. 司政部及其下属机构
14. 经济部及其下属机构
15. 外交部及其下属机构
16. 内政部及其下属机构
17. 农业部及其下属机构
18. 国家法院管理局

[18]非军事物资包含在本附件第 3 部分。

19. Lietuvos kariuomenė ir jos padaliniai (Lithuanian Armed Forces and structure thereof)[19]
20. Generalinė prokuratūra (The General Public Prosecutor's Office)
21. Valstybės kontrolė (State Control)
22. Lietuvos bankas (Bank of Lithuania)
23. Specialiųjų tyrimų tarnyba (Special Investigation Service)
24. Konkurencijos taryba (Competition Council)
25. Lietuvos gyventojų genocido ir rezistencijos tyrimo centras (Genocide and Resistance Research Centre of Lithuania)
26. Nacionalinė sveikatos taryba (National Health Council)
27. Moterų ir vyrų lygių galimybių kontrolieriaus tarnyba (Office of the Equal Opportunities Ombudsman)
28. Vaiko teisių apsaugos kontrolieriaus įstaiga (Children's Rights Ombudsmen Institution)
29. Seimo kontrolierių įstaiga (State Audit Office)
30. Valstybinė lietuvių kalbos komisija (State Commission of the Lithuanian Language)
31. Valstybinė paminklosaugos komisija (State Commission for Cultural Heritage Protection)
32. Vertybinių popierių komisija (Lithuanian Security Commission)
33. Vyriausioji rinkimų komisija (Central Electoral Committee)
34. Vyriausioji tarnybinės etikos komisija (Chief Commission of Official Ethics)
35. Etninės kultūros globos taryba (Council for the Protection of Ethnic Culture)
36. Žurnalistų etikos inspektoriaus tarnyba (Office of the Inspector of Journalists' Ethics)
37. Valstybės saugumo departamentas (State Security Department)
38. Valstybinė kainų ir energetikos kontrolės komisija (National Control Commission for Prices and Energy)
39. Vyriausioji administracinių ginčų komisija (Chief Administrative Disputes Commission)
40. Mokestinių ginčų komisija (Commission on Tax Disputes)
41. Valstybinė lošimų priežiūros komisija (State Gambling Supervisory Commission)
42. Lietuvos archyvų departamentas (Lithuanian Archives Department)
43. Europos teisės departamentas (European Law Department)
44. Lietuvos mokslo taryba (The Lithuanian Council of Science)
45. Ginklų fondas (Weaponry Fund)

[19] Non-warlike materials contained in Part (3) of this Annex.

19. 立陶宛武装部队及其机构[19]
20. 总检察长办公室
21. 国家调控局
22. 立陶宛银行
23. 特别调查局
24. 竞争委员会
25. 立陶宛种族灭绝和抵抗运动研究中心
26. 国民健康委员会
27. 机会平等巡视官办公室
28. 儿童权利巡视官机构
29. 国家审计办公室
30. 立陶宛国家语言委员会
31. 国家文化遗产保护委员会
32. 立陶宛安全委员会
33. 中央选举委员会
34. 公务员道德规范主任委员会
35. 民族文化保护理事会
36. 新闻记者道德规范监察办公室
37. 国家安全局
38. 国家价格和能源调控委员会
39. 主要行政争议处理委员会
40. 税收争端委员会
41. 国家赌博监督委员会
42. 立陶宛档案局
43. 欧洲法律局
44. 立陶宛科学委员会
45. 军备基金

[19]非军事物资包含在本附件第 3 部分。

46. Lietuvos valstybinis mokslo ir studijų fondas (Lithuanian State Science and Studies Foundation)
47. Informacinės visuomenės plėtros komitetas (Information Society Development Committee)
48. Kūno kultūros ir sporto departamentas (Lithuanian State Department of Physical Culture and Sport)
49. Ryšių reguliavimo tarnyba (Lithuanian Telecommunications Regulator)
50. Statistikos departamentas (Department of Statistics)
51. Tautinių mažumų ir išeivijos departamentas (Department of National Minorities and Lithuanians Living Abroad)
52. Valstybinė atominės energetikos saugos inspekcija (State Nuclear Safety Inspectorate)
53. Valstybinė duomenų apsaugos inspekcija (State Data Protection Inspectorate)
54. Valstybinė maisto ir veterinarijos tarnyba (State Food and Veterinary Service)
55. Valstybinė ligonių kasa (State Patients' Fund)
56. Valstybinė tabako ir alkoholio kontrolės tarnyba (State Tobacco and Alcohol Control Service)
57. Viešųjų pirkimų tarnyba (Public Procurement Office)
58. Lietuvos Aukščiausiasis Teismas (The Supreme Court of Lithuania)
59. Lietuvos apeliacinis teismas (The Court of Appeal of Lithuania)
60. Lietuvos vyriausiasis administracinis teismas (The Supreme Administrative Court of Lithuania)
61. Apygardų teismai (County Courts of Lithuania)
62. Apygardų administraciniai teismai (County Administrative Courts of Lithuania)
63. Apylinkių teismai (District Courts of Lithuania).

46.　立陶宛国家科学研究基金会

47.　信息社会发展委员会

48.　立陶宛国家体育运动局

49.　立陶宛电信管理机构

50.　统计局

51.　少数民族和海外立陶宛人事务局

52.　国家核安全监察局

53.　国家资料保护监察局

54.　国家食品和兽医局

55.　国家患者基金

56.　国家烟酒控制局

57.　公共采购办公室

58.　立陶宛最高法院

59.　立陶宛上诉法院

60.　立陶宛最高行政法院

61.　立陶宛地方法院

62.　立陶宛地方行政法院

63.　立陶宛地区法院

LUXEMBOURG - LUXEMBOURG - LUXEMBURGO

(La version française fait foi)

1. Ministère du Budget: Service Central des Imprimés et des Fournitures de l'Etat;
2. Ministère de l'Agriculture: Administration des Services Techniques de l'Agriculture;
3. Ministère de l'Education Nationale: Lycées d'Enseignement Secondaire et d'Enseignement Secondaire Technique;
4. Ministère de la Famille et de la Solidarité Sociale: Maisons de Retraite;
5. Ministère de la Force Publique: Armée[20] - Gendarmerie - Police;
6. Ministère de la Justice: Etablissements Pénitientiaires;
7. Ministère de la Santé Publique: Hôpital Neuropsychiatrique;
8. Ministère des Travaux Publics: Bâtiments Publics - Ponts et Chaussées;
9. Ministère des Communications: Centre Informatique de l'Etat
10. Ministère de l'Environnement: Administration de l'Environnement.

[20] Matériel non-militaire figurant dans la partie (3) de la présente annexe.

卢森堡

(仅以法文为准)

1. 预算部：国家印刷和供应品服务中心
2. 农业部：农业技术服务管理局
3. 国民教育部：中等教育和中等技术教育
4. 家庭和社会团结部：福利院
5. 公共武装部： 军队[20]– 法国警察部队—警察
6. 司法部：监狱设施
7. 公共卫生部：精神病院
8. 公共事业部：公共建筑—土木工程司
9. 通知部：国家信息中心
10. 环境部：环境管理局

[20]非军事物资包含在本附件第 3 部分。

HUNGARY – HONGRIE - HUNGRÍA

(Authentic in the English language only)

1. Belügyminisztérium (Ministry of the Interior)
2. Egészségügyi, Szociális és Családügyi Minisztérium (Ministry of Health, Social and Family Affairs)
3. Foglalkoztatáspolitikai és Munkaügyi Minisztérium (Ministry of Employment Policy and Labour Affairs)
4. Földművelésügyi és Vidékfejlesztési Minisztérium (Ministry of Agriculture and Rural Development)
5. Gazdasági és Közlekedési Minisztérium (Ministry of Economy and Transport)
6. Gyermek-, Ifjúsági és Sportminisztérium (Ministry of Children, Youth and Sports)
7. Honvédelmi Minisztérium (Ministry of Defence)[21]
8. Igazságügyi Minisztérium (Ministry of Justice)
9. Informatikai és Hírközlési Minisztérium (Ministry of Informatics and Communications)
10. Környezetvédelmi és Vízügyi Minisztérium (Ministry of Environment and Water Management)
11. Külügyminisztérium (Ministry of Foreign Affairs)
12. Miniszterelnöki Hivatal (Prime Minister's Office)
13. Nemzeti Kulturális Örökség Minisztériuma (Ministry of Cultural Heritage)
14. Oktatási Minisztérium (Ministry of Education)
15. Pénzügyminisztérium (Ministry of Finance)
16. Központi Szolgáltatási Főigazgatóság (Central Services Directorate)

[21] Non-warlike materials contained in Part (3) of this Annex.

匈牙利

(仅以英文为准)

1. 内政部
2. 卫生、社会和家庭部
3. 就业政策和劳动事务部
4. 农业和乡村发展部
5. 国家经济和交通部
6. 儿童、青年和体育部
7. 国防部[21]
8. 司法部
9. 信息和通信部
10. 环境和水利部
11. 外交部
12. 总理办公室
13. 文化遗产部
14. 教育部
15. 财政部
16. 中央服务局

[21]非军事物资包含在本附件第 3 部分。

MALTA – MALTE - MALTA

(Authentic in the English language only)

1. Uffiċċju tal-President (Office of the President)
2. Uffiċċju ta' l-Iskrivan tal-Kamra tad-Deputati (Office of the Clerk to the House of Representatives)
3. Uffiċċju tal-Prim Ministru (Office of the Prime Minister)[22]
4. Ministeru għall-Politika Soċjali (Ministry for Social Policy)
5. Ministeru ta' l-Edukazzjoni (Ministry of Education)
6. Ministeru tal-Finanzi u l-Affarijiet Ekonomiċi (Ministry of Finance and Economic Affairs)
7. Ministeru tar-Riżorsi u l-Infrastruttura (Ministry for Resources and Infrastructure)
8. Ministeru tat-Turiżmu (Ministry for Tourism)
9. Ministeru għat-Trasport u Komunikazzjoni (Ministry for Transport and Communications)
10. Ministeru tal-Ġustizzja u l-Intern (Ministry for Justice and Home Affairs)
11. Ministeru għall-Affarijiet Rurali u l-Ambjent (Ministry for Rural Affairs and the Environment)
12. Ministeru għal Għawdex (Ministry for Gozo)
13. Ministeru tas-Saħħa (Ministry of Health)
14. Ministeru ta' l-Affarijiet Barranin (Ministry of Foreign Affairs)
15. Ministeru għat-Teknoloġija ta' l-Informazzjoni u Investiment (Ministry for Information Technology and Investment)
16. Ministeru għaż-Żgħażagħ u l-Kultura (Ministry for Youth and the Arts)

[22] Procurement for the Armed Forces of Malta: non-warlike materials contained in Part (3) of this Annex.

马耳他

(仅以英文为准)

1. 总统府
2. 众议院职员办公室
3. 总理府[22]
4. 社会政策部
5. 教育部
6. 财政和经济事务部
7. 资源和基础设施部
8. 旅游部
9. 交通和通信部
10. 司法和家庭事务部
11. 乡村事务和环境部
12. 戈佐岛部
13. 卫生部
14. 外交部
15. 信息技术和投资部
16. 青年和艺术部

[22]马耳他武装部队采购：非军事物资包含在本附件第 3 部分。

NETHERLANDS - PAYS BAS - PAÍSES BAJOS

(Authentic in the English Language only)

List of entities

Ministries and central governmental bodies

1.	MINISTRY OF GENERAL AFFAIRS	MINISTERIE VAN ALGEMENE ZAKEN
	Advisory Council on Government Policy	Bureau van de Wetenschappelijke Raad voor het Regeringsbeleid
	National Information Office	Rijksvoorlichtingsdienst (Directie voorlichting, RVD-DV; Directie toepassing communicatie-techniek, RVD-DTC)
2.	MINISTRY OF THE INTERIOR	MINISTERIE VAN BINNENLANDSE ZAKEN
	Government Personnel Information System Service	Dienst Informatievoorziening Overheidspersoneel
	Public Servants Medical Expenses Agency	Dienst Ziektekostenvoorziening Overheidspersoneel
	Central Archives	Centrale Archiefselectiedienst
		Binnenlandse Veiligheidsdienst (BVD)
	Netherlands Institute for Firemen and Combatting Calamities	Nederlands Instituut voor Brandweer en Rampenbestrijding (NIBRA)
	Netherlands Bureau for Exams of Firemen	Nederlands Bureau Brandweer Examens (NBBE)
	National Institue for Selection and Education of Policemen	Landelijk Selectie en Opleidingsinstituut Politie (LSOP)
	25 Individual Police Regions	25 Afzonderlijke politieregio's
	National Police Forces	Korps Landelijke Politiediensten
3.	MINISTRY OF FOREIGN AFFAIRS	MINISTERIE VAN BUITENLANDSE ZAKEN
	SNV Organisation for Development Cooperation and Awareness	SNV, Organisatie voor Ontwikkelingssamenwerking en Bewustwording
	CBI, Centre for promotion of import from developing countries	CBI, Centrum tot Bevordering van de Import uit Ontwikkelingslanden

荷兰

(仅以英文为准)

实体清单

各部和中央政府机构

1. 总务部

政府政策咨询委员会

国家信息办公室

2. 内政部

政府个人信息系统局

公务员医疗费用局

中央档案室

荷兰消防抗灾局

荷兰消防考试局

荷兰警察选拔和教局

25 个警区

国家警察部队

3. 外交部

发展组织

促进自发展中国家进口中心

4.	MINISTRY OF DEFENCE[23]	MINISTERIE VAN DEFENSIE
	Central Organisation, Ministry of Defense	Centrale organisatie van het ministerie van Defensie
	Staff, Defense Interservice Command	Staf Defensie Interservice Commando (DICO)
	Defense telematics Agency (establishment of this new service is expected to take place on 1 September 1997)	Defensie telematica Organisatie (DTO)
	Duyverman Computer Centre	Duyverman Computer Centrum (DCC)
	(This service will be part of DTO and will consequently loose, as from 1 January 1998, its status as independent procurement service)	
	Central Directorate, Defense Infrastucture Agency	Centrale directie van de Dienst Gebouwen, Werken en Terreinen
	The individual regional directorates of the Defence Infrastructure Agency	De afzonderlijke regionale directies van de Dienst Gebouwen, Worken en Terreinen
	Directorate of material Royal Netherlands Navy	Directie materieel Koninklijke Marine
	Directorate of material Royal Netherlands Army	Directie materieel Koninklijke Landmacht
	Information Technology Support Centre, Royal Netherlands Army	Dienstcentrum Automatisering Koninklijke Landmacht
	Directorate of material Royal Netherlands Airforce	Directie materieel Koninklijke Luchtmacht
	Defense Pipeline Organisation	Defensie Pijpleiding Organisatie
5.	MINISTRY OF ECONOMIC AFFAIRS	MINISTERIE VAN ECONOMISCHE ZAKEN
	Economic Investigation Agency	Economische Controledienst
	Central Plan Bureau	Centraal Planbureau
	Netherlands Central Bureau of Statistics	Centraal Bureau voor de Statistiek
	Senter	Senter
	Industrial Property Office	Bureau voor de Industriële Eigendom
	Central Licensing Office for Import and Export	Centrale Dienst voor de In- en Uitvoer
	State Supervision of Mines	Staatstoezicht op de Mijnen

[23] Non-warlike materials contained in Part (3) of this Annex.

4. 国防部[23]

国防部办公厅

各军种司令部参谋部

国防部信息技术局 (该新机构预计 1997 年 9 月 1 日设立)

杜瓦曼电脑中心(该机构将成为国防部信息技术局一部分，从而自 1998 年 1 月 1 日起不再具有独立采购服务地位)

国防基础设施局中央局

国防基础设施局各地区局

荷兰皇家海军物资局

荷兰皇家陆军物资局

荷兰皇家陆军信息技术支持中心

荷兰皇家空军物资局

国防部信息传递机构

5. 经济事务部

经济调查局

中央计划局

荷兰中央统计局

创新和永续发展局

工业产权办公室

中央进出口许可办公室

国家矿业监督局

[23]非军事物资包含在本附件第 3 部分。

6.	MINISTRY OF FINANCE	MINISTERIE VAN FINANCIËN
	Directorates of the State Tax Department	Directies der Rijksbelastingen
	State Tax Department/Fiscal Intelligence and Information Department	Belastingdienst/FIOD
	State Tax Department/Computer Centre	Belastingdienst/Automatiseringscentrum
	State Tax Department/Training	Belastingdienst/Opleidingen
7.	MINISTRY OF JUSTICE	MINISTERIE VAN JUSTITIE
	Service for judicial institutions	Dienst justitiële inrichtingen
	Service prevention, Youth protection and rehabilitation	Dienst preventie, Jeugd bescherming en reclassering
	Service Administration of justice	Dienst rechtspleging
	Central Debt Collection Agency of the Ministry of Justice	Centraal Justitie Incassobureau
	National Police Services Force	Korps Landelijke Politiediensten
	Immigration and Naturalisation Service	Immigratie- en Naturalisatiedienst
	Public Prosecutor	Openbaar Ministerie
8.	MINISTRY OF AGRICULTURE, NATURE MANAGEMENT AND FISHERIES	MINISTERIE VAN LANDBOUW, NATUURBEHEER EN VISSERIJ
		Dienst Landelijke Service bij Regelingen (LASER)
	Game Fund	Jachtfonds
	National Inspection Service for Animals and Animal Protection	Rijksdienst voor de Keuring van Vee en Vlees (RVV)
	Plant Protection Service	Plantenziektenkundige Dienst (PD)
	National Forest Service	Staatsbosbeheer (SBB)
	General Inspection Service	Algemene Inspectiedienst (AID)
		Dienst Landinrichting Beheer Landbouwgronden (LBL)
	Agricultural Research Service	Dienst Landbouwkundig Onderzoek (DLO)
	National Fisheries Research Institute	Rijksinstituut voor Visserijonderzoek (RIVO-DLO)
	Government Institute for Quality Control of Agricultural Products	Rijkskwaliteit Instituut voor Land- en Tuinbouwprodukten (RILJIT-DLO)
	National Institute for Nature Management	Instituut voor Bos- en Natuuronderzoek
		De afzonderlijke Regionale Beleidsdirecties

6. 财政部

国家税务局

国家税务司/财政情报和信息司

国家税务司/计算机中心

国家税务司/培训处

7. 司法部

司法机构局

预防、青年保护和安置局

司法行政管理局

司法部中央债务代收中心

国家警察部队

移民和归化局

检察官办公室

8. 农业、自然管理和渔业部

狩猎基金

国家动物和动物保护监察局

植物保护局

国家森林局

总监察局

农业研究局

国家渔业研究所

政府农产品质量控制机构

国家自然管理机构

9.	MINISTRY OF EDUCATION, CULTURE AND SCIENCE	MINISTERIE VAN ONDERWIJS, CULTUUR EN WETENSCHAPPEN
	Netherlands State Institute for War Documentation	Rijksinstituut voor Oorlogsdocumentatie
	Public Record Office	Rijksarchiefdienst
	Council for Education	Onderwijsraad
	Advisory Council for Science and Technology Policy	Adviesraad voor het Wetenschap en Technologiebeleid
	Central Financial Entities	Centrale Financiën Instellingen
	Inspection of Education	Onderwijsinspectie
	National Institute for Ancient Monuments	Rijksdienst voor de Monumentenzorg
	National Institute for Archeological Soil Exploration	Rijksdienst Oudheidkundig Bodemonderzoek
	Council for Cultural Heritage	Raad voor Cultuur
10.	MINISTRY OF SOCIAL AFFAIRS AND EMPLOYMENT	MINISTERIE VAN SOCIALE ZAKEN EN WERKGELEGENHEID
11.	MINISTRY OF TRANSPORT, PUBLIC WORKS AND WATER MANAGEMENT	MINISTERIE VAN VERKEER EN WATERSTAAT
	Directorate-General for Civil Aviation	Directoraat-Generaal Rijksluchtvaartdienst
	Directorate-General for Navigation and Maritime Affairs	Directoraat-Generaal Scheepvaart en Maritieme Zaken
	Directorate-General for Transport	Directoraat-Generaal Vervoer
	Directorate-General for Public Works and Water Management	Directoraat-Generaal Rijkswaterstaat
	Telecommunications and Post Department	Hoofddirectie Telecommunicatie en Post
	Royal Netherlands Meteorological Institute	Koninklijk Nederlands Meteorologisch Instituut
	Central Services	Centrale Diensten
	The individual regional directories of Water Management	De afzonderlijke regionale directies van Rijkswaterstaat
	The individual specialised services of Water Management	De afzonderlijke specialistische diensten van Rijkswaterstaat
	Service for Construction	Bouwdienst
	Geometric Service	Meetkundige dienst

9. 教育、文化和科学部

荷兰国家战争文献研究所

公共档案办公室

教育委员会

科技政策咨询委员会

中央财务机构

教育监察局

国家古迹协会

国家考古地质勘测研究院

文化遗产理事会

10. 社会事务和就业部

11. 交通、公共工程和水管理部

民用航空管理总局

航海与海事总局

运输总局

公共工程和水管理总局

通信和邮政司

荷兰皇家气象研究所

中央服务局

各地区水管理理事会

各水管理专业局

工程局

地理测量局

	Advisory Council for Traffic and Transport	Adviesdienst Verkeer en Vervoer
	National Institute for Coastal and Marine Management	Rijksinstituut voor Kust en Zee
	National Institute for Sweet Water Management and Waste Water Treatment	Rijksinstituut voor Integraal Zoetwaterbeheer en Afvalwaterbehandeling
12.	MINISTRY OF HOUSING, PHYSICAL PLANNING AND ENVIRONMENT	MINISTERIE VAN VOLKSHUISVESTING, RUIMTELIJKE ORDENING EN MILIEUBEHEER
	Directorate-General for Environment Management	Directoraat-Generaal Milieubeheer
	Directorate-General for Public Housing	Directoraat-Generaal van de Volkshuisvesting
	Government Buildings Agency	Rijksgebouwendienst
	National Physical Planning Agency	Rijksplanologische Dienst
13.	MINISTRY OF WELFARE, HEALTH AND CULTURAL AFFAIRS	MINISTERIE VAN VOLKSGEZONDHEID, WELZIJN EN SPORT
	Inspection Health Protection	Inspectie Gezondheidsbescherming
	Inspection Public Health	Inspectie Gezondheidszorg
	Veterinary Inspection	Veterinaire Inspectie
	Inspectorate for Child and Youth Care and Protection Services	Inspectie Jeugdhulpverlening en Jeugdbescherming
	National Institute of Public Health and Environmental Protection	Rijksinstituut voor de Volksgezondheid en Milieuhygiëne (RIVM)
	Social and Cultural Planning Office	Sociaal en Cultureel Planbureau
	Agency to the College for Assessment of Pharmaceuticals	Agentschap t.b.v. het College ter Beoordeling van Geneesmiddelen
14.	SECOND CHAMBER OF THE STATES GENERAL	TWEEDE KAMER DER STATEN-GENERAAL
15.	FIRST CHAMBER OF THE STATES GENERAL	EERSTE KAMER DER STATEN-GENERAAL
16.	CABINET FOR NETHERLANDS ANTILLEAN AND ARUBAN AFFAIRS	KABINET VOOR NEDERLANDS-ANTILLIAANSE EN ARUBAANSE ZAKEN
17.	COUNCIL OF STATE	RAAD VAN STATE
18.	NETHERLANDS COURT OF AUDIT	ALGEMENE REKENKAMER

交通和运输咨询委员会

国家沿海和海事研究所

国家淡水管理和污水处理研究所

12. 住房、体育和环境部

环境管理总局

公共住房总局

政府建筑局

国家体育规划局

13. 福利、卫生 文化事务部

健康保障监察局

公共卫生监察局

动物监察局

儿童和青年关心和保护监察局

国家公共卫生和环境保护机构

社会和文化规划办公室

药品评估机构管理局

14. 下议院

15. 上议院

16. 荷兰、安替列群岛与阿鲁巴岛事务内阁

17. 国家委员会

18. 荷兰审计法院

19.	NATIONAL OMBUDSMAN	NATIONALE OMBUDSMAN
20.	CHANCELLERY OF THE NETHERLANDS ORDER	KANSELARIJ DER NEDERLANDSE ORDEN
21.	THE QUEEN'S CABINET	KABINET DER KONINGIN

19. 国家巡视官

20. 荷兰法令大臣官邸

21. 女王内阁

AUSTRIA - AUTRICHE - AUSTRIA

(Authentic in the English language only)

(A) Present coverage of entities:

1.		Federal Chancellery	Bundeskanzleramt
2.		Federal Ministry for Foreign Affairs	Bundesministerium für auswärtige Angelegenheiten
3.		Federal Ministry of Labour, health and social affairs	Bundesministerium für arbeit, Gesundheit und soziales
4.		Federal Ministry of Finance	Bundesministerium für Finanzen
	(a)	Procurement Office	Amtswirtschaftsstelle
	(b)	Division III/1 (procurement of technical appliances, equipments and goods for the customs guard)	Abteilung III/1 (Beschaffung von technischen Geräten, Einrichtungen und Sachgütern für die Zollwache)
	(c)	Federal EDP-Office (procurement of the Federal Ministry of Finance and of the Federal Office of Accounts)	Bundesrechenamt (EDV-Bereich des Bundesministeriums für Finanzen und des Bundesrechenamtes)
5.		Federal Ministry for Environment, Youth and Family – Procurement Office	Bundesministerium für Umwelt, Jugend und Familie, Amtwirtschaftsstelle
6.		Federal Ministry for Economic Affairs	Bundesministerium für wirtschaftliche Angelegenheiten, Amtswirtschaftsstelle
7.		Federal Ministry of Internal Affairs	Bundesministerium für Inneres
	(a)	Division I/5 (Procurement Office)	Abteilung I/5 (Amtswirtschaftsstelle)
	(b)	Division I/6 [procurement of goods (other than those procured by Division II/3) for the Federal Police]	Abteilung I/6 (Beschaffung aller Sachgüter für die Bundespolizei soweit sie nicht von der Abteilung II/3 beschafft werden)
	(c)	EDP-Centre (procurement of electronical data processing machines (hardware))	EDV-Zentrale (Beschaffung von EDV-"Hardware")
	(d)	Division II/3 (procurement of technical appliances and equipments for the Federal Police)	Abteilung II/3 (Beschaffung von technischen Geräten und Einrichtungen für die Bundespolizei)
	(e)	Division II/5 (procurement of technical appliances and equipment for the Federal Provincial Police)	Abteilung II/5 (Beschaffung von technischenGeräten und Einrichtungen für die Bundesgendarmerie)

奥地利

(仅以英文为准)

(A) 实体目前涵盖范围：

1. 联邦总理府

2. 联邦外交部

3. 联邦劳工、卫生和社会事务部

4. 联邦财政部

(a) 采购办公室

(b) III/1 处(关警用技术装置、设备和货物的采购)

(c) 联邦电子数据处理办公室 (联邦财政部和联邦统制局的采购)

5. 联邦环境、青年和家庭部—采购办公室

6. 联邦经济事务部

7. 联邦内政部

(a) I/5 处 (采购办公室)

(b) I/6 处 [联邦警察用货物的采购 (II/3 处采购的货物除外)]

(c) 电子数据处理中心 (电子数据处理机(硬件)的采购)

(d) II/3 处(联邦警察用技术装置和设备的采购)

(e) II/5 处 (州联邦警察用采购技术装置和设备的采购)

2007 年 1 月 1 日 (WT/Let/556)

	(f)	Division II/19 (procurement of equiment for supervision of road traffic)	Abteilung II/19 (Beschaffung von Einrichtungen zur Überwachung des Straβ enverkehrs)
	(g)	Divsion II/21 (procurement of aircraft)	Abteilung II/21 (Beschaffung von Flugzeugen)
8.		Federal Ministry for Justice – Procurement Office	Bundesministerium für Justiz, Amtswirtschaftsstelle
9.		Federal Ministry of Defence[24]	Bundesministerium für Landesverteidigung (Nichtkriegsmaterial wie in Annex I, Teil 3 angeführt)
10.		Federal Ministry of Agriculture and Forestry	Bundesministerium für Land- und Forstwirtschaft
11.		Federal Ministry of Education and Cultural Affairs	Bundesministerium für Unterricht und kulturelle Angelegenheiten
12.		Federal Ministry for Science and Transport	Bundesministerium für Wissenschaft und Verkehr
13.		Austrian Central Statistical Office	Österreichisches Statistisches Zentralamt
14.		Austrian Federal Academy of Public Administration	Verwaltungsakademie des Bundes
15.		Federal Office of Metrology and Surveying	Bundesamt für Eich- und Vermessungswesen
16.		Federal Institute for Testing and Research, Arsenal (BVFA)	Bundesforschungs- und Prüfzentrum Arsenal
17		Austro control GES. M.B.H. - Austrian office for civil aviation	Austro Control GES. M.B.H. - Österreichische Gesellschaft für Zivilluftfahrt
18.		Federal Institute for Testing of Motor Vehicles	Bundesprüfanstalt für Kraftfahrzeuge
19.		Post and Telecom Austria	Post und Telecom Austria Aktiengesellschaft

(B) All other central public authorities including their regional and local sub-divisions provided that they do not have an industrial or commercial character.

[24] Non-warlike materials contained in Part (3) of this Annex.

(f) II/19 处 (道路交通监督设备的采购)

(g) II/21 处 (航空器的采购)

8. 联邦司法部—采购办公室

9. 联邦国防部[24]

10. 联邦农业和林业部

11. 联邦教育和文化事务部

12. 联邦科学和运输部

13. 奥地利中央统计办公室

14. 奥地利联邦公共行政管理学院

15. 联邦计量和勘测办公室

16. 联邦阿森纳测试和研究所

17 奥地利空中监管中心—奥地利民用航空办公室

18. 联邦机动车测试研究所

19. 奥地利邮政电信局

(B) 所有其他中央公共机构，含其地区和地方分支机构，只要此类机构不具产业或商业性质。

[24]非军事物资包含在本附件第 3 部分。

POLAND – POLOGNE - POLONIA

(Authentic in the English language only)

1. Kancelaria Prezydenta RP (Chancellery of the President of the Republic of Poland)
2. Kancelaria Sejmu RP (Chancellery of the Sejm)
3. Kancelaria Senatu RP (Chancellery of the Senate)
4. Sąd Najwyższy (Supreme Court)
5. Naczelny Sąd Administracyjny (Supreme Administrative Court)
6. Trybunał Konstytucyjny (Constitutional Court)
7. Najwyższa Izba Kontroli (Supreme Chamber of Control)
8. Biuro Rzecznika Praw Obywatelskich (Office of the Ombudsman)
9. Krajowa Rada Radiofonii i Telewizji (National Broadcasting Council)
10. Generalny Inspektor Ochrony Danych Osobowych (Inspector General for the Protection of Personal Data)
11. Państwowa Komisja Wyborcza (State Election Commission)
12. Krajowe Biuro Wyborcze (National Election Office)
13. Państwowa Inspekcja Pracy (National Labour Inspectorate)
14. Biuro Rzecznika Praw Dziecka (Office of the Children's Rigths Ombudsman)
15. Kancelaria Prezesa Rady Ministrów (Prime Minister's Chancellery)
16. Ministerstwo Finansów (Ministry of Finance)
17. Ministerstwo Gospodarki Pracy i Polityki Społecznej (Ministry of Economy, Labour and Social Policy)
18. Ministerstwo Kultury (Ministry of Culture)
19. Ministerstwo Nauki i Informatyzacji (Ministry of Science and Informatisation)
20. Ministerstwo Obrony Narodowej (Ministry of National Defence)[25]
21. Ministerstwo Rolnictwa i Rozwoju Wsi (Ministry of Agriculture and Rural Development)
22. Ministerstwo Skarbu Państwa (Ministry of the State Treasury)
23. Ministerstwo Sprawiedliwości (Ministry of Justice)
24. Ministerstwo Infrastruktury (Ministry of Infrastructure)
25. Ministerstwo Środowiska (Ministry of Environment)

[25] Non-warlike materials contained in Part (3) of this Annex.

波兰

(仅以英文为准)

1. 波兰共和国总统府
2. 色姆(下院)
3. 上院
4. 最高法院
5. 最高行政法院
6. 宪法法院
7. 最高审计院
8. 巡视官办公室
9. 国家广播理事会
10. 个人信息保护检察长
11. 国家选举委员会
12. 国家选举办公室
13. 国家劳动监察局
14. 儿童权利保障巡视官
15. 总理府
16. 财政部
17. 经济、劳动和社会政策部
18. 文化部
19. 科学和信息化部
20. 国防部[25]
21. 农业和乡村发展部
22. 国库部
23. 司法部
24. 基础设施部
25. 环境部

[25]非军事物资包含在本附件第 3 部分。

2007 年 1 月 1 日 (WT/Let/556)

26. Ministerstwo Spraw Wewnętrznych i Administracji (Ministry of Internal Affairs and Administration)
27. Ministerstwo Spraw Zagranicznych (Ministry of Foreign Affairs)
28. Ministerstwo Zdrowia (Ministry of Health)
29. Ministerstwo Edukacji Narodowej i Sportu (Ministry of National Education and Sport)
30. Urząd Komitetu Integracji Europejskiej (Office of the Committee for European Integration)
31. Rządowe Centrum Studiów Strategicznych (Government Centre for Strategic Studies)
32. Agencja Restrukturyzacji i Modernizacji Rolnictwa (Agency for Restructuring and Modernisation of Agriculture)
33. Agencja Rynku Rolnego (Agriculture Market Agency)
34. Agencja Własności Rolnej Skarbu Państwa (State Treasury Agricultural Property Agency)
35. Narodowy Fundusz Zdrowia (National Health Fund)
36. Polska Akademia Nauk (Polish Academy of Science)
37. Polskie Centrum Akredytacji (Polish Acreditation Centre)
38. Polski Komitet Normalizacyjny (Polish Committee for Standardisation)
39. Rządowe Centrum Legislacji (Government Legislation Centre)
40. Zakład Ubezpieczeń Społecznych (Social Insurance Office)
41. Komisja Nadzoru Ubezpieczeń i Funduszy Emerytalnych (Insurance and Pension Funds Supervisiory Commission)
42. Komisja Papierów Wartościowych i Giełd (Polish Securities and Exchange Commission)
43. Główny Urząd Miar (Main Office of Measures)
44. Urząd Patentowy Rzeczpospolitej Polskiej (Patent Office of the Republic of Poland)
45. Urząd Regulacji Energetyki (The Energy Regulatory Authority of Poland)
46. Urząd do Spraw Kombatantów i Osób Represjonowanych (Office for Military Veterans and Victims of Repression)
47. Generalna Dyrekcja Dróg Krajowych i Autostrad (The General Directorate of National Roads and Motorways)
48. Urząd Transportu Kolejowego (Office for Railroad Transport)
49. Urząd Głównego Inspektora Transportu Drogowego (Office of the Main Inspector of Road Transport)
50. Główny Urząd Geodezji i Kartografii (The Main Office of Geodesy and Cartography)

26. 内政和行政管理部
27. 外交部
28. 卫生部
29. 国民教育和体育部
30. 欧洲一体化委员会办公室
31. 政府战略研究中心
32. 农业重组和现代化局
33. 农业市场局
34. 国库农业产权局
35. 国家健康基金
36. 波兰国家科学院
37. 波兰认证中心
38. 波兰标准化委员会
39. 政府立法中心
40. 社会保险局
41. 保险和养老基金监管委员会
42. 波兰证券交易委员会
43. 计量总局
44. 波兰共和国专利办公室
45. 波兰能源管理局
46. 退伍和伤残军人管理办公室
47. 国家道路和高速公路总局
48. 铁路运输局
49. 道路运输检察长办公室
50. 测绘总局

51. Główny Urząd Nadzoru Budowlanego (The Main Office for Construction Supervision)
52. Urząd Lotnictwa Cywilnego (The Main Office for Civil Aviation)
53. Urząd Regulacji Telekomunikacji i Poczty (Office for Telecommunication Regulation and Post)
54. Naczelna Dyrekcja Archiwów Państowych (The Main Directorate for National Archives)
55. Kasa Rolniczego Ubezpieczenia Społecznego (Farmers Social Security Fund)
56. Główny Inspektorat Inspekcji Ochrony Roślin i Nasiennictwa (The Main Inspectorate for the Inspection of Plant and Seeds Protection)
57. Główny Inspektorat Jakości Handlowej Artykułów Rolno-Spożywczych (The Main Inspectorate of Commercial Quality of Agri-Food Products)
58. Główny Inspektorat Weterynarii (The Main Veterinary Inspectorate)
59. Komenda Główna Państwowej Straży Pożarnej (The Chief Command of the National Fire-guard)
60. Komenda Główna Policy (The Chief Police Command)
61. Komenda Główna Straży Granicznej (The Chief Boarder Guards Command)
62. Urząd do Spraw Repatriacji i Cudzoziemców (Office for Repatriation and Foreigners)
63. Urząd Zamówień Publicznych (Public Procurement Office)
64. Wyższy Urząd Górniczy (Main Mining Office)
65. Główny Inspektorat Ochrony Środowiska (The Main Inspectorate for Environment Protection)
66. Państwowa Agencja Atomistyki (State Atomic Agency)
67. Główny Inspektorat Farmaceutyczny (Main Pharmaceutical Inspectorate)
68. Główny Inspektorat Sanitarny (Main Sanitary Inspectorate)
69. Agencja Bezpieczeństwa Wewnętrznego (Internal Security Agency)
70. Agencja Wywiadu (Foreign Intelligence Agency)
71. Główny Urząd Statystyczny (Main Statistical Office)
72. Urząd Ochrony Konkurencji i Konsumentów (Office for Competition and Consumer Protection)
73. Urząd Służby Cywilnej (Civil Service Office)
74. Instytut Pamięci Narodowej – Komisja Ścigania Zbrodni Przeciwko Narodowi Polskiemu (National Remembrance Institute – Commission for the Prosecution of Crimes Against the Polish Nation)

51. 建筑监督总局
52. 民用航空总局
53. 电信管理和邮政办公室
54. 国家档案总局
55. 农民社会保险基金
56. 植物和种子保护监察总局
57. 农业食品质量监察总局
58. 兽医监察总局
59. 国家消防队总司令部
60. 警察总司令部
61. 边防警卫总司令部
62. 归国人员和外国人事务办公室
63. 公共采购办公室
64. 采矿管理总局
65. 环境保护监察总局
66. 国家原子能机构
67. 药品监察总局
68. 卫生监察总局
69. 国内安全机构
70. 外国情报机构
71. 国家统计总局
72. 竞争和消费者保护办公室
73. 行政事务办公室
74. 国家纪念协会–波兰叛国罪起诉委员会

75. Państwowa Agencja Inwestycji Zagranicznych (State Foreign Investment Agency)
76. Polska Konfederacja Sportu (Polish Confederation of Sport)
77. Narodowy Bank Polski (National Bank of Poland)
78. Narodowy Fundusz Ochrony Środowiska i Gospodarki Wodnej (The National Fund for Environmental Protection and Water Management)
79. Państwowy Fundusz Rehabilitacji Osób Niepełnosprawnych (State Fund for the Rehabilitation of the Disabled)
80. Polskie Centrum Badań I Certyfikacji (Polish Centre for Testing and Certification)
81. Agencja Mienia Wojskowego (Agency for Military Property)[26]

[26] Non-warlike materials contained in Part (3) of this Annex.

75. 国家外国投资机构
76. 波兰运动联合会
77. 波兰国家银行
78. 国家环境保护和水管理基金会
79. 国家残疾人安置基金
80. 波兰测试和认证中心
81. 军用物资局[26]

[26]非军事物资包含在本附件第 3 部分。

PORTUGAL - PORTUGAL - PORTUGAL

(Authentic in the English language only)

1.	PRIME MINISTER'S OFFICE	PRESIDÊNCIA DO CONSELHO DE MINISTROS
	Secretariat-General, Prime Minister's Office	Secretaria-Geral da Presidéncia do Conselho de Ministros
	High Commissioner for Imigration and Ethnic Minorities	Alto Comissário para a Imigraçao e Minorias Étnicas
	High Commissioner for the Questions on Equality Promotion and Family	Alto Comissário para as Questões da Promoção da Igualdade e da Familia
	Legal Centre	Centro Juridico-CEJUR
	Government Computer Network Management Centre	Centro de Gestão da Rede Informática do Governo
	Commission for Equality and Women's Rights	Comissão para a Igualdade e para os Direitos das Mulheres
	Economic and Social Council	Conselho Económico e Social
	High Council on Administration and Civil Service	Conselho Superior da Administração e da Função Pública
	Ministerial Department on Planning, Studies and Support	Gabinete de Apoio, Estudos e Planeamento
	Ministerial Department with Special Responsibility for Macao	Gabinete de Macau
	Ministerial Department responsible for Community Service by Conscientious Objectors	Gabinete do Serviço Cívico e dos Objectores de Consciência
	Ministerial Department for European Affairs	Gabinete dos Assuntos Europeus
	Secretariat for Administrative Modernization	Secretariado para a Modernisação Administrativa
	High Council on Sports	Conselho Superior do Desporto
2.	MINISTRY OF HOME AFFAIRS	MINISTÉRIO DA ADMINISTRAÇAO INTERNA
	Secretariat-General	Secretaria-Geral
	Legal Service	Auditoria Jurídica
	Directorate-General for Roads	Direcção-Geral de Viação

葡萄牙

(仅以英文为准)

1.　总理府

总理府总秘书长

移民和少数民族高级专员

平等促进和家庭问题高级专员

法律中心

政府计算机网络管理中心

平等和妇女权利委员会

经济和社会理事会

行政管理和行政事务高级理事会

计划、研究和支持部

澳门特别职能部

拒服兵役人员社区服务部

欧洲事务部

行政管理现代化秘书处

体育高级理事会

2.　内政部

总秘书处

法律局

道路总局

	Ministerial Department responsible for Studies and Planning	Gabinete de Estudos e Planeamento de Instalações
	Ministerial Department for European Affairs	Gabinete dos Assuntos Europeus
	National Fire Service	Gabinete Nacional Sirene
	Republican National Guard	Guarda Nacional Republicana
	Civilian Administrations	Governos Civis
	Police	Polícia de Segurança Pública
	General Inspectorate on Internal Administration	Inspecção-Geral da Administração Interna
	Technical Secretariat for Electoral Matters	Secretariado técnico dos Assuntos para e Processo Eleitoral
	Customs and Immigration Department	Serviço de Estrangeiros e Fronteiras
	Intelligence and Security Department	Serviço de Informaçoões de Segurança
3.	MINISTRY OF AGRICULTURE, OF RURAL DEVELOPMENT AND FISHERIES	MINISTÉRIO DA AGRICULTURA, DO DESENVOLVIMENTO RURAL E DAS PESCAS
	Secretariat-General	Secretaria-Geral
	Legal Service	Auditoria Jurídica
	Environment Audit Office	Auditor do Ambiente
	National Council of Agriculture, Rural Development and Fisheries	Conselho Nacional da Agricultura, do Desenvolvimiento Rural et das Pescas
	Directorate-General for Forests	Direcção-Geral das Florestas
	Directorate-General for Fisheries and Agriculture	Direcção-Geral das Pescas e Agricultura
	Directorate-General for Rural Development	Direcção-Geral do Desenvolvimento Rural
	Directorate-General for Control of Food Quality	Direcção-Geral de Fiscalização e Controlo da Qualidade Alimentar
	Institute for Hydraulic questions, Rural Engineering and Enviroment	Instituto de Hidráulica, Engenharia Rural e Ambiente
	Directorate-General for Culture Protection	Direcção-Geral de Protecção das Culturas
	Directorate-General of Veterinary	Direcção-Geral de Veterinária
	Regional Directorates for Agriculture (7)	Direcções Regionais de Agriculture (7)

研究和计划部

欧洲事务部

国家消防局

共和国国家卫队

民政局

警察

国内行政管理监察总局

选举事务技术秘书处

海关和移民司

情报和安全司

3. 农业、乡村发展和渔业部

总秘书处

法律局

环境审计办公室

国家农业、乡村发展和渔业理事会

森林总局

渔业和农业总局

乡村发展总局

食品质量控制总局

水利、乡村工程和环境研究所

文化保护总局

兽医总局

地区农业局 (7 个)

	Ministerial Department for Planning and Agri-food Policy	Gabinete de Planeamento e Política Agroalimentar
	General Inspectorate and Audit Office (Management Audits)	Inspecção-Geral e Auditoria de Gestão
	General Inspectorate for fisheries	Inspecção-Geral das Pescas
	Equestrian National Service	Serviço Nacional Coudêlico
	National Laboratory for Veterinary Research	Laboratório Nacional de Investigação Veterinária
4.	MINISTRY OF THE ENVIRONMENT	MINISTÉRIO DO AMBIENTE
	Secretariat-General	Secretaria-Geral
	Directorate-General for Environment	Direcção-Geral do Ambiente
	Regional Directorates for Environment (5)	Direcções Regionais do Ambiente (5)
5.	MINISTRY OF SCIENCE AND TECHNOLOGY	MINISTÉRIO DA CIÊNCIA E DA TECNOLOGIA
	Secretariat-General	Secretaria-Geral
	Legal Service	Auditoria Jurídica
	High Council for Science and Technology	Conselho Superior da Ciência e Tecnologia
	Ministerial Department for Scientific Policy and Technology	Gabinete coordenador da Politica Cientifica e Tecnologia
6.	MINISTRY OF CULTURE	MINISTÉRIO DA CULTURA
	Secretariat-General	Secretaria-Geral
	Regional Directorates for Culture (6)	Delegações Regionais da Cultura (6)
	Ministerial Department for International Relations	Gabinete das Relações Internacionais
	Ministerial Department for Copyright	Gabinete do Direito de Autor
	General Inspectorate for Cultural Activities	Inspecção-Geral das Actividades Culturais
7.	MINISTRY OF DEFENCE	MINISTÉRIO DA DEFESA NACIONAL
	Secretariat-General of the Ministry of Defence	Secretaria-Geral do Ministério da Defesa Nacional
	Legal Service	Auditoria Jurídica

计划和农业食品政策部

监察总局和审计办公室 (管理审计)

渔业监察总局

国家骑士局

国家兽医研究实验室

4. 环境部

总秘书处

环境总局

地区环境局(5 个)

5. 科技部

总秘书处

法律局

科学技术高级理事会

科学政策和技术部

6. 文化部

总秘书处

地区文化局 (6 个)

国际关系部

版权部

文化活动监察总局

7. 国防部

国防部总秘书处

法律局

	English	Portuguese
	Directorate-General for the Navy	Direcção-Geral da Marinha
	Directorate-General for Armaments and Defence Equipments	Direcção-Geral de Armamento e Equipamento de Defesa
	Directorate-General for Infrastructure	Direcção-Geral de Infra-Estruturas
	Directorate-General for Personnel	Direcção-Geral de Pessoal
	Directorate-General for National Defence Policy	Direcção-Geral de Política de Defesa Nacional
	National Security Authority	Autoridade Nacional de Segurança
	General-Inspectorate of Armed Forces	Inspecção-Geral das Forças Armadas
	National Defence Institute	Instituto da Defesa Nacional
	Council of Defence Science and Technology	Conselho de Ciência et Técnologia da Defesa
	Council of Chiefs of Staff	Conselho da Chefes de Estado Maior
	Military Police	Policia Judiciária Militar
	Maritime Authority System	Sistema de Autoridade Marítima
	Hydrographic Institute	Instituto Hidrográfico
	Alfeite Arsenal	Arsenal do Alfeite
	Chief of Staff of the Armed Forces	Estado Maior General das Forças Armadas
	Chief of Staff of the Army	Estado Maior do Exército
	Chief of Staff of the Navy	Estado Maior da Armada
	Chief of Staff of the Air Force	Estado Maior da Força Aéria
	Commission on International Law of the Sea	Comissão do Direito Marítimo Internacional
	Defence and Military Information Service	Serviço de Informações de Defesa e Militares
	Portuguese Commission of Military History	Comissão Portuguesa da História Militar
8.	MINISTRY OF ECONOMY	MINISTÉRIO DA ECONOMIA
	Secretariat-General	Secretaria-Geral
	Commission for the Imposition of Sanctions in Advertising Matters	Comissão de Aplicação de Coimas em Matéria de Publicidade
	Commission for Emergency Energy Planning	Comissão de Planeamento Energético de Emergência
	Commission for Emergency Industrial Planning	Comissão de Planeamento Industrial de Emergência
	Council of Competition	Conselho da Concorrência

海军总局

武器装备和防御设备总局

基础设施总局

人事总局

国防政策总局

国家安全局

武装部队监察总局

国防研究所

国防科技理事会

参谋长理事会

宪兵队

港务监督体系

水文地理研究所

阿尔费蒂兵工厂

武装部队参谋长

陆军参谋长

海军参谋长

空军参谋长

国际海洋法委员会

防务和军事情报局

葡萄牙军队历史委员会

8. 经济部

总秘书处

处罚广告品委员会

紧急能源计划委员会

紧急工业计划委员会

竞争理事会

	Council of Financial Securities	Conselho de Garantías Financeiras
	Sectoral Councils for Industry, Construction, Energy, Trade and Tourism	Conselhos Sectoriais da Indústria, da Construção, da Energia, do Comércio e do Turismo
	National Council of Quality	Conselho Nacional da Qualidade
	Directorate-General for Trade and Competition	Direcção-Geral do Comércio e da Concorrência
	Directorate-General for Energy	Direcção-Geral da Energia
	Directorate-General for Industry	Direcção-Geral da Indústria
	Directorate-General for Tourism	Direcção-Geral do Turismo
	Regional Delegations	Delegações Regionais
	Ministerial Department for Studies and Economic Prospective	Gabinete de Estudos e Prospectiva Económica
	Directorate-General for International Economic Relations	Direcção-Geral das Relações Económicas Internacionais
	General Inspectorate for Economic Activities	Inspecção-Geral das Actividades Económicas
	General Inspectorate for Gambling	Inspecção-Geral de Jogos
	Council for the Economic Development	Conselho para o Desenvolvimento Económico
9.	MINISTRY OF EDUCATION	MINISTÉRIO DA EDUCAÇÃO
	Secretariat-General	Secretaria-Geral
	Social Security Fund	Caixa da Previdência
	Education National Council	Conselho Nacional de Educação
	Council of Directors-General	Conselho de Directores Gerais
	Department for Primary Education	Departamento de Educação Básica
	Department for Educational Resources Management	Departamento de Gestão dos Recursos Educativos
	Department for Secondary Education	Departamento do Ensino Secundário
	Department for Higher Education	Departamento do Ensino Superior
	Regional Directorates for Education (5)	Direcções Regionais de Educação (5)
	University Stadium of Lisbon	Estádio Universitário de Lisboa
	Nursery, Primary and Secondary Education Establishments	Estabelecimentos de Educação Pré-Escolar e dos Ensinos Básico e Secundário
	Ministerial Department of Scholar Sport	Gabinete Coordenador do Desporto Escolar

金融证券理事会

工业、建筑、能源、贸易与旅游部门理事会

国家质量理事会

贸易和竞争总局

能源总局

工业总局

旅游总局

地区代表团

研究和经济预期部

国际经济关系总局

经济活动监察总局

博彩监察总局

经济发展理事会

9. 教育部

总秘书处

社会保险基金

国家教育理事会

局长理事会

初等教育司

教育资源管理司

中等教育司

高等教育司

地区教育局(5 个)

里斯本大学体育馆

托儿所、初等和中等教育设施

教师运动部

	Ministerial Department of European Affairs and International Relations	Ganinete dos Assuntos Europeus e Relações Internacionais
	General Inspectorate of Education	Inspecção-Geral da Educação
	Ministerial Department for Financial Management	Gabinete de Gestão Financeira
	Ministerial Department for Prospective and Planning	Departamento de Avaliação, Prospectiva e Planeamento
10.	MINISTRY OF EQUIPMENT, PLANNING, AND TERRITORIAL ADMINISTRATION	MINISTÉRIO DO EQUIPAMENTO, DO PLANEAMENTO E DA ADMINISTRAÇÃO DO TERRITÓRIO
	Secretariat-General	Secretaria-Geral
	Legal Service	Auditoria Jurídica
	Environment Service	Auditoria Ambiental
	Commission for Support to Rehabilitation of the Territorial Administration	Comissão de Apoio à Restruturação da Administração do Território
	Regional Coordination Committees	Comissões de Coordenação Regional
	Commission for Planning of Emergency Maritime Transport	Comissão de Planeamento do Transporte Maritímo de Emergência
	Council for Public and Particular Works Contracts	Conselho de Mercados de Obras Públicas e Particulares
	High Council for Telecommunications	Conselho Superior de Telecomunicações
	Department for Prospective and Planning	Departamento de Prospectiva e Planeamento
	Directorate General for Autarquic Administration	Direcção-Geral da Administração Autárquica
	Directorate General for Civil Aviation	Direcção-Geral da Aviação Civil
	Directorate General for Ports, Navigation and Maritime Transport	Direcção-Geral de Portos, Navegação e Transportes Marítimos
	Directorate General for Regional Development	Direcção-Geral do Desenvolvimento Regional
	Directorate General for Territorial Planning and Urban Development	Direcção-Geral do Ordenamento do território e do Desenvolvimento Urbano
	Directorate General for National Buildings and Monuments	Direcção-Geral dos Edificios e Monumentos Nacionais
	Directorate General for Land Transport	Direcção-Geral dos Transportes Terrestres

欧洲事务和国际关系部

教育监察总局

财政管理部

预期和计划部

10. 设备、计划和领土管理部

总秘书处

法律局

环境局

支持恢复领土管委员会

地区协调委员会

紧急海运计划委员会

公共和特殊工程合同理事会

通信高级理事会

预期和计划司

市政管理总局

民用航空总局

港口、航空和海运总局

地区发展总局

领土规划和城市发展总局

国家建筑和纪念物总局

陆路运输总局

	Ministerial Department for Investment Coordination	Gabinete de Coordenção dos Investimentos e do Financiamento
	Ministerial Department for European Issues and External Relations	Gabinete para os Assuntos Europeus e Relações Externas
	General Inspectorate of the Ministry of Equipment, Planning and Territorial Administration	Inspecção-Geral do Ministério do Equipamento, do Planeamento e da Administraçao do Território
	High Council for Public Works and Transport	Conselho Superior de Obras Públicas e Transportes
11.	MINISTRY OF FINANCE	MINISTÉRIO DAS FINANÇAS
	Secretariat-General	Secretaria-Geral
	Directorate-General for Customs and Special Taxes on Consumption	Direcção-Geral das Alfândegas e dos Impostos Especiais sobre o consumo
	Directorate-General for European Studies and International Relations	Direcção-Geral de Assuntos Europeus e Relações Internacionais
	Directorate-General for Studies	Direcção-Geral de Estudos e Previsão
	Directorate-General for Informatics and Support to Taxation and Customs Services	Direcção-Geral de Informática e Apoio aos Serviços Tributários e Aduaneiros
	Directorate-General for the Protection of Civil Servants-ADSE	Direcção-Geral de Protecção Social aos Funcionários e Agentes de Administração Pública-ADSE
	Directorate-General for the Budget	Direcção-Geral do Orçamento
	Directorate-General of Patrimony	Direcção-Geral do Património
	Directorate-General for the Treasury	Direcção-Geral do Tesouro
	Directorate-General for Taxation	Direcção-Geral dos Impostos
	General Inspectorate for Finance	Inspecção-Geral de Finanças
	Institute for Information Technology	Instituto de Informática
	Customs Stabilization Fund	Fundo de Estabilização Aduaneiro
	Taxation Stabilization Fund	Fundo de Estabilização Tributário
	Public Debt Regularization Fund	Fundo de Regularizaçao da Dívida Pública
12.	MINISTRY OF JUSTICE	MINISTÉRIO DA JUSTIÇA
	Secretariat-General	Secretaria-Geral
	Legal Service	Auditoria Jurídica

投资协调部

欧洲问题和对外关系部

设备、计划与领土管理部监察总局

公共工程和运输高级理事会

11. 财政部

总秘书处

关税和特别消费税总局

欧洲研究和国际关系总局

研究总局

税收和关税服务信息和支持总局

公务员保护总局

预算总局

遗产总局

国库总局

税收总局

财政监察总局

信息技术研究所

海关平准基金

税收平准基金

公债规范基金会

12. 司法部

总秘书处

法律局

	Directorate-General for Fighting Against Corruption, Fraud and Economic-Financial Infractions	Direcção Central para o Combate à Corrupçao, Fraudes e Infracções Económico-Financeiras
	Directorate-General for Registers and Other Official Documents	Direcção-Geral dos Registros e Notariado
	Directorate-General for Computerized Services	Direcção-Geral dos Serviços de Informática
	Directorate-General for Judiciary Services	Direcção-Geral dos Serviços Judiciários
	Directorate-General for the Prison Service	Direcção-Geral dos Serviços Prisionais
	Directorate-General for the Protection and Care of Minors Prison Establishments	Direcção-Geral dos Serviços Tutelares de Menores
	Ministerial Department responsible for European Law	Gabinete de Direito Europeu
	Ministerial Department responsible for Documentation and Comparative Law	Gabinete de Documentação e Direito Comparado
	Ministerial Department responsible for Studies and Planning	Gabinete de Estudos e Planeamento
	Ministerial Department responsible for Financial Management	Gabinete de Gestão Financeira
	Ministerial Department responsible for Planning and Coordinating Drug Control	Gabinete de Planeamento e Coordenação do Combate à Droga
	Criminal Investigation Department	Polícia Judiciária
	Social Services	Serviços Sociais
	National Police and Forensic Science Institute	Instituto Nacional de Polícia e Ciências Criminais
	Forensic Medicine Institutes	Serviços Médico-Legais
	Legal Courts	Tribunais Judiciais
	The High Council of the Judiciary	Conselho Superior de Magistratura
	Public Prosecutor office	Ministério Público
13.	MINISTRY OF FOREIGN AFFAIRS	MINISTÉRIO DOS NEGÓCIOS ESTRANGEIROS
	Secretariat-General	Secretaria-Geral
	Legal Affairs Department	Departamento dos Assuntos Jurídicos

反腐败、反欺诈和经济金融违规总局

注册和其他官方文件总局

计算机化服务总局

司法服务总局

监狱服务总局

保护和关心未成年人监狱设施总局

欧洲法律部

文献和比较法律部

研究和计划部

财务管理部

毒品控制计划和协调部

犯罪调查司

社会服务

国家警察和司法学研究所

法医研究所

法院

审判官高级理事会

检察官办公室

13. 外交部

总秘书处

法律事务司

	Interministerial Commission for Cooperation	Comissão Interministerial para a cooperação
	Interministerial Commission for Community Affairs	Comissão Interministerial para os Assuntos Comunitários
	Interministerial Commission for Migration and Portuguese Communities	Comissão Interministerial as Migraçoes e Comunidades Portuguesas
	Council of Portuguese Communities	Conselho das Comunidades Portuguesas
	Directorate-General for Bilateral Relations	Direcção-Geral das Relações Bilaterais
	Directorate-General for Foreign Policy	Direcção-Geral de Política Externa
	Directorate-General for Community Affairs	Direcção-Geral dos Assuntos Comunitários
	Directorate-General for Consular Affairs and Portuguese Communities	Direcção-Geral dos Assuntos Consulares e Communidades Portuguesas
	Directorate-General for Multilateral Affairs	Direcção-Geral dos Assuntos Multilaterais
	Ministerial Department por Information and Press	Gabinete de Informação e Imprensa
	Diplomatic and Consular Inspectorate	Inspecção Diplomática e Consular
	Diplomatic Institute	Instituto Diplomático
14.	MINISTRY FOR QUALIFICATION AND EMPLOYMENT	MINISTÉRIO PARA A QUALIFICAÇÃO E O EMPREGO
	Secretariat-General	Secretaria-Geral
	Interministerial Commission for Employment	Comissão Interministerial para o Emprego
	National Council for Health and Safety in the workplace	Conselho Nacional de Higiene e Segurança no Trabalho
	Statistics Department	Departamento de Estatística
	Studies and Planning Department	Departamento de Estudos e Planeamento
	European Social Fund Department	Departamento para os Assuntos do Fundo Social Europeu
	Department of European Affairs and External Relations	Departamento para os Assuntos Europeus e Relações Externas
	Directorate-General for Employment and Vocational Training	Direcção-Geral do Emprego e Formação Profissional

部际合作委员会

部际社区事务委员会

部际移民和葡萄牙社团委员会

葡萄牙社团理事会

双边关系总局

外交政策总局

社区事务总局

领事事务和葡萄牙社区总局

多边事务总局

信息和新闻部

外交和领事监察局

外交学会

14. 资格和就业部

总秘书处

部际就业委员会

国家劳动场所健康和安全理事会

统计司

研究和计划司

欧洲社会基金司

欧洲事务和对外关系司

就业和职业培训总局

	Directorate-General for Labour Conditions	Direcção-Geral das Condições de Trabalho
	Legal Department	Gabinete Jurídico
	Centre for Scientific and Tecnical Information	Centro de Informação Científica e Técnica
15.	MINISTRY OF HEALTH	MINISTÉRIO DA SAÚDE
	Secretariat-General	Secretaria-Geral
	Department for Studies and Health Planning	Departamento de Estudos e Planeamento da Saúde
	Health Human Resource Department	Departamento de Recursos Humanos da Saúde
	Directorate-General for Health Installations & Equipment	Direcção-Geral das instalações e Equipamentos da Saúde
	Directorate-General for Health	Direcção-Geral da Saúde
	General Inspectorate of Health	Inspecção-Geral da Saúde
	Institutes of General Clinics	Institutos de Clínica Geral
	National Health Council	Conselho Nacional de Saúde
16.	MINISTRY OF SOLIDARITY AND SOCIAL SECURITY	MINISTÉRIO DA SOLIDARIEDADE E SEGURANÇA SOCIAL
	Secretariat-General	Secretaria-Geral
	National Council for Social Economy	Conselho Nacional para a Economia Social
	National Council for third-age policy	Conselho Nacional para a Política de Terceira Idade
	National Council for Rehabilitation and Integration of Dissable People	Conselho nacional para a Reabilitação e Integração das pessoas com Deficiência
	Department of Statistics, Studies and Planning	Departamento de Estatística, Estudos e Planeamento
	Ministerial Department for European Affairs and International Relations	Gabinete de Assuntos Europeus e de Relações Internacionais
	Directorate-General for Social Works	Direcção-Geral da Acção Social
	Directorate-General for Social Security Schemes	Direcção-Geral dos Regimes de Segurança Social
	General Inspectorate for Social Security	Inspecção-Geral da Segurança Social
	Social Observatory	Observatório Social

劳工条件总局

法律司

科技信息中心

15. 卫生部

总秘书处

研究和卫生计划司

卫生人力资源司

卫生设施和设备总局

卫生总局

卫生监察总局

全科门诊研究所

国家卫生理事会

16. 团结和社会保险部

总秘书处

国家社会经济理事会

国家第三时期政策理事会

国家残疾人康复和安置理事会

统计、研究和计划司

欧洲事务和国际关系部

社会福利工作总局

社会保险方案总局

社会保险监察总局

天文台

17.	PRESIDENCY OF THE REPUBLIC Secretariat-General of the Presidency of the Republic	PRESIDÊNCIA DA REPÚBLICA Secretaria-Geral da Presidência da República
18.	CONSTITUTIONAL COURT	TRIBUNAL CONSTITUCIONAL
19.	COURT OF AUDITORS Directorate-General of the Court of Auditors	TRIBUNAL DE CONTAS Direcção-Geral do Tribunal de Contas
20.	OMBUDSMAN	PROVEDORIA DE JUSTIÇA

17. 共和国总统府

共和国总统府总秘书处

18. 宪法法院

19. 审计法院

审计法院总局

20. 巡视官

ROMANIA – ROUMANIE – RUMANÍA

(Authentic in the English language only)

1. Administraţia Prezidenţială (Presidential Administration)
2. Senatul României (Romanian Senate)
3. Camera Deputaţilor (Chamber of Deputies)
4. Înalta Curte de Casaţie şi Justiţie (Supreme Court)
5. Curtea Constituţională (Constitutional Court)
6. Consiliul Legislativ (Legislative Council)
7. Curtea de Conturi (Court of Accounts)
8. Consiliul Superior al Magistraturii (Superior Council of Magistracy)
9. Parchetul General de pe langa Inalta Curte de Casatie si Justitie (General Prosecutor's Office attached to the Supreme Court)
10. Secretariatul General al Guvernului (General Secretariat of the Government)
11. Cancelaria Primului-Ministru (Chancellery of the Prime-Minister)
12. Ministerul Afacerilor Externe (Ministry of Foreign Affairs)
13. Ministerul Integrării Europene (Ministry of European Integration)
14. Ministerul Finanţelor Publice (Ministry of Public Finance)
15. Ministerul Justiţiei (Ministry of Justice)
16. Ministerul Apărării Naţionale (Ministry of National Defence[27])
17. Ministerul Administraţiei şi Internelor (Ministry of Administration and Interior)
18. Ministerul Muncii, Solidarităţii Sociale şi Familiei (Ministry of Labour, Social Solidarity and Family)
19. Ministerul Economiei şi Comerţului (Ministry of Economy and Commerce)
20. Ministerul Agriculturii, Pădurii şi Dezvoltării Rurale (Ministry of Agriculture, Forest and Rural Development)
21. Ministerul Transporturilor, Construcţiilor şi Turismului (Ministry of Transport, Constructions and Tourism)
22. Ministerul Educaţiei şi Cercetării (Ministry of Education and Research)
23. Ministerul Sanatatii Publice (Ministry of Public Health)

[27] Non-warlike materials contained in Part (3) of this Annex.

罗马尼亚

(仅以英文为准)

1. 总统府
2. 罗马尼亚参议院
3. 众议院
4. 最高法院
5. 宪法法院
6. 立法委员会
7. 审计法院
8. 行政长官最高议会
9. 最高法院总检察官办公室
10. 政府总秘书处
11. 总理府
12. 外交部
13. 欧洲一体化部
14. 公共财政部
15. 司法部
16. 国防部[27]
17. 行政管理和内政部
18. 劳工、社会团结和家庭部
19. 经济和商业部
20. 农业、林业和乡村发展部
21. 运输、建设和旅游部
22. 教育和研究部
23. 公共健康部

[27]非军事物资包含在本附件第 3 部分。

24. Ministerul Culturii şi Cultelor (Ministry of Culture and Religious Affairs)
25. Ministerul Comunicaţiilor şi Tehnologiei Informaţiilor (Ministry of Communications and Information Technology)
26. Ministerul Mediului şi Gospodăririi Apelor (Ministry of Environment and Water Management)
27. Ministerul Public (Public Ministry)
28. Serviciul Român de Informaţii (Romanian Intelligence Service)
29. Serviciul Român de Informaţii Externe (Romanian Foreign Intelligence Service)
30. Serviciul de Protecţie şi Pază (Protection and Guard Service)
31. Serviciul de Telecomunicaţii Speciale (Special Telecommunications Service)
32. Consiliul Naţional al Audiovizualului (The National Audiovisual Council)
33. Directia Naţionala Anticorupţie (National Anti-corruption Department)
34. Inspectoratul General de Politie (General Inspectorate of Police)
35. Autoritatea Nationala pentru Reglementarea si Monitorizarea Achizitiilor Publice (National Authority for Regulating and Monitoring Public Procurement)
36. Autoritatea Naţională de Reglementare în Comunicaţii (National Authority for Communications Regulation)
37. Autoritatea Nationala de Reglementare pentru Serviciile Publice de Gospodarie Comunala (National Authority for Regulating the Public Services and Rural Administration)
38. Autoritatea Naţională Sanitară Veterinară şi pentru Siguranţa Alimentelor (Sanitary Veterinary and Food Safety National Authority)
39. Autoritatea Naţională pentru Protecţia Consumatorilor (National Authority for Consumer Protection)
40. Autoritatea Navala Română (Romanian Naval Authority)
41. Autoritatea Feroviară Română (AFER) (Romanian Railway Authority)
42. Autoritatea Rutieră Română (ARR) (Romanian Road Authority)
43. Autoritatea Naţională pentru Protecţia Copilului şi Adopţie (National Authority for Child Protection and Adoption)
44. Autoritatea Naţională pentru Persoanele cu Handicap (National Authority for Disabled Persons)
45. Autoritatea Nationala pentru Turism (National Authority for Tourism)
46. Agenţia pentru Strategii Guvernamentale (Agency of Governmental Strategies)

24. 文化和宗教事务部
25. 通信和信息技术部
26. 环境和水管理部
27. 公共事务部
28. 罗马尼亚情报局
29. 罗马尼亚外国情报局
30. 保护和防卫局
31. 特殊电信局
32. 国家视听理事会
33. 国家反贪污局
34. 警察监察总局
35. 国家公共采购管理和监督局
36. 国家通信管理局
37. 国家公共服务和乡村管理局
38. 国家兽医和食品安全局
39. 国家消费者保护局
40. 罗马尼亚海军
41. 罗马尼亚铁路局
42. 罗马尼亚公路局
43. 国家儿童保护和收养局
44. 国家残疾人事务局
45. 国家旅游局
46. 政府战略局

47. Agenţia Naţională a Medicamentului (National Medicines Agency)
48. Agenţia Naţională pentru Sport (National Agency for Sport)
49. Agenţia Naţională pentru Ocuparea Fortei de Munca (National Agency for Employment)
50. Agenţia Naţională de Reglementare în Domeniul Energiei (National Agency for Power Regulation)
51. Agenţia Română pentru Conservarea Energiei (Romanian Agency for Power Conservation)
52. Agenţia Naţională pentru Resurse Minerale (National Agency for Mineral Resources)
53. Agenţia Română pentru Investiţii Străine (Romanian Agency for Foreign Investment)
54. Agenţia Naţională pentru Întreprinderi Mici şi Mijlocii şi Cooperaţie (National Agency for Small and Medium-Sized Entreprises and Cooperation)
55. Agenţia Naţională a Funcţionarilor Publici (National Agency of Public Civil Servants)
56. Agenţia Naţională de Administrare Fiscală (National Agency of Fiscal Administration)

47. 国家药品局

48. 国家体育局

49. 国家就业局

50. 国家电力管理局

51. 国家电力保护局

52. 国家矿产资源局

53. 国家外国投资局

54. 国家中小企业和合作局

55. 国家公务员局

56. 国家财政管理局

SLOVENIA – SLOVENIE - ESLOVENIA

(Authentic in the English language only)

1. Predsednik Republike Slovenije (President of the Republic of Slovenia)
2. Državni zbor (The National Assembly)
3. Državni svet (The National Council)
4. Varuh človekovih pravic (The Ombudsman)
5. Ustavno sodišče (The Constitutional Court)
6. Računsko sodišče (The Court of Audits)
7. Državna revizijska komisja (The National Review Commission)
8. Slovenska akademija znanosti in umetnosti (The Slovenian Academy of Science and Art)
9. Vladne službe (The Government Services)
10. Ministrstvo za finance (Ministry of Finance)
11. Ministrstvo za notranje zadeve (Ministry of Internal Affairs)
12. Ministrstvo za zunanje zadeve (Ministry of Foreign Affairs)
13. Ministrstvo za obrambo (Ministry of Defence)[28]
14. Ministrstvo za pravosodje (Ministry of Justice)
15. Ministrstvo za gospodarstvo (Ministry of the Economy)
16. Ministrstvo za kmetijstvo, gozdarstvo in prehrano (Ministry of Agriculture, Forestry and Food)
17. Ministrstvo za promet (Ministry of Transport)
18. Ministrstvo za okolje, prostor in energijo (Ministry of Environment, Spatial Planning and Energy)
19. Ministrstvo za delo, družino in socialne zadeve (Ministry of Labour, Family and Social Affairs)
20. Ministrstvo za zdravje (Ministry of Health)
21. Ministrstvo za informacijsko družbo (Ministry of Information Society)
22. Ministrstvo za šolstvo, znanost in šport (Ministry of Education, Science and Sport)
23. Ministrstvo za kulturo (Ministry of Culture)
24. Vrhovno sodišče Republike Slovenije (The Supreme Court of the Republic of Slovenia)
25. Višja sodišča (Higher Courts)

[28] Non-warlike materials contained in Part (3) of this Annex.

斯洛文尼亚

(仅以英文为准)

1. 斯洛文尼亚共和国总统
2. 国民大会
3. 国务委员会
4. 巡视官
5. 宪法法院
6. 审计法院
7. 国家审查委员会
8. 斯洛文尼亚科学和艺术学院
9. 政府服务局
10. 财政部
11. 内政部
12. 外交部
13. 国防部[28]
14. 司法部
15. 经济部
16. 农业、林业和食品部
17. 交通部
18. 环境、空间规划和能源部
19. 劳动、家庭和社会事务部
20. 卫生部
21. 信息社会部
22. 教育、科学和体育部
23. 文化部
24. 斯洛文尼亚共和国最高法院
25. 高等法院

[28]非军事物资包含在本附件第 3 部分。

26. Okrožna sodišča (District Courts)
27. Okrajna sodišča (County Courts)
28. Vrhovno tožilstvo Republike Slovenije (The Supreme Prosecutor of the Republic of Slovenia)
29. Okrožna državna tožilstva (Districts' State Prosecutors)
30. Družbeni pravobranilec Republike Slovenije (Social Attorney of the Republic of Slovenia)
31. Državno pravobranilstvo Republike Slovenije (National Attorney of the Republic of Slovenia)
32. Upravno sodišče Republike Slovenije (Administrative Court of the Republic of Slovenia)
33. Senat za prekrške Republike Slovenije (Senat of Minor Offenses of the Republic of Slovenia)
34. Višje delovno in socialno sodišče v Ljubljani (Higher Labour and Social Court)
35. Delovna sodišča (Labour Courts)
36. Sodniki za prekrške (Judges of Minor Offenses)
37. Upravne enote (Local Administration Units)

26. 地区法院
27. 地方法院
28. 斯洛文尼亚共和国最高检察官
29. 地方国家检察官
30. 斯洛文尼亚共和国社会律师
31. 斯洛文尼亚共和国国家律师
32. 斯洛文尼亚共和国行政法院
33. 斯洛文尼亚共和国未成年人犯罪中心
34. 高等劳资和社会法院
35. 劳资争议法院
36. 未成年人犯罪法官
37. 地方行政机构

SLOVAKIA – SLOVAQUIE - ESLOVAQUIA

(Authentic in the English language only)

1. Ministries and other State administration authorities (not exhaustive list):

2. Kancelária Prezidenta Slovenskej republiky (The Office of the President of the Slovak Republic)

3. Národná rada Slovenskej republiky (National Council of the Slovak Republic)

4. Úrad vlády Slovenskej republiky (The Office of the Government of the Slovak Republic)

5. Ministerstvo zahraničných vecí Slovenskej republiky (Ministry of Foreign Affairs)

6. Ministerstvo hospodárstva Slovenskej republiky (Ministry of Economy of the Slovak Republic)

7. Ministerstvo obrany Slovenskej republiky (Ministry of Defence of the Slovak Republic)[29]

8. Ministerstvo vnútra Slovenskej republiky (Ministry of the Interior of the Slovak Republic)

9. Ministerstvo financií Slovenskej republiky (Ministry of Finance of the Slovak Republic)

10. Ministerstvo kultúry Slovenskej republiky (Ministry of Culture of the Slovak Republic)

11. Ministerstvo zdravotníctva Slovenskej republiky (Ministry of Health of the Slovak Republic)

12. Ministerstvo práce, sociálnych vecí a rodiny Slovenskej republiky (Ministry of Labour, Social Affairs and Family of the Slovak Republic)

13. Ministerstvo školstva Slovenskej republiky (Ministry of Education of the Slovak Republic)

14. Ministerstvo spravodlivosti Slovenskej republiky (Ministry of Justice of the Slovak Republic)

15. Ministerstvo životného prostredia Slovenskej republiky (Ministry of Environment of the Slovak Republic)

16. Ministerstvo pôdohospodárstva Slovenskej republiky (Ministry of Agriculture of the Slovak Republic)

17. Ministerstvo dopravy, pôšt a telekomunikácií Slovenskej republiky (Ministry of Transport, Posts and Telecommunication of the Slovak Republic)

[29] Non-warlike materials contained in Part (3) of this Annex.

斯洛伐克

(仅以英文为准)

1. 各部和其他国家行政机构(非详尽清单)：

2. 斯洛伐克共和国总统办公室

3. 斯洛伐克共和国国务委员会

4. 斯洛伐克共和国政府办公厅

5. 外交部

6. 斯洛伐克共和国经济部

7. 斯洛伐克共和国国防部[29]

8. 斯洛伐克共和国内政部

9. 斯洛伐克共和国财政部

10. 斯洛伐克共和国文化部

11. 斯洛伐克共和国卫生部

12. 斯洛伐克共和国劳工、社会事务和家庭部

13. 斯洛伐克共和国教育部

14. 斯洛伐克共和国司法部

15. 斯洛伐克共和国环境部

16. 斯洛伐克共和国农业部

17. 斯洛伐克共和国运输、邮政和通信部

[29] 非军事物资包含在本附件第 3 部分。

18. Ministerstvo výstavby a regionálneho rozvoja Slovenskej republiky (Ministry of Construction and Regional Development of the Slovak Republic)

19. Ústavný súd Slovenskej republiky (Constitutional Court of the Slovak Republic)

20. Najvyšší súd Slovenskej republiky (Supreme Court of the Slovak Republic)

21. Generálna prokuratúra Slovenskej republiky (Public Prosecution of the Slovak Republic)

22. Najvyšší kontrolný úrad Slovenskej republiky (Supreme Audit Office of the Slovak Republic)

23. Protimonopolný úrad Slovenskej republiky (Antimonopoly Office of the Slovak Republic)

24. Úrad pre verejné obstarávanie (Office for Public Procurement)

25. Štatistický úrad Slovenskej republiky (Statistical Office of the Slovak Republic)

26. Úrad geodézie, kartografie a katastra Slovenskej republiky (Office of the Land Register of the Slovak Republic)

27. Úrad pre normalizáciu, metrológiu a skúšobníctvo Slovenskej republiky (Office of Standards, Metrology and Testing of the Slovak Republic)

28. Telekomunikačný úrad Slovenskej republiky (Telecommunications Office of the Slovak Republic)

29. Úrad priemyselného vlastníctva Slovenskej republiky (Industrial Property Office of the Slovak Republic)

30. Úrad pre finančný trh (Office for the Finance Market)

31. Národný bezpečnostný úrad (National Security Office)

32. Poštový úrad (Post Office)

33. Úrad na ochranu osobných údajov (Office for Personal Data Protection)

34. Kancelária verejného ochrancu práv (Ombudsman's Office)

18. 斯洛伐克共和国建筑和地区发展部

19. 斯洛伐克共和国宪法法院

20. 斯洛伐克共和国最高法院

21. 斯洛伐克共和国公诉法院

22. 斯洛伐克共和国最高审计局

23. 斯洛伐克共和国反垄断办公室

24. 公共采购办公室

25. 斯洛伐克共和国统计局

26. 斯洛伐克共和国土地注册局

27. 斯洛伐克共和国标准、计量和检测局

28. 斯洛伐克共和国电信局

29. 斯洛伐克共和国工业产权局

30. 金融市场办公室

31. 国家证券办公室

32. 邮政局

33. 个人数据保护办公室

34. 巡视官办公室

FINLAND - FINLANDE - FINLANDIA

(Authentic in the English language only)

1.	OFFICE OF THE CHANCELLOR OF JUSTICE	OIKEUSKANSLERINVIRASTO
2.	MINISTRY OF TRADE AND INDUSTRY	KAUPPA-JA TEOLLISUUSMINISTERIÖ
	National Consumer Administration	Kuluttajavirasto
	National Food Administration	Elintarvikevirasto
	Office of Free Competition	Kilpailuvirasto
	Council of Free Competition	Kilpailuneuvosto
	Office of the Consumer Ombudsman	Kuluttaja-asiamiehen toimisto
	Consumer Complaint Board	Kuluttajavalituslautakunta
	National Board of Patents and Registration	Patentti- ja rekisterihallitus
3.	MINISTRY OF TRANSPORT AND COMMUNICATIONS	LIIKENNEMINISTERIÖ
	Telecommunications Administration Centre	Telehallintokeskus
4.	MINISTRY OF AGRICULTURE AND FORESTRY	MAA- JA METSÄTALOUSMINISTERIÖ
	National Land Survey of Finland	Maanmittauslaitos
5.	MINISTRY OF JUSTICE	OIKEUSMINISTERIÖ
	The Office of the Data Protection Ombudsman	Tietosuojavaltuutetun toimisto
	Courts of Law	Tuomioistuinlaitos – Korkein oikeus – Korkein hallinto-oikeus – Hovioikeudet – Käräjäoikeudet – Lääninoikeudet – Markkinatuomioistuin – Työtuomioistuin – Vakuutusoikeus – Vesioikeudet
	Prison Administration	Vankeinhoitolaitos
6.	MINISTRY OF EDUCATION	OPETUSMINISTERIÖ
	National Board of Education	Opetushallitus
	National Office of Film Censorship	Valtion elokuvatarkastamo

芬兰

(仅以英文为准)

1. 司法大臣办公室

2. 贸易和工业部

   国家消费者管理局
   国家食品管理局
   自由竞争办公室
   自由竞争理事会
   消费者巡视官办公室
   消费者投诉局
   国家专利和注册局

3. 交通和通信部

   通信管理中心

4. 农业和林业部

   芬兰国家土地勘测局

5. 司法部

   数据保护巡视官办公室
   法院
   监狱管理局

6. 教育部

   国家教育局
   国家电影审查局

7.	MINISTRY OF DEFENCE[30]	PUOLUSTUSMINISTERIÖ
	Defence Forces	Puolustusvoimat
8.	MINISTRY OF THE INTERIOR	SISÄASIAINMINISTERIÖ
	Population Register Centre	Väestörekisterikeskus
	Central Criminal Police	Keskusrikospoliisi
	Mobile Police	Liikkuva poliisi
	Frontier Guard	Rajavartiolaitos
9.	MINISTRY OF SOCIAL AFFAIRS AND HEALTH	SOSIAALI- JA TERVEYSMINISTERIÖ
	Unemployment Appeal Board	Työttömyysturvalautakunta
	Appeal Tribunal	Tarkastuslautakunta
	National Agency for Medicines	Lääkelaitos
	National Board of Medicolegal Affairs	Terveydenhuollon oikeusturvakeskus
	State Accident Office	Tapaturmavirasto
	Finnish Centre for Radiation and Nuclear Safety	Säteilyturvakeskus
	Reception Centres for Asylum Seekers	Valtion turvapaikan hakijoiden vastaanotto-keskukset
10.	MINISTRY OF LABOUR	TYÖMINISTERIÖ
	National Conciliators' Office	Valtakunnansovittelijain toimisto
	Labour Council	Työneuvosto
11.	MINISTRY FOR FOREIGN AFFAIRS	ULKOASIAINMINISTERIÖ
12.	MINISTRY OF FINANCE	VALTIOVARAINMINISTERIÖ
	State Economy Controller's Office	Valtiontalouden tarkastusvirasto
	State Treasury Office	Valtiokonttori
		Valtion työmarkkinalaitos
		Verohallinto
		Tullihallinto
		Valtion vakuusrahasto
13.	MINISTRY OF ENVIRONMENT	YMPÄRISTÖMINISTERIÖ
	National Board of Waters and Environment	Vesi- ja ympäristöhallitus

[30] Non-warlike materials contained in Part (3) of this Annex.

7. 国防部[30]

国防部队

8. 内政部

人口登记中心
中央刑事警察
机动警察
边防警卫

9. 社会事务和卫生部

失业申诉局
申诉仲裁机构
国家医品局
国家法医事务局
国家事故处理局
芬兰辐射和核安全中心
避难者接待中心

10. 劳工部

国家调解办公室
劳动委员会

11. 外交部

12. 财政部

国家经济管理办公室
国库办公室

13. 环境部

国家水资源和环境局

[30]非军事物资包含在本附件第 3 部分。

SWEDEN - SUÈDE -SUECIA

(Authentic in the English language only)

Royal Academy of Fine Arts	Akademien för de fria konsterna
Public Law-Service Offices (26)	Allmänna advokatbyråerna (26)
National Board for Consumer Complaints	Allmänna reklamationsnämnden
National Board of Occupational Safety and Health	Arbetarskyddsstyrelsen
Labour Court	Arbetsdomstolen
National Agency for Government Employers	Arbetsgivarverket
National Institute for Working Life	Arbetslivsinstitutet
National Labour Market Board	Arbetsmarknadsstyrelsen
Board of Occupational Safety and Health for Government Employees	Arbetsmiljönämnd, statliga sektorns
Museum of Architecture	Arkitekturmuseet
National Archive of Recorded Sound and Moving Images	Arkivet för ljud och bild
The Office of the Childrens' Ombudsman	Barnombudsmannen
Swedish Council on Technology Assessment in Health Care	Beredning för utvärdering av medicinsk metodik, statens
Royal Library	Biblioteket, Kungliga
National Board of Film Censors	Biografbyrå, statens
Dictionary of Swedish Biography	Biografiskt lexikon, svenskt
Swedish Accounting Standards Board	Bokföringsnämnden
National Housing Credit Guarantee Board	Bostadskreditnämnd, statens (BKN)
National Housing Board	Boverket
National Council for Crime Prevention	Brottsförebyggande rådet
Criminal Victim Compensation and Support Authority	Brottsoffermyndigheten
Council for Building Research	Byggforskningsrådet
Central Committee for Laboratory Animals	Centrala försöksdjursnämnden
National Board of Student Aid	Centrala studiestödsnämnden
Data Inspection Board	Datainspektionen
Ministries (Government Departments)	Departementen
National Courts Administration	Domstolsverket
National Electrical Safety Board	Elsäkerhetsverket
Export Credits Guarantee Board	Exportkreditnämnden

瑞典

(仅以英文为准)

皇家美术学院
公共法律服务办公室(26 个)
国家消费者投诉局
国家职业安全和健康局
劳资争议法院
国家雇主局
国家职业生活学会
国家劳动力市场局
政府雇员职业安全和健康局
建筑博物馆
国家录音录像档案馆
儿童巡视官办公室
瑞典卫生健康技术评估委员会
皇家图书馆
国家电影审查局
瑞典传记辞典
瑞典会计标准局
国家住房信贷担保局
国家住宅局
国家预防犯罪理事会
犯罪受害者赔偿和支持局
建筑研究理事会
实验室动物中央委员会
国家助学金局
数据监察局
各部 (政府部门)
国家法院管理局
国家电力安全局
出口信贷担保局

Financial Supervisory Authority	Finansinspektionen
National Board of Fisheries	Fiskeriverket
Aeronautical Research Institute	Flygtekniska försöksanstalten
National Institute of Public Health	Folkhälsoinstitutet
Council for Planning and Co-ordination of Research	Forskningsrådsnämnden
National Fortifications Administration	Fortifikationsverket
	Förhandlare (K 1996:01) för statens köp av färjetrafik till och från Gotland
National Conciliators' Office	Förlikningsmannaexpedition, statens
National Defence Research Establishment	Försvarets forskningsanstalt
Defence Material Administration	Försvarets materielverk
National Defence Radio Institute	Försvarets radioanstalt
Swedish Museums of Military History	Försvarshistoriska museer, statens
National Defence College	Försvarshögskolan
The Swedish Armed Forces	Försvarsmakten
Social Insurance Offices	Försäkringskassorna
Geological Survey of Sweden	Geologiska undersökning, Sveriges
Geotechnical Institute	Geotekniska institut, statens
The National Rural Development Agency	Glesbygdsverket
Graphic Institute and the Graduate School of Communications	Grafiska institutet och institutet för högre kommunikations- och reklamutbildning
The Swedish Broadcasting Commission	Granskningsnämnden för Radio och TV
Swedish Government Seamen's Service	Handelsflottans kultur- och fritidsråd
Ombudsman for the Disabled	Handikappombudsmannen
Board of Accident Investigation	Haverikommission, statens
Courts of Appeal (6)	Hovrätterna (6)
Council for Research in the Humanities and Social Sciences	Humanistisk-samhällsvetenskapliga forskningsrådet
Regional Rent and Tenancies Tribunals (12)	Hyres- och arendenämnder (12)
Remand Prisons (28)	Häktena (28)
Committee on Medical Responsibility	Hälso- och sjukvårdens ansvarsnämnd
National Agency for Higher Education	Högskoleverket
Supreme Court	Högsta domstolen
Register Authority for Floating Charges	Inskrivningsmyndigheten för företagsinteckningar

金融监督局
国家渔业司
航空研究所
国家公共卫生研究所
研究规划和协调理事会
国家防御工事管理局
国家调解办公室
国家国防研究机构
防务物资管理局
国防无线电研究所
瑞典军事历史博物馆
国防大学
瑞典武装部队
社会保险办公室
瑞典地质勘测
地球技术研究所
国家乡村发展局
图像研究所和通信研究所
瑞典广播委员会
瑞典政府海员服务局
残疾人巡视官
事故调查局
上诉法院(6 个)
人文学科和社会科学研究理事会
地区出租和租赁法院(12 个)
押候监狱 (28 个)
医疗责任委员会
国家高等教育局
最高法院
浮动担保登记局

National Institute for Psycho-Social Factors and Health	Institut för psykosocial miljömedicin, statens
National Institute for Regional Studies	Institut för regionalforskning, statens
Swedish Institute of Space Physics	Institutet för rymdfysik
Swedish Immigration Board	Invandrarverk, statens
Swedish Board of Agriculture	Jordbruksverk, statens
Office of the Chancellor of Justice	Justitiekanslern
Office of the Equal Opportunities Ombudsman	Jämställdhetsombudsmannen
National Judicial Board of Public Lands and Funds	Kammarkollegiet
Administrative Courts of Appeal (4)	Kammarrätterna (4)
National Chemicals Inspectorate	Kemikalieinspektionen
National Board of Trade	Kommerskollegium
Swedish Transport and Communications Research Board	Kommunikationsforskningsberedningen
National Franchise Board for Environment Protection	Koncessionsnämnden för miljöskydd
National Institute of Economic Research	Konjunkturinstitutet
Swedish Competition Authority	Konkurrensverket
College of Arts, Crafts and Design	Konstfack
College of Fine Arts	Konsthögskolan
National Art Museums	Konstmuseer, statens
Arts Grants Committee	Konstnärsnämnden
National Art Council	Konstråd, statens
National Board for Consumer Policies	Konsumentverket
Armed Forces Archives	Krigsarkivet
National Laboratory of Forensic Science	Kriminaltekniska laboratorium, statens
Correctional Regional Offices (6)	Kriminalvårdens regionkanslier (6)
National/Local Institutions (68)	Kriminalvårdsanstalterna (68)
National Paroles Board	Kriminalvårdsnämnden
National Prison and Probation Administration	Kriminalvårdsstyrelsen
Enforcement Services (24)	Kronofogdemyndigheterna (24)
National Council for Cultural Affairs	Kulturråd, statens
Swedish Coast Guard	Kustbevakningen
Nuclear-Power Inspectorate	Kärnkraftsinspektion, statens
National Land Survey	Lantmäteriverket
Royal Armoury	Livrustkammaren/Skoklosters slott/ Hallwylska museet

国家心理社会因素和健康研究所
国家地区研究所
瑞典空间物理研究所
瑞典移民局
瑞典农业局
司法大臣办公室
平等机会巡视官办公室
公共土地和基金司法局
上诉行政法院 (4 个)
国家化工品监察局
国家贸易局
瑞典运输和通信研究局
国家环境保护全民委员会
国家经济研究所
瑞典竞争管理局
工艺设计美术学院
美术学院
国家美术博物馆
艺术资助委员会
国家美术理事会
国家消费者政策局
武装部队档案局
国家司法科学实验室
地区纠正犯罪办公室 (6 个)
国家/地方协会 (68 个)
国家假释局
国家监狱和缓刑管理局
强制执行局 (24 个)
国家文化事务理事会
瑞典海岸警卫队
核能监察局
国家土地勘测局
皇家军械库

National Food Administration	Livsmedelsverk, statens
The National Gaming Board	Lotteriinspektionen
Medical Products Agency	Läkemedelsverket
County Labour Boards (24)	Länsarbetsnämnderna (24)
County Administrative Courts (24)	Länsrätterna (24)
County Administrative Boards (24)	Länsstyrelserna (24)
National Government Employee Salaries and Pensions Board	Löne- och pensionsverk, statens
Market Court	Marknadsdomstolen
Medical Research Council	Medicinska forskningsrådet
Swedish Meteorological and Hydrological Institute	Meteorologiska och hydrologiska institut, Sveriges
Armed Forces Staff and War College	Militärhögskolan
Swedish National Collections of Music	Musiksamlingar, statens
Museum of Natural History	Naturhistoriska riksmuseet
Natural Science Research Council	Naturvetenskapliga forskningsrådet
National Environmental Protection Agency	Naturvårdsverket
Scandinavian Institute of African Studies	Nordiska Afrikainstitutet
Nordic School of Public Health	Nordiska hälsovårdshögskolan
Nordic Institute for Studies in Urban and Regional Planning	Nordiska institutet för samhällsplanering
Nordic Museum	Nordiska museet, stiftelsen
Swedish Delegation of the Nordic Council	Nordiska rådets svenska delegation
Recorders Committee	Notarienämnden
National Board for Intra Country Adoptions	Nämnden för internationella adoptionsfrågor
National Board for Public Procurement	Nämnden för offentlig upphandling
National Fund for Administrative Development	Statens förnyelsefond
Swedish National Committee for Contemporary Art Exhibitions Abroad	Nämnden för utställning av nutida svensk konst i utlandet
National Board for Industrial and Technical Development	Närings- och teknikutvecklingsverket (NUTEK)

国家食品管理局
国家博彩局
医疗产品局
省劳工局(24 个)
省行政法院(24 个)
省行政管理局(24 个)
国家雇员工资和养老金局
市场法院
医学研究理事会
瑞典气象水文研究所
武装参谋和军事学院
瑞典国家音乐博物馆
自然历史博物馆
自然科学研究理事会
国家环境保护局
斯堪的纳维亚非洲研究所
北欧公共健康学院
北欧城市和地区规划研究所
北欧博物馆
北欧理事会瑞典代表团
专职法官委员会
国内收养局
国家公共采购局
国家行政发展基金
瑞典当代艺术国外展览国家委员会
国家工业和技术发展局

Office of the Ethnic Discrimination Ombudsman; Advisory Committee on Questions Concerning Ethnic Discrimination	Ombudsmannen mot etnisk diskriminering; nämnden mot etnisk diskriminering
Court of Patent Appeals	Patentbesvärsrätten
Patents and Registration Office	Patent- och registreringsverket
Co-ordinated Population and Address Register	Person- och adressregisternämnd, statens
Swedish Polar Research Secretariat	Polarforskningssekretariatet
Press Subsidies Council	Presstödsnämnden
National Library for Psychology and Education	Psykologisk-pedagogiska bibliotek, statens
The Swedish Radio and TV Authority	Radio- och TV-verket
Governmental Central Services Office	Regeringskansliets förvaltningsavdelning
Supreme Administrative Court	Regeringsrätten
Central Board of National Antiquities and National Historical Museums	Riksantikvarieämbetet och statens historiska museer
National Archives	Riksarkivet
Bank of Sweden	Riksbanken
Administration Department of the Swedish Parliament	Riksdagens förvaltningskontor
The Parliamentary Ombudsmen	Riksdagens ombudsmän, JO
The Parliamentary Auditors	Riksdagens revisorer
National Social Insurance Board	Riksförsäkringsverket
National Debt Office	Riksgäldskontoret
National Police Board	Rikspolisstyrelsen
National Audit Bureau	Riksrevisionsverket
National Tax Board	Riksskatteverket
Travelling Exhibitions Service	Riksutställningar, Stiftelsen
Office of the Prosecutor-General	Riksåklagaren
National Space Board	Rymdstyrelsen
Council for Working Life Research	Rådet för arbetslivsforskning
National Rescue Services Board	Räddningsverk, statens
Regional Legal-aid Authority	Rättshjälpsmyndigheten
National Board of Forensic Medicine	Rättsmedicinalverket
Sami (Lapp) School Board Sami (Lapp) Schools	Sameskolstyrelsen och sameskolor
National Maritime Administration	Sjöfartsverket
National Maritime Museums	Sjöhistoriska museer, statens

种族歧视巡视官办公室；种族
歧视问题咨询委员会
专利上诉法院
专利和注册局
协调人口和地址登记
瑞典极地研究秘书处
报刊补贴理事会
国家心理学和教育图书馆
瑞典广播和电视局
政府中央服务办公室
最高行政法院
国家文物和国家历史博物馆总局
国家档案馆
瑞典银行
瑞典议会管理局
议会巡视官
议会审计局
国家社会保险局
国债办公室
国家警察局
国家审计局
国家税务局
巡回展览局
总检察官办公室
国家空间局
职业生活研究理事会
国家营救服务局
地区法律援助局
国家法医局
拉普兰学校董事会
拉普兰人学校
国家海事管理局
国家海洋博物馆

Local Tax Offices (24)	Skattemyndigheterna (24)
Swedish Council for Forestry and Agricultural Research	Skogs- och jordbrukets forskningsråd, SJFR
National Board of Forestry	Skogsstyrelsen
National Agency for Education	Skolverk, statens
Swedish Institute for Infectious Disease Control	Smittskyddsinstitutet
National Board of Health and Welfare	Socialstyrelsen
Swedish Council for Social Research	Socialvetenskapliga forskningsrådet
National Inspectorate of Explosives and Flammables	Sprängämnesinspektionen
Statistics Sweden	Statistiska centralbyrån
Agency for Administrative Development	Statskontoret
National Institute of Radiation Protection	Strålskyddsinstitut, statens
Swedish International Development Cooperation Authority	Styrelsen för internationellt utvecklings-samarbete, SIDA
National Board of Psychological Defence and Conformity Assessment	Styrelsen för psykologiskt försvar
Swedish Board for Accreditation	Styrelsen för ackreditering och teknisk kontroll
Swedish Institute	Svenska Institutet, stiftelsen
Library of Talking Books and Braille Publications	Talboks- och punktskriftsbiblioteket
Swedish Research Council for Engineering Sciences	Teknikvetenskapliga forskningsrådet
National Museum of Science and Technology	Tekniska museet, stiftelsen
District and City Courts (97)	Tingsrätterna (97)
Judges Nomination Proposal Committee	Tjänsteförslagsnämnden för domstolsväsendet
Armed Forces' Enrolment Board	Totalförsvarets pliktverk
Swedish Board of Customs	Tullverket
Swedish Tourist Authority	Turistdelegationen
The National Board of Youth Affairs	Ungdomsstyrelsen
Universities and University Colleges	Universitet och högskolor
Aliens Appeals Board	Utlänningsnämnden
National Seed Testing and Certification Institute	Utsädeskontroll, statens

地方税务办公室 (24 个)
瑞典林业和农业研究理事会
国家森林局
国家教育局
瑞典传染病控制研究所
国家卫生和福利局
瑞典社会研究理事会
国家易燃易爆物品监察局
瑞典统计局
行政发展局
国家辐射保护研究所
瑞典国际发展合作局
国家心理防卫和合格评定局
瑞典认证局
瑞典学院
有声读物和盲文出版物图书馆
瑞典工程科学研究理事会
国家科学技术博物馆
区和市法院 (97 个)
法官任命提案委员会
武装部队入伍局
瑞典海关局
瑞典旅游局
国家青年事务局
大学和学院
外侨上诉局
国家种子检验和认证研究所

National Water Supply and Sewage Tribunal	Vatten- och avloppsnämnd, statens
National Agency for Higher Education	Verket för högskoleservice (VHS)
National Veterinary Institute	Veterinärmedicinska anstalt, statens
Swedish National Road and Transport Research Institute	Väg- och transportforskningsinstitut, statens
National Plant Variety Board	Växtsortnämnd, statens
Labour Inspectorate	Yrkesinspektionen
Public Prosecution Authorities incl. County Public Prosecution Authority and District Prosecution Authority	Åklagarmyndigheterna inkl. läns- och distriktsåklagarmyndigheterna
National Board of Civil Emergency Preparedness	Överstyrelsen för civil beredskap

国家水供应和污水法院

国家高等教育局

国家兽医学院

瑞典国家道路和运输研究所

国家植物多样性局

劳动监察局

公诉机构，包括省公诉机构和区公诉机构

国家国民应急准备局

UNITED KINGDOM - ROYAUME-UNI - REINO UNIDO

(Authentic in the English language only)

1. CABINET OFFICE

   Civil Service College
   Office of Public Services
   The Buying Agency
   Parliamentary Counsel Office
   Central Comuter and Telecommunications Agency (CCTA)

2. CENTRAL OFFICE OF INFORMATION

3. CHARITY COMMISSION

4. CROWN PROSECUTION SERVICE

5. CROWN ESTATE COMMISSIONERS (VOTE EXPENDITURE ONLY)

6. CUSTOMS AND EXCISE DEPARTMENT

7. DEPARTMENT FOR INTERNATIONAL DEVELOPMENT

8. DEPARTMENT FOR NATIONAL SAVINGS

9. DEPARTMENT FOR EDUCATION AND EMPLOYMENT

   Higher Education Funding Council for England
   Office of Manpower Economics

10. DEPARTMENT OF HEALTH

   Central Council for Education and Training in Social Work
   Dental Practice Board
   English National Board for Nursing, Midwifery and Health Visitors
   National Health Service Authorities and Trusts
   Prescription Pricing Authority
   Public Health Laboratory Service Board
   U.K. Central Council for Nursing, Midwifery and Health Visiting

11. DEPARTMENT OF NATIONAL HERITAGE

   British Library
   British Museum
   Historic Buildings and Monuments Commission for England (English Heritage)

英国

(仅以英文为准)

1. 内阁办公室
   行政事务学院
   公共服务办公室
   采购局
   内阁律师办公室
   中央计算机和电信机构
2. 中央信息办公室
3. 慈善委员会
4. 皇家检察总署
5. 皇家财产专员 (仅限选举支出)
6. 关税和税务部
7. 国际发展部
8. 国民储蓄管理部
9. 教育和就业部
   英格兰高等教育基金理事会
   人力经济办公室
10. 卫生部
    社会工作教育和培训中央理事会
    口腔医生局
    英格兰国家护理、助产和卫生访视员局
    国家卫生服务局和财团
    处方药定价局
    公共卫生实验服务局
    英国中央护理、助产和卫生访视理事会
11. 国家遗产部
    英国图书馆
    大英博物馆
    英格兰历史建筑和纪念物委员会(英格兰遗产)

2007 年 1 月 1 日 (WT/Let/556)

Imperial War Museum
Museums and Galleries Commission
National Gallery
National Maritime Museum
National Portrait Gallery
Natural History Museum
Royal Commission on Historical Manuscripts
Royal Commission on Historical Monuments of England
Royal Fine Art Commission (England)
Science Museum
Tate Gallery
Victoria and Albert Museum
Wallace Collection

12. DEPARTMENT OF SOCIAL SECURITY

Medical Boards and Examining Medical Officers (War Pensions)
Regional Medical Service
Independent Tribunal Service
Disability Living Allowance Advisory Board
Occupational Pensions Board
Social Security Advisory Committee

13. DEPARTMENT OF THE ENVIRONMENT

Building Research Establishment Agency
Commons Commission
Countryside Commission
Valuation tribunal
Rent Assessment Panels
Royal Commission on Environmental Pollution

14. DEPARTMENT OF THE PROCURATOR GENERAL AND TREASURY SOLICITOR

Legal Secretariat to the Law Officers

15. DEPARTMENT OF TRADE AND INDUSTRY

National Weights and Measures Laboratory
Domestic Coal Consumers' Council
Electricity Committees
Gas Consumers' Council
Central Transport Consultative Committees

帝国战争博物馆
博物馆和美术馆委员会
国家美术馆
国家海洋博物馆
国家肖像美术馆
自然历史博物馆
皇家历史手稿委员会
皇家英格兰历史纪念物委员会
皇家美术委员会 (英格兰)
科学博物馆
泰特美术馆
维多利亚和阿尔伯特博物馆
华莱士收藏馆

12. 社会保险部

医疗委员会和检查军医 (战争养老金)
地区医疗局
独立仲裁局
残疾人生活津贴咨询委员会
职业养老金局
社会保险咨询委员会

13. 环境部

建筑研究所
下院委员会
乡村委员会
估价仲裁机构
出租估价委员会
皇家环境污染委员会

14. 财政部法律局长和政府法制局

检察官法律秘书处

15. 贸易和工业部

国家度量衡实验室
国内煤炭消费者理事会
电力委员会
煤气消费者理事会
中央运输咨询委员会

Monopolies and Mergers Commission
Patent Office
Employment Appeal Tribunal
Industrial Tribunals

16. DEPARTMENT OF TRANSPORT

Coastguard Services

17. EXPORT CREDITS GUARANTEE DEPARTMENT

18. FOREIGN AND COMMONWEALTH OFFICE

Wilton Park Conference Centre

19. GOVERNMENT ACTUARY'S DEPARTMENT

20. GOVERNMENT COMMUNICATIONS HEADQUARTERS

21. HOME OFFICE

Boundary Commission for England
Gaming Board for Great Britain
Inspectors of Constabulary
Parole Board and Local Review Committees

22. HOUSE OF COMMONS

23. HOUSE OF LORDS

24. INLAND REVENUE, BOARD OF

25. INTERVENTION BOARD FOR AGRICULTURAL PRODUCE

26. LORD CHANCELLOR'S DEPARTMENT

Combined Tax Tribunal
Council on Tribunals
Immigration Appellate Authorities
Immigration Adjudicators
Immigration Appeal Tribunal
Lands Tribunal
Law Commission
Legal Aid Fund (England and Wales)
Pensions Appeal Tribunals
Public Trust Office
Office of the Social Security Commissioners

垄断和并购委员会
专利办公室
就业上诉仲裁机构
工业仲裁机构

16.　交通部
海岸监察局

17.　出口信用担保部

18.　外交和英联邦事务部
威尔顿公园会议中心

19.　政府精算部

20.　政府通信总局

21.　内政部
英格兰边境委员会
大不列颠博彩局
警察稽查
假释局和地方审查委员会

22.　下议院

23.　上议院

24.　国内税收局

25.　农产品管理局

26.　大法官部
复合税仲裁机构
仲裁机构理事会
移民上诉局
移民裁判机构
移民上诉机构
土地上诉机构
法律委员会
法律援助基金会(英格兰和威尔士)
养老金上诉机构
公共信托办公室
社会保险专员办公室

2007 年 1 月 1 日 (WT/Let/556)

Supreme Court Group (England and Wales)
Court of Appeal – Criminal
Circuit Offices and Crown, County and Combined Courts (England & Wales)
Transport Tribunal

27. MINISTRY OF AGRICULTURE, FISHERIES AND FOOD

Agricultural Dwelling House Advisory Committees
Agricultural Land Tribunals
Agricultural Wages Board and Committees
Cattle Breeding Centre
Plant Variety Rights Office
Royal Botanic Gardens, Kew

28. MINISTRY OF DEFENCE[31]

Meteorological Office
Procurement Executive

29. NATIONAL AUDIT OFFICE

30. NATIONAL INVESTMENT AND LOANS OFFICE

31. NORTHERN IRELAND COURT SERVICE

Coroners Courts
County Courts
Court of Appeal and High Court of Justice in Northen Ireland
Crown Court
Enforcement of Judgements Office
Legal Aid Fund
Magistrates Court
Pensions Appeals Tribunals

32. NORTHERN IRELAND, DEPARTMENT OF AGRICULTURE

33. NORTHERN IRELAND, DEPARTMENT OF ECONOMIC DEVELOPMENT

34. NORTHERN IRELAND, DEPARTMENT OF EDUCATION

35. NORTHERN IRELAND, DEPARTMENT OF THE ENVIRONMENT

36. NORTHERN IRELAND, DEPARTMENT OF FINANCE AND PERSONNEL

37. NORTHERN IRELAND, DEPARTMENT OF HEALTH AND SOCIAL SERVICES

[31] Non-warlike materials contained in Part (3) of this Annex.

最高法院团(英格兰和威尔士)
上诉法院—刑事
巡视办公室和皇家、郡和联合法院(英格兰和威尔士)
运输上诉机构

27. 农业、渔业和食品部
农地住屋咨询委员会
农业土地上诉机构
农业工资局和委员会
畜牧中心
植物新品种权利办公室
皇家植物园

28. 国防部[31]
气象办公室
采购执行中心

29. 国家审计局

30. 国家投资和贷款办公室

31. 北爱尔兰法院服务局
验尸官法院
郡法院
北爱尔兰上诉法院和最高法院
刑事法院
判决执行处
法律援助基金
治安法院
养老金上诉机构

32. 北爱尔兰，农业部

33. 北爱尔兰，经济发展部

34. 北爱尔兰，教育部

35. 北爱尔兰，环境部

36. 北爱尔兰，财政和人事部

37. 北爱尔兰，卫生和社会服务部

[31]非军事物资包含在本附件第 3 部分。

38. NORTHERN IRELAND OFFICE

Crown Solicitor's Office
Department of the Director of Public Prosecutions for Northern Ireland
Northern Ireland Forensic Science Laboratory
Office of Chief Electoral Officer for Northern Ireland
Police Authority for Northern Ireland
Probation Board for Northern Ireland
State Pathologist Service

39. OFFICE OF FAIR TRADING

40. OFFICE FOR NATIONAL STATISTICS

National Health Service Central Register

41. OFFICE OF THE PARLIAMENTARY COMMISSIONER FOR ADMINISTRATION AND HEALTH SERVICE COMMISSIONERS

42. PAYMASTER GENERAL'S OFFICE

43. POSTAL BUSINESS OF THE POST OFFICE

44. PRIVY COUNCIL OFFICE

45. PUBLIC RECORD OFFICE

46. REGISTRY OF FRIENDLY SOCIETIES

47. ROYAL COMMISSION ON HISTORICAL MANUSCRIPTS

48. ROYAL HOSPITAL, CHELSEA

49. ROYAL MINT

50. SCOTLAND, CROWN OFFICE AND PROCURATOR

Fiscal Service

51. SCOTLAND, REGISTERS OF SCOTLAND

52. SCOTLAND, GENERAL REGISTER OFFICE

53. SCOTLAND, LORD ADVOCATE'S DEPARTMENT

54. SCOTLAND, QUEEN'S AND LORD TREASURER'S REMEMBRANCER

38. 北爱尔兰事务部

政治律师办公室

北爱尔兰公诉总长办公室

北爱尔兰法律科学实验室

北爱尔兰首席选举官员办公室

北爱尔兰警察局

北爱尔兰假释局

国家病理局

39. 公平贸易署

40. 国家统计局

国家卫生服务中央注册中心

41. 议会行政专员和卫生专员办公室

42. 总支付办公室

43. 邮政局邮政业务中心

44. 枢密院

45. 历史档案馆

46. 互助会注册处

47. 皇家历史手稿委员会

48. 皇家医院

49. 皇家铸币厂

50. 苏格兰皇家办事处和检察官

财务局

51. 苏格兰，苏格兰注册局

52. 苏格兰，注册总局

53. 苏格兰，检察总长

54. 苏格兰，女王和贵族债务官

55. SCOTTISH COURTS ADMINISTRATION

Accountant of Court's Office
Court of Justiciary
Court of Session
Lands Tribunal for Scotland
Pensions Appeal Tribunals
Scottish Land Court
Scottish Law Commission
Sheriff Courts
Social Security Commissioners' Office

56. THE SCOTTISH OFFICE CENTRAL SERVICES

57. THE SCOTTISH OFFICE AGRICULTURE AND FISHERIES DEPARTMENT:

Crofters Commission
Red Deer Commission
Royal Botanic Garden, Edinburgh

58. THE SCOTTISH OFFICE INDUSTRY DEPARTMENT

59. THE SCOTTISH OFFICE EDUCATION DEPARTMENT

National Galleries of Scotland
National Library of Scotland
National Museums of Scotland
Scottish Higher Education Funding Council

60. THE SCOTTISH OFFICE ENVIRONMENT DEPARTMENT

Rent Assesment Panel and Committees
Royal Commission on the Ancient and Historical Monuments of Scotland
Royal Fine Art Commission for Scotland

61. THE SCOTTISH OFFICE HOME AND HEALTH DEPARTMENTS

HM Inspectorate of Constabulary
Local Health Councils
National Board for Nursing, Midwifery and Health Visiting for Scotland
Parole Board for Scotland and Local Review Committees
Scottish Council for Postgraduate Medical Education
Scottish Crime Squad
Scottish Criminal Record Office
Scottish Fire Service Training School
Scottish National Health Service Authorities and Trusts
Scottish Police College

55. 苏格兰法院管理局
法院总会计师办公室
刑事法院
民事法院
苏格兰土地仲裁机构
养老金上诉仲裁机构
苏格兰土地法院
苏格兰法律委员会
地方法院
社会保险专员办公室
56. 苏格兰中央服务办公室
57. 苏格兰农业和渔业部
佃农委员会
麋鹿委员会
爱丁堡皇家植物园
58. 苏格兰工业部
59. 苏格兰教育部
苏格兰国家美术馆
苏格兰国家图书馆
苏格兰国家博物馆
苏格兰高等教育基金理事会
60. 苏格兰环境部
租金评估小组和委员会
苏格兰古代和历史纪念物皇家委员会
苏格兰皇家美术委员会
61. 苏格兰内政和卫生部
皇家警务监察局
地方卫生理事会
苏格兰护理、助产和卫生访视局
苏格兰假释局和地方审查委员会
苏格兰研究生医学教育理事会
苏格兰犯罪总局
苏格兰刑事档案办公室
苏格兰消防培训学校
苏格兰国民健康服务局和财团
苏格兰警察学院

62. SCOTTISH RECORD OFFICE

63. HM TREASURY

64. WELSH OFFICE

Royal Commission of Ancient and Historical Monuments in Wales
Welsh National Board for Nursing, Midwifery and Health Visiting
Local Government Boundary Commission for Wales
Valuation Tribunals (Wales)
Welsh Higher Education Finding Council
Welsh National Health Service Authorities and Trusts
Welsh Rent Assessment Panels

62. 苏格兰档案局
63. 财政部
64. 威尔士事务部

威尔士古代和历史纪念物皇家委员会

威尔士护理、助产和卫生访视局

威尔士地方政府边境委员会

估价裁判机构 (威尔士)

威尔士高等教育基金理事会

威尔士国民健康服务局和财团

威尔士租金评估小组

3. List of supplies and equipment purchased by Ministries of Defence in Belgium, Bulgaria, Czech Republic, Denmark, Germany, Estonia, Greece, Spain, France, Ireland, Italy, Cyprus, Latvia, Lithuania, Luxembourg, Hungary, Malta, the Netherlands, Austria, Poland, Portugal, Romania, Slovenia, Slovakia, Finland, Sweden and the United Kingdom that are covered by the Agreement

Chapter 25: Salt, sulphur, earths and stone, plastering materials, lime and cement

Chapter 26: Metallic ores, slag and ash

Chapter 27: Mineral fuels, mineral oils and products of their distillation, bituminous substances, mineral waxes

except:
ex 27.10: special engine fuels (except Austria)
heating and engine fules (only Austria)

Chapter 28: Inorganic chemicals, organic and inorganic compounds of precious metals, of rare-earth metals, of radio-active elements and isotopes

except:
ex 28.09: explosives
ex 28.13: explosives
ex 28.14: tear gas
ex 28.28: explosives
ex 28.32: explosives
ex 28.39: explosives
ex 28.50: toxic products
ex 28.51: toxic products
ex 28.54: explosives

Chapter 29: Organic chemicals

except:
ex 29.03: explosives
ex 29.04: explosives
ex 29.07: explosives
ex 29.08: explosives
ex 29.11: explosives
ex 29.12: explosives
ex 29.13: toxic products
ex 29.14: toxic products

3. 本协定所涵盖的比利时、保加利亚、捷克、丹麦、德国、爱沙尼亚、希腊、西班牙、法国、爱尔兰、意大利、塞浦路斯、拉脱维亚、立陶宛、卢森堡、匈牙利、马耳他、荷兰、奥地利、波兰、葡萄牙、罗马尼亚、斯洛文尼亚、斯洛伐克、芬兰、瑞典和英国国防部所采购的供应品和设备清单

第 25 章： 盐；硫磺；泥土及石料；石膏料、石灰及水泥

第 26 章： 矿砂、矿渣及矿灰

第 27 章： 矿物燃料、矿物油及其蒸馏产品；沥青物质；矿物蜡

除：
ex 27.10：特殊发动机燃料(奥地利除外)
加热用和发动机燃料(仅限奥地利)

第 28 章： 无机化学品；贵金属、稀土金属、放射性元素及其同位素的有机及无机化合物

除：
ex 28.09：爆炸物
ex 28.13：爆炸物
ex 28.14：催泪瓦斯
ex 28.28：爆炸物
ex 28.32：爆炸物
ex 28.39：爆炸物
ex 28.50：有毒物品
ex 28.51：有毒物品
ex 28.54：爆炸物

第 29 章： 有机化学品

除：
ex 29.03：爆炸物
ex 29.04：爆炸物
ex 29.07：爆炸物
ex 29.08：爆炸物
ex 29.11：爆炸物
ex 29.12：爆炸物
ex 29.13：有毒物品
ex 29.14：有毒物品

ex 29.15: toxic products
ex 29.21: toxic products
ex 29.22: toxic products
ex 29.23: toxic products
ex 29.26: explosives
ex 29.27: toxic products
ex 29.29: explosives

Chapter 30: Pharmaceutical products

Chapter 31: Fertilizers

Chapter 32: Tanning and dyeing extracts, tannings and their derivatives, dyes, colours, paints and varnishes, putty, fillers and stoppings, inks

Chapter 33: Essential oils and resinoids, perfumery, cosmetic or toilet preparations

Chapter 34: Soap, organic surface-active agents, washing preparations, lubricating preparations, artificial waxes, prepared waxes polishing and scouring preparations, candles and similar articles, modelling pastes and 'dental waxes'

Chapter 36 Explosives, pyrotechnic products, matches, pyrophoric alloys, certain combustible perparations (only Austria and Sweden)

except (only Austria)
ex 36.01: propellent powders
ex 36.02: prepared explosives
ex 36.04: detonators
ex 36.08: explosives

Chapter 35: Albuminoidal substances, glues, enzymes

Chapter 37: Photographic and cinematographic goods

Chapter 38: Miscellaneous chemical products

except:
ex 38.19: toxic products (Not for Sweden)

Chapter 39: Artificial resins and plastic materials, cellulose esters and ethers, articles thereof

except:
ex 39.03: explosives (Not for Sweden)

ex 29.15：有毒物品
ex 29.21：有毒物品
ex 29.22：有毒物品
ex 29.23：有毒物品
ex 29.26：爆炸物
ex 29.27：有毒物品
ex 29.29：爆炸物

第 30 章： 药品

第 31 章： 肥料

第 32 章： 鞣料浸膏及染料浸膏；鞣酸及其衍生物；染料、颜料及其他着色料；油漆及清漆；油灰及其他类似胶粘剂；墨水、油墨

第 33 章： 清油及香膏；芳香料制品及化妆盥洗品

第 34 章： 肥皂、有机表面活性剂、洗涤剂、润滑剂、人造蜡、调制蜡、光洁剂、蜡烛及类似品、塑型用膏、“牙科用蜡”及牙科用熟石膏制剂

第 36 章： 炸药；烟火制品；火柴；引火合金；易燃材料制品(仅限奥地利和瑞典)

除(仅限奥地利)
ex 36.01：发射药
ex 36.02：配制炸药
ex 36.04：雷管
ex 36.08：爆炸物

第 35 章： 蛋白类物质；改性淀粉；胶；酶

第 37 章： 照相及电影用品

第 38 章： 杂项化学产品

除：
ex 38.19：有毒物品(瑞典除外)

第 39 章： 塑料及其制品

除：
ex 39.03：爆炸物(瑞典除外)

Chapter 40: Rubber, synthetic rubber, factice, and articles thereof

except:
ex 40.11: bullet-proof tyres (Not for Sweden)

Chapter 41: Raw hides and skins (other than furskins) and leather: (Not for Austria)

Chapter 42: Articles of leather, saddlery and harness, travel goods, handbags and similar containers, articles of animal gut (other than silk-worm gut): (Not for Austria)

Chapter 43: Furskins and artificial fur, manufactures thereof

Chapter 44: Wood and articles of wood, wood charcoal: (Not for Austria)

Chapter 45: Cork and articles of cork

Chapter 46: Manufactures of straw of esparto and of other plaiting materials, basketware and wickerwork

Chapter 47: Paper-making material

Chapter 48: Paper and paperboard, articles of paper pulp, of paper or of paperboard: (Not for Austria)

Chapter 49: Printed books, newspapers, pictures and other products of the printing industry, manuscripts, typescripts and plans: (Not for Austria)

Chapter 65: Headgear and parts thereof

except (only Austria):
ex 65.05: military headgear

Chapter 66: Umbrellas, sunshades, walking-sticks, whips, riding-crops and parts thereof

Chapter 67: Prepared feathers and down and articles made of feathers or of down, artificial flowers, articles of human hair

Chapter 68: Articles of stone, of plaster, of cement, of asbestos, of mica and of similar materials

Chapter 69: Ceramic products

Chapter 70: Glass and glassware

第 40 章： 橡胶及其制品

除：
ex 40.11：防弹轮胎(瑞典除外)

第 41 章： 生皮(毛皮除)及皮革(奥地利除外)

第 42 章： 皮革制品；鞍具及挽具；旅行用品、手提包及类似容器；动物肠线(蚕胶丝除外)制品(奥地利除外)

第 43 章： 毛皮、人造毛皮及其制品

第 44 章： 木及木制品；木炭(奥地利除外)

第 45 章： 软木及软木制品

第 46 章： 稻草、秸秆、针茅或其他编结材料制品；篮筐及柳条编结品

第 47 章： 纸制品

第 48 章： 纸与纸板；纸浆、纸或纸板制品(奥地利除外)

第 49 章： 书籍、报纸、印刷图画及其他印刷品；手稿、打字稿及设计图纸(奥地利除外)

第 65 章： 帽类及其零件

除：(仅限奥地利)
ex 65.05：军帽

第 66 章： 雨伞、阳伞、手杖、鞭子、马鞭及其零件

第 67 章： 已加工羽毛、羽绒及其制品；人造花；人发制品

第 68 章： 石料、石膏、水泥、石棉、云母及类似材料的制品

第 69 章： 陶瓷制品

第 70 章： 玻璃及其制品

Chapter 71:	Pearls, precious and semi-precious stones, precious metals, rolled precious metals, and articles thereof; imitation jewellery
Chapter 72:	Coins (only Austria and Sweden)
Chapter 73:	Iron and steel and articles thereof
Chapter 74:	Copper and articles thereof
Chapter 75:	Nickel and articles thereof
Chapter 76:	Aluminium and articles thereof
Chapter 77:	Magnesium and beryllium and articles thereof
Chapter 78:	Lead and articles thereof
Chapter 79:	Zinc and articles thereof
Chapter 80:	Tin and articles thereof
Chapter 81:	Other base metals employed in metallurgy and articles thereof
Chapter 82:	Tools, implements, cutlery, spoons and forks, of base metal, parts thereof except: ex 82.05: tools (Not for Austria) ex 82.07: tools, parts ex 82.08: hand tools (only Austria)
Chapter 83:	Miscellaneous articles of base metal
Chapter 84:	Boilers, machinery and mechanical appliances, parts thereof except: ex 84.06: engines ex 84.08: other engines ex 84.45: machinery ex 84.53: automatic data-processing machines (Not for Austria) ex 84.55: parts of machines under heading No 84.53 (Not for Austria and Sweden) ex 84.59: nuclear reactors (Not for Austria and Sweden)

第 71 章：　天然或养殖珍珠、宝石或半宝石、贵金属、包贵金属及其制品；仿首饰；

第 72 章：　钱币(仅限奥地利和瑞典)

第 73 章：　钢铁制品

第 74 章：　铜及其制品

第 75 章：　镍及其制品

第 76 章：　铝及其制品

第 77 章：　镁和铍及其制品

第 78 章：　铅及其制品

第 79 章：　锌及其制品

第 80 章：　锡及其制品

第 81 章：　其他贱金属、金属陶瓷及其制品

第 82 章：　贱金属工具、器具、利口器、餐匙、餐叉及其零件

除：
ex 82.05：工具(奥地利除外)
ex 82.07：工具零件
ex 82.08：手动工具(仅限奥地利)

第 83 章：　贱金属杂项制品

第 84 章：　核反应堆、锅炉、机器、机械器具及零件

除：
ex 84.06：发动机
ex 84.08：其他发动机
ex 84.45：机械
ex 84.53：自动数据处理机(奥地利除外)
ex 84.55：8453 所列机器零件(奥地利和瑞典除外)
ex 84.59：核反应堆(奥地利和瑞典除外)

Chapter 85: Electrical machinery and equipment, parts thereof

except:
ex 85.03: electric cells and batteries (only Austria)
ex 85.13: telecommunication equipment
ex 85.15: transmission apparatus

Chapter 86: Railway and tramway locomotives, rolling-stock and parts thereof; railway and tramway tracks fixtures and fittings, traffic signalling equipment of all kinds (not electrically powered)

except:
ex 86.02: armoured locomotives, electric
ex 86.03: other armoured locomotives
ex 86.05: armoured wagons
ex 86.06: repair wagons
ex 86.07: wagons

Chapter 87: Vehicles, other than railway or tramway rolling-stock, and parts thereof

except:
ex 87.08: tanks and other armoured vehicles
ex 87.01: tractors
ex 87.02: military vehicles
ex 87.03: breakdown lorries
ex 87.09: motorcycles
ex 87.14: trailers

Chapter 88: Aircraft and parts thereof (only Austria)

Chapter 89: Ships, boats and floating structures

except:
ex 89.01: warships (only Austria)
ex 89.01 A: warships (except Austria)
ex 89.03: floating structures (only Austria)

Chapter 90: Optical, photographic, cinematographic, measuring, checking, precision, medical and surgical instruments and apparatus, parts thereof

except:
ex 90.05: binoculars
ex 90.13: miscellaneous instruments, lasers
ex 90.14: telemeters
ex 90.28: electrical and electronic measuring instruments
ex 90.11: microscopes (Not for Sweden and Austria)

第 85 章：　电机、电气设备及其零件

除：
ex 85.03：电池(仅限奥地利)
ex 85.13：电信设备
ex 85.15：传送设备

第 86 章：　铁道及电车道机车、车辆及其零件；铁道及电车道轨道固定装置及其零件、附件；各种机械(包括电动机械)交通信号设备

除：
ex 86.02：装甲机车，电动
ex 86.03：其他装甲机车
ex 86.05：装甲无蓬货车
ex 86.06：修理用无蓬货车
ex 86.07：无蓬货车

第 87 章：　车辆及其零件、附件，但铁道及电车道车辆除外

除：
ex 87.08：坦克及其他装甲车辆
ex 87.01：拖拉机
ex 87.02：军用车辆
ex 87.03：救援车辆
ex 87.09：摩托车
ex 87.14：拖车

第 88 章：　航空器、航天器及其零件(仅限奥地利)

第 89 章：　船舶及浮动结构体

除：
ex 89.01：军舰(仅限奥地利)
ex 89.01A：军舰(奥地利除外)
ex 89.03：浮动结构体(仅限奥地利)

第 90 章：　光学、照相、电影、计量、检验、医疗或外科用仪器及设备、精密仪器及设备

除：
ex 90.05：望远镜
ex 90.13：未列名仪器，激光器
ex 90.14：测距仪
ex 90.28：电气电子测量仪
ex 90.11：显微镜(瑞典和奥地利除外)

ex 90.17: medical instruments (Not for Sweden and Austria)
ex 90.18: mechano-therapy appliances (Not for Sweden and Austria)
ex 90.19: orthopaedic appliances (Not for Sweden and Austria)
ex 90.20: X-ray apparatus (Not for Sweden and Austria)

Chapter 91: Clocks and watches and parts thereof

Chapter 92: Musical instruments, sound recorders or reproducers, television image and sound recorders or reproducers, parts and accessories of such articles

Chapter 94: Furniture and parts thereof, bedding, mattresses, mattress supports, cushions and similar stuffed furnishings

except:
ex 94.01 A: aircraft seats (Not for Austria)

Chapter 95: Articles and manufactures of carving or moulding material

Chapter 96: Brooms, brushes, powder-puffs and sieves

Chapter 97: Toys, games and sport requisites, parts thereof (only Austria and Sweden)

Chapter 98: Miscellaneous manufactured articles

ex 90.17：医疗仪器(瑞典和奥地利除外)
ex 90.18：热疗设备(瑞典和奥地利除外)
ex 90.19：整容设备(瑞典和奥地利除外)
ex 90.20：X 光设备(瑞典和奥地利除外)

第 91 章： 钟表及其零件

第 92 章： 乐器及其零件、附件；录音机及放声机、电视图像、声音的录制和重放设备及零件、附件

第 94 章： 家具；寝具、褥垫、弹簧床垫、软坐垫及类似的填充制品

除：
ex 94.01A：航空器座椅(奥地利除外)

第 95 章： 雕刻或模塑材料制品

第 96 章： 帚、刷子、粉扑和筛子

第 97 章： 玩具、游戏品、运动用品及其零件、附件(仅限奥地利和瑞典)

第 98 章： 杂项制品

2007 年 1 月 1 日 (WT/Let/556)

3. LISTE DES MATÉRIELS ACHETÉS PAR LES MINISTÈRES DE LA DÉFENSE DE LA BELGIQUE, BULGARIE, RÉPUBLIQUE TCHÉQUE, DANEMARK, ALLEMAGNE, ESTONIE, GRÉCE, ESPAGNE, FRANCE, IRLANDE, ITALIE, CHYPRE, LETTONIE, LITUANIE, LUXEMBOURG, HONGRIE, MALTE, PAYS-BAS, AUTRICHE, POLOGNE, PORTUGAL, ROUMANIE, SLOVENIE, SLOVAQUIE, FINLANDE, SUEDE ET ROYAUME-UNI, ET SOUMIS À L'ACCORD

Chapitre 25: Sel, soufre, terres et pierres, plâtres, chaux et ciments

Chapitre 26: Minerais métallurgiques, scories et cendres

Chapitre 27: Combustibles minéraux, huiles minérales et produits de leur distillation, matières bitumineuses, cires minérales

à l'exception de:
ex 27.10: carburant spéciaux (sauf pour l'Autriche)
fuel-oils de chauffage et carburants (seulement pour l'Autriche)

Chapitre 28: Produits chimiques inorganiques, composés inorganiques ou organiques de métaux précieux, d'éléments radio-actifs, de métaux des terres rares et d'isotopes

à l'exception de:
ex 28.09: explosifs
ex 28.13: explosifs
ex 28.14: gaz lacrymogènes
ex 28.28: explosifs
ex 28.32: explosifs
ex 28.39: explosifs
ex 28.50: produits toxicologiques
ex 28.51: produits toxicologiques
ex 28.54: explosifs

Chapitre 29: Produits chimiques organiques

à l'exception de:
ex 29.03: explosifs
ex 29.04: explosifs
ex 29.07: explosifs
ex 29.08: explosifs
ex 29.11: explosifs
ex 29.12: explosifs
ex 29.13: produits toxicologiques

ex 29.14: produits toxicologiques
ex 29.15: produits toxicologiques
ex 29.21: produits toxicologiques
ex 29.22: produits toxicologiques
ex 29.23: produits toxicologiques
ex 29.26: explosifs
ex 29.27: produits toxicologiques
ex 29.29: explosifs

Chapitre 30: Produits pharmaceutiques

Chapitre 31: Engrais

Chapitre 32: Extraits tannants et tinctoriaux, tanins et leur dérivés, matières colorantes, couleurs, peintures, vernis et teintures, mastics, encres

Chapitre 33: Huiles essentielles et sésinoides, produits de parfumerie ou de toilette et cosmétiques

Chapitre 34: Savons, produits organiques tensio-actifs, préparations pour lessives, préparations lubrifiantes, cires artificielles, cires préparées, produits d'entretien, bougies et articles similaires, pâtes à modeler et "cires pour l'art dentaire"

Chapitre 35: Matières albuminoïdes, colles, enzymes

Chapitre 36 Poudres et explosifs, articles de pyrotechnie, allumettes, alliages pyrophoriques, matières inflammables (seulement pour l'Autriche and Suède)

à l'exception de (seulement pour l'Autriche)
ex 36.01: poudres à tirer
ex 36.02: explosifs préparés
ex 36.04: détonateurs
ex 36.08: explosifs

Chapitre 37: Produits photographiques et cinématographiques

Chapitre 38: Produits divers des industries chimiques

à l'exception de:
ex 38.19: produits toxicologiques (sauf pour la Suède)

Chapitre 39: Matières plastiques artificielles, éthers et esters de la cellulose, résines artificielles et ouvrages en ces matières

à l'exception de:
ex 39.03: explosifs (sauf pour la Suède)

Chapitre 40: Caoutchouc naturel ou synthétique, factice pour caoutchouc et ouvrages en caoutchouc

à l'exception de:
ex 40.11: pneus pour automobiles (sauf pour la Suède)

Chapitre 41: Peaux and cuirs: (sauf pour l'Autriche)

Chapitre 42: Ouvrages en cuir, articles de bourrellerie et de sellerie, articles de voyage, sacs à main et contenants similaires, ouvrages en boyaux: (sauf pour l'Autriche)

Chapitre 43: Pelleteries et fourrures, pelleteries factices

Chapitre 44: Bois, charbon de bois et ouvrages en bois: (sauf pour l'Autriche)

Chapitre 45: Liège et ouvrages en liège

Chapitre 46: Ouvrages de sparterie et de vannerie

Chapitre 47: Matières servant à la fabrication du papier

Chapitre 48: Papier et cartons, ouvrages en pâte de cellulose, en papier et en carton: (sauf pour l'Autriche)

Chapitre 49: Articles de librairie et produits des arts graphiques: (sauf pour l'Autriche)

Chapitre 65: Coiffures et parties de coiffures

à l'exception de (seulement pour l'Autriche):
ex 65.05: coiffures militaires

Chapitre 66: Parapluies, parasols, cannes, fouets, cravaches et leurs parties

Chapitre 67: Plumes et duvet apprêtés et articles en plumes ou en duvet, fleurs artificielles, ouvrages en cheveux

Chapitre 68: Ouvrages en pierres, plâtre, ciment, amiante, mica et matières analogues

Chapitre 69: Produits céramiques

Chapitre 70: Verres et ouvrages en verre

Chapitre 71: Perles fines, pierres gemmes et similaires, métaux précieux, plaqués ou doublés de métaux précieux et ouvrages en ces matières; bijouterie de fantaisie

Chapitre 72: Monnaies (seulement pour l'Autriche et la Suède)

Chapitre 73: Fonte, fer et acier

Chapitre 74: Cuivre

Chapitre 75: Nickel

Chapitre 76: Aluminium

Chapitre 77: Magnésium, béryllium

Chapitre 78: Plomb

Chapitre 79: Zinc
Chapitre 80: Etain

Chapitre 81: Autres métaux communs

Chapitre 82: Outillage, articles de coutellerie et couverts de table, en métaux communs

à l'exception de:
ex 82.05: outillage (sauf Autriche)
ex 82.07: pieces d'outillage
ex 82.08: outillage à main (seulement pour l'Autriche)

Chapitre 83: Ouvrages divers en métaux communs

Chapitre 84: Chaudières, machines, appareils et engins mécaniques

à l'exception de:
ex 84.06: moteurs
ex 84.08: autres propulseurs
ex 84.45: machines
ex 84.53: machines automatiques de traitement de l'information (sauf pour l'Autriche)
ex 84.55: pièces No 84.53 (sauf pour l'Autriche et la Suède)
ex 84.59: réacteurs nucléaires (sauf pour l'Autriche et la Suède)

Chapitre 85: Machines et appareils électriques et objets servant à des usages électrotechniques

à l'exception de:
ex 85.03: piles électriques (seulement pour l'Autriche)
ex 85.13: télécommunication
ex 85.15: appareils de transmission

Chapitre 86: Véhicules et matériel pour voies ferrées, appareils de signalisation non électriques pour voies de communication

à l'exception de:
ex 86.02: locomotives blindées
ex 86.03: autres locoblindés
ex 86.05: wagons blindés
ex 86.06: wagons ateliers
ex 86.07: wagons

Chapitre 87: Voitures automobiles, tracteurs, cycles et autres véhicules terrestres

à l'exception de:
ex 87.08: chars et automobiles blindés
ex 87.01: tracteurs
ex 87.02: véhicules militaires
ex 87.03: voitures de dépannage
ex 87.09: motocycles
ex 87.14: remorques

Chapitre 88: Navigation aérienne (seulement pour l'Autriche)

Chapitre 89: Navigation maritime et fluviale

à l'exception de:
ex 89.01: bateaux de guerre (seulement pour l'Autriche)
ex 89.01A: bateaux de guerre (sauf pour l'Autriche)
ex 89.03: engins flottants (seulement pour l'Autriche)

Chapitre 90: Instruments et appareils d'optique, de photographie et de cinématographie, de mesure, de vérification, de précision, instruments et appareils médico-chirurgicaux

à l'exception de:
ex 90.05: jumelles
ex 90.13: instruments divers, lasers
ex 90.14: télèmetres
ex 90.28: instruments de mesures électriques ou électroniques
ex 90.11: microscopes (sauf pour l'Autriche et la Suède)
ex 90.17: instruments médicaux (sauf pour l'Autriche et la Suède)
ex 90.18: appareils de mécanothérapie (sauf pour l'Autriche et la Suède)
ex 90.19: appareils d'orthopédie (sauf pour l'Autriche et la Suède)
ex 90.20: appareils rayon X (sauf pour l'Autriche et la Suède)

Chapitre 91: Horlogerie

Chapitre 92: Instruments de musique, appareils d'enregistrement ou de reproduction du son; appareils d'entregistrement ou de reproduction des images et du son en télévision, parties et accessoires de ces instruments et appareils

Chapitre 94: Meubles, mobilier médico-chirurgigal, articles de literie et similaires

à l'exception de:
ex 94.01A: sièges d'aérodynes (sauf pour l'Autriche)

Chapitre 95: Matières à tailler et à mouler, à l'état travaillé (y compris les ouvrages)

Chapitre 96: Ouvrages de brosserie et pinceaux, balais, houppes et articles de tamiserie

Chapitre 97: Jouets, jeux, articles pour divertissements et pour sports (seulement pour l'Autriche and Suède)

Chapitre 98: Ouvrages divers

3. LISTA DE MATERIALES COMPRADOS POR LOS MINISTERIOS DE DEFENSA DE BÉLGICA, BULGARIA, REPÚBLICA CHECA, DINAMARCA, ALEMANIA, ESTONIA, GRECIA, ESPAÑA, FRANCIA, IRLANDA, ITALIA, CHIPRE, LETONIA, LITUANIA, LUXEMBURGO, HUNGRÍA, MALTA, PAÍSES BAJOS, AUSTRIA, POLONIA, PORTUGAL, ROMANIA, ESLOVENIA, ESLOVAQUIA, FINLANDIA, SUECIA Y EL REINO UNIDO, Y SUJETOS AL ACUERDO

Capítulo 25: Sal, azufre, tierras y piedras, yesos, cales y cementos

Capítulo 26: Minerales metalúrgicos, escorias, cenizas

Capítulo 27: Combustibles minerales, aceites minerales y productos de su destilación, materias bituminosas, ceras minerales

excepto:
ex 27.10: carburantes especiales (salvo Austria)
combustibles para calefacción y carburantes (solamente Austria)

Capítulo 28: Productos químicos inorgánicos, compuestos inorgánicos u orgánicos de metales preciosos, de elementos radioactivos, de metales de las tierras raras y de isótopos

excepto:
ex 28.09: explosivos
ex 28.13: explosivos
ex 28.14: gases lacrimógenos
ex 28.28: explosivos
ex 28.32: explosivos
ex 28.39: explosivos
ex 28.50: productos tóxicos
ex 28.51: productos tóxicos
ex 28.54: explosivos

Capítulo 29: Productos químicos orgánicos

excepto:
ex 29.03: explosivos
ex 29.04: explosivos
ex 29.07: explosivos
ex 29.08: explosivos
ex 29.11: explosivos
ex 29.12: explosivos
ex 29.13: productos tóxicos
ex 29.14: productos tóxicos

ex 29.15: productos tóxicos
ex 29.21: productos tóxicos
ex 29.22: productos tóxicos
ex 29.23: productos tóxicos
ex 29.26: explosivos
ex 29.27: productos tóxicos
ex 29.29: explosivos

Capítulo 30: Productos farmacéuticos

Capítulo 31: Abonos

Capítulo 32: Extractos curtientes y tintóreos, taninos y sus derivados, materias colorantes, colores, pinturas, barnices y tintes, mástiques, tintas

Capítulo 33: Aceites esenciales y resinoides, productos de perfumería o de tocador y cosméticos

Capítulo 34: Jabones, productos orgánicos tensoactivos, preparaciones para lavar, preparaciones lubricantes, ceras artificiales, ceras preparadas, productos para lustrar y pulir, bujías y artículos análogos, pastas para modelar, y "ceras para el arte dental"

Capítulo 35: Materias albuminoides y colas, enzimas

Capítulo 36 Pólvoras y explosivos, artículos de pirotecnia, fósforos, aleaciones pirofóricas, materias inflamables (solamente Austria y Suecia)

excepto (solamente Austria)
ex 36.01: pólvoras de proyección
ex 36.02: explosivos preparados
ex 36.04: detonadores
ex 36.08: explosivos

Capítulo 37: Productos fotográficos y cinematográficos

Capítulo 38: Productos diversos de las industrias químicas

excepto:
ex 38.19: productos tóxicos (salvo Suecia)

Capítulo 39: Materias plásticas artificiales, éteres y ésteres de la celulosa, resinas artificiales y manufacturas de estas materias

excepto:
ex 39.03: explosivos (salvo Suecia)

Capítulo 40: Caucho natural o sintético, caucho facticio y manufacturas de caucho

excepto:
ex 40.11: neumáticos a prueba de bala (salvo Suecia)

Capítulo 41: Pieles y cuero: (salvo Austria)

Capítulo 42: Manufacturas de cuero, artículos de guarnicionería y talabartería, artículos de viaje, bolsos de mano y continentes similares, manufacturas de tripas: (salvo Austria)

Capítulo 43: Peletería y confecciones de peletería, peletería facticia

Capítulo 44: Madera, carbón vegetal y manufacturas de madera: (salvo Austria)

Capítulo 45: Corcho y sus manufacturas

Capítulo 46: Manufacturas de espartería y cestería

Capítulo 47: Materias utilizadas en la fabricación de papel

Capítulo 48: Pepel y cartón, manufacturas de pasta de celulosa, de papel y de cartón: (salvo Austria)

Capítulo 49: Artículos de librería y productos de las artes gráficas: (salvo Austria)

Capítulo 65: Sombreros y demás tocados y sus partes componentes

excepto (solamente Austria):
ex 65.05: sombreros, gorras y demás tocados militares

Capítulo 66: Paraguas, quitasoles, bastones, látigos, fustas y sus partes componentes

Capítulo 67: Plumas y plumón preparados y artículos de pluma o de plumón, flores artificiales, manufacturas de cabellos

Capítulo 68: Manufacturas de piedra, yeso, cemento, amianto, mica y materias análogas

Capítulo 69: Productos cerámicos

Capítulo 70: Vidrio y manufactura de vidrio

Capítulo 71: Perlas finas, piedras preciosas y semipreciosas y similares, metales preciosos, chapados de metales preciosos y manufacturas de estas materias, bisutería de fantasía

Capítulo 72: Monedas (solamente Austria y Suecia)

Capítulo 73: Fundición, hierro y acero

Capítulo 74: Cobre

Capítulo 75: Níquel

Capítulo 76: Aluminio

Capítulo 77: Magnesio, berilio (glucinio)

Capítulo 78: Plomo

Capítulo 79: Zinc

Capítulo 80: Estaño
Capítulo 81: Otros metales comunes

Capítulo 82: Herramientas, artículos de cuchillería y cubiertos de mesa, de metales comunes

excepto:
ex 82.05: herramientas (salvo Austria)
ex 82.07: piezas de herramientas
ex 82.08: herramientas de mano (solamente Austria)

Capítulo 83: Manufacturas diversas de metales comunes

Capítulo 84: Calderas, máquinas, aparatos y artefactos mecánicos

excepto:
ex 84.06: motores
ex 84.08: otros propulsores
ex 84.45: máquinas
ex 84.53: máquinas automáticas para tratamiento de la información (salvo Austria)
ex 84.55: piezas de las máquinas de la partida 84.53 (salvo Austria y Suecia)
ex 84.59: reactores nucleares (salvo Austria y Suecia)

Capítulo 85: Máquinas y aparatos eléctricos y objetos destinados a usos electrotécnicos

excepto:
ex 85.03: pilas eléctricas (solamente Austria)
ex 85.13: telecomunicaciones
ex 85.15: aparatos transmisores

Capítulo 86: Vehículos y material para vías férreas, aparatos non eléctricos de señalización para vías de comunicación

excepto:
ex 86.02: locomotoras blindadas
ex 86.03: las demás locomotoras de maniobra blindadas
ex 86.05: vagones blindados
ex 86.06: vagones talleres
ex 86.07: vagones

Capítulo 87: Vehículos automóviles, tractores, velocípedos y otros vehículos terrestres

excepto:
ex 87.08: carros y automóviles blindados
ex 87.01: tractores
ex 87.02: vehículos militares
ex 87.03: coches para arreglo de averías
ex 87.09: motociclos
ex 87.14: remolques

Capítulo 88: Navegación aérea (solamente Austria)

Capítulo 89: Navegación marítima y fluvial

excepto:
ex 89.01: buques de guerra (solamente Austria)
ex 89.01 A: buques de guerra (salvo Austria)
ex 89.03: artefactos flotantes (solamente Austria)

Capítulo 90: Instrumentos y aparatos de óptica, de fotografía y de cinematografía, de medida, de comprobación y de precisión, instrumentos y aparatos médico-quirúrgicos,

excepto:
ex 90.05: gemelos
ex 90.13: instrumentos diversos, lasers
ex 90.14: telémetros
ex 90.28: instrumentos de medida eléctricos o electrónicos
ex 90.11: microscopios (salvo Austria y Suecia)
ex 90.17: instrumentos de medicina (salvo Austria y Suecia)
ex 90.18: aparatos de mecanoterapia (salvo Austria y Suecia)
ex 90.19: aparatos de ortopedia (salvo Austria y Suecia)
ex 90.20: aparatos de rayos X (salvo Austria y Suecia)

Capítulo 91: Relojería

Capítulo 92: Instrumentos de música, aparatos para el registro y la reproducción del sonido o para el registro y reproducción en televisión de imágenes y sonido, partes y acessorios de esos instrumentos y aparatos

Capítulo 94: Muebles, mobiliario médico-quirúrgico, artículos de cama y similares

excepto:
ex 94.01 A: asientos para aeronaves (salvo Austria)

Capítulo 95: Materias para talla y moldeo, labradas (incluidas las manufacturas)

Capítulo 96: Manufacturas de cepillería, pinceles, escobas, plumeros, borlas y cedazos

Capítulo 97: Juguetes, juegos, artículos para recreo y para deportes (salvo Austria y Suecia)

Capítulo 98: Manufacturas diversas

EUROPEAN COMMUNITIES
COMMUNAUTES EUROPEENNES
COMUNIDADES EUROPEAS

ANNEX 2- ANNEXE 2 - ANEXO 2

Entities which Procure in Accordance with the Provisions of this Agreement
Entités qui passent des marchés conformément aux dispositions du présent accord
Entidades que se rigen en sus contratos por las disposiciones del presente acuerdo

SUPPLIES / FOURNITURES / SUMINISTROS

Thresholds:	SDR 200,000
Valeurs de seuil:	DTS 200 000
Valores de umbral:	DEG 200.000

SERVICES / SERVICES / SERVICIOS
specified in Annex 4 / spécifiés dans l'Annexe 4 / detallados en el Anexo 4

Thresholds:	SDR 200,000
Valeurs de seuil:	DTS 200 000
Valores de umbral:	DEG 200.000

WORKS / TRAVAUX / OBRAS
specified in Annex 5 / spécifiés dans l'Annexe 5 / detalladas en el Anexo 5

Thresholds:	SDR 5,000,000
Valeurs de seuil:	DTS 5 000 000
Valores de umbral:	DEG 5.000.000

LIST OF ENTITIES / LISTE DES ENTITÉS / LISTA DE LAS ENTIDADES:

1. CONTRACTING AUTHORITIES OF THE REGIONAL OR LOCAL PUBLIC AUTHORITIES;
POUVOIRS ADJUDICATEURS DES COLLECTIVITÉES TERRITORIALES;
PODERES ADJUDICADORES DE LOS ENTES PÚBLICOS TERRITORIALES:

2. BODIES GOVERNED BY PUBLIC LAW AS DEFINED IN DIRECTIVE 93/37;
LES ORGANISMES DE DROIT PUBLIC TELS QUE DÉFINIS PAR LA DIRECTIVE 93/37;
LOS ORGANISMOS DE DERECHO PÚBLICO SEGÚN LA DEFINICIÓN DE LA DIRECTIVA 93/37:

- A "**body governed by public law**" means any body

欧洲共同体

附件 2

依照本协定条款进行采购的实体

供应品

门槛金额: 200,000 特别提款权

服务
附件 4 列出

门槛金额: 200,000 特别提款权

工程
附件 5 列出

门槛金额: 5,000,000 特别提款权

实体清单:

1. 地区或地方政府缔约机关;

2. 按照 93/37 号指令所定义的受公法管辖的机构;

- 一“受公法管辖的机构”指一机构:

2000 年 3 月 1 日 (WT/Let/330)

  - established for the specific purpose of meeting needs in the general interest, not having an industrial or commercial character, and

  - having legal personality, and

  - financed, for the most part, by the State, or regional or local authorities, or other bodies governed by public law, or subject to management supervision by those bodies, orhaving an administrative, managerial or supervisory board; more than half of whose members are appointed by the State, regional or local authorities or by other bodies governed by public law.

  The lists of bodies and categories of bodies governed by public law which fulfill the criteria referred to are set out in Annex I to Directive 93/37. These lists are indicative only (see Official Journal of the European Communitities n° L 199/56, 09.08.1993 and n° C 241/228, 29.08.1994).

- On entend par "**organisme de droit public**" tout organisme:

  - créé pour satisfaire spécifiquement des besoins d'intérêt général ayant un caractère autre qu'industriel ou commercial, et

  - doté de la personalité juridique, et

  - dont l'activité et financée majoritairement par l'Etat, les collectivités territoriales ou d'autres organismes de droit public, soit la gestion est soumise à un contrôle par ces derniers, soit l'organe d'administration, de direction ou de surveillance est composé de membres dont plus de la moitié est désignée par l'Etat, les collectivités territoriales ou d'autres organismes de droit public.

  Les listes des organismes et des catégories d'organismes de droit public qui remplissent les ces critères figurent à l'annexe I de la Directive 93/37. Ces listes sont uniquement indicatives (voir Journal officiel des Communautés Européennes n° L 199/54, 09.08.1993 et n° C 241/228, 29.08.1994).

- "**Organismo de derecho público**" cualquier organismo:

  - creado para satisfacer específicamente necesidades de interés general que no tengan carácter industrial o mercantil, y

  - dotado de personalidad jurídica, y

  - cuya actividad esté mayoritariamente financiada por el Estado, los entes territoriales u otros organismos de derecho público, o bien, cuya gestion se halle sometida a un control por parte de estos últimos, o bien, cuyo órgano de administración, de dirección o de vigilancia esté compuesto por miembros de los cuales más de la mitad sean nombrados por el Estado los entes territoriales u otros organismos de derecho público.

- 为满足符合公共利益的需求这一特定目的而建立，不具产业或商业性质；
- 具有法人资格，且
- 主要由国家、地区或地方政府机构或由公法管辖的其他机构提供经费，或者接受上述机构的管理监督，或者设有行政、管理或监督委员会，委员会成员一半以上由国家、地区或地方政府机构或受公法管辖的其他机构任命。

满足所指标准的受公法管辖的机构和机构类型清单列入 93/37 号指令附件 1 中。清单仅为指示性质(请见 1993 年 9 月 8 日 L199/56 号《欧洲共同体公报》和 1994 年 8 月 29 日 C241/228 号《欧洲共同体公报》)。

2000 年 3 月 1 日 (WT/Let/330)

En el Anexo I a la Directive 93/37 figuran las listas de los organismos y de las categorías de organismos de derecho público que reúnen estos criterios. Estas listas son únicamente indicativas (véase Diario Oficial de las Comunidades Europeas Official n° L 199/56, 09.08.1993 y n° C 241/228, 29.08.1994).

EUROPEAN COMMUNITIES
COMMUNAUTES EUROPEENNES
COMUNIDADES EUROPEAS

ANNEX 3- ANNEXE 3 - ANEXO 3

Entities which Procure in Accordance with the Provisions of this Agreement
Entités qui passent des marchés conformément aux dispositions du présent accord
Entidades que se rigen en sus contratos por las disposiciones del presente acuerdo

SUPPLIES / FOURNITURES / SUMINISTROS

Thresholds:	SDR 400,000
Valeurs de seuil:	DTS 400 000
Valores de umbral:	DEG 400.000

SERVICES / SERVICES / SERVICIOS
specified in Annex 4 / spécifiés dans l'Annexe 4 / detallados en el Anexo 4

Thresholds:	SDR 400,000
Valeurs de seuil:	DTS 400 000
Valores de umbral:	DEG 400.000

WORKS / TRAVAUX / OBRAS
specified in Annex 5 / spécifiés dans l'Annexe 5 / detalladas en el Anexo 5

Thresholds:	SDR 5,000,000
Valeurs de seuil:	DTS 5 000 000
Valores de umbral:	DEG 5.000.000

1 March 2000 (WT/Let/330)

欧洲共同体

附件 3

依照本协定条款进行采购的实体

供应品

门槛金额: 400,000 特别提款权

服务
附件 4 列出

门槛金额: 400,000 特别提款权

工程
附件 5 列出

门槛金额: 5,000,000 特别提款权

2000 年 3 月 1 日 (WT/Let/330)

List of Entities */ Liste des entités / Lista de las entidades*:

The contracting entities within the meaning of Article 2 of Directive 93/38/EEC which are public authorities or public undertakings and which have as one of their activities any of those referred to below or any combination thereof:

(a) the provision or operation of fixed networks intended to provide a service to the public in connection with the production, transport or distribution of drinking water or the supply of drinking water to such networks;

(b) the provision or operation of fixed networks intended to provide a service to the public in connection with the production, transport or distribution of electricity or the supply of electricity to such networks;

(c) the provision of airport or other terminal facilities to carriers by air;

(d) the provision of maritime or inland port or other terminal facilities to carriers by sea or inland waterway;

(e) the operation of networks providing a service to the public in the field of urban transport by railway [1], automated systems,tramway, trolley bus, bus or cable in accordance with Directive 93/38/EEC.

The public authorities or public undertakings listed in Annex I (production, transport or distribution of drinking water), Annex II (production, transport or distribution of electricity), Annex VII (contracting entities in the field of urban railway, tramway, trolley bus or bus services), Annex VIII (contracting entities in the field of airport facilities) and Annex IX (contracting entities in the field of maritime or inland port or other terminal facilities) of Directive 93/38/EEC fulfill the criteria set out above. Those lists are indicative only (see Official Journal of the European Communitities n° L 199/84, 09.08.1993 and n° C 241/228, 29.08.1994).

List of Entities / ***Liste des entités*** */ Lista de las entidades*:

Les autorités adjudicatrices au sens de l'article 2 de la directive 93/38/CEE qui sont des pouvoirs publics ou des entreprises publiques et qui exercent une des activités visées ci-dessous ou plusieurs de ces activités:

(a) la mise à disposition ou l'exploitation de réseaux fixes destinés à fournir un service au public dans le domaine de la production, du transport ou de la distribution d'eau potable ou l'alimentation de ces réseaux en eau potable;

[1] Not including the entities listed in Annex VI of Directive 93/38/EEC (copy attached)

实体清单：

欧洲经济共同体 93/38 号指令第 2 条意义内、属政府机构或公共企业且其至少一项活动属下列任何一项或多项的缔约实体：

(a) 提供或经营固定网络，旨在向公众提供与饮用水的生产、输送或配送有关的服务或与向此类网络供应饮用水有关的服务；

(b) 提供或经营固定网络，旨在向公众提供与电力的生产、输送或配送有关的服务或与向此类网络供应电力有关的服务；

(c) 向空运承运人提供机场或其他航空站；

(d) 向海运或内河航道承运人提供海港或内陆港口或其他港口设施；

(e) 依照 93/38/EEC指令，经营固定网络，在城市运输领域通过铁路[1]、自动系统、有轨电车、无轨电车、公共汽车或缆车向公众提供服务。

列入欧洲经济共同体 93/38 号指令附件 1(生产、输送或配送饮用水)、附件 2(生产、输送或配送电力)、附件 7(城市铁路、无轨电车、有轨电车或公共汽车服务领域中的缔约实体)、附件 8(机场设施领域中的缔约实体)和附件 9(海港或内陆港口或其他港口设施领域中的缔约实体)满足以上所列条件。这些清单仅为例示性质(请见 1993 年 9 月 8 日 L199/84 号《欧洲共同体公报》和 1994 年 8 月 29 日 C241/228 号《欧洲共同体公报》)。

[1] 不含 93/38/EEC 指令(附后)附件 6 中所列实体。

(b) la mise à disposition ou l'exploitation de réseaux fixes destinés à fournir un service au public dans le domaine de la production, du transport ou de la distribution d'électricité ou l'alimentation de ces réseaux en électricité;

(c) la mise à disposition des transporteurs aériens des aéroports ou d'autres terminaux de transport;

(d) la mise à disposition des transporteurs maritimes ou fluviaux des ports maritimes ou intérieurs ou d'autres terminaux de transport;

(e) la exploitation de réseaux destinés à fournir un service au public dans le domaine du transport urbain par chemin de fer[2], systèmes automatiques, tramway, trolleybus ou autobus ou câble, en accord avec la directive 93/38/CEE.

Les pouvoirs publics ou autorités publiques énumérées aux annexes I (production, transport ou distribution d'eau potable), II (production, transport ou distribution d'électricité), VII (entités adjudicatrices dans le domaine des services de chemin de fer), VIII (entités adjudicatrices dans le domaine des installations aéroportuaires) et IX (entités adjudicatrices dans le domaine des installations portuaires maritimes ou intérieures ou autres terminaux) de la directive 93/38 répondent aux critères énoncés ci-dessus. Ces listes sont uniquement indicatives (voir Journal officiel des Communautés Européennes n° L 199/54, 09.08.1993 et n° C 241/228, 29.08.1994).

List of Entities / Liste des entités / ***Lista de las entidades*****:**

Las entidades contractantes según el sentido del artículo 2 de la directiva 93/38/CEE que sean poderes públicos o empresas públicas y que realicen alguna de la actividades contempladas en los párrafos siguientes o varias de estas actividades:

(a) la puesta a disposición o la explotación de redes fijas que presten un servicio al público en relación con la producción, transporte o distribución de agua potable o el suministro de agua potable a dichas redes;

(b) la puesta a disposición o la explotación de redes fijas que presten un servicio al público en relación con la producción, transporte o distribución de electricidad o el suministro de electricidad a dichas redes;

(c) la puesta a disposición de los transportistas aéreos de los aeropuertos o de otras terminales de transporte;

(d) la puesta a disposición de los transportistas marítimos o fluviales de los puertos marítimos o interiores o de otras terminales de transporte;

(e) la explotación de redes que presten un servicio público en el campo del transporte urbano por ferrocarril[3], sistemas automáticos, tranvía, trolebús, autobús o cable.

---

[2] Ne sont pas inclus les entités énumérées dans l'annexe VI de la directive 93/38/CEE (copie annexée)

[3] No se incluyen las entidades enumeradas en el anexo VI de la directiva 93/38/CEE (copia anexa)

Las entidades contractantes enumeradas en los anexos I (producción, transporte o distribución de agua potable), II (producción, transporte o distribución de electricidad), VII (entidades contractantes del sector de los servicios de ferrocarriles urbanos, tranvías, trolebuses o autobuses), VIII (entidades contractantes del sector de los aeropuertos) y IX (entidades contractantes del sector de los puertos marítimos o fluviales u otras terminales) de la directiva 93/38/CEE reúnen los criterios enunciados anteriormente. Estas listas son únicamente indicativas (véase Diario Oficial de las Comunidades Europeas Official n° L 199/56, 09.08.1993 y n° C 241/228, 29.08.1994).

1 March 2000 (WT/Let/330)

EUROPEAN COMMUNITIES
COMMUNAUTES EUROPEENNES
COMUNIDADES EUROPEAS

Directive 93/37

As mentioned in Appendix I - Annex 2 of the GPA

1 January 2007 (WT/Let/556)

欧洲共同体

93/37 号指令

GPA 附录 1 的附件 2 中提及

2007 年 1 月 1 日(WT/Let/556)

ANNEX I

LISTS OF BODIES AND CATEGORIES OF BODIES GOVERNED BY PUBLIC LAW REFERRED TO IN ARTICLE 1(b)

I. BELGIUM

Bodies:

- Archives générales du Royaume et Archives de l'État dans les Provinces - Algemeen Rijksarchief en Rijksarchief in de Provinciën,
- Conseil autonome de l'enseignement communautaire - Autonome Raad van het Gemeenschapsonderwijs,
- Radio et télévision belges, émissions néerlandaises - Belgische Radio en Televisie, Nederlandse uitzendingen,
- Belgisches Rundfunk- und Fernsehzentrum der Deutschsprachigen Gemeinschaft (Centre de radio et télévision belge de la Communauté de langue allemande - Centrum voor Belgische Radio en Televisie voor de Duitstalige Gemeenschap),
- Bibliothèque royale Albert Ier - Koninklijke Bibliotheek Albert I,
- Caisse auxiliaire de paiement des allocations de chômage - Hulpkas voor Werkloosheidsuitkeringen,
- Caisse auxiliaire d'assurance maladie-invalidité - Hulpkas voor Ziekte- en Invaliditeits verzekeringen,
- Caisse nationale des pensions de retraite et de survie - Rijkskas voor Rust- en Overlevingspensioenen,
- Caisse de secours et de prévoyance en faveur des marins naviguant sous pavillon belge - Hulp- en Voorzorgskas voor -Zeevarenden onder Belgische Vlag,
- Caisse nationale des calamités - Nationale Kas voor de Rampenschade,
- Caisse spéciale de compensation pour allocations familiales en faveur des travailleurs de l'industrie diamantaire - Bijzondere Verrekenkas voor Gezinsvergoedingen ten bate van de Arbeiders der Diamantnijverheid,
- Caisse spéciale de compensation pour allocations familiales en faveur des travailleurs de l'industrie du bois - Bijzondere Verrekenkas voor Gezinsvergoedingen ten bate van Arbeiders in de Houtnijverheid,
- Caisse spéciale de compensation pour allocations familiales en faveur des travailleurs occupés dans les entreprises de batellerie - Bijzondere Verrekenkas voor Gezinsvergoedingen ten bate van Arbeiders der Ondernemingen voor Binnenscheepvaart,
- Caisse spéciale de compensation pour allocations familiales en faveur des travailleurs occupés dans les entreprises de chargement, déchargement et manutention de marchandises dans les ports débarcadères, entrepôts et stations (appelée habituellement «Caisse spéciale de compensation pour allocations familiales des régiones maritimes») - Bijzondere Verrekenkas voor Gezinsvergoedingen ten bate van de Arbeiders gebezigd door Ladings- en Lossingsondernemingen en door de Stuwadoors in de Havens, Losplaatsen, Stapelplaatsen en Stations (gewoonlijk genoemd: Bijzondere Compensatiekas voor kindertoeslagen van de zeevaartgewesten),
- Centre informatique pour la Région bruxelloise - Centrum voor Informatica voor het Brusselse Gewest,

附录 1

第 1 条(b)款所述的受公法管辖的机构和机构类别清单

一、 比利时

机构:

- 皇家总档案馆和各省国家档案馆
- 语区教育自治委员会
- 比利时无线电广播电台和电视台、转播荷兰的电视节目
- 德语语区比利时广播和电视台中心
- 阿尔贝一世皇家图书馆
- 失业津贴偿付辅助基金
- 疾病—残疾保险辅助基金
- 国家退休及人寿基金
- 比利时海员援助和互助基金
- 国家灾害基金
- 钻石产业劳动者家庭补助金特别补偿基金
- 木材制造业劳动者家庭补助金特别补偿基金
- 内河航运企业劳动者家庭补助金特别补偿基金
- 在停靠港口，仓库和车站里面的货物装卸和搬运公司工作的劳动者的家庭补助金特别补偿基金(通常称为“海洋地区家庭补助金特别补偿基金”)
- 布鲁塞尔大区计算机中心

2007 年 1 月 1 日(WT/Let/556)

- Commissariat général de la Communauté flamande pour la coopération internationale - Commissariaat-generaal voor Internationale Samenwerking van de Vlaamse Gemeenschap,
- Commissariat général pour les relations internationales de la Communauté française de Belgique - Commissariaat-generaal bij de Internationale Betrekkingen van de Franse Gemeenschap van België,
- Conseil central de l'économie - Centrale Raad voor het Bedrijfsleven,
- Conseil économique et social de la Région wallonne - Sociaal-economische Raad van het Waals Gewest,
- Conseil national du travail - Nationale Arbeidsraad,
- Conseil supérieur des classes moyennes - Hoge Raad voor de Middenstand,
- Office pour les travaux d'infrastructure de l'enseignement subsidié - Dienst voor Infrastructuurwerken van het Gesubsidieerd Onderwijs,
- Fondation royale - Koninklijke Schenking,
- Fonds communautaire de garantie des bâtiments scolaires - Gemeenschappelijk Waarborgfonds voor Schoolgebouwen,
- Fonds d'aide médicale urgente - Fonds voor Dringende Geneeskundige Hulp,
- Fonds des accidents du travail - Fonds voor Arbeitsongevallen,
- Fonds des maladies professionnelles - Fonds voor Beroepsziekten,
- Fonds des routes - Wegenfonds,
- Fonds d'indemnisation des travailleurs licenciés en cas de fermeture d'entreprises - Fonds tot Vergoeding van de in geval van Sluiting van Ondernemingen Ontslagen Werknemers,
- Fonds national de garantie pour la réparation des dégâts houillers - Nationaal Waarborgfonds inzake Kolenmijnschade,
- Fonds national de retraite des ouvriers mineurs - Nationaal Pensioenfonds voor Mijnwerkers,
- Fonds pour le financement des prêts à des États étrangers - Fonds voor Financiering van de Leningen aan Vreemde Staten,
- Fonds pour la rémunération des mousses enrôlés à bord des bâtiments de pêche - Fonds voor Scheepsjongens aan Boord van Vissersvaartuigen,
- Fonds wallon d'avances pour la réparation des dommages provoqués par des pompages et des prises d'eau souterraine - Waals Fonds van Voorschotten voor het Herstel van de Schade veroorzaakt door Grondwaterzuiveringen en Afpompingen,
- Institut d'aéronomie spatiale - Instituut voor Ruimte-aëronomie,
- Institut belge de normalisation - Belgisch Instituut voor Normalisatie,
- Institut bruxellois de l'environnement - Brussels Instituut voor Milieubeheer,
- Institut d'expertise vétérinaire - Instituut voor Veterinaire Keuring,
- Institut économique et social des classes moyennes - Economisch en Sociaal Instituut voor de Middenstand,
- Institut d'hygiène et d'épidémiologie - Instituut voor Hygiëne en Epidemiologie,
- Institut francophone pour la formation permanente des classes moyennes - Franstalig Instituut voor Permanente Vorming voor de Middenstand,
- Institut géographique national - Nationaal Geografisch Instituut,
- Institut géotechnique de l'État - Rijksinstituut voor Grondmechanica,
- Institut national d'assurance maladie-invalidité - Rijksinstituut voor Ziekte- en Invaliditeitsverzekering,
- Institut national d'assurances sociales pour travailleurs indépendants - Rijksinstituut voor de Sociale Verzekeringen der Zelfstandigen,
- Institut national des industries extractives - Nationaal Instituut voor de Extractiebedrijven,

- 弗拉芒语语区国际合作联络总局
- 比利时法语语区国际关系联络总局
- 中央经济委员会
- 瓦隆大区社会经社委员会
- 国家劳工委员会
- 中产阶级高级委员会
- 资助教学基础设施工程办公室
- 皇家基金会
- 语区学校建筑保障基金
- 紧急医疗救济基金
- 劳动事故基金
- 职业病基金
- 公路基金
- 企业倒闭解雇员工赔偿基金
- 煤矿损害修复国家保障基金
- 矿工退休国家基金
- 外国借贷融资基金
- 在渔船上招募的见习水手报酬基金
- 瓦隆大区泵送和抽取地下水引起的损失预先赔偿基金
- 空间高层大气研究所
- 比利时标准化研究所
- 布鲁塞尔环境研究所
- 兽医鉴定研究所
- 中产阶级经济社会研究所
- 卫生和流行病学研究所
- 法语中产阶级终生教育研究所
- 国家地理研究所
- 国家地质工学研究所，
- 疾病—残疾保险国家研究所
- 独立劳动者社会保险国家研究所
- 国家采掘工业研究所

- Institut national des invalides de guerre, anciens combattants et victimes de guerre - Nationaal Instituut voor Oorlogsinvaliden, Oudstrijders en Oorlogsslachtoffers,
- Institut pour l'amélioration des conditions de travail - Instituut voor Verbetering van de Arbeidsvoorwaarden,
- Institut pour l'encouragement de la recherche scientifique dans l'industrie et l'agriculture - Instituut tot Aanmoediging van het Wetenschappelijk Onderzoek in Nijverheid en Landbouw,
- Institut royal belge des sciences naturelles - Koninklijk Belgisch Instituut voor Natuurwetenschappen,
- Institut royal belge du patrimoine artistique - Koninklijk Belgisch Instituut voor het Kunstpatrimonium,
- Institut royal de météorologie - Koninklijk Meteorologisch Instituut,
- Enfance et famille - Kind en Gezin,
- Compagnie des installations maritimes de Bruges - Maatschappij der Brugse Zeevaartinrichtingen,
- Mémorial national du fort de Breendonck - Nationaal Gedenkteken van het Fort van Breendonck,
- Musée royal de l'Afrique centrale - Koninklijk Museum voor Midden-Afrika,
- Musées royaux d'art et d'histoire - Koninklijke Musea voor Kunst en Geschiedenis,
- Musées royaux des beaux-arts de Belgique - Koninklijke Musea voor Schone Kunsten van België,
- Observatoire royal de Belgique - Koninklijke Sterrenwacht van België,
- Office belge de l'économie et de l'agriculture - Belgische Dienst voor Bedrijfsleven en Landbouw,
- Office belge du commerce extérieur - Belgische Dienst voor Buitenlandse Handel,
- Office central d'action sociale et culturelle au profit des membres de la communauté militaire - Centrale Dienst voor Sociale en Culturele Actie ten behoeve van de Leden van de Militaire Gemeenschap,
- Office de la naissance et de l'enfance - Dienst voor Borelingen en Kinderen,
- Office de la navigation - Dienst voor de Scheepvaart,
- Office de promotion du tourisme de la Communauté française - Dienst voor de Promotie van het Toerisme van de Franse Gemeenschap,
- Office de renseignements et d'aide aux familles des militaires - Hulp- en Informatiebureau voor Gezinnen van Militairen,
- Office de sécurité sociale d'outre-mer - Dienst voor Overzeese Sociale Zekerheid,
- Office national d'allocations familiales pour travailleurs salariés - Rijksdienst voor Kinderbijslag voor Werknemers,
- Office national de l'emploi - Rijksdienst voor de Arbeidsvoorziening,
- Office national des débouchés agricoles et horticoles - Nationale Dienst voor Afzet van Land - en Tuinbouwprodukten,
- Office national de sécurité sociale - Rijksdienst voor Sociale Zekerheid,
- Office national de sécurité sociale des administrations provinciales et locales - Rijksdienst voor Sociale Zekerheid van de Provinciale en Plaatselijke Overheidsdiensten,
- Office national des pensions - Rijksdienst voor Pensioenen,
- Office national des vacances annuelles - Rijksdienst voor de Jaarlijkse Vakantie,
- Office national du lait - Nationale Zuiveldienst,
- Office régional bruxellois de l'emploi - Brusselse Gewestelijke Dienst voor Arbeidsbemiddeling,

- 战争残疾人、退伍军人和战争受害者国家研究所
- 改善工作条件研究所
- 工农业科研促进研究所
- 比利时自然科学皇家研究所
- 比利时艺术遗产皇家研究所
- 皇家气象研究所
- 儿童和家庭
- 布鲁日海运设施公司
- 布伦东克要塞国家纪念馆
- 皇家中非博物馆
- 皇家历史和艺术博物馆
- 皇家比利时美术博物馆
- 皇家比利时天文台
- 比利时农业和经济办公室
- 比利时外贸办公室
- 国家军队成员社会文化活动中心
- 儿童和生育办公室
- 航海办公室
- 法语语区旅游促进办公室
- 军人家属家庭援助和咨询办公室
- 海外社会保险办公室
- 国家工薪劳动者家庭补助中心
- 国家就业办公室
- 国家园艺和农业销售办公室
- 国家社保中心
- 省级和地方社保中心
- 国家养老金中心
- 国家年度假期办公室
- 国家乳业办公室
- 布鲁塞尔大区就业办公室

- Office régional et communautaire de l'emploi et de la formation - Gewestelijke en Gemeenschappelijke Dienst voor Arbeidsvoorziening en Vorming,
- Office régulateur de la navigation intérieure - Dienst voor Regeling der Binnenvaart,
- Société publique des déchets pour la Région flamande - Openbare Afvalstoffenmaatschappij voor het Vlaams Gewest,
- Orchestre national de Belgique - Nationaal Orkest van België,
- Organisme national des déchets radioactifs et des matières fissiles - Nationale Instelling voor Radioactief Afval en -Splijtstoffen,
- Palais des beaux-arts - Paleis voor Schone Kunsten,
- Pool des marins de la marine marchande - Pool van de Zeelieden ter Koopvaardij,
- Port autonome de Charleroi - Autonome Haven van Charleroi,
- Port autonome de Liège - Autonome Haven van Luik,
- Port autonome de Namur - Autonome Haven van Namen,
- Radio et télévision belges de la Communauté française - Belgische Radio en Televisie van de Franse Gemeenschap,
- Régie des bâtiments - Regie der Gebouwen,
- Régie des voies aériennes - Regie der Luchtwegen,
- Régie des postes - Regie der Posterijen,
- Régie des télégraphes et des téléphones - Regie van Telegraaf en Telefoon,
- Conseil économique et social pour la Flandre - Sociaal-economische Raad voor Vlaanderen,
- Société anonyme du canal et des installations maritimes de Bruxelles - Naamloze Vennootschap Zeekanaal en-Haveninrichtingen van Brussel,
- Société du logement de la Région bruxelloise et sociétés agréées - Brusselse Gewestelijke Huisvestingsmaatschappij en erkende maatschappijen,
- Société nationale terrienne - Nationale Landmaatschappij,
- Théâtre royal de la Monnaie - De Koninklijke Muntschouwburg,
- Universités relevant de la Communauté flamande - Universiteiten afhangende van de Vlaamse Gemeenschap,
- Universités relevant de la Communauté française - Universiteiten afhangende van de Franse Gemeenschap,
- Office flamand de l'emploi et de la formation professionnelle - Vlaamse Dienst voor Arbeidsvoorziening en Beroepsopleiding,
- Fonds flamand de construction d'institutions hospitalières et médico-sociales - Vlaams Fonds voor de Bouw van Ziekenhuizen en Medisch-Sociale Instellingen,
- Société flamande du logement et sociétés agréées - Vlaamse Huisvestingsmaatschappij en erkende maatschappijen,
- Société régionale wallonne du logement et sociétés agréées - Waalse Gewestelijke Maatschappij voor de Huisvesting en erkende maatschappijen,
- Société flamande d'épuration des eaux - Vlaamse Maatschappij voor Waterzuivering,
- Fonds flamand du logement des familles nombreuses - Vlaams Woningfonds van de Grote Gezinnen.

Categories:

- les centres publics d'aide sociale,
- les fabriques d'église (church councils).

- 地区和语区就业培训办公室
- 内河航运监管办公室
- 弗拉芒大区废品公司(国有)
- 比利时国家交响乐团
- 国家可裂变物质和放射性残渣机构
- 美术宫
- 商船海员联营
- 沙勒鲁瓦自治港
- 列日自治港
- 那幕尔自治港
- 比利时法语语区无线电广播电台和电视台
- 住房的政府经营
- 航空航线的政府经营
- 邮政政府经营
- 电报和电话的政府经营
- 弗拉芒社会经济委员会
- 布鲁塞尔运河和航海设施股份有限公
- 布鲁塞尔大区住房公司和相关获授权的公司
- 国家土地公司
- 莫奈皇家歌剧院
- 隶属于弗拉芒语区的大学
- 隶属于法语语区的大学
- 弗拉芒就业和职业培训办公室
- 弗拉芒医疗机构和社会医疗建设基金
- 弗拉芒住房公司和相关获授权的公司
- 瓦隆大区住房公司和相关获授权的公司
- 弗拉芒净化水公司
- 弗拉芒人口多的家庭的住房基金

类别:

- 社会救济中心
- 教堂财产(管理委员会)

II. DENMARK

Bodies:

- Københavns Havn,
- Danmarks Radio,
- TV 2/Danmark,
- TV2 Reklame A/S,
- Danmarks Nationalbank,
- A/S Storebæltsforbindelsen,
- A/S Øresundsforbindelsen (alene tilslutningsanlæg i Danmark),
- Københavns Lufthavn A/S,
- Byfornyelsesselskabet København,
- Tele Danmark A/S with subsidiaries:
- Fyns Telefon A/S,
- Jydsk Telefon Aktieselskab A/S,
- Kjøbenhavns Telefon Aktieselskab,
- Tele Sønderjylland A/S,
- Telecom A/S,
- Tele Danmark Mobil A/S.

Categories:

- De kommunale havne (municipal ports),
- Andre Forvaltningssubjekter (other public administrative bodies).

III. GERMANY

1. Legal persons governed by public law

Authorities, establishments and foundations governed by public law and created by federal, State or local authorities in particular in the following sectors:

1.1. Authorities

- Wissenschaftliche Hochschulen und verfaßte Studentenschaften (universities and established student bodies),
- berufsständige Vereinigungen (Rechtsanwalts-, Notar-, Steuerberater-, Wirtschaftsprüfer-, Architekten-, Ärzte- und Apothekerkammern) (professional associations representing lawyers, notaries, tax consultants, accountants, architects, medical practitioners and pharmacists),
- Wirtschaftsvereinigungen (Landwirtschafts-, Handwerks-, Industrie- und Handelskammern, Handwerksinnungen, Handwerkerschaften) (business and trade associations: agricultural and craft associations, chambers of industry and commerce, craftmen's guilds, tradesmen's associations),

二、 丹麦

机构:
- 哥本哈根港口
- 丹麦广播电台
- 丹麦电视台二台
- 电视电视台二台广播频道
- 丹麦国民银行
- 丹麦电讯
- 丹麦声讯 (丹麦唯一批准的)
- 哥本哈根机场
- 哥本哈根城市再建设公司
- 丹麦电信公司及子公司
- 费恩斯电话公司
- 日德兰电话私人有限公司
- 哥本哈根电话私人有限公司
- 南日德兰地区电话公司
- 电信公司
- 丹麦移动通信公司

类别:
- 城市港口
- 其他行政管理机构

三、 德国

1. 受公法管辖的法人

由联邦、州或地方政府设立、受公法管辖的政府机构、公共机构和基金会，特别在下列部门：

1.1. 政府机构

- 大学和常设学生团体
- 专业协会，代表律师、公证人、税务顾问、会计师、建筑师、执业医师和药剂师
- 商业与贸易协会：农业和手工业协会、工业和商业协会、手工业同业公会、手工业者协会

- Sozialversicherungen (Krankenkassen, Unfall- und Rentenversicherungsträger) (social security institutions: health, accident and pension insurance funds), kassenärztliche Vereinigungen (associations of panel doctors),
- Genossenschaften und Verbände (cooperatives and other associations).

1.2. Establishments and foundations

Non-industrial and non-commercial establishments subject to state control and operating in the general interest, particularly in the following fields:

- Rechtsfähige Bundesanstalten (federal institutions having legal capacity),
- Versorgungsanstalten und Studentenwerke (pension organizations and students' unions),
- Kultur-, Wohlfahrts- und Hilfsstiftungen (cultural, welfare and relief foundations).

2. Legal persons governed by private law

Non-industrial and non-commercial establishments subject to State control and operating in the general interest (including kommunale Versorgungsunternehmen, municipal utilities), particularly in the following fields:

- Gesundheitswesen (Krankenhäuser, Kurmittelbetriebe, medizinische Forschungseinrichtungen, Untersuchungs- und Tierkörperbeseitigungsanstalten) (health: hospitals, health resort establishments, medical research institutes, testing and carcase-disposal establishments),
- Kultur (öffentliche Bühnen, Orchester, Museen, Bibliotheken, Archive, zoologische und botanische Gärten) (culture: public theatres, orchestras, museums, libraries, archives, zoological and botanical gardens),
- Soziales (Kindergärten, Kindertagesheime, Erholungseinrichtungen, Kinder- und Jugendheime, Freizeiteinrichtungen, Gemeinschafts- und Bürgerhäuser, Frauenhäuser, Altersheime, Obdachlosenunterkünfte) (social welfare: nursery schools, children's playschools, rest-homes, children's homes, hostels for young people, leisure centres, community and civic centres, homes for battered wives, old people's homes, accommodation for the homeless),
- Sport (Schwimmbäder, Sportanlagen und -einrichtungen) (sport: swimming baths, sports facilities),
- Sicherheit (Feuerwehren, Rettungsdienste) (safety: fire brigades, other emergency services),
- Bildung (Umschulungs-, Aus-, Fort- und Weiterbildungseinrichtungen, Volkshochschulen) (education: training, further training and retraining establishments, adult evening classes),
- Wissenschaft, Forschung und Entwicklung (Großforschungseinrichtungen, wissenschaftliche Gesellschaften und Vereine, Wissenschaftsförderung) (science, research and development: large-scale research institutes, scientific societies and associations, bodies promoting science),
- Entsorgung (Straßenreinigung, Abfall- und Abwasserbeseitigung) (refuse and garbage disposal services: street cleaning, waste and sewage disposal),
- Bauwesen und Wohnungswirtschaft (Stadtplanung, Stadtentwicklung, Wohnungsunternehmen, Wohnraumvermittlung) (building, civil engineering and housing: town planning, urban development, housing enterprises, housing agency services),

- 社会保险：健康、意外伤害和养老保险基金；医保指定医生协会
- 合作社和其他协会

1.2. 公共机构和基金会

受州控制、为公共利益运营的非工业和非商业性机构，特别在以下领域：

- 具有法定资格的联邦机构
- 养老院和学生会
- 文化、福利和救济基金会

2. 受私法管辖的法人

受州控制、为公共利益运营的非工业和非商业性机构，(包括市政公用事业)，特别在以下领域：

- 卫生：医院、疗养院、医疗研究机构、检验与动物尸体处理机构
- 文化：公共剧院、乐团、博物馆、图书馆、档案馆、动物和植物园
- 社会福利：幼儿园、托儿所、疗养院、儿童之家、青年旅社、休闲中心、社区和市民中心、受虐妻子之家、老年人之家、无家可归者收容所
- 运动：游泳池、运动设施
- 安全：消防队、其他应急服务
- 教育：培训、进修和再培训机构、成人夜校
- 科学、研究和开发：大型研究机构、科学社团和协会、科学促进机构
- 垃圾废物处理服务：街道清洁、废物和污水处理
- 建筑、土木工程和住房：城镇规划、城市开发、住房企业、住房代理机构

2007 年 1 月 1 日(WT/Let/556)

- Wirtschaft (Wirtschaftsförderungsgesellschaften) (economy: organizations promoting economic development),
- Friedhofs- und Bestattungswesen (cemeteries and burial services),
- Zusammenarbeit mit den Entwicklungsländern (Finanzierung, technische Zusammenarbeit, Entwicklungshilfe, Ausbildung) (cooperation with developing countries: financing, technical cooperation, development aid, training).

IV. GREECE

Categories:

Other legal persons governed by public law whose public works contracts are subject to State control.

V. SPAIN

Categories:

- Entidades Gestoras y Servicios Comunes de la Seguridad Social (administrative entities and common services of the health and social services)
- Organismos Autónomos de la Administración del Estado (independent bodies of the national administration)
- Organismos Autónomos de las Comunidades Autónomas (independent bodies of the autonomous communities)
- Organismos Autónomos de las Entidades Locales (independent bodies of local authorities)
- Otras entidades sometidas a la legislación de contratos del Estado español (other entities subject to Spanish State legislation on procurement).

VI. FRANCE

Bodies:

1. National public bodies:

1.1. with scientific, cultural and professional character:

- Collège de France,
- Conservatoire national des arts et métiers,
- Observatoire de Paris.

1.2. Scientific and technological:

- Centre national de la recherche scientifique (CNRS),
- Institut national de la recherche agronomique,
- Institut national de la santé et de la recherche médicale,
- Institut français de recherche scientifique pour le développement en coopération (ORSTOM).

- 经济：经济发展促进组织
- 墓地与殡葬服务
- 与发展中国家合作：融资、技术合作、发展援助、培训

四、 希腊

类别:

公共工程合同受国家控制的、受公法管辖的其他法人。

五、 西班牙

类别:

- 行政管理实体、医疗和社会服务等公共服务
- 国家行政机关的独立机构
- 自治社区的独立机构
- 地方政府的独立机构
- 其他受西班牙关于采购的国家法律管辖的实体

六、 法国

机构:

1. 国家公共机构:

1.1. 科学、文化和专业性质:

- 法兰西学院
- 国家艺术和手工艺博物馆
- 巴黎天文台

1.2. 科学和技术性质:

- 国家科学研究中心
- 国家农科所
- 国家卫生和医学研究院
- 法国发展合作科研所

1.3. with administrative character:

- Agence nationale pour l'emploi,
- Caisse nationale des allocations familiales,
- Caisse nationale d'assurance maladie des travailleurs salariés,
- Caisse nationale d'assurance vieillesse des travailleurs salariés,
- Office national des anciens combattants et victimes de la guerre,
- Agences financières de bassins.

Categories:

1. National public bodies:

- universités (universities),
- écoles normales d'instituteurs (teacher training colleges).

2. Administrative public bodies at regional, departmental and local level:

- collèges (secondary schools),
- lycées (secondary schools),
- établissements publics hospitaliers (public hospitals),
- offices publics d'habitations à loyer modéré (OPHLM) (public offices for low-cost housing).

3. Groupings of territorial authorities:

- syndicats de communes (associations of local authorities),
- districts (districts),
- communautés urbaines (municipalities),
- institutions interdépartementales et interrégionales (institutions common to more than one Département and interregional institutions).

VII. IRELAND

Bodies:

- Shannon Free Airport Development Company Ltd,
- Local Government Computer Services Board,
- Local Government Staff Negotiations Board,
- Córas Tráchtála (Irish Export Board),
- Industrial Development Authority,
- Irish Goods Council (Promotion of Irish Goods),
- Córas Beostoic agus Feola (CBF) (Irish Meat Board),
- Bord Fáilte Éireann (Irish Tourism Board),
- Údarás na Gaeltachta (Development Authority for Gaeltacht Regions),
- An Bord Pleanála (Irish Planning Board).

1.3. 行政管理性质：

- 国家就业署
- 国家家庭补助金管理局
- 国家工薪职工疾病保险管理局
- 国家工薪职工养老保险管理局
- 国家退伍军人及战争伤残人员署
- 流域地区金融署

类别:

1. 国家公共机构：

- 大学
- 师范学校

2. 地区、省和地方行政管理公共机构:

- 中学
- 公立中学
- 公立医院
- 廉租房公共管理局

3. 地方政府的分类：

- 地方政府的协会
- 区
- 城市
- 跨省和大区机构

七、 爱尔兰

机构:

- 香农自由空港开发有限责任公司
- 地方政府计算机服务局
- 地方政府员工谈判局
- 爱尔兰出口局
- 工业发展局
- 爱尔兰商品理事会(爱尔兰商品促进)
- 爱尔兰肉类局
- 爱尔兰旅游局
- 爱尔兰语地区发展局
- 爱尔兰规划局

2007 年 1 月 1 日(WT/Let/556)

Categories:

- Third level Educational Bodies of a Public Character,
- National Training, Cultural or Research Agencies,
- Hospital Boards of a Public Character,
- National Health & Social Agencies of a Public Character,
- Central & Regional Fishery Boards.

VIII. ITALY

Bodies:

- Agenzia per la promozione dello sviluppo nel Mezzogiorno.

Categories:

- Enti portuali e aeroportuali (port and airport authorities),
- Consorzi per le opere idrauliche (consortia for water engineering works),
- Le università statali, gli istituti universitari statali, i consorzi per i lavori interessanti le università (State universities, State university institutes, consortia for university development work),
- Gli istituti superiori scientifici e culturali, gli osservatori astronomici, astrofisici, geofisici o vulcanologici (higher scientific and cultural institutes, astronomical, astrophysical, geophysical or vulcanological oberservatories),
- Enti di ricerca e sperimentazione (organizations conducting research and experimental work),
- Le istituzioni pubbliche di assistenza e di beneficenza (public welfare and benevolent institutions),
- Enti che gestiscono forme obbligatorie di previdenza e di assistenza (agencies administering compulsory social security and welfare schemes),
- Consorzi di bonifica (land reclamation consortia),
- Enti di sviluppo o di irrigazione (development or irrigation agencies),
- Consorzi per le aree industriali (associations for industrial areas),
- Comunità montane (groupings of municipalities in mountain areas),
- Enti preposti a servizi di pubblico interesse (organizations providing services in the public interest),
- Enti pubblici preposti ad attività di spettacolo, sportive, turistiche e del tempo libero (public bodies engaged in -entertainment, sport, tourism and leisure activities),
- Enti culturali e di promozione artistica (organizations promoting culture and artistic activities).

IX. LUXEMBOURG

Categories:

- Les établissements publics de l'État placés sous la surveillance d'un membre du gouvernement (public establishments of the State placed under the supervision of a member of the Government),

类别:
- 公立性质的三级教育机构
- 国家培训 、文化和研究机构
- 公立性质的医院
- 公立性质的国家卫生与社会事务机构
- 中央与地方渔业署

八、 意大利

机构:
- 南部开发促进机构

类别:
- 口岸和空港管理机构
- 水利工程公会
- 国立大学、国立学院、大学发展工作公会
- 高等科学和文化机构、天文、天体物理、地球物理或火山观测台
- 开展研究和实验工作的组织
- 公共福利和慈善机构
- 管理强制性社会保险和福利计划的机构
- 土地复垦公会
- 发展或灌溉机构
- 工业领域的协会
- 山区城市团体
- 为公共利益而提供服务的组织
- 从事娱乐、运动、旅游和休闲活动的公共机构
- 促进文化的艺术活动的组织

九、 卢森堡

类别:
- 处于一政府组成机构监督之下的国家公共机构

- Les établissements publics placés sous la surveillance des communes (public establishments placed under the supervision of the communes),
- Les syndicats de communes créés en vertu de la loi du 14 février 1900 telle qu'elle a été modifiée par la suite (associations of communes created under the law of 14 February 1900 as subsequently modified).

X. THE NETHERLANDS

Bodies:
- De Nederlandse Centrale Organisatie voor Toegepast Natuurwetenschappelijk Onderzoek (TNO) en de daaronder ressorterende organisaties.

Categories:
- De waterschappen (administration of water engineering works),
- De instellingen van wetenschappelijk onderwijs vermeld in artikel 8 van de Wet op het Wetenschappelijk Onderwijs (1985), de academische ziekenhuizen (Institutions for scientific education, as listed in Article 8 of the Scientific Education Act (1985)) wet op het Wetenschappelijk Onderwijs (1985) (teaching hospitals).

XI. PORTUGAL

Categories:
- Estabelecimentos públicos de ensino investigaçaço científica e saúde (public establishments for education, scientific research and health),
- Institutos públicos sem carácter comercial ou industrial (public institutions without commercial or industrial character),
- Fundaçöes públicas (public foundations),
- Administraçöes gerais e juntas autonómas (general administration bodies and independent councils).

XII. THE UNITED KINGDOM

Bodies:
- Central Blood Laboratories Authority,
- Design Council,
- Health and Safety Executive,
- National Research Development Corporation,
- Public Health Laboratory Services Board,
- Advisory, Conciliation and Arbitration Service,
- Commission for the New Towns,
- Development Board For Rural Wales,
- English Industrial Estates Corporation,
- National Rivers Authority,
- Northern Ireland Housing Executive,

- 处于市镇监督下的公共机构
- 根据 1900 年 2 月 14 日及随后修改的法律建立的市镇联合会

十、 荷兰

机构:

- 荷兰中央应用科学研究组织和其附属组织

类别:

- 水利工程管理机构
- 《1985 年科学教育法》第 8 条所列科学教育机构(医学院)

十一、 葡萄牙

类别:

- 教育、科研和卫生性质的公共机构
- 非商业或工业性质的公共机构
- 公共基金会
- 一般行政管理机构和独立理事会

十二、 英国

机构:

- 中央血站实验室管理局
- 设计理事会
- 健康和安全管理局
- 国家研究发展公司
- 公共卫生实验室管理局
- 咨询、协调和仲裁局
- 新市镇委员会
- 威尔士乡村发展局
- 英国工业业公司
- 国家河流管理局
- 北爱尔兰房屋管理局

2007 年 1 月 1 日(WT/Let/556)

- Scottish Enterprise,
- Scottish Homes,
- Welsh Development Agency.

Categories:
- Universities and polytechnics, maintained schools and colleges,
- National Museums and Galleries,
- Research Councils,
- Fire Authorities,
- National Health Service Authorities,
- Police Authorities,
- New Town Development Corporations,
- Urban Development Corporations.

XIII. AUSTRIA

All bodies subject to budgetary supervision by the 'Rechnungshof' (audit authority) not having an industrial or commercial character.

XIV. FINLAND

Public or publicly controlled entities or undertakings not having an industrial or commercial character.

XV. SWEDEN

All non-commercial bodies whose procurement is subject to supervision by the National Board for Public Procurement.

XVI. CZECH REPUBLIC

- Fond národního majetku (National Property Fund)
- Pozemkový fond (Land Fund)
- and other state funds
- Česká národní banka (Czech National Bank)
- Česká televize (Czech Television)
- Český rozhlas (Czech Radio)
- Rada pro rozhlasové a televizní vysílání (The Council for Radio and Television Broadcasting)
- Česká konsolidační agentura (Czech Consolidation Agency)
- Health insurance agencies
- Universities

and other legal entities established by a special Act which for their operation and in compliance with budget regulations use money from the state budget, state funds, contributions of international institutions, district authority budget, or budgets of self-governing territorial divisions.

- 苏格兰工商委员会
- 苏格兰住房局
- 威尔士发展局

类别：

- 大学和理工学院、公立学校和学院
- 国家博物馆和美术馆
- 研究理事会
- 消防管理机构
- 国家卫生服务管理机构
- 警察管理机构
- 新市镇发展公司
- 城市发展公司

十三、 奥地利

所有受审计管理机构预算监督的不具工业或商业性质的机构。

十四、 芬兰

不具工业或商业性质的公共实体或公共控制的实体。

十五、 瑞典

受国家公共采购局管辖的所有非商业性质的机构。

十六、 捷克

- 国家房地产基金
- 土地基金
- 其他国家基金
- 捷克国家银行
- 捷克电视台
- 捷克广播电台
- 广播电视委员会
- 捷克不良资产托管局
- 健康保险机构
- 大学

以及根据一有关其运营的特殊法并以符合预算法规的方式设立的、经费来自国家预算、国家基金、国际机构捐款、地区政府预算或自治领地预算的其他法律实体。

2007 年 1 月 1 日(WT/Let/556)

XVII. ESTONIA

Bodies:

- Eesti Kunstiakadeemia (Estonian Academy of Arts)
- Eesti Liikluskindlustuse Fond (Estonian Traffic Insurance Foundation)
- Eesti Muusikaakadeemia (Estonian Academy of Music)
- Eesti Põllumajandusülikool (Estonian Agricultural University)
- Eesti Raadio (Estonian Radio)
- Eesti Teaduste Akadeemia (Estonian Academy of Sciences)
- Eesti Televisioon (Estonian Television)
- Hoiuste Tagamise Fond (Deposit Guarantee Fund)
- Hüvitusfond (Compensation Fund)
- Kaitseliidu Peastaap (The Defence League Headquarters)
- Keemilise ja Bioloogilise Füüsika Instituut (National Institute of Chemical Physics and Biophysics)
- Keskhaigekassa (Central Health Insurance Fund)
- Kultuurkapital (Cultural Endowment of Estonia)
- Notarite Koda (The Chamber of Notaries)
- Rahvusooper Estonia (Estonian National Opera)
- Rahvusraamatukogu (National Library of Estonia)
- Tallinna Pedagoogikaülikool (Tallinn Pedagogical University)
- Tallinna Tehnikaülikool (Tallinn Technical University)
- Tartu Ülikool (University of Tartu)

Categories:

- Other legal persons governed by public law whose public works contracts are subject to State control

XVIII. CYPRUS

- Αρχή Ανάπτυξης Ανθρώπινου Δυναμικού Κύπρου (Human Resource Development Authority)
- Αρχή Κρατικών Εκθέσεων (Cyprus State Fair Authority)
- Επιτροπή Σιτηρών Κύπρου (Cyprus Grain Commission)
- Επιστημονικό Τεχνικό Επιμελητήριο Κύπρου (Scientific and Technical Chamber of Cyprus)
- Θεατρικός Οργανισμός Κύπρου (National Theatre of Cyprus)
- Κυπριακός Οργανισμός Αθλητισμού (Cyprus Sports Organisation)
- Κυπριακός Οργανισμός Τουρισμού (Cyprus Tourism Organization)
- Κυπριακός Οργανισμός Αναπτύξεως Γης (Cyprus Land Development Corporation)
- Οργανισμός Γεωργικής Ασφαλίσεως (Agricultural Insurance Organisation)
- Οργανισμός Κυπριακής Γαλακτοκομικής Βιομηχανίας (Cyprus Milk Industry Organisation)
- Οργανισμός Νεολαίας Κύπρου (Youth Board of Cyprus)
- Οργανισμός Χρηματοδοτήσεως Στέγης (Housing Finance Corporation)
- Συμβούλια Αποχετεύσεων (Sewerage Boards)
- Συμβούλια Σφαγείων (Slaughterhouse Boards)
- Σχολικές Εφορίες (School Boards)
- Χρηματιστήριο Αξιών Κύπρου (Cyprus Stock Exchange)
- Επιτροπή Κεφαλαιαγοράς Κύπρου (Cyprus Securities and Exchange Commission)

十七、 爱沙尼亚

机构:
- 爱沙尼亚艺术学院
- 爱沙尼亚交通保险基金会
- 爱沙尼亚音乐学院
- 爱沙尼亚农业大学
- 爱沙尼亚广播电台
- 爱沙尼亚科学院
- 爱沙尼亚电视台
- 储蓄保证基金
- 补偿基金
- 保护联盟总部
- 国家化学物理和生物物理研究所
- 中央健康保险基金
- 爱沙尼亚文化禀赋基金
- 公证协会
- 爱沙尼亚国家歌剧院
- 爱沙尼亚国家图书馆
- 塔林师范大学
- 塔林理工大学
- 塔尔图大学

类别:
- 公共工程合同受国家控制的、受公法管辖的其他法人。

十八、 塞浦路斯

- 人力资源开发管理局
- 塞浦路斯国家展览局
- 塞浦路斯谷物委员会
- 塞浦路斯科技商会
- 塞浦路斯国家剧院组织
- 塞浦路斯运动组织
- 塞浦路斯旅游组织
- 塞浦路斯土地开发公司
- 农业保险组织
- 塞浦路斯奶业组织
- 塞浦路斯青年组织
- 住房金融公司
- 污水局
- 屠宰局
- 学校董事会
- 塞浦路斯股票交易所
- 塞浦路斯证券交易委员会

- Πανεπιστήμιο Κύπρου (University of Cyprus)
- Κεντρικός Φορέας Ισότιμης Κατανομής Βαρών (Central Agency for Equal Distribution of Burdens)
- Αρχή Ραδιοτηλεόρασης Κύπρου – Cyprus Radio-Television Authority

XIX. LATVIA

Categories:

- Bezpeļņas organizācijas, kuras nodibinājusi valsts vai pašvaldība un kuras tiek finansētas no valsts vai pašvaldības budžeta (Non-profit-making organisations established by the State or a local government and which the State budget or a local government budget finances)
- Specializētie bērnu sociālās aprūpes centri (Specialised social care centres for children)
- Specializētie valsts sociālās aprūpes pansionāti (Specialised State social care homes for old people)
- Specializētie valsts sociālās aprūpes un rehabilitācijas centri (Specialised State social care and rehabilitation centres)
- Valsts bibliotēkas (State libraries)
  Valsts muzeji (State museums)
- Valsts teātri (State theatres)
- Valsts un pašvaldību aģentūras (State and local government agencies)
- Valsts un pašvaldību pirmsskolas izglītības iestādes, kuras reģistrētas Izglītības un zinātnes ministrijas izglītības iestāžu reģistrā (State and local government pre-school education institutions registered in the Register of Education Institutions at the Ministry of Education and Science)
- Valsts un pašvaldību interešu izglītības iestādes, kuras reģistrētas Izglītības un zinātnes ministrijas izglītības iestāžu reģistrā (State and local government institutions of hobby/interest education registered in the Register of Education Institutions at the Ministry of Education and Science)
- Valsts un pašvaldību profesionālās ievirzes izglītības iestādes, kuras reģistrētas Izglītības un zinātnes ministrijas izglītības iestāžu reģistrā (State and local government vocational education institutions registered in the Register of Education Institutions at the Ministry of Education and Science)
- Valsts un pašvaldību vispārējās izglītības iestādes, kuras reģistrētas Izglītības un zinātnes ministrijas izglītības iestāžu reģistrā (State and local government general education institutions registered in the Register of Education Institutions at the Ministry of Education and Science)
- Valsts un pašvaldību pamata un vidējās profesionālās izglītības iestādes un koledžas, kuras reģistrētas Izglītības un zinātnes ministrijas izglītības iestāžu reģistrā (State and local government basic and secondary vocational education institutions and colleges (first level higher professional education institutions) registered in the Register of Education Institutions at the Ministry of Education and Science)
- Valsts un pašvaldību augstākās izglītības iestādes, kuras reģistrētas Izglītības un zinātnes ministrijas izglītības iestāžu reģistrā (State and local government higher education institutions registered in the Register of Education Institutions at the Ministry of Education and Science)
- Valsts zinātniskās institūcijas (State scientific reasearch entities)
- Valsts veselības aprūpes iestādes (State health care establishments)
- Citi publisko tiesību subjekti, kuru darbība nav saistīta ar komercdarbību (Other bodies governed by public law not having a commercial character)

- 塞浦路斯大学
- 负担公平分配中央机构
- 塞浦路斯广播电视管理局

十九、 拉脱维亚

类别:

- 国家或地方政府设立、由国家或地方预算提供资金的非营利组织
- 专业儿童关爱中心
- 专业国家老年人关爱之家
- 专业国家关爱和康复中心
- 国家图书馆

  国家博物馆
- 国家剧院
- 国家和地方政府机构
- 在教育和科学部教育机构登记处登记的国家和地方政府学前教育机构
- 在教育和科学部教育机构登记处登记的国家和地方政府爱好/兴趣教育机构
- 在教育和科学部教育机构登记处登记的国家和地方政府职业教育机构
- 在教育和科学部教育机构登记处登记的国家和地方政府普通教育机构
- 在教育和科学部教育机构登记处登记的国家和地方政府基础和中等职业教育机构及学院(一级高等专业教育机构)
- 在教育和科学部教育机构登记处登记的国家和地方政府高等教育机构
- 国家科研实体
- 国家健康保健机构
- 其他受公法管辖的、不具商业性质的机构

XX. LITHUANIA

All bodies not having an industrial or commercial character whose procurement is subject to supervision by the Public Procurement Office under the Government of the Republic of Lithuania.

XXI. HUNGARY

Bodies:

- a megyei, illetőleg a regionális fejlesztési tanács (county and regional development council), az elkülönített állami pénzalap kezelője (managing bodies of the separate state fund), a társadalombiztosítás igazgatási szerve (social security administration body)
- a köztestület (public-law corporation) és a köztestületi költségvetési szerv (budgetary organ of a public-law corporation), valamint a közalapítvány (public foundation)
- a Magyar Távirati Iroda Részvénytársaság (Hungarian News Agency Plc.), a közszolgálati műsorszolgáltatók (public service broadcasters), valamint azok a köz-műsorszolgáltatók, amelyek működését többségében közpénzből finanszírozzák (public broadcasters financed mainly from the public budget)
- az Állami Privatizációs és Vagyonkezelő Részvénytársaság (Hungarian Privatization and State Holding Company)
- a Magyar Fejlesztési Bank Részvénytársaság (Hungarian Development Bank Plc.), az a gazdálkodó szervezet, melyben a Magyar Fejlesztési Bank Részvénytársaság ellenőrző részesedéssel rendelkezik (business organisations on which the Hungarian Development Bank Plc. exercises a dominant influence).

Categories:

- egyes központi és önkormányzati költségvetési szervek (certain budgetary organs)
- alapítvány (foundation), társadalmi szervezet (civil society organisations), közhasznú társaság (public benefit company), biztosító egyesület (insurance association), víziközmű-társulat (public utility water works association)
- business organisations established for the purpose of meeting needs in the general interest and controlled by public entities or financed mainly from the public budget.

XXII. MALTA

1. Kunsill Malti għall-Iżvilupp Ekonomiku u Soċjali (Malta Council for Economic and Social Development)
2. Awtorità tax-Xandir (Broadcasting Authority)
3. MITTS Ltd. (Malta Information Technology and Training Services Ltd.)
4. Awtorità għas-Saħħa u s-Sigurta' fuq il-Post tax-Xogħol (Occupational Health and Safety Authority)
5. Awtorità tad-Djar (Housing Authority)
6. Korporazzjoni għax-Xogħol u t-Taħrig (Employment and Training Corporation)
7. Fondazzjoni għ as-Servizzi għ all-Ħ arsien Soċjali (Foundation for Social Welfare Services)
8. Sedqa
9. Appoġġ
10. Kummissjoni Nazzjonali Persuni b'Diżabilita` (National Commission for Persons with Disability)

二十、 立陶宛

受立陶宛共和国政府公共采购办公室监督的所有不具工业或商业性质的机构。

二十一、匈牙利

机构:

- 州和地区发展理事会
  独立国家基金管理机构
  社会保险管理机构
- 公法法人公司
  公法法人公司的预算机构
  公共基金会
- 匈牙利通讯社
  公共服务广播公司
  主要由财政预算提供经费的公共广播公司
- 匈牙利私有化和国有控股有限公司
- 匈牙利开发银行
  匈牙利开发银行对其拥有重要影响的商业组织

类别:

- 某些预算机构
- 基金会、民权社会组织
  公益公司、保险协会
  公用事业供水工程协会
- 为满足公共利益需求而设立的、受公共实体控制或主要由公共预算提供经费的商业组织

二十二、马耳他

1. 马耳他经济和社会发展理事会
2. 广播管理局
3. 马耳他信息技术和培训服务有限公司
4. 职业健康和安全管理局
5. 住房管理局
6. 就业和培训公司
7. 社会公益服务基金会
8. 马耳他国家禁毒和反酗酒局
9. 马耳他国家儿童和家庭社会福利局
10. 国家残疾人委员会

11. Bord tal-Koperattivi (Cooperatives Board)
12. Fondazzjoni għaċ-Ċentru tal-Kreativita` (Foundation for the Centre of Creativity)
13. Orkestra Nazzjonali (National Orchestra)
14. Kunsill Malti għax-Xjenza u Teknoloġija (Malta Council for Science and Technology)
15. Teatru Manoel (Manoel Theatre)
16. Dar il-Mediterran għall-Konferenzi (Mediterranean Conference Centre)
17. Bank Ċentrali ta' Malta (Central Bank of Malta)
18. Awtorità għas-Servizzi Finanzjarji ta' Malta (Malta Financial Services Authority)
19. Borża ta' Malta (Malta Stock Exchange)
20. Awtorità dwar il-Lotteriji u l-Logħob (Lotteries and Gaming Authority)
21. Awtorità ta' Malta dwar ir-Riżorsi (Malta Resources Authority)
22. Kunsill Konsultattiv dwar l-Industrija tal-Bini (Building Industry Consultative Council)
23. Istitut għall-Istudju tat-Turiżmu (Institute of Tourism Studies)
24. Awtorità tat-Turiżmu ta' Malta (Malta Tourism Authority)
25. Awtorità ta' Malta dwar il-Komunikazzjoni (Malta Communications Authority)
26. Korporazzjoni Maltija għall-Iżvilupp (Malta Development Corporation)
27. Istitut għall-Promozzjoni ta' l-Intrapriżi Żgħar (IPSE Ltd)
28. Awtorità ta' Malta dwar l-Istandards (Malta Standards Authority)
29. Awtorità ta' Malta ta' l-Istatistika (Malta Statistics Authority)
30. Laboratorju Nazzjonali ta' Malta (Malta National Laboratory)
31. Metco Ltd
32. MGI / Mimcol
33. Maltapost plc
34. Gozo Channel Co Ltd
35. Awtorità ta' Malta dwar l-Ambjent u l-Ippjanar (Malta Environment and Planning Authority)
36. Fondazzjoni għ as-Servizzi Mediċi (Foundation for Medical Services)
37. Sptar Zammit Clapp (Zammit Clapp Hospital)
38. Ċentru Malti għ all-Arbitraġġ (Malta Arbitration Centre)
39. Kunsilli Lokali (Local Councils)

XXIII. POLAND

1. Uniwersytety i szkoły wyższe, wyższe szkoły pedagogiczne, ekonomiczne, rolnicze, artystyczne, teologiczne m.in. (Universities and academic schools, pedagogical, economics, agricultural, artistic, theological academic schools, etc.)

- Uniwersytet w Białymstoku (University of Białystok)
- Uniwersytet Gdański (University of Gdańsk)
- Uniwersytet Śląski (University of Silesia in Katowice)
- Uniwersytet Jagielloński w Krakowie (Jagiellonian University in Cracow)
- Uniwersytet Kardynała Stefana Wyszyńskiego (The Cardinal Stefan Wyszyński University in Warsaw)
- Katolicki Uniwersytet Lubelski (The Catholic University of Lublin)
- Uniwersytet Marii Curie-Skłodowskiej (The Maria-Curie Skłodowska University in Lublin)
- Uniwersytet Łódzki (University of Łódź)
- Uniwersytet Opolski (University of Opole)
- Uniwersytet im. Adama Mickiewicza (The Adam Mickiewicz University in Poznań)
- Uniwersytet Mikołaja Kopernika (The Nicholas Copernicus University in Toruń)
- Uniwersytet Szczeciński (University of Szczecin)

11. 合作社局
12. 创造力中心基金会
13. 国家乐团
14. 马耳他科技理事会
15. 蒙诺哥剧院
16. 地中海会议中心
17. 马耳他中央银行
18. 马耳他金融服务局
19. 马耳他股票交易所
20. 彩票和博彩管理局
21. 马耳他资源管理局
22. 建筑业咨询理事会
23. 旅游学院
24. 马耳他旅游局
25. 马耳他通信局
26. 马耳他发展公司
27. 小企业促进协会
28. 马耳他标准局
29. 马耳他统计局
30. 马耳他国家图书馆
31. 马耳他对外贸易公司
32. 马耳他政府投资有限公司
33. 马耳他邮政局
34. 戈左航道有限公司
35. 马耳他环境和规划局
36. 医疗服务基金会
37. 扎米特克拉普医院
38. 马耳他仲裁中心
39. 地方理事会

二十三、波兰

1. 大学和学院、教育、经济、农业、艺术、神学院等
- 比亚维斯托克大学
- 格但斯克大学
- 卡托维兹赛里西亚大学
- 克拉科夫雅盖隆大学
- 华沙市红衣主教大学
- 天主教卢布林大学
- 卢布林居民夫人大学
- 罗兹大学
- 奥波莱大学
- 波兹南密茨凯维奇大学
- 托伦哥白尼大学
- 什丘钦大学

- Uniwersytet Warmińsko-Mazurski w Olsztynie (University of Warmia and Mazury in Olsztyn)
- Uniwersytet Warszawski (University of Warsaw)
- Uniwersytet Wrocławski (University of Wrocław)
- Uniwersytet Zielonogórski (University of Zielona Góra)
- Akademia Techniczno-Humanistyczna w Bielsku-Białej (Academy of Humanities and Technics in Bielsko Biała)
- Akademia Górniczo-Hutnicza im. St. Staszica w Krakowie (The Stanisław Staszic University of Mining and Metallurgy)
- Politechnika Białostocka (Technical University of Białystok)
- Politechnika Częstochowska (Technical University of Częstochowa)
- Politechnika Gdańska (Technical University of Gdańsk)
- Politechnika Koszalińska (Technical University of Koszalin)
- Politechnika Krakowska (Technical University of Cracow)
- Politechnika Lubelska (Technical University of Lublin)
- Politechnika Łódzka (Technical University of Łódź)
- Politechnika Opolska (Technical University of Opole)
- Politechnika Poznańska (Technical University of Poznań)
- Politechnika Radomska im. Kazimierza Pułaskiego (The Kazimierz Puławski Technical University in Radom)
- Politechnika Rzeszowska im. Ignacego Łukasiewicza (The Ignacy Łukasiewicz Technical University in Rzeszów)
- Politechnika Szczecińska (Technical University of Szczecin)
- Politechnika Śląska (Technical University of Silesia in Gliwice)
- Politechnika Świętokrzyska (Technical University of Świętokrzyskie in Kielce)
- Politechnika Warszawska (Technical University of Warsaw)
- Politechnika Wrocławska (Technical University of Wroclaw)
- Akademia Morska w Gdyni (Gdynia Maritime University)
- Wyższa Szkoła Morska w Szczecinie (Maritime University Szczecin)
- Akademia Ekonomiczna im. Karola Adamieckiego w Katowicach (The Karol Adamiecki University of Economics in Katowice)
- Akademia Ekonomiczna w Krakowie (University of Economics in Kraków)
- Akademia Ekonomiczna w Poznaniu (University of Economics in Poznań)
- Szkoła Główna Handlowa (Warsaw School of Economics)
- Akademia Ekonomiczna im.Oskara Langego we Wrocławiu (The Oscar Lange University of Economics in Wrocław)
- Akademia Bydgoska im. Kazimierza Wielkiego (The Kazimierz Wielki University of Economics in Bydgoszcz)
- Akademia Pedagogiczna im. KEN w Krakowie (Pedagogical University in Cracow)
- Akademia Pedagogiki Specjalnej im. Marii Grzegorzewskiej (The Maria Grzegorzewska University of Special Pedagogy in Warsaw)
- Akademia Podlaska w Siedlcach (Podlaska Academy in Siedlce)
- Akademia Świętokrzyska im. Jana Kochanowskiego w Kielcach (The Jan Kochanowski Swiętokrzyska Academy in Kielce)
- Pomorska Akademia Pedagogiczna w Słupsku (Pomeranian Pedagogical Academy in Slupsk)

1 January 2007 (WT/Let/556)

- 奥尔什丁瓦尔密亚和玛祖里大学
- 华沙大学
- 弗罗茨瓦夫大学
- 绿山城大学
- 别尔斯—科比亚瓦人文与技术学院
- 斯坦尼斯拉夫—斯塔斯齐克矿冶大学
- 比亚威斯托克理工大学
- 琴斯托霍瓦理工大学
- 格但斯克理工大学
- 科沙林理工大学
- 克拉科夫理工大学
- 卢布林理工大学
- 罗兹理工大学
- 奥波莱理工大学
- 波兹南理工大学
- 拉多姆市卡兹米尔兹·普瓦斯基理工大学
- 热舒夫市依格纳茨·武卡谢维奇科技大学
- 什丘钦理工大学
- 格利维采市赛里西亚理工大学
- 凯尔采圣十字理工大学
- 华沙理工大学
- 弗罗茨瓦夫理工大学
- 格丁尼亚海事大学
- 什丘钦海事大学
- 卡托维兹市卡罗尔经济大学
- 科拉克夫经济大学
- 波兹南经济大学
- 华沙经济学院
- 弗罗茨瓦夫市奥斯卡·兰格尔经济大学
- 比德哥什市卡兹米尔兹·韦尔基经济大学
- 克拉科夫市师范大学
- 华沙玛利亚·格泽高泽乌斯卡特殊教育大学
- 谢德尔采市波德拉斯卡学院
- 凯尔采市简·科察诺乌斯基·斯维托兹斯卡学院
- 斯武普斯克市波美拉尼亚师范学院

- Wyższa Szkoła Filozoficzno-Pedagogiczna "Ignatianum" w Krakowie (School of Philosophy and Pedagogy "Ignatianum" in Cracow)
- Wyższa Szkoła Pedagogiczna im.Tadeusza Kotarbińskiego w Zielonej Górze (The Tadeusz Kotarbiński Pedagogy School in Zielona Góra)
- Wyższa Szkoła Pedagogiczna w Częstochowie (Pedagogy School in Częstochowa)
- Wyższa Szkoła Pedagogiczna w Rzeszowie (Pedagogy School in Rzeszów)
- Akademia Techniczno-Rolnicza im. J. J. Śniadeckich w Bydgoszczy (The J.J. Śniadeckich Technical and Agricultural Academy in Bydgoszcz)
- Akademia Rolnicza im.Hugona Kołłątaja w Krakowie (The Hugo Kołłątaj Agricultural University in Cracow)
- Akademia Rolnicza w Lublinie (Agricultural University of Lublin)
- Akademia Rolnicza im. Augusta Cieszkowskiego w Poznaniu (The August Cieszkowski Agricultural University in Poznań)
- Akademia Rolnicza w Szczecinie (Agricultural University of Szczecin)
- Szkoła Główna Gospodarstwa Wiejskiego w Warszawie (Warsaw Agricultural University)
- Akademia Rolnicza we Wrocławiu (Agricultural University of Wrocław)
- Akademia Medyczna w Białymstoku (Medical Academy of Białystok)
- Akademia Medyczna im. Ludwika Rydygiera w Bydgoszczy (The Ludwik Rydygier Medical Academy in Bydgoszcz)
- Akademia Medyczna w Gdańsku (Medical Academy of Gdańsk)
- Śląska Akademia Medyczna w Katowicach (Medical Academy of Silesia in Katowice)
- Collegium Medicum Uniwersytetu Jagiellońskiego w Krakowie (The Collegium Medicum Jagiellonian University in Cracow)
- Akademia Medyczna w Lublinie (Medical Academy of Lublin)
- Akademia Medyczna w Łodzi (Medical Academy of Łódź)
- Akademia Medyczna im. Karola Marcinkowskiego w Poznaniu (The Karol Marcinkowski Medical Academy in Poznań)
- Pomorska Akademia Medyczna w Szczecinie (Pomeranian Academy of Medicine in Szczecin)
- Akademia Medyczna w Warszawie (Medical Academy of Warsaw)
- Akademia Medyczna im. Piastów Śląskich we Wrocławiu (The Piastów Sląskich Medical Academy in Wroclaw)
- Centrum Medyczne Kształcenia Podyplomowego (Medical Centre for Post-graduate Training)
- Chrześcijańska Akademia Teologiczna w Warszawie (Christian Theological Academy in Warsaw)
- Papieski Wydział Teologiczny w Poznaniu (Pope's Theological Department in Poznań)
- Papieski Fakultet Teologiczny we Wrocławiu (Pope's Theological Faculty in Wrocław)
- Papieski Wydział Teologiczny w Warszawie (Pope's Theological Department in Warsaw)
- Akademia Marynarki Wojennej im. Bohaterów Westerplatte w Gdyni (Naval University of Gdynia named for Westerplatte's Heroes)
- Akademia Obrony Narodowej (National Defence Academy)
- Wojskowa Akademia Techniczna im. Jarosława Dąbrowskiego w Warszawie (The Jarosław Dąbrowski Technical Military Academy in Warsaw)
- Wojskowa Akademia Medyczna im. Gen. Dyw. Bolesława Szareckiego w Łodzi (The gen. Bolesław Szarecki Medical Military Academy in Łódź)

- 克拉科夫市伊格内修斯哲学与师范学校
- 绿山城塔德乌斯科塔宾斯基师范学校
- 琴斯托霍瓦师范学校
- 热舒夫师范学校
- 比得哥什市斯尼阿德克技术与农学院
- 克拉科夫市雨果·科拉塔基农业大学
- 卢布林农业大学
- 克拉科夫市波兹南农业大学
- 什丘钦农业大学
- 华沙农业大学
- 弗罗茨瓦夫农业大学
- 比亚韦斯托克医学院
- 比德格什市路德维克瑞迪基尔医学院
- 格但斯克医学院
- 卡托维兹市西里西亚医学院
- 克拉科夫市贾基洛尼亚大学
- 卢布林医学院
- 罗兹医学院
- 波兹南卡罗尔·马辛科沃斯基医学院
- 什丘钦市波美拉尼亚医药学院
- 华沙医学院
- 弗罗茨瓦夫彼亚斯托斯拉斯科基医学院
- 研究生医疗培训中心
- 华沙基督学院
- 波兹南教皇神学部
- 弗罗茨瓦夫教皇神学院
- 华沙教皇神学部
- 纪念韦斯特布拉德英雄的格丁尼亚海军大学
- 国防学院
- 华沙雅罗斯瓦夫·栋布洛斯维基军事理工学院
- 罗兹市博莱斯瓦·斯乍莱科基将军军事医学院

- Wyższa Szkoła Oficerska im. Tadeusza Kościuszki we Wrocławiu (The Tadeusz Kościuszko Military Academy in Wrocław)
- Wyższa Szkoła Oficerska Wojsk Obrony Przeciwlotniczej im. Romualda Traugutta (The Romuald Traugutt Anti-Aircraft Forces Academy)
- Wyższa Szkoła Oficerska im. gen. Józefa Bema w Toruniu (The gen. J. Bem Military Academy in Toruń)
- Wyższa Szkoła Oficerska Sił Powietrznych w Dęblinie (Air Forces Military Academy in Dęblin)
- Wyższa Szkoła Policji w Szczytnie (Police High School in Szczytno)
- Szkoła Główna Służby Pożarniczej w Warszawie (The Main School of Fire Service in Warsaw)
- Akademia Muzyczna im. Feliksa Nowowiejskiego w Bydgoszczy (The Feliks Nowowiejski Academy of Music in Bydgoszcz)
- Akademia Muzyczna im. Stanisława Moniuszki w Gdańsku (The Stanisław Moniuszko Academy of Music in Gdańsk)
- Akademia Muzyczna im. Karola Szymanowskiego w Katowicach (The Karol Szymanowski Academy of Music in Katowice)
- Akademia Muzyczna w Krakowie (Academy of Music in Cracow)
- Akademia Muzyczna im. Grażyny i Kiejstuta Bacewiczów w Łodzi (The Grażyna i Kiejstut Bacewicz Academy of Music in Łódź)
- Akademia Muzyczna im. Ignacego Jana Paderewskiego w Poznaniu (The Ignacy Jan Paderewski Academy of Music in Poznań)
- Akademia Muzyczna im. Fryderyka Chopina w Warszawie (The Fryderyk Chopin Academy of Music in Warsaw)
- Akademia Muzyczna im. Karola Lipińskiego we Wrocławiu (The Karol Lipiński Academy of Music in Wrocław)
- Akademia Sztuk Pięknych w Gdańsku (The Academy of Fine Arts in Gdańsk)
- Akademia Sztuk Pięknych w Katowicach (The Academy of Fine Arts in - Katowice)Akademia Sztuk Pięknych im. Jana Matejki w Krakowie (The Jan Matejko Academy of Fine Arts in Cracow)
- Akademia Sztuk Pięknych im. Władysława Strzemińskiego w Łodzi (The Władysław Strzemiński Academy of Fine Arts in Łódź)
- Akademia Sztuk Pięknych w Poznaniu (The Academy of Fine Arts in Poznań)
- Akademia Sztuk Pięknych w Warszawie (The Academy of Fine Arts in Warsaw)
- Akademia Sztuk Pięknych we Wrocławiu (The Academy of Fine Arts in Wrocław)
- Państwowa Wyższa Szkoła Teatralna im. Ludwika Solskiego w Krakowie (The Ludwik Solski State Higher Theatre School in Cracow)
- Państwowa Wyższa Szkoła Filmowa, Telewizyjna i Teatralna im. Leona Schillera w Łodzi (The Leon Schiller State Higher Film, Television and Theatre School in Łódź)
- Akademia Teatralna im. Aleksandra Zelwerowicza w Warszawie (The Aleksander Zelwerowicz Academy of Theatre in Warsaw)
- Akademia Wychowania Fizycznego i Sportu im. Jędrzeja Śniadeckiego w Gdańsku (The Jędrzej Śniadecki Academy of Physical Education and Sport in Gdańsk)
- Akademia Wychowania Fizycznego w Katowicach (Academy of Physical Education in Katowice)

- 弗罗茨瓦夫市塔德乌斯·科斯修斯科军事学院
- 罗穆尔德·特罗哥特防空部队学院
- 托伦市贝姆将军事学院
- 登布林市空军军事学院
- 什奇特诺市高等警察学校
- 华沙消防学校
- 比得歌什菲利克斯·诺沃维杰斯基音乐学院
- 格但斯克斯坦尼斯洛·莫纽斯兹科音乐学院
- 卡托维兹市卡罗尔·斯兹马诺乌斯基音乐学院
- 克拉科夫市音乐学院
- 罗兹市格拉兹纳·基斯塔特·巴西维兹音乐学院
- 波兹南伊格纳西·简·帕德热维斯基音乐学院
- 华沙弗雷德里克·肖邦音乐学院
- 弗罗茨瓦夫市卡罗尔·利平斯克音乐学院
- 格但斯克艺术学院
- 卡托维兹市艺术学院，克拉科夫市简·马特基科艺术学院
- 罗兹市乌拉德迪斯洛·斯特泽敏斯基艺术学院
- 波兹南艺术学院
- 华沙艺术学院
- 弗罗茨瓦夫市艺术学院
- 克拉科夫市路德维克·索尔斯基国立高等戏剧学校
- 罗兹市利昂·希勒国立高等电影、电视和戏剧学校
- 华沙市亚历克山德·泽尔维洛维克兹戏剧学院
- 格但斯克杰迪泽·斯尼亚德克基体育和运动学院
- 卡托维兹体育教育学院

- Akademia Wychowania Fizycznego im. Bronisława Czecha w Krakowie (The Bronisław Czech Academy of Physical Education in Cracow)
- Akademia Wychowania Fizycznego im. Eugeniusza Piaseckiego w Poznaniu (The Eugeniusz Piasecki Academy of Physical Education in Poznań)
- Akademia Wychowania Fizycznego Józefa Piłsudskiego w Warszawie (The Józef Piłsudski Academy of Physical Education in Warsaw)
- Akademia Wychowania Fizycznego we Wrocławiu (Academy of Physical Education in Wroclaw)

2. Państwowe i samorządowe instytucje kultury (national and self- governing cultural institutions)
3. Parki narodowe (national parks)
4. Agencje państwowe działające w formie spółek (national agencies acting in the form of companies)
5. Państwowe Gospodarstwo Leśne "Lasy Państwowe " ("State Forests" National Forest Holding)
6. Podstawowe, gimnazjalne i ponadgimnazjalne szkoły publiczne (public primary and secondary schools)
7. Publiczni nadawcy radiowi i telewizyjni (public radio and TV broadcasters)

- Telewizja Polska S. A. (Polish TV)
- Polskie Radio S. A. (Polish Radio)

8. Publiczne muzea, teatry, biblioteki i inne publiczne placówki kultury m.in.: (public museums, theatres, libraries, other public cultural institutions, etc.)

- Narodowe Centrum Kultury w Warszawie (National Centre for Culture in Warsaw)
- Zachęta – Państwowa Galeria Sztuki w Warszawie (Zachęta – State Gallery of Art in Warsaw)
- Centrum Sztuki Współczesnej – Zamek Ujazdowski w Warszawie (Centre for Contemporary Art – Ujazdowski Castle in Warsaw)
- Centrum Rzeźby Polskiej w Orońsku (Centre for Polish Sculpture in Orońsk)
- Międzynarodowe Centrum Kultury w Krakowie (International Culture Centre Cracow)
- Centrum Międzynarodowej Współpracy Kulturalnej – Instytut Adama Mickiewicza w Warszawie (Centre for International Cutural Cooperation – Adam Mickiewicz Institute in Warsaw)
- Dom Pracy Twórczej w Wigrach (House for Artistic Works in Wigry)
- Dom Pracy Twórczej w Radziejowicach (House for Artistic Works in Radziejowice)
- Biblioteka Narodowa w Warszawie (National Library in Warsaw)
- Naczelna Dyrekcja Archiwów Państwowych (Directorate of the Polish State's Archives)
- Muzeum Narodowe w Krakowie (National Museum in Cracow)
- Muzeum Narodowe w Poznaniu (National Museum in Poznań)
- Muzeum Narodowe w Warszawie (National Museum in Warsaw)
- Zamek Królewski w Warszawie – Pomnik Historii i Kultury Narodowej (Royal Castle in Warsaw – National History and Culture Monument)
- Zamek Królewski na Wawelu Państwowe Zbiory Sztuki w Krakowie (Royal Castle Wawel National Collections of Art in Cracow)
- Muzeum Żup Krakowskich w Wieliczce (Cracow Salt-mine Museum in Wieliczka)
- Państwowe Muzeum Auschwitz-Birkenau w Oświęcimiu (State Museum Auschwitz-Birkenau in Oświęcim)
- Państwowe Muzeum na Majdanku w Lublinie (State Museum Majdanek in Lublin)

- 克拉科夫市布若尼斯洛捷克体育学院
- 波兹南市尤金尼斯兹・皮阿塞克基体育学院
- 弗罗茨瓦夫乔泽夫・皮尔苏德斯基体育学院
- 弗罗茨瓦夫体育学院

2. 国家和自营文化机构
3. 国家公园
4. 以公司形式运营的国家机构
5. “国家森林”国家森林控股有限公司
6. 公立小学和中学
7. 公共广播和电视台

- 波兰电视台
- 波兰广播电台

8. 公共博物馆、剧院、图书馆、其他公共文化机构等：

- 华沙国家文化中心
- 扎切塔—华沙国家美术馆
- 当代艺术中心—华沙乌亚兹多夫斯基城堡
- 奥龙斯库市波兰雕塑中心
- 克拉科夫市国际文化中心
- 国际文化合作中心—华沙亚当・密茨凯维奇研究所
- 维格雷市艺术作品屋
- 拉济科维采市艺术作品馆
- 华沙国家图书馆
- 波兰国家档案局
- 克拉科夫市国家博物馆
- 波兹南国家博物馆
- 华沙国家博物馆
- 华沙皇宫—国家历史和文化纪念物
- 克拉科夫市国家艺术收藏馆
- 克拉科夫市维利奇卡盐矿博物馆
- 奥斯威辛—比克瑙国家博物馆
- 卢布林马伊达内克国家博物馆

- Muzeum Stutthof w Sztutowie (Museum Stutthof in Sztutowo)
- Muzeum Zamkowe w Malborku (Castle Museum in Marlbork)
- Centralne Muzeum Morskie w Gdańsku (Central Maritime Museum)
- Muzeum "Łazienki Królewskie" – Zespół Pałacowo-Ogrodowy w Warszawie (Museum "Łazienki Królewskie" – Palace-garden Complex in Warsaw)
- Muzeum Pałac w Wilanowie (Palace-museum in Wilanów)
- Muzeum Wojska Polskiego (Museum for Polish Armed Forces)
- Teatr Narodowy w Warszawie (National Theatre in Warsaw)
- Narodowy Stary Teatr im. Heleny Modrzejewskiej w Krakowie (The Helena Modrzejewska Old Theatre in Cracow)
- Teatr Wielki – Opera Narodowa w Warszawie (Great Theatre – National Opera in Warsaw)
- Filharmonia Narodowa w Warszawie (National Philharmonic Hall in Warsaw)

9. Publiczne placówki naukowe, jednostki badawczo- rozwojowe oraz inne placówki badawcze (Public research institutions, research and development institutions and other research institutions)

XXIV. SLOVENIA

- občine (local communities)
- javni zavodi s področja vzgoje, izobraževanja ter športa (public institutes in the area of child care, education and sport)
- javni zavodi s področja zdravstva (public institutes in the area of health care)
- javni zavodi s področja socialnega varstva (public institutes in the area of social security)
- javni zavodi s področja kulture (public institutes in the area of culture)
- javni zavodi s področja raziskovalne dejavnosti (public institutes in the area of science and research)
- javni zavodi s področja kmetijstva in gozdarstva (public institutes in the area of agriculture and forestry)
- javni zavodi s področja okolja in prostora (public institutes in the area of environment and spatial planning)
- javni zavodi s področja gospodarskih dejavnosti (public institutes in the area of economic activities)
- javni zavodi s področja malega gospodarstva in turizma (public institutes in the area of small enterprises and tourism)
- javni zavodi s področja javnega reda in varnosti (public institutes in the area of public order and security)
- agencije (agencies)
- skladi socialnega zavarovanja (social security funds)
- javni skladi na ravni države in na ravni občin (public funds at the level of the central government and local communities)
- Družba za avtoceste v RS (Motorway Company in the Republic of Slovenia)
- Pošta Slovenije (The Post Office of Slovenia)

- 施图托沃夫市施图特霍夫博物馆
- 马尔堡城堡博物馆
- 中央海事博物馆
- 瓦金基博物馆—华沙皇宫—花园综合体
- 维拉努夫博物馆
- 波兰军队博物馆
- 华沙国家剧院
- 克拉科夫市海伦娜•莫杰耶芙斯卡旧剧院
- 大剧院—华沙国家歌剧院
- 华沙国家交响乐厅

9. 公共研究机构、研究与开发机构和其他研究机构

二十四、斯洛文尼亚

- 当地社区
- 儿童保健、教育和运动领域的公共机构
- 卫生保健领域的公共机构
- 社会保险领域的公共机构
- 文化领域的公共机构
- 科学和研究领域的公共机构
- 农业和林业领域公共机构
- 环境和空间规划领域的公共机构
- 经济活动领域的公共机构
- 小型企业和旅游领域的公共机构
- 公共秩序和安全领域的公共机构
- 代理机构
- 社会保险基金
- 中央政府和地方社区一级的公共基金
- 斯洛文尼亚共和国中的高速公路公司
- 斯洛文尼亚邮政局

XXV. SLOVAKIA

The procuring entity is defined in Article 3 §1 of Act No. 263/1999 Z. z. on Public Procurement, as amended, as:

1. an organisation financed by the State budget (e.g. ministries, other state administration authorities) or co-financed by the State budget (e.g. universities, colleges) and by a State goal-specific fund
2. a self-governed region, a municipality, an organisation of a self-governed region or municipality financed or co-financed by the same
3. a health insurance agency
4. a legal entity established by law as a public institution (e.g. Slovenská televízia, Slovenský rozhlas, Sociálna poisťovňa)
5. National Property Fund of the Slovak Republic
6. Slovak Land Fund
7. association of legal entities which was formed by the procuring entities stated in items (1) to (3)".

XXVI. BULGARIA

Bodies:

- Икономически и социален съвет (Economic and Social Council)
- Национален осигурителен институт (National Social Security Institute)
- Национална здравноосигурителна каса (National Health Insurance Fund)
- Български червен кръст (Bulgarian Red Cross)
- Българска академия на науките (Bulgarian Academy of Sciences)
- Национален център за аграрни науки (National Centre for Agrarian Science)
- Български институт за стандартизация (Bulgarian Institute for Standardisation)
- Българско национално радио (Bulgarian National Radio)
- Българска национална телевизия (Bulgarian National Television)

Categories:

- Държавни предприятия по смисъла на чл.62, ал.3 от Търговския закон (обн., ДВ, бр.48/18.6.1991) (State undertakings within the meaning of Article 62(3) of the Commercial Law (published in State Gazette No 48/18.6.1991)).
- Държавни висши училища, създадени в съответствие с чл.13 на Закона за висшето образование (обн., ДВ, бр.112/27.12.1995) (State Universities, established pursuant to Article 13 of the Law on the Higher Education (published in State Gazette No 112/27.12.1995)).
- Културни институти по смисъла на Закона за закрила и развитие на културата (обн., ДВ, бр.50/1.6.1999) (Cultural institutes within the meaning of the Law on Culture Protection and Development (published in State Gazette No 50/1.6.1999)).
- Държавни или общински лечебни заведения по чл. 3, ал. 1 от Закона за лечебните заведения (обн., ДВ, бр.62/9.7.1999) (State or municipal medical institutions referred to in Article 3(1) of the Law on Medical Institutions (published in State Gazette No 62/9.7.1999)).

二十五、斯洛伐克

经修订的 263/1999 Z. z.号关于公共采购的法法律第 1.3 条将采购实体定义为：

1. 由国家预算提供经费的组织(如各部、其他国家行政机关)，或由国家预算和国家特定目标基金共同提供经费的组织(如大学、学院)
2. 自治地区、自治市、由自治地区或自治市中由自治地区或自治市提供经费或部分经费的组织
3. 健康保险机构
4. 依法作为公共机构设立的法律实体(如斯洛伐克电视台、斯洛伐克广播电台、社会保险)
5. 斯洛伐克共和国房地产基金
6. 斯洛伐克土地基金
7. (1)至 (3)项所述采购实体组成的法律实体联合会

二十六、保加利亚

机构：

- 经济和社会理事会
- 国家社会保险机构
- 国家健康保险基金
- 保加利亚红十字会
- 保加利亚科学院
- 国家土地科学中心
- 保加利亚标准化机构
- 保加利亚国家广播电台
- 保加利亚国家电视台

类别：

- 属 1991 年 6 月 18 日 48 号国家公报中公布的《商业法》第 62(3)条意义的国家企业
- 根据 1995 年 12 月 27 日 112 号国家公报公布的《高等教育法》第 13 条设立的国立大学
- 属 1999 年 6 月 1 日 50 号国家公报公布的《文化保护与发展法》意义内的文化机构。
- 1999 年 7 月 9 日 62 号国家公报公布的《医疗机构法》第 3(1)条所指的国家或城市医疗机构

- Лечебни заведения по чл. 5, ал. 1 от Закона за лечебните заведения (обн., ДВ, бр.62/9.7.1999) (Medical institutions referred to in Article 5(1) of the Law on Medical Institutions (published in State Gazette No 62/9.7.1999)).
- Юридически лица с нестопанска цел за осъществяване на общественополезна дейност по смисъла на Закона за юридическите лица с нестопанска цел (обн., ДВ, бр.81/6.10.2000), които отговарят на условията по §1, т.1 на Закона за обществените поръчки (обн., ДВ, бр. 28/6.4.2004) (Legal persons of a non-commercial character established for the purpose of meeting needs of general interest pursuant to the Law on Legal Persons of a Non-commercial Character (published in State Gazette No 81/6.10.2000), and satisfying the conditions of §1, item 1 of the Public Procurement Law (published in State Gazette No 28/6.4.2004)).

XXVII. ROMANIA

Bodies:

- Academia Română (Romanian Academy)
- Biblioteca Naţională (National Library)
- Institutul Cultural Român (Romanian Cultural Institute)
- Institutul European din România (European Institute from Romania)
- Institutul de Memorie Culturală (Institute for Cultural Memory)
- Agenţia Naţională "Socrates" (National Agency "Socrates")
- Centrul European UNESCO pentru Învăţământul Superior (CEPES) (UNESCO European Center for Higher Education)
- Comisia Naţională a României pentru UNESCO (National Romanian Commission for UNESCO)
- Societatea Română de Radiodifuziune (Romanian Broadcasting Company)
- Societatea Română de Televiziune (Romanian Television Company)
- Societatea Naţională pentru Radiocomunicaţii (National Radiocommunication Company)
- Oficiul Naţional al Cinematografiei (National Cinematography Office)
- Studioul de Creaţie Cinematografică (Studio of Cinematographic Creation)
- Arhiva Naţională de Filme (National Film Archive)
- Oficiul Naţional pentru Documentare şi Expoziţii de Artă (National Office for Documentation and Art Exhibition)
- Corul Naţional de Cameră "Madrigal" (National Chamber Choir Madrigal)
- Inspectoratul muzicilor militare (Institute of Military Music)
- Palatul Naţional al Copiilor (National Children Palace)
- Oficiul Naţional al Burselor de Studii în Străinătate (National Office for Scolarships Abroad)
- Agenţia Socială a Studenţilor (Social Agency of Students)
- Comitetul Olimpic Român (Romanian Olympic Committee)
- Centrul Român pentru Promovarea Cooperării Europene în Domeniul Tineretului (EUROTIN) (Romanian Agency for European Youth Cooperation)
- Centrul de Informare şi Consultanţă pentru Tineret (INFOTIN) (Youth Information and Counselling Center)
- Centrul de Studii şi Cercetări pentru Probleme de Tineret (CSCPT) (Youth Studies and Research Center)

- 1999 年 7 月 9 日 62 号国家公报公布的《医疗机构法》第 5(1)条所指的医疗机构
- 根据 2000 年 10 月 6 日 81 号国家公报公布的《非商业性质法人法》、为满足普遍利益而设立并满足 2004 年 6 月 4 日 28 号国家公报公布的《公共采购法》第 1 章第 1 项的条件的非商业性质法人

二十七、罗马尼亚

机构:

- 罗马尼亚学院
- 国家图书馆
- 罗马尼亚文化学院
- 罗马尼亚欧洲学院
- 文化记忆研究院
- “苏格拉底”国家委员会
- 联合国教科文组织高等教育欧洲中心
- 罗马尼亚国家联合国教科文组织委员会
- 罗马尼亚广播公司
- 罗马尼亚电视公司
- 国家广播通讯公司
- 国家电影摄影办公室
- 电影摄影创意工作室
- 国家电影档案
- 国家文献和艺术展览办公室
- 罗马尼亚牧歌合唱团
- 军乐协会
- 国家少年宫
- 国家海外奖学金办公室
- 大学生管理局
- 罗马尼亚奥林匹克委员会
- 罗马尼亚欧洲青年合作促进中心
- 青年信息和咨询中心
- 青年学习和研究中心

- Centrul de Cercetări pentru Probleme de Sport (CCPS) (Center for Sport Research)
- Societatea Naţională de Cruce Roşie (Romanian National Red Cross Society)
- Consiliul Naţional pentru Combaterea Discriminării (National Council for Combatting Discrimination)
- Secretariatul de Stat pentru Problemele Revoluţionarilor din Decembrie 1989
- (State Secretariat for December 1989 Revolutionaries' Problems)
- Secretariatul de Stat pentru Culte (State Secretariat for Cults)
- Agenţia Naţională pentru Locuinţe (National Agency for Housing)
- Casa Naţională de Pensii şi Alte Drepturi de Asigurări Sociale (National House of Pension and Other Social Insurance Rights)
- Casa Naţională de Asigurări de Sănătate (National House of Health Insurance)
- Inspecţia Muncii (Labour Inspection)
- Oficiul Central de Stat pentru Probleme Speciale (Central State Office for Special Problems)
- Inspectoratul General pentru Situaţii de Urgenţă (General Inspectorate for Emergency Situations)
- Agenţia Naţională de Consultanţă Agricolă (National Agency for Agricultural Counselling)
- Agenţia Naţională pentru Ameliorare şi Reproducţie în Zootehnie (National Agency for Improvement and Zootechnic Reproduction)
- Laboratorul Central pentru Carantină Fitosanitară (Central Laboratory of Phytosanitary Quarantine)
- Laboratorul Central pentru Controlul Calităţii Seminţelor (Central Laboratory for Seeds Quality Control)
- Institutul pentru Controlul Produselor Biologice şi Medicamentelor de Uz Veterinar (Institute for the Control of Veterinary Biologicals and Medicines)
- Institutul de Igienă şi Sănătate Publică şi Veterinară (Hygiene Institute of Veterinary Public Health)
- Institutul de Diagnostic şi Sănătate Animală (Institute for Diagnosis and Animal Health)
- Institutul de Stat pentru Testarea şi Înregistrarea Soiurilor (State Institute for Variety Testing and Registration)
- Banca de Resurse Genetice Vegetale (Genetical Vegetal Resources Bank)
- Institutul Diplomatic Roman (Romanian Diplomatic Institute)
- Administraţia Naţională a Rezervelor de Stat (National Administration of State Reserves)
- Agenţia Naţională pentru Dezvoltarea şi Implementarea Programelor de Reconstrucţie a Zonelor Miniere (National Agency for the Development and the Implementation of the Mining Regions Reconstruction Programs)
- Agenţia Naţională pentru Substanţe şi Preparate Chimice Periculoase (National Agency for Dangerous Chemical Substances)
- Agenţia Naţională de Control al Exporturilor Strategice şi al Interzicerii Armelor Chimice (National Agency for the Control of Strategic Exports and Prohibition of Chemical Weapons)
- Agenţia Naţională pentru Supravegherea Radioactivităţii Mediului (National Agency for Environment Radioactivity Surveillance)
- Administraţia Rezervaţiei Biosferei "Delta Dunării" Tulcea (Administration of Natural Biosphere Reservation-"Danube Delta"-Tulcea)

- 运动研究中心
- 罗马尼亚国家红十字会
- 国家反歧视理事会
- 1989 年 12 月革命者问题国家秘书处
- 国家宗教事务秘书处
- 国家住房局
- 国家养老金和其他社会保险权利公共机构
- 国家医疗保险公共机构
- 劳动监察局
- 国家专门问题中央办公室
- 紧急情况监察总局
- 国家农业咨询局
- 国家畜牧改良和繁殖局
- 植物卫生检疫中央实验室
- 种子质量控制中央实验室
- 控制生物制品和兽医药品研究所
- 公共和兽医卫生健康研究所
- 诊断和动物健康研究所
- 国家品种测试和注册研究所
- 植物基因资源库
- 罗马尼亚外交学会
- 国家储备管理局
- 国家矿区重建计划制定和执行署
- 国家危险化学物质管理局
- 国家战略出口控制和禁止化学武器局
- 国家环境放射性监督局
- 图尔恰“多瑙河三角洲”自然生物圈保护区管理局

- Regia Naţională a Pădurilor (ROMSILVA) (National Forests Administration)
- Administraţia Naţională Apele Române (Romanian Waters National Administration)
- Administratia Nationala de Meteorologie (National Administration of Meteorology)
- Comisia Naţională pentru Reciclarea Materialelor (National Commission for Materials Recycling)
- Comisia Naţională pentru Controlul Activităţilor Nucleare (National Commission for Nuclear Activity Control)
- Agenţia Naţională pentru Ştiinţă, Tehnologie şi Inovare (National Agency for Science, Technology and Innovation)
- Agenţia Naţională pentru Comunicaţii şi Informatică (National Agency for Communication and Informatics)
- Inspectoratul General pentru Comunicaţii şi Tehnologia Informaţiei (General Inspectorate for Communication and Information Technology)
- Oficiul pentru Administrare şi Operare al Infrastructurii de Comunicaţii (Office for Administration and Operation of the Data Communication Infrastructure)
- Inspecţia de Stat pentru Controlul Cazanelor, Recipientelor sub Presiune şi Instalaţiilor de Ridicat (State Inspection for the Control of Boilers, Pressure Vessels and Hoisting Equipment)
- Centrul Român pentru Pregătirea şi Perfecţionarea Personalului din Transporturi Navale – CERONAV (Romanian Center for Instruction and Training of Personnel engaged in Naval Transport)
- Inspectoratul Navigaţiei Civile (INC) (Inspectorate for Civil Navigation)
- Societatea de Servicii de Management Feroviar SMF SA (Society for Railway Management Services)
- Societatea de Administrare Active Feroviare SAAF SA (Society for Railway Assets Administration)
- Regia Autonomă Registrul Auto Român (Autonomous Regie - Romanian Auto Register)
- Agenţia Spaţială Română (Romanian Space Agency)
- Şcoala Superioară de Aviaţie Civilă (Superior School of Civil Aviation)
- Aeroclubul României (Romanian Aeroclub)
- Centrul de pregătire pentru Personalul din Industrie Buşteni (TrainingCenter for the Staff in Industry Busteni)
- Centrul Român de Comerţ Exterior (Romanian Center of Foreign Trade)
- Centrul de Formare şi Management pentru Comerţ Bucureşti (Management and Formation Center for Commerce Bucureşti)
- Agenţia de Cercetare pentru Tehnică şi Tehnologii Militare (Research Agency for Military Technics and Technology)
- Asociaţia Română de Standardizare (ASRO) (Romanian Association of Standardization)
- Asociaţia de Acreditare din România (RENAR) (Romanian Accreditation Association)
- Comisia Naţională de Prognoză (CNP) (National Commission for Prognosis)
- Institutul Naţional de Statistică (INS) (National Institute for Statstics)
- Consiliul Concurenţei (CC) (Competition Council)
- Comisia Naţională a Valorilor Mobiliare (CNVM) (National Commission for Transferable Securities)
- Consiliul Economic şi Social (CES) (Economic and Social Council)
- Oficiul Participaţiilor Statului şi Privatizării în Industrie (Office of State Participation and Privatization in Industry)

- 国家森林管理局
- 罗马尼亚国家水务局
- 国家气象管理局
- 国家物资回收委员会
- 国家核活动控制委员会
- 国家科学、技术和创新局
- 通信和信息化监察总局
- 通讯与信息技术监察总局
- 数据通信基础设施管理和运营办公室
- 国家锅炉、压力容器和起重设备监察局
- 罗马尼亚航运人员教育和培训中心
- 民航监察局
- 铁道管理服务协会
- 铁路资产管理局
- 罗马尼亚汽车登记处
- 罗马尼亚航天局
- 民用航空高等学校
- 罗马尼亚航空俱乐部
- 布什泰尼工业员工培训中心
- 罗马尼亚对外贸易中心
- 布加勒斯特贸易管理和制订中心
- 军事工艺和技术研究局
- 罗马尼亚标准化协会
- 罗马尼亚认证协会
- 国家预测委员会
- 国家统计学会
- 竞争理事会
- 国家可转让证券委员会
- 经济和社会理事会
- 工业领域国家参与和私有化办公室

- Agenţia Domeniilor Statului (Agency of State Domains)
- Oficiul Naţional al Registrului Comerţului (National Trade Register Office)
- Autoritatea pentru Valorificarea Activelor Statului (AVAS) (Authority for State Assets Recovery)
- Oficiul National de Prevenire şi Combatere a Spălării Banilor (ONPCSB) (National Office for Preventing and Combatting Money Laundering)
- Consiliul Naţional pentru Studierea Arhivelor Securităţii (National Council for Study of the Securitate Archives)
- Avocatul Poporului (People's Attorney)
- Autoritatea Electorala Permanenta (Permanent Electoral Authority)
- Institutul Naţional de Administraţie (INA) (National Institute of Administration)
- Inspectoratul Naţional pentru Evidenţa Persoanelor (National Inspectorate for Persons' Record)
- Oficiul de Stat pentru Invenţii şi Mărci (OSIM) (State Office for Inventions and Trademarks)
- Oficiul Român pentru Drepturile de Autor (ORDA) (Romanian Office for Author Rights)
- Oficiul Naţional pentru Protejarea Patrimoniului (National Office for Patrimony Protection)
- Agentia Nationala Antidrog (National Antidrug Agency)
- Biroul Român de Metrologie Legală (Romanian Bureau of Legal Metrology)
- Inspecţia de Stat în Construcţii (State Inspection in Construction)
- Compania Naţională de Investiţii (Natonal Company for Investements)
- Compania Naţională de Autostrăzi şi Drumuri Naţionale (Romanian National Company of Motorways and National Roads)
- Agentia Nationala de Cadastru si Publicitate Imobiliara (National Agency for Cadastre and Real Estate Advertising)
- Direcţia topografică militară (Department of Military Topography)
- Administratia Nationala a Îmbunătăţirilor Funciare (National Administration of Land Improvements)
- Garda Financiară (Financial Guard)
- Garda Naţională de Mediu (National Guard for Environment)
- Institutul Naţional de Expertize Criminalistice (National Institute for Criminological Expertise)
- Institutul Naţional al Magistraturii (National Institute of Magistracy)
- Institutul Naţional pentru Pregătirea şi Perfecţionarea Magistraţilor (National Institute for Magistrates' Professional Training)
- Institutul Naţional de Criminologie (National Institute of Criminology)
- Centrul de Pregătire şi Perfecţionare a Grefierilor şi a Celuilalt Personal Auxiliar de Specialitate (Training Center for Courtclerks and Other Auxiliary Specialised Personnel)
- Direcţia Generală a Penitenciarelor (General Directorate for Penitentiaries)
- Oficiul Registrului Naţional al Informaţiilor Secrete de Stat (National Register Office of State Secret Information)
- Autoritatea Nationala a Vămilor (National Customs Authority)
- Regia Autonomă "Administraţia Zonei Libere Constanţa-Sud" (Autonomous Regie "Free Zone Administration Constanţa-Sud")
- Regia Autonomă "Administraţia Zonei Libere Brăila" (Autonomous Regie “Free Zone Administration Brăila”)

- 国有领土管理局
- 国家贸易注册办公室
- 国家资产收回管理局
- 国家预防和打击洗钱办公室
- 国家保安部队档案研究理事会
- 人民律师协会
- 常设选举局
- 国家行政协会
- 国家个人记录监察局
- 国家发明和商标办公室
- 罗马尼亚著作权办公室
- 国家遗产保护办公室
- 国家禁毒局
- 罗马尼亚法定计量局
- 国家建设监察局
- 国家投资公司
- 罗马尼亚国家高速公路和国家公路公司
- 国家地籍和房地产广告局
- 军事测绘局
- 国家土地改良局
- 金融防范局
- 国家环境保护局
- 国家犯罪学知识研究院
- 国家地方行政官学会
- 国家地方行政官培训学会
- 国家犯罪学研究院
- 书记员和其他专业辅助人员培训中心
- 监狱监察总局
- 国家保密信息登记办公室
- 国家海关局
- 南康斯坦察自由区管理局
- 布勒伊拉自由区管理局

- Regia Autonomă "Administraţia Zonei Libere Galaţi" (Autonomous Regie "Free Zone Administration Galaţi")
- Regia Autonomă "Administraţia Zonei Libere Sulina" (Autonomous Regie "Free Zone Administration Sulina")
- Regia Autonomă "Administraţia Zonei Libere Giurgiu" (Autonomous Regie "Free Zone Administration Giurgiu")
- Regia Autonomă "Administraţia Zonei Libere Curtici" (Autonomous Regie "Free Zone Administration Curtici")
- Banca Naţională a României (National Bank of Romania)
- Regia Autonomă "Monetăria Statului" (Autonomous Regie "State Mint of Romania")
- Regia Autonomă "Imprimeria Băncii Naţionale" (Autonomous Regie "Printing House of the National Bank")
- Regia Autonomă "Imprimeria Naţională" (Autonomous Regie "National Printing House")
- Regia Autonomă "Monitorul Oficial" (Autonomous Regie "Official Gazette")
- Regia Autonomă "Rasirom" (Autonomous Regie "Rasirom")
- Regia Autonomă "Unifarm" Bucureşti (Autonomous Regie "Unifarm" Bucureşti)
- Regia Autonomă "România Film" (Autonomous Regie "Romania Film")
- Compania Naţională "Loteria Română" (National Company "Romanian Lottery")
- Compania Naţională "Romtehnica" (National Company "Romtehnica")
- Compania Naţională "Romarm" (National Company "Romarm")
- Regia Autonomă "Romavia" (Autonomous Regie "Romavia")
- Agenţia Naţională de Presă ROMPRES (National News Agency ROMPRES)
- Regia Autonomă "Editura Didactică şi Pedagogică" (Autonomous Regie "Didactic and Pedagogical Publishing House")
- Regia Autonomă "Administraţia Patrimoniului Protocolului de Stat" (Autonomous Regie "Administration of State Patrimony and Protocol")
- Institute şi centre de cercetare (Research institutes and centers)
- Instituţii de învăţământ de stat (Education state institutes)
- Universităţi de stat (State Universities)
- Muzee (Museums)
- Biblioteci de stat (State Libraries)
- Teatre de stat, opere, operete, filarmonica, centre şi case de cultură (State Theaters, operas, philharmonic orchestras, cultural houses and centers)
- Reviste (Magazines)
- Edituri (Publishing houses)
- Inspectorate şcolare, de cultură, de culte (School , culture and cults inspectorates)
- Complexuri, federaţii şi cluburi sportive (Sport federations and clubs)
- Spitale, sanatorii, policlinici, dispensare, centre medicale, institute medico-legale, staţii ambulanţă (Hospitals, sanatoriums, clinics, medical units, legal-medical institutes, ambulance stations)

- 加拉茨自由区管理局
- 苏利纳自由区管理局
- 久贝加自由区管理局
- 库尔蒂奇自由区管理局
- 罗马尼亚国家银行
- 罗马尼亚铸币厂
- 国家银行印刷厂
- 国家印刷所
- 官方公报
- 拉西若姆自治区
- 布勒加斯特统一农场自治区
- 罗马尼亚电影公司
- 罗马尼亚国家彩票公司
- 国家 Romtehnica 公司
- 国家 Romarm 公司
- 罗迈维亚自治区
- 罗马尼亚国家通讯社
- 教学和教育出版社
- 国家遗产和礼仪管理局
- 研究所和研究中心
- 国家教育机构
- 国立大学
- 博物馆
- 国家图书馆
- 国家剧院、歌剧院、交响乐团、文化馆和文化中心
- 杂志
- 出版社
- 学校、文化和宗教监察机构
- 运动联合会和俱乐部
- 医院、疗养院、诊所、医疗队、法医研究所、救护站

- Unităţi de asistenţă socială (Social assistance units)
- Tribunale (Tribunals)
- Judecătorii (Law Courts)
- Curţi de apel (Courts of Appeal)
- Penitenciare (Penitentiaries)
- Parchetele de pe lângă instanţele judecătoreşti (Prosecutor's Offices)
- Unităţi militare (Military units)
- Instanţe militare (Military courts)
- Inspectorate de Politie (Police Inspectorates)
- Centre de odihnă (Rest Houses)".
- Comisa de Supraveghere a Asigurarilor (CSA) (Insurance Supervisory Commission)
- Comisa de Supraveghere a Sistemului de Pensii Private (Private Pension System Supervisory Commission).

In addition to the entities listed in Annex I of Directive 93/37/EEC (pages 92-101 of document GPA/W/51), the following entities shall be regarded as bodies governed by public law within the sense of such Directive:

Austria: "Austrian State Printing Office"

Denmark: "Copenhagen Hospital Corporation" ("Hovedstandens Sygehusfaellesskab")

Ireland: "Forbas"; "Forbairt"

Luxembourg: "L'entreprise des Postes et Télécomunications (Postal business only)"

Portugal:

"INGA (National Agricultural Intervention and Guarantee Institute/Instituto Nacional de Intervenção e Garantia Agrícola)"

"Institute for the Consumer / Instituto do Consumidor"

"Institute for Meteorology / Instituto de Meteorologia"

"Institute for Natural Conservation / Instituto da Conservação da Natureza"

"Water Institute / Instituto da Agua"

"ICEP / Instituto de Comércio Externo de Portugal"

"Portuguese Blood Institute / Instituto do Sangue"

United Kingdom: "Ordnance Survey"

- 社会援助机构
- 仲裁机构
- 法院
- 上诉法院
- 监狱
- 检察官办公室
- 军事单位
- 军事法庭
- 警察监察
- 招待所
- 保险监督委员会
- 私人养老金系统监督委员会

除欧洲经济共同体 93/37 号指令附件 1(GPA/W/51 号文件第 92-101 页)所列实体外，下列实体应视为该指令含义内的受公法管辖的机构：

奥地利： “奥地利国家印刷办公室”

丹麦： “哥本哈根医院公司”

爱尔兰： “爱尔兰企贸科技创新政策咨询委员会”； “爱尔兰企贸科技创新政策署”

卢森堡： “邮政和电信企业(仅限邮政业务)”

葡萄牙：

“国家农业干预和担保协会”

“消费者协会”

“国家气象学会”

“国家自然保护学会”

“水资源学会”

“葡萄牙外贸学会”

“葡萄牙血液学会”

英国： “陆军测量局”

2007 年 1 月 1 日 (WT/Let/556)

EUROPEAN COMMUNITIES
COMMUNAUTES EUROPEENNES
COMUNIDADES EUROPEAS

Directive 93/38

As mentioned in Appendix I - Annex 3 of the GPA

1 January 2007 (WT/Let/556)

欧洲共同体

93/38 号指令

GPA 附录 1 的附件 3 中提及

2007 年 1 月 1 日 (WT/Let/556)

ANNEX I

PRODUCTION, TRANSPORT OR DISTRIBUTION OF DRINKING WATER

BELGIUM

Entity set up pursuant to the décret du 2 juillet 1987 de la région wallonne érigeant en entreprise régionale de production et d'adduction d'eau le service du ministère de la région chargé de la production et du grand transport d'eau.

Entity set up pursuant to the arrêté du 23 avril 1986 portant constitution d'une société wallonne de distribution d'eau.

Entity set up pursuant to the arrêté du 17 juillet 1985 de l'exécutif flamand portant fixation des statuts de la société flamande de distribution d'eau.

Entities producing or distributing water and set up pursuant to the loi relative aux intercommunales du 22 décembre 1986.

Entities producing or distributing water set up pursuant to the code communal, article 47 *bis*, *ter et quater* sur les régies communales.

DENMARK

Entities producing or distributing water referred to in Article 3, paragraph 3 of lovbekendtgøelse om vandforsyning m.v. af 4 juli 1985.

GERMANY

Entities producing or distributing water pursuant to the Eigenbetriebsverordnungen or Eigenbetriebsgesetze of the Länder (Kommunale Eigenbetriebe).

Entities producing or distributing water pursuant to the Gesetze Huber die Kommunale Gemeinschaftsarbeit oder Zusammenarbeit of the Länder.

Entities producing water pursuant to the Gesetz über Wasser- und Bodenverbände vom 10 Februar 1937 and the erste Verordnung über Wasser- und Bodenverbände vom 3 September 1937.

(Regiebetriebe) producing or distributing water pursuant to the Kommunalgesetze and notably with the Gemeindeordnungen der Länder.

Entities set up pursuant to the Aktiengesetz vom 6 September 1965, zuletzt geändert am 19 Dezember 1985 or GmbH-Gesetz vom 20 Mai 1898, zuletzt geändert am 15 Mai 1986, or having the legal status of a Kommanditgesellschaft, producing or distributing water on the basis of a special contract with regional or local authorities.

附录 1

饮用水的生产、输送和配送

比利时

根据瓦隆大区 1987 年 7 月 2 日关于将负责水生产和大规模输送的政府部门设立为水生产和输送的地区性公司的法令设立的实体。

根据 1986 年 4 月 23 日由瓦隆水配送公司组成的法令设立的实体。

根据 1985 年 7 月 17 日关于确定弗拉芒区水配送公司章程的行政法令设立的实体。

根据 1986 年 12 月 22 日关于市镇间事务的法律设立的生产或配送水的实体。

根据与市镇管理有关的市镇法规第 47 条之二第 3 和 4 款设立的生产或配送水的实体。

丹麦

1985 年 7 月 4 日颁布的《水法》第 3 条第 3 款所指的水生产或配送实体。

德国

根据各联邦州个体经营法规(地方个体经营)生产或配送水的实体。

根据各联邦州地方集体劳动或合作法规生产或配送水的实体。

根据 1937 年 2 月 10 日颁布的《水及土地协会法》及 1937 年 9 月 3 日颁布的《水及土地协会法第 1 条例》生产水的实体。

根据各州地方法规、特别是乡镇法规，生产或配送水的国营企业。

根据 1965 年 9 月 6 日颁布并于 1985 年 12 月 19 日修订的《股份法》或 1898 年 5 月 20 日颁布关于 1986 年 5 月 15 日修订的《有限公司法》设立的实体，或具有限合伙公司法律地位的，根据与地区或地方政府机关签订的专门合同生产或配送水的实体。

GREECE

The Water Company of Athens / *Εταιρεία Ύδρευσης – Αποχέτευσης Πρωτευούσης* (Etaireia Ydrefsιs Apochetefsιs Protevoysis) set up pursuant to Law 1068/80 of 23 August 1980.

The Water Company of Salonica / *Οργισμός Ύδρευσης Θεσσαλονίκης* (Organismos Ydrefsιs Thessalonikis) operating pursuant to Presidential Decree 61/1988.

The Water Company of Voios / *Εταιρεία Ύδρευσης Βόλου* (Etaireia Ydrefsιs Voloy) operating pursuant to Law 890/1979.

Municipal companies / *Δημοτικές Επιχειρήσεις ύδρευσης - αποχέτευσης* (Dimotikes Epicheiriseis ydrefsis apochetefsis) producing or distributing water and set up pursuant to Law 1059/80 of 23 August 1980.

Associations of local authorities / *Σύνδεσμοι ύδρευσης* (Syndesmoi ydrevsys) operating pursuant to the Code of local authorities *Κώδικας Δήμων και Κοινοτήτων* (Kodikas Dimon Kai Koinotiton) implemented by Presidential Decree 76/1985.

SPAIN

- Entities producing or distributing water pursuant to *Ley no 7/1985 de 2 de abril de 1985. Reguladora de las Bases del Régimen local* and to *Decreto Real no 781/1986 Texto Refundido Régimen local.*

- Canal de Isabel II. *Ley de la Comunidad Autónoma de Madrid de 20 de diciembre de 1984.*

- Mancomunidad de los Canales de Taibilla, *Ley de 27 de abril de 1946.*

FRANCE

Entities producing or distributing water pursuant to the:

dispositions générales sur les régies, code des communes L 323-1 à L 328-8, R 323-1 à R 323-6 (dispositions générales sur les régies); or

code des communes L 323-8 R 323-4 [régies directes (ou de fait)]; or

décret-loi du 28 décembre 1926, règlement d'administration publique du 17 février 1930, code des communes L 323-10 à L 323-13, R 323-75 à 323-132 (régies à simple autonomie financière); or

code des communes L 323-9, R 323-7 à R 323-74, décret du 19 octobre 1959 (régies à personnalité morale et à autonomie financière); or

code des communes L 324-1 à L 324-6, R 324-1 à R 324-13 (gestion déléguée, concession et affermage); or

jurisprudence administrative, circulaire intérieure du 13 décembre 1975 (gérance); or

希腊

根据 1980 年 8 月 23 日 1068/80 号法律成立的雅典水公司。

根据 61/1988 号总统令经营的萨洛尼卡水公司。

根据 890/1979 号法律经营的维奥斯水公司。

根据 1980 年 8 月 23 日 1059/80 号法律生产或配送水的城市公司。

根据依据 76/1985 号总统令实施的当地政府法典经营的当地政府协会。

西班牙

- 根据 1985 年 4 月 2 日颁布的 1985/7 号法律，地方政府对基地的监管规定以及地方政府根据 1986/781 号法令指定的当地规定，生产或配送水的实体。
- 根据 1984 年 12 月 20 日颁布的马德里自治区法律规定的伊莎贝尔二世运河水公司。
- 根据 1946 年 4 月 27 日法令规定的泰利维亚运河联合体。

法国

根据以下法律生产或配送水的实体：

经营管理总则、市镇法典 L 323-1 至 L 328-8、 R 323-1 至 R 323-6；或

市镇法典 L 323-8 和 R 323-4[直接(或事实)管理]；或

1926 年 12 月 28 日法令、1930 年 2 月 17 日国家行政管理条例、市镇法规 L 323-10 至 L 323-13、 R 323-75 至 323-132(直接独立核算管理)；或

市镇法典 L 323-9、R 323-7 至 R 323-74，1959 年 10 月 19 日法令(法人和核算独立管理)；或

市镇法规 L 324-1 至 L 324-6、 R 324-1 至 R 324-13(授权管理、特许权和租赁)；或

司法行政裁决和 1975 年 12 月 13 日内部通知(管理)；或

code des communes R 324-6, circulaire intérieure du 13 décembre 1975 (régie intéressée); or

circulaire intérieure du 13 décembre 1975 (exploitation aux risques et périls); or

décret du 20 mai 1955, loi du 7 juillet 1983 sur les sociétés d'économie mixte (participation à une société d'économie mixte); or

code des communes L 322-1 À L 322-6, R 322-1 À R 322-4 (dispositions communes aux régies, concessions et affermages).

IRELAND

Entities producing or distributing water pursuant to the Local Government (Sanitary Services) Act 1878 to 1964.

ITALY

Entities producing or distributing water pursuant to the *Testo unico delle leggi sull'assunzione diretta dei pubblici servizi da parte dei comuni e delle province approvato con Regio Decreto 15 ottobre 1925, n. 2578 and to Decreto del P.R. n. 902 del 4 ottobre 1986.*

Ente Autonomo Acquedotto Pugliese set up pursuant to *RDL 19 ottobre 1919, n. 2060.*

Ente Acquedotti Siciliani set up pursuant to *leggi regionali 4 settembre 1979, n. 2/2 e 9 agosto 1980, n. 81.*

Ente Sardo Acquedotti e Fognature set up pursuant to *legge 5 luglio 1963 n. 9.*

LUXEMBOURG

Local authorities distributing water.

Associations of local authorities producing or distributing water set up pursuant to the *loi du 14 février 1900 concernant la création des syndicats de communes telle qu'elle a été modifiée et complétée par la loi du 23 décembre 1958 et par la loi du 29 juillet 1981* and pursuant to *the loi du 31 juillet 1962 ayant pour objet le renforcement de l'alimentation en eau potable du grand-duché du Luxembourg à partir du réservoir d'Esch-sur-Sûre.*

NETHERLANDS

Entities producing or distributing water pursuant to the *Waterleidingwet van 6 april 1957, amended by the wetten van 30 juni 1967, 10 september 1975, 23 juni 1976, 30 september 1981, 25 januari 1984, 29 januari 1986.*

市镇法规 R 324-6、1975 年 12 月 13 日内部通知(有关管理部分)；或

1975 年 12 月 13 日的内部通知(有关自负盈亏经营部分)；或

关于公私合营公司(加入一家公私合营公司)的 1983 年 7 月 7 日法令，1955 年 5 月 20 日法令；或

市镇法典 L 322-1 至 L 322-6、 R 322-1 至 R 322-4(管理、特许权和租赁共同规定)。

爱尔兰

根据《地方政府(卫生服务)法》1878 至 1964 生产或配送水的实体。

意大利

根据 1925 年 10 月 15 日皇家法令批准、1986 年 10 月 12 日共和国法令修订的《省市公共服务直接选举法》规定生产或配送水的实体。

根据 1919 年 10 月 19 日 2060 号 RDL 成立的水厂管理机构。

根据 1979 年 9 月 4 日法律和 1980 年 8 月 9 日 81 号法令成立的西西里水厂管理机构。

根据 1963 年 7 月 5 日 9 号法律建立的撒丁岛水厂和排水管理机构。

卢森堡

配送水的当地政府机构。

根据由 1958 年 12 月 23 日和 1981 年 7 月 29 日的法律，对 1900 年 2 月 14 日的关于建立市镇联合会法律作了修改和补充，并依照以加强从埃斯克—绍尔蓄水池起的卢森堡大公国饮用水的供应为目的 1962 年 7 月 31 日的法律设立的水生产和配送当地政府机构联合会。

荷兰

根据 1957 年 4 月 6 日颁布、后于 1967 年 6 月 30 日、1975 年 9 月 10 日、1976 年 6 月 23 日、1981 年 9 月 30 日、1984 年 1 月 25 日和 1986 年 1 月 29 日修订的《水资源管理法》的规定，生产或配送水的实体。

PORTUGAL

Empresa Pública das Águas Livres producing or distributing water pursuant to the *Decreto-Lei no 190/81 de 4 de Julho de 1981.*

Local authorities producing or distributing water.

UNITED KINGDOM

Water companies producing or distributing water pursuant to *the Water Acts 1945 and 1989.*

The Central Scotland Water Development Board producing water and the water authorities producing or distributing water pursuant to the *Water (Scotland) Act 1980.*

The Department of the Environment for Northern Ireland responsible for producing and distributing water pursuant to the *Water and Sewerage (Northern Ireland) Order 1973.*

AUSTRIA

Entities of local authorities (Gemeinden) and associations of local authorities (Gemeindeverbände) producing, transporting or distributing drinking water pursuant to *the Wasserversorgungsgesetze of the nine Länder.*

FINLAND

Entities producing, transporting or distributing drinking water pursuant to *Article 1 of Laki yleisistä vesi- ja viemärilaitoksista (982/77) of 23 December 1977.*

SWEDEN

Local authorities and municipal companies which produce, transport or distribute drinking water pursuant to *lagen (1970:244) om allmänna vatten- och avloppsanläggningar.;*

CZECH REPUBLIC

All producers, shippers or distributors of drinking water that provide their services to the public (section 2 b) of Act No. 199/1994 Sb. on Public Procurement).

ESTONIA

Entities operating pursuant to Article 5 of the Public Procurement Act (RT I 2001, 40, 224) and Article 14 of the Competition Act (RT I 2001, 56 332).

CYPRUS

The Water Boards, distributing water in municipal and other areas pursuant to the Water Supply (Municipal and Other Areas) Law, Cap. 350. (Τα Συμβούλια Υδατοπρομήθειας που διανέμουν νερό σε δημοτικές και άλλες περιοχές, δυνάμει του περί Υδατοπρομήθειας Δημοτικών και Άλλων Περιοχών Νόμου, Κεφ. 350).

葡萄牙

根据 1981 年 7 月 4 日 190/81 号法令设立的生产或配送水的自来水有限公司。

生产或配送水的地方政府机构。

英国

根据 1945 年和 1989 年《水法》生产或配送水的水务公司。

根据 1980 年《(苏格兰)水法》生产水的苏格兰中央水开发局和生产或配送水的水务机构。

北爱尔兰环境部根据 1973 年(北爱尔兰)《水和污水令》负责生产和配送水。

奥地利

根据《9 联邦州供水法》生产、**输送**或配送饮用水的地方政府机构实体和地方政府机构的协会。

芬兰

根据 1977 年 12 月 23 日《公共用水和管道公司法》(982/77 号)第 1 条生产、输送或配送饮用水的实体。

瑞典

根据《公共供水和污水处理设施法》 (1970:244 号) 的规定生产、输送或配送饮用水的地方政府机构和城市公司。

捷克

根据 199/1994 号关于公共采购的法律第 2b 节，所有向公众提供服务的饮用水生产者、运输者或配送者。

爱沙尼亚

根据《公共采购法》(RT I 2001, 40, 224)第 5 条和《竞争法》(RT I 2001, 56 332)第 14 条经营的实体。

塞浦路斯

根据(城市和其他地区)《水供应法》第 350 章在城市和其他地区配送水的供水局。

2007 年 1 月 1 日 (WT/Let/556)

LATVIA

Public entities of local governments producing and distributing drinking water to the fixed networks intended to provide a service to the public.

LITHUANIA

Entities producing, transporting and distributing drinking water pursuant to the Lietuvos Respublikos geriamojo vandens įstatymas (Žin., 2001, Nr. 64-2327) and Lietuvos Respublikos vandens įstatymas (Žin., 1997, Nr. 104-2615) and being in compliance with the provisions of Lietuvos Respublikos viešųjų pirkimų įstatymas (Žin., 2002, Nr. 118-5296).

HUNGARY

Entities producing, transporting or distributing water pursuant to Act LVII of 1995 on water management (1995. évi LVII. törvény a vízgazdálkodásról).

MALTA

Korporazzjoni għas-Servizzi ta" l-Ilma (Water Services Corporation).

POLAND

Przedsiębiorstwa wodociągowo-kanalizacyjne w rozumieniu ustawy z dnia 7 czerwca 2001 r. o zbiorowym zaopatrzeniu w wodę i zbiorowym odprowadzaniu ścieków prowadzące działalność gospodarczą w zakresie zbiorowego zaopatrzenia w wodę lub zbiorowego odprowadzania ścieków. (Water-supply and sewage enterprises within the meaning of the Act of 7 June 2001 on the collective water supply and discharge of wastewater).

SLOVENIA

Podjetja, ki črpajo, izvajajo prenos ali dobavo pitne vode, skladno s koncesijskim aktom, izdanim na podlagi Zakona o varstvu okolja (Uradni list RS, 32/93, 1/96) in odloki občin. (Entities producing, transporting or distributing drinking water, in accordance with the concession act granted pursuant to the Environment Protection Act (Official Journal of the Republic of Slovenia, 32/93, 1/96) and the decisions issued by the municipalities).

SLOVAKIA

The procuring entity is defined in Article 3 §2 and §3 of Act No. 263/1999 Z. z. on Public Procurement, as amended, as a legal entity which deals in water management by producing and operating the public distribution of drinking water, operates public sewerage or sewage works (e.g. Západoslovenské vodárne a kanalizácie, Stredoslovenské vodárne a kanalizácie, Východoslovenské vodárne a kanalizácie).

拉脱维亚

向为公众提供服务的固定网络生产和配送饮用水的地方政府公共实体。

立陶宛

根据《立陶宛饮用水法》(2001 年，64-2327 号)和《立陶宛水法》(1997 年，104-2615 号)并符合《立陶宛公共采购法》(2002 年，118-5296 号)规定的生产、输送和配送饮用水的实体。

匈牙利

根据关于水资源管理的 1995 年 57 号法生产、输送或配送水的实体。

马耳他

水服务公司。

波兰

属 2001 年 6 月 7 日关于集中水供应和废水处理的法律意义的水供应和污水处理企业。

斯洛文尼亚

根据依照《环境保护法》(《斯洛文尼亚共和国公报》32/93、1/96 号)签署的特许法和各城市做出的决定，生产、输送或配送饮用水的实体。

斯洛伐克

经修订的 263/1999 Z. z.号关于政府采购的法律第 3.2 和 3.3 条将采购实体定义为，通过生产饮用水和经营饮用水的公共配送而从事水务管理的法律实体，或经营公共污水处理或污水处理工程的法律实体。(如西斯洛伐克自来水和管道公司、中斯洛伐克自来水和管道公司、东斯洛伐克自来水和管道公司)。

<u>2007 年 1 月 1 日 (WT/Let/556)</u>

BULGARIA

"В И К – Батак" – ЕООД, Батак
"В и К – Белово" – ЕООД, Белово
"Водоснабдяване и канализация Берковица" – ЕООД, Берковица
"Водоснабдяване и канализация" – ЕООД, Благоевград
"В и К – Бебреш" – ЕООД, Ботевград
"Инфрастрой" – ЕООД, Брацигово
"Водоснабдяване" – ЕООД, Брезник
"Водоснабдяване и канализация" – ЕАД, Бургас
"Бързийска вода" – ЕООД, Бързия
"Водоснабдяване и канализация" – ООД, Варна
"ВиК-Златни пясъци" – ООД, Варна
"Водоснабдяване и канализация Йовковци" – ООД, Велико Търново
"Водоснабдяване, канализация и териториален водоинженеринг" – ЕООД, Велинград
"ВИК" – ЕООД, Видин
"Водоснабдяване и канализация" – ООД, Враца
"В И К" – ООД, Габрово
"В И К" – ООД, Димитровград
"Водоснабдяване и канализация" – ЕООД, Добрич
"Водоснабдяване и канализация – Дупница" – ЕООД, Дупница
"Водоснабдяване и канализация" – ООД, Исперих
"В И К – Кресна" – ЕООД, Кресна
"Меден кладенец" – ЕООД, Кубрат
"ВИК" – ООД, Кърджали
"Водоснабдяване и канализация" – ООД, Кюстендил
"Водоснабдяване и канализация" – ООД, Ловеч
"В и К – Стримон" – ЕООД, Микрево
"Водоснабдяване и канализация" – ООД, Монтана
"Водоснабдяване и канализация – П" – ЕООД, Панагюрище
"Водоснабдяване и канализация" – ООД, Перник
"В И К" – ЕООД, Петрич
"Водоснабдяване, канализация и строителство" – ЕООД, Пещера
"Водоснабдяване и канализация" – ЕООД, Плевен
"Водоснабдяване и канализация" – ЕООД, Пловдив
"Водоснабдяване–Дунав" – ЕООД, Разград
"ВКТВ" – ЕООД, Ракитово
"Водоснабдяване и канализация" – ООД, Русе
"УВЕКС" – ЕООД, Сандански
"Водоснабдяване и канализация" – ЕАД, Свищов
"Бяла" – ЕООД, Севлиево
"Водоснабдяване и канализация" – ООД, Силистра
"В и К" – ООД, Сливен
"Водоснабдяване и канализация" – ЕООД, Смолян
"Софийска вода" – АД, София

保加利亚

巴塔市自来水和管道有限公司
别罗沃市自来水和管道有限公司
别尔科维察市自来水和管道有限公司
布拉格耶夫格勒市自来水和管道有限公司
鲍代夫市自来水和管道有限公司
博拉奇科沃市基础设施建设有限公司
博雷茨涅克市自来水有限公司
布尔加斯市自来水和管道有限公司
巴茨伊亚市自来水有限公司
瓦尔纳市自来水和管道有限公司
瓦尔纳市金沙滩自来水和管道有限公司
约夫克夫察市自来水和管道有限公司
维林格勒市自来水、管道和水利有限公司
维丁市自来水和管道有限公司
瓦尔纳市自来水和管道有限公司
加布罗沃市自来水和管道有限公司
迪米特洛夫格勒市自来水和管道有限公司
多布里奇市自来水和管道有限公司
多普尼察市自来水和管道有限公司
伊斯佩里市自来水和管道有限公司
克雷斯纳市自来水和管道有限公司
库布拉特市自来水和管道有限公司
卡得加里市自来水和管道有限公司
库斯腾迪尔市自来水和管道有限公司
洛维奇市自来水和管道有限公司
米克雷沃市自来水和管道有限公司
摩塔纳市自来水和管道有限公司
巴纳久里什泰市自来水和管道有限公司
佩罗尼克市自来水和管道有限公司
佩特里奇市自来水和管道有限公司
佩什代拉市自来水、管道和建筑公司
普列文市自来水和管道有限公司
普罗夫迪夫市自来水和管道有限公司
拉茨格勒市自来水有限公司
拉奇托沃市自来水有限公司
鲁塞市自来水和管道有限公司
桑丹斯基市自来水有限公司
斯维什托夫自来水和管道有限公司
塞夫列沃市自来水有限公司
斯列斯特拉市自来水和管道有限公司
斯列文自来水和管道有限公司
斯莫良自来水和管道有限公司
索非亚市自来水有限公司

"Водоснабдяване и канализация" – ЕООД, София
"Стамболово" – ЕООД, Стамболово
"Водоснабдяване и канализация" – ЕООД, Стара Загора
"Водоснабдяване и канализация-С" – ЕООД, Стрелча
"Водоснабдяване и канализация – Тетевен" – ЕООД, Тетевен
"В и К – Стенето" – ЕООД, Троян
"Водоснабдяване и канализация" – ООД, Търговище
"Водоснабдяване и канализация" – ЕООД, Хасково
"Водоснабдяване и канализация" – ООД, Шумен
"Водоснабдяване и канализация" – ЕООД, Ямбол

ROMANIA

Departamente ale autorităţilor locale şi companii care produc, transportă şi distribuie apă (departments of the local authorities and companies that produce, transport and distribute water):

- S.C. APA-C.T.T.A. S.A. Alba Iulia, Alba
- S.C. APA - C.T.T.A. Filiala Alba Iulia S.A., Alba-Iulia, Alba
- S.C. APA-C.T.T.A. S.A. Filiala Blaj, Blaj, Alba
- Compania de Apă Arad, Arad
- S.C. Aquaterm AG" 98 S.A. Curtea de Argeş, Argeş
- S.C APA Canal 2000 S.A. Piteşti, Argeş
- S.C.APA Canal S.A. Oneşti, Bacău
- Compania de Apă-Canal, Oradea, Bihor
- R.A.J.A. Aquabis Bistriţa, Bistriţa-Năsăud
- SC APA Grup SA Botoşani, Botoşani
- Compania de Apă, Braşov Braşov
- R.A. "APA", Brăila, Brăila
- SC Ecoaquasa Sucursala Călăraşi, Călăraşi, Călăraşi
- S.C. Compania de Apă Someş S.A., Cluj, Cluj-Napoca
- S.C. Aquasom S.A. Dej, Cluj
- Regia Autonomă Judeţeană de Apă, Constanţa, Constanţa
- R.A.G.C. Târgovişte, Dâmboviţa
- R.A. APA Craiova, Craiova, Dolj
- S.P. Apă-Canal S.A., Baileşti, Dolj
- R.A. Apei - Valea Jiului, Petroşani, Hunedoara
- S.C. Apa - Prod S.A. Deva, Hunedoara
- R.A.J.A.C. Iaşi, Iaşi
- Directia Apă-Canal, Paşcani, Iaşi
- Societatea Nationala a Apelor Minerale (SNAM)

索非亚市自来水和管道有限公司
斯坦博罗沃市自来水有限公司
旧扎果拉市自来水和管道有限公司
斯特雷特察市自来水和管道有限公司
台特文市自来水和管道有限公司
特罗扬市自来水和管道有限公司
塔尔戈维什泰自来水和管道有限公司
哈斯特沃市自来水和管道有限公司
舒门市自来水和管道有限公司
扬博尔市自来水和管道有限公司

罗马尼亚

生产、输送和配送水的地方政府部门和公司：

- 阿尔巴市阿尔巴尤利亚 C.T.T.A.水公司
- 阿尔巴市 C.T.T.A 水公司阿尔巴尤利亚分公司
- 阿尔巴市 C.T.T.A.水公司布拉日分公司
- 阿拉德县阿帕公司
- 阿尔杰什县库尔列什—德—阿尔杰什 Aquaterm AG" 98 公司
- 阿尔杰什县皮特什蒂水道 2000 公司
- 巴克乌县奥内什蒂水道公司
- 比霍尔县奥拉迪亚水道公司
- 比斯特里察—讷瑟乌德县 R.A.J.A. Aquabis 公司
- 博托沙尼县水集团公司
- 布勒依拉县水公司
- 布勒依拉县国营水公司
- 克勒拉什县 Ecoaquasa 分公司
- 克鲁日县克鲁日—纳波卡市克鲁日水公司
- 克鲁日县德日 Aquasom 公司
- 康斯坦察省水公司
- 登博维察县特尔戈维什特 R.A.G.C 公司
- 多尔日县克拉约瓦克拉约瓦水公司
- 多尔日县巴依雷什蒂水道公司
- 胡内多瓦拉县佩特罗香鹫谷水公司
- 胡内多瓦拉县德瓦水生产公司
- 雅西县雅西 RA.J.A.C 公司
- 雅西县帕什卡尼水道公司
- 国家矿泉水公司

ANNEX II

PRODUCTION, TRANSPORT OR DISTRIBUTION OF ELECTRICITY

BELGIUM

Entities producing, transporting or distributing electricity pursuant to *article 5: Des régies communales et intercommunales of the loi du 10 mars 1925 sur les distributions d'énergie électrique.*

Entities transporting or distributing electricity pursuant to *the loi relative aux intercommunales du 22 décembre 1986.*

EBES, Intercom, Unerg and other entities producing, transporting or distributing electricity and granted a concession for distribution pursuant to *article 8 - les concessions communales et intercommunales of the loi du 10 mars 1952 sur les distributions d'énergie électrique.*

The Société publique de production d'électricité (SPÉ).

DENMARK

Entities producing or transporting electricity on the basis of a licence pursuant to *§3, stk. 1, of the lov nr. 54 af 25. februar 1976 om elforsyning, jf. bekendtgørelse nr. 607 af 17.december 1976 om elforsyningslovens anvendelsesområde.*

Entities distributing electricity as defined *in §3, stk. 2, of the lov nr. 54 af 25. februar 1976 om elforsyning, jf. bekendtgørelse nr. 607 af 17. december 1976 om elforsyningslovens anvendelsesområde* and on the basis of authorizations for expropriation pursuant to *Articles 10 to 15 of the lov om elektriske stærkstrømsanlæg, jf lovbekendtgørelse nr. 669 af 28. december 1977.*

GERMANY

Entities producing, transporting or distributing electricity as defined *in §2 Absatz 2 of the Gesetz zur Förderung der Energiewirtschaft (Energiewirtschaftsgesetz) of 13 December 1935. Last modified by the Gesetz of 19 December 1977, and auto-production of electricity so far as this is covered by the field of application of the Directive pursuant to Article 2, paragraph 5.*

GREECE

Δημόσια Επιχείρηση Ηλεκτρισμού (Dimosia Epicheirisi Ilektrismoy) (Public Power Corporation) set up pursuant to the law 1468 of 2 August 1950 Περί ιδρύσεως Δημοσίας Επιχειρήσεως Ηλεκτρισμού (*Peri idryseos Dimosias Epicheiriseos Ilektrismoy)*, and operating pursuant *to the law 57/85:Δομή ρόλος και τρόπος διοίκησης και λειτουργίας της κοινωνικοποιημένης Δημόσιας Επιχείρησης Ηλεκτρισμού (Domi, rolos kai tropos dioksis kai leitoyrgias tis koinonikopoiimenis Dimosias Epicheiriseos Ilektrismoy).*

附录 2

电力的生产、输送或配送

比利时

根据 1925 年 3 月 10 日关于电力能源分配有关的市镇和市镇之间的管理法律第 5 条设立的生产、输送和配送电力的实体。

根据 1986 年 12 月 22 日关于市镇间事务的法律设立的生产、输送和配送电力的实体。

根据 1952 年 3 月 10 日与电力输送有关的法律第 8 条设立的 EBES 公司、Intercom 公司、Unerg 公司和其他生产、输送或配送电力并被授予特许经营权的实体。

国营电力生产公司。

丹麦

根据 1976 年 2 月 25 日 54 号关于电力供应的法律第 1 条第 3 款和 1976 年 12 月 17 日关于电力供应法适用范围的 607 号条例授予的许可生产或输送电力的实体。

根据 1976 年 2 月 25 日 54 号关于电力供应的法律第 2 条第 3 款、1976 年 12 月 17 日关于电力供应法适用范围的 607 号条例和 1977 年 12 月 28 日关于 669 号条例电力生产企业第 10 至 15 条所获得的授权，从事电力配送的实体。

德国

根据 1935 年 12 月 13 日颁布的《能源经济促进法》第 2 条第 2 款定义的生产、输送或配送电力的实体。经 1977 年 12 月 19 日最新修订的法律，并根据第 2 条第 5 款涵盖在本指令适用范围内的自动生产电力的实体。

希腊

根据 1950 年 8 月 2 日 1468 号关于建立公共电力事业的法律设立并根据 57/85 号关于管理和经营公共电力的法律进行经营的公共电力公司。

SPAIN

Entities producing, transporting or distributing electricity pursuant to *Article 1 of the Decreto de 12 de marzo de 1954, approving the Reglamento de verificaciones eléctricas y regularidad en el suministro de energía and pursuant to Decreto 2617/1966, de 20 de octubre, sobre autorizacíon administrativa en materia le instalaciones eléctricas.*

Red Eléctrica de España SA, set up pursuant to *Real Decreto 91/1985 de 23 de enero.*

FRANCE

Électricité de France, set up and operating pusuant to *the loi 46/6288 du 8 avril 1946 sur la nationalisation de l'éelectricité et du gaz.*

Entities (sociétés d'économie mixte or réegies) distributing electricity and referred to in *article 23 of the loi 48/1260 du 12 août 1948 portant modification des lois 46/6288 du 8 avril 1946 et 46/2298 du 21 octobre 1946 sur la nationalisation de l'électricitée et du gaz.*

Compagnie nationale du Rhône.

IRELAND

The Electricity Supply Board (ESB) set up and operating pursuant to *the Electricity Supply Act 1927.*

ITALY

Ente nazionale per l'energia elettrica set up pursuant to *legge n.. 1643, 6 dicembre 1962 approvato con Decreto n.1720, 21 dicembre 1965.*

Entities operating on the basis of a concession pursuant to *article 4, n.5 or 8 of legge 6 dicembre 1962, n.1643 - Istituzione dell'Ente nazionale per la energia elettrica e trasferimento ad esso delle imprese esercenti le industrie elettriche.*

Entities operating on the basis of concession pursuant to *article 20 of Decreto del Presidente delle Repubblica 18 marzo 1965, n. 342 norme integrative della legge 6 dicembre 1962, n. 1643 e norme relative al coordinamento e all'esercizio delle attività elettriche esercitate da enti ed imprese diverse dell'Ente nazionale per l'énergia elettrica.*

LUXEMBOURG

Compagnie grand-ducale d'électricité de Luxembourg, producing or distributing electricity pursuant to *the convention du 11 novembre 1927 concernant l'établissement et l'exploitation des réseaux de distribution d'énergie électrique dans le grand-duché du Luxembourg approuvée par la loi du 4 janvier 1928.*

Société électrique de l'Our (SEO).

Syndicat de Communes SIDOR.

西班牙

根据 1954 年 3 月 12 日颁布的《关于能源供给电力检查及监管规定》第 1 条，以及 1966 年 10 月 20 日颁布的 2617/1966 号关于电力设施原材料许可的法令，从事电力的生产、输送或配送的实体。

根据 1985 年 1 月 23 日颁布的 91/1985 号法令设立的西班牙电网公司。

法国

根据 1946 年 4 月 8 日 46/6288 号关于能源和煤气的国有化的法律建立和运营的法国电力公司。

根据 1946 年 4 月 8 日 46/6288 号与电力和煤气国有化有关的法律、1946 年 10 月 21 日 46/2298 号法律条文修改和 1948 年 8 月 12 日 48/1260 号法律条文第 23 款的配送电力的实体(公私合营公司或官营)。

罗讷省国营公司。

爱尔兰

根据《1927 年电力供应法》成立和经营的供电局。

意大利

根据 1962 年 12 月 6 日 1643 号法律、1965 年 12 月 21 日 1720 号法令批准设立的国营电力公司。

根据 1962 年 12 月 6 日 1643 号法律第 4 条第 5 或 8 段—国家电力研究所及经营电力工业的企业转让经营—获得特许经营权运营的实体。

根据 1965 年 3 月 18 日共和国 342 号总统令第 20 条，1962 年 12 月 6 日 1643 号法律附则中关于国家电力公司不同组织和公司电力活动的协调和运作的规定运营的实体。

卢森堡

根据由 1928 年 1 月 4 日法律批准的涉及到卢森堡大公国的电力能源配送网的建立和经营的 1927 年 11 月 11 日协议而成立的生产和配送电力的卢森堡电力公司。

法国兴业电气公司。

SIDOR 市镇联合会。

NETHERLANDS

Elektriciteitsproduktie Oost-Nederland.

Elektriciteitsbedrijf Utrecht-Noord-Holland-Amsterdam (UNA).

Elektriciteitsbedrijf Zuid-Holland (EZH)

Elektriciteitsproduktiemaatschappij Zuid-Nederland (EPZ).

Provinciale Zeeuwse Energie Maatschappij (PZEM).

Samenwerkende Elektriciteitsbedrijven (SEP).

Entities distributing electricity on the basis of a licence (vergunning) granted by the provincial authorities pursuant to the Provinciewet.

PORTUGAL

Electricidade de Portugal (EDP) , set up pursuant to the *Decreto-Lei no 502/76 de 30 de Junho de 1976.*

Entities distributing electricity pursuant to *artigo 1o do Decreto-Lei no 344-B/82 de 1 de Setembro de 1982, amended by Decreto-Lei no 297/86 de 19 de Setembro de 1986*. Entities producing electricity pursuant to *Decreto Lei no 189/88 de 27 de Maio de 1988.*

Independent producers of electricity pursuant to *Decreto Lei n o 189/88 de 27 de Maio de 1988.*

Empresa de Electricidade dos Açores - EDA, EP, created pursuant to the *Decreto Regional no 16/80 de 21 de Agosto de 1980.*

Empresa de Electricidade da Madeira, EP, created pursuant to the *Decreto-Lei no 12/74 de 17 de Janeiro de 1974 and regionalized pursuant to the Decreto-Lei no 31/79 de 24 de Fevereiro de 1979, Decreto-Lei no91/79 de 19 de Abril de 1979.*

UNITED KINGDOM

Central Electricity Generating (CEGB), and the Areas Electricity Boards producing, transporting or distributing electricity pursuant to the Electricity Act 1947 and the Electricity Act 1957.

The North of Scotland Hydro-Electricity Board (NSHB), producing, transporting and distributing electricity pursuant to the Electricity (Scotland) Act 1979.

The South of Scotland Electricity Board (SSEB) producing, transporting and distributing electricity pursuant to the Electricity (Scotland) Act 1979.

The Northern Ireland Electricity Service (NIES), set up pursuant to the Electricity Supply (Northern Ireland) Order 1972.

荷兰

东荷兰电力生产公司。

乌得勒支—北荷兰—阿姆斯特丹电力生产公司。

南荷兰电气公司。

南荷兰电力生产公司。

泽兰省能源协会。

合作电力公司。

由省级机关根据国家法律授予许可从事电力配送的实体。

葡萄牙

葡萄牙电力公司，根据 1976 年 6 月 30 日 502/76 号法令设立。

电力配送实体，根据 1982 年 9 月 1 日 344-B/82 号法令设立，该法令经 1986 年 9 月 19 日 297/86 号法令修订。电力生产实体，根据 1988 年 5 月 27 日 189/88 号法令设立。

独立电力生产商，根据 1988 年 5 月 27 日 189/88 号法令设立。

亚速尔群岛电力公司，根据 1980 年 8 月 21 日 16/80 号区域法令设立。

马德拉电力公司，根据 1974 年 1 月 17 日 12/74 号法令设立，并根据 1979 年 2 月 24 日 31/79 号法令和 1979 年 4 月 19 日 91/79 号法令进行区域管理。

英国

中央发电局或地方电力局，根据《1947 年电力法》和《1957 年电力法》生产、输送或配送电力。

北苏格兰水电局，根据《1979 年(苏格兰)电力法》生产、输送或配送电。

南苏格兰电力局，根据《1979 年(苏格兰)电力法》生产、输送或配送电力。

北爱尔兰电力局，根据 1972 年《(北爱尔兰)供电令》设立。

AUSTRIA

Entities producing, transporting or distributing electricity pursuant to *the second Verstaatlichungsgesetz (BGBl. Nr. 81/1947), and the Elektrizitätswirtschaftsgesetz (BGBl. Nr. 260/1975), including the Elektrizitätswirtschaftsgesetze of the nine Länder.*

FINLAND

Entities producing, transporting or distributing electricity on the basis of a concession pursuant to *Article 27 of Sähkoelaki (319/79) of 16 March 1979.*

SWEDEN

Entities which transport or distribute electricity on the basis of a concession pursuant to *lagen (1902:71 s. 1) innefattande vissa bestämmelser om elektriska anläggningar.*

CZECH REPUBLIC

The contracting authority is defined in section 2 b) of Act. No. 199/1994 Sb. on Public Procurement as České energetické závody, a.s. (Czech Power Works, producer) and 8 regional distribution companies: Středočeská energetická a.s. (Central-Bohemian Power Company), Východočeská energetická, a.s. (East-Bohemian Power Company), Severočeská energetická a.s. (North-Bohemian Power Company), Západočeská energetická, a.s. (West-Bohemian Power Company), Jihočeská a.s. (South-Bohemian Power Company), Pražské energetické závody, a.s. (Prague´s Power Works), Jihomoravská energetická, a.s. (South-Moravian Company), Severomoravská energetická, a.s. (North Moravian Power Company); these entities produce or transport electricity on the basis of the Energy Act No. 458/2000 Sb.

ESTONIA

Entities operating pursuant to Article 5 of the Public Procurement Act (RT I 2001, 40, 224) and Article 14 of the Competition Act (RT I 2001, 56 332).

CYPRUS

The Electricity Authority of Cyprus established by the Electricity Development Law, Cap. 171. (Η Αρχή Ηλεκτρισμού Κύπρου που εγκαθιδρύθηκε από τον περί Αναπτύξεως Ηλεκτρισμού Νόμο, Κεφ. 171).

LATVIA

Valsts akciju sabiedrība "Latvenergo" (State public limited liability company "Latvenergo").

奥地利

根据第 2 部《国有化法》(联邦法律公报 81/1947 号)和《电力经济法》(联邦法律公报 260/1975 号)，包括《9 联邦州电力经济法》，生产、输送或配送电力的实体。

芬兰

根据依据 1979 年 3 月 16 日 Sähkoelaki (319/79 号)第 27 条给予的特许经营权生产、输送或配送电力的实体。

瑞典

根据依据法律(1902:71 s.1 号)中包含的某些关于电力装置的条款给予的特许经营权的输送或配送电力的实体。

捷克

缔约实体如 199/1994 号关于公共政府采购的法律第 2 b)节中所定义，指捷克电厂(生产者)及 8 个地区配送公司：中捷克州电力股份公司、东捷克州电力股份公司、北捷克州电力股份公司、西捷克州电力股份公司、南捷克州电力股份公司、布拉格电厂、南摩拉维亚电力公司、北摩拉维亚电力公司，这些实体根据 458/2000 Sb 号《能源法》生产或输送电力。

爱沙尼亚

根据《公共采购法》(RT I 2001, 40, 224)第 5 条和《竞争法》(RT I 2001, 56 332)第 14 条经营的实体。

塞浦路斯

根据《电力发展法》第 171 章设立的塞浦路斯电力局。

拉脱维亚

Latvenergo 国有公共有限责任公司。

LITHUANIA

Entities producing, transporting or distributing electricity pursuant to the Lietuvos Respublikos elektros energetikos įstatymas (Žin., 2000, Nr. 66-1984) and being in compliance with the provisions of Lietuvos Respublikos viešuju pirkimų istatymas (Žin., 2002, Nr. 118-5296).
Valstybės įmonė Ignalinos atominė elektrinė (State Enterprise Ignalina Nuclear Power Plant) set up pursuant to the Lietuvos Respublikos branduolinės energijos įstatymas (Žin., 1996, Nr. 119-2771).

HUNGARY

Entities producing, transporting or distributing electricity on the basis of an authorisation pursuant to Act CX of 2001 on electricity (2001. évi CX. törvény a villamos energiáról).

MALTA

Korporazzjoni Enemalta (Enemalta Corporation).

POLAND

Przedsiębiorstwa energetyczne w rozumieniu ustawy z dnia 10 kwietnia 1997 r. Prawo energetyczne (Energy enterprises within the meaning of the Act of 10 April 1997 "Energy Law").

SLOVENIA

ELES- Elektro Slovenija, podjetja, ki proizvajajo električno energijo, skladno z Energetskim zakonom (Uradni list RS, 79/99), podjetja, ki izvajajo transport električne energije, skladno z Energetskim zakonom (Uradni list RS, 79/99), podjetja, ki dobavljajo električno energijo, skladno z Energetskim zakonom (Uradni list RS, 79/99) (ELES- Elektro Slovenija; entities producing, transporting or distributing electricity pursuant to the Energy Act (Official Journal of the Republic of Slovenia, 79/99)).

SLOVAKIA

The procuring entity is defined in Article 3 §2 and §3 of Act No. 263/1999 Z. z. on Public Procurement, as amended, as a legal entity which deals in energy sectors by generating, purchasing and distributing electricity and by transmitting electricity (Act No. 70/1998 Z. z. as amended – e.g. Slovenské elektrárne a.s., Regionálne rozvodné závody).

立陶宛

根据《立陶宛电力能源法》(2000 年，66-1984 号)生产、输送或配送电力、并符合《立陶宛公共采购法》(2002 年，118-5296 号)规定的实体。
根据《立陶宛核能源法》(1996 年， 119-2771 号)设立的立陶宛国家伊格纳林纳核电站。

匈牙利

根据依据 2001 年 110 号《电力法》的规定给予的授权生产、输送或配送电力的实体。

马耳他

马耳他能源公司。

波兰

属 1997 年 4 月 10 日《能源法》意义内的能源企业。

斯洛文尼亚

根据《能源法》(《斯洛文尼亚共和国公报》79/99 号)，斯洛文尼亚电力公司及生产、输送或配送电力的实体。

斯洛伐克

经修订的 263/1999 Z. z.号关于公共采购的法律第 3.2 和 3.3 条将采购实体定义为，通过生产、购买和配送电力以及输送电力而在能源部门经营的实体(经修订的 70/1998 Z. z.号法案，如斯洛伐克电力股份公司、地区电力输送公司)。

2007 年 1 月 1 日 (WT/Let/556)

BULGARIA

Лица, които притежават лицензия за производство, пренос, разпределение, обществена доставка или обществено снабдяване с електрическа енергия в съответствие с чл.39, ал.1 на Закона за енергетиката (обн., ДВ, бр.107/9.12.2003) (Entities licensed for production, transport, distribution, public delivery or public supply of electricity pursuant to Article 39(1) of the Law on Energy (published in State Gazette No 107/9.12.2003)) (Национална електрическа компания (НЕК) - National Electric Company (NEK)).

ROMANIA

– "Societatea Comercială de Producere a Energiei Electrice Hidroelectrica – SA Bucureşti" (Commercial Company for Electric Power Production Hidroelectrica – SA Bucureşti)
– "Societatea Naţională Nuclearelectrica – SA" (National Company Nuclaerectrica – SA)
– "Societatea Comercială de Producere a Energiei Electrice şi Termice Termoelectrica SA" (Commercial Company for Electric Power and Thermal Energy Production Termoelectrica SA)
– "S.C. Electrocentrale Deva SA" (SC Power Stations Deva SA)
– "S.C. Electrocentrale Bucureşti SA" (SC Power Stations Bucharest SA)
– "S.C. Electrocentrale Galaţi SA" (SC Power Stations Galati SA)
– "S.C. Electrocentrale Termoelectrica SA" (SC Power Stations Termoelectrica SA)
– "Societatea Comercială Complexul Energetic Rovinari" (Commercial Company Rovinari Energy Complex)
– "Societatea Comercială Complexul Energetic Turceni" (Commercial Company Turceni Energy Complex)
– "Societatea Comercială Complexul Energetic Craiova" (Commercial Company Craiova Energy Complex)
– "Compania Naţională de Transport a Energiei Electrice Transelectrica – SA Bucureşti" (National Power Grid Company Transelectrica SA)
– "Societatea Comercială de Distribuţie şi Furnizare a Energiei Electrice Electrica – SA Bucureşti" (Commercial Company for Electricity Distribution and Supply Electrica – SA Bucharest) :
    - S.C. Filiala de Distribuţie şi Furnizare a energiei electrice "Electrica BANAT" SA (Electricity Distribution and Supply Branch "Electrica BANAT" SA)
    - S.C. Filiala de Distribuţie şi Furnizare a energiei electrice "Electrica DOBROGEA" SA (Electricity Distribution and Supply Branch "Electrica DOBROGEA" SA SC)
    - S.C. Filiala de Distribuţie şi Furnizare a energiei electrice "Electrica MOLDOVA" SA (SC Electricity Distribution and Supply Branch "Electrica MOLDOVA" SA)
    - S.C. Filiala de Distribuţie şi Furnizare a energiei electrice "Electrica MUNTENIA SUD" SA (SC Electricity Distribution and Supply Branch "Electrica MUNTENIA SUD" SA)
    - S.C. Filiala de Distribuţie şi Furnizare a energiei electrice "Electrica MUNTENIA NORD" SA (SC Electricity Distribution and Supply Branch "Electrica MUNTENIA NORD" SA)
    - S.C. Filiala de Distribuţie şi Furnizare a energiei electrice "Electrica OLTENIA" SA (SC Electricity Distribution and Supply Branch "Electrica OLTENIA" SA)
    - S.C. Filiala de Distribuţie şi Furnizare a energiei electrice "Electrica TRANSILVANIA SUD" SA (SC Electricity Distribution and Supply Branch "Electrica TRANSILVANIA SUD" SA)
    - S.C. Filiala de Distribuţie şi Furnizare a energiei electrice "Electrica TRANSILVANIA NORD" SA" (SC Electricity Distribution and Supply Branch "Electrica TRANSILVANIA NORD" SA).

保加利亚

国家电力公司，根据 107/9.12.2003 号国家公报公布的《能源法》第 39(1)条获得许可生产、输送、配送、公开交付或公开供应电力的实体。

罗马尼亚

– 布加勒斯特水力发电商业公司
– 国家核电公司
– 电力和热能发电商业公司
– 德瓦商业发电站
– 布加勒斯特商业发电站
– 加拉茨商业发电站
– 电力和热能发电商业公司发电站
– 罗维纳里发电联合企业
– 图尔切尼发电联合企业
– 克拉约瓦发电联合企业
– 布加勒斯特电力输送公司
– 布加勒斯特电力配送和供应商业公司：
    - 巴纳特电力配送和供应分公司
    - 多布罗加电力配送和供应分公司
    - 摩尔多瓦电力配送和供应分公司
    - 蒙泰尼亚电力配送和供应分公司
    - 北蒙泰尼亚电力配送和供应分公司
    - 奥泰尼亚电力配送和供应分公司
    - 南兰西瓦尼亚电力配送和供应分公司
    - 北兰西瓦尼亚电力配送和供应分公司

2007 年 1 月 1 日 (WT/Let/556)

ANNEX VII

CONTRACTING ENTITIES IN THE FIELD OF URBAN RAILWAY, TRAMWAY, TROLLEYBUS OR BUS SERVICES

BELGIUM

Societé nationale des chemins de fer vicinaux (SNCV)/Nationale Maatschappij van Buurtspoorwegen (NMB)

Entities providing transport services to the public on the basis of a contract granted by SNCV pursuant to *Articles 16 and 21 of the arrêté du 30 déecembre 1946 relatif aux transports rémunérés de voyageurs par route effectuées par autobus et par autocars.*

Sociétée des transports intercommunaux de Bruxelles (STIB),

Maatschappij van het Intercommunaal Vervoer te Antwerpen (MIVA),

Maatschappij van het Intercommunaal Vervoer te Gent (MIVG),

Société des transports intercommunaux de Charleroi (STIC),

Société des transports intercommunaux de la région liégeoise (STIL),

Société des transports intercommunaux de l'agglomération verviétoise (STIAV), and other entities set up pursuant to *the loi relative à la création de sociétés de transports en commun urbains/Wet betreffende de oprichting van maatschappijen voor stedelijk gemeenschappelijk vervoer of 22 February 1962.*

Entities providing transport services to the public on the basis of a contract with STIB pursuant to *Article 10* or with other transport entities pursuant to *Article 11 of the arrêté royal 140 du 30 déecembre 1982 relatif aux mesures d'assainissement applicables à certains organismes d'intérêt public dépendant du ministère des communications.*

DENMARK

Danske Statsbaner (DSB)

Entities providing bus services to the public (almindelig rutekørsel) on the basis of an authorization pursuant to lov nr. 115 af 29 marts 1978 om buskørsel.

GERMANY

Entities providing, on the basis of an authorization, short-distance transport services to the public (Öffen tlichen Personennahverkehr) pursuant to *the Personenbeförderungsgesetz vom 21 März 1961, as last amended on 25 July 1989.*

附件 7

城市铁路、有轨电车、无轨电车或公共汽车服务领域中的缔约实体

比利时

国营郊区铁路国营公司。

根据国营郊区铁路国营公司依据 1946 年 12 月 30 日关于公共汽车和大客车旅客有偿运输法令第 16 和 21 条授予的合同、向向公众提供运输服务的实体。

布鲁塞尔市公交运输公司。

安特卫普市公交公司。

根特市公交公司。

沙勒鲁瓦市公交公司。

列日地区公交公司。

韦尔维耶公交公司，其他根据 1962 年 2 月 22 日关于城市运输公司设立的法律设立的实体。

根据依据 1982 年 12 月 30 日与关于隶属于交通部的某些公共利益机构的整顿措施的 140 号皇家法令第 10 条，与布鲁塞尔市公交运输公司签订有关合同向公众提供运输服务的实体，或是根据上述法令第 11 条的建立的其他实体。

丹麦

丹麦国家铁路。

根据依据 1978 年 3 月 29 日 115 号关于公共汽车运输的法律给予的授权向公众提供公共汽车服务的实体。

德国

根据依据 1961 年 5 月 21 日颁布并于 1989 年 7 月 25 日最新修订的《人员运输法》给予的授权，向公众提供公共短途运输服务的实体。

2007 年 1 月 1 日 (WT/Let/556)

GREECE

Ηλεκτροκίνητα Λεωφορεια Περιοχής Αθηνών–Πειραιώς (Ilektrokinita Leoforeia Periochis Athinon-Peiraios, Electric buses of the Athens - Piraeus area) operating pursuant to *decree 768/1970 and law 588/1977.*

ΗλεκτρικοίΣιδηρόδρομοι Αθηνών–Πειραιώς (Ilektrikoi Sidorodromoi Athinion-Peiraios, Athen-Piraeus electric railways) operating pursuant to *laws 352/1976 and 588/1977.*

Επιχείρηση Αστικών ΣυγκοινωνιώνEpicheirisi Ostikon Sygkoinion. (Enterprise of urban transport) operating pursuant to *law 588/1977.*

Κοινό Ταμείο Εισπράζεως Λεωφορείω Koino (Tameio Eisprazeos Leoforeion, Joint receipts fund of buses) operating pursuant to *decree 102/1973.*

ΡΟΔΑ (Δημοτική Επιχειίρηση Λεωφορείων Ρόδου) (Diomtiki Epicheirisi Leoforeion) Roda: Municipal bus enterprise in Rhodes.

Οργανισμός Αστικών Συγκοινωνιών Θεσσαλονίκης Organismos Astikon Sygkoinion Thessalonikis. (Urban transport organization of Thessaloniki) operating pursuant to *decree 3721/1957* and *law 716/1980.*

SPAIN

Entities providing transport services to the public pursuant to the *Ley de Régimen local.*

Corporacíon metropolitana de Madrid.

Corporacíon metropolitana de Barcelona.

Entities providing urban or inter-urban bus services to the public pursuant to *Articles 113 to 118 of the Ley de Ordenacíon de Transportes Terrestres de 31 de julio de 1987.*

Entities providing bus services to the public, pursuant to Article 71 of *the Ley de Ordinacíon de Transportes Terrestres de 31 de julio de 1987.*

FEVE, RENFE (or Empresa Nacional de Transportes de Viajeros por Carretera) providing bus services to the public pursuant to *the Disposiciones adicionales. Primera, de la Ley de Ordenacíon de Transportes Terrestres de 31 de julio de 1957.*

Entities providing bus services to the public pursuant to Disposiciones Transitorias, Tercera, *de la Ley de Ordenacíon de Transportes Terrestres de 31 de julio de 1957.*

希腊

雅典—比雷埃夫斯地区电动公共汽车，根据 768/1970 号令和 588/1977 号法律运营。

雅典—比雷埃夫斯电气铁路，根据 352/1976 号和 588/1977 号法律运营。

根据 588/1977 号法律经营的城市运输企业。

根据 102/1973 号令经营的公共汽车联合基金。

罗得市政公共汽车公司。

萨洛尼市港城市运输组织，根据 3721/1957 号令和 716/1980 号法律运营。

西班牙

根据地方政府法律提供运输服务的实体。

马德里地铁公司。

巴塞罗那地铁公司。

根据 1987 年 7 月 31 日颁布的《地面交通管理法》第 113-118 条向公众提供城际公共汽车服务的实体。

根据 1987 年 7 月 31 日颁布的《地面交通管理法》第 71 条向公众提供公共汽车服务的实体。

根据 1987 年 7 月 31 日颁布的《地面交通管理法》附件 1 的规定，向公众提供服务的西班牙窄轨铁路公司、西班牙国家铁路网公司(或西班牙国家公路客运公司)。

根据 1987 年 7 月 31 日颁布的《地面交通管理法》附件 3 的规定，向公众提供公共汽车服务的实体。

FRANCE

Entities providing transport services to the public pursuant to article 7-11 of *the loi no 82-1153 du 30 décembre 1982, transports intérieurs, orientation*.

Régie autonome des transports parisiens, Société nationale des chemins de fer français, APTR, and other entities providing transport services to the public on the basis of an *authorization granted by the syndicat des transports parisiens pursuant to the ordonnance de 1959 et ses décrets d'application relatifs à l'organisation des transports de voyageurs dans la réegion parisienne.*

IRELAND

Iarnrod Éiréann (Irish Rail).

Bus Éireann (Irish Bus).

Bus Átha Cliath (Dublin Bus).

Entities providing transport services to the public pursuant to the amended Road Transport Act 1932.

ITALY

Entities providing transport services of a concession pursuant *to Legge 28 settembre 1939, n. 1822 - Disciplina degli autoservizi di linea (autolinee per viaggiatori, bagagli e pacchi agricoli in regime di concessione all'industria privata) - Article 1 as modified by Article 45 of Decreto del Preisidente della Repubblica 28 giugno 1955, n. 771.*

Entities providing transport services to the public pursuant to *Article 1 (15) of Regio Decreto 15 ottobre 1925, n. 2578 - Approvazione del Testo unico della legge sull'assunzione diretta del pubblici servizi da parte dei comuni e delle province.*

Entities operating on the basis of a concession pursuant to *Article 242 or 255 of Regio Decreto 9 maggio 1912, n. 1447, che approva il Testo unico delle disposizioni di legge per le ferrovie concesse all'industria privata, le tramvie a trazione meccanica e gli automobili.*

Entities or local authorities operating on the basis of a concession pursuant to *Article 4 of Legge 14 giugno 1949, n. 410, concorso dello Stato per la riattivazione dei pubblici servizi di trasporto in concessione.*

Entities operating on the basis of a concession pursuant to *Article 14 of Legge 2 agosto 1952, n. 1221 - Provvedimenti per l'esercizio ed il potenziamento di ferrovie e di altre linee di trasporto in regime di concessione.*

LUXEMBOURG

Chemins de fer du Luxembourg (CFL).

Service communal des autobus municipaux de la ville de Luxembourg.

法国

根据 1982 年 12 月 30 日 82-1153 号法律中的第 7-11 条内部运输方计设立的向公众提供运输服务的实体。

巴黎交通运输自治管理公司、法国铁路国营公司、公路运输业联合会和根据巴黎运输联合会依据与巴黎地区的旅客运输组织有关的应用法令给予的授权设立的为公众提供运输服务的其他实体。

爱尔兰

爱尔兰铁路服务公司。

爱尔兰公共汽车服务公司。

都柏林公共汽车服务公司。

根据经修订的《1932 年道路运输法》向公众提供运输服务的实体。

意大利

根据依据 1939 年 9 月 28 日 1822 号的关于公共汽车服务纪律的法令(在私营产业特许经营体制内旅客公共汽车线路)第 1 条，经 1955 年 6 月 28 日 771 号共和国总统法令第 45 条修订，获得的特许经营权提供运输服务的实体。

根据 1925 年 10 月 15 日 2578 号地区法令—批准各省市直接使用公共服务的法律文本—第 1(15)条向公众提供运输服务的实体。

根据依据 1912 年 5 月 9 日 144 号法律第 242 或 255 条关于批准私有铁路、有轨电车和商业运营汽车的法律文本获得的特许经营权运营的实体。

根据依据 1949 年 6 月 14 日 410 号法律第 4 条关于恢复公共运输服务的国家竞争条款获得的特许经营权运营的实体或当地机构。

根据依据 1952 年 8 月 2 日 1221 号法律第 14 条关于铁路和其他运输路线运营和升级条款获得的特许经营权运营的实体。

卢森堡

卢森堡铁路。

卢森堡城市的市镇公共汽车的社区服务。

Transports intercommunaux du canton d'Esch-sur-Alzette (TICE).

Bus service undertakings operating pursuant to the reglement grand-ducal du 3 février 1978 concernant les conditions d'octroi des autorisations d'établissement et d'exploitation des services de transports routiers réguliers de personnes rémunérées.

NETHERLANDS

Entities providing transport services to the public pursuant to *Chapter II (Openbaar vervoer) of the Wet Personenvervoer van 12 maart 1987.*

PORTUGAL

Rodoviaria Nacional, EP.

Companhia Carris de ferro de Lisboa.

Metropolitano de Lisboa, EP.

Serviços de Transportes Colectivos do Porto.

Serviços Municipalizados de Transporte do Barreiro.

Serviços Municipalizados de Transporte de Aveiro.

Serviços Municipalizados de Transporte de Braga.

Serviços Municipalizados de Transporte de Coimbra.

Serviços Municipalizados de Transporte de Portalegre.

UNITED KINGDOM

Entities providing bus services to the public pursuant to the London Regional Transport Act 1984.

Glasgow Underground.

Greater Manchester Rapid Transit Company.

Docklands Light Railway.

London Underground Ltd.

British Railways Board.

Tyne and Wear Metro.

阿尔泽特河畔埃施县各市镇间共同拥有的交通运输。

根据依据 1978 年 2 月 3 日关于设立和从事旅客道路运输授权的条件的大公条例运营的公共汽车服务企业。

荷兰

根据 1987 年 3 月 12 日《客运法》第 2 章(运输部分)向公众提供运输服务的实体。

葡萄牙

葡萄牙国营巴士

里斯本公路和轮渡运输网

里斯本地铁

波尔图公交网

巴雷鲁地方运输管理机构

阿维罗当地运输管理机构

布拉加当地运输管理机构

科英布拉当地运输管理机构

波塔格莱雷区当地运输管理机构

英国

根据 1984 年《伦敦地区运输法》向公众提供公共汽车服务的实体

格拉斯哥地铁网

大曼彻斯特捷运公司

伦敦港区轻轨

伦敦地铁有限公司

英国铁路局

泰恩—威尔地铁

2007 年 1 月 1 日 (WT/Let/556)

AUSTRIA

Entities providing transport services pursuant *to the Eisenbahngesetz 1957 (BGBl. Nr. 60/1957) and the Kraftfahrliniengesetz 1952 (BGBl. Nr. 84/1952*).

FINLAND

Public or private entities operating bus services according to *"Laki (343/91) luvanvaraisesta henkilöliikenteestae tiellä" and Helsingin kaupungin liikennelaitos/Helsingfors stads trafikverk (Helsinki Transport Board*), which provides metro and tramway services to the public.

SWEDEN

Entities operating urban railway or tramway services according to *lagen (1978:438) om huvudmannaskap för viss kollektiv persontrafik and lagen (1990:1157) om jaernvägssäkerhet*. Public or private entities operating a trolley bus or bus service in accordance with the *lagen (1978:438) om huvudmannaskap för viss kollektiv persontrafik and lagen (1983:293) om yrkestrafik.*

CZECH REPUBLIC

Any operator of public transport systems and providers of services to the public in rail, tramway, trolleybus or bus transport (section 2 b) of Act No. 199/1994 Sb. on Public Procurement).

ESTONIA

Entities operating pursuant to Article 5 of the Public Procurement Act (RT I 2001, 40, 224) and Article 14 of the Competition Act (RT I 2001, 56 332).

LATVIA

Public entities which provide passenger transportation services in the following cities by bus, trolleybus, tram: Rīga, Jūrmala, Liepāja, Daugavpils, Jelgava, Rēzekne, Ventspils.

LITHUANIA

Entities providing urban trolleybus, bus or cable services to the public i accordance with the Lietuvos Respublikos kelių transporto kodeksas (Žin., 1996, Nr. 119-2772) and being in compliance with the provisions of Lietuvos Respublikos viešųjų pirkimų įstatymas (Žin., 2002, Nr. 118-5296).

HUNGARY

Entities providing road transport services to the public on the basis of Act I of 1988 on road transport (1988. évi I. törvény a közúti közlekedésről) and on the basis of an authorisation pursuant to Decree No 89/1988. (XII. 20.) MT of the Council of Ministers on road transport services and on operation of road vehicles (89/1988. (XII. 20.) MT rendelet a közúti közlekedési szolgáltatásokról és a közúti járművek üzemben tartásáról).

奥地利

根据《1957 年铁路法》(联邦法律公报 60/1957 号)和《1952 年动力运营线路法》(联邦法律公报 84/1952 号)提供运输服务的实体。

芬兰

根据《道路运输许可法》(343/91 号)提供公共汽车服务的公共或私营实体，及向公众提供地铁和有轨电车服务的赫尔辛基运输局。

瑞典

根据《公共客运所有权法》(1978:438 号)和《铁路安全法》 (1990:1157 号)经营城市铁路或有轨电车服务的实体。根据《公共客运所有权法》(1978:438 号)和《专业交通法》(1983:293 号)经营无轨电车或公共汽车服务的公共或私人实体。

捷克

根据第 199/1994 Sb.关于公共采购的法令第 2 b 节，公共交通系统的任何运营商及向公众提供铁路、有轨电车、无轨电车或公共汽车服务的提供商。

爱沙尼亚

根据《公共采购法》(RT I 2001, 40, 224)第 5 条和《竞争法》(RT I 2001, 56 332)第 14 条运营的实体。

拉脱维亚

在下列城市通过公共汽车、无轨电车、有轨电车提供客运服务的公共实体：里加、朱马拉、利耶帕亚、陶格夫匹尔斯、叶尔加瓦、雷泽克内、文茨皮尔斯。

立陶宛

根据《立陶宛道路交通法》(1996 年，119-2772 号) 并以符合《立陶宛公共采购法》(2002 年， 118-5296 号)规定的方式，提供城市无轨电车、公共汽车或缆车服务的实体。

匈牙利

根据 1988 年关于道路运输的 1 号法律并根据依据部长理事会 89/1988 号关于道路运输服务和道路车辆运营的法令给予的授权，向公众提供道路运输服务的实体。

Entities providing railway transport services to the public on the basis of Act XCV of 1993 on railways (1993. évi XCV. törvény a vasútról) and on the basis of an authorisation pursuant to Decree No 15/2002. (II. 27.) KöViM of the Minister of Transport and Water Management on licensing of railway undertakings (15/2002. (II. 27.) KöViM rendelet a vasútvállallatok működésének engedélyezéséről).

MALTA

L-Awtorita` dwar it-Trasport ta' Malta (Malta Transport Authority).

POLAND

Podmioty świadczące usługi w zakresie miejskiego transportu kolejowego, działające na podstawie koncesji wydanej zgodnie z ustawą z dnia 27 czerwca 1997 r. o transporcie kolejowym (Dz.U. Nr 96, poz.591 ze zm.).(Entities providing services in the field of urban railway transport, acting on the basis of the Act of 27 June 1997 on railway transport (Dz. U. Nr 96, poz. 591 as amended).

Podmioty świadczące usługi dla ludności w zakresie miejskiego transportu autobusowego działające na podstawie zezwolenia zgodnie z ustawą z dnia 6 września 2001 r. o transporcie drogowym (Dz.U.Nr 125, poz. 1371 ze zm.) oraz podmioty świadczące usługi dla ludności w zakresie miejskiego transportu (Entities providing services for the public in the field of urban bus transport, acting on the basis of the licence issued under the Act of 6 September 2001 on road transport (Dz. U. Nr 125, poz. 1371 as amended) and entities providing service for the public in the field of urban transport.

SLOVENIA

Podjetja, ki opravljajo javni mestni avtobusni prevoz, skladno z Zakonom o prevozih v cestnem prometu (Uradni list RS, 72/94, 54/96, 48/98 in 65/99).(Companies providing public urban bus transport in accordance with Road Transport Traffic Act (Official Gazette of the Republic of Slovenia, nos. 72/94, 54/96, 48/98 and 65/99)).

SLOVAKIA

The procuring entity is defined in Article 3 §2 and §3 of Act No. 263/1999 Z. z. on Public Procurement, as amended, as a legal entity which deals in road transport, by operating scheduled public bus transport, and transport on the railways (Act No. 164/1996 Z. z. as amended, Act No. 168/1996 Z. z. as amended – e.g.
Železnice Slovenskej republiky /ŽSR/
Železničná spoločnosť a.s.
Dopravný podnik Bratislava, a.s.
Dopravný podnik mesta Žiliny, a.s.
Dopravný podnik mesta Prešov, a.s.
Dopravný podnik mesta Košíc, a.s.
Banskobystrická dopravná spoločnosť, a.s.).

根据依据交通和水利部关于铁路企业许可的 15/2002 号令给予的授权，并根据 1993 年 95 号关于铁路的法律，向公众提供铁路运输服务的实体。

马耳他

马耳他运输管理局

波兰

根据经修订的 1997 年 6 月 27 日关于铁路运输的法律(Dz. U. Nr 96, poz. 591)，在城市铁路运输领域提供服务的实体。

根据依据经修订的 2001 年 9 月 6 日关于道路运输的法律(Dz. U. Nr 125, poz. 1371)给予的许可，在城市公共汽车领域向公众提供服务的实体，以及在城市运输领域向公众提供服务的实体。

斯洛文尼亚

根据《道路运输交通法》(《斯洛文尼亚共和国公报》72/94、54/96、48/98 和 65/99 号)提供城市公共汽车运输服务的公司。

斯洛伐克

经修订的 263/1999 Z. z.号关于公共采购的法律第 3.2 和 3.3 条将采购实体定义为，通过按照时刻表经营公共汽车运输和铁路运输而从事道路运输的法律实体(经 164/1996 Z. z.号法和 168/1996 Z. z.号修订，例如：
斯洛伐克铁路局
斯洛伐克铁路股份公司
布拉迪斯拉发运输股份公司
日利纳运输股份公司
普雷绍夫运输股份公司
科希策运输股份公司
班斯卡—比斯特里察运输股份公司)。

BULGARIA

"Метрополитен" ЕАД София,
"Столичен електротранспорт" ЕАД София,
"Столичен автотранспорт" ЕАД, София,
"Бургасбус" ЕООД, Бургас,
"Градски транспорт" ЕАД, Варна,
"Тролейбусен транспорт" ЕООД, Враца,
"Общински пътнически транспорт" ЕООД, Габрово,
"Автобусен транспорт" ЕООД, Добрич,
"Тролейбусен транспорт" ЕООД, Добрич,
"Тролейбусен транспорт" ЕООД, Пазарджик,
"Тролейбусен транспорт" ЕООД, Перник,
"Автобусни превози" ЕАД, Плевен,
"Тролейбусен транспорт" ЕООД, Плевен,
"Градски транспорт Пловдив" ЕАД, Пловдив,
"Градски транспорт" ЕООД, Русе,
"Пътнически превози" ЕАД, Сливен,
"Автобусни превози" ЕООД, Стара Загора,
"Тролейбусен транспорт" ЕООД, Хасково.

ROMANIA

SC Transport cu Metroul Bucureşti "METROREX" SA (Bucharest Subway Transport Company "Metrorex" SA),
Regii autonome locale de transport urban de călători (local independent urban passenger transport operators)".

保加利亚

索非亚市地铁有限公司
索非亚市电力配送有限公司
索非亚市汽车运输有限公司
布尔加斯市“布尔加斯巴士”有限公司
瓦尔纳市城市交通有限公司
瓦尔纳市无轨电车运输有限公司
加布罗沃市市政公共交通有限公司
多布里奇市巴士交通有限公司
多布里奇市无轨电车运输有限公司
帕察勒德耶克市无轨电车运输有限公司
佩罗尼克市无轨电车运输有限公司
普列文巴士交通有限公司
普列文巴士无轨电车运输有限公司
普罗夫迪夫市城际交通有限公司
鲁塞市城际交通有限公司
斯列文公共交通运输有限公司
旧扎果拉果市巴士交通有限公司
哈斯科沃市无轨电车运输有限公司

罗马尼亚

布加勒斯特地铁运输公司
地方城市客运独立运营商

ANNEX VIII

CONTRACTING ENTITIES IN THE FIELD OF AIRPORT FACILITIES

BELGIUM

Régie des voies aériennes set up pursuant to the *arrêté-loi du 20 novembre 1946 portant création de la réegie des voies aéeriennes amended by arrCetBe royal du 5 octobre 1970 portant refonte du statut de la régle des voies aériennes.*

DENMARK

Airports operating on the basis of an authorization pursuant to *§ 55, stk. 1, lov om luftfart, jf. lovbekendtgørelse nr. 408 af 11. september 1985.*

GERMANY

Airports as defined *in Article 38 Absatz 2 no of the Luftverkehrszulassungsordnung vom 19 März 1979, as last amended by the Verordnung vom 21 Juli 1986.*

GREECE

Airports operating pursuant to law 517/1931 setting up the civil aviation service Υπηρεσία Πολιτικής Αεροπορίας(ΥΠΑ)(Ypiresia Politikis Aeroporias (YPA)).

International airports operating pursuant to *presidential decree 647/981.*

SPAIN

Airports managed by Aeropuertos Nacionales operating pursuant to *the Real Decreto 278/1982 de 15 de octubre de 1982.*

FRANCE

Aéroports de Paris operating pursuant *to titre V, articles L 251-1 à 252-1 du code de l'aviation civile.*

Aéroport de Bâle - Mulhouse, set up pursuant *to the convention franco-suisse du 4 juillet 1949.*

Airports as defined *in article L 270-1, code de l'aviation civile.*

Airports operating pursuant to *the cahier de charges type d'une concession d'aéroport, décret du 6 mai 1955.*

Airports operating on the basis of a convention d'exploitation pursuant to *article L/221, code de l'aviation civile.*

附录 8

机场设施领域的缔约实体

比利时

根据 1946 年 11 月 20 日关于航空航线管理的法律—法令(包含 1970 年 10 月 5 日关于航空航线管理的修订法令有关内容)进行航空路线的管理。

丹麦

根据依据 1985 年 9 月 11 日 408 号《航空法》第 55 条第 1 款给予的授权运营的机场。

德国

根据 1979 年 3 月 19 日颁布、1986 年 7 月 21 日最新修订的《航空许可条例》第 38 条第 2 款定义的机场。

希腊

根据 517/1931 号关于民用航空管理局设立民航服务的法律进行运营的机场。

根据 647/981 号总统令运营的国际机场。

西班牙

根据 1982 年 10 月 15 日颁布的 278/1982 号法令由国家机场管理部门管理的机场。

法国

根据《民航法典》L 251-1 至 252-1 条标题 5 运营的巴黎机场。

根据 1949 年 7 月 4 日法国—瑞士协议设立的巴莱—米卢斯机场。

《民航法典》L 270-1 条定义的机场。

根据依据 1955 年 5 月 6 日法令给予的特许经营权运营的机场。

根据依照《民航法典》L/221 条签订的协议运营的机场。

2007 年 1 月 1 日 (WT/Let/556)

IRELAND

Airports of Dublin, Cork and Shannon managed by Aer Rianta - Irish Airports.

Airports operating on the basis of a Public use License granted, pursuant to *the Air Navigation and Transport Act No 23 1936, the Transport Fuel and Power Transfer of Departmental, Administration and Ministerial Functions Order 1959 (SI No 125 of 1959) and the Air Navigation (Aerodromes and Visual Ground Aids) Order 1970 (SI No 291 of 1970).*

ITALY

Civil Stat. airports (aerodroal civili istituiti dallo Stato referred to in *Article 692 of the Codice della navigazione, Regio Decreto 30 marzo 1942, n. 327.*

Entities operating airport facilities on the basis of a concession granted pursuant to *Article 694 of the Codice della navigazione, Regio Decreto 30 marzo 1942, n. 327.*

LUXEMBOURG

Aéroport de Findel.

NETHERLANDS

Airports operating pursuant to Articles 18 and following of *the Luchtvaartwet of 15 January 1958, amended on 7 June 1978.*

PORTUGAL

Airports managed by Aeroportos de Navegaçao Aérea (ANA), EP pursuant to *Decreto-Lei no 246/79.*

Aeroporto do Funchal and Aeroporto de Porto Santo, regionalized pursuant to the *Decreto-Lei no 284/81.*

UNITED KINGDOM

Airports managed by British Airports Authority plc.

Airports which are public limited companies (plc) pursuant to the Airports Act 1986.

FINLAND

Airports managed by "Ilmailulaitos/Luftfartsverket" pursuant to *Ilmailulaki (595/64).*

SWEDEN

Publicly owned and operated airports in accordance with *lagen (1957:297) om luftfart.*

Privately owned and operated airports with an exploitation permit under the act, where this permit corresponds to the criteria of Article 2 (3) of the Directive.';

爱尔兰

由爱尔兰机场管理局管理的都柏林、科克和香农机场。.

根据依据 1936 年 23 号《空中导航和运输法》、1959 年《运输、燃料和权利(部门管理和部门职能移交》令(SI1959 年 125 号)以及 1970 年《空中导航令》(航空站和可视地面辅助设备)(1970 年 SI 291 号)给予的公共使用许可运营的机场。

意大利

根据 1942 年 3 月 30 日 327 号皇家法令《航空法》第 692 条所指的民用机场。

根据依据 1942 年 3 月 30 日 327 号皇家法令《航空法》第 694 条授予的特许经营权经营机场设施的实体。

卢森堡

芬德尔机场

荷兰

根据 1958 年 1 月 15 日颁布、1978 年 6 月 7 日修订的《航空法》第 18 条规定运营的机场。

葡萄牙

根据 246/79 号法令规定由机场管理公司管理的机场。

根据 284/81 号法令规定的丰沙尔机场和圣港岛地区机场。

英国

英国机场管理局公共有限公司管理的机场。

根据 1986 年《机场法》属公共有限责任公司的机场。

芬兰

根据《民航法》(595/64 号)规定由民航/航空局管理的机场。

瑞典

根据《航空法》(1957:297 号)规定的公有和运营的机场。

持有法案项下的使用许可的私有和运营的机场，该许可对应指令第 2 (3)条的标准。

2007 年 1 月 1 日 (WT/Let/556)

CZECH REPUBLIC

Operators of airports (section 2 b) of Act No. 199/1994 Sb. on Public Procurement).

ESTONIA

Entities operating pursuant to Article 5 of the Public Procurement Act (RT I 2001, 40, 224) and Article 14 of the Competition Act (RT I 2001, 56 332).

LATVIA

Valsts akciju sabiedrība "Latvijas gaisa satiksme" (State public limited liability company "Latvijas gaisa satiksme").
Valsts akciju sabiedrība ""Starptautiskā lidosta "Rīga"" (State public limited liability company "International airport "Rīga"").

LITHUANIA

Airports operating pursuant to the Lietuvos Respublikos aviacijos įstatymas (Žin., 2000, Nr. 94-2918) and Lietuvos Respublikos civilinės aviacijos įstatymas (Žin., 2000, Nr 66-1983).
Valstybės įmonė "Oro navigacija" (state enterprise "Oro navigacija") operating pursuant to the Lietuvos Respublikos aviacijos įstatymas (Žin., 2000, Nr. 94-2918) and Lietuvos Respublikos civilinės aviacijos įstatymas (Žin., 2000, Nr. 66-1983).
Other entities operating in the field of airport facilities and being in compliance with the provisions of Lietuvos Respublikos viešųjų pirkimų įstatymas (Žin., 2002, Nr. 118-5296).

HUNGARY

Airports operating on the basis of an authorisation pursuant to Act XCVII of 1995 on air traffic (1995. évi XCVII. törvény a légiközlekedésről).
Budapest Ferihegy International Airport managed by the Budapest Ferihegy International Airport Operator Plc. (Budapest Ferihegy Nemzetközi Repülőtér managed by Budapest Ferihegy Nemzetközi Repülőtér Üzemeltetési Rt.) on the basis of Act XVI of 1991 on concessions (1991. évi XVI. törvény a koncesszióról), Act XCVII of 1995 on air traffic (1995. évi XCVII. törvény a légiközlekedésről), Decree No 45/2001. (XII. 20.) KöViM of the Minister of Transport and Water Management on winding-up the Air Traffic and Airport Administration and establishing HungaroControl Hungarian Air Navigation Services (45/2001. (XII. 20.) KöViM rendelet a Légiforgalmi és Repülőtéri Igazgatóság megszüntetéséről és a HungaroControl Magyar Légiforgalmi Szolgálat létrehozásáról).

MALTA

L-Ajruport Internazzjonali ta" Malta (Malta International Airport).

POLAND

Przedsiębiorstwo Państwowe "Porty Lotnicze" (the state enterprise "Polish Airports").

捷克

199/1994 号关于公共政府采购的法律第 2 b 节中项下的机场运营商。

爱沙尼亚

根据《公共采购法》(RT I 2001, 40, 224)第 5 条和《竞争法》(RT I 2001, 56 332)第 14 条经营的实体。

拉脱维亚

拉脱维亚航空公共有限责任公司
里加国际机场公共有限责任公司

立陶宛

根据《立陶宛航空法》(2000 年，94-2918 号) 和《立陶宛商用航空法》(2000 年，66-1983 号)运营的机场。
根据《立陶宛航空法》(2000 年，94-2918 号) 和《立陶宛商用航空法》(2000 年，66-1983 号)运营的立陶宛国家航空公司。
符合《立陶宛公共采购法》(2002 年，118-5296 号)规定、在机场设施领域运营的其他实体。

匈牙利

根据依据 1995 年 97 号《空中交通法》获得的授权运营的机场。
布达佩斯费里海吉国际机场运营公共有限公司根据 1991 年 16 号关于特许经营权的法律、1995 年 97 号关于空中交通的法律、交通和水利部关于空中交通管制和机场管理以及关于建立匈牙利航空服务公司的 45/2001 号令管理的布达佩斯费里海吉国际机场。

马耳他

马耳他国际机场

波兰

国有企业波兰机场

SLOVENIA

Javna civilna letališča, skladno z Zakonom o letalstvu (Uradni list RS, 18/01). Public civil airports that operate in accordance with Civil Aviation Act (Official Gazette of the Republic of Slovenia, no. 18/01).

SLOVAKIA

The procuring entity is defined in Article 3 §2 and §3 of Act No. 263/1999 Z. z. on Public Procurement, as amended, as a legal entity which deals in civil aviation by establishing and operating public airports and ground aviation facilities (Act No. 143/1998 Z.z. as amended – e.g. Airports – Letisko M.R. Štefánika, Letisko Košice – Barca, Letisko Poprad – Tatry, Letisko Sliač, Letisko Piešťany – managed by Slovenská správa letísk /Slovak Airports Administration/ and operating on the basis of a licence issued by Ministry of Transport, Posts and Telecommunications of the Slovak Republic pursuant to § 32 Act No. 143/1998 Z. z. on Civil Aviation).

BULGARIA

– Главна дирекция "Гражданска въздухоплавателна администрация" (General Directorate "Civil Aviation Administration")
– ДП "Ръководство на въздушното движение"
– Летищни оператори на граждански летища за обществено ползване, определени от Министерския съвет в съответствие с чл.43, ал.3 на Закона на гражданското въздухоплаване (обн., ДВ, бр.94/1.12.1972) (Airport operators of civil airports for public use determined by the Council of Ministers pursuant to Article 43(3) of the Civil Aviation Law (published in State Gazette No 94/1.12.1972):

ROMANIA

– Compania Naţională "Aeroportul Internaţional Henri Coandă Bucureşti" – SA (National Company "International Airport Henri Coandă Bucharest" – SA)
– Societatea Naţională "Aeroportul Internaţional Bucureşti – Băneasa" – SA (National Company "International Airport Bucharest – Baneasa" – SA)
– Societatea Naţională "Aeroportul Internaţional Constanţa" – SA (National Company "International Airport Constanţa" – SA)
– Societatea Naţională "Aeroportul Internaţional Timişoara – Traian Vuia" – SA (National Company "International Airport Timişoara – Traian Vuia" – SA)
– Regia Autonomă "Administraţia Română a Serviciilor de Trafic Aerian – ROMATSA" (Autonomous Regie "Romanian Air Traffic Services Administration - ROMATSA")
– Regia Autonomă "Autoritatea Aeronautică Civilă Română" (Autonomous Regie "Romanian Civil Aviation Authority")

斯洛文尼亚

根据《民航法》(《斯洛文尼亚共和国公报》18/01 号)运营的公共民用机场。

斯洛伐克

经修订的 263/1999 Z. z.号关于公共采购的法律第 3.2 和 3.3 条将采购实体定义为，通过建立和运营公共机场和地面航空设施从事民航业务的法律实体。（经修订的 143/1998 Z.z.号法案，如斯洛伐克民航局/斯洛伐克机场管理局管理、并根据运输、邮政和电信部依据 143/1998 Z. z.号《民航法》第 32 条授予的许可运营的什捷法尼克机场、科希策机场、波普拉德机场、斯里阿奇机场和皮耶什佳尼机场)。

保加利亚

- 保加利亚民航总局。
- 保加利亚空中管理局。
- 部长会议根据 94/1.12.1972 号国家公报发布的《民航法》第 43(3)条指定用于公共用途的民用机场的机场运营商。

罗马尼亚

- 国企—布加勒斯特亨利康达国际机场
- 国企—布加勒斯特—伯尼亚萨国际机场
- 国企—康斯坦察国际机场
- 国企—蒂米什瓦拉—特拉扬武亚国际机场
- 罗马尼亚空中交通服务管理局
- 罗马尼亚民用航空管理局

– Aeroporturile aflate în subordinea consiliilor locale (The airports subordinate to Local Councils) :
  - Regia Autonomă Aeroportul Arad (Autonomous Regie Arad Airport)
  - Regia Autonomă Aeroportul Bacău (Autonomous Regie Bacău Airport)
  - Regia Autonomă Aeroportul Baia Mare (Autonomous Regie Baia Mare Airport)
  - Regia Autonomă Aeroportul Caransebeş (Autonomous Regie Caransebeş Airport)
  - Regia Autonomă Aeroportul Cluj-Napoca (Autonomous Regie Cluj - Napoca Airport)
  - Regia Autonomă Aeroportul Craiova (Autonomous Regie Craiova Airport)
  - Regia Autonomă Aeroportul Iaşi (Autonomous Regie Iaşi Airport)
  - Regia Autonomă Aeroportul Oradea (Autonomous Regie Oradea Airport)
  - Regia Autonomă Aeroportul Satu-Mare (Autonomous Regie Satu - Mare Airport)
  - Regia Autonomă Aeroportul Sibiu (Autonomous Regie Sibiu Airport)
  - Regia Autonomă Aeroportul Suceava (Autonomous Regie Suceava Airport)
  - Regia Autonomă Aeroportul Târgu Mureş (Autonomous Regie Târgu Mureş Airport)
  - Regia Autonomă Aeroportul Tulcea (Autonomous Regie Tulcea Airport).

- 地方理事会管理的机场：
  - 阿拉德机场
  - 巴克乌机场
  - 巴亚马雷机场
  - 卡兰塞贝什机场
  - 克卢日—纳波卡机场
  - 克拉约瓦机场
  - 雅西机场
  - 奥拉迪亚机场
  - 萨图—马雷机场
  - 锡比乌机场
  - 苏恰瓦机场
  - 特尔古穆列什机场
  - 图尔恰机场

ANNEX IX

CONTRACTING ENTITIES IN THE FIELD OF MARITIME OR INLAND PORT OR OTHER TERMINAL FACILITIES

BELGIUM

- Société anonyme du canal et des installations maritimes de Bruxelles.
- Port autonome de Liége.
- Port autonome de Namur.
- Port autonome de Charleroi.
- Port de la ville de Gand.
- La Compagnie des installations maritimes de Bruges - Maatschappij der Brugse haveninrichtingen.
- Société intercommunale de la rive gauche de l'Escaut - Intercommunale maatschappij van de linker Scheldeoever (Port d'Anvers).
- Port de Nieuwport.
- Port d'Ostende.

DENMARK

- Ports as defined in *Article 1, I to III of the bekendtgyrelse nr. 604 af 16 december 1985 om hvilke havne der er omfattet af lov om trafikhavne, jf. lov nr. 239 af 12 maj 1976 om trafikhavne.*

GERMANY

- Seaports owned totally or partially by territorial authorities (Länder, Kreise, Gemeinden).
- Inland ports subject to *the Hafenordnung pursuant to the Wassergesetze der Länder*.

GREECE

- Οργαυισμός Λψένος Πειραιώς Piraeus port (Organismos Limenos Peiraios) set up pursuant to *Emergency Law 1559/1950 and Law 1630/1951.*
- Οργαυισμός Λψένος Θεσαλονίκης Thessaloniki port (Organismos Limenos Thessalonikis) set up pursuant to *decree N.A. 2251/1953.*

附件 9

海港、内河港或其他港口设施领域的缔约实体

比利时

- 布鲁塞尔运河和海运设施股份有限公司
- 列日自治港
- 那慕尔自治港
- 沙勒鲁瓦自治港
- 根特港
- 布鲁日海运设施公司
- 斯凯尔特河左岸各市镇间共有公司
- 尼尔波特港
- 奥斯坦德港

丹麦

- 港口如 1976 年 5 月 12 日 239 号法令《运输港口法》和 1985 月 12 月 16 日《关于<运输港口法>涉及港口的决议》第 1 条第 1 至 3 部分所定义。

德国

- (州、县、乡镇)地方政府机构全部或部分拥有的海港。
- 根据各州《水法》、受《港口条例》管辖的内河港。

希腊

- 根据 1559/1950 号《紧急状态法》与 1630/1951 号法设立的比雷埃夫斯港。
- 根据 2251/1953 号令设立的萨洛尼卡港。

2007 年 1 月 1 日 (WT/Let/556)

- Other ports governed by presidential *decree 649/1977 (NA. 649/1977) Εποπτεία, οργάνωσηλειτουργίας, διοικητκός έλεγχος λψένων (Epopteia, organosi leitoyrgias dioktitikos elenchos limeron, supervision, organization of functioning and administrative control).*

SPAIN

- Puerto de Huelva set up pursuant to *the Decreto de 2 de octubre de 1969, no 2380/69. Puertos y Faros. Otorga Régimen de Estatuto de Autonomía al Puerto de Huelva.*

- Puerto de Barcelona set up pursuant to *the Decreto de 25 de agosto de 1978, no 2407/78, Puertos y Faros. Otorga al de Barcelona Régimen de Estatuto de Autonomía.*

- Puerto de Bilbao set up pursuant to *the Decreto de 25 de agosto de 1978, no 2048/78. Puertos y Faros. Otorga al de Bilbao Régimen de Estatuto de Autonomía.*

- Puerto de Valencia set up pursuant to the Decreto de 25 de agosto de 1978, no 2409/78. Puertos y Faros. Otorga al de Valençia Régimen de Estatuto de Autonomía.

- Juntas de Puertos operating pursuant to *the Lei 27/68 de 20 de junio de 1968 &; Puertos y Faros. Juntas de Puertos y Estatutos de Autonomía* and to *the Decreto de 9 de abril de 1970, no 1350/70. Juntas de Puertos. Reglamento.*

- Ports managed by the Comisíon Administrativa de Grupos de Puertos, operating pursuant to *the Ley 27/68 de 20 de junio de 1968, Decreto 1958/78 de 23 de junio de 1978 and Decreto 571/81 de 6 de mayo de 1981.*

- Ports listed in the *Real Decreto 989/82 de 14 de mayo de 1982. Puertos. Clasificacíon de los de interés general.*

FRANCE

- Port autonome de Paris set up pursuant to *loi 68/917 du 24 octobre 1968 relative au port autonome de Paris.*

- Port autonome de Strasbourg set up pursuant to *the convention du 20 mai 1923 entre l'BEtat et la ville de Strasbourg relative à la constitution du port rhénan de Strasbourg et à l'exécution de travaux d'extension de ce port, approved by the loi du 26 avril 1924.*

- Other inland waterway ports set up or managed pursuant to *article 6 (navigation intérieure) of the décret 69-140 du 6 février 1969 relatif aux concessions d'outillage public dans les ports maritimes.*

- Ports autonomes operating pursuant to *articles L 111-1 et suivants of the code des ports maritimes.*

- Ports non autonomes operating pursuant to *articles R 121-1 et suivants of the code des ports maritimes.*

- 649/1997 号总统令管辖的其他港口。

西班牙

- 韦尔瓦港口，根据 1969 年 10 月 2 日颁布的 2380/69 号关于港口及灯塔的法令设立，该法令授予韦尔瓦港自治权。

- 巴塞罗那港口，根据 1978 年 8 月 25 日颁布的 2407/78 号关于港口及灯塔的法令设立，该法令授予巴塞罗那港自治权。

- 毕尔巴鄂港口，根据 1978 年 8 月 25 日颁布的 2408/78 号关于港口及灯塔的法令设立，该法令授予毕尔巴鄂港自治权。

- 瓦伦西亚港口，根据 1978 年 8 月 25 日颁布的 2409/78 号关于港口及灯塔的法令设立，该法令授予瓦伦西亚港自治权所设立的。

- 根据 1968 年 6 月 20 日颁布的 27/68 号《关于港口及灯塔、港口委员会及自治条理的法律》以及 1970 年 4 月 9 日颁布的关于港口委员会的 1350/70 号法令成立的港口委员会。

- 根据 1968 年 6 月 20 日颁布的 27/68 号法律、1978 年 6 月 23 日颁布的 1958/78 号法令以及 1981 年 5 月 6 日颁布的 571/81 号法令，由港口集合管理委员会管理的港口。

- 根据 1982 年 5 月 14 日颁布的 989/82 号关于港口、普通用语分类的法律所列出的港口。

法国

- 巴黎自治港，根据与巴黎自治港有关的 1968 年 10 月 24 日 68/917 号法律设立。

- 斯特拉斯堡自治港，根据 1924 年 4 月 26 日法令批准的与斯特拉斯堡莱茵河港的设立及该港口的延伸工程的实施有关的国家和斯特拉斯堡城市之间 1923 年 5 月 20 日协议设立。

- 根据与海港的公共设备特许权有关的 1969 年 2 月 6 日 69-140 法令第 6 条(内河航运)设立和管理的其他内河水道。

- 根据海港法典 L 111-1 条及其他条款运营的自治港。

- 根据海港法典 L 121-1 条及其他条款运营的非自治港。

- Ports managed by regional authorities (départements) or operating pursuant to a concession granted by the regional authorities (départements) pursuant to *article 6 of the loi 86-663 du 22 juillet 1983 complétant la loi 83-8 du 7 janvier 1983 relative à la répartition de compétences entre les communes, départements et l'Etat.*

IRELAND

- Ports operating pursuant to *the Harbour Acts 1946 to 1976.*

- Port of Dun Laoghaire operating pursuant to *the State Harbours Act 1924.*

- Port of Rosslare Harbour operating pursuant to *the Finguard and Rosslare Railways and Harbours Act 1899.*

ITALY

- State ports and other ports managed by the Capitaneria di Porto pursuant to *the Codice della navigazione, Regio Decreto 30 marzo 1942, n. 32.*

- Autonomous ports (enti portuali) set up by special laws pursuant to *Article 19 of the Codice della navigazione, Regio Decreto 30 marzo 1942, n. 327.*

LUXEMBOURG

Port de Mertert set up and operating pursuant to *loi du 22 juillet 1963 relative à l'aménagement et à l'exploitation d'un port fluvial sur la Moselle.*

NETHERLANDS

Havenbedrijven, set up and operating pursuant to *the Gemeentewet van 29 juni 1851.*

Havenschap Vlissingen, set up by *the wet van 10 september 1970 houdende een gemeenschappelijke regeling tot oprichting van het Havenschap Vlissingen.*

Havenschap Terneuzen, set up by *the wet van 8 april 1970 houdende een gemeenschappelijke regeling tot oprichting van het Havenschap Terneuzen.*

Havenschap Delfzijl, set up by *the wet van 31 juli 1957 houdende een gemeenschappelijke regeling tot oprichting van het Havenschap Delfzijl.*

Industrie- en havenschap Moerdijk, set up by *gemeenschappelijke regeling tot oprichting van het Industrie- en havenschap Moerdijk van 23 oktober 1970, approved by Koninklijke Besluit nr. 23 van 4 maart 1972.*

- 根据由大区(省)当局批准的特许权，根据由与国家、省、市镇的职权分配有关的 1983 年 1 月 7 日 83-8 法律进行补充的 1983 年 7 月 22 日 86-663 法律第 6 条的规定，由地区(省)政府机构管理或运营的港口。

爱尔兰

- 根据 1946 年至 1976 年《港口法》运营的港口。
- 根据 1994 年《国家港口法》运营的邓莱里港。
- 根据 1899 年《芬加德和罗斯莱尔铁路和港口法》运营的罗斯莱尔港。

意大利

- 根据 1942 年 3 月 30 日 32 号皇家法令批准的《航海法》规定管理的的国家港口和其他港口。
- 根据 1942 年 3 月 30 日 327 号皇家法令批准的《航海法》第 19 条的特别法律建立的自治港(港口管理局)。

卢森堡

根据与摩泽尔省上的河港治理和开发有关的 1963 年 7 月 22 日的法律建立和运营的枚尔特尔特港

荷兰

根据 1851 年 6 月 29 日市政府法案设立和运营的港口公司。

弗利辛恩港，根据 1970 年 9 月 10 日关于设立弗利辛恩港的通则设立。

泰尔纳曾港，根据 1970 年 4 月 8 日关于设立泰尔纳曾港的通则设立。

代尔夫宰尔港，根据 1957 年 7 月 31 日关于设立代尔夫宰尔港的通则设立。

穆尔代克工业区和港，根据 1970 年 10 月 23 日制定、1972 年 4 月 23 日皇家法令批准的关于设立穆尔代克工业区和港口的通则设立。

PORTUGAL

Porto do Lisboa set up pursuant to *Decreto Real do 18 de Fevereiro de 1907 and operating pursuant to Decreto-Lei no 36976 de 20 de Julho de 1948.*

Porto do Douro e Leixões set up pursuant to *Decreto-Lei n o 36977 de 20 de Julho de 1948.*

Porto de Sines set up pursuant to *Decreto-Lei no 508/77 de 14 de Dezembro de 1977.*

Portos de Setúbal, Aveiro, Figueira de Foz, Viana do Castelo, Portimão e Faro operating pursuant to *the Decreto-Lei no 37754 de 18 de Fevereiro de 1950.*

UNITED KINGDOM

Harbour Authorities within the meaning of *Section 57 of the Harbours Act 1964 providing port facilities to carriers by sea or inland waterway.*

AUSTRIA

Inland ports owned totally or partially by Länder and/or Gemeinden.

FINLAND

Ports operating pursuant to *Laki kunnallisista satamajärjestyksistä ja liikennemaksuista (955/76).*

Saimaa Canal (Saimaan kanavan hoitokunta).

SWEDEN

Ports and terminal facilities according to *lagen (1983:293) om inrättande, utvidgning och avlysning av allmän farled och allmän hamn, the förordningen (1983:744) om trafiken paa Göta kanal.*

AUSTRIA

Austro Control GmbH

Entities as defined in *Articles 60 to 80 of the Luftfahrtgesetz 1957 (BGBl. Nr. 253/1957).*

CZECH REPUBLIC

Operators of harbours (section 2 b) of Act No. 199/1994 Sb. on Public Procurement).

ESTONIA

Entities operating pursuant to Article 5 of the Public Procurement Act (RT I 2001, 40, 224) and Article 14 of the Competition Act (RT I 2001, 56 332).

葡萄牙

里斯本港，根据 1907 年 2 月 18 日法令设立并根据 1948 年 7 月 20 日 36976 号法令运营。

杜罗—莱伊拉尚伊斯港，根据 1948 年 7 月 20 日 36977 号法令设立。

锡尼什港，根据 1977 年 12 月 14 日 508/77 号法令设立。

塞图巴尔、阿维罗、菲盖拉达福什、维亚纳堡区和法鲁港，根据 1950 年 2 月 18 日 37754 号法令设立。

英国

属 1964 年《港口法》第 57 节定义的、向海运和内河水道承运人提供港口设施服务的港口管理局。

奥地利

联邦州和/或乡镇全部或部分拥有的内河港。

芬兰

根据《1957 年城市港口体系和运费法》(955/76 号)运营的港口。

塞马湖运河公司

瑞典

根据《建设、扩大和取消公共航道和公共港口法》(1983:293 号) 和《约塔运河交通管理规定》(1983:744) 运营的港口和港口设施。

奥地利

奥地利航空管理局。

1957 年《航空法》 (联邦法律公报 253/1957 号)第 60 至 80 条定义的实体。

捷克

199/1994 Sb.号关于公共采购的法律第 2.b 节项下的港口运营商。

爱沙尼亚

根据《公共采购法》(RTI 2001, 40, 224)第 5 条和《竞争法》(RT I 2001, 56 332)第 14 条经营的实体。

2007 年 1 月 1 日 (WT/Let/556)

CYPRUS

The Cyprus Ports Authority established by the Cyprus Ports Authority Law of 1973 (Η Αρχή Λιμένων Κύπρου, που εγκαθιδρύθηκε από τον περί Αρχής Λιμένων Κύπρου Νόμο του 1973).

LATVIA

Authorities, which govern ports in accordance with the law "Likums par ostām":
Rīgas brīvostas pārvalde (Rīga free port authority)
Ventspils brīvostas pārvalde (Ventspils free port authority)
Liepājas ostas pārvalde (Liepāja port authority)
Salacgrīvas ostas pārvalde (Salacgrīva port authority)
Skultes ostas pārvalde (Skulte port authority)
Lielupes ostas pārvalde (Lielupe port authority)
Engures ostas pārvalde (Engure port authority)
Mērsraga ostas pārvalde (Mērsrags port authority)
Pāvilostas pārvalde (Pāvilosta port authority)
Rojas ostas pārvalde (Roja port authority).

LITHUANIA

Valstybės įmonė "Klaipėdos valstybinio jūrų uosto direkcija" (state enterprise "Klaipėda State Seaport Authority") operating pursuant to the Lietuvos Respublikos Klaipėdos valstybinio jūrų uosto įstatymas (Žin., 1996, Nr. 53-1245).
Valstybės įmonė "Vidaus vandens kelių direkcija" (state enterprise "Inland Waterways Administration") operating pursuant to the Lietuvos Respublikos vidaus vandenų transporto kodeksas (Žin., 1996, Nr. 105-2393).
Other entities operating in the field of maritime or inland port or other terminal facilities and being in compliance with the provisions of Lietuvos Respublikos viešųjų pirkimų įstatymas (Žin., 2002, Nr. 118-5296).

HUNGARY

Public ports operated fully or partially by the State pursuant to Act XLII of 2000 on water transport (2000. évi XLII. törvény a vízi közlekedésről).

MALTA

L-Awtorita' Marittima ta' Malta (Malta Maritime Authority).

POLAND

Podmioty zajmujące się zarządzaniem portami morskimi lub śródlądowymi i udostępnianiem ich przewoźnikom morskim i śródlądowym. (Entities operating in the field of management of sea ports or inland harbours and letting them for use to sea and inland carriers.).

塞浦路斯

根据 1973 年《塞浦路斯港管理局法》设立的塞浦路斯港管理局。

拉脱维亚

根据《港口法》管理港口的机构：
里加自由港管理局
文茨皮尔斯自由港管理局
利耶帕亚港管理局
萨拉茨格里瓦港管理局
斯库尔特港管理局
利耶卢佩港管理局
恩古雷港管理局
梅尔斯拉格斯港管理局
帕维洛斯塔港管理局
罗亚港务管理局

立陶宛

克莱佩达港口管理局，根据《立陶宛国有克莱佩达港口法》(1996 年，53-1245 号)运营。
立陶宛国家内陆水域运输管理局，根据《立陶宛内陆水域运输法》(1996 年，105-2393 号)运营。
符合《立陶宛公共采购法》(2002 年，118-5296 号)规定的、在海港、内河港或其他港口设施领域运营的其他实体。

匈牙利

根据 2000 年 42 号《水路运输法》由国家全部或部分运营的公共港口。

马耳他

马耳他海事管理局

波兰

在海港或内河港管理领域运营，并允许海运和内陆运输承运人使用的实体。

SLOVENIA

Morska pristanišča v državni ali delni lasti države, ko opravljajo gospodarsko javno službo, skladno s Pomorskim zakonikom (Uradni list RS, 26/01). (Sea ports in full or partial state ownership when performing economic public service in accordance with the Maritime Code (Official Gazette of the Republic of Slovenia, no. 26).

SLOVAKIA

The procuring entity is defined in Article 3 §2 and §3 of Act No. 263/1999 Z. z. on Public Procurement, as amended, as a legal entity which deals in inland navigation by maintaining the waterways and by establishing and maintaining public ports and waterway facilities (Act No. 338/2000 Z. z.– e.g. Prístav Bratislava, Prístav Komárno, Prístav Štúrovo)."

BULGARIA

ДП "Пристанищна инфраструктура"

Лицата, които по силата на специални или изключителни права осъществяват експлоатация на цяло или част от пристанище за обществен транспорт с национално значение, посочено в Приложение № 1 към чл.103а на Закона за морските пространства, вътрешните водни пътища и пристанищата на Република България (обн., ДВ, бр.12/11.02.2000) (Entities which on the bases of special or exclusive rights perform exploitation of ports for public transport with national importance or parts thereof, listed in Annex No 1 to Article 103a of the Law on Maritime Space, Inland Waterways and Ports of the Republic of Bulgaria (published in State Gazette No 12/11.02.2000):

Лицата, които по силата на специални или изключителни права осъществяват експлоатация на цяло или част от пристанище за обществен транспорт с регионално значение, посочено в Приложение № 2 към чл.103а на Закона за морските пространства, вътрешните водни пътища и пристанищата на Република България (обн., ДВ, бр.12/11.02.2000) (Entities which on the bases of special or exclusive rights perform exploitation of ports for public transport with regional importance or parts thereof, listed in Annex No 2 to Article 103a of the Law on Maritime Space, Inland Waterways and Ports of the Republic of Bulgaria (published in State Gazette No 12/11.02.2000):

斯洛文尼亚

根据《海事法》(《斯洛文尼亚共和国公报》26 号)提供公共经济服务时全部或部分国有的海港。

斯洛伐克

经修订的 263/1999 Z. z.号关于公共采购的法律第 3.2 和 3.3 条将采购实体定义为，通过维护水道和通过建立和维护公共港口和水道设施从事内河航运的法律实体。(338/2000 Z. z.号法，如布拉迪斯拉发港口、科玛尔诺港口、施图罗沃港口)。

保加利亚

保加利亚港口管理局。

根据 12/11.02.2000 号国家公报公布的《保加利亚共和国海域、内陆河和港口法》第 103a 条附件 1 所列的、根据特权或独占权利用具有国家重要性的港口或其一部分进行公共运输的实体。

根据 12/11.02.2000 号国家公报公布的《保加利亚共和国海域、内陆河和港口法》第 103a 条附件 2 所列的、根据特权或独占权利用具有地区重要性的港口或其一部分进行公共运输的实体。

ROMANIA

Compania Naţională "Administraţia Porturilor Maritime" SA Constanţa (National Company "Administration of Maritime Ports" SA Constanţa)
Compania Naţională "Administraţia Canalelor Navigabile SA" (National Company "Administration of Maritime Ports" SA Constanţa)
Compania Naţională de Radiocomunicaţii Navale "RADIONAV" SA (National Company of Naval Radiocommunications "RADIONAV" SA)
Regia Autonomă "Administraţia Fluvială a Dunării de Jos" (Autonomous Regie "River Administration of Lower Danube")
Compania Naţională "Administraţia Porturilor Dunării Maritime" (National Company "Maritime Danube Ports Administration")
Compania Naţională "Administraţia Porturilor Dunării Fluviale" SA (National Company "River Danube Ports Administration")
Agenţia Română de Intervenţii şi Salvare Navală – ARISN (Romanian Agency forInterventions and Naval Rescue - ARISN)
Porturile: Sulina, Brăila, Zimnicea şi Turnul-Măgurele (Ports : Sulina, Brăila, Zimnicea and Turnul-Măgurele).

罗马尼亚

康斯坦察港务管理局
康斯坦察运河港务管理局
国家海军无线电公司
多瑙河下游管理局
多瑙河港海事管理局
多瑙河港务管理局
罗马尼亚邮政和海运管理局
港口：苏利纳、布勒依拉、齐姆尼恰和图尔努—马古雷莱

2007 年 1 月 1 日 (WT/Let/556)

EUROPEAN COMMUNITIES
COMMUNAUTÉS EUROPÉENNES
COMUNIDADES EUROPEAS

ANNEX 4- ANNEXE 4 - ANEXO 4

Services / Services / Servicios

Of the Universal List of Services, as contained in document MTN.GNS/W/120, the following services are included:

Subject	*CPC Reference No.*
Maintenance and repair services	6112, 6122, 633, 886
Land transport services, including armoured car services, and courier services, except transport of mail	712 (except 71235), 7512, 87304
Air transport services of passengers and freight, except transport of mail	73 (except 7321)
Transport of mail by land, except rail, and by air	71235, 7321
Telecommunications services	752* (except 7524, 7525, 7526)
Financial services	ex 81
(a) Insurance services	812, 814
(b) Banking and investments services**	
Computer and related services	84
Accounting, auditing and bookkeeping services	862
Market research and public opinion polling services	864
Management consulting services and related services	865, 866***
Architectural services; engineering services and integrated engineering services, urban planning and landscape architectural services; related scientific and technical consulting services; technical testing and analysis services	867
Advertising services	871
Building-cleaning services and property management services	874, 82201 - 82206
Publishing and printing services on a fee or contract basis	88442
Sewage and refuse disposal; sanitation and similar services	94

1 March 2000 (WT/Let/330)

欧洲共同体

附件 4

服务

包括载于 MTN.GNS/W/120 号文件的服务通用清单中的下列服务：

事项	*CPC 参考号*
维护和修理服务	6112、6122、633、886
陆路运输服务，包括装甲车服务和速递服务：邮件运输除外	712(不含 71235)、7512、87304
航空客运和货运服务，邮件运输除外	73(不含 7321)
陆地和航空邮件运输，铁路运输除外	71235, 7321
电信服务	752* (不含 7524、7525、7526)
金融服务	ex 81
(a) 保险服务 (b) 银行与投资服务**	812、814
计算机及相关服务	84
会计、审计和簿记服务	862
市场调研和民意测验服务	864
管理咨询服务及相关服务	865、866***
建筑设计服务；工程服务与集中工程服务、城市规划和景观设计服务；相关科技咨询服务；技术咨询服务；技术测试和分析服务	867
广告服务 建筑物清洁服务与物业管理服务	871 874、82201-82206
收费或合同基础上的出版和印刷服务	88442
排污及废物处理；卫生及类似服务	94

2000 年 3 月 1 日 (WT/Let/330)

Notes to Annex 4

* except voice telephony, telex, radiotelephony, paging and satellite services.

** except contracts for financial services in connection with the issue, sale, purchase or transfer of securities or other financial instruments, and central bank services. In Finland payments from governmental entities (expenses) shall be transacted through a certain credit institution (Postipankki Ltd) or through the Finnish Postal Giro System. In Sweden, payments to and from governmental agencies shall be transacted through the Swedish Postal Giro System (Postgiro).

*** except arbitration and conciliation services.

附件 4 注释

* 语音通信、电传、无线电话、寻呼及卫星服务除外。

** 关于证券或其他金融工具的发行、销售、购买或转让的金融服务合同及中央银行服务合同除外。在芬兰，政府实体的付款(开支)应通过某一信用机构(芬兰邮政银行)办理或通过芬兰邮政电子转账系统办理。在瑞典，向政府机构付款或政府机构的付款应通过瑞典邮政电子转账系统办理(邮政划拨)。

*** 仲裁和调解服务除外

2000 年 3 月 1 日 (WT/Let/330)

De la Liste universelle des services contenue dans le document MTN.GNS/W/120, les services suivants sont inclus:

Désignation des services	*Numéro de référence CPC*
Services d'entretien et de réparation	6112, 6122, 633, 886
Services de transport terrestre, y compris les services de véhicules blindés et les services de courrier, à l'exclusion des transport de courrier	712 (except 71235), 7512, 87304
Services de transports aériens: transport de voyageurs et de marchandises, à l'exclusion des transports de courrier	73 (except 7321)
Transport de courrier par transport terrestre, à l'exclusion du transport ferroviaire, et par air	71235, 7321
Services de télécommunications	752* (except 7524, 7525, 7526)
Services financiers	ex 81
(a) Services d'assurance	812, 814
(b) Services bancaires et d'investissement**	
Services informatiques et services connexes	84
Services comptables, d'audit et de tenue de livres	862
Services d'études de marché et de sondages	864
Services de conseil en gestion et services connexes	865, 866***
Services d'architecture; services d'ingénierie et services intégrés d'ingénierie; services d'aménagement urbain et d'architecture paysagère; services connexes de consultations scientifiques et techniques; services d'essais et d'analyses techniques	867
Services de publicité	871
Services de nettoyage de bâtiments et services de gestion de propriétés	874, 82201 - 82206
Services de publication et d'impression sur la base d'une redevance ou sur une base contractutelle	88442
Services de voirie et d'enlèvement des ordures: services d'assainis-sement et services analogues	94

Notes de l'Annexe 4

* à l'exclusion des services de téléphonie vocale, de télex, de radiotéléphonie, d'appel unilatéral sans transmission de parole, ainsi que des services de transmission par satellite.

** à l'exclusion des marchés des services financiers relatifs à l'émission, à l'achat, à la vente et au transfert de titres ou d'autres instruments financiers, ainsi que des services prestés par des banques centrales. In Finland payments from governmental entities (expenses) shall be transacted through a certain credit institution (Postipankki Ltd) or through the Finnish Postal Giro System. In Sweden, payments to and from governmental agencies shall be transacted through the Swedish Postal Giro System (Postgiro).

*** à l'exclusion des services d'arbitrage et de conciliation.

De la Lista universal de servicios contenida en el documento MTN.GNS/W/120, se incluyen los servicios siguientes:

Servicios	*Número de referencia CCP*
Servicios de mantenimiento y de reparación	6112, 6122, 633, 886
Servicios de transporte por vía terrestre, incluidos servicios de furgones blindados y servicios de mensajería, excepto transporte de correo	712 (except 71235), 7512, 87304
Servicios de transporte aéreo de pasajeros y carga, excepto transporte de correo	73 (except 7321)
Transporte de correo por vía terrestre, excepto transporte por ferrocarril, y por vía aérea	71235, 7321
Servicios de telecomunicación	752* (except 7524, 7525, 7526)
Servicios financieros	ex 81
(a) Servicios de seguros	812, 814
(b) Servicios bancarios y de inversiones**	
Servicios informaticos y servicios conexos	84
Servicios de contabilidad, auditoría et teneduría de libros	862
Servicios de investigación de estudios y encuestas de opinión pública	864
Servicios de consultores de dirección y servicios conexos	865, 866***
Servicios de arquitectura; servicios de ingeniería y servicios integrados de ingeniería; servicios de planificación urbana y servicios de arquitectura paisajista; servicios conexos de consultores en ciencia y tecnología; servicios de ensayos y análisis técnicos	867
Servicios de publicidad	871
Servicios de limpieza de edificios y servicios de administración de bienes raíces	874, 82201 - 82206
Servicios editoriales y de imprenta, por tarifa o por contrato	88442

Servicios	*Número de referencia CCP*
Alcantarillado y eliminación de desperdicios: servicios de saneamiento y servicios similares	94

Notas del Anexo 4

* exceptuando los servicios de telefonía vocal, de télex, de radiotelefonía, de llamada unilateral sin transmisión de palabra, así como los servicios de transmisión por satélite.

** exceptuando los contratos de servicios financieros relativos a la emisión, compra, venta y transferencia de títulos u otros instrumentos financieros, y los servicios prestados por los bancos centrales. In Finland payments from governmental entities (expenses) shall be transacted through a certain credit institution (Postipankki Ltd) or through the Finnish Postal Giro System. In Sweden, payments to and from governmental agencies shall be transacted through the Swedish Postal Giro System (Postgiro).

*** exceptuando los servicios de arbitraje y conciliación.

EUROPEAN COMMUNITIES
COMMUNAUTÉS EUROPÉENNES
COMUNIDADES EUROPEAS

ANNEX 5- ANNEXE 5 - ANEXO 5

Construction Services / Services de construction / Servicios de construcción

Definition:

A construction services contract is a contract which has as its objective the realization by whatever means of civil or building works, in the sense of Division 51 of the Central Product Classification.

Définition:

Un marché de services de construction est un marché qui a pour objet la réalisation, par quelque moyen que ce soit, des travaux de bâtiment ou génie civil, au sens de la Division 51 de la Classification centrale de produits.

Definición:

Un contrato de servicios de construción es un contrato que tiene por objeto la realización, por cualquier medio, de una obra de construcción de edificios e ingeniería civil, en el sentido de la División 51 de la Clasificación Central de Productos.

欧洲共同体

附件 5

建筑服务

定义：

建筑服务合同是指根据《中央产品分类》第 51 类，以通过任何土木或建筑工程手段实现目的的合同。

2000 年 3 月 1 日 (WT/Let/330)

***List of Division 51, CPC** / Liste de la division 51, CPC / Lista de la división 51, CCP*

Group	Class	Subclass	Title	Corresponding ISCI
SECTION 5			CONSTRUCTION WORK AND CONSTRUCTIONS: LAND	
DIVISION 51			CONSTRUCTION WORK	
511			Pre-erection work at construction sites	
	5111	51110	Site investigation work	4510
	5112	51120	Demolition work	4510
	5113	51130	Site formation and clearance work	4510
	5114	51140	Excavating and earthmoving work	4510
	5115	51150	Site preparation work for mining	4510
	5116	51160	Scaffolding work	4520
512			Construction work for buildings	
	5121	51210	For one- and two-dwelling buildings	4520
	5122	51220	For multi-dwelling buildings	4520
	5123	51230	For warehouses and industrial buildings	4520
	5124	51240	For commercial buildings	4520
	5125	51250	For public entertainment buildings	4520
	5126	51260	For hotel, restaurant and similar buildings	4520
	5127	51270	For educational buildings	4520
	5128	51280	For health buildings	4520
	5129	51290	For other buildings	4520
513			Construction work for civil engineering	

CPC 第 51 类清单

组	级	次级	名称	对应的国际产业标准分类
部门 5			建筑工程	
类 51			建筑工地的准备工作	
511			工作调查工作	
	5111	51110	拆除工作	4510
	5112	51120	工地形成和清扫工作	4510
	5113	51130	挖土和运土工作	4510
	5114	51140	采矿场地的准备工作	4510
	5115	51150	搭脚手架工作	4510
	5116	51160	建筑工程	4520
512			建筑物的建筑工作	
	5121	51210	一两幢住宅建筑物	4520
	5122	51220	多幢住宅建筑物	4520
	5123	51230	仓库和工业用建筑物	4520
	5124	51240	商业用建筑物	4520
	5125	51250	公共娱乐建筑物	4520
	5126	51260	旅馆、餐馆和类似建筑物	4520
	5127	51270	教育用建筑物	4520
	5128	51280	医用建筑物	4520
	5129	51290	其他建筑物	4520
513			土木工程的建筑工作	

2000 年 3 月 1 日 (WT/Let/330)

Group	Class	Subclass	Title	Corresponding ISCI
	5131	51310	For highways (except elevated highways), street, roads, railways and airfield runways	4520
	5132	51320	For bridges, elevated highways, tunnels and subways	4520
	5133	51330	For waterways, harbours, dams and other water works	4520
	5134	51340	For long distance pipelines, communication and power lines (cables)	4520
	5135	51350	For local pipelines and cables; ancillary works	4520
	5136	51360	For constructions for mining and manufacturing	4520
	5137		For constructions for sport and recreation	
		51371	For stadia and sports grounds	4520
		51372	For other sport and recreation installations (e.g. swimming pools, tennis courts, golf courses)	4520
	5139	51390	For engineering works n.e.c.	4520
514	5140	51400	Assembly and erection of prefabricated constructions	4520
515			Special trade construction work	
	5151	51510	Foundation work, including pile driving	4520
	5152	51520	Water well drilling	4520
	5153	51530	Roofing and water proofing	4520
	5154	51540	Concrete work	4520
	5155	51550	Steel bending and erection (including welding)	4520
	5156	51560	Masonry work	4520

1 March 2000 (WT/Let/330)

组	级	次级	名称	对应的国际产业标准分类
	5131	51310	公路(高架公路除外)、街道、道路、铁路和机场跑道	4520
	5132	51320	桥梁、高架公路、隧道和地铁	4520
	5133	51330	水道、港口、堤坝和其他水利工程	4520
	5134	51340	长距离管道、通信和电力线(电缆)	4520
	5135	51350	市内管道和电缆；辅助工程	4520
	5136	51360	矿业和制造业用建筑	4520
	5137		体育和娱乐用建筑	
		51371	露天体育场、运动场地	4520
		51372	其他体育和娱乐设施(如游泳池、网球场、高尔夫球场)	4520
	5139	51390	其他未另列明的土木工程	4520
514	5140	51400	预制构件的组装和装配服务	4520
515			特种行业建筑工程	
	5151	51510	基础工作，包括打桩	4520
	5152	51520	水井钻探	4520
	5153	51530	盖屋顶和防水	4520
	5154	51540	混凝土服务	4520
	5155	51550	钢制品的成形和安装(包括焊接)	4520
	5156	51560	砖石工程	4520

Group	Class	Subclass	Title	Corresponding ISCI
	5159	51590	Other special trade construction work	4520
516			Installation work	
	5161	51610	Heating, ventilation and air conditioning work	4530
	5162	51620	Water plumbing and drain laying work	4530
	5163	51630	Gas fitting construction work	4530
	5164		Electrical work	
		51641	Electrical wiring and fitting work	4530
		51642	Fire alarm construction work	4530
		51643	Burglar alarm system construction work	4530
		51644	Residential antenna construction work	4530
		51649	Other electrical construction work	4530
	5165	51650	Insulation work (electrical wiring, water,heat, sound)	4530
	5166	51660	Fencing and railing construction work	4530
	5169		Other installation work	
		51691	Lift and escalator construction work	4530
		51699	Other installation work n.e.c.	4530
517			Building completion and finishing work	
	5171	51710	Glazing work and window glass installation work	4540
	5172	51720	Plastering work	4540
	5173	51730	Painting work	4540
	5174	51740	Floor and wall tiling work	4540

组	级	次级	名称	对应的国际产业标准分类
	5159	51590	其他特种行业建筑工程	4520
516			安装工程	
	5161	51610	安装工程	4530
	5162	51620	供暖、通风和空调设备安装工作 供暖、通风和空调设备安装工作	4530
	5163	51630	水管道工程和下水道安装工作	4530
	5164		燃气设备安装工作	
		51641	电气设备安装工程	4530
		51642	电线和电气设备安装工作	4530
		51643	火警装置安装工作	4530
		51644	防盗报警系统安装工作	4530
		51649	住宅天线装置安装工作	4530
	5165	51650	其他电气设备安装工作	4530
	5166	51660	绝缘装置安装工作(电线、水、热、声)	4530
	5169		栅栏和围栏安装工作	
		51691	其他安装工作	4530
		51699	升降机和自动电梯安装工作	4530
517			建筑物竣工和修整工程	
	5171	51710	玻璃装配工作和窗玻璃安装工作	4540
	5172	51720	粉刷工作	4540
	5173	51730	油漆工作	4540
	5174	51740	地面和墙面贴砖工作	4540

Group	Class	Subclass	Title	Corresponding ISCI
	5175	51750	Other floor laying, wall covering and wall papering work	4540
	5176	51760	Wood and metal joinery and carpentry work	4540
	5177	51770	Interior fitting decoration work	4540
	5178	51780	Ornamentation fitting work	4540
	5179	51790	Other building completion and finishing work	4540
518	5180	51800	Renting services related to equipment for construction or demolition of buildings or civil engineering works, with operator	4550

组	级	次级	名称	对应的国际产业标准分类
	5175	51750	其他地面铺设、墙面涂料和贴壁纸工作	4540
	5176	51760	木制和金属制细木作及木作工作	4540
	5177	51770	内部装置装饰工作	4540
	5178	51780	装饰安装工作	4540
	5179	51790	其他建筑物竣工和修整工程	4540
518	5180	51800	配有技师的建筑物或土木工程建造或拆除设备租赁服务	4550

List of Division 51, CPC / ***Liste de la division 51, CPC*** / *Lista de la división 51, CCP*

Groupe	Classe	Sous-classe	Titre	Correspondance ISCI
SECTION 5				
DIVISION 51			TRAVAUX DE CONSTRUCTION	
511			Travaux de préparation des sites et chantiers de construction	
512			Travaux d'entreprises générales de construction de bâtiments	
513			Travaux d'entreprises générales de construction d'ouvrages de génie civil	
514			Assemblage et construction d'ouvrages préfabriqués	
515			Travaux d'entreprises de construction spécialisées	
516			Travaux de pose d'installations et de montage	
517			Travaux d'achèvement et de finition des bâtiments	
518			Autres services	

List of Division 51, CPC / Liste de la division 51, CPC / ***Lista de la división 51, CCP***

Grupo	Clase	Subclase	Titulo	Corresponden-cia ISCI
SECTION 5				
DIVISION 51			TRABAJOS DE CONSTRUCCION	
511			Preparación de solares de construcción	
512			Construcción de inmuebles	
513			Obras de ingeniería civil	
514			Ensamblaje y construcción de obras prefabricadas	
515			Obras de empresas de construcción especializadas	
516			Obras de instalación y de montaje	
517			Obras de decoración y acabado	
518			Otros servicios	

1 March 2000 (WT/Let/330)

GENERAL NOTES AND DEROGATIONS FROM THE PROVISIONS OF ARTICLE III OF APPENDIX I OF THE EC

General Notes and Derogations from the Provisions of Article III

1. The EC will not extend the benefits of this Agreement:

- as regards the award of contracts by entities listed in Annex 2 to the suppliers and service providers of Canada;

- as regards the award of contracts, other than for supplies, listed in Annex 2 to the suppliers and service providers of the USA;

- as regards the award of contracts by entities listed in Annex 3 paragraph

  (a) (water) to the suppliers and service providers of Canada and the USA,

  (b) (electricity) to the suppliers and service providers of Canada, and Japan,

  (c) (airports) to the suppliers and service providers of Canada, Korea and the USA,

  (d) (ports) to the suppliers and service providers of Canada,

  (e) (urban transport) to the suppliers and service providers of Canada, Japan, Korea and the USA; to the suppliers and service providers of Israel, as regards bus services,

  until such time as the EC has accepted that the Parties concerned give comparable and effective access for EC undertakings to the relevant markets;

- to service providers of Parties which do not include service contracts for the relevant entities in Annexes 1 to 3 and the relevant service category under Annexes 4 and 5 in their own coverage.

2. The provisions of Article XX shall not apply to suppliers and service providers of:

- Israel, Japan and Korea in contesting the award of contracts by entities listed under Annex 2 paragraph 2, until such time as the EC accepts that they have completed coverage of sub-central entities;

- Japan, Korea and the USA in contesting the award of contracts to a supplier or service provider of Parties other than those mentioned, which are small or medium sized enterprises under the relevant provisions of EC law, until such time as the EC accepts that they no longer operate discriminatory measures in favour of certain domestic small and minority businesses;

11 January 2003 (WT/Let/438)

欧共体附录 1 总注释及对第 3 条规定的背离

总注释及对第 3 条规定的背离

1. 欧共体在下列方面不将本协定利益给予下列参加方：

- 对于附件 2 中所列实体授予的合同，本协定利益不给予加拿大供应商和服务提供者；

- 对于附件 2 所列除供应品外的合同的授予，本协定利益不给予美国供应商和服务提供者；

- 对于附件 3 所列实体授予的合同：

  (a) (水)本协定利益不给予美国和加拿大供应商和服务提供者；

  (b) (电力)本协定利益不给予加拿大和日本供应商和服务提供者；

  (c) (机场)本协定利益不给予加拿大、韩国和美国供应商和服务提供者；

  (d) (港口)本协定利益不给予加拿大供应商和服务提供者；

  (e) (城市交通)本协定利益不给予加拿大、日本、韩国和美国供应商和服务提供者；不给予以色列供应商和服务提供者在公共汽车服务方面的利益，

  直至欧共体已经认为有关参加方给予欧共体企业对于相关市场的对等和有效的准入机会；

- 本协定利益不给予在其承诺范围内未对附件 1 至 3 中相关实体包含相关服务合同和未在附件 4 和 5 中包括相关服务类别的参加方的服务提供者。

2. 第 20 条不适用于下列参加方的供应商和服务提供者：

- 以色列、日本和韩国，在竞争附件 2 第 2 款下所列实体所授予的合同时，直至欧共体认为他们的次中央实体范围已经完整时止；

- 日本、韩国和美国，在竞争将合同授予已提及的参加方供应商或服务提供者之外的一属欧共体相关规定所定义的小型或中型企业的供应商或服务提供者时，直至欧共体认为他们不再采取有利于某些国内小型和少数族裔企业的歧视性措施时止;

2003 年 1 月 11 日(WT/Let/438)

- Israel, Japan and Korea in contesting that award of contracts by EC entities, whose value is less than the threshold applied for the same category of contracts awarded by these Parties.

3. Until such time as the EC has accepted that the Parties concerned provide access for EC suppliers and service providers to their own markets, the EC will not extend the benefits of this Agreement to suppliers and service providers of:

- Canada, as regards procurement of FSC 36, 70 and 74 (special industry machinery, general purpose automatic data processing equipment, software, supplies and support equipment (except 7010 ADPE configurations), office machines, visible record equipment and ADP equipment);

- Canada, as regards procurement of FSG 58 (communications, protection and coherent radiation equipment) and the USA as regards air traffic control equipment;

- Korea and Israel as regards procurement by entities listed in Annex 3 paragraph (b), as regards procurement of HS Nos 8504, 8535, 8537 and 8544 (electrical transformers, plugs, switches and insulated cables); and for Israel, HS Nos. 8501, 8536 and 902830;

- the USA, as regards procurement by entities listed in Annex 3 paragraph (d), as regards procurement of dredging services and procurement related to shipbuilding;

- Canada and the USA as regards contracts for good or service components of contracts which, although awarded by an entity covered by this Agreement, are not themselves subject to this Agreement.

4. The Agreement shall not apply to contracts awarded under:

- an international agreement and intended for the joint implementation or exploitation of a project by the signatory States;

- an international agreement relating to the stationing of troops;

- the particular procedure of an international organization.

5. The Agreement shall not apply to procurement of agricultural products made in furtherance of agricultural support programmes and human feeding programmes.

6. Contracts awarded by entities in Annexes 1 and 2 in connection with activities in the fields of drinking water, energy, transport or telecommunications, are not included.

7. This Agreement shall not apply to contracts awarded by entities in Annex 3:

- for the purchase of water and for the supply of energy or of fuels for the production of energy;

- 以色列、日本和韩国，在竞争欧共体实体授予的合同时，其价值低于这些参加方所授予的相同类别合同所适用的门槛金额。

3. 在欧共体已经认为有关参加方对欧共体供应商和服务供应者提供进入其各自市场的机会之前，欧共体不将本协定的利益给予下列参加方供应商和服务提供者：

- 加拿大，对于 FSC 36、70 和 74 的采购(特殊工业机械；通用自动化处理设备、软件、耗材和配套设备(7010 自动化处理系统结构除外)；办公设备、显露式记录设备和自动化处理设备；

- 加拿大，对于 FSC 58 的采购(通信、探测和相干辐射设备)及美国，对于空中交通管制设备的采购；

- 以色列和韩国，对于附件 3(b)款所列实体关于协调制度编码 HS8504、8535、8537 和 8544(变压器、插头、开关和绝缘电缆)的采购；以色列，关于协调制度编码 HS8501、8536 和 902830 的采购；

- 美国，对于附件 3 第(a)款所列实体关于疏浚服务的采购和与造船有关的采购；

- 加拿大和美国，对于虽由本协定所涵盖一实体授予、但其货物或服务组成部分本身不受本协定管辖的合同。

4. 本协定不适用于根据下列内容授予的合同：

- 旨在由签署国联合执行或开发一项目的国际协定；

- 与军队驻扎有关的国际协定；

- 国际组织的特定程序。

5. 本协定不适用于为促进农业支持计划和人类供给计划而采购的农产品。

6. 不包括附件 1 和 2 中实体授予的与饮用水、能源、运输或通信领域活动有关的合同。

7. 本协定不适用于附件 3 中实体所授予的下列合同：

- 为购买水而授予的合同和为供应能源或为生产能源而供应燃料；

2003 年 1 月 11 日(WT/Let/438)

- for purposes other than the pursuit of their activities as described in this Annex or for the pursuit of such activities in a non-member country;

- for purposes of re-sale or hire to third parties, provided that the contracting entity enjoys no special or exclusive right to sell or hire the subject of such contracts and other entities are free to sell or hire it under the same conditions as the contracting entity.

8. This Agreement shall not be applicable to contracts:

- for the acquisition or rental of land, existing buildings, or other immovable property or concerning rights thereon;

- for the acquisition, development, production or co-production of programme material by broadcasters and contracts for broadcasting time.

9. This Agreement shall not be applicable to the award of service contracts by Spanish entities listed in Annex 3 before 1 January 1997 or to the award of contracts by Greek or Portuguese entities listed in Annex 3 before 1 January 1998.

10. The provision of services, including construction services, in the context of procurement procedures according to this Agreement is subject to the conditions and qualifications for market access and national treatment as will be required by Austria in conformity with her commitments under the GATS.

11. This Agreement shall not apply to contracts awarded to an entity in Finland which itself is a contracting authority within the meaning of the Public Procurement Act: "Laki julkisista hankinnoista" (1505/92), or in Sweden within the meaning of the "Lag om offentlig upphandling" (1992:1528), on the basis of an exclusive right which it enjoys pursuant to a law, regulation or administrative provision or to contracts of employment in Finland and Sweden.

12. When a specific procurement may impair important national policy objectives, the Finnish or Swedish Governments may consider it necessary in singular procurement cases to deviate from the principle of national treatment in the Agreement. A decision to this effect will be taken at Cabinet level. Finland also reserves its position with regard to the application of this Agreement to the Åland Islands (Ahvenanmaa).

- 所授予合同的目的不是为了从事本附件所述活动或为在一非成员国从事此类活动；

- 为再销售或向第三方出租，但条件是缔约实体不享受销售或出租此类合同客体的特殊或专用权，且其他实体有权根据与缔约实体相同的条件销售或出租此类合同客体。

8. 对于附件 4，本协定不适用于下列合同：

- 购买或租赁土地、现有建筑物或其他不动产或涉及相关权利的合同，无论通过何种出资方式；

- 广播电台购买、开发、制作或联合制作节目内容的合同和播放时间的合同。

9. 本协定不适用于附件 3 中所列西班牙实体在 1997 年 1 月 1 日前或附件 3 中所列希腊或葡萄牙实体在 1998 年 1 月 1 日前授予的服务合同。

10. 在根据本协定所进行的采购程序中，服务的提供，包括建筑服务的提供，需遵守奥地利依照其在 GATS 项下的承诺所要求的关于市场准入和国民待遇的条件和资格。

11. 本协定不适用于给予芬兰一本身属《公共采购法》(1505/92)意义内的缔约机构的实体的合同，或给予瑞典一本身属《公共采购法》(1992:1528)意义内的缔约机构的实体的合同，此类实体根据一法律、法规或行政规定或芬兰和瑞典的雇佣合同享有专用权。

12. 如一特定采购可能损害国家重要政策目标，则芬兰或瑞典政府可考虑有必要在一单一采购案中背离本协定中的国民待遇原则。有关决定将由内阁一级做出。芬兰还保留对本协定适用于奥兰群岛的立场。

2003 年 1 月 11 日(WT/Let/438)

NOTES GENERALES ET DEROGATIONS AUX DISPOSITIONS DE L'ARTICLE III DE L'APPENDICE I DE LA CE

Notes générales et dérogations aux dispositions de l'article III

1. La CE n'étendra pas le bénéfice des dispositions de cet accord:

- en ce qui concerne les marchés passés par les entités mentionnées à l'Annexe 2 aux fournisseurs et aux prestataires de services du Canada;

- en ce qui concerne les marchés passés, à l'exception des fournitures, énumérés à l'annexe 2 aux fournisseurs et aux prestataires de services des États-Unis;

- en ce qui concerne les marchés passés par les entités énumérées à l'annexe 3 paragraphes

  (a) (eau), aux fournisseurs et aux prestataires de services du Canada et des États-Unis,

  (b) (électricité), aux fournisseurs et aux prestataires de services du Canada, et du Japon,

  (c) (aéroports), aux fournisseurs et aux prestataires de services du Canada, de la Corée et des États-Unis,

  (d) (ports), aux fournisseurs et aux prestataires de services du Canada,

  (e) (transport urbain), aux fournisseurs et aux prestataires de services du Canada, du Japon, de la Corée et des États-Unis d'Amérique; aux producteurs et fournisseurs de service d'Israël, pour ce qui est des services de transport de voyageurs par autobus,

  tant qu'elle n'aura pas constaté que les Parties concernées assurent aux entreprises de la CE un accès comparable et effectif aux marchés considérés;

- aux prestataires de services des Parties qui n'incluent pas, dans leurs propres listes, les marchés de services passés par les entités mentionnées aux Annexes 1 à 3 et concernant les catégories de services visées aux Annexes 4 et 5.

2. Les dispositions de l'article XX ne sont pas applicables aux fournisseurs et aux prestataires de services des pays suivants:

- Israël, Japon et Corée en ce qui concerne les recours intentés contre l'adjudication de marchés par les entités mentionnées à l'annexe 2 paragraphe 2, tant que la CE n'a pas constaté que ces pays ont complété la liste des entités sous-centrales;
- Japon, Corée et États-Unis en ce qui concerne les recours intentés contre l'adjudication de marchés à un fournisseur ou à un prestataire de services d'autres

parties, lorsque ledit fournisseur est une entreprise petite ou moyenne au sens du droit communautaire, tant que la CE n'aura pas constaté que ces pays n'appliquent plus de mesures discriminatoires pour favoriser certaines petites entreprises nationales ou certaines entreprises nationales détenues par les minorités;

- Israël, Japon et Corée en ce qui concerne les recours intentés contre l'adjudication par des entités de la CE de marchés dont la valeur est inférieure au seuil appliqué à la même catégorie de marchés par lesdites Parties.

3. Tant que la CE n'aura pas constaté que les Parties concernées assurent l'accès de leurs marchés aux fournisseurs et aux prestataires de services de la CE, elle n'étendra pas le bénéfice des dispositions du présent accord aux fournisseurs et aux prestataires de services des pays suivants:

- Canada, en ce qui les marchés portant sur les produits relevant des n° 36, 70 et 74 de la FSC (machines industrielles spéciales, matériel d'informatique général, logiciel, fournitures et matériel auxiliaire (sauf 7010 configurations d'équipement de traitement automatique des données), machines de bureau, matériel de bureaumatique et d'informatique de bureau;

- Canada, en ce qui concerne les marchés portant sur les produits relevant du FSG 58 (matériel de communications, matériel de détection des radiations et d'émission de rayonnement cohérent) et États-Unis en ce qui concerne les équipements de contrôle du trafic aérien;

- Corée et Israël en ce qui concerne les marchés passés par les entités énumérées à l'annexe 3 paragraphe (b), pour les produits relevant des n° 8504, 8535, 8537 et 8544 du SH (transformateurs électriques, prises de courant, interrupteurs et câbles isolés); et Israël en ce qui concerne les produits relevant des n° 8501, 8536 et 902830 du SH;

- États-Unis, en ce qui concerne les marchés passés par les entités énumérées à l'annexe 3 paragraphe (d), en ce qui concerne l'acquisition des services de dragage et l'acquisition relative à la construction navale;

- Canada et États-Unis en ce qui concerne les marchés de fournitures et de services entrant dans le cadre de marchés qui, tout en étant passés par une entité relevant du champ d'application du présent accord, ne sont pas eux-mêmes soumis à ce dernier.

4. Le présent accord n'est pas applicable aux marchés passés en vertu:

- d'un accord international et portant sur la réalisation ou l'exploitation en commun d'un ouvrage par les Etats signataires;

- d'un accord international conclu en relation avec le stationnement des troupes;

- de la procédure spécifique d'une organisation internationale.

5. Le présent accord n'est pas applicable aux marchés des produits agricoles passés en application des programmes de soutien à l'agriculture ou de programmes d'aide alimentaire.

11 January 2003 (WT/Let/438)

6. Les marchés passés par les entités mentionnées aux annexes 1 et 2 dans les secteurs de l'eau potable, de l'énergie, du transport ou des télécommunications, ne sont pas inclus.

7. Le présent accord n'est pas applicable aux marchés passés par les entités mentionnées à l'annexe 3:

- pour l'acquisition d'eau et la fourniture d'énergie ou de combustibles destinés à la production d'énergie;

- à des fins autres que la poursuite de leurs activités selon la description donnée dans cette annexe ou pour la poursuite de ces activités dans un pays tiers;

- à des fins de revente ou de location à des tiers, lorsque l'entité adjudicatrice ne bénéficie d'aucun droit spécial ou exclusif pour vendre ou louer l'objet de ces marchés et lorsque d'autres entités peuvent librement le vendre ou le louer dans les mêmes conditions que l'entité adjudicatrice.

8. Le présent accord n'est pas applicable aux marchés passés:

- pour l'acquisition ou la location de terrains, de bâtiments existants, ou d'autres biens immeubles ou qui concernent des droits sur ces biens;

- pour l'acquisition, le développement, la production ou la coproduction du matériel destiné à la radiodiffusion et la télédiffusion et des contrats de temps d'émission.

9. Le présent accord n'est pas applicable à la passation des marchés de service par les entités espagnoles énumérées à l'annexe 3 avant le 1er janvier 1997 ou à la passation des marchés par les entités grecques ou portugaises énumérées à l'annexe 3 avant le 1er janvier 1998.

10. La prestation des services, y compris les services de construction, dans le contexte des procédures de passation de marchés en vertu cet accord est soumise aux conditions et aux qualifications pour l'accès au marché et le traitement national exigées par l'Autriche conformément à ses engagements sous l'AGCS.

11. Cet accord n'est pas applicable aux marchés attribués à une entité en Finlande qui est elle-même un pouvoir adjudicateur au sens de la loi sur les marchés publics: "Laki julkisista hankinnoista" (1505/92), ou en Suède au sens de la "Lag om offentlig upphandling" (1992:1528), sur la base d'un droit exclusif dont elle bénéficie en vertu des dispositions législatives, réglementaires ou administratives ou en vertu des contrats de travail en Finlande ou Suède.

12. Lorsqu'une acquisition spécifique peut altérer des objectifs politiques nationaux importants, les gouvernements finlandais et suédois pourront considérer nécessaire de s'écarter du principe de traitement national de l'Accord dans des cas particuliers. Une telle décision sera prise au niveau du Cabinet. La Finlande réserve également sa position en ce qui concerne l'application de cet accord aux îles Åland (Ahvenanmaa).

11 January 2003 (WT/Let/438)

NOTAS Y DEROGACIONES GENERALES DE LO PREVISTO EN EL ARTÍCULO III DEL APÉNDICE I DE LA CE

Notas y derogaciones generales de lo previsto en el artículo III

1. La CE no concederá los beneficios de este Acuerdo:

- por lo que se refiere a la adjudicación de los contratos por las entidades enumeradas en el anexo 2 a los proveedores y a los prestadores de servicios de Canadá;

- por lo que se refiere a la adjudicación de los contratos, con excepción de contratos de suministros, enumerados en el anexo 2 a los proveedores y a los prestadores de servicios de los EE.UU.;

- por lo que se refiere a la adjudicación de los contratos por entidades enumeradas en el anexo 3 párrafos

  (a) (agua), a los proveedores y a los prestadores de servicios de Canadá y de los EE.UU.,

  (b) (electricidad), a los proveedores y a los prestadores de servicios de Canadá y Japón,

  (c) (aeropuertos), a los proveedores y a los prestadores de servicios de Canadá, Corea y los EE.UU.,

  (d) (puertos), a los proveedores y a los prestadores de servicios de Canadá,

  (e) (transporte urbano), a los proveedores y a los prestadores de servicios de Canadá, Japón, Corea y los EE.UU.; a los proveedores en general y a los proveedores de servicios de Israel, respecto de los servicios de autobús,

  hasta que la CE haya aceptado que las partes afectadas garantizan un acceso comparable y efectivo de empresas de la Comunidad a los mercados pertinentes;

- a los prestadores de servicios de las Partes que no incluyen los contratos de servicio adjudicados por las entidades enumeradas en anexos 1 a 3 y la categoría pertinente de servicio conforme a los anexos 4 y 5 en su propia cobertura.

2. Lo previsto en el artículo XX no se aplicará a los proveedores y a los prestadores de servicios de los siguiente países:

- Israel, Japón y Corea por lo que se refiere a la impugnación de la adjudicación de contratos por las entidades enumeradas en el anexo 2 párrafo 2°, hasta que la CE acepte que estos países han completado su cobertura de entidades subcentrales;

- Japón, Corea y los EE.UU. por lo que se refiere a la impugnación de la adjudicación de los contratos a un proveedor o a un prestador de servicios de las otras Partes, que sean empresas pequeñas o medianas conforme a las disposiciones pertinentes del derecho comunitario, hasta que la CE acepte que ya no aplican medidas discriminatorias a favor de ciertas pequeñas empresas y ciertas empresas de minoría;

- Israel, Japón y Corea por lo que se refiere a la impugnación de la adjudicación de los contratos por las entidades de la CE cuyo valor es inferior al umbral aplicable en la misma categoría de contratos por estas partes.

3. Hasta que la CE haya aceptado que las partes afectadas proporcionan el acceso de los proveedores y los prestadores de servicios de la CE a sus propios mercados, la CE no concederá los beneficios de este Acuerdo a los proveedores y a los prestadores de servicios de los países siguientes:

- Canadá, por lo que se refiere a la adquisición de FSC 36, 70 y 74 (maquinaria industrial especial, material general de proceso de datos automáticos, soporte lógico, suministros y material auxiliar (excepto 7010 configuraciones ADPE), máquinas de oficina, material de ofimática y de informática de oficina);

- Canadá, por lo que se refiere a la adquisición de FSG 58 (material de comunicaciones, material de detección de radiaciones y de emisión de radiación coherente) y los EE.UU. por lo que se refiere al material de control de tráfico aéreo;

- Corea e Israel por lo que se refiere a la adquisición por entidades enumeradas en el anexo 3 párrafo (b), por lo que se refiere a la adquisición de nos. 8504, 8535, 8537 y 8544 HS (transformadores eléctricos, enchufes, interruptores y cables aislantes); y para Israel, nos. 8501, 8536 y 902830 HS;

- los EE.UU., por lo que se refiere a la adquisición por entidades enumeradas en el anexo 3 párrafo (d), por lo que se refiere a la adquisición de servicios de dragado y a la adquisición relacionada con la construcción naval;

- Canadá y los EE.UU. por lo que se refiere a los contratos de bienes o de servicios componentes de contratos que, aunque sean concedidos por una entidad cubierta por este Acuerdo, no están ellos mismos sujetos a este Acuerdo.

4. El presente Acuerdo no se aplicará a los contratos adjudicados en virtud de:

- un acuerdo internacional destinado a la ejecución o explotación conjunta de un proyecto por los Estados signatarios;

- un acuerdo internacional relativo al estacionamiento de tropas;

- un procedimiento específico de una organización internacional.

5. El presente Acuerdo no se aplicará a la adquisición de productos agrícolas hecha en aplicación de programas de ayuda a la agricultura y de programas de ayuda alimentaria.

6. Los contratos adjudicados por las entidades en los anexos 1 y 2 con respecto a actividades en los sectores del agua potable, la energía, el transporte o las telecomunicaciones, no están incluidos.

7. El presente Acuerdo no se aplicará a los contratos que las entidades enumeradas en el anexo 3 adjudiquen:

- para la compra de agua y para el suministro de energía o de combustibles destinados a la producción de energía;

- para fines distintos de la prosecución de sus actividades según lo descrito en este anexo o para la prosecución de tales actividades en un país tercero;

- a efectos de reventa o arrendamiento a terceros siempre y cuando la entidad contratante no goce de derechos especiales o exclusivos de venta o arrendamiento del objeto de dichos contratos, y existan otras entidades que puedan venderlos o arrendarlos libremente en las mismas condiciones que la entidad contratante.

8. El presente Acuerdo no será aplicable a contratos:

- para la adquisición o el arrendamiento de terrenos, edificios ya existentes, u otros bienes inmuebles o relativos a derechos sobre estos bienes;

- para la adquisición, el desarrollo, la producción o coproducción de material de programa por emisores de ondas y contratos de tiempo de emisión.

9. El presente Acuerdo no será aplicable a la adjudicación de contratos de servicio por entidades españolas enumeradas en el anexo 3 antes del 1 de enero de 1997 o a la adjudicación de los contratos por entidades griegas o portuguesas enumeradas en el anexo 3 antes del 1 de enero de 1998.

10. La prestación de servicios, incluidos los servicios de construcción, en el contexto de los procedimientos de contratación en virtud este Acuerdo está sujeta a las condiciones y calificaciones para el acceso al mercado y el trato nacional requeridas por Austria de conformidad con sus compromisos bajo el ACCS.

11. Este Acuerdo no se aplicará a los contratos adjudicados a una entidad en Finlandia que sea a su vez una entidad adjudicadora en el sentido de la Ley de Contratación Pública: "Hankinnoista de julkisista Laki" (1505/92), o en Suecia en el sentido del "Lag om offentlig upphandling" (1992:1528), basándose en un derecho exclusivo del que goce en virtud de disposiciones legales, reglamentarias o administrativas, o en virtud de un contrato laboral en Finlandia y Suecia.

12. Cuando una adquisición específica puede alterar objetivos importantes de política nacional, los gobiernos finés o sueco podrán considerar necesario desviarse en casos concretos del principio del trato nacional del Acuerdo. Decisiones de este tipo se tomarán a nivel de gabinete. Finlandia también se reserva su posición por lo que se refiere a la aplicación de este Acuerdo a las islas Aland (Ahvenanmaa).

HONG KONG, CHINA
中国香港

HONG KONG, CHINA

ANNEX 1

Government Entities which Procure in Accordance With the Provisions of this Agreement

Supplies

Threshold: 130,000 SDR for goods and services other than construction services
5,000,000 SDR for construction services

List of Entities:

1. Agriculture, Fisheries and Conservation Department
2. Architectural Services Department
3. Audit Commission
4. Auxiliary Medical Services
5. Buildings Department
6. Census and Statistics Department
7. Civil Aid Services
8. Civil Aviation Department
9. Civil Engineering and Development Department
10. Companies Registry
11. Correctional Services Department
12. Customs and Excise Department
13. Department of Health
14. Department of Justice
15. Drainage Services Department
16. Electrical and Mechanical Services Department
17. Environmental Protection Department
18. Fire Services Department
19. Food and Environmental Hygiene Department
20. Government Flying Service
21. Government Laboratory
22. Government Logistics Department
23. Government Property Agency
24. Government Secretariat
25. Highways Department
26. Home Affairs Department
27. Hong Kong Monetary Authority
28. Hong Kong Observatory
29. Hong Kong Police Force (including Hong Kong Auxiliary Police Force)
30. Immigration Department
31. Independent Commission Against Corruption
32. Information Services Department

9 March 2005 (WT/Let/491)

中国香港

附件 1

依照本协定条款进行采购的政府实体

供应品

门槛金额： 130,000 特别提款权，货物及除建筑服务外的服务
5,000,000 特别提款权，建筑服务

实体清单：

1. 渔农自然护理署
2. 建筑署
3. 审计署
4. 医疗辅助队
5. 屋宇署
6. 政府统计处
7. 民众安全服务队
8. 民航处
9. 土木工程拓展署
10. 公司注册处
11. 惩教署
12. 香港海关
13. 卫生署
14. 律政司
15. 渠务署
16. 机电工程署
17. 环境保护署
18. 消防处
19. 食物环境卫生署
20. 政府飞行服务队
21. 政府化验所
22. 政府物流服务署
23. 政府产业署
24. 政府总部
25. 路政署
26. 民政事务局
27. 香港金融管理局
28. 香港天文台
29. 香港警察(含香港辅助警察队)
30. 入境事务处
31. 廉政公署
32. 政府新闻处

2005 年 3 月 9 日 (WT/Let/491)

33. Inland Revenue Department
34. Intellectual Property Department
35. Invest Hong Kong
36. Joint Secretariat for the Advisory Bodies on Civil Service and Judicial Salaries and Conditions of Service
37. Judiciary
38. Labour Department
39. Land Registry
40. Lands Department
41. Legal Aid Department
42. Leisure and Cultural Services Department
43. Marine Department
44. Office of the Ombudsman
45. Office of the Telecommunications Authority
46. Official Receiver's Office
47. Planning Department
48. Post Office
49. Public Service Commission
50. Radio Television Hong Kong
51. Rating and Valuation Department
52. Registration and Electoral Office
53. Secretariat, Independent Police Complaints Council
54. Secretariat, University Grants Committee
55. Social Welfare Department
56. Student Financial Assistance Agency
57. Television and Entertainment Licensing Authority
58. Trade and Industry Department
59. Transport Department
60. Treasury
61. Water Supplies Department

33. 税务局
34. 知识产权局
35. 投资推广署
36. 公务及司法人员薪俸及服务条件咨询委员会联合秘书处
37. 司法机构
38. 劳工处
39. 土地注册处
40. 地政总署
41. 法律援助署
42. 康乐及文化事务署
43. 海事处
44. 申诉专员公署
45. 电讯管理局
46. 破产管理处
47. 规划署
48. 邮政局
49. 公务员叙用委员会
50. 香港电台
51. 差饷物业估价署
52. 选举事务处
53. 独立监察警方处理投诉委员会秘书处
54. 大学教育资助委员会秘书处
55. 社会福利署
56. 学生资助办事处
57. 影视及娱乐事务管理处
58. 工业贸易署
59. 运输署
60. 库务署
61. 水务署

2005 年 3 月 9 日 (WT/Let/491)

ANNEX 2

Government Entities which Procure in Accordance With the Provisions of this Agreement

Hong Kong, China has no Annex 2 entities.

9 March 2005 (WT/Let/491)

附件 2

依照本协定条款进行采购的政府实体

中国香港无附件 2 实体。

2005 年 3 月 9 日 (WT/Let/491)

ANNEX 3

All Other Entities which Procure in Accordance With the Provisions of this Agreement

Threshold: 400,000 SDR for supplies and services other than construction services

5,000,000 SDR for construction services

List of Entities:

1. Housing Authority and Housing Department
2. Hospital Authority
3. Airport Authority
4. MTR Corporation Limited
5. Kowloon-Canton Railway Corporation

6 January 2001 (WT/Let/370)

附件 3

依照本协定条款进行采购的所有其他实体

门槛金额： 400,000 特别提款权，货物及除建筑服务外的服务
5,000,000 特别提款权，建筑服务

实体清单：

1. 房屋委员会及房屋署
2. 医院管理局
3. 机场管理局
4. 港铁公司
5. 九广铁路公司

2001 年 1 月 6 日 (WT/Let/370)

ANNEX 4

Services

The following services, classified according to the United Nations Central Product Classification (CPC) Code on Goods and Services, will be covered:

		CPC
1.	*Computer and Related Services*	
-	Data base and processing services	843+844
-	Maintenance and repair service of office machinery and equipment including computers	845
-	Other Computer Services	849
2.	*Rental/Leasing Services Without Operators*	
-	Relating to ships	83103
-	Relating to aircraft	83104
-	Relating to other transport equipment	83101+83102+83105
-	Relating to other machinery and equipment	83106+83109
3.	*Other Business Services*	
Maintenance and repair of equipment (not including maritime vessels, aircraft or other transport equipment)		633+8861-8866
Market Research & Public Opinion Polling Services		864
Security Services		87304
Building-Cleaning Services		874
Advertising Services		871
4.	*Courier Services*	
5.	*Telecommunications Services*	(Provisions of certain types of service may require licensing under the Telecommunication Ordinance)
Value-added telecommunications services		7523, 843
Basic telecommunications services		7521, 7529
Telecommunications-related services		754

1 March 2000 (WT/Let/330)

附件 4

服务

下列依照联合国《中央产品分类》编码分类的服务将涵盖其中：

CPC

1. *计算机及相关服务*

- 数据库和处理服务	843+844
- 办公机器和设备维护和修理服务，包括计算机	845
- 其他计算机服务	849

2. *无操作人员的租赁服务*

- 船舶租赁	83103
- 航空器租赁	83104
- 其他运输设备租赁	83101+83102+83105
- 其他机器设备租赁	83106+83109

3. *其他商业服务*

设备维护和修理 (不包括船舶、航空品或其他运输设备）	633+8861-8866
市场调研和民意测验服务	864
保安服务	87304
建筑物清洁服务	874
广告服务	871

4. *速递服务*

5. *电信服务* (某种类型服务的提供可能需要根据《电讯条例》获得许可)

增值电信服务	7523、843
基础电信服务	7521, 7529
电信相关服务	754

2000 年 3 月 1 日 (WT/Let/330)

6.	*Environmental Services*	
-	Sewage services	9401
-	Refuse disposal services	9402
7.	*Financial Services*	ex 81
-	All Insurance and Insurance-Related Services	(exceptions are set out in paragraph 5 of General Conditions)
-	Banking and other financial services	
8.	*Transport Services*	
-	Air transportation services (excluding transportation of mail)	731, 732, 734
-	Road transport services	712, 6112, 8867

6. *环境服务*

-	排污服务	9401
-	废物处理服务	9402

7. *财政服务* ex 81

-	所有保险和保险相关服务	(例外列于普遍条件第 5 款中)
-	银行和其他金融服务	

8. *运输服务*

-	航空运输服务 (不含邮件运输)	731、732、734
-	道路交通服务	712、6112、8867

2000 年 3 月 1 日 (WT/Let/330)

ANNEX 5

Construction Services

Definition:

A construction services contract is a contract which has as its objective the realization by whatever means of civil or building works, in the sense of Division 51 of the Central Product Classification (CPC).

List of Division 51 CPC

All services of Division 51 of the CPC

Threshold: 5,000,000 SDR

附件 5

建筑服务

定义：

建筑服务合同是指根据《中央产品分类》第 51 类，以通过任何土木或建筑工程手段实现目的的合同。

CPC 第 51 类清单：

CPC 第 51 类包含的所有服务。

门槛金额： 5,000,000 特别提款权

2000 年 3 月 1 日 (WT/Let/330)

GENERAL CONDITIONS APPLICABLE TO ENTITIES AND SERVICES SPECIFIED IN ANNEXES 1 TO 5

1. Notwithstanding anything in the Annexes 1-5, the Agreement shall not apply to:

   - All consultancy and franchise arrangements

   - Transportation of mail by air

   - Statutory insurances including third party liability in respect of vehicles and vessels and employer's liability insurance in respect of employees

   - Purchase of office or residential accommodation by the Government Property Agency.

2. Operators of telecommunications services may require licensing under the Telecommunication Ordinance. Operators applying for the licences are required to be established in Hong Kong under the Companies Ordinance.

3. Hong Kong, China shall not be obliged to permit the supply of such services cross-border, or through commercial presence or the presence of natural persons.

4. The following services are excluded from the Financial Services under Annex 4

   1. *CPC 81402*

      Insurance and pension consultancy services

   2. *CPC 81339*

      Money broking

   3. *CPC 8119+81323*

      Asset management, such as cash or portfolio management, all forms of collective investment management, pension fund management, custodial depository and trust services.

   4. *CPC 81339 or 81319*

      Settlement and clearing services for financial assets, including securities, derivative products, and other negotiable instruments.

适用于附件 1 至 5 所列实体和服务的普遍条件

1. 尽管有附件 1 至 5 的规定，但是本协定并不适用于：

   - 所有咨询和特许经营安排
   - 邮件的航空运输
   - 法定保险，包括涉及车辆和船舶的第三方责任险和涉及雇员的雇主责任险
   - 政府产业署购买的办公或住宅用房。

2. 电信服务运营商可能需要根据《电讯条例》获得许可。申请该许可的运营商需要根据《公司条例》在香港设立。

3. 不得要求中国香港允许通过跨境提供此类服务、或通过商业存在或自然人存在提供此类服务。

4. 下列服务不包括在附件 4 中的金融服务内：

   1. *CPC 81402*

      保险和退休金咨询服务

   2. *CPC 81339*

      货币经纪

   3. *CPC 8119+81323*

      资产管理，如现金或证券管理、各种形式的集体投资管理、养老基金管理、保管、存款和信托服务。

   4. *CPC 81339 或 81319*

      金融资产的结算和清算，包括证券、衍生产品和其他可转让票据。

2005 年 3 月 9 日 (WT/Let/491)

5. *CPC 8131 or 8133*

Advisory and other auxiliary financial services on all the activities listed in subparagraphs 5(a)(v) to (xvi) in the Annex on Financial Services in the General Agreement on Trade in Services, including credit reference and analysis, investment and portfolio research and advice, advice on acquisitions and on corporate restructuring and strategy.

6. *CPC 81339+81333+81321*

Trading for own account or for account of customers, whether on an exchange, in an over-the-counter market or otherwise, the following:

- money market instruments (cheques, bills, certificate of deposits, etc.)
- foreign exchange
- derivative products including, but not limited to futures and options
- exchange rate and interest rate instruments, including products such as swaps, forward rate agreement, etc.
- transferable securities
- other negotiable instruments and financial assets, including bullion.

9 March 2005 (WT/Let/491)

5. *CPC 8131 或 8133*

就《服务贸易总协定》中《关于金融服务的附件》第 5 款(a)项(v)至(xvi)目中所列的所有活动提供咨询和其他附属金融服务，包括信用调查和分析、投资和资产组合的研究和咨询、收购咨询、公司重组和策略咨询。

6. *CPC 81339+81333+81321*

交易市场、公开市场或场外交易市场的自行交易或代客交易：

- 货币市场工具(包括支票、汇票、存单)
- 外汇
- 衍生产品，包括但不仅限于期货和期权
- 汇率和利率工具，包括换汇和远期利率协议等产品
- 可转让证券
- 其他可转让票据和金融资产，包括金银条块。

ICELAND
冰岛

ICELAND

(Authentic in the English language only)

ANNEX 1

Entities which Procure in Accordance With the Provisions of this Agreement

Supplies
Threshold: SDR 130,000

Services (specified in Annex 4)
Threshold: SDR 130,000

Works (specified in Annex 5)
Threshold: SDR 5,000,000

List of Entities:

The following central government entities including:

Central purchasing entities not having an industrial or commercial character governed by Act no. 63/1970 on the arrangement of public works contracts, and Act no. 52/1987, on government procurement, as amended.

The entities in charge of government procurement are the following bodies:
Ríkiskaup (State Trading Center)
Framkvæmdasýslan (Government Construction Contracts)
Vegagerð ríkisins (Public Road Administration)
Siglingastofnun (Icelandic Maritime Administration)

28 April 2001 (WT/Let/396)

冰岛

(仅以英文为准)

附件 1

依照本协定条款进行采购的实体

供应品
门槛金额: 130,000 特别提款权

服务 (附件 4 中列明)
门槛金额: 130,000 特别提款权

工程 (附件 5 中列明)
门槛金额: 5,000,000 特别提款权

实体清单:

下列中央政府采购实体包括:

受经修正的关于公共工程合同安排的 63/1970 号法和关于政府采购的 52/1987 号法管辖、不具产业或商业性质的中央采购实体。

负责政府采购的实体为下列机构:
国家贸易中心
政府建筑合同管理局
公用道路管理局
冰岛海事管理局

2001 年 4 月 28 日 (WT/Let/396)

ANNEX 2

Entities which Procure in Accordance
With the Provisions of this Agreement

Supplies
Threshold: SDR 200,000

Services (specified in Annex 4)
Threshold: SDR 200,000

Works (specified in Annex 5)
Threshold: SDR 5,000,000

List of Entities:

1. Contracting local public authorities, including all municipalities.

2. Public bodies at the local level not having an industrial or commercial character.

28 April 2001 (WT/Let/396)

附件 2

依照本协定条款进行采购的实体

供应品
门槛金额: 200,000 特别提款权

服务 (附件 4 中列明)
门槛金额: 200,000 特别提款权

工程 (附件 5 中列明)
门槛金额: 5,000,000 特别提款权

实体清单:

1. 缔约地方政府，包括所有城市。

2. 地方一级不具产业或商业性质的公共机构。

2001 年 4 月 28 日 (WT/Let/396)

ANNEX 3

Other Entities which Procure in Accordance
With the Provisions of this Agreement

Supplies
Threshold: SDR 400,000

Services (specified in Annex 4)*
Threshold: SDR 400,000

Works (specified in Annex 5)
Threshold: SDR 5,000,000

List of Sectors:

1. *The electricity sector*:

Landvirkjun (The National Power Company), *lög nr. 42/1983.*
Rafmagnsveitur ríkisins (The State Electric Power Works), *orkulög nr. 58/1967*
Orkuveita Reykjavíkur (Reykjavík Energy).
Orkubú Vestfjarða (Vestfjord Power Company), *lög nr. 66/1976.*
Other entities producing, transporting or distributing electricity pursuant to *orkulög nr. 58/1967.*

2. *Urban transport*:

Strætisvagnar Reykjavíkur (The Reykjavík Municipal Bus Service).
Almenningsvagnar bs.
Other Municipal bus services.

3. *Airports*:

Flugmálastjórn (Directorate of Civil Aviation)

4. *Ports*:

Siglingastofnun, (Icelandic Maritime Administration).
Other entities operating pursuant to *Hafnalög nr. 23/1994.*

5. *Water supply*:**

Public entities producing or distributing drinking water pursuant to *lög nr 81/1991, um vatnsveitur sveitarfélaga.*

28 April 2001 (WT/Let/396)

附件 3

依照本协定条款进行采购的其他实体

供应品
门槛金额: 400,000 特别提款权

服务 (附件 4 中列明) *
门槛金额: 400,000 特别提款权

工程 (附件 5 中列明)
门槛金额: 5,000,000 特别提款权

部门清单:

1. *电力部门*:

国家电力公司，*42/1983 号法*
州电力工程公司，*58/1967 号法*
雷克雅未克能源公司
韦斯特峡湾电力公司，*66/197 号法*
根据 *58/1967 号法*生产、传输或配送电力的其他实体

2. *城市交通*:

雷克雅未克城市公共汽车服务
公共汽车服务
其他城市公共汽车服务

3. *机场*:

民用航空管理局

4. *港口*:
冰岛海事管理局
根据 *23/1994 号法*运营的其他实体。

5. *供水*: **
根据*有关社区供水的 81/1991 号法*生产或分配饮用水的公用事业实体。

2001 年 4 月 28 日 (WT/Let/396)

Notes to Annex 3

* This Agreement shall not apply to service contracts which:

(a) a contracting entity awards to an affiliated undertaking;

(b) are awarded by a joint venture formed by a number of contracting entities for the purpose of carrying out a relevant activity within the meaning of paragraphs 1-5 of this Annex to one of those contracting entities or to an undertaking which is affiliated with one of these contracting entities;

Provided that at least 80 per cent of the average turnover of that undertaking with respect to services arising within the EEA for the three preceding years derives from the provision of such services to undertakings with which it is affiliated. When more than one undertaking affiliated with the contracting entity provides the same service or similar services, the total turnover deriving from the provision of services by those undertakings shall be taken into account.

** The supply of drinking water and electricity to networks which provide a service to the public by a contracting entity other than a public authority shall not be considered as a relevant activity within the meaning of paragraphs 1 and 5 of Annex 3 where:

- the production of drinking water or electricity by the entity concerned takes place because its consumption is necessary for carrying out an activity other than that referred to in paragraphs 1 and 5 of this Annex; and

- supply to the public network depends only on the entity's own consumption and has not exceeded 30 per cent of the entity's total production of drinking water or energy, having regard to the average for the preceding three years, including the current year.

附件 3 注释

*　本定不适用于下列服务合同：

(a)　一缔约实体授予其附属企业的服务合同；

(b)　由一若干缔约实体组成的、旨在从事本附件第 1 至 5 款意义内的活动的合资企业授予这些缔约实体之一或一附属于这些缔约实体之一的企业的服务合同；

但条件是该企业在欧洲经济区内所产生的服务以往 3 年的平均营业额至少 80%来自该企业向其所附属企业提供此类服务。如该缔约实体超过一家以上的附属企业提供相同或类似服务，则应考虑这些企业从提供此类服务所获全部营业额。

**　在下列情形下，一不属政府机构的缔约实体向为公众提供服务的网络供应饮用水和电力的行为，不得视为属附件 3 第 1 至 5 款意义内的相关活动：

- 有关实体生产饮用水或电力属因其消费系为从事本附件第 1 至 5 款所指活动以外的活动所必需；且

- 向公共网络供应仅取决于该实体自身消费，且未超过该实体饮用水或能源总产量的 30%，指以往 3 年(含当年)的平均值。

2001 年 4 月 28 日 (WT/Let/396)

ANNEX 4

Services

Of the Universal List of Services, as contained in document MTN.GNS/W/120, the following services are included:*

Subject	*CPC Reference N*
Maintenance and repair services	6112, 6122, 633, 886
Land transport services, including armoured car services, and courier services, except transport of mail	712 (except 71235), 7512, 87304
Air transport services of passengers and freight, except transport of mail	73 (except 7321)
Transport of mail by land, except rail, and by air	71235, 7321
Telecommunications services	752** (except 7524, 7525, 7526)
Financial services	ex 81
(a) Insurance services	812, 814
(b) Banking and investment services***	
Computer and related services	84
Accounting, auditing and bookkeeping services	862
Market research and public opinion polling services	864
Management consulting services and related services	865, 866****
Architectural services; engineering services and integrated engineering services, urban planning and landscape architectural services; related scientific and technical consulting services; technical consulting services; technical testing and analysis services	867
Advertising services	871
Building-cleaning services and property management services	874, 82201-82206

28 April 2001 (WT/Let/396)

附件 4

服务

包括载于 MTN.GNS/W/120 号文件的服务通用清单中的下列服务：*

事项	*CPC 参考号*
维护和修理服务	6112、6122、633、886
陆路运输服务,包括装甲车服务和速递服务，邮件运输除外	712(不含 71235)、7512、87304
航空客运和货运服务,邮件运输除外	73(不含 7321)
陆地和航空邮件运输，铁路运输除外	71235, 7321
电信服务	752 ** (不含 7524、7525、7526)
金融服务	ex 81
(a) 保险服务 (b) 银行与投资服务 ***	812、814
计算机及相关服务	84
会计、审计和簿记服务	862
市场调研和民意测验服务	864
管理咨询服务及相关服务	865、866 ****
建筑设计服务；工程服务与集中工程服务、 城市规划和景观设计服务； 相关科技咨询服务； 技术咨询服务； 技术测试和分析服务	867
广告服务	871
建筑物清洁服务与物业管理服务	874、82201-82206

2001 年 4 月 28 日 (WT/Let/396)

Subject	*CPC Reference N*
Publishing and printing services on a fee or contract basis	88442
Sewage and refuse disposal; sanitation and similar services	94

Notes to Annex 4

* except for services which entities have to procure from another entity pursuant to an exclusive right established by a published law, regulation or administrative provision

** except voice telephony, telex, radiotelephony, paging and satellite services

*** except contracts for financial services in connection with the issue, sale, purchase, or transfer of securities or other financial instruments, and central bank services

**** except arbitrations and conciliation services

28 April 2001 (WT/Let/396)

事项	*CPC 参考号*
收费或合同基础上的出版和印刷服务	88442
排污及废物处理；卫生及类似服务	94

附件 4 注释

* 一实体根据一已公布的法律、法规或管理规定所确定的专用权必须向另一实体购买的服务除外

** 语音通信、电传、无线电话、寻呼及卫星服务除外

*** 关于证券或其他金融工具的发行、销售、购买或转让的金融服务合同及中央银行服务合同除外

**** 仲裁和调解服务除外

2001 年 4 月 28 日 (WT/Let/396)

ANNEX 5

Construction Services

Definition:

A construction service contract is a contract which has as its objective the realization by whatever means of civil or building works, in the sense of Division 51 of the Central Product Classification (CPC).

List of Division 51, CPC:

All public works/construction services of Division 51.

附件 5

建筑服务

定义:

建筑服务合同是指根据《中央产品分类》第 51 类，以通过任何土木或建筑工程手段实现目的的合同。

CPC 第 51 类清单:

CPC 51 类包含的所有服务。

2001 年 4 月 28 日 (WT/Let/396)

GENERAL NOTES AND DEROGATIONS FROM THE PROVISIONS OF ARTICLE III

1. Iceland will not extend the benefits of this Agreement:

- as regards the award of contracts by entities listed in Annex 2 to the suppliers and service providers of Canada;

- as regards the award of contracts, other than for supplies, listed in Annex 2 to the suppliers and service providers of the USA;

- as regards the award of contracts by entities listed in Annex 3 paragraph

  (1) (electricity), to the suppliers and service providers of Canada, Singapore and Japan;

  (2) (urban transport), to the suppliers and service providers of Canada, Japan, Korea and the USA;

  (3) (airports), to the suppliers and service providers of Canada, Korea and the USA;

  (4) (ports), to the suppliers and service providers of Canada;

  (5) (water), to the suppliers and service providers of Canada and the USA;

until such time as Iceland has accepted that the Parties concerned give comparable and effective access for Icelandic undertakings to the relevant markets;

- to service providers of Parties which do not include the relevant service contracts for the relevant entities in Annexes 1 to 3 and the relevant service category under Annexes 4 and 5 in their own coverage.

2. The provisions of Article XX shall not apply to suppliers and service providers of:

- Japan and Korea in contesting the award of contracts by entities listed under Annex 2, paragraph 2, until such time as Iceland accepts that they have completed coverage of sub-central entities;

- Japan and Korea in contesting the award of contracts to a supplier or service provider of Parties other than those mentioned, which are small or medium-sized enterprises under the relevant provisions in Iceland, until such time as Iceland accepts that they no longer operate discriminatory measures in favour of certain domestic small and minority businesses;

- Israel, Japan and Korea in contesting the award of contracts by Icelandic entities, whose value is less than the threshold applied for the same category of contracts awarded by these Parties.

11 January 2003 (WT/Let/438)

总注释及对第 3 条规定的背离

1. 冰岛在下列方面不将本协定利益给予下列参加方：

- 对于附件 2 中所列实体授予的合同，本协定利益不给予加拿大供应商和服务提供者；

- 对于附件 2 所列除供应品外的合同的授予，本协定利益不给予美国供应商和服务提供者；

- 对于附件 3 条款中所列实体授予的合同：

  (1) (电力)，本协定利益不给予加拿大、新加坡和日本供应商和服务提供者;

  (2) (城市交通)，本协定利益不给予加拿大、日本、韩国和美国供应商和服务提供者;

  (3) (机场)，本协定利益不给予加拿大、韩国和美国供应商和服务提供者;

  (4) (港口)，本协定利益不给予加拿大供应商和服务提供者;

  (5) (水)，本协定利益不给予加拿大和美国供应商和服务提供者;

直至冰岛已经认为有关参加方给予冰岛企业对于相关市场的对等和有效的准入机会。

- 本协定利益不给予在其各自承诺范围中未对附件 1 至 3 中相关实体包括相关服务合同和未在附件 4 和 5 中包括相关服务类别的参加方的服务提供者。

2. 第 20 条规定不适用于下列参加方的供应商和服务提供者：

- 日本和韩国，在竞争附件 2 第 2 款下所列实体授予的合同时，直至冰岛认为他们的次中央实体范围已经完整时止；

- 日本和韩国，在竞争将合同授予已提及的参加方供应商或服务提供者之外的一属冰岛相关规定所定义的小型或中型企业的供应商或服务提供者时，直至冰岛认为他们不再采取有利于某些国内小型和少数族裔企业的歧视性措施时止;

- 以色列、日本和韩国，在竞争冰岛实体授予的合同时，其价值低于这些参加方所授予的相同类别合同所适用的门槛金额。

2003 年 1 月 11 日(WT/Let/438)

3. Until such time as Iceland has accepted that the Parties concerned provide access for Icelandic suppliers and service providers to their own markets, Iceland will not extend the benefits of this Agreement to suppliers and service providers of:

- Canada as regards procurement of FSC 58 (communications, protection and coherent radiation equipment) and the USA as regards air traffic control equipment;

- Israel and Korea as regards procurement by entities listed in Annex 3, paragraph 1, as regards procurement of HS Nos 8504, 8535, 8537 and 8544 (electrical transformers, plugs, switches and insulated cables); and for Israel, HS Nos 8501, 8536 and 902830;

- Canada and the USA as regards contracts for good or service components of contracts which, although awarded by an entity covered by this Agreement, are not themselves subject to this Agreement.

4. Contracts awarded by entities in Annexes 1 and 2 in connection with activities in the fields of drinking water, energy, transport or telecommunications, are not included.

5. With regard to Annex 3, this Agreement shall not apply to the following contracts:

- contracts which the contracting entities under paragraph 5 award for the purchase of water;

- contracts which the contracting entities under paragraph 1 award for the supply of energy or of fuels for the production of energy;

- contracts which the contracting entities award for purposes other than the pursuit of their activities as described in this Annex or for the pursuit of such activities in a non-EEA country;

- contracts awarded for purposes of re-sale or hire to third parties provided that the contracting entity enjoys no special or exclusive right to sell or hire the subject of such contracts and that other entities are free to sell or hire it under the same conditions as the contracting entity;

- contracting entities exercising activities in the bus transportation sector where other entities are free to offer the same services in the same geographical area and under substantially the same conditions.

6. With regard to Annex 4, this Agreement shall not apply to the following:

- contracts for the acquisition or rental, by whatever financial means, of land, existing buildings, or other immovable property or concerning rights thereon;

- contracts for the acquisition, development, production or co-production of programme material by broadcasters and contracts for broadcasting time;

3. 在冰岛已经认为有关参加方对冰岛供应商和服务提供者提供进入其各自市场的机会之前，冰岛不将本协定的利益给予下列参加方的供应商和服务提供者：

- 加拿大，对于 FSC 58 的采购(通信、侦测和相干辐射设备)及美国，对于空中交通管制设备的采购；

- 以色列和韩国，对于附件 3 第 1 款中所列实体关于协调制度编码 HS8504、8535、8537 和 8544(变压器、插头、开关和绝缘电缆)的采购；以色列，关于协调制度编码 HS8501、8536 和 902830 的采购；

- 加拿大和美国，对于虽由本协定所涵盖一实体授予、但其货物或服务组成部分本身不受本协定管辖的合同。

4. 不包括附件 1 和 2 中实体授予的与在饮用水、能源、运输或通信领域活动有关的合同。

5. 对于附件 3，本协定不适用于下列合同：

- 第 5 款下缔约实体为购买水而授予的合同；

- 第 1 款下缔约实体为供应能源或为生产能源而供应燃料而授予的合同；

- 缔约实体所授予的合同目的不是为了从事本附件所述活动或为在一非欧洲经济区国家从事此类活动而授予的合同；

- 为再销售或向第三方出租而授予的合同，但条件是缔约实体不享受销售或出租此类合同客体的特殊或专用权，且其他实体有权根据与该缔约实体相同的条件销售或出租此类合同客体：

- 在公共汽车运输部门从事活动的缔约实体，而其他实体有权在同一地理区域以实质相同的条件提供相同服务。

6. 对于附件 4，本协定不适用于下列合同：

- 购买或租赁土地、现有建筑物或其他不动产或涉及相关权利的合同，无论通过何种出资方式；

- 广播电台购买、开发、制作或联合制作节目内容的合同和播放时间的合同；

2003 年 1 月 11 日(WT/Let/438)

- contracts awarded to an entity which is itself a contracting authority within the meaning of the Public Procurement Act: "Lög um opinber innkaup (52/1997) and Regulation (302/1996) on the basis of an exclusive right which it enjoys pursuant to a published law, regulation or administrative provision;

- contracts of employment.

7. The Agreement shall not apply to contracts awarded under:

- an international agreement and intended for the joint implementation or exploitation of a project by the signatory States;

- an international agreement relating to the stationing of troops;

- the particular procedure of an international organization.

8. The Agreement shall not apply to procurement of agricultural products made in furtherance of agricultural support programmes and human feeding programmes.

11 January 2003 (WT/Let/438)

- 给予一本身属《公共采购法》(52/1997)和法规(302/1996)意义内的缔约机构的实体的合同，该实体根据已公布的法律、法规或管理规定享有专用权；

- 雇佣合同。

7. 本协定不适用于在下列情况下授予的合同：

- 旨在由签署国联合执行或开发一项目的国际协定；

- 与军队驻扎有关的国际协定；

- 国际组织的特定程序。

8. 本协定不适用于为促进农业支持计划和人类供给计划而采购的农产品。

2003 年 1 月 11 日(WT/Let/438)

ISRAEL
以色列

ISRAEL

(Authentic in the English language only)

ANNEX 1

Central Government Entities which Procure in Accordance With the Provisions of this Agreement

Supplies	*Threshold*: 130,000 SDR
Services (specified in Annex 4)	*Threshold*: 130,000 SDR
Construction (specified in Annex 5)	*Threshold*: 8,500,000 SDR; during the period beginning from 1 January 2006 until 31 December 2008, the threshold shall be set at 5,000,000 SDR

List of Entities:

House of Representatives (the Knesset)
Prime Minister's Office
Ministry of Agriculture and Rural Development
Ministry of Communications
Ministry of Construction and Housing
Ministry of Education, Culture and Sport
Ministry of National Infrastructures excluding Fuel Authority
Ministry of the Environment
Ministry of Finance
Civil Service Commission
Ministry of Foreign Affairs
Ministry of Health (1)
Ministry of Immigrants Absorption
Ministry of Industry, Trade and Labour
Ministry of the Interior
Ministry of Justice
Ministry of Social Affairs
Ministry of Science and Technology
Ministry of Tourism
Ministry of Transport
Office of the State Comptroller and Ombudsman

13 February 2006 (WT/Let/513)

以色列

(仅以英文为准)

附件 1

依照本协定条款进行采购的中央政府实体

供应品 *门槛金额：* 130,000 特别提款权

服务(附件 4 中列明) *门槛金额：* 130,000 特别提款权

建筑(附件 5 中列明) *门槛金额：* 8,500,000 特别提款权；在自 2006 年 1 月 1 日起至 2008 年 12 月 31 日止的时期内，门槛金额应定为 5,000,000 特别提款权

实体清单

众议院(以色列国会)
总理办公室
农业和乡村发展部
交通部
建设和住房部
教育、文件和体育部
国家基础设施部，不含燃料管理局
环境部
财政部
文职委员会
外交部
卫生部(1)
移民接收部
工业、贸易和劳工部
内政部
司法部
社会事务部
科技部
旅游部
运输部
审计长和调查官办公室

2006 年 2 月 13 日 (WT/Let/513)

Note to Annex 1

(1) *Ministry of Health - Excepted Products*

- Insulin and infusion pumps
- Audiometers
- Medical dressings (bandages, adhesive tapes excluding gauze bandages and gauze pads)
- Intravenous solution
- Administration sets for transfusions
- Scalp vein sets
- Hemi-dialysis and blood lines
- Blood packs
- Syringe needles

附件 1 注释

(1) *卫生部—例外产品*

- 胰岛素和输液泵
- 听度计
- 医用敷料 (绷带、胶布，不包括纱布绷带和纱布衬垫)
- 静脉溶液
- 输血用系列器材
- 头皮针
- 血液透析和输血管
- 血袋
- 皮下注射针头

2005 年 12 月 21 日 (WT/Let/507)

ANNEX 2

Sub-Central Government Entities which Procure in Accordance With the Provisions of this Agreement

Supplies	*Threshold*: 250,000 SDR
Services (specified in Annex 4)	*Threshold*: 250,000 SDR
Construction (specified in Annex 5)	*Threshold*: 8,500,000 SDR; during the period beginning from 1 January 2006 until 31 December 2008, the threshold shall be set at 5,000,000 SDR

List of Entities:

Municipalities of Jerusalem, Tel-Aviv and Haifa

Local Government Economic Services Ltd.

13 February 2006 (WT/Let/513)

附件 2

依照本协定条款进行采购的次中央政府实体

供应品 *门槛金额:* 250,000 特别提款权

服务(附件 4 中列明) *门槛金额:* 250,000 特别提款权

建筑(附件 5 中列明) *门槛金额:* 8,500,000 特别提款权；在自 2006 年 1 月 1 日起至 2008 年 12 月 31 日止的时期内，门槛金额应定为 5,000,000 特别提款权

实体清单:

耶路撒冷、特拉维夫及海法市政府

地方政府经济服务有限公司

2006 年 2 月 13 日 (WT/Let/513)

ANNEX 3

All Other Entities which Procure in Accordance
With the Provisions of this Agreement

Supplies — *Threshold*: 355,000 SDR

Services (specified in Annex 4) — *Threshold*: 355,000 SDR

Construction (specified in Annex 5) — *Threshold*: 8,500,000 SDR; during the period beginning from 1 January 2006 until 31 December 2008, the threshold shall be set at 5,000,000 SDR

List of Entities:

Israel Airports Authority
Israel Ports Development and Assets Company Ltd. (1)
Ashdod Port Company Ltd. (1)
Haifa Port Company Ltd. (1)
Eilat Port Company Ltd. (1)
Israel Railways Limited (1)
Israel Broadcasting Authority
Israel Educational Television
Israel Postal Company Ltd.
The Israel Electric Corp. Ltd. (1) (2a)
Mekorot Water Co. Ltd.
Sports' Gambling Arrangement Board
The Standards Institution of Israel
National Insurance Institute of Israel
All entities operating in the field of urban transport, except those operating in the field of bus services (2b)

Notes to Annex 3

(1) Procurement of cables is excluded.

(2a) Excluded products: cables (H.S. 8544), electro-mechanic meters (ex. H.S. 9028), transformers (H.S. 8504), disconnectors and switchers (H.S. 8535-8537), electric motors (H.S. 8501).

(2b) With regard to procurement by entities operating in the field of urban transport, except those operating in the field of bus services, this Agreement shall apply only to goods and services, including construction services, of the European Community.

Israel is willing to negotiate the opening of procurement by entities operating in the field of urban transport, except those operating in the field of bus services, to other Parties to the Agreement under the condition of reciprocity.

26 September 2006 (WT/Let/550)

附件 3

依照本协定条款进行采购的所有其他实体

供应品 *门槛金额:* 355,000 特别提款权

服务 (附件 4 中列明) *门槛金额:* 355,000 特别提款权

建筑 (附件 5 中列明) *门槛金额:* 8,500,000 特别提款权；在自 2006 年 1 月 1 日起至 2008 年 12 月 31 日止的时期内，门槛金额应定为 5,000,000 特别提款权

实体清单:

以色列机场管理局
以色列港口发展和资产有限公司 (1)
阿什杜德港口有限公司(1)
埃拉特港口有限公司(1)
以色列铁路有限公司(1)
以色列广播管理局
以色列教育电视台
以色列邮政有限公司
以色列电力有限公司(1) (2a)
麦克罗特水务有限公司
体育彩票管理局
以色列标准协会
以色列全国保险协会
在城市交通领域运营的所有实体，在公共汽车服务领域运营的实体除外(2b)

附件 3 注释

(1)　不包括电缆采购。

(2a)　排除的产品：电缆(HS8544)、电机仪表(ex HS9028)、变压器(HS8504)、分离器和开关(HS8535-8537)、电动机(HS 8501)。

(2b)　对于在城市交通领域运营的实体所进行的采购，在公共汽车服务领域运营的实体除外，本协定仅适用于欧共体的货物和服务，包括建筑服务。

以色列愿意与其他参加方在对等条件下就开放在城市交通领域运营的实体的采购进行谈判，在公共汽车服务领域运营的实体除外。

2006 年 9 月 26 日 (WT/Let/550)

ANNEX 4

Services

Of the Universal List of Services, as contained in document MTN.GNS/W/120, the following services are included:

CPC	*Description*
6112, 6122, 633, 886	Maintenance and repair services
641	Hotel and similar accommodation services
642-3	Food and beverage serving services
712	Land transport services
73	Passenger transportation services
7471	Travel agency and tour operator services
752	Telecommunications services
821	Real estate services involving own or leased property
83106 to 83109	Leasing or rental services concerning machinery and equipment without operator only
83203 to 83209	Leasing or rental services concerning personal and household goods only
84	Computer and related services
861	Legal services (advisory services on foreign and international law only)
862	Accounting, auditing and bookkeeping services
863	Taxation services (excluding legal services)
864	Market research and public opinion
865-6	Management consulting
867	Architectural services; engineering services and integrated engineering services, urban planning and landscape architectural services; related scientific and technical consulting services; technical testing and analysis services

附件 4

服务

包括载于 MTN.GNS/W/120 号文件的服务通用清单中的下列服务：

CPC	*描述*
6112、6122、633、886	维护和修理服务
641	旅馆和类似住宿服务
642-3	餐饮服务
712	陆路运输服务
73	客运服务
7471	旅行社和旅游经营者服务
752	电信服务
821	涉及自有或租赁房地产的服务
83106 至 83109	仅限无操作人员的机械和设备的租赁或出租服务
83203 至 83209	仅限个人和家庭用品的租赁或出租服务
84	计算机及相关服务
861	法律服务(仅限关于外国和国际法的咨询服务)
862	会计、审计和簿记服务
863	税收服务(不含法律服务)
864	市场调研和民意测验
865-6	管理咨询
867	建筑设计服务；工程服务与集中工程服务、城市规划和景观设计服务；相关科技咨询服务;技术咨询服务；技术测试和分析服务

2005 年 12 月 21 日 (WT/Let/507)

871	Advertising services
874, 82201-82206	Building-cleaning services and property management services
876	Packaging services
8814	Services incidental to forestry and logging, including forest management
883	Services incidental to mining, including drilling and field services
88442	Publishing and printing services on a fee or contract basis
887	Services incidental to energy distribution
9401-5	Environmental services

Note to Annex 4

The offer regarding services (including construction) is subject to the limitation and conditions specified in Israel's schedule of the GATS.

21 December 2005 (WT/Let/507)

871	广告服务
874、82201-82206	建筑物清洁服务和资产管理服务
876	包装服务
8814	林业和伐木附带服务，包括林业管理
883	在收费或合同基础上的与采矿业有关的服务
88442	在收费或合同基础上的印刷和出版服务
887	与能源分配有关的服务
9401-5	环境服务

附件 4 注释

关于服务的出价(包括建筑)应受以色列 GATS 减让表中列明的限制和条件管辖。

2005 年 12 月 21 日(WT/Let/507)

ANNEX 5

Construction Services

Definition:

A construction services contract is a contract which has as its objective the realization by whatever means of civil or building works, in the sense of Division 51 of the Central Product Classification.

Threshold: 8,500,00 SDR; during the period beginning from 1 January 2006 until 31 December 2008, the threshold shall be set at 5,000,000 SDR

List of construction services offered

CPC	*Description*
511	Pre-erection work at construction sites
512	Construction work for buildings
513	Construction work for civil engineering
514	Assembly and erection of prefabricated construction
515	Special trade construction work
516	Installation work
517	Building completion and finishing work
518	Renting services related to equipment for construction

附件 5

建筑服务

定义:

建筑服务合同是指根据《中央产品分类》第 51 类，以通过任何土木或建筑工程手段实现目的的合同。

门槛金额: 8,500,000 特别提款权；在自 2006 年 1 月 1 日起至 2008 年 12 月 31 日止的时期内，门槛金额应定为 5,000,000 特别提款权

建筑服务出价清单

CPC	*描述*
511	建筑工地的准备工作
512	建筑物的建筑工作
513	土木工程的建筑工作
514	预制构件的组装和装配
515	特种行业建筑工程
516	安装工程
517	建筑物竣工和修整工程
518	与建筑设备有关的租赁服务

2005 年 12 月 21 日 (WT/Let/507)

GENERAL NOTES

(1) The Agreement shall not apply to contracts awarded for purposes of re-sale or hire to third parties, provided that the contracting entity enjoys no special or exclusive right to sell or hire the subject of such contracts and other entities are free to sell or hire it under the same conditions as the contracting entity.

(2) The Agreement shall not apply to contracts for the purchase of water and for the supply of energy and of fuels for the production of energy.

(3) The Agreement shall not apply to the acquisition or rental of land, buildings or other immovable property, or concerning rights thereon.

1 March 2000 (WT/Let/330)

总注释

(1) 本协定不适用于为向第三方再销售或出租而授予的合同，但条件是缔约实体不享受销售或出租此类合同客体的特殊或专属权，且其他实体有权根据与缔约实体相同的条件销售或出租此类合同客体。

(2) 本协定不适用于为购买水及为提供能源和为提供用于生产能源的燃料的合同。

(3) 本协定不适用于购买或租赁土地、建筑物或其他不动产或涉及相关的权利。

2000 年 3 月 1 日 (WT/Let/330)

NOTE

Offset

1. Having regard to Article XVI and to general policy considerations regarding development, Israel may operate provisions which require the limited incorporation of domestic content, offset procurement or transfer of technology, in the form of objective and clearly defined conditions for participation in procedures for the award of contracts, which do not discriminate between other Parties.

This shall be done under the following terms:

(a) Israel shall ensure that its entities indicate the existence of such conditions in their tender notices and specify them clearly in the contract documents.

(b) Suppliers will not be required to purchase goods that are not offered on competitive terms, including price and quality, or to take any action which is not justified from a commercial standpoint.

(c) Offsets in any form may be required up to 35 per cent of the contract going down to 30 per cent after five years, 28 per cent after ten years and 20 per cent after 13 years, beginning from the date Israel implements the Agreement.

2. (a) At the end of each period mentioned in paragraph 1(c), Israel will submit a report concerning the implementation of this Note.

(b) When the level of the offset has reached 20 per cent, Israel will consult with the Parties to this Agreement on the level of the use of offset by Israel. The review shall take into consideration *inter alia* general and economic developments in Israel, its trade balance, the actual performance within the framework of this Agreement and the views of the other Parties.

21 December 2005 (WT/Let/507)

注释

补偿

1. 考虑到第 16 条和有关发展的总体政策考虑，以色列可以以不在其他参加方之间造成歧视的参加合同授予程序的客观和明确定义的条件的形式，使用要求有限比例的本国含量、补偿采购或技术转让的规定。

此点应根据下列条件实施：

(a) 以色列应保证其采购实体在其招标通知中注明此类条件的存在，并在合同文件中明确列出。

(b) 不得要求供应商购买以非竞争条件提供的货物，包括价格和质量，或采取任何从商业角度无法证明合理的行动。

(c) 任何形式的补偿可最高达合同的 35%，自以色列实施本协定之日起 5 年后降至 30%，10 年后降至 28%，13 年后降至 20%。

2. (a) 在第 1 款(c)项所指每一期限末，以色列将提交一份关于实施本注释的报告。

(b) 待补偿水平达到 20%后，以色列将就其所使用补偿的水平与本协定参加方进行磋商。审议应特别考虑以色列的总体发展和经济发展情况、其贸易平衡、本协定框架内的实际表现以及其他参加方的观点。

2005 年 12 月 21 日(WT/Let/507)

JAPAN
日本

JAPAN

(Authentic in the English language only)

ANNEX 1

Central Government Entities which Procure in Accordance with the Provisions of this Agreement

Supplies

Threshold:

130 thousand SDR

List of Entities:

All entities covered by the Accounts Law as follows:

- House of Representatives
- House of Councillors
- Supreme Court
- Board of Audit
- Cabinet
- National Personnel Authority
- Cabinet Office
- Imperial Household Agency
- National Public Safety Commission (National Police Agency)
- Financial Services Agency
- Ministry of Internal Affairs and Communications
- Ministry of Justice
- Ministry of Foreign Affairs
- Ministry of Finance
- Ministry of Education, Culture, Sports, Science and Technology
- Ministry of Health, Labour and Welfare
- Ministry of Agriculture, Forestry and Fisheries
- Ministry of Economy, Trade and Industry
- Ministry of Land, Infrastructure, Transport and Tourism
- Ministry of Environment
- Ministry of Defense

Services

Threshold:

Construction services: 4,500 thousand SDR

Architectural, engineering and other technical services covered by this Agreement:
450 thousand SDR

Other services: 130 thousand SDR

List of Entities which procure the services, specified in Annex 4:

All entities covered by the Accounts Law as follows:

- House of Representatives
- House of Councillors
- Supreme Court
- Board of Audit
- Cabinet
- National Personnel Authority
- Cabinet Office
- Imperial Household Agency
- National Public Safety Commission (National Police Agency)

21 March 2009 (WT/Let/641)

日本

(仅以英文为准)

附件 1

依照本协定条款进行采购的中央政府实体

供应品

门槛金额:

130,000 特别提款权

实体清单:

《会计法》涵盖的所有实体如下:

- 众议院
- 参议院
- 最高法院
- 会计检察院
- 内阁
- 人事院
- 内阁府
- 宫内厅
- 国家公安委员会
(警察厅)
- 金融厅
- 总务省
- 法务省
- 外务省
- 财务省
- 文部科学省
- 厚生劳动省
- 农林水产省
- 经济产业省
- 国土交通省
- 环境省
- 防卫省

服务

门槛金额:

建筑服务: 4,500,000 特别提款权

本协定涵盖的建筑设计、工程及其他技术服务:
450,000 特别提款权

其他服务: 130,000 特别提款权

采购附件 4 所列服务的实体清单:

《会计法》涵盖的所有实体如下:

- 众议院
- 参议院
- 最高法院
- 会计检察院
- 内阁
- 人事院
- 内阁府
- 宫内厅
- 国家公安委员会
(警察厅)

2009 年 3 月 21 日 (WT/Let/641)

***Services** (cont'd)*

- Financial Services Agency
- Ministry of Internal Affairs and Communications
- Ministry of Justice
- Ministry of Foreign Affairs
- Ministry of Finance
- Ministry of Education, Culture, Sports, Science and Technology
- Ministry of Health, Labour and Welfare
- Ministry of Agriculture, Forestry and Fisheries
- Ministry of Economy, Trade and Industry
- Ministry of Land, Infrastructure and Transport
- Ministry of Environment
- Ministry of Defense

Notes to Annex 1

1. Entities covered by the Accounts Law include all their internal sub-divisions, independent organs, attached organizations and other organizations and local branch offices provided for in the National Government Organization Law and the Law establishing the Cabinet Office.

2. Products and services procured with a view to resale or with a view to use in the production of goods for sale are not included.

3. This Agreement shall not apply to contracts to be awarded to co-operatives or associations in accordance with laws and regulations existing at the time of the entry into force of this Agreement for Japan.

4. This Agreement will generally apply to procurement by the Ministry of Defense of the following Federal Supply Classification (FSC) categories subject to the Japanese Government determinations under the provisions of Article XXIII, paragraph 1:

FSC	*Description*
22	Railway Equipment
24	Tractors
32	Woodworking Machinery and Equipment
34	Metalworking Machinery
35	Service and Trade Equipment
36	Special Industry Machinery
37	Agricultural Machinery and Equipment
38	Construction, Mining, Excavating, and Highway Maintenance Equipment
39	Materials Handling Equipment
40	Rope, Cable, Chain, and Fittings
41	Refrigeration, Air Conditioning, and Air Circulating Equipment
43	Pumps and Compressors
45	Plumbing, Heating and Sanitation Equipment
46	Water Purification and Sewage Treatment Equipment
47	Pipe, Tubing, Hose, and Fittings
48	Valves
51	Hand Tools
52	Measuring Tools
55	Lumber, Millwork, Plywood and Veneer
61	Electric Wire, and Power and Distribution Equipment
62	Lighting Fixtures and Lamps
65	Medical, Dental, and Veterinary Equipment and Supplies
6630	Chemical Analysis Instruments
6635	Physical Properties Testing Equipment
6640	Laboratory Equipment and Supplies
6645	Time Measuring Instruments
6650	Optical Instruments
6655	Geophysical and Astronomical Instruments

服务(续)

- 金融厅
- 总务省
- 法务省
- 外务省
- 财务省
- 文部科学省
- 厚生劳动省
- 农林水产省
- 经济产业省
- 国土交通省
- 环境省
- 防卫省

附件 1 注释

1. 《会计法》所涵盖实体包括《国家行政组织法》和《内阁府设置法》规定的所有内部机构、独立机构、附属组织及其他组织和当地分支机构。

2. 不包括用于转售目的的货物和服务或用于生产供销售的货物的货物和服务。

3. 本协定不适用于依照本协定对日本生效时已存在的法律授予合作社或协会的合同。

4. 本协定通常适用于防卫省对下列《联邦产品分类》(FSC)类别的采购，取决于日本政府根据第 23 条第 1 款所做决定：

FSC	*描述*
22	铁路设备
24	拖拉机
32	木工机器和设备
34	金属加工机器
35	服务和交易设备
36	特别工业机器
37	农业机器和设备
38	建筑、采矿、开凿和公路维护设备
39	材料处理设备
40	粗绳、电缆、链条和配件
41	冷却、空调和空气循环装备
43	泵和压缩机
45	管道、加热和卫生设备
46	水净化和污水处理设备
47	水管和配件
48	阀
51	手工工具
52	测量工具
55	木材、木制品、胶合板和饰面板
61	电线及电力传输设备
62	照明器材和灯
65	内科、牙科和兽医设备和耗材
6630	化学分析仪器
6635	物理性质测试设备
6640	实验室设备和耗材
6645	计时测量仪器
6650	光学仪器
6655	地球物理学和天文学仪器

FSC	*Description (cont'd)*
6660	Meteorological Instruments and Apparatus
6670	Scales and Balances
6675	Drafting, Surveying, and Mapping Instruments
6680	Liquid and Gas Flow, Liquid Level, and Mechanical Motion Measuring Instruments
6685	Pressure, Temperature, and Humidity Measuring and Controlling Instruments
6695	Combination and Miscellaneous Instruments
67	Photographic Equipment
68	Chemicals and Chemical Products
71	Furniture
72	Household and Commercial Furnishings and Appliances
73	Food Preparation and Serving Equipment
74	Office Machines and Visible Record Equipment
75	Office Supplies and Devices
76	Books, Maps, and Other Publications
77	Musical Instruments, Phonographs, and Home-type Radios
79	Cleaning Equipment and Supplies
80	Brushes, Paints, Sealers, and Adhesives
8110	Drums and Cans
8115	Boxes, Cartons, and Crates
8125	Bottles and Jars
8130	Reels and Spools
8135	Packaging and Packing Bulk Materials
85	Toiletries
87	Agricultural Supplies
93	Non-metallic Fabricated Materials
94	Non-metallic Crude Materials
99	Miscellaneous

FSC	*描述(续)*
6660	气象学仪品和装置
6670	天平
6675	绘图、测量和测绘仪器
6680	液体和气体流动、液面及机械运动测量仪器
6685	压力、温度和湿度测量和控制仪器
6695	组合和杂项仪器
67	摄影设备
68	化学药品和化工品
71	家具
72	家用和商用家具和器械
73	食品加工和供餐设备
74	办公设备和可视记录设备
75	办公用品和装置
76	图书、地图和其他出版物
77	乐器、留声机和家用收音机
79	清洁设备和耗材
80	刷子、油漆、封条和粘合剂
8110	桶
8115	盒子、硬纸盒和板条箱
8125	瓶和罐
8130	卷轴
8135	包装和包装粒状材料
85	盥洗用品
87	农用品
93	非金属制品
94	非金属原料
99	杂项制品

2004 年 10 月 17 日 (WT/Let/483)

ANNEX 2

Sub-Central Government Entities which Procure in Accordance with the Provisions of this Agreement

Supplies

Threshold:

200 thousand SDR

List of Entities:

All prefectural governments entitled "To", "Do", "Fu" and "Ken", and all designated cities entitled "Shitei-toshi", covered by the Local Autonomy Law as follows:

- Hokkaido
- Aomori-ken
- Iwate-ken
- Miyagi-ken
- Akita-ken
- Yamagata-ken
- Fukushima-ken
- Ibaraki-ken
- Tochigi-ken
- Gunma-ken
- Saitama-ken
- Chiba-ken
- Tokyo-to
- Kanagawa-ken
- Niigata-ken
- Toyama-ken
- Ishikawa-ken
- Fukui-ken
- Yamanashi-ken
- Nagano-ken
- Gifu-ken
- Shizuoka-ken
- Aichi-ken
- Mie-ken
- Shiga-ken
- Kyoto-fu
- Osaka-fu
- Hyogo-ken
- Nara-ken
- Wakayama-ken
- Tottori-ken
- Shimane-ken
- Okayama-ken
- Hiroshima-ken
- Yamaguchi-ken
- Tokushima-ken
- Kagawa-ken
- Ehime-ken
- Kochi-ken
- Fukuoka-ken
- Saga-ken
- Nagasaki-ken
- Kumamoto-ken
- Oita-ken
- Miyazaki-ken
- Kagoshima-ken
- Okinawa-ken
- Osaka-shi
- Nagoya-shi
- Kyoto-shi
- Yokohama-shi
- Kobe-shi
- Kitakyushu-shi
- Sapporo-shi
- Kawasaki-shi
- Fukuoka-shi
- Hiroshima-shi
- Sendai-shi
- Chiba-shi

Services

Threshold:

Construction services: 15,000 thousand SDR

Architectural, engineering and other technical services covered by this Agreement:
1,500 thousand SDR

Other services: 200 thousand SDR

1 March 2000 (WT/Let/330)

附件 2

依照本协定条款进行采购的次中央政府实体

供应品

门槛金额:

200,000 特别提款权

实体清单:

《地方会计法》涵盖的所有名为“都”、“道”、“府”、“县”的地方政府和名为“指定都市”的指定城市如下:

- 北海道
- 青森县
- 岩手县
- 宫城县
- 秋田县
- 山形县
- 福岛县
- 茨城县
- 枥木县
- 群马县
- 埼玉县
- 千叶县
- 东京道
- 神奈川县
- 新潟县
- 富山县
- 石川县
- 福井县
- 山梨县
- 长野县
- 岐阜县
- 静冈县
- 爱知县
- 三重县
- 滋贺县
- 京都府
- 大阪府
- 兵库县
- 奈良县
- 和歌山县
- 鸟取县
- 岛根县
- 冈山县
- 广岛县
- 山口县
- 德岛县
- 香川县
- 爱媛县
- 高知县
- 福冈县
- 佐贺县
- 长崎县
- 熊本县
- 大分县
- 宫崎县
- 鹿儿岛县
- 冲绳县
- 大阪市
- 名古屋市
- 京都市
- 横滨市
- 神户市
- 北九州市
- 札幌市
- 川崎市
- 福冈市
- 广岛市
- 仙台市
- 千叶市

服务

门槛金额:

建筑服务: 15,000,000 特别提款权

本协定涵盖的建筑设计、工程及其他技术服务:
1,500,000 特别提款权

其他服务: 200,000 特别提款权

2000 年 3 月 1 日 (WT/Let/330)

***Services** (cont'd)*

List of Entities which procure the services, specified in Annex 4:

All prefectural governments entitled "To", "Do", "Fu" and "Ken", and all designated cities entitled "Shitei-toshi", covered by the Local Autonomy Law as follows:

- Hokkaido
- Aomori-ken
- Iwate-ken
- Miyagi-ken
- Akita-ken
- Yamagata-ken
- Fukushima-ken
- Ibaraki-ken
- Tochigi-ken
- Gunma-ken
- Saitama-ken
- Chiba-ken
- Tokyo-to
- Kanagawa-ken
- Niigata-ken
- Toyama-ken
- Ishikawa-ken
- Fukui-ken
- Yamanashi-ken
- Nagano-ken
- Gifu-ken
- Shizuoka-ken
- Aichi-ken
- Mie-ken
- Shiga-ken
- Kyoto-fu
- Osaka-fu
- Hyogo-ken
- Nara-ken
- Wakayama-ken
- Tottori-ken
- Shimane-ken
- Okayama-ken
- Hiroshima-ken
- Yamaguchi-ken
- Tokushima-ken
- Kagawa-ken
- Ehime-ken
- Kochi-ken
- Fukuoka-ken
- Saga-ken
- Nagasaki-ken
- Kumamoto-ken
- Oita-ken
- Miyazaki-ken
- Kagoshima-ken
- Okinawa-ken
- Osaka-shi
- Nagoya-shi
- Kyoto-shi
- Yokohama-shi
- Kobe-shi
- Kitakyushu-shi
- Sapporo-shi
- Kawasaki-shi
- Fukuoka-shi
- Hiroshima-shi
- Sendai-shi
- Chiba-shi

Notes to Annex 2

1. "To", "Do", "Fu", "Ken" and "Shitei-toshi" covered by the Local Autonomy Law include all internal sub-divisions, attached organizations and branch offices of all their governors or mayors, committees and other organizations provided for in the Local Autonomy Law.

2. Products and services procured with a view to resale or with a view to use in the production of goods for sale are not included.

3. This Agreement shall not apply to contracts to be awarded to co-operatives or associations in accordance with laws and regulations existing at the time of the entry into force of this Agreement for Japan.

4. This Agreement shall not apply to contracts which the entities award for purposes of their daily profit-making activities which are exposed to competitive forces in markets. This note shall not be used in a manner which circumvents the provisions of this Agreement.

5. Procurement related to operational safety of transportation is not included.

6. Procurement related to the production, transport or distribution of electricity is not included.

1 March 2000 (WT/Let/330)

服务(续)

采购附件 4 所列服务的实体清单：

《地方会计法》涵盖的所有名为“都”、“道”、“府”、“县”的地方政府和名为“指定都市”的指定城市如下：

- 北海道
- 青森县
- 岩手县
- 宫城县
- 秋田县
- 山形县
- 福岛县
- 茨城县
- 枥木县
- 群马县
- 埼玉县
- 千叶县
- 东京道
- 神奈川县
- 新潟县
- 富山县
- 石川县
- 福井县
- 山梨县
- 长野县
- 岐阜县
- 静冈县
- 爱知县
- 三重县
- 滋贺县
- 京都府
- 大阪府
- 兵库县
- 奈良县
- 和歌山县
- 鸟取县
- 岛根县
- 冈山县
- 广岛县
- 山口县
- 德岛县
- 香川县
- 爱媛县
- 高知县
- 福冈县
- 佐贺县
- 长崎县
- 熊本县
- 大分县
- 宫崎县
- 鹿儿岛县
- 冲绳县
- 大阪市
- 名古屋市
- 京都市
- 横滨市
- 神户市
- 北九州市
- 札幌市
- 川崎市
- 福冈市
- 广岛市
- 仙台市
- 千叶市

附件 2 注释

1. 《地方会计法》涵盖的所有“都”、“道”、“府”、“县”包括《地方会计法》规定的所有内部机构、附属组织和所有县知府或市长办公室的分支机构、委员会和其他组织。

2. 不包括用于转售目的的货物和服务或用于生产供销售的货物的货物和服务。

3. 本协定不适用于依照本协定对日本生效时已存在的法律授予合作社或协会的合同。

4. 本协定不适用于实体为了处于市场竞争中的日常盈利活动而授予的合同。本条注释不得以规避本协定条款的方式实施。

5. 不包括与运输的操作安全有关的采购。

6. 不包括与电力的生产、输送或配送有关的采购。

2000 年 3 月 1 日 (WT/Let/330)

JAPAN

ANNEX 3

All Other Entities which Procure in Accordance with the Provisions of this Agreement

Supplies

Threshold:

130 thousand SDR

List of Entities:

1. Group A

- Japan Water Agency
- Japan Regional Development Corporation
- Japan Railway Construction Public Corporation (a)(d)
- Narita International Airport Corporation
- East Nippon Expressway Company Limited
- Central Nippon Expressway Company Limited
- West Nippon Expressway Company Limited
- Metropolitan Expressway Company Limited
- Hanshin Expressway Company Limited
- Honshu-Shikoku Bridge Expressway Company Limited
- Japan Expressway Holding and Debt Repayment Agency
- Urban Development Corporation (a)
- Japan Science and Technology Agency
- Japan Atomic Energy Agency (b)
- Japan Environmental Safety Corporation
- Japan International Cooperation Agency
- Welfare and Medical Service Agency
- Government Pension Investment Fund
- Agriculture and Livestock Industries Corporation
- Japan Oil, Gas and Metals National Corporation (c)
- Japan Small and Medium Enterprise Corporation
- Japan Post
- Japan Labour Health and Welfare Organization
- Employment and Human Resources Development Organization of Japan
- Okinawa Development Finance Corporation
- Japan Finance Corporation
- Housing Loan Corporation
- Japan Finance Corporation for Municipal Enterprises
- Development Bank of Japan
- Tokyo Metro Co. Ltd. (a)
- Japan Tobacco Inc.
- Hokkaido Railway Company (a)
- East Japan Railway Company (a)
- Central Japan Railway Company (a)
- West Japan Railway Company (a)
- Shikoku Railway Company (a)
- Kyushu Railway Company (a)
- Japan Freight Railway Company (a)
- Nippon Telegraph and Telephone Co. (f)
- Nippon Telegraph and Telephone East Co. (f)
- Nippon Telegraph and Telephone West Co. (f)
- Northern Territories Issue Association
- National Consumer Affairs Center of Japan
- RIKEN (b)
- Environmental Restoration and Conservation Agency
- Fund for the Promotion and Development of the Amami Islands
- Japan Foundation
- Japan Student Services Organization

26 May 2009 (WT/Let/643)

日本

附件 3

依照本协定条款进行采购的所有其他实体

供应品

门槛金额:

130,000 特别提款权

实体清单:

1. A 组

- 独立行政法人水资源机构
- 地方振兴整备公团
- 日本铁路建设公团 (a) (d)
- 成田国际机场株式会社
- 东日本高速公路株式会社
- 中日本高速公路株式会社
- 西日本高速公路株式会社
- 首都高速公路株式会社
- 阪神高速公路株式会社
- 本州-四国联络高速公路株式会社
- 日本高速公路保有和债务返还机构
- 都市基盘整备公团 (a)
- 独立行政法人科学技术振兴机构
- 日本原子能研究开发机构 (b)
- 日本环境安全事业株式会社
- 独立行政法人国际协力机构
- 独立行政法人福祉医疗机构
- 年金公积金管理运用独立行政法人
- 独立行政法人农畜产业振兴机构
- 独立行政法人石油天然气金属矿物资源机构 (c)
- 独立行政法人中小企业综合实业团
- 日本邮政公社
- 独立行政法人劳动者健康福祉机构
- 独立行政法人雇用和能力开发机构
- 冲绳振兴开发金融公库
- 日本政策金融公库
- 住宅金融公库
- 公营企业金融公库
- 日本政策投资银行
- 东京地铁株式会社 (a)
- 日本烟草产业株式会社
- 北海道旅客铁道株式会社 (a)
- 东日本旅客铁道株式会社 (a)
- 中日本旅客铁道株式会社(a)
- 西日本旅客铁道株式会社 (a)
- 四国旅客铁道株式会社(a)
- 九州旅客铁道株式会社(a)
- 日本货物铁道株式会社 (a)
- 日本电信电话株式会社(f)
- 东日本电信电话株式会社 (f)
- 西日本电信电话株式会社 (f)
- 独立行政法人北方领土问题对策协会
- 独立行政法人国民生活中心
- 独立行政法人理化学研究所(b)
- 独立行政法人环境再生保全机构
- 独立行政法人奄美群岛振兴开发基金
- 独立行政法人国际交流基金
- 独立行政法人学生支援机构

2009 年 5 月 26 日 (WT/Let/643)

***Supplies** (cont'd)*

- Japan Arts Council
- Japan Society for the Promotion of Science
- University of the Air Foundation
- National Agency for the Advancement of Sports and Health
- Social Insurance Medical Fee Payment Fund
- National Center for Persons with Severe Intellectual Disabilities, Nozominosono
- Japan Racing Association
- Mutual Aid Association of Agriculture, Forestry and Fishery Corporation Personnel
- The National Association of Racing
- Farmers' Pension Fund
- Keirin Promotion Association (A juridical person designated as such pursuant to the Bicycle Racing Law)
- Japan External Trade Organization
- Motorcycle Racing Promotion Association (A juridical person designated as such pursuant to the Auto Racing Law)
- New Energy and Industrial Technology Development Organization
- Japan National Tourist Organization
- The Japan Institute for Labour Policy and Training
- Mutual Aid Fund for Official Casualties and Retirement of Volunteer Firemen
- Corporation for Advanced Transport and Technology (e)
- The Promotion and Mutual Aid Corporation for Private Schools of Japan
- Organization for Workers' Retirement Allowance Mutual Aid

2. Group B

- National Archives of Japan
- Communications Research Laboratory
- National Research Institute of Fire and Disaster
- National Research Institute of Brewing
- National Center for University Entrance Examinations
- National Institute of Special Needs Education
- National Institution for Youth Education
- National Women's Education Center
- The National Institute for Japanese Language
- National Science Museum
- National Institute for Materials Science
- National Research Institute for Earth Science and Disaster Prevention
- National Aerospace Laboratory of Japan
- National Institute of Radiological Sciences
- National Museum of Art
- National Institutes for Cultural Heritage
- National Center for Teachers' Development
- National Institute of Health and Nutrition
- National Institute of Industrial Safety
- National Institute of Industrial Health
- Food and Agricultural Materials Inspection Center
- National Center for Seeds and Seedlings
- National Livestock Breeding Center
- National Agriculture and Food Research Organization
- National Fisheries University
- National Institute of Agrobiological Sciences
- National Institute for Agro-Environmental Sciences
- Japan International Research Center for Agricultural Sciences
- Forestry and Forest Products Research Institute
- Fisheries Research Agency
- Research Institute of Economy, Trade and Industry
- National Center for Industrial Property Information and Training
- Nippon Export and Investment Insurance
- National Institute of Advanced Industrial Science and Technology
- National Institute of Technology and Evaluation
- Public Works Research Institute
- Building Research Institute

4 December 2008 (WT/Let/637/Corr.1)

供应品 (续)

- 独立行政法人日本艺术文化振兴会
- 独立行政法人日本学术振兴会
- 放送大学学园
- 独立行政法人日本体育振兴中心
- 社会保险诊疗报酬支付基金
- 独立行政法人国立重度智力障碍者综合设施希望园
- 日本中央赛马会
- 农林渔业团体职员共济组合
- 地方赛马全国协会
- 独立行政法人农民退休金基金
- 日本自行车振兴会(根据《自行车竞赛法》指定的行政法人)
- 独立行政法人日本贸易振兴机构
- 日本小型自动车振兴会(根据《自动车竞赛法》指定的行政法人)
- 独立行政法人新能源产业技术综合开发机构
- 独立行政法人国际观光振兴机构
- 独立行政法人劳动政策研究培训机构
- 消防员等公共灾害补偿互助基金
- 运输设施整备事业团 (e)
- 日本私立学校振兴互助事业团
- 独立行政法人劳动者退休金互助机构

2. B 组

- 独立行政法人国立公文馆
- 独立行政法人通讯综合研究所
- 独立行政法人消防研究中心
- 独立行政法人酒类综合研究所
- 独立行政法人大学入学考试中心
- 独立行政法人国立特殊教育综合研究所
- 独立行政法人国立青少年教育振兴机构
- 独立行政法人国立女性教育会馆
- 独立行政法人国立国语研究所
- 独立行政法人国立科学博物馆
- 独立行政法人物质材料研究机构
- 独立行政法人防灾科学技术研究所
- 独立行政法人航空宇宙技术研究所
- 独立行政法人放射线医学综合研究所
- 独立行政法人国立美术馆
- 独立行政法人文化财产研究所
- 独立行政法人教员培训中心
- 独立行政法人国立健康营养研究所
- 独立行政法人产业安全研究所
- 独立行政法人产业医学综合研究所
- 独立行政法人农林水产消费安全技术中心
- 独立行政法人种苗管理中心
- 独立行政法人家畜改良中心
- 独立行政法人农业食品产业技术综合研究机构
- 独立行政法人水产大学
- 独立行政法人农业生物资源研究所
- 独立行政法人农业环境技术研究所
- 独立行政法人国际农林水产业研究中心
- 独立行政法人森林综合研究所
- 独立行政法人水产综合研究中心
- 独立行政法人经济产业研究所
- 独立行政法人工业产权信息培训馆
- 独立行政法人日本贸易保险
- 独立行政法人产业技术综合研究所
- 独立行政法人产品评估技术基础机构
- 独立行政法人土木研究所
- 独立行政法人建筑研究所

2008 年 12 月 4 日 (WT/Let/637/Corr.1)

Supplies *(cont'd)*

- National Traffic Safety and Environment Laboratory
- National Maritime Research Institute
- Port and Airport Research Institute
- Electronic Navigation Research Institute
- Civil Engineering Research Institute of Hokkaido
- Marine Technical Education Agency
- National Institute for Sea Training
- Civil Aviation College
- National Institute for Environmental Studies
- Labor Management Organization for USFJ Employees
- National Agency for Vehicle Inspection
- National Statistics Center
- Japan Mint
- National Printing Bureau
- Japan Nuclear Energy Safety Organization
- National Hospital Organization
- National University Corporation
- Inter-University Research Institute Corporation
- Institute of National Colleges of Technology, Japan
- National Institution for Academic Degrees and University Evaluation
- Center for National University Finance and Management

Services

Threshold:

Construction services:
4,500 thousand SDR for Japan Post in Group A
15,000 thousand SDR for all other entities in Group A
4,500 thousand SDR for entities in Group B

Architectural, engineering and other technical services covered by this Agreement:
450 thousand SDR

Other services: 130 thousand SDR

List of Entities which procure the services, specified in Annex 4:

1. Group A

- Japan Water Agency
- Japan Regional Development Corporation
- Japan Railway Construction Public Corporation (a)(d)
- Narita International Airport Corporation
- East Nippon Expressway Company Limited
- Central Nippon Expressway Company Limited
- West Nippon Expressway Company Limited
- Metropolitan Expressway Company Limited
- Hanshin Expressway Company Limited
- Honshu-Shikoku Bridge Expressway Company Limited
- Japan Expressway Holding and Debt Repayment Agency
- Urban Development Corporation (a)
- Japan Science and Technology Agency
- Japan Atomic Energy Agency (b)
- Japan Environmental Safety Corporation
- Japan International Cooperation Agency
- Welfare and Medical Service Agency
- Government Pension Investment Fund
- Agriculture and Livestock Industries Corporation
- Japan Oil, Gas and Metals National Corporation (c)
- Japan Small and Medium Enterprise Corporation
- Japan Post
- Japan Labour Health and Welfare Organization
- Employment and Human Resources Development Organization of Japan
- Okinawa Development Finance Corporation
- Japan Finance Corporation
- Housing Loan Corporation
- Japan Finance Corporation for Municipal Enterprises
- Development Bank of Japan
- Tokyo Metro Co. Ltd. (a)
- Japan Tobacco Inc. (g)
- Hokkaido Railway Company (a)(g)
- East Japan Railway Company (a)(g)
- Central Japan Railway Company (a)(g)
- West Japan Railway Company (a)(g)
- Shikoku Railway Company (a)(g)
- Kyushu Railway Company (a)(g)

26 May 2009 (WT/Let/643)

供应品（续）

- 独立行政法人交通安全环境研究所
- 独立行政法人海上技术安全研究所
- 独立行政法人港口机场技术研究所
- 独立行政法人电子航法研究所
- 独立行政法人北海道开发土木研究所
- 独立行政法人海技大学
- 独立行政法人航海训练所
- 独立行政法人航空大学
- 独立行政法人国立环境研究所
- 独立行政法人驻军等劳动者劳务管理机构
- 汽车检查独立行政法人
- 独立行政法人统计中心
- 独立行政法人造币局
- 独立行政法人国立印刷局
- 独立行政法人原子能安全基础设施机构
- 独立行政法人国立医院机构
- 独立行政法人国立大学法人
- 大学共同利用机构法人
- 独立行政法人国立高等专门学校机构
- 独立行政法人大学评估与学位授予机构
- 独立行政法人国立大学财政和经营中心

服务

门槛金额：

建筑服务：
4,500,000 特别提款权 A 组日本邮政公社
15,000,000 特别提款权 A 组所有其他实体
4,500,000 特别提款权 B 组实体

本协定涵盖的建筑设计、工程及
其他技术服务：
450,000 特别提款权

其他服务*：130,000 特别提款权*

采购附件 4 中所列服务的实体清单：

1. A 组

- 独立行政法人水资源机构
- 地方振兴整备公团
- 日本铁道建设公团(a) (d)
- 成田国际机场株式会社
- 东日本高速公路株式会社
- 中日本高速公路株式会社
- 西日本高速公路株式会社
- 首都高速公路株式会社
- 阪神高速公路株式会社
- 本州-四国联络高速公路株式会社
- 日本高速公路保有和债务返还机构
- 都市基盘整备公团 (a)
- 独立行政法人科学技术振兴机构
- 日本原子能研究开发机构 (b)
- 日本环境安全事业株式会社
- 独立行政法人国际协力机构
- 独立行政法人福祉医疗机构
- 年金公积金管理运用独立行政法人
- 独立行政法人农畜产业振兴机构
- 独立行政法人石油天然气金属矿物资源机构 (c)
- 独立行政法人中小企业综合事业团
- 日本邮政公社
- 独立行政法人劳动者健康福祉机构
- 独立行政法人雇用和能力开发机构
- 冲绳振兴开发金融公库
- 日本政策金融公库
- 住宅金融公库
- 公营企业金融公库
- 日本政策投资银行
- 东京地铁株式会社 (a)
- 日本烟草产业株式会社(g)
- 北海道旅客铁道株式会社 (a) (g)
- 东日本旅客铁道株式会社 (a) (g)
- 中日本旅客铁道株式会社(a) (g)
- 西日本旅客铁道株式会社 (a) (g)
- 四国旅客铁道株式会社(a) (g)
- 九州旅客铁道株式会社(a) (g)

2009 年 5 月 26 日 (WT/Let/643)

***Services** (cont'd)*

- Japan Freight Railway Company (a)(g)
- Nippon Telegraph and Telephone Co. (f)(g)
- Nippon Telegraph and Telephone East Co. (f)(g)
- Nippon Telegraph and Telephone West Co. (f)(g)
- Northern Territories Issue Association
- National Consumer Affairs Center of Japan
- RIKEN (b)
- Environmental Restoration and Conservation Agency
- Fund for the Promotion and Development of the Amami Islands
- Japan Foundation
- Japan Student Services Organization
- Japan Arts Council
- Japan Society for the Promotion of Science
- University of the Air Foundation
- National Agency for the Advancement of Sports and Health
- Social Insurance Medical Fee Payment Fund
- National Center for Persons with Severe Intellectual Disabilities, Nozominosono
- Japan Racing Association
- Mutual Aid Association of Agriculture, Forestry and Fishery Corporation Personnel
- The National Association of Racing
- Farmers' Pension Fund
- Keirin Promotion Association (A juridical person designated as such pursuant to the Bicycle Racing Law)
- Japan External Trade Organization
- Motorcycle Racing Promotion Association (A juridical person designated as such pursuant to the Auto Racing Law)
- New Energy and Industrial Technology Development Organization
- Japan National Tourist Organization
- The Japan Institute for Labour Policy and Training
- Mutual Aid Fund for Official Casualties and Retirement of Volunteer Firemen
- Corporation for Advanced Transport and Technology (e)
- The Promotion and Mutual Aid Corporation for Private Schools of Japan
- Organization for Workers' Retirement Allowance Mutual Aid

2. Group B

- National Archives of Japan
- Communications Research Laboratory
- National Research Institute of Fire and Disaster
- National Research Institute of Brewing
- National Center for University Entrance Examinations
- National Institute of Special Needs Education
- National Institution for Youth Education
- National Women's Education Center
- The National Institute for Japanese Language
- National Science Museum
- National Institute for Materials Science
- National Research Institute for Earth Science and Disaster Prevention
- National Aerospace Laboratory of Japan
- National Institute of Radiological Sciences
- National Museum of Art
- National Institutes for Cultural Heritage
- National Center for Teachers' Development
- National Institute of Health and Nutrition
- National Institute of Industrial Safety
- National Institute of Industrial Health
- Food and Agricultural Materials Inspection Center
- National Center for Seeds and Seedlings
- National Livestock Breeding Center
- National Agriculture and Food Research Organization
- National Fisheries University
- National Institute of Agrobiological Sciences
- National Institute for Agro-Environmental Sciences
- Japan International Research Center for Agricultural Sciences
- Forestry and Forest Products Research Institute

4 December 2008 (WT/Let/637/Corr.1)

服务(续)

- 日本货物铁道株式会社 (a) (g)
- 日本电信电话株式会社(f) (g)
- 东日本电信电话株式会社(f) (g)
- 西日本电信电话株式会社(f) (g)
- 独立行政法人北方领土问题对策协会
- 独立行政法人国民生活中心
- 独立行政法人理化学研究所(b)
- 独立行政法人环境再生保全机构
- 独立行政法人奄美群岛振兴开发基金
- 独立行政法人国际交流基金
- 独立行政法人学生支援机构
- 独立行政法人日本艺术文化振兴会
- 独立行政法人日本学术振兴会
- 放送大学学园
- 独立行政法人日本体育振兴中心
- 社会保险诊疗报酬支付基金
- 独立行政法人国立重度智力障碍者综合设施希望园
- 日本中央赛马会
- 农林渔业团体职员共济组合
- 地方赛马全国协会
- 独立行政法人农民退休金基金
- 日本自行车振兴会(根据《自行车竞赛法》指定的行政法人)
- 独立行政法人日本贸易振兴机构
- 日本小型自动车振兴会(根据《自动车竞赛法》指定的行政法人)
- 独立行政法人新能源产业技术综合开发机构
- 独立行政法人国际观光振兴机构
- 独立行政法人劳动政策研究培训机构
- 消防员等公共灾害补偿互助基金
- 运输设施整备事业团 (e)
- 日本私立学校振兴互助事业团
- 独立行政法人劳动者退休金互助机构

2. B 组

- 独立行政法人国立公文馆
- 独立行政法人通讯综合研究所
- 独立行政法人消防研究中心
- 独立行政法人酒类综合研究所
- 独立行政法人大学入学考试中心
- 独立行政法人国立特殊教育综合研究所
- 独立行政法人国立青少年教育振兴机构
- 独立行政法人国立女性教育会馆
- 独立行政法人国立国语研究所
- 独立行政法人国立科学博物馆
- 独立行政法人物质材料研究机构
- 独立行政法人防灾科学技术研究所
- 独立行政法人航空宇宙技术研究所
- 独立行政法人放射线医学综合研究所
- 独立行政法人国立美术馆
- 独立行政法人文化财产研究所
- 独立行政法人教员培训中心
- 独立行政法人国立健康营养研究所
- 独立行政法人产业安全研究所
- 独立行政法人产业医学综合研究所
- 独立行政法人农林水产消费安全技术中心
- 独立行政法人种苗管理中心
- 独立行政法人家畜改良中心
- 独立行政法人农业食品产业技术综合研究机构
- 独立行政法人水产大学
- 独立行政法人农业生物资源研究所
- 独立行政法人农业环境技术研究所
- 独立行政法人国际农林水产业研究中心
- 独立行政法人森林综合研究所

2008 年 12 月 4 日 (WT/Let/637/Corr.1)

Services (cont'd)

- Fisheries Research Agency
- Research Institute of Economy, Trade and Industry
- National Center for Industrial Property Information and Training
- Nippon Export and Investment Insurance
- National Institute of Advanced Industrial Science and Technology
- National Institute of Technology and Evaluation
- Public Works Research Institute
- Building Research Institute
- National Traffic Safety and Environment Laboratory
- National Maritime Research Institute
- Port and Airport Research Institute
- Electronic Navigation Research Institute
- Civil Engineering Research Institute of Hokkaido
- Marine Technical Education Agency
- National Institute for Sea Training
- Civil Aviation College
- National Institute for Environmental Studies
- Labor Management Organization for USFJ Employees
- National Agency for Vehicle Inspection
- National Statistics Center
- Japan Mint
- National Printing Bureau
- Japan Nuclear Energy Safety Organization
- National Hospital Organization
- National University Corporation
- Inter-University Research Institute Corporation
- Institute of National Colleges of Technology, Japan
- National Institution for Academic Degrees and University Evaluation
- Center for National University Finance and Management

Notes to Annex 3

1. Products and services procured with a view to resale or with a view to use in the production of goods for sale are not included.

2. This Agreement shall not apply to contracts to be awarded to co-operatives or associations in accordance with laws and regulations existing at the time of the entry into force of this Agreement for Japan.

3. This Agreement shall not apply to contracts which the entities in Group A award for purposes of their daily profit-making activities which are exposed to competitive forces in markets. This note shall not be used in a manner which circumvents the provisions of this Agreement.

4. Notes to specific entities:

(a) Procurement related to operational safety of transportation is not included.

(b) Procurement which could lead to the disclosure of information incompatible with the purpose of the Treaty on the Non-Proliferation of Nuclear Weapons or with international agreements on intellectual property rights is not included. Procurement for safety-related activities aiming at utilization and management of radioactive materials and responding to emergencies of nuclear installation is not included.

(c) Procurement related to geological and geophysical survey is not included.

(d) Procurement of advertising services, construction services and real estate services is not included.

(e) Procurement of ships to be jointly owned with private companies is not included.

(f) Procurement of public electrical tele-communications equipment and of services related to operational safety of telecommunications is not included.

(g) Procurement of the services specified in Annex 4, other than construction services, is not included.

---

26 May 2009 (WT/Let/643)

服务(续)

- 独立行政法人水产综合研究中心
- 独立行政法人经济产业研究所
- 独立行政法人工业产权信息培训馆
- 独立行政法人日本贸易保险
- 独立行政法人产业技术综合研究所
- 独立行政法人产品评估技术基础机构
- 独立行政法人土木研究所
- 独立行政法人建筑研究所
- 独立行政法人交通安全环境研究所
- 独立行政法人海上技术安全研究所
- 独立行政法人港口机场技术研究所
- 独立行政法人电子航法研究所
- 独立行政法人北海道开发土木研究所
- 独立行政法人海技大学
- 独立行政法人航海训练所
- 独立行政法人航空大学
- 独立行政法人国立环境研究所
- 独立行政法人驻军等劳动者劳务管理机构
- 汽车检查独立行政法人
- 独立行政法人统计中心
- 独立行政法人造币局
- 独立行政法人国立印刷局
- 独立行政法人原子能安全基础设施机构
- 独立行政法人国立医院机构
- 独立行政法人国立大学法人
- 大学共同利用机构法人
- 独立行政法人国立高等专门学校机构,
- 独立行政法人大学评估与学位授予机构
- 独立行政法人国立大学财政和经营中心

附件 3 注释

1. 不包括用于转售目的的货物和服务或用于生产供销售的货物的货物和服务。

2. 本协定不适用于依照本协定对日本生效时已存在的法律授予合作社或协会的合同。

3. 本协定不适用于实体为了处于市场竞争中的日常盈利活动而授予的合同。本条注释不得以规避本协定条款的方式实施。

4. 对特定实体的注释:

(a) 不包括与运输的运营安全有关的采购。

(b) 不包括有可能导致与《不扩散核武器条约》或关于知识产权的国际协定目前不一致的信息披露的采购。不包括旨在使用和管理放射物质和对核设施的紧急状况做出反应的与安全有关的活动的采购。

(c) 不包括与地质和地球物理测量有关的采购。

(d) 不包括广告服务、建筑服务和房地产服务的采购。

(e) 不包括将与私营公司共同所有的船只的采购。

(f) 不包括公共电子通信设备的采购和与电信运营安全有关的服务的采购。

(g) 不包括附件 4 所列除建筑服务之外的服务的采购。

2009 年 5 月 26 日 (WT/Let/643)

ANNEX 4

Services

Of the Universal List of Services, as contained in document MTN.GNS/W/120, the following services are included:

(Provisional Central
Product Classification
(CPC), 1991)

- 51 Construction work
- 6112 Maintenance and repair services of motor vehicles[Note 1]
- 6122 Maintenance and repair services of motorcycles and snowmobiles[Note 1]
- 712 Other land transport services (except 71235 Mail transportation by land)
- 7213 Rental services of sea-going vessels with operator
- 7223 Rental services of non-sea-going vessels with operator
- 73 Air transport services (except 73210 Mail transportation by air)
- 748 Freight transport agency services
- 7512 Courier services[Note 2]
- Telecommunications services

-- MTN.GNS/W/120	- Corresponding CPC	
-- 2.C.h.	- 7523	Electronic mail;
-- 2.C.i.	- 7521	Voice mail;
-- 2.C.j.	- 7523	On-line information and data base retrieval;
-- 2.C.k.	- 7523	Electronic data interchange (EDI);
-- 2.C.l.	- 7529	Enhanced facsimile services;
-- 2.C.m.	- 7523	Code and protocol conversion; and
-- 2.C.n.	- 7523	On-line information and/or data processing (including transaction processing)

- 84 Computer and related services
- 864 Market research and public opinion polling services
- 867 Architectural, engineering and other technical services[Note 3]
- 871 Advertising services
- 87304 Armoured car services
- 874 Building-cleaning services
- 88442 Publishing and printing services[Note 4]
- 886 Repair services incidental to metal products, machinery and equipment
- 94 Sewage and refuse disposal, sanitation and other environmental protection services

附件 4

服务

包括载于 MTN.GNS/W/120 号文件的服务通用清单中的下列服务：

(临时中央
产品分类
(CPC), 1991)

- 51 建筑工程
- 6112 机动车的保养和修理服务[注1]
- 6122 摩托车和雪地用汽车的保养和修理服务[注1]
- 712 其他陆路运输服务(71235 陆路邮件运输服务除外)
- 7213 配备驾驶员的远洋船出租服务
- 7223 配备驾驶员的非远洋船出租服务
- 73 空运服务(73210 邮件空运服务除外)
- 748 货运代理行服务
- 7512 速递服务[注2]
- 电信服务
  - -- MTN.GNS/W/120 号文件
    - 相应 CPC
  - -- 2.C.h. - 7523 电子邮件服务；
  - -- 2.C.i. - 7521 语音邮件服务；
  - -- 2.C.j. - 7523 在线信息和数据调用服务；
  - -- 2.C.k. - 7523 电子数据交换服务(EDI)；
  - -- 2.C.l. - 7529 增值传真服务；
  - -- 2.C.m. - 7523 编码和规程转换服务；及
  - -- 2.C.n. - 7523 在线信息和/或数据处理 (包括传输处理)
- 84 计算机及相关服务
- 864 市场调研和民意测验服务
- 867 建筑设计、工程及其他技术服务[注3]
- 871 广告服务
- 87304 装甲车服务
- 874 建筑物清洁服务
- 88442 出版和印刷服务[注4]
- 886 从属金属制品、机械和设备的修理服务
- 94 污水和垃圾处置、卫生及其他环境保护服务

2000 年 3 月 1 日 (WT/Let/330)

Notes to Annex 4

1. Maintenance and repair services are not included with respect to those motor vehicles, motorcycles and snowmobiles which are specifically modified and inspected to meet regulations of the entities.

2. Courier services are not included with respect to letters.

3. Architectural, engineering and other technical services related to construction services, with the exception of the following services when procured independently, are included:

   - Final design services of CPC 86712 Architectural design services;
   - CPC 86713 Contract administration services;
   - Design services consisting of one or a combination of final plans, specifications and cost estimates of either CPC 86722 Engineering design services for the construction of foundations and building structures, or CPC 86723 Engineering design services for mechanical and electrical installations for buildings, or CPC 86724 Engineering design services for the construction of civil engineering works; and
   - CPC 86727 Other engineering services during the construction and installation phase.

4. Publishing and printing services are not included with respect to materials containing confidential information.

附件 4 注释

1. 保养和修理服务不包括为经专门改造和检查以满足实体规定的机动车、摩托车和雪地车。

2. 不包括信件的速递服务。

3. 包括与建筑服务有关的建筑设计、工程和其他技术服务，但下列服务如单独采购则不包括在内：

- CPC 86712 建筑设计服务所含最终设计服务；
- CPC 86713 合同管理服务；
- 下列服务项下由一个或一组最终计划、规格和估价组成的设计服务：CPC 86722 地基和建筑结构的建筑工程设计服务、或CPC 86723 建筑物的机械和电力安装工程设计服务、或CPC 86724 土木工程建筑的建筑工程设计服务；以及
- CPC 86727 建筑和安装阶段其他工程服务。

4. 不包括含机密信息材料的出版和印刷服务。

2000 年 3 月 1 日 (WT/Let/330)

ANNEX 5

Construction Services

Definition:

A construction services contract is a contract which has as its objective the realization by whatever means of civil or building works, in the sense of Division 51 of the Central Product Classification (CPC).

List of Division 51, CPC:

All services listed in Division 51.

Threshold: 4,500 thousand SDR for entities set out in ANNEX 1;
15,000 thousand SDR for those in ANNEX 2;
4,500 thousand SDR for Japan Post in Group A in ANNEX 3;
15,000 thousand SDR for all other entities in Group A in ANNEX 3; and
4,500 thousand SDR for entities in Group B in ANNEX 3.

附件 5

建筑服务

定义：

建筑服务合同是指根据《中央产品分类》第 51 类，以通过任何土木或建筑工程手段实现目的的合同。

CPC 第 51 类清单：

CPC 51 类包含的所有服务。

门槛金额： 4,500,000 特别提款权, 附件 1 所列实体；
15,000,000 特别提款权，附件 2 中实体；
4,500,000 特别提款权，附件 3 中 A 组日本邮政公社；
15,000, 000 特别提款权，附件 3 中 A 组所有其他实体；及
4,500,000 特别提款权，附件 3 中 B 组实体。

2003 年 10 月 14 日 (WT/Let/452/Rev.1)

GENERAL NOTES

1. For goods and services (including construction services) of Canada and suppliers of such goods and services, this Agreement does not apply to procurement by the entities listed in Annexes 2 and 3 (except for Japan Post in Group A and the entities in Group B set out in Annex 3).

2. In case Parties do not apply Article XX to suppliers or service providers of Japan in contesting the award of contract by entities, Japan may not apply the Article to suppliers or service providers of the Parties in contesting the award of contracts by the same kind of entities.

总注释

1. 对于加拿大的货物和服务(包括建筑服务)及此类货物和服务的提供者，本协定不适用于附件 2 和 3(附件 3 中 A 组日本邮政公社和 B 组实体除外)所列实体进行的采购。

2. 如果在竞争实体授予的合同时，参加方不对日本的供应品或服务提供者适用第 20 条，则日本可以在竞争同类企业授予的合同时，对该参加方的供应品或服务提供者不适用该条款。

2003 年 10 月 14 日 (WT/Let/452/Rev.1)

KOREA
韩国

KOREA

(Authentic in the English language only)

ANNEX 1

Central Government Entities which Procure in Accordance with the Provisions of this Agreement

Supplies

Threshold: 130,000 SDR

List of Entities:

- Board of Audit and Inspection
- Office of the Prime Minister
- Ministry of Gender Equality
- Ministry of Strategy and Finance
- Financial Services Commission
- Ministry of Unification
- Ministry of Public Administration and Security
- Ministry of Government Legislation
- Ministry of Patriots and Veterans Affairs
- Ministry of Foreign Affairs and Trade
- Ministry of Justice
- Ministry of National Defense
- Ministry of Education, Science and Technology
- Ministry of Culture, Sports and Tourism
- Cultural Heritage Administration
- Ministry for Food, Agriculture, Forestry and Fisheries
- Ministry of Knowledge Economy
- Ministry for Health, Welfare and Family Affairs
- Korea Food and Drug Administration
- Ministry of Labor
- Ministry of Land, Transport and Maritime Affairs
- Ministry of Environment
- Public Procurement Service (limited to purchases for entities in this list only. Regarding procurement for entities in Annex 2 and Annex 3 in this list, the coverages and thresholds for such entities thereunder shall be applied.)

20 July 2009 (WT/Let/649)

韩国

(仅以英文为准)

附件 1

依照本协定条款进行采购的中央实体

供应品

门槛金额: 130,000 特别提款权

实体清单:

- 监查院
- 总理室
- 女性部
- 企划财政部
- 金融服务委员会
- 统一部
- 行政安全部
- 法制处
- 国家报勋处
- 外交通商部
- 法务部
- 国防部
- 教育科学技术部
- 文化部
- 文化财厅
- 农水产食品部
- 知识经济部
- 保健福祉家庭部
- 食药厅
- 劳动部
- 国土海洋部
- 环境部
- 调达厅(仅限于为本清单中实体所进行的采购。对于为附件 2 和附件 3 中实体进行的采购，应适用该两附件中规定的范围和门槛金额。)

2009 年 7 月 20 日(WT/Let/649)

- National Tax Service
- Customs Service
- National Statistical Office
- Korea Meteorological Administration
- National Police Agency (except purchases for the purpose of maintaining public order, as provided in Article XXIII of the Code.)
- Supreme Prosecutors' Office
- Military Manpower Administration
- Rural Development Administration
- Forest Service
- Korean Intellectual Property Office
- Small and Medium Business Administration
- Korea Coast Guard (except purchases for the purpose of maintaining public order, as provided in Article XXIII of the Agreement.)

Services

Threshold: 130,000 SDR

List of Entities which Procure Services Specified in Annex 4:

Same as "Supplies" section

Construction Services

Threshold: 5,000,000 SDR

List of Entities which Procure Services Specified in Annex 5:

Same as "Supplies" section

Notes to Annex 1

1. The above central government entities include their subordinate linear organizations, special local administrative organs, and attached organs as prescribed in the Government Organization Act of the Republic of Korea.

2. This Agreement does not apply to the products and services procured with a view to resale or to use in the production of goods or provision of services for sale.

23 May 2006 (WT/Let/543)

- 国税厅
- 关税厅
- 统计厅
- 气象厅
- 警察厅(根据第 23 条规定，为维持公共秩序而进行的采购除外)
- 最高检察官办公室
- 兵务厅
- 农村振兴厅
- 山林厅
- 特许厅
- 中小企业厅
- 海洋警察厅 (根据第 23 条规定，为维持公共秩序而进行的采购除外)

服务

门槛金额: 130,000 特别提款权

采购附件 4 所列服务的实体清单：

同"供应品"部分

建筑服务

门槛金额: 5,000,000 特别提款权

采购附件 5 所列服务的实体清单：

同"供应品"部分

附件 1 注释

1. 以上中央政府实体包括其直属组织、特别地方管理机构及《韩国政府组织法》所规定的附属机构。

2. 本协定不适用于为再销售或为用于供销售的货物的生产或服务的提供的货物和服务的采购。

2006 年 5 月 23 日(WT/Let/543)

3. This Agreement does not apply to the single tendering procurement and set-asides for small- and medium-sized businesses according to the Act Relating to Contracts to which the State is a Party and its Presidential Decree, and the procurement of agricultural, fishery and livestock products according to the Foodgrain Management Law, the Law Concerning Marketing and Price Stabilization of Agricultural and Fishery Products, and the Livestock Law.

4. This Agreement does not apply to the procurement of satellites according to the Aviation and Space Industry Development Promotion Law for five years from its entry into force for Korea.

5. The Defense Logistics Agency shall be considered as part of the Ministry of National Defense. Subject to the decision of the Korean Government under the provisions of paragraph 1, Article XXIII, for MND purchases, this Agreement will generally apply to the following FSC categories only, and for services and construction services listed in Annex 4 and Annex 5, it will apply only to those areas which are not related to national security and defense.

FSC	*Description*
2510	Vehicular cab, body, and frame structural components
2520	Vehicular power transmission components
2540	Vehicular furniture and accessories
2590	Miscellaneous vehicular components
2610	Tires and tubes, pneumatic, nonaircraft
2910	Engine fuel system components, nonaircraft
2920	Engine electrical system components, nonaircraft
2930	Engine cooling system components, nonaircraft
2940	Engine air and oil filters, strainers and cleaners, nonaircraft
2990	Miscellaneous engine accessories, nonaircraft
3020	Gears, pulleys, sprockets and transmission chain
3416	Lathes
3417	Milling machines
3510	Laundry and dry cleaning equipment
4110	Refrigeration equipment
4230	Decontaminating and impregnating equipment
4520	Space heating equipment and domestic water heaters
4940	Miscellaneous maintenance and repair shop specialized equipment
5120	Hand tools, nonedged, nonpowered
5410	Prefabricated and portable buildings
5530	Plywood and veneer
5660	Fencing, fences and gates
5945	Relays and solenoids
5965	Headsets, handsets, microphones and speakers
5985	Antennae, waveguide, and related equipment
5995	Cable, cord, and wire assemblies: communication equipment
6505	Drugs and biologicals
6220	Electric vehicular lights and fixtures

3. 本协定不适于根据《国家合同法》及其总统法令进行的单一招标采购和为中小企业预留的采购，以及根据《谷物管理法》、《农渔畜产品销售和价格稳定法》及《牲畜法》对农渔畜产品的采购。

4. 本协定在其对韩国生效起 5 年内不适用于根据《航天和空间产业发展促进法》对卫星的采购。

5. 防卫事业厅应视为国防部的一部分。对于国防部的采购，本协定通常仅适用于下列 FSC 类别，取决于韩国政府根据第 23 条第 1 款规定所做决定，对于附件 4 和附件 5 中所列服务和建筑服务，本协定仅适用于与国家安全和防卫无关的领域。

FSC	*描述*
2510	车身结构部件
2520	机动车动力驱动部件
2540	机动车内饰和配件
2590	其他各种车辆部件
2610	非飞行器用的轮胎和内胎
2910	非航空用发动机燃料系统部件
2920	非航空用发动机电子系统部件
2930	非航空用发动机冷却系统部件
2940	非航空用发动机过滤器
2990	其他各种非航空用发动机配件
3020	齿轮滑车扣链齿和链条
3416	车床
3417	铣床
3510	洗衣和干洗装置
4110	冷却装置
4230	除污设备
4520	暖气和加热器
4940	其他各种装置
5120	非动力无刃手工工具
5410	预制安装和手提式物件
5530	夹板和薄木片
5660	围墙和门
5945	继电器
5965	耳机、电话听筒, 喇叭筒
5985	天线波导装置
5995	海底电缆
6505	药和生物产品
6220	车灯

6840	Pest control agents disinfectants
6850	Miscellaneous chemical, specialties
7310	Food cooking, baking, and serving equipment
7320	Kitchen equipment and appliances
7330	Kitchen hand tools and utensils
7350	Table ware
7360	Sets, kits, outfits, and modules food preparation and serving
7530	Stationery and record forms
7920	Brooms, brushes, mops, and sponges
7930	Cleaning and polishing compounds and preparations
8110	Drums and cans
9150	Oils and greases: cutting, lubricating, and hydraulic
9310	Paper and paperboard

6840	消毒剂
6850	其他化学品
7310	食物烹饪烘焙设备
7320	厨房设备器械
7330	厨房手工具和器具
7350	餐具
7360	供餐设备
7530	文具
7920	扫帚、刷子、墩布和海绵
7930	清洁、抛光机
8110	鼓和罐子
9150	油、水性油脂
9310	纸和卡片纸

ANNEX 2

Sub-Central Government Entities which Procure in Accordance With the Provisions of this Agreement

Supplies

Threshold: 200,000 SDR

List of Entities:

- Seoul Metropolitan Government
- Busan Metropolitan City
- Daegu Metropolitan City
- Incheon Metropolitan City
- Gwangju Metropolitan City
- Daejeon Metropolitan City
- Gyonggi-do
- Gang-won-do
- Chungcheongbuk-do
- Chungcheongnam-do
- Gyeongsangbuk-do
- Gyeongsangnam-do
- Jeollabuk-do
- Jeollanam-do
- Jeju Special Self-Governing Province

Services

Threshold: 200,000 SDR

List of Entities which Procure Services Specified in Annex 4:

Same as "Supplies" section

Construction Services

Threshold: SDR 15,000,000

List of Entities which Procure Services Specified in Annex 5:

Same as "Supplies" section

附件 2

依照本协定条款进行采购的次中央政府实体

供应品

门槛金额: 200,000 特别提款权

实体清单：

- 首尔特别市
- 釜山市
- 大邱市
- 仁川市
- 光州市
- 大田市
- 京畿道
- 江原道
- 忠清北道
- 忠清南道
- 庆尚北道
- 庆尚南道
- 全罗北道
- 全罗南道
- 济州特别自治道

服务

门槛金额: 200,000 特别提款权

采购附件 4 所列服务的实体清单：

同“供应品”部分

建筑服务

门槛金额: 15,00,000 特别提款权

采购附件 5 所列服务的实体清单：

同“供应品”部分

2009 年 7 月 20 日(WT/Let/649)

Notes to Annex 2

1. The above sub-central administrative government entities include their subordinate organizations under direct control and offices as prescribed in the Local Autonomy Law of the Republic of Korea.

2. This Agreement does not apply to the products and services procured with a view to resale or to use in the production of goods or provision of services for sale.

3. This Agreement does not apply to the single tendering procurement and set-asides for small- and medium-sized businesses according to the Act Relating to Contracts to which the Local Government is a Party and its Presidential Decree.

4. This Agreement does not apply to the procurement of satellites according to the Aviation and Space Industry Development Promotion Law for five years from its entry into force for Korea.

20 July 2009 (WT/Let/649)

附件 2 注释

1. 以上次中央政府实体包括其直接控制的附属组织及《韩国政府组织法》所规定的机构。

2. 本协定不适用于为再销售或为用于供销售的货物的生产或服务的提供的货物和服务的采购。

3. 本协定不适于根据《地方政府合同法》及其总统法令进行的单一招标采购和为中小企业预留的采购。

4. 本协定在其对韩国生效起 5 年内不适用于根据《航天和空间产业发展促进法》对卫星的采购。

2009 年 7 月 20 日(WT/Let/649)

ANNEX 3

All Other Entities which Procure in Accordance
With the Provisions of this Agreement

Supplies

Threshold: 450,000 SDR

List of Entities:

- Korea Development Bank
- Industrial Bank of Korea
- Korea Minting and Security Printing Corporation
- Korea Electric Power Corporation (except purchases of products in the categories of HS Nos. 8504, 8535, 8537 and 8544)
- Korea Coal Corporation
- Korea Resources Corporation
- Korea National Oil Corporation
- Korea Trade-Investment Promotion Agency
- Korea Highway Corporation
- Korea National Housing Corporation
- Korea Water Resources Corporation
- Korea Land Corporation
- Korea Rural Community and Agricultural Corporation
- Korea Agro-Fisheries Trade Corporation
- Korea National Tourism Organization
- Korea Workers' Compensation and Welfare Service
- Korea Gas Corporation
- Korea Railroad Corporation

Construction Services

Threshold: 15,000,000 SDR

List of Entities which Procure Services Specified in Annex 5:

Same as "Supplies" section

20 July 2009 (WT/Let/649)

附件 3

依照本协定规定进行采购的所有其他实体

供应品

门槛金额: 450,000 特别提款权

实体清单:

- 韩国产业银行
- 韩国中小企业银行
- 韩国造币公社
- 韩国电力公社(HS 8504、8535、8537 和 8544 项下产品的采购除外)
- 韩国煤炭公社
- 大韩矿业振兴公社
- 韩国石油公社
- 大韩贸易投资振兴公社
- 韩国道路公社
- 韩国住宅公社
- 韩国水资源公社
- 韩国土地开发公社
- 韩国农渔村公社
- 韩国农水产品流通公社
- 韩国观光公社
- 韩国勤劳福祉公团
- 韩国天然气公社
- 韩国铁道公社

建筑服务

门槛金额: 15,000,000 特别提款权

采购附件 5 所列服务的实体清单:

同“供应品”部分

2009 年 7 月 20 日(WT/Let/649)

Notes to Annex 3

1. This Agreement does not apply to the products and services procured with a view to resale or to use in the production of goods or provision of services for sale.

2. This Agreement does not apply to the single tendering procurement and set-asides for small- and medium-sized businesses according to the Act Relating to the Public Entities' Operation and the Rules Relating to the Public Enterprises and Quasi-Government Entities' Contracting Matters.

3. This Agreement does not apply to the procurement of satellites according to the Aviation and Space Industry Development Promotion Law for five years from its entry into force for Korea.

20 July 2009 (WT/Let/649)

附件 3 注释

1. 本协定不适用于为再销售或为用于供销售的货物的生产或服务的提供的货物和服务的采购。

2. 本协定不适于根据《公共实体运营法》和《关于公共企业及准政府实体合同事项的规定》进行的单一招标采购和为中小企业预留的采购。

3. 本协定在其对韩国生效起 5 年内不适用于根据《航天和空间产业发展促进法》对卫星的采购。

2009 年 7 月 20 日(WT/Let/649)

ANNEX 4

Services

Of the Universal List of Services, as contained in document MTN.GNS/W/120, the following services are included (others being excluded):

GNS/W/120	***CPC***	***Description***
1.A.b.	862	Accounting, auditing and bookkeeping services
1.A.c.	863	Taxation services
1.A.d.	8671	Architectural services
1.A.e.	8672	Engineering services
1.A.f.	8673	Integrated engineering services
1.A.g.	8674	Urban planning and landscape architectural services
1.B.a.	841	Consultancy services related to the installation of computer hardware
1.B.b.	842	Software implementation services
1.B.c.	843	Data processing services
1.B.d.	844	Data base services
1.B.e.	845	Maintenance and repair services of office machinery and equipment (including computers)
1.E.a.	83103	Rental/leasing services without operators relating to ships
1.E.b.	83104	Rental/leasing services without operators relating to aircraft
1.E.c.	83101, 83105*	Rental/leasing services without operators relating to other transport equipment (only passenger vehicles for less than fifteen passengers)
1.E.d.	83106, 83108, 83109	Rental/leasing services without operators relating to other machinery and equipment
	83107	Rental/leasing services without operator relating to construction machinery and equipment
1.F.a.	8711, 8719	Advertising agency services
1.F.b.	864	Market research and public opinion polling services
1.F.c.	865	Management consulting services
1.F.d.	86601	Project management services
1.F.e.	86761*	Composition and purity testing and analysis services (only inspection, testing and analysis services of air, water, noise level and vibration level)

20 July 2009 (WT/Let/649)

附件 4

服务

包括载于 MTN.GNS/W/120 号文件的服务通用清单中的下列服务(其他服务排除在外)：

GNS/W/120	*CPC*	*描述*
1.A.b.	862	会计、审计和簿记服务
1.A.c.	863	税收服务
1.A.d.	8671	建筑设计服务
1.A.e.	8672	工程服务
1.A.f.	8673	集中工程服务
1.A.g.	8674	城市规划和园林建筑服务
1.B.a.	841	与计算机硬件安装有关的咨询服务
1.B.b.	842	软件执行服务
1.B.c.	843	数据处理服务
1.B.d.	844	数据库服务
1.B.e.	845	办公用机械和设备，包括计算机的保养和修理服务
1.E.a.	83103	不配备技师的船只租赁或出租服务
1.E.b.	83104	不配备驾驶员的航空器租赁或出租服务
1.E.c.	83101、83105*	不配备驾驶员的私人汽车租赁或出租服务(仅限载客15人以下的客车)
1.E.d.	83106、83108, 83109	不配备技师的其他机械和设备的租赁或出租服务
	83107	不配备技师的建筑机械和设备的租赁或出租服务
1.F.a.	8711、8719	广告服务
1.F.b.	864	市场调研和民意测验服务
1.F.c.	865	管理咨询服务
1.F.d.	86601	项目管理服务
1.F.e.	86761*	成分和纯度检验和分析服务 (仅限空气、水、噪度级和震动级的检验和分析服务)

2009 年 7 月 20 日 (WT/Let/649)

GNS/W/120	CPC	Description
	86764	Technical inspection services
1.F.f.	8811*, 8812*	Consulting services relating to agriculture and animal husbandry
	8814*	Services incidental to forestry (excluding aerial fire fighting and disinfection)
1.F.g.	882*	Consulting services relating to fishing
1.F.h.	883*	Consulting services relating to mining
1.F.m.	86751, 86752	Related scientific and technical consulting services
1.F.n.	633, 8861	Maintenance and repair of equipment
	8862, 8863	
	8864, 8865	
	8866	
1.F.p.	875	Photographic services
1.F.q.	876	Packaging services
1.F.r.	88442*	Printing (screen printing, gravure printing, and services relating to printing)
1.F.s.	87909*	- Stenography services
		- Convention agency services
1.F.t.	87905	Translation and interpretation services
2.C.j.	7523*	On-line information and data-base retrieval
2.C.k.	7523*	Electronic data interchange
2.C.l.	7523*	Enhanced/value-added facsimile services including store and forward, store and retrieve
2.C.m.	-	Code and protocol conversion
2.C.n.	843*	On-line information and/or data processing (including transaction processing)
2.D.a.	96112*, 96113*	Motion picture and video tape production and distribution services (excluding those services for cable TV broadcasting)
2.D.e.	-	Record production and distribution services (sound recording)
6.A.	9401*	Refuse water disposal services (only collection and treatment services of industrial waste water)
6.B.	9402*	Industrial refuse disposal services (only collection, transport, and disposal services of industrial refuse)
6.D.	9404*, 9405*	Cleaning services of exhaust gases and noise abatement

1 March 2000 (WT/Let/330)

GNS/W/120	*CPC*	*描述*
	86764	技术检查服务
1.F.f.	8811*、8812*	与农业和从属畜牧业有关的咨询服务
	8814*	从属林业的服务 (不含空中灭火和消毒)
1.F.g.	882*	与渔业有关的咨询服务
1.F.h.	883*	与采矿有关的咨询服务
1.F.m.	86751、86752	相关科技咨询服务
1.F.n.	633、8861	设备的保养和修理服务
	8862、8863	
	8864、8865	
	8866	
1.F.p.	875	摄影服务
1.F.q.	876	包装服务
1.F.r.	88442*	印刷(丝网印刷、凹版印刷及与印刷有关的服务)
1.F.s.	87909*	- 速记服务
		- 会议代理服务
1.F.t.	87905	笔译和口译服务
2.C.j.	7523*	在线信息和数据调用服务
2.C.k.	7523*	电子数据交换服务
2.C.l.	7523*	增值传真服务，包括储存和发送、储存和调用
2.C.m.	-	编码和规程转换服务
2.C.n.	843*	在线信息和/或数据处理(包括传输处理)
2.D.a.	96112*、96113*	电影和录像的制作和发行服务(不含为有线电视播放提供的服务)
2.D.e.	-	录音制作和发行服务(声音录制)
6.A.	9401*	排污服务(仅限工业废水的收集和处理服务)
6.B.	9402*	工业废物处理服务(仅限工业废物的收集、运输和处理服务)
6.D.	9404*、9405*	废气的清除服务和消声服务

2000 年 3 月 1 日(WT/Let/330)

GNS/W/120	*CPC*	*Description*
		services (services other than construction work services)
	9406*, 9409*	Environmental testing and assessment services (only environmental impact assessment services)
11.A.b.	7212*	International transport, excluding cabotage
11.A.d.	8868*	Maintenance and repair of vessels
11.F.b.	71233*	Transportation of containerized freight, excluding cabotage
11.H.c	748*	Freight transport agency services - Maritime agency services - Maritime freight forwarding services - Shipping brokerage services - Air cargo transport agency services - Customs clearance services
11.I.	-	Freight forwarding for rail transport

Note to Annex 4

Asterisks (*) designate "part of" as described in detail in the Revised Conditional Offer of the Republic of Korea Concerning Initial Commitments on Trade in Services.

1 March 2000 (WT/Let/330)

GNS/W/120	*CPC*	*描述*
		(建筑工程服务以外的服务)
	9406*、9409*	环境检验和评估服务(仅限环境影响评估服务)
11.A.b.	7212*	国际运输，不含国内交通运输权
11.A.d.	8868*	船舶保养和修理
11.F.b.	71233*	集装箱货运输，不含国内交通运输权
11.H.c	748*	货运代理服务
		- 海运代理服务
		- 海运转运服务
		- 船舶代理服务
		- 空运代理服务
		- 清关服务
11.I.	-	铁路运输货运转运服务

附件 4 注释

星号 (*) 指“部分”，在韩国关于服务贸易最初承诺的有条件修改出价中详述。

2000 年 3 月 1 日(WT/Let/330)

ANNEX 5

Construction Services

Definition:

A construction services contract is a contract which has as its objective the realization by whatever means of civil or building works, in the sense of Division 51 of the Central Product Classification.

Threshold: 5,000,000 SDR for entities set out in Annex 1
15,000,000 SDR for entities set out in Annex 2
15,000,000 SDR for entities set out in Annex 3

List of construction services offered:

CPC	*Description*
511	Pre-erection work at construction sites
512	Construction work for buildings
513	Construction work for civil engineering
514	Assembly and erection of prefabricated construction
515	Special trade construction work
516	Installation work
517	Building completion and finishing work

附件 5

建筑服务

定义：

建筑服务合同是指根据《中央产品分类》第 51 类，以通过任何土木或建筑工程手段实现目的的合同。

门槛金额: 5,000,000 特别提款权，附件 1 所列实体
15,000,000 特别提款权，附件 2 所列实体
15,000,000 特别提款权，附件 3 所列实体

建筑服务出价清单：

CPC	描述
511	建筑工地的准备工作
512	建筑物的建筑工作
513	土木工程的建筑工作
514	预制构件的组装和装配
515	特种行业建筑工程
516	安装工程
517	建筑物竣工和修整工程

2000 年 3 月 1 日 (WT/Let/330)

GENERAL NOTES

1. Korea will not extend the benefits of this Agreement

   (a) as regards the award of contracts by the National Railroad Administration,

   (b) as regards procurement for airports by the entities listed in Annex 1,

   (c) as regards procurement for urban transportation (including subways) by the entities listed in Annexes 1 and 2

   to the suppliers and service providers of member States of the European Communities, Austria, Norway, Sweden, Finland and Switzerland, until such time as Korea has accepted that those countries give comparable and effective access for Korean undertakings to their relevant markets.

2. For goods and services (including construction services) of Canada and suppliers of such goods and services, this Agreement does not apply to procurement by the entities listed in Annexes 2 and 3. Korea is prepared to amend this note at such time as coverage with respect to these Annexes can be resolved with Canada.

3. A service listed in Annex 4 is covered with respect to a particular party only to the extent that such party has included that service in its Annex 4.

1 March 2000 (WT/Let/330)

总注释

1. 韩国在下列方面：

    (a) 对于国家铁路局授予的合同，

    (b) 对于附件 1 所列实体关于机场的采购，

    (c) 对于附件 1 和 2 所列实体关于城市交通(包括地铁)的采购，

    不将本协定的利益给予欧共体成员国、奥地利、挪威、瑞典、芬兰和瑞士的供应商和服务提供者，直至韩国认为这些国家给予韩国企业对于相关市场的对等和有效的准入机。

2. 对于加拿大的货物和服务(包括建筑服务)及此类货物和服务的提供者，本协定不适用于由附件 2 和 3 中所列实体进行的采购。韩国准备在能够与加拿大解决这些附件的涵盖范围之时修改本注释。

3. 对于附件 4 中所列一服务，仅在一特定参加方已将该服务纳入其附件 4 中时，方针对该参加方而涵盖其中。

2000 年 3 月 1 日 (WT/Let/330)

LIECHTENSTEIN
列支敦士登

LIECHTENSTEIN

(Authentic in the English language only)

ANNEX 1

Central Government Entities which Procure in Accordance With the Provisions of this Agreement

Supplies	*Threshold:*	SDR 130,000
Services (specified in Annex 4)	*Threshold:*	SDR 130,000
Construction services (specified in Annex 5)	*Threshold:*	SDR 5,000,000

List of Entities:

Government of the Principality of Liechtenstein

Note to Annex 1

The Agreement shall not apply to contracts awarded by contracting authorities in the field of drinking water, energy, transport or telecommunications.

1 March 2000 (WT/Let/330)

列支敦士登

(仅以英文为准)

附件 1

依照本协定条款进行采购的中央政府实体

供应品	*门槛金额:*	130,000 特别提款权
服务 (附件 4 中列明)	*门槛金额:*	130,000 特别提款权
建筑服务(附件 5 中列明)	*门槛金额:*	5,000,000 特别提款权

实体清单:

列支敦士登公国政府

注释 1 注释

本协定不适用于缔约机构所授予的与在饮用水、能源、运输或电信领域活动有关的合同。

2000 年 3 月 1 日 (WT/Let/330)

ANNEX 2

Sub-Central Entities which Procure in Accordance With the Provisions of this Agreement

Supplies	*Threshold:*	SDR 200,000
Services (specified in Annex 4)	*Threshold:*	SDR 200,000
Construction services (specified in Annex 5)	*Threshold:*	SDR 5,000,000

List of Entities:

1. Public Authorities at local level

2. Bodies governed by public law and not having an industrial or commercial character at the local level.

Note to Annex 2

The Agreement shall not apply to contracts awarded by contracting authorities in connection with activities in the field of drinking water, energy, transport or telecommunications.

1 March 2000 (WT/Let/330)

附件 2

依照本协定条款进行采购的次中央政府实体

供应品 *门槛金额：* 200,000 特别提款权

服务 (附件 4 中列明) *门槛金额：* 200,000 特别提款权

建筑服务(附件 5 中列明) *门槛金额：* 5,000,000 特别提款权

实体清单：

1. 地方一级政府机构；

2. 地方一级受公法管辖、不具产业或商业性质的机构。

附件 2 注释

本协定不适用于缔约机构所授予的与在饮用水、能源、运输或电信领域活动有关的合同。

2000 年 3 月 1 日 (WT/Let/330)

ANNEX 3

All Other Entities which Procure in Accordance With the Provisions of this Agreement

Supplies	*Threshold:*	SDR 400,000
Services	*Threshold:*	SDR 400,000
Works (specified in Annex 5)	*Threshold:*	SDR 5,000,000

List of Entities:

The contracting entities which are public authorities[1] or public undertakings[2] and which have as at least one of their activities any of those referred to below:

1. the provision or operation of fixed networks intended to provide a service to the public in connection with the production, transport or distribution of drinking water or the supply of drinking water to such networks (as specified under title I);

2. the provision or operation of fixed networks intended to provide a service to the public in connection with the production, transport or distribution of electricity or the supply of electricity to such networks (as specified under title II);

---

[1]Public authorities means the State, regional or local authorities, bodies governed by public law, or associations formed by one or more of such authorities or bodies governed by public law. A body is considered to be governed by public law where it:

- is established for the specific purpose of meeting needs in the general interest, not being of an industrial or commercial nature;

- has legal personality; and

- is financed for the most part by the State, or regional or local authorities, or other bodies governed by public law, or is subject to management supervision by those bodies, or has an administrative, managerial or supervisory board more than half of whose members are appointed by the State, regional or local authorities, or other bodies governed by public law.

[2]Public undertakings means any undertaking over which the public authorities may exercise directly or indirectly a dominant influence by virtue of their ownership of it, their financial participation therein, or the rules which govern it. A dominant influence on the part of the public authorities shall be presumed when these authorities, directly or indirectly, in relation to an undertaking:

- hold the majority of the undertaking's subscribed capital; or

- control the majority of the votes attaching to shares issued by the undertaking; or

- can appoint more than half of the members of the undertaking's administrative, managerial or supervisory body.

1 March 2000 (WT/Let/330)

附件 3

依照本协定条款进行采购的所有其他实体

供应品 *门槛金额：* 400,000 特别提款权

服务 *门槛金额：* 400,000 特别提款权

工程(附件 5 中列明) *门槛金额：* 5,000,000 特别提款权

实体清单：

属政府机构[1]或公共企业[2]且其至少一项活动属下列任何一项之一的缔约实体：

1. 提供或经营固定网络，旨在向公众提供与饮用水的生产、输送或配送有关的服务或与向此类网络供应饮用水有关的服务(以下标题 I 中列明)；

2. 提供或经营固定网络，旨在向公众提供与电力的生产、输送或配送有关的服务或与向此类网络供应电力有关的服务(以下标题 II 中列明)；

---

[1] 政府机构指受公法管辖的国家、地区或地方政府机构，或由一个或更多此类受公法管辖的机构构成的协会。在下列情况下，一机构被视为受公法管辖：

- 为满足符合公共利益的需求这一特定目而设立，不具产业或商业性质；
- 具有法人资格；且
- 主要由国家、地区或地方政府机构或由受公法管辖的其他机构提供经费，或者接受上述机构的管理监督，或者设有行政、管理或监督委员会，委员会成员一半以上由国家、地区或地方政府机构或受公法管辖的其他机构任命。.

[2] 公共企业指任何企业，公共机构可直接或间接通过对其的所有权、对其的资金参与或管辖其的规定而施加主要影响。如政府机构对于一企业直接或间接：

- 持有该企业已认缴资本的大多数；或
- 控制该企业发行股票所附加的投票权的大多数；或
- 可任命该企业行政、管理或监督机构的半数以上成员，

则该政府机构应被认定具有主要影响。

2000 年 3 月 1 日 (WT/Let/330)

3. the operation of fixed networks providing a service to the public in the field of transport by urban railway, automated systems, tramway, trolleybus, bus or cable (as specified under title III);
4. the exploitation of a geographical area for the purpose of the provision of airport or other terminal facilities to carriers by air (as specified under title IV);

5. the exploitation of a geographical area for the purpose of the provision of inland port or other terminal facilities to carriers by sea or inland waterway (as specified under title V).

I. Production, transport or distribution of drinking water

Public authorities and public undertakings producing, transporting and distributing drinking water. Such public authorities and public undertakings are operating under local legislation or under individual agreements based thereupon.

- Gruppenwasserversorgung Liechtensteiner Oberland

- Gruppenwasserversorgung Liechtensteiner Unterland

II. Production, transport or distribution of electricity

Public authorities and public undertakings for the production, transport and distribution of electricity operating on the basis of authorizations for expropriation pursuant to the "Gesetz vom 16. Juni 1947 betreffend die "Liechtensteinischen Kraftwerke" (LKWG)".

- Liechtensteinische Kraftwerke

III. Contracting entities in the field of urban railway, automated systems, tramway, trolley bus, bus or cable services

Liechtensteinische Post-, Telefon- und Telegrafenbetriebe (PTT)

according to "Vertrag vom 9. Januar 1978 zwischen dem Fürstentum Liechtenstein und der Schweizerischen Eidgenossenschaft über die Besorgung der Post- und Fernmeldedienste im Fürstentum Liechtenstein durch die Schweizerischen Post-, Telefon- und Telegrafenbetriebe (PTT).

IV. Contracting entities in the field of airport facilities

None

3. 经营固定网络，旨在在运输领域通过城市铁路、自动化系统、有轨电车、无轨电车、公共汽车或缆车向公众提供服务(以下标题 III 中列明)；

4. 开发一地理区域，旨在向空运承运人提供机场或其他航空站(以下标题 IV 中列明)；

5. 开发一地理区域，以向海运或内河航道承运人提供内陆港口或其他港口设施(以下标题 V 中列明)。

I. 饮用水的生产、输送或配送

生产、输送和配送饮用水的政府机构和公共企业。此类政府机构和公共企业根据当地立法或据此订立的单独协定运营。

- 上列支敦士登供水集团公司
- 下列支敦士登供水集团公司

II. 电力生产、输送或配送

根据“1947 年 6 月 16 日关于列支敦士登电厂的法律”，从事电力生产、输送或配送的政府机构和公共企业：

- 列支敦士登电厂

III. 城市铁路、自动化系统、有轨电车、无轨电车、公共汽车或缆车服务方面的缔约实体

列支敦士登邮政、电话和电报局

根据列支敦士登公国与瑞士联邦之间于 1978 年 1 月 9 日签订的协议，列支敦士登公国境内的邮政服务、远程通信服务由瑞士邮政、电话和电报企业提供。

IV. 机场设施领域的缔约实体

无

2000 年 3 月 1 日 (WT/Let/330)

Notes to Annex 3

This Agreement shall not apply:

1. to contracts which the contracting entity awards for purposes other than the pursuit of their activities as described in this Annex.

2. to contracts awarded for purposes of re-sale or hire to third parties, provided that the contracting entity enjoys no special or exclusive right to sell or hire the subject of such contracts and other entities are free to sell or hire it under the same conditions as the contracting entity.

3. to contracts for the purchase of water.

4. to contracts of contracting entities other than a public authority exercising the supply of drinking water or electricity to networks which provide a service to the public, if they produce these services by themselves and consume them for the purpose of carrying out other activities than those described under this Annex under I and II and provided that the supply to the public network depends only on the entity's own consumption and does not exceed 30 per cent of the entity's total production of drinking water or energy, having regard to the average for the preceding three years.

5. to contracts for the supply of energy or of fuels for the production of energy.

6. to contracts awarded by contracting entities providing a bus service if other entities are free to offer the same service either in general or in a specific geographical area and under the same conditions.

1 March 2000 (WT/Let/330)

附件 3 注释

本协定不适用于：

1. 缔约实体不是为了从事本附件所述其活动而授予的合同。

2. 为再销售或向第三方出租而授予的合同，但条件是缔约实体不享受销售或出租此类合同客体的特殊或专用权，且其他实体有权根据与该缔约实体相同的条件销售或出租此类合同客体。

3. 购买水的合同。

4. 向为公众提供服务的网络供应饮用水和电力、且不属政府机构的缔约实体的合同，如此类实体自己生产这些服务，为从事本附件标题 I 和 II 下所述活动之外的活动而消费这些服务，且向公共网络供应仅取决于该实体自身消费，未超过该实体饮用水或能源总产量的 30%，指以往 3 年的平均值。

5. 供应能源或为生产能源而供应燃料的合同。

6. 提供公共汽车服务的缔约实体所授予的合同，如其他实体有权普遍或在某一特定地理区域以相同条件提供相同服务。

2000 年 3 月 1 日 (WT/Let/330)

ANNEX 4

Services

The following services from the services sectoral classification list contained in document MTN.GNS/W/120 are included:

Subject	
Maintenance and repair services	6112, 6122, 633, 886
Land transport services, including armoured car services, and courier services, except transport of mail	712 (except 71235), 7512, 87304
Air transport services of passengers and freight, except transport of mail	73 (except 7321)
Transport of mail by land, except rail, and by air	71235, 7321
Telecommunications services	752[1]
Financial services	ex 81
(a) Insurance services	812, 814
(b) Banking and investment services[2]	
Computer and related services	84
Accounting, auditing and bookkeeping services	862
Market research and public opinion polling services	864
Management consulting services and related services	865, 866[3]
Architectural services; engineering services and integrated engineering services, urban planning and landscape architectural services; related scientific and technical consulting services; technical testing and analysis services	867

[1]Except voice telephony, telex, radiotelephony, paging and satellite services

[2]Except contracts for financial services in connection with the issue, sale, purchase, or transfer of securities or other financial instruments, and central bank services

[3]Except arbitration and conciliation services

附件 4

服务

包括下列取自 MTN.GNS/W/120 号文件所载服务部门分类清单的服务：

事项	
维护和修理服务	6112、6122、633、886
陆路运输服务、 包括装甲车服务和 速递服务、邮件运输除外	712(不含 71235)、 7512、87304
航空客运和货运服务、 邮件运输除外	73(不含 7321)
陆地和航空邮件运输、铁路运输除外	71235、7321
电信服务	752[1]
金融服务	ex 81
(a) 保险服务 (b) 银行与投资服务[2]	812、814
计算机及相关服务	84
会计、审计和簿记服务	862
市场调研和民意测验服务	864
管理咨询服务及相关服务	865、866[3]
建筑设计服务；工程服务与集中工程服务、 城市规划和景观设计服务； 相关科技咨询服务; 技术咨询服务； 技术测试和分析服务	867

[1]语音通信、电传、无线电话、寻呼及卫星服务除外。

[2]关于证券或其他金融工具的发行、销售、购买或转让的金融服务合同及中央银行服务合同除外。

[3]仲裁和调解服务除外。

2000 年 3 月 1 日 (WT/Let/330)

Advertising services	871
Building-cleaning services and property management services	874, 82201-82206
Publishing and printing services on a fee or contract basis	88442
Sewage and refuse disposal; sanitation and similar services	94

Notes to Annex 4

The Agreement shall not apply to:

1. service contracts awarded to an entity which is itself a procuring entity listed in Annex 1 or 2 on the basis of an exclusive right which it enjoys pursuant to a published law, regulation or administrative provision.

2. service contracts which a contracting entity awards to an affiliated undertaking or which are awarded by a joint venture formed by a number of contracting entities for the purpose of carrying out an activity within the meaning of Annex 3 or to an undertaking which is affiliated with one of these contracting entities. At least 80 per cent of the average turnover of that undertaking for the preceding three years has to derive from the provision of such services to undertakings with which it is affiliated. Where more than one undertaking affiliated with the contracting entity provides the same service, the total turnover deriving from the provision of services by those undertakings shall be taken into account.

3. contracts for the acquisition or rental, by whatever means, of land, existing buildings, or other immovable property or concerning rights thereon.

4. to contracts of employment.

5. for the acquisition, development, production or co-production of programme material by broadcasters and contracts for broadcasting time.

1 March 2000 (WT/Let/330)

广告服务	871
建筑物清洁服务与 物业管理服务	874、82201-82206
收费或合同基础上的出版和印刷服务	88442
排污及废物处理；卫生及类似服务	94

附件 4 注释

本协定不适用于：

1. 授予一列入附件 1 或 2 中、根据一已公布的法律、法规或管理规定享有专用权的采购实体的服务合同。

2. 一缔约实体授予一附属企业的服务合同或由一若干缔约实体组成的、旨在从事附件 3 意义内的活动的合资企业授予的服务合同、或授予一附属于这些缔约实体之一的企业的服务合同。该企业以往 3 年平均营业额的至少 80%应来自于该企业向其所附属的企业提供此类服务。如该缔约实体的附属企业超过一家以上提供相同或服务，则应考虑这些企业从提供服务中所获全部营业额。

3. 购买或租赁土地、现有建筑物或其他不动产或涉及相关权利的合同、无论通过何种方式。

4. 雇佣合同。

5. 广播电台购买、开发、制作或联合制作节目内容的合同和播放时间的合同。

2000 年 3 月 1 日(WT/Let/330)

ANNEX 5

Construction Services

Definition:

A construction services contract is a contract which has as its objective the realization by whatever means of civil or building works, in the sense of Division 51 of the Central Product Classification.

List of Division 51, CPC:

General construction work for buildings	512
General construction work for civil engineering	513
Installation and assembly work	514 + 516
Building completion and finishing work	517
Other	511 + 515 + 518

附件 5

建筑服务

定义:

建筑服务合同是指根据《中央产品分类》第 51 类，以通过任何土木或建筑工程手段实现目的的合同。

CPC 第 51 类清单:

建筑物的建筑工作	512
土木工程的建筑工作	513
组装和安装工程	514 + 516
建筑物竣工和修整工程	517
其他	511 + 515 + 518

2000 年 3 月 1 日 (WT/Let/330)

GENERAL NOTES AND DEROGATIONS FROM THE PROVISIONS OF ARTICLE III

1. The Principality of Liechtenstein will not extend the benefits of this Agreement:

- as regards the award of contracts by entities listed in Annex 2 to the suppliers and service providers of Canada and the United States of America,

- as regards the award of contracts by entities listed in Annex 3 in the following sectors:
  - water: to the suppliers and service providers of Canada and the United States of America;

  - electricity: to the suppliers and service providers of Canada, Japan and the United States of America;

  - urban transport: to the suppliers and service providers of Canada, Israel, Japan, Korea and the United States of America

until such time as the Principality of Liechtenstein has accepted that the Parties concerned give comparable and effective access for undertakings of the Principality of Liechtenstein to the relevant markets;

- to service providers of Parties which do not include service contracts for the relevant entities in Annexes 1 to 3 and the relevant service category under Annexes 4 and 5 in their own coverage.

2. The provisions of Article XX shall not apply to suppliers and service providers of:

- Israel, Japan and Korea in contesting the award of contracts by bodies governed by public law and not having an industrial or commercial character listed in Annex 2, paragraph 2, until such time as the Principality of Liechtenstein accepts that they have completed coverage of sub-central entities;

- Canada, Japan, Korea and the United States of America in contesting the award of contracts to a supplier or service provider of Parties other than those mentioned, which are small- or medium-sized enterprises under the relevant provisions of the law of Liechtenstein until such time as the Principality of Liechtenstein accepts that they no longer operate discriminatory measures in favour of certain domestic small and minority businesses;

- Israel, Japan and Korea in contesting the award of contracts by entities of the Principality of Liechtenstein, whose value is less than the threshold applied for the same category of contracts awarded by these Parties.

总注释及对第 3 条规定的背离

1. 列支敦士登公国在下列方面不将本协定利益给予下列参加方：

- 对于附件 2 中所列实体授予的合同，本协定利益不给予加拿大和美国供应商和服务提供者；

- 对于附件 3 所列实体在下列部门授予的合同：

  - 水：本协定利益不给予加拿大和美国供应商和服务提供者;

  - 电：本协定利益不给予加拿大、日本和美国供应商和服务提供者;

  - 城市交通：本协定利益不给予加拿大、以色列、日本、韩国和美国供应商和服务提供者；

直至列支敦士登公国已经认为有关参加方给予列支敦士登公国企业对于相关市场的对等和有效的准入机会。

- 本协定利益不给予在其各自承诺范围中未对附件 1 至 3 中相关实体包括相关服务合同和未在附件 4 和 5 中包括相关服务类别的参加方的服务提供者。

2. 第 20 条不适用于下列参加方的供应商和服务提供者：

- 以色列、日本和韩国，在竞争附件 2 第 2 款下所列实体授予的合同时，直到列支敦士登公国认为他们的次中央实体的涵盖范围已经完整时止；

- 加拿大、日本、韩国和美国，在竞争将合同授予已提及的参加方供应商或服务提供者之外的一属列支敦士登相关规定所定义的小型或中型企业的供应商或服务提供者时，直至列支敦士登公国认为他们不再采取有利于某些国内小型和少数族裔企业的歧视性措施时止;

- 以色列、日本和韩国，在竞争列支敦士登公国实体授予的合同时，其价值低于这些参加方所授予的相同类别合同所适用的门槛金额。

2000 年 3 月 1 日 (WT/Let/330)

3. Until such time as the Principality of Liechtenstein has accepted that the Parties concerned provide access for suppliers and service providers to their own markets, the Principality of Liechtenstein will not extend the benefits of this Agreement to suppliers and service providers of:

- Canada, as regards procurement of FSC 36, 70 and 74 (special industry machinery; general purpose automatic data processing equipment, software, supplies and support equipment (except 7010 ADPE configurations); office machines, visible record equipment and ADP equipment);

- Canada, as regards procurement of FSC 58 (communications, protection and coherent radiation equipment) and the United States of America as regards air traffic control equipment;

- Korea and Israel as regards procurement by entities listed in Annex 3, paragraph (B) as regards procurement of HS Nos 8504, 8535, 8537 and 8544 (electrical transformers, plugs, switches and insulated cables); and for Israel, HS Nos 8501, 8536 and 902830;
- Canada and the United States of America as regards contracts for good or service components of contracts which, although awarded by an entity covered by this Agreement, are not themselves subject to this Agreement.

4. The Agreement shall not apply to contracts awarded under:

- an international agreement and intended for the joint implementation or exploitation of a project by signatory States;

- the particular procedure of an international organization.

5. The Agreement shall not apply to procurement of agricultural products made in furtherance of agricultural support programmes and human feeding programmes.

6. The provision of services, including construction services, in the context of procurement procedures according to this Agreement is subject to the conditions and qualifications for market access and national treatment as will be required by the Principality of Liechtenstein in conformity with its commitments under the GATS.

1 March 2000 (WT/Let/330)

3. 在列支敦士登公国已经认为有关参加方对供应商和服务提供者提供进入其各自市场的机会之前，列支敦士登公国不将本协定的收益给予下列参加方的供应商和服务提供者：

- 加拿大，对于 FSC 36、70 和 74 的采购(特殊工业机械；通用自动化处理设备、软件、耗材和配套设备(7010 自动化处理系统结构除外)；办公设备、显露式记录设备和自动化处理设备；

- 加拿大，对于 FSC 58 的采购(通信、探测和相干辐射设备)及美国，对于空中交通管制设备的采购；

- 以色列和韩国，对于附件 3 B 款所列实体关于协调制度编码 HS8504、8535、8537 和 8544(变压器、插头、开关和绝缘电缆)的采购；以色列，关于协调制度编码 HS8501、8536 和 902830 的采购；

- 加拿大和美国，对于虽由本协定所涵盖实体授予、但其货物或服务组成部分本身不受本协定管辖的合同。

4. 本协定不适用于在下列情况下授予的合同：

- 旨在由签署国联合执行或开发一项目的国际协定；

- 国际组织的特定程序。

5. 本协定不适用于为促进农业支持计划和人类供给计划而采购的农产品。

6. 在根据本协定所进行的采购程序中，服务的提供，包括建筑服务的提供，需遵守列支敦士登公国依照其 GATS 项下承诺所要求的关于市场准入和国民待遇的条件和资格。

2000 年 3 月 1 日(WT/Let/330)

NETHERLANDS WITH RESPECT TO ARUBA
荷属阿鲁巴

THE KINGDOM OF THE NETHERLANDS WITH RESPECT TO ARUBA

(Authentic in the English language only)

ANNEX 1

Central Government Entities which Procure in Accordance with the Provisions of this Agreement

Supplies	*Threshold:*	SDR 130,000
Services	*Threshold:*	SDR 130,000
Works	*Threshold:*	SDR 5,000,000

List of Entities:

Ministry of General Affairs;
Ministry of Public Works and Health;
Ministry of Transport and Communication;
Ministry of Welfare;
Ministry of Justice and Sport;
Ministry of Finance;
Ministry of Economic Affairs.

1 March 2000 (WT/Let/330)

荷属阿鲁巴

(仅以英文为准)

附件 1

依照本协定条款进行采购的中央政府实体

供应品	*门槛金额:*	130,000 特别提款权
服务	*门槛金额:*	130,000 特别提款权
工程	*门槛金额:*	5,000,000 特别提款权

实体清单:

总务部;
公共工程和健康部;
交通运输部;
福利部;
司法和体育部;
财政部;
经济事务部。

2000 年 3 月 1 日 (WT/Let/330)

ANNEX 2

Sub-Central Entities which Procure in Accordance with the Provisions of this Agreement

Non-applicable for Aruba (Aruba does not have any Sub-central Governments).

附件 2

依照本协定条款进行采购的次中央实体

不适用于阿鲁巴(阿鲁巴没有任何次中央政府)。

2000 年 3 月 1 日 (WT/Let/330)

ANNEX 3

Other Entities which Procure in Accordance
with the Provisions of this Agreement

Supplies *Threshold:* SDR 400,000

Services *Threshold:* SDR 400,000

Works *Threshold:* SDR 5,000,000

List of Entities:

Water en Energiebedrijf N.V. (Water and Energy Company);
Aruba Ports Authority N.V.;
Arubus N.V. (Public Transport Company);
Setar (Telecommunications Company);
Airport Authority N.V.;
Findacion Caspa Comunidad Arbubano (Public Housing).

1 March 2000 (WT/Let/330)

附件 3

依照本协定条款进行采购的其他实体

供应品 *门槛金额：* 400,000 特别提款权

服务 *门槛金额：* 400,000 特别提款权

工程 *门槛金额：* 5,000,000 特别提款权

实体清单：

水力和能源公司；
阿鲁巴港口管理局；
公共运输部；
电信公司；
机场管理局；
公共住房管理局。

ANNEX 4

Services

List of Services	*CPC*
Legal services	861
Accountancy	862
Taxation services	863
Engineering services	8672
Computer services	841
Management consulting services	865
Franchising	8929
Insurance	812, 814
Banking and securities trade	811, 813
Hotel lodging services	6411
Entertainment services	9619
Recreation park and beach services	96491
Sporting services	9641
Shipping (freight and passenger transport)	72
Maritime auxiliary services: cargo handling	74
Freight transport: agency services/freight forwarding	74
Maritime auxiliary services: storage/warehousing	74
Road transport	71231, 71234, 71239

1 March 2000 (WT/Let/330)

附件 4

服务

服务清单	*CPC*
法律服务	861
会计	862
税收服务	863
工程服务	8672
计算机服务	841
管理咨询服务	865
特许经营服务	8929
保险	812、814
银行和证券交易	811、813
旅馆住宿服务	6411
娱乐服务	9619
游乐园和海滩服务	96491
体育服务	9641
水运服务	72
海运辅助服务：货物装卸	74
货运代理行服务	74
海运辅助服务：存储和仓储服务	74
道路运输	71231、71234、71239

ANNEX 5

Construction Services

List of Construction Services	*CPC*
Construction work for buildings	512

附件 5

建筑服务

建筑服务清单	*CPC*
建筑物的建筑工作	512

2000 年 3 月 1 日 (WT/Let/330)

NORWAY
挪威

NORWAY

(Authentic in the English language only)

ANNEX 1

Entities which Procure in Accordance
With the Provisions of this Agreement

Supplies
Threshold: SDR 130,000

Services (specified in Annex 4)
Threshold: SDR 130,000

Works (specified in Annex 5)
Threshold: SDR 5,000,000

List of Entities:

The following central government entities including:

Statsministerens kontor	**Office of the Prime Minister**
Barne - og familiedepartementet	**Ministry of Children and Family Affairs**
Barneombudet	Commissioner for Children
Forbrukerombudet	Consumer Ombudsman
Forbrukerrådet	Consumer Council
Likestillingsombudet	Equal Status Ombud
Likestillingsrådet	Equal Status Council
Statens Adopsjonskontor	Government Adoption Office
Statens Institutt for Forbruksforskning	National Institute for Consumer Research
Finans- og tolldepartementet	**Ministry of Finance**
Kredittilsynet	The Banking, Insurance and Securities Commission of Norway
Skattedirektoratet	Directorate of Taxes
Oljeskattekontoret	Petroleum Tax Office
Toll- og avgiftsdirektoratet	Directorate of Customs and Excise
Fiskeridepartementet	**Ministry of Fisheries**
Fiskeridirektoratet	Directorate of Fisheries
Havforskningsinstituttet	Institute of Marine Research

1 March 2000 (WT/Let/330)

挪威

(仅以英文为准)

附件 1

依照本协定条款进行采购的实体

供应品
门槛金额: 130,000 特别提款权

服务 (附件 4 列明)
门槛金额: 130,000 特别提款权

工程 (附件 5 列明)
门槛金额: 5,000,000 特别提款权

实体清单:

包括下列中央政府实体:

首相办公室

儿童和家庭事务部

儿童专员
消费者巡视官
消费者委员会
平等地位巡视官
平等地位委员会
政府收养办公室
全国消费者研究所

财政部

挪威银行、保险和证券委员会
税务局
石油税办公室
海关和消费税局

渔业部

渔业局
海洋研究所

2000 年 3 月 1 日(WT/Let/330)

Kystdirektoratet	Coast Directorate
Forsvarsdepartementet*	**Ministry of Defence***
Forsvarets bygningstjeneste	Norwegian Defence Construction Service
Forsvarets Forskningsinstitutt*	Norwegian Defence Research Establishment*
Forsvarets Overkommando*	Headquarters Defence Command Norway*
Forsvarets tele- og datatjeneste	Norwegian Defence Communications and Data Services Administration
Haerens Forsyningskommando*	Army Material Command*
Luftforsvarets Forsyningskommando*	Airforce Material Command*
Sjøforsvarets Forsyningskommando*	Navy Material Command*
Forsvarets Sanitet*	Norwegian Defence Medical Service*
Justis- og politidepartementet	**Ministry of Justice (and the Police)**
Brønnøysundregisterene	The Brønnøysund Register Centre
Datatilsynet	The Data Inspectorate
Direktoratet for sivilt beredskap	The Directorate for Civil Defence and Emergency Planning
Riksadvokaten	Director General of Public Prosecutions
Statsadvokatembetene	Offices of the District Public Prosecutor
Politiet	Police Services
Kirke,- utdannings- og forskningsdepartementet	**Ministry of Education, Research and Church Affairs**
Bispedømmerådet	Diocesan Council
Det norske meteoroligiske institutt	Norwegian Meteorological Institute
Kirkerådet	National Council of the Church of Norway
Lærarutdanningsrådet	Teacher Training Council
Nidarosdomens restaureringsarbeider	The Restoration Workshop of Nidaros Cathedral
Norsk Utenrikspolitisk Institutt	Norwegian Institute of International Affairs
Norsk Voksenpedagogisk Forskningsinstitutt	Norwegian Institute of Adult Education
Riksbibliotektjenesten	National Office for Research and Special Libraries
Samisk Utdanningsråd	Sami Education Council

Kommunal- og arbeidsdepartementet Ministry of Local Government and Labour

Arbeidsdirektoratet	Directorate of Labour
Arbeidsforskningsinstituttet	Work Research Institute
Direktoratet for arbeidstilsynet	Norwegian Directorate of Labour Inspection
Direktoratet for Brann og Eksplosjonsvern	Directorate for Fire and Explosion Prevention

1 March 2000 (WT/Let/330)

海岸局

国防部*

挪威防务工程局
挪威防务研究机构*
挪威防务司令部*
挪威防务通信和数据服务管理局
陆军物资司令部*
空军物资司令部*
海军物资司令部*
挪威防务医疗局*

司法部 (及警察局)

布伦尼注册中心
数据监察局
民防和应急计划局
刑事检控专员
区检察官办公室
警察局

教育、研究和教堂事务部

宗教委员会
挪威气象研究所
挪威国家教堂委员会
教师培训委员会
修复尼德罗斯大教堂办公室
挪威国际事务研究所
挪威成人教育研究所
国家研究和特种图书馆办公室
萨米教育委员会

地方政府和劳动部

劳动局
劳动研究所
挪威劳动监察局
消防和防爆局

2000 年 3 月 1 日(WT/Let/330)

Produkt- og elektrisitetstilsynet	The Norwegian Directorate for Product and Electrical Safety
Produktregisteret	The Product Register
Statens Bygningstekniske Etat	National Office of Building Technology and Administration
Utlendingsdirektoratet	Directorate of Immigration
Kulturdepartementet	**Ministry of Cultural Affairs**
Norsk Filminstitutt	National Film Board
Norsk Kulturråd	Norwegian Cultural Council
Norsk Språkråd	Norwegian Language Council
Riksarkivet	National Archives of Norway
Statsarkivene	National Archives
Rikskonsertene	Norwegian State Foundation for National Promotion of Music
Statens Bibliotektilsyn	Norwegian Directorate of Public and School Libraries
Statens Filmkontroll	National Board of Film Censors
Statens Filmsentral	National Film Board
Landbruksdepartementet	**Ministry of Agriculture**
Reindriftsadministrasjonen	Directorate for Reindeer Husbandry
Statens dyrehelsetilsyn	Norwegian Animal Health Authority
Statens forskningsstasjoner i Landbruk	Norwegian State Agricultural Research Stations
Statens landbrukstilsyn	Norwegian Agricultural Inspection Service
Statens Næringsmiddeltilsyn	The Norwegian Food Control Authority
Veterinærinstituttet	National Veterinary Institute
Miljøverndepartementet	**Ministry of the Environment**
Direktoratet for Naturforvaltning	Directorate of Nature Management
Norsk Polarinstitutt	Norwegian Polar Research Institute
Riksantikvaren	Directorate for Cultural Heritage
Statens Forurensingstilsyn	State Pollution Control Authority
Statens Kartverk	Norwegian Mapping Authority
Nærings-og handelsdepartementet	**Ministry of Trade and Industry**
Bergvesenet	Directorate of Mining
Justervesenet	Norwegian Metrology and Accreditation Service
Norges Geologiske Undersøkelse	Geological Survey of Norway
Statens Veiledningskontor for oppfinnere	Norwegian Government Consultative Office for Inventors
Sjøfartsdirektoratet	Norwegian Maritime Directorate
Skipsregistrene	Norwegian International Ship Register
Styret for det industrielle rettsvern	Norwegian Patent Office

1 March 2000 (WT/Let/330)

挪威产品和电气安全局
产品注册局
国家建筑技术和管理办公室
移民局

文化事务部

国家电影局
挪威文化委员会
挪威语言委员会
挪威档案局
国家档案局
国家音乐促进基金会
挪威公共和学校图书馆局
国家电影审查局
国家电影局

农业部

驯鹿畜牧局
挪威动物健康局
挪威国家农业研究站
挪威农业检验局
挪威食品管理局
国家兽医所

环境部

自然管理局
挪威极地研究院
文化遗产局
国家污染控制局
挪威测绘局

贸易和工业部

矿务局
挪威计量和认证委员会
地质勘测局
挪威政府发明者咨询办公室
挪威海事局
挪威国际船舶注册中心
挪威专利局

Olje- og energidepartementet	**Ministry of Oil and Energy**
Norges vassdrags- og energiverk	Norwegian Water Resources and Energy Administration
Oljedirektoratet	Norwegian Petroleum Directorate
Planleggings- og samordningsdepartementet	**Ministry of National Planning and Coordination**
Fylkesmannsembetene	The County Governors
Konkurransetilsynet	Norwegian Competition Authority
Prisdirektoratet	The Price Directorate
Statens Forvaltningstjeneste	Government Administration Services
Statens Informasjonstjeneste	Norwegian Central Information Service
Statsbygg	The Directorate of Public Construction and Property
Statskonsult	Directorate of Public Management
Samferdselsdepartementet	**Ministry of Transport and Communication**
Postdirektoratet	Norway Post
Statens teleforvaltning	Norwegian Telecommunications Authority
Statens vegvesen	Public Roads Administration
Sosialdepartementet	**Ministry of Health and Social Affairs**
Statens helsetilsyn	Norwegian Board of Health
Statens Institutt for Folkehelse	National Institute of Public Health
Radiumhospitalet	Norwegian Radium Hospital
Rikshospitalet	National Hospital
Rikstrygdeverket	National Insurance Administration
Rusmiddeldirektoratet	Directorate for the Prevention of Alcohol and Drug Problems
Statens Helseundersøkelser	National Health Screening Service
Statens Institutt for alkohol- og narkotikaforskning	National Institute for Alcohol and Drug Research
Statens Legemiddelkontroll	Norwegian Medicines Control Authority
Statens Strålevern	Norwegian Radiation Protection Authority
Statens Tobakkskaderåd	National Council on Smoking and Health
Utenriksdepartementet	**Ministry of Foreign Affairs**
Direktoratet for utviklingshjelp	Directorate for Development Cooperation
Stortinget	**The Storting**
Stortingets ombudsmann for	Stortingets Ombudsman for Public

1 March 2000 (WT/Let/330)

石油和能源部

挪威水资源和能源管理局
挪威石油管理局

全国规划和协调部

郡长
挪威竞争局
物价局
政府行政服务局
挪威中央信息服务局
公共建筑和财产局
公共管理局

交通和通信部

挪威邮政局
挪威电信局
公共道路管理局

卫生和社会事务部

挪威卫生委员会
国家公共卫生研究所
挪威放射医院
国立医院
国家保险管理局
预防酗酒和吸毒局
国家体检局
国家酒精和毒品研究所
挪威药品控制局
挪威预防放射管理局
国家吸烟和健康委员会

外交部

合作发展局

挪威议会

挪威议会公共管理巡视官

2000 年 3 月 1 日(WT/Let/330)

forvaltningen - Sivilombudsmannen	Administration
Riksrevisjonen	Office of the Auditor General
Domstolene	**Courts of Law**

Note to Annex 1

Procurement by defence entities (marked with an "*") covers products falling under the CCCN chapters specified in the General Notes.

总审计长办公室

法院

附件 1 注释

防务实体(“*”号标出)进行的采购涵盖总注释中列明的 CCCN 章节项下的产品。

2000 年 3 月 1 日(WT/Let/330)

ANNEX 2

Entities which Procure in Accordance
With the Provisions of this Agreement

Supplies
Threshold: SDR 200,000

Services (specified in Annex 4)
Threshold: SDR 200,000

Works (specified in Annex 5)
Threshold: SDR 5,000,000

List of Entities:

1. Contracting authorities of the regional or local public authorities (all counties (19) and municipalities (435)).

2. Bodies governed by public law, or associations formed by one or more such authorities or bodies governed by public law[1], including:

Norsk Rikskringkastning	The Norwegian Broadcasting Corporation
Norges Bank	Norges Bank
Statistisk Sentralbyrå	Statistics Norway
Norges Forskningsråd	Research Council of Norway
Statens Pensjonskasse	Norwegian Public Service Pension Fund
Garanti-instituttet for Eksportkreditt	Norwegian Guarantee Institute for Export Credit

[1] A body is considered to be governed by public law when it:

- is established for the specific purpose of meeting needs in the general interest, not being of a commercial or industrial nature, and
- has legal personality, and
- is financed for the most part by the State, or regional or local authorities, or other bodies governed by public law, or is subject to management supervision by those bodies, or has an administrative, managerial or supervisory board more than half of whose members are appointed by the State, regional or local authorities, or other bodies governed by public law.

1 March 2000 (WT/Let/330)

附件 2

依照本协定条款进行采购的实体

供应品
门槛金额: 200,000 特别提款权

服务 (附件 4 列明)
门槛金额: 200,000 特别提款权

工程 (附件 5 列明)
门槛金额: 5,000,000 特别提款权

实体清单:

1. 地区或地方政府缔约机构(所有郡(19 个)和市(435 个))。

2. 受公法管辖的机构或由一个或多个受公法管辖的机构组成的协会[1]，包括：

   挪威广播公司
   挪威央行
   挪威统计局
   挪威研究理事会
   挪威退休基金管理局
   挪威出口信贷保险公司

[1] 在下列情况下，一机构被视为受公法管辖：

- 为满足符合公共利益的需求这一特定目的而设立，不具产业或商业性质；
- 具有法人资格；且
- 主要由国家、地区或地方政府机构或由受公法管辖的其他机构提供经费，或者接受上述机构的管理监督，或者设有行政、管理或监督委员会，委员会成员一半以上由国家、地区或地方政府机构或受公法管辖的其他机构任命。

2000 年 3 月 1 日 (WT/Let/330)

Categories:

- *Statsbanker (State Banks)*

- *Universiteter og Høyskoler etter lov av 16. juni 1989 nr. 77 (Universities and Colleges)*

- *Publicly owned and operated museums*

分类:

- *央行*
- *大学和学院*
- *公共所有的博物馆*

2000 年 3 月 1 日 (WT/Let/330)

ANNEX 3

Other Entities which Procure in Accordance
With the Provisions of this Agreement

Supplies
Threshold: SDR 400,000

Services (specified in Annex 4)*
Threshold: SDR 400,000

Works (specified in Annex 5)
Threshold: SDR 5,000,000

List of Sectors:

1. *The electricity sector*:**

Public entities producing, transporting or distributing electricity pursuant to Lov om bygging og drift av elektriske anlegg (LOV 1969-06-19), Lov om erverv av vannfall, bergverk og annen fast eiendom m.v., Kap. I, jf. kap. V (LOV 19-17-24 16, kap. I), or Vassdragsreguleringsloven (LOV 1917-12-14 17) or Energiloven (LOV 1990-06-29 50).

2. *Urban transport*:

Public entities which have as one of their activities the operation of networks providing a service to the public in the field of transport by automated systems, urban railway, tramway, trolley bus, bus or cable according to Lov om anlegg og drift av jernbane, herunder sporvei, tunellbane og forstadsbane m.m. (LOV 1993-06-11 100), or Lov om samferdsel (LOV 1976-06-04 63) or Lov om anlegg av taugbaner og løipestrenger (LOV 1912-06-14 1).

3. *Airports*:

Public entities providing airport facilities pursuant to Lov om luftfart (LOV 1960-12-16 1).

Luftfartsverket National Civil Aviation Administration

4. *Ports*:

Public entities operating pursuant to Havneloven (LOV 1984-06-08 51).

5. *Water supply*:**

Public entities producing or distributing water pursuant to Forskrift om Drikkevann og Vannforsyning (FOR 1951 - 09-28).

附件 3

依照本协定条款进行采购的其他实体

供应品
门槛金额: 200,000 特别提款权

服务 (附件 4 列明) *
门槛金额: 200,000 特别提款权

工程 (附件 5 列明)
门槛金额: 5,000,000 特别提款权

部门清单:

1. *电力部门*: **

   根据 1969 年 6 月 19 日《电力设备建设与运营法》、1917 年 12 月 14 日《开发瀑布、矿山与其他不动产相关法》和 1917 年 12 月 14 日《水资源法》等生产、传输或配送电力公司。

2. *城市交通*:

   根据 1993 年 6 月 11 日《铁路建设与运营法(包括有轨电车、地下铁路和市郊铁路)》、1976 年 6 月 4 日《交通法》、1912 年 6 月 14 日《道路建设法》 等通过自动系统、城市铁路、有轨电车、无轨电车、公共汽车或缆车等向公众提供交通服务的公司。

3. *机场*:

   根据 1960 年 12 月 16 日《航空法》提供机场的公司。

   国家民航管理局

4. *港口*:

   根据 1984 年 6 月 8 日《港口法》提供港口的公司。

5. *供水*: **

   根据 1951 年 9 月 28 日《饮水与供水条例》生产或配送水的公司。

Notes to Annex 3

* This Agreement shall not apply to service contracts which:

(a) a contracting entity awards to an affiliated undertaking;

(b) are awarded by a joint venture formed by a number of contracting entities for the purpose of carrying out a relevant activity within the meaning of paragraphs 1-5 of this Annex to one of those contracting entities or to an undertaking which is affiliated with one of these contracting entities;

provided that at least 80 per cent of the average turnover of that undertaking with respect to services arising within the EEA for the three preceding years derives from the provision of such services to undertakings with which it is affiliated. When more than one undertaking affiliated with the contracting entity provides the same service or similar services, the total turnover deriving from the provision of services by those undertakings shall be taken into account.

** The supply of drinking water and electricity to networks which provide a service to the public by a contracting entity other than a public authority shall not be considered as a relevant activity within the meaning of paragraphs 1 and 5 of Annex 3 where:

- the production of drinking water or electricity by the entity concerned takes place because its consumption is necessary for carrying out an activity other than that referred to in paragraphs 1 and 5 of this Annex, and

- supply to the public network depends only on the entity's own consumption and has not exceeded 30 per cent of the entity's total production of drinking water or energy, having regard to the average for the preceding three years, including the current year.

附件 3 注释

*　本定不适用于下列服务合同：

(a)　一缔约实体授予其附属企业的服务合同；

(b)　由一若干缔约实体组成的、旨在从事本附件第 1 至 5 款意义内的活动的合资企业授予这些缔约实体之一或一附属于这些缔约实体之一的企业的服务合同；

但条件是该企业在欧洲经济区内所产生的服务以往 3 年的平均营业额至少 80%来自该企业向其所附属企业提供此类服务。如该缔约实体超过一家以上的附属企业提供相同或类似服务，则应考虑这些企业从提供此类服务所获全部营业额。

**　在下列情形下，一不属政府机构的缔约实体向为公众提供服务的网络供应饮用水和电力的行为，不得视为属附件 3 第 1 至 5 款意义内的相关活动：

- 有关实体生产饮用水或电力属因其消费系为从事本附件第 1 至 5 款所指活动以外的活动所必需；且

- 向公共网络供应仅取决于该实体自身消费，且未超过该实体饮用水或能源总产量的 30%，指以往 3 年(含当年)的平均值。

2000 年 3 月 1 日 (WT/Let/330)

ANNEX 4

Services

Of the Universal List of Services, as contained in document MTN.GNS/W/120, the following services are included:*

Subject	*CPC Reference N*
Maintenance and repair services	6112, 6122, 633, 886
Land transport services, including armoured car services, and courier services, except transport of mail	712 (except 712235), 7512, 87304
Air transport services of passengers and freight, except transport of mail	73 (except 7321)
Transport of mail by land, except rail, and by air	71235, 7321
Telecommunications services	752** (except 7524, 7525, 7526)
Financial services	ex 81
(a) Insurance services (b) Banking and investment services***	812, 814
Computer and related services	84
Accounting, auditing and bookkeeping services	862
Market research and public opinion polling services	864
Management consulting services and related services	865, 866****
Architectural services; engineering services and integrated engineering services, urban planning and landscape architectural services; related scientific and technical consulting services; technical consulting services; technical testing and analysis services	867
Advertising services	871
Building-cleaning services and property management services	874, 82201-82206

1 March 2000 (WT/Let/330)

附件 4

服务

包括载于 MTN.GNS/W/120 号文件的服务通用清单中的下列服务：*

事项	*CPC 参考号*
维护和修理服务	6112、6122、633、886
陆路运输服务, 包括装甲车服务和速递服务，邮件运输除外	712(不含 71235)、7512、87304
航空客运和货运服务,邮件运输除外	73(不含 7321)
陆地和航空邮件运输，铁路运输除外	71235、7321
电信服务	752 ** (不含 7524、7525、7526)
金融服务	ex 81
(a) 保险服务 (b) 银行与投资服务 ***	812、814
计算机及相关服务	84
会计、审计和簿记服务	862
市场调研和民意测验服务	864
管理咨询服务及相关服务	865、866 ****
建筑设计服务；工程服务与集中工程服务、城市规划和景观设计服务； 相关科技咨询服务; 技术咨询服务； 技术测试和分析服务	867
广告服务	871
建筑物清洁服务与物业管理服务	874、82201-82206

2000 年 3 月 1 日 (WT/Let/330)

Subject	*CPC Reference N*
Publishing and printing services on a fee or contract basis	88442
Sewage and refuse disposal; sanitation and similar services	94

Notes to Annex 4

* except for services which entities have to procure from another entity pursuant to an exclusive right established by a published law, regulation or administrative provision
** except voice telephony, telex, radiotelephony, paging and satellite services
*** except contracts for financial services in connection with the issue, sale, purchase, or transfer of securities or other financial instruments, and central bank services
**** except arbitrations and conciliation services

事项	*CPC 参考号*
收费或合同基础上的出版和印刷服务	88442
排污及废物处理；卫生及类似服务	94

附件 4 注释

*	一实体根据一已公布的法律、法规或管理规定所确定的专用权必须向另一实体购买的服务除外
**	语音通信、电传、无线电话、寻呼及卫星服务除外
***	关于证券或其他金融工具的发行、销售、购买或转让的金融服务合同及中央银行服务合同除外
****	仲裁和调解服务除外

ANNEX 5

Construction Services

Definition:

A construction service contract is a contract which has as its objective the realization by whatever means of civil or building works, in the sense of Division 51 of the Central Product Classification (CPC).

List of Division 51, CPC:

All public works/construction services of Division 51.

附件 5

建筑服务

定义：

建筑服务合同是指根据《中央产品分类》第 51 类，以通过任何土木或建筑工程手段实现目的的合同。

CPC 第 51 类清单：

CPC 51 类包含的所有服务。

2000 年 3 月 1 日 (WT/Let/330)

GENERAL NOTES AND DEROGATIONS FROM THE PROVISIONS OF ARTICLE III

1. Norway will not extend the benefits of this Agreement:

- as regards the award of contracts by entities listed in Annex 2 to the suppliers and service providers of Canada;

- as regards the award of contracts, other than for supplies, listed in Annex 2 to the suppliers and service providers of the USA;

- as regards the award of contracts by entities listed in Annex 3 paragraph

(1) (electricity), to the suppliers and service providers of Canada, Singapore and Japan;

(2) (urban transport), to the suppliers and service providers of Canada, Israel, Japan, Korea and the USA;

(3) (airports), to the suppliers and service providers of Canada, Korea and the USA;

(4) (ports), to the suppliers and service providers of Canada;

(5) (water), to the suppliers and service providers of Canada and the USA;

until such time as Norway has accepted that the Parties concerned give comparable and effective access for Norwegian undertakings to the relevant markets;

- to service providers of Parties which do not include the relevant service contracts for the relevant entities in Annexes 1 to 3 and the relevant service category under Annexes 4 and 5 in their own coverage.

2. The provisions of Article XX shall not apply to suppliers and service providers of:

- Israel, Japan and Korea in contesting the award of contracts by entities listed under Annex 2, paragraph 2, until such time as Norway accepts that they have completed coverage of sub-central entities;

- Japan, Korea and the USA in contesting the award of contracts to a supplier or service provider of Parties other than those mentioned, which are small or medium-sized enterprises under the relevant provisions in Norway, until such time as Norway accepts that they no longer operate discriminatory measures in favour of certain domestic small and minority businesses;

- Israel, Japan and Korea in contesting the award of contracts by Norwegian entities, whose value is less than the threshold applied for the same category of contracts awarded by these Parties.

11 January 2003 (WT/Let/438)

总注释及对第 3 条规定的背离

1. 挪威在下列方面不将本协定利益给予下列参加方：

- 对于附件 2 中所列实体授予的合同，本协定利益不给予加拿大供应商和服务提供者；

- 对于附件 2 所列除供应品外的合同的授予，本协定利益不给予美国供应商和服务提供者；

- 对于附件 3 所列实体授予的合同：

  (1) (电力)，本协定利益不给予加拿大、新加坡和日本供应商和服务提供者；

  (2) (城市交通)，本协定利益不给予加拿大、日本、韩国和美国供应商和服务提供者;

  (3) (机场)，本协定利益不给予加拿大、韩国和美国供应商和服务提供者;

  (4) (港口)，本协定利益不给予加拿大供应商和服务提供者;

  (5) (水)，本协定利益不给予美国和加拿大供应商和服务提供者;

直至挪威已经认为有关参加方给予挪威企业对于相关市场的对等和有效的准入机会。

- 本协定利益不给予在其各自承诺范围内未对附件 1 至 3 中相关实体包含相关服务合同和未在附件 4 和 5 中包括相关服务类别的参加方的服务提供者。

2. 第 20 条不适用于下列参加方的供应商和服务提供者：

- 以色列、日本和韩国，在竞争附件 2 第 2 款下所列实体所授予的合同时，直至挪威认为他们的次中央实体范围已经完整时止；

- 日本、韩国和美国，在竞争将合同授予已提及的参加方供应商或服务提供者之外的一属挪威相关规定所定义的小型或中型企业的供应商或服务提供者时，直至挪威认为他们不再采取有利于某些国内小型和少数族裔企业的歧视性措施时止;

- 以色列、日本和韩国，在竞争挪威实体授予的合同时，其价值低于这些参加方所授予的相同类别合同所适用的门槛金额。

2003 年 1 月 11 日 (WT/Let/438)

3. Until such time as Norway has accepted that the Parties concerned provide access for Norwegian suppliers and service providers to their own markets, Norway will not extend the benefits of this Agreement to suppliers and service providers of:

- Canada as regards procurement of FSC 36, 70 and 74 (special industry machinery; general purpose automatic data processing equipment, software, supplies and support equipment (except 7010 ADPE configurations); office machines, visible record equipment and ADP equipment);

- Canada as regards procurement of FSC 58 (communications, protection and coherent radiation equipment) and the USA as regards air traffic control equipment.

- Israel and Korea as regards procurement by entities listed in Annex 3, paragraph 1, as regards procurement of HS Nos 8504, 8535, 8537 and 8544 (electrical transformers, plugs, switches and insulated cables); and for Israel, HS Nos 8501, 8536 and 902830;

- Canada and the USA as regards contracts for good or service components of contracts which, although awarded by an entity covered by this Agreement, are not themselves subject to this Agreement.

4. Contracts awarded by entities in Annexes 1 and 2 in connection with activities in the fields of drinking water, energy, transport or telecommunications, are not included.

5. With regard to Annex 3, this Agreement shall not apply to the following contracts:

- contracts which the contracting entities under paragraph 5 award for the purchase of water;

- contracts which the contracting entities under paragraph 1 award for the supply of energy or of fuels for the production of energy;

- contracts which the contracting entities award for purposes other than the pursuit of their activities as described in this Annex or for the pursuit of such activities in a non-EEA country;

- contracts awarded for purposes of re-sale or hire to third parties provided that the contracting entity enjoys no special or exclusive right to sell or hire the subject of such contracts and that other entities are free to sell or hire it under the same conditions as the contracting entity;

- contracting entities exercising activities in the bus transportation sector where other entities are free to offer the same services in the same geographical area and under substantially the same conditions.

3. 在挪威已经认为有关参加方对挪威供应商和服务提供者提供进入其各自市场的机会之前，挪威不将本协定的利益给予下列参加方的供应商和服务提供者：

- 加拿大，对于 FSC 36、70 和 74 的采购(特殊工业机械；通用自动化处理设备、软件、耗材和配套设备(7010 自动化处理系统结构除外)；办公设备、显露式记录设备和自动化处理设备；

- 加拿大，对于 FSC 58 的采购(通信、探测和相干辐射设备)及美国，对于空中交通管制设备的采购；

- 以色列和韩国，对于附件 3 第 1 款所列实体关于协调制度编码 HS8504、8535、8537 和 8544(变压器、插头、开关和绝缘电缆)的采购；以色列，关于协调制度编码 HS8501、8536 和 902830 的采购；

- 加拿大和美国，对于虽由本协定所涵盖一实体授予、但其货物或服务组成部分本身不受本协定管辖的合同。

4. 不包括附件 1 和 2 中实体授予的与饮用水、能源、运输或通信领域活动有关的合同。

5. 对于附件 3，本协定不适用于下列合同：

- 第 5 款下缔约实体为购买水而授予的合同；

- 第 1 款下缔约实体为供应能源或为生产能源而供应燃料而授予的合同；

- 缔约实体所授予的合同目的不是为了从事本附件所述活动或为在一非欧洲经济区国家从事此类活动而授予的合同；

- 为再销售或向第三方出租而授予的合同，但条件是缔约实体不享受销售或出租此类合同客体的特殊或专用权，且其他实体有权根据与缔约实体相同的条件销售或出租此类合同客体；

- 在公共汽车运输部门从事活动的缔约实体，而其他实体有权在同一地理区域以实质相同的条件提供相同服务。

6. With regard to Annex 4, this Agreement shall not apply to the following:

- contracts for the acquisition or rental, by whatever financial means, of land, existing buildings, or other immovable property or concerning rights thereon;

- contracts for the acquisition, development, production or co-production of programme material by broadcasters and contracts for broadcasting time;

- contracts awarded to an entity which is itself a contracting authority within the meaning of the Public Procurement Act: "Lov om offentlige anskaffelser m.v." (LOV 1992-11-27 116) on the basis of an exclusive right which it enjoys pursuant to a published law, regulation or administrative provision;

- contracts of employment.

7. The Agreement shall not apply to contracts awarded under:

- an international agreement and intended for the joint implementation or exploitation of a project by the signatory States;

- an international agreement relating to the stationing of troops;

- the particular procedure of an international organization.

8. The Agreement shall not apply to procurement of agricultural products made in furtherance of agricultural support programmes and human feeding programmes.

9. The thresholds in the Annexes will be applied so as to conform with the public procurement thresholds of the EEA agreement.

10. This Agreement does not apply to procurement subject to secrecy or other particular restrictions with regard to the safety of the realm.

11. When a specific procurement may impair important national policy objectives, the Norwegian Government may consider it necessary in singular procurement cases to deviate from the principle of national treatment in the Agreement. A decision to this effect will be taken at the Norwegian Cabinet level.

12. Norway reserves its position with regard to the application of this Agreement to Svalbard, Jan Mayen Island and Norways Antarctic possessions.

Defence Entities:

Procurement by defence entities (marked with an "*" in Annex 1) covers the following:

Chapter 25: Salt; sulphur; earths and stone; plastering materials, lime and cement
Chapter 26: Metallic ores, slag and ash

11 January 2003 (WT/Let/438)

6. 对于附件 4，本协定不适用于下列合同：

- 购买或租赁土地、现有建筑物或其他不动产或涉及相关权利的合同，无论通过何种出资方式；
- 广播电台购买、开发、制作或联合制作节目内容的合同和播放时间的合同；
- 合同所授予的一实体根据已公布的法律、法规或管理规定享有专属权，因而其本身属 1992 年 11 月 27 日《公共采购法》意义内的缔约机构；
- 雇佣合同。

7. 本协定不适用于根据下列内容授予的合同：

- 旨在由签署国联合执行或开发一项目的国际协定；
- 与军队驻扎有关的国际协定；
- 国际组织的特定程序。

8. 本协定不适用于为促进农业支持计划和人类供给计划而采购的农产品。

9. 附件中门槛金额的适用将符合 EEA 协定中公共采购的门槛金额。

10. 本协定不适用于受到涉及本王国安全的秘密或其他特定限制所管辖的采购。

11. 如一特定采购可能损害重要国家政策目标，则挪威政府可以认为有必要在一单一采购案中背离本协定中的国民待遇原则。有关决定将由挪威内阁一级做出。

12. 挪威保留有关将本协定适用于斯瓦尔巴特群岛、扬马延岛和挪威北极领土的立场。

防务实体:

防务实体(附件 1 中以“*”号标出)进行的采购涵盖下列产品：

第 25 章： 盐；硫磺；泥土及石料；石膏料、石灰及水泥
第 26 章： 矿砂、矿渣及矿灰

2003 年 1 月 11 日 (WT/Let/438)

Chapter 27: Mineral fuels, mineral oils and products of their distillation; bituminous substances; mineral waxes
except:
ex 27.10 special engine fuels

Chapter 28: Inorganic chemicals; organic and inorganic compounds of precious metals, of rare earth metals, of radio-active elements and of isotopes
except:
ex 28.09 explosives
ex 28.13 explosives
ex 28.14 tear gas
ex 28.28 explosives
ex 28.32 explosives
ex 28.39 explosives
ex 28.50 toxic products
ex 28.51 toxic products
ex 28.54 explosives

Chapter 29: Organic chemicals
except:
ex 29.03 explosives
ex 29.04 explosives
ex 29.07 explosives
ex 29.08 explosives
ex 29.11 explosives
ex 29.12 explosives
ex 29.13 toxic products
ex 29.14 toxic products
ex 29.15 toxic products
ex 29.21 toxic products
ex 29.22 toxic products
ex 29.23 toxic products
ex 29.26 explosives
ex 29.27 toxic products
ex 29.29 explosives

Chapter 30: Pharmaceutical products

Chapter 31: Fertilizers

Chapter 32: Tanning and dyeing extracts; tannins and their derivatives; dyes, colours, paints and varnishes, putty, fillers and stoppings, inks

Chapter 33: Essential oils and resinoids; perfumery, cosmetics and toilet preparations

Chapter 34: Soap, organic surface-active agents, washing preparations, lubricating preparations, artificial waxes, prepared waxes, polishing and scouring preparations, candles and similar articles, modelling pastes and "dental waxes"

Chapter 35: Albuminoidal substances; glues; enzymes

Chapter 37: Photographic and cinematographic goods

Chapter 38: Miscellaneous chemical products
except:
ex 38.19 toxic products

第 27 章：　矿物燃料、矿物油及其蒸馏产品；沥青物质；矿物蜡
除：
ex 27.10　特殊发动机燃料
第 28 章：　无机化学品；贵金属、稀土金属、放射性元素及其同位素的有机及无机化合物
除：
ex 28.09　爆炸物
ex 28.13　爆炸物
ex 28.14　催泪瓦斯
ex 28.28　爆炸物
ex 28.32　爆炸物
ex 28.39　爆炸物
ex 28.50　有毒物品
ex 28.51　有毒物品
ex 28.54　爆炸物
第 29 章：　有机化学品
除：
ex 29.03　爆炸物
ex 29.04　爆炸物
ex 29.07　爆炸物
ex 29.08　爆炸物
ex 29.11　爆炸物
ex 29.12　爆炸物
ex 29.13　有毒物品
ex 29.14　有毒物品
ex 29.15　有毒物品
ex 29.21　有毒物品
ex 29.22　有毒物品
ex 29.23　有毒物品
ex 29.26　爆炸物
ex 29.27　有毒物品
ex 29.29　爆炸物
第 30 章：　药品
第 31 章：　肥料
第 32 章：　鞣料浸膏及染料浸膏；鞣酸及其衍生物；染料、颜料及其他着色料；油漆及清漆；油灰及其他类似胶粘剂；墨水、油墨
第 33 章：　清油及香膏；芳香料制品及化妆盥洗品
第 34 章：　肥皂、有机表面活性剂、洗涤剂、润滑剂、人造蜡、调制蜡、光洁剂、蜡烛及类似品、塑型用膏、“牙科用蜡”及牙科用熟石膏制剂
第 35 章：　蛋白类物质；改性淀粉；胶；酶炸药；
第 37 章：　照相及电影用品
第 38 章：　杂项化学产品
除：
ex 38.19　有毒物品

2003 年 1 月 11 日 (WT/Let/438)

Chapter 39:	Artificial resins and plastic materials, cellulose esters and ethers, articles thereof except: ex 39.03 explosives
Chapter 40:	Rubber, synthetic rubber, factice, and articles thereof except: ex 40.11 bullet-proof tyres
Chapter 41:	Raw hides and skins (other than furskins) and leather
Chapter 42:	Articles of leather; saddlery and harness; travel goods, handbags and similar containers; articles of animal gut (other than silk-worm gut)
Chapter 43:	Furskins and artificial fur; manufactures thereof
Chapter 44:	Wood and articles of wood; wood charcoal
Chapter 45:	Cork and articles of cork
Chapter 46:	Manufactures of straw of esparto and of other plaiting materials; basketware and wickerwork
Chapter 47:	Paper-making material
Chapter 48:	Paper and paperboard; articles of paper pulp, of paper or of paperboard
Chapter 49:	Printed books, newspapers, pictures and other products of the printing industry; manuscripts, typescripts and plans
Chapter 65:	Headgear and parts thereof
Chapter 66:	Umbrellas, sunshades, walking-sticks, whips, riding-crops and parts thereof
Chapter 67:	Prepared feathers and down and articles made of feathers or of down; artificial flowers; articles of human hair
Chapter 68:	Articles of stone, of plaster, of cement, of asbestos, of mica and of similar materials
Chapter 69:	Ceramic products
Chapter 70:	Glass and glassware
Chapter 71:	Pearls, precious and semi-precious stones, precious metals, rolled precious metals, and articles thereof; imitation jewellery
Chapter 73:	Iron and steel and articles thereof
Chapter 74:	Copper and articles thereof
Chapter 75:	Nickel and articles thereof
Chapter 76:	Aluminium and articles thereof
Chapter 77:	Magnesium and beryllium and articles thereof
Chapter 78:	Lead and articles thereof
Chapter 79:	Zinc and articles thereof
Chapter 80:	Tin and articles thereof
Chapter 81:	Other base metals employed in metallurgy and articles thereof
Chapter 82:	Tools, implements, cutlery, spoons and forks, of base metal; parts thereof except: ex 82.05 tools ex 82.07 tools, parts
Chapter 83:	Miscellaneous articles of base metal
Chapter 84:	Boilers, machinery and mechanical appliances; parts thereof except: ex 84.06 engines ex 84.08 other engines ex 84.45 machinery ex 84.53 automatic data-processing machines ex 84.55 parts of machines under heading 84.53 ex 84.59 nuclear reactors

11 January 2003 (WT/Let/438)

第 39 章： 塑料及其制品
除：
ex 39.03 爆炸物
第 40 章： 橡胶及其制品
除：
ex 40.11 防弹轮胎
第 41 章： 生皮(毛皮除)及皮革
第 42 章： 皮革制品；鞍具及挽具；旅行用品、手提包及类似容器；动物肠线(蚕胶丝除外)制品
第 43 章： 毛皮、人造毛皮及其制品
第 44 章： 木及木制品；木炭
第 45 章： 软木及软木制品
第 46 章： 稻草、秸秆、针茅或其他编结材料制品；篮筐及柳条编结品
第 47 章： 纸制品
第 48 章： 纸与纸板；纸浆、纸或纸板制品
第 49 章： 书籍、报纸、印刷图画及其他印刷品；手稿、打字稿及设计图纸
第 65 章： 帽类及其零件
第 66 章： 雨伞、阳伞、手杖、鞭子、马鞭及其零件
第 67 章： 已加工羽毛、羽绒及其制品；人造花；人发制品
第 68 章： 石料、石膏、水泥、石棉、云母及类似材料的制品
第 69 章： 陶瓷制品
第 70 章： 玻璃及其制品
第 71 章： 天然或养殖珍珠、宝石或半宝石、贵金属、包贵金属及其制品；仿首饰；硬币
第 73 章： 钢铁制品
第 74 章： 铜及其制品
第 75 章： 镍及其制品
第 76 章： 铝及其制品
第 77 章： 镁和铍及其制品
第 78 章： 铅及其制品
第 79 章： 锌及其制品
第 80 章： 锡及其制品
第 81 章： 其他贱金属、金属陶瓷及其制品
第 82 章： 贱金属工具、器具、利口器、餐匙、餐叉及其零件
除：
ex 82.05 工具
ex 82.07 工具零件
第 83 章： 贱金属杂项制品
第 84 章： 核反应堆、锅炉、机器、机械器具及零件
除：
ex 84.06 发动机
ex 84.08 其他发动机
ex 84.45 机械
ex 84.53 自动数据处理机
ex 84.55 8453 所列机器零件
ex 84.59 核反应堆

2003 年 1 月 11 日 (WT/Let/438)

Chapter 85: Electrical machinery and equipment; parts thereof
except:
ex 85.13 telecommunication equipment
ex 85.15 transmission apparatus

Chapter 86: Railway and tramway locomotives, rolling-stock and parts thereof
except:
ex 86.02 armoured locomotives, electric
ex 86.03 other armoured locomotives
ex 86.05 armoured wagons
ex 86.06 repair wagons
ex 86.07 wagons

Chapter 87: Vehicles, other than railway or tramway rolling-stock, and parts thereof
except:
ex 87.01 tractors
ex 87.02 military vehicles
ex 87.03 breakdown lorries
ex 87.08 tanks and other armoured vehicles
ex 87.09 motorcycles
ex 87.14 trailers

Chapter 89: Ships, boats and floating structures
except:
ex 89.01A warships

Chapter 90: Optical, photographic, cinematographic, measuring, checking, precision, medical and surgical instruments and apparatus; parts thereof
except:
ex 90.05 binoculars
ex 90.13 miscellaneous instruments, lasers
ex 90.14 telemeters
ex 90.28 electrical and electronic measuring instruments
ex 90.11 microscopes
ex 90.17 medical instruments
ex 90.18 mechano-therapy appliances
ex 90.19 orthopaedic appliances
ex 90.20 X-ray apparatus

Chapter 91: Clocks and watches and parts thereof

Chapter 92: Musical instruments; sound recorders or reproducers; television image and sound recorders or reproducers; parts and accessories of such articles

Chapter 94: Furniture and parts thereof; bedding, mattresses, mattress supports, cushions and similar stuffed furnishings
except:
ex 94.01A aircraft seats

Chapter 95: Articles and manufactures of carving or moulding material

Chapter 96: Brooms, brushes, powder-puffs and sieves

Chapter 98: Miscellaneous manufactured articles

11 January 2003 (WT/Let/438)

第 85 章： 电机、电气设备及其零件
除：
ex 85.13 电信设备
ex 85.15 传送设备

第 86 章： 铁道及电车道机车、车辆及其零件
除：
ex 86.02 装甲机车，电动
ex 86.03 其他装甲机车
ex 86.05 装甲无蓬货车
ex 86.06 修理用无蓬货车
ex 86.07 无蓬货车

第 87 章： 车辆及其零件、附件，但铁道及电车道车辆除外
除：
ex 87.01 拖拉机
ex 87.02 军用车辆
ex 87.03 救援车辆
ex 87.08 坦克及其他装甲车辆
ex 87.09 摩托车
ex 87.14 拖车

第 89 章： 船舶及浮动结构体
除：
ex 89.01A 军舰

第 90 章： 光学、照相、电影、计量、检验、医疗或外科用仪器及设备、精密仪器及设备
除：
ex 90.05 望远镜
ex 90.13 未列名仪器，激光器
ex 90.14 测距仪
ex 90.28 电气电子测量仪
ex 90.11 显微镜
ex 90.17 医疗仪器
ex 90.18 热疗设备
ex 90.19 整容设备
ex 90.20 X 光设备

第 91 章： 钟表及其零件

第 92 章： 乐器及其零件、附件

第 94 章： 家具；寝具、褥垫、弹簧床垫、软坐垫及类似的填充制品
除：
ex 94.01A 航空器座椅

第 95 章： 雕刻或模塑材料制品

第 96 章： 帚、刷子、粉扑和筛子

第 98 章： 杂项制品

2003 年 1 月 11 日 (WT/Let/438)

SINGAPORE
新加坡

SINGAPORE

ANNEX 1

Central Government Entities which Procure in Accordance with the Provisions of this Agreement

Goods	*Threshold:*	SDR 130,000
Services (specified in Annex 4)	*Threshold:*	SDR 130,000
Construction (specified in Annex 5)	*Threshold:*	SDR 5,000,000

List of Entities:

Auditor-General's Office
Attorney-General's Office
Cabinet Office
Istana
Judicature
Ministry of Transport
Ministry of Community Development and Sports
Ministry of Education
Ministry of Environment
Ministry of Finance
Ministry of Foreign Affairs
Ministry of Health
Ministry of Home Affairs
Ministry of Information, Communications and the Arts
Ministry of Manpower
Ministry of Law
Ministry of National Development
Ministry of Trade and Industry
Parliament
Presidential Councils
Prime Minister's Office
Public Service Commission
Ministry of Defence

This Agreement will generally apply to purchases by the Singapore Ministry of Defence of the following FSC categories (others being excluded) subject to the Government of Singapore's determinations under the provision of Article XXIII, paragraph 1.

11 August 2002 (WT/Let/429)

新加坡

附件 1

依照本协定条款进行采购的中央政府实体

货物	*门槛金额:*	130,000 特别提款权
服务(附件 4 中列明)	*门槛金额:*	130,000 特别提款权
建筑(附件 5 中列明)	*门槛金额:*	5,000,000 特别提款权

实体清单:

审计署
总检察署
内阁办公室
总统府
司法部
交通部
社会发展及体育部
教育部
环境部
财政部
外交部
卫生部
内政部
新闻、通讯及艺术部
人力部
律政部
国家发展部
贸易及工业部
国会
总统理事会
总理公署
公共服务委员会
国防部

本协定通常适用于新加坡国防部对下列 FSC 类别(其他类别除外)的采购，取决于新加坡政府根据第 23 条第 1 款的规定所做决定。

2002 年 8 月 11 日 (WT/Let/429)

FSC	*Description*
22	Railway Equipment
23	Ground Effect Vehicles, Motor Vehicles, Trailers and Cycles
24	Tractors
25	Vehicular Equipment Components
26	Tires and Tubes
29	Engine Accessories
30	Mechanical Power Transmission Equipment
31	Bearings
32	Woodworking Machinery and Equipment
34	Metalworking Machinery
35	Service and Trade Equipment
36	Special Industry Machinery
37	Agricultural Machinery and Equipment
38	Construction, Mining, Excavating and Highway Maintenance Equipment
39	Materials Handling Equipment
40	Rope, Cable, Chain and Fittings
41	Refrigeration, Air Conditioning and Air Circulating Equipment
42	Fire Fighting, Rescue and Safety Equipment
43	Pumps and Compressors
44	Furnace, Steam Plant and Drying Equipment
45	Plumbing, Heating and Sanitation Equipment
46	Water Purification and Sewage Treatment Equipment
47	Pipe, Tubing, Hose and Fittings
48	Valves
51	Handtools
52	Measuring Tools
53	Hardware and Abrasives
54	Prefabricated Structures and Scaffolding
55	Lumber, Millwork, Plywood and Veneer
56	Construction and Building Materials
61	Electric Wire, and Power and Distribution Equipment
62	Lighting, Fixtures and Lamps
63	Alarm, Signal and Security Detection Systems
65	Medical, Dental and Veterinary Equipment and Supplies
67	Photographic Equipment
68	Chemicals and Chemical Products
69	Training Aids and Devices
70	General Purpose Automatic Data Processing Equipment, Software, Supplies and Support Equipment
71	Furniture
72	Household and Commercial Furnishings and Appliances
73	Food Preparation and Serving Equipment
74	Office Machines, Text Processing Systems and Visible Record Equipment
75	Office Supplies and Devices
76	Books, Maps and other Publications
77	Musical Instruments, Phonographs and Home-Type Radios
78	Recreational and Athletic Equipment

11 August 2002 (WT/Let/429)

FSC	*描述*
22	铁路设备
23	地面效应车、机动车辆、拖车和自行车
24	拖拉机
25	机动车部件
26	轮胎和内胎
29	发动机配件
30	机械动力传输设备
31	轴承
32	木工机器和设备
34	金属加工设备
35	服务和销售设备
36	特殊工业机器
37	农业机器和设备
38	建筑、采矿、开凿和公路维护设备
39	材料处理设备
40	粗绳、电缆、链条和配件
41	冷却、空调和空气循环装备
42	消防、援救和安全设备
43	泵和压缩机
44	火炉、蒸气设备、烘干设备和核反应堆
45	管道、加热和卫生设备
46	水净化和污水处理设备
47	管和配件
48	阀
51	维护和修理商店设备
52	手工工具
53	硬件和研磨剂
54	预制件和脚手架
55	木材、木制品、胶合板和饰面板
56	建筑材料
61	电线及电力传输设备
62	照明器材和灯
63	警报、信号和探测系统
65	内科、牙科和兽医设备和耗材
67	摄影设备
68	化学药品和化工品
69	教具和训练器材
70	自动化处理设备软件、耗材和配套设备
71	家具
72	家用和商业家具和器械
73	食品加工和供餐设备
74	办公设备
75	办公用品和装置
76	书、地图和其他出版物
77	乐器、留声机和家用收音机
78	娱乐和运动器材

2002 年 8 月 11 日(WT/Let/429)

79 Cleaning Equipment and Supplies
80 Brushes, Paints, Sealers and Adhesives
81 Containers, Packaging and Packing Supplies
83 Textiles, Leather, Furs, Apparel and Shoe Findings, Tents and Flags
84 Clothing, Individual Equipment, and Insignia
85 Toiletries
87 Agricultural Supplies
88 Live Animals
89 Subsistence
91 Fuels, Lubricants, Oils and Waxes
93 Non-metallic Fabricated Materials
94 Non-metallic Crude Materials
95 Metal Bars, Sheets and Shapes
96 Ores, Minerals, and their Primary Products
99 Miscellaneous

Notes to Annex 1:

1. The Agreement shall not apply to any procurement in respect of:

   (a) construction contracts for chanceries abroad and headquarters buildings made by the Ministry of Foreign Affairs; and

   (b) contracts made by the Internal Security Department, Criminal Investigation Department, Security Branch and Central Narcotics Bureau of the Ministry of Home Affairs as well as procurement that have security considerations made by the Ministry.

2. The Agreement shall not apply to any procurement made by a covered entity on behalf of a non-covered entity.

11 August 2002 (WT/Let/429)

79 清洁设备和耗材
80 刷子、油漆、封条和粘合剂
81 容器、包装材料和包装用品
83 纺织品、皮革、毛皮、服装和鞋子、帐篷、旗
84 服装、个人装备和勋章
85 盥洗用品
87 农业供给
88 活动物
89 食物
91 燃料、润滑剂、油和蜡
93 非金属制品
94 非金属原料
95 金属棒、片和型材
96 矿石、矿物及其初级产品
99 杂项制品

附件 1 注释：

1. 本协定不适用于以下方面的任何采购：

(a) 外交部订立的国外档案馆和总部建筑物建筑合同；及

(b) 内务部下设的国内安全司、罪犯调查司、安全机构及中央毒品局订立的合同以及该部所进行的含有安全考虑的采购。

2. 本协定不适用于一涵盖实体代表一非涵盖实体进行的任何采购。

2002 年 8 月 11 日 (WT/Let/429)

ANNEX 2

Sub-Central Entities which Procure in Accordance with the Provisions of the Agreement

Non-applicable for Singapore (Singapore does not have any Sub-central Governments).

1 March 2000 (WT/Let/330)

附件 2

依照本协定条款进行采购的次中央实体

不适用于新加坡 (新加坡没有次中央政府)。

2000 年 3 月 1 日 (WT/Let/330)

ANNEX 3

All other Entities which Procure in Accordance with the Provisions of this Agreement

Goods	*Threshold:*	SDR 400,000
Services (specified in Annex 4)	*Threshold:*	SDR 400,000
Construction (specified in Annex 5)	*Threshold:*	SDR 5,000,000

List of Entities:

Agency for Science, Technology and Research
Board of Architects
Civil Aviation Authority of Singapore
Building and Construction Authority
Economic Development Board
Housing and Development Board
Info–communications Development Authority of Singapore
Inland Revenue Authority of Singapore
International Enterprise Singapore
Land Transport Authority of Singapore
Jurong Town Corporation
Maritime and Port Authority of Singapore
Monetary Authority of Singapore
Nanyang Technological University
National Parks Board
National University of Singapore
Preservation of Monuments Board
Professional Engineers Board
Public Transport Council
Sentosa Development Corporation
Singapore Broadcasting Authority
Singapore Tourism Board
Standards, Productivity and Innovation Board
Urban Redevelopment Authority

Note to Annex 3:

1. The Agreement shall not apply to any procurement made by a covered entity on behalf of a non-covered entity.

11 August 2002 (WT/Let/429)

附件 3

依照本协定条款进行采购的所有其他实体

货物	*门槛金额:*	400,000 特别提款权
服务(附件 4 中列明)	*门槛金额:*	400,000 特别提款权
建筑(附件 5 中列明)	*门槛金额:*	5,000,000 特别提款权

实体清单:

科学、技术与研究局
建筑师局
新加坡民用航空局
建设局
经济发展局
建屋发展局
新加坡资讯通信发展局
新加坡国内税务局
新加坡国际企业发展局
新加坡交通管理局
裕廊镇管理局
新加坡海事和港务局
新加坡金融管理局
南洋理工大学
国家公园局
新加坡国立大学
古迹保存局
专业工程师局
公共交通理事会
圣陶沙发展公司
新加坡广播管理局
新加坡旅游局
标准、生产力及创新局
市区重建局

附件 3 注释:

1. 本协定不适用于一涵盖实体代表一非涵盖实体进行的任何采购。

2002 年 8 月 11 日 (WT/Let/429)

ANNEX 4

Services

The following services as contained in document MTN.GNS/W/120 are offered (others being excluded):

Threshold: SDR 130,000 for entities as set out in Annex 1
SDR 400,000 for entities as set out in Annex 3

CPC	*Description*
862	Accounting, Auditing and Book-keeping Services
8671	Architectural Services
865	Management Consulting Services
874	Building-Cleaning Services
641-643	Hotels and Restaurants (incl. catering)
74710	Travel Agencies and Tour Operators
7472	Tourist Guide Services
843	Data Processing Services
844	Database Services
932	Veterinary Services
84100	Consultancy Services Related to the Installation of Computer Hardware
84210	Systems and Software Consulting Services
87905	Translation and Interpretation Services
7523	Electronic Mail
7523	Voice Mail
7523	On-Line Information and Database Retrieval
7523	Electronic Data Interchange
96112	Motion Picture or Video Tape Production Services
96113	Motion Picture or Video Tape Distribution Services
96121	Motion Picture Projection Services
96122	Video Tape Projection Services
96311	Library Services
8672	Engineering Services
7512	Courier Services
-	Biotechnology Services
-	Exhibition Services
-	Commercial Market Research
-	Interior Design Services, Excluding Architecture
-	Professional, Advisory and Consulting Services Relating to Agriculture, Forestry, Fishing and Mining, Including Oilfield Services

附件 4

服务

包含在 MTN.GNS/W/120 号文件中的下列服务列入出价(其他服务除外)：

门槛金额: 对于附件 1 所列实体为 130,000 特别提款权
对于附件 3 所列实体为 400,000 特别提款权

CPC	*描述*
862	会计、审计和簿记服务
8671	建筑设计服务
865	管理咨询服务
874	建筑物清洁服务
641-643	旅馆和餐馆 (包括饮食服务)
74710	旅行社和旅游经营者
7472	导游服务
843	数据处理服务
844	数据库服务
932	兽医服务
84100	与计算机硬件安装有关的咨询服务
84210	系统和软件咨询服务
89705	笔译和口译服务
7523	电子邮件
7523	语音邮件
7523	在线信息和数据库调用服务
7523	电子数据交换
96112	电影和录像的制作
96113	电影和录像的发行
96121	电影放映服务
96122	录像放映服务
96311	图书馆服务
8672	工程服务
7512	速递服务
-	生物科技服务
-	展览服务
-	商业市场研究
-	室内设计服务,不包括建筑设计
-	与农业、林业、渔业和采矿业有关的专业咨询服务，包括油田服务

2000 年 3 月 1 日 (WT/Let/330)

Notes to Annex 4:

1. The offer regarding services is subject to the limitations and conditions specified in the Government of Singapore's offer under the GATS negotiations.

2. The Agreement shall not apply to any procurement made by a covered entity on behalf of a non-covered entity.

附件 4 注释：

1. 有关服务的出价需遵守新加坡政府在 GATS 谈判中规定的限制和条件。

2. 本协定不适用于一涵盖实体代表一非涵盖实体进行的任何采购。

2000 年 3 月 1 日 (WT/Let/330)

ANNEX 5

Construction Services

The following construction services in the sense of Division 51 of the Central Product Classification as contained in document MTN.GNS/W/120 are offered (others being excluded):

Threshold: SDR 5,000,000 for entities as set out in Annex 1
SDR 5,000,000 for entities as set out in Annex 3

List of construction services offered:

CPC	*Description*
512	General construction work for buildings
513	General construction work for civil engineering
514, 516	Installation and assembly work
517	Building completion and finishing work
511, 515, 518	Others

Notes to Annex 5:

1. The offer regarding construction services is subject to the limitations and conditions specified in the Government of Singapore's offer under the GATS negotiations.

2. The Agreement shall not apply to any procurement made by a covered entity on behalf of a non-covered entity.

1 March 2000 (WT/Let/330)

附件 5

建筑服务

下列包含在 MTN.GNS/W/120 号文件中《中央产品分类》第 51 类中的建筑服务列入出价(其他服务除外)：

门槛金额：　对于附件 1 所列实体为 5,000,000 特别提款权
对于附件 3 所列实体为 5,000,000 特别提款权

列入出价的建筑服务：

CPC	*描述*
512	建筑物的建筑工作
513	土木工程的建筑工作
514、516	组装和安装工程
517	建筑物竣工和修整工程
511、515、518	其他

附件 5 注释：

1. 有关建筑服务的出价需遵守新加坡政府在 GATS 谈判中规定的限制和条件。

2. 本协定不适用于一涵盖实体代表一非涵盖实体进行的任何采购。

2000 年 3 月 1 日 (WT/Let/330)

GENERAL NOTE:

1. Taking into account the concerns expressed by GPA Members, Singapore will review its current compulsory registration system with the view to removing any unintended effects of discrimination and of limited tendering in its open tender system that the existing registration system may have on GPA Members within a period of three years after its accession.

1 March 2000 (WT/Let/330)

总注释：

1.　考虑到 GPA 成员所表达的关注，新加坡将在加入后 3 年时间内审查其现行强制注册制度，以期消除现行注册制度在公开投标体制中可能对 GPA 成员非故意造成的任何歧视和有限招标效果。

2000 年 3 月 1 日 (WT/Let/330)

SWITZERLAND
瑞士

SUISSE

(La version française fait foi)

ANNEXE 1

Entités du gouvernement fédéral qui passent des marchés conformément aux dispositions du présent accord

Fournitures	*Valeur de seuil:*	130 000 DTS
Services (spécifiés à l'Annexe 4)	*Valeur de seuil:*	130 000 DTS
Services de construction (spécifiés à l'Annexe 5)	*Valeur de seuil:*	5 000 000 DTS

Liste des entités couvrant tous les Départements fédéraux suisses:

1. Chancellerie fédérale (CF):

   Chancellerie fédérale
   Bibliothèque centrale du Parlement et de l'Administration fédérale
   Préposé fédéral à la protection des données
   Services du Parlement

2. Département fédéral des affaires étrangères (DFAE):

   Secrétariat général du Département fédéral des affaires étrangères
   Direction du développement et de la coopération
   Direction du droit international public
   Direction politique
   Secrétariat d'État du Département fédéral des affaires étrangères

3. Département fédéral de l'intérieur (DFI):

   Secrétariat général du Département fédéral de l'intérieur
   Archives fédérales
   Bureau fédéral de l'égalité entre femmes et hommes
   Conseil des écoles polytechniques fédérales
   Écoles polytechniques fédérales et établissements annexes
   Groupement de la science et de la recherche
   Institut fédéral de recherches sur la forêt, la neige et le paysage
   Institut fédéral pour l'aménagement, l'épuration et la protection des eaux
   Institut Paul Scherrer
   Institut suisse de météorologie
   Laboratoire fédéral d'essai des matériaux et de recherches

29 September 2000 (WT/Let/356)

瑞士

(仅以法文为准)

附件 1

依照本协定条款进行采购的中央政府实体

供应品 *门槛金额:* 130 000 特别提款权

服务(附件 4 中列明) *门槛金额:* 130 000 特别提款权

建筑服务 (附件 5 中列明) *门槛金额:* 5 000 000 特别提款权

瑞士政府部门名单:

1. 联邦办公厅:

联邦办公厅
议会及联邦机构中央图书馆
资料保护联邦办公室
议会行政处

2. 外交部:

外交部总秘书处
发展合作局
国际公法局
政治局
外交事务总局

3. 内政部:

内政部总秘书处
联邦档案室
男女平等联邦办公室
联邦高等理工学院
联邦高等理工学院及其附属机构
科学研究组织
联邦森林、雪地及地形研究中心
联邦水资源装置制造、净化、保护研究中心
瑞士国立研究机构
瑞士气象研究所
材料研究联邦实验室

2000 年 9 月 29 日(WT/Let/356)

Office fédéral de l'assurance militaire[1]
Office fédéral de l'éducation et de la science
Office fédéral de la culture
Office fédéral de la santé publique
Office fédéral de la statistique
Office fédéral des assurances sociales

4. Département fédéral de la justice et police (DFJP):

Secrétariat général du Département fédéral de la justice et police
Institut suisse de droit comparé
Institut suisse de la propriété intellectuelle
Ministère public de la Confédération
Office fédéral de la justice
Office fédéral de la police
Office fédéral de l'aménagement du territoire
Office fédéral de métrologie
Office fédéral des assurances privées
Office fédéral des étrangers
Office fédéral des réfugiés

5. Département fédéral de la défense, de la protection de la population et des sports (DDPS):

Secrétariat général du Département fédéral de la défense, de la protection de la population et des sports[1]
Administration centrale du groupement de l'armement[1]
Commandement des écoles d'état-major et de commandants[1]
Commandement du Corps des gardes fortification[1]
État-Major de l'instruction opérative[1]
État-Major général[1]
Groupe de l'état-major général[1]
Groupe de la logistique de l'état-major général[1]
Groupe de la promotion de la paix et de la coopération en matière de sécurité[1]
Groupe de la Direction de l'instruction des forces terrestres[1]
Groupe de la planification de l'état-major général[1]
Groupe de l'aide au commandement de l'état-major général[1]
Groupe des affaires sanitaires de l'état-major général[1]
Groupe des opérations de l'état-major général[1]
Groupe des opérations des forces aériennes[1]
Groupe du personnel de l'armée de l'état-major général[1]
Groupe du personnel enseignant des forces terrestres[1]
Groupe des renseignements de l'état-major général[1]
Office de l'auditeur en chef[1]
Office des exploitations des forces terrestres[1]
Office fédéral de la protection civile[1]
Office fédéral de la topographie
Office fédéral de l'instruction des forces aériennes[1]

[1] Pour les marchés passés par les offices du Département militaire fédéral mentionnés, voir liste des matériels civils de la défense et de la protection civile en annexe. (Il en est de même de l'Administration fédérale des douanes en ce qui concerne l'équipement des gardes frontière et des douaniers.)

联邦军人保险办公室[1]
教育科学局
文化局
公共卫生局
联邦统计局
社会保险局

4. 联邦司法警察部：

联邦司法警察部总秘书处
瑞士比较法律局
瑞士知识产权局
联邦公共事务局
联邦司法局
联邦警察局
联邦领土整治局
联邦计量局
联邦私人保险事务局
联邦外国人局
联邦难民局

5. 联邦人口、体育和民防部：

联邦人口、体育和民防部总秘书处[1]
总装备部[1]
参谋院校指挥部[1]
要塞防御指挥部[1]
军事行动参谋部[1]
总参谋部[1]
总参谋部突击队[1]
总参谋部后勤部队[1]
安全问题维和合作部队[1]
陆军指挥突击队[1]
总参谋部规划组[1]
总参谋部协同指挥组[1]
总参谋部医疗救助队[1]
总参谋部军事行动分队[1]
空军行动分队[1]
总参谋部队人事组[1]
陆军教官组[1]
总参谋部情报组[1]
主要办案员办公室[1]
陆军扩大战果办公室[1]
国民保护联邦办公室[1]
地形学联邦办公室
空军指挥联邦办公室[1]

[1] 对于上述联邦军事部门各机构的采购，请见附件中防务和民防用非军事设备清单。(该清单同样适用于联邦海关管理局采购的边防警卫和海关官员人员用装备)。

Office fédéral des armes de combat[1]
Office fédéral des armes et des services d'appui[1]
Office fédéral des armes et des services de la logistique[1]
Office fédéral des exploitations des forces aériennes[1]
Office fédéral des systèmes d'armes des forces aériennes et des systèmes de commandement[1]
Office fédéral des systèmes d'armes et des munitions[1]
Office fédéral du matériel d'armée et des constructions[1]
Office fédéral du sport
Services centraux de l'état-major général[1]
Services centraux des forces aériennes[1]
Services centraux des forces terrestres[1]

6. Département fédéral des finances (DFF):

Secrétariat général du Département fédéral des finances
Administration fédérale des contributions
Administration fédérale des douanes[1]
Administration fédérale des finances
Caisse fédérale d'assurance
Commission fédérale des banques
Contrôle fédéral des finances
Monnaie officielle de la Confédération suisse
Office fédéral de l'informatique
Office fédéral des constructions et de la logistique
Office fédéral du personnel
Régie fédérale des alcools

7. Département fédéral de l'économie (DFE):

Secrétariat général du Département fédéral de l'économie
Commission de la concurrence
Office fédéral de l'agriculture
Office fédéral de la formation professionnelle et de la technologie
Office fédéral du logement
Office fédéral pour l'approvisionnement économique du pays
Office vétérinaire fédéral
Secrétariat d'État à l'économie
Surveillance des prix

---

[1] Pour les marchés passés par les offices du Département militaire fédéral mentionnés, voir liste des matériels civils de la défense et de la protection civile en annexe. (Il en est de même de l'Administration fédérale des douanes en ce qui concerne l'équipement des gardes frontière et des douaniers.)

作战部队联邦办公室[1]
武器勤务支持联邦办公室[1]
武器后勤服务联邦办公室[1]
空军扩大战果联邦办公室[1]
空军及指挥系统武器制度联邦办公室[1]
武器和军需物资系统联邦办公室[1]
武器和建筑材料联邦办公室[1]
体育运动联邦办公室
总指挥中心[1]
空军总指挥中心[1]
陆军总指挥中心[1]

6. 联邦财政部：

联邦财政部总秘书处
联邦税务局
联邦海关总署[1]
联邦财政局
联邦保险基金会
联邦银行委员会
联邦财政监督处
瑞士联邦官方铸币厂
联邦电子信息局
联邦建筑及后勤保障局
联邦人事办公室
联邦酒类专卖局

7. 联邦经济部：

联邦经济部总秘书处
竞争委员会
联邦农业局
联邦职业培训与技术局
联邦住房局
联邦物资供应局
联邦兽医局
国家经济总局
物价监督局

[1] 对于上述联邦军事部门各机构的采购，请见附件中防务和民防用非军事设备清单。(该清单同样适用于联邦海关管理局采购的边防警卫和海关官员人员用装备)。

8. Département fédéral de l'environment, des transports, de l'énergie et de la communication (DETEC):

Secrétariat général du Département fédéral de l'environnement, des transports, de l'énergie et de la communication
Commission fédérale de la communication
La Poste[2]
Office fédéral de la communication
Office fédéral de l'aviation civile
Office fédéral de l'économie des eaux
Office fédéral de l'énergie
Office fédéral de l'environnement, des forêts et du paysage
Office fédéral des routes
Office fédéral des transports

[2] Pour autant que l'entité ne soit pas en concurrence avec des entreprises auxquelles le présent accord n'est pas applicable.

8. 联邦环境、交通、能源和通信部：

联邦环境、交通、能源和通信部总秘书处
联邦通信委员会
联邦邮政总局[2]
联邦通信局
联邦民航局
联邦水域经济局
联邦能源局
联邦环境、国家森林局
联邦公路局
联邦运输局

[2] 以该实体不与本协定未涵盖企业进行竞争为限。

Note relative à l'annexe 1

Le présent accord ne s'applique pas aux marchés passés par des entités énumérées dans cette annexe et portant sur des activités dans les secteurs de l'eau potable, de l'énergie, des transports ou des télécommunications.

Liste des matériels civils de la défense et de la protection civile soumis à l'accord

Chapitre 25: Sel; soufre; terres et pierres; plâtres; chaux et ciments

Chapitre 26: Minerais métallurgiques, scories et cendres

Chapitre 27: Combustibles minéraux, huiles minérales et produits de leur distillation; matières bitumineuses; cires minérales

Chapitre 28: Produits chimiques inorganiques; composés inorganiques ou organiques de métaux précieux, d'éléments radioactifs, de métaux des terres rares et d'isotopes

à l'exception de:

ex 28.09 : explosifs
ex 28.13 : explosifs
ex 28.14 : gaz lacrymogènes
ex 28.28 : explosifs
ex 28.32 : explosifs
ex 28.39 : explosifs
ex 28.50 : produits toxicologiques
ex 28.51 : produits toxicologiques
ex 28.54 : explosifs

Chapitre 29: Produits chimiques organiques

à l'exception de:

ex 29.03 : explosifs
ex 29.04 : explosifs
ex 29.07 : explosifs
ex 29.08 : explosifs
ex 29.11 : explosifs
ex 29.12 : explosifs
ex 29.13 : produits toxicologiques
ex 29.14 : produits toxicologiques
ex 29.15 : produits toxicologiques
ex 29.21 : produits toxicologiques
ex 29.22 : produits toxicologiques
ex 29.23 : produits toxicologiques
ex 29.26 : explosifs
ex 29.27 : produits toxicologiques
ex 29.29 : explosifs

附件 1 注释

本协定不适用于本附件所列实体所授予的与在饮用水、能源、运输或电信领域的活动有关的合同。

受本协定管辖的防务和民防用非军事设备清单

第 25 章：　盐；硫磺；泥土及石料；石膏料、石灰及水泥

第 26 章：　矿砂、矿渣及矿灰

第 27 章：　矿物燃料、矿物油及其蒸馏产品；沥青物质；矿物蜡

第 28 章：　无机化学品；贵金属、稀土金属、放射性元素及其同位素的有机及无机化合物

除：

ex 28.09：爆炸物
ex 28.13：爆炸物
ex 28.14：催泪瓦斯
ex 28.28：爆炸物
ex 28.32：爆炸物
ex 28.39：爆炸物
ex 28.50：有毒物品
ex 28.51：有毒物品
ex 28.54：爆炸物

第 29 章：　有机化学品

除：

ex 29.03：爆炸物
ex 29.04：爆炸物
ex 29.07：爆炸物
ex 29.08：爆炸物
ex 29.11：爆炸物
ex 29.12：爆炸物
ex 29.13：有毒物品
ex 29.14：有毒物品
ex 29.15：有毒物品
ex 29.21：有毒物品
ex 29.22：有毒物品
ex 29.23：有毒物品
ex 29.26：爆炸物
ex 29.27：有毒物品
ex 29.29：爆炸物

Chapitre 30:	Produits pharmaceutiques
Chapitre 31:	Engrais
Chapitre 32:	Extraits tannants ou tinctoriaux; tanins et leurs dérivés; matières colorantes, couleurs, peintures, vernis et teintures, mastics, encres
Chapitre 33:	Huiles essentielles et résinoïdes; produits de parfumerie ou de toilette et cosmétiques
Chapitre 34:	Savons, produits organiques tensio-actifs, préparations pour lessives, préparations lubrifiantes, cires artificielles, cires préparées, produits d'entretien, bougies et articles similaires, pâtes à modeler et "cires pour l'art dentaire"
Chapitre 35:	Matières albuminoïdes; colles, enzymes
Chapitre 36:	Poudres et explosifs; articles de pyrotechnie; allumettes; alliages pyrophoriques; matières inflammables *à l'exception de*: ex 36.01 : poudres ex 36.02 : explosifs préparés ex 36.04 : détonateurs ex 36.08 : explosifs
Chapitre 37:	Produits photographiques et cinématographiques
Chapitre 38:	Produits divers des industries chimiques *à l'exception de*: ex 38.19 : produits toxicologiques
Chapitre 39:	Matières plastiques artificielles, éthers et esters de la cellulose, résines artificielles et ouvrages en ces matières *à l'exception de*: ex 39.03 : explosifs
Chapitre 40:	Caoutchouc naturel ou synthétique, factice pour caoutchouc et ouvrages en caoutchouc *à l'exception de*: ex 40.11 : pneus
Chapitre 43:	Pelleteries et fourrures, pelleteries factices

第 30 章：　药品

第 31 章：　肥料

第 32 章：　鞣料浸膏及染料浸膏；鞣酸及其衍生物；染料、颜料及其他着色料；油漆及清漆；油灰及其他类似胶粘剂；墨水、油墨

第 33 章：　清油及香膏；芳香料制品及化妆盥洗品

第 34 章：　肥皂、有机表面活性剂、洗涤剂、润滑剂、人造蜡、调制蜡、光洁剂、蜡烛及类似品、塑型用膏、“牙科用蜡”及牙科用熟石膏制剂

第 35 章：　蛋白类物质；改性淀粉；胶；酶炸药；

第 36 章：　炸药；烟火制品；火柴；引火合金；易燃材料制品

除：

ex 36.01：发射药
ex 36.02：配制炸药
ex 36.04：雷管
ex 36.08：爆炸物

第 37 章：　照相及电影用品

第 38 章：　杂项化学产品

除：

ex 38.19：有毒物品

第 39 章：　塑料及其制品

除：

ex 39.03：爆炸物

第 40 章：　橡胶及其制品

除：

ex 40.11：防弹轮胎

第 43 章：　毛皮、人造毛皮及其制品

Chapitre 44:	Bois, charbon de bois et ouvrages en bois
Chapitre 45:	Liège et ouvrages en liège
Chapitre 46:	Ouvrages de sparterie et de vannerie
Chapitre 47:	Matières servant à la fabrication du papier
Chapitre 48:	Papiers et cartons; ouvrages en pâte de cellulose, en papier et en carton
Chapitre 49:	Articles de librairie et produits des arts graphiques
Chapitre 65:	Coiffures et parties de coiffures
Chapitre 66:	Parapluies, parasols, cannes, fouets, cravaches et leurs parties
Chapitre 67:	Plumes et duvet apprêtés et articles en plumes ou en duvet; fleurs artificielles; ouvrages en cheveux
Chapitre 68:	Ouvrages en pierres, plâtre, ciment, amiante, mica et matières analogues
Chapitre 69:	Produits céramiques
Chapitre 70:	Verre et ouvrages en verre
Chapitre 71:	Perles fines, pierres gemmes et similaires, métaux précieux, plaqués ou doublés de métaux précieux et ouvrages en ces matières; bijouterie de fantaisie
Chapitre 73:	Fonte, fer et acier
Chapitre 74:	Cuivre
Chapitre 75:	Nickel
Chapitre 76:	Aluminium
Chapitre 77:	Magnésium, beryllium (glucinium)
Chapitre 78:	Plomb
Chapitre 79:	Zinc
Chapitre 80:	Etain
Chapitre 81:	Autres métaux communs
Chapitre 82:	Outillage; articles de coutellerie et couverts de table, en métaux communs
Chapitre 83:	Ouvrages divers en métaux communs

第 44 章：　木及木制品；木炭

第 45 章：　软木及软木制品

第 46 章：　稻草、秸秆、针茅或其他编结材料制品；篮筐及柳条编结品

第 47 章：　纸制品

第 48 章：　纸与纸板；纸浆、纸或纸板制品

第 49 章：　书籍、报纸、印刷图画及其他印刷品；手稿、打字稿及设计图纸

第 65 章：　帽类及其零件

第 66 章：　雨伞、阳伞、手杖、鞭子、马鞭及其零件

第 67 章：　已加工羽毛、羽绒及其制品；人造花；人发制品

第 68 章：　石料、石膏、水泥、石棉、云母及类似材料的制品

第 69 章：　陶瓷制品

第 70 章：　玻璃及其制品

第 71 章：　天然或养殖珍珠、宝石或半宝石、贵金属、包贵金属及其制品；仿首饰；硬币

第 73 章：　钢铁制品

第 74 章：　铜及其制品

第 75 章：　镍及其制品

第 76 章：　铝及其制品

第 77 章：　镁和铍及其制品

第 78 章：　铅及其制品

第 79 章：　锌及其制品

第 80 章：　锡及其制品

第 81 章：　其他贱金属、金属陶瓷及其制品

第 82 章：　贱金属工具、器具、利口器、餐匙、餐叉及其零件

第 83 章：　贱金属杂项制品

2000 年 9 月 29 日(WT/Let/356)

Chapitre 84: Chaudières, machines, appareils et engins mécaniques

Chapitre 85: Machines et appareils électriques et objets servant à des usages électrotechniques

à l'exception de:

ex 85.03 : Piles électriques
ex 85.13 : Télécommunications
ex 85.15 : Appareils de transmission

Chapitre 86: Véhicules et matériaux pour voies ferrées; appareils de signalisation non électriques pour voies de communication

à l'exception de:

ex 86.02 : Locomotives blindées
ex 86.03 : autres locoblindées

ex 86.05 : Wagons blindés
ex 86.06 : Wagons ateliers
ex 86.07 : Wagons

Chapitre 87: Voitures automobiles, tracteurs, cycles et autres véhicules terrestres

à l'exception de:

87.08 : Cars et automobiles blindés
ex 87.02 : Camions lourds
ex 87.09 : Motocycles
ex 87.14 : Remorques

Chapitre 88: Navigation aérienne

à l'exception de:

ex 88.02 : Avions

Chapitre 89: Navigation maritime et fluviale

Chapitre 90: Instruments et appareils d'optique, de photographie et de cinématographie, de mesure, de vérification, de précision; instruments et appareils médico-chirurgicaux

à l'exception de:

ex 90.05 : Jumelles
ex 90.13 : Instruments divers, lasers
ex 90.14 : Télémètres
ex 90.28 : Instruments de mesure électriques ou électroniques

Chapitre 91: Horlogerie

第 84 章： 核反应堆、锅炉、机器、机械器具及零件

第 85 章： 电机、电气设备及其零件

除；

ex 85.03：电池
ex 85.13：电信设备
ex 85.15：传送设备

第 86 章： 铁道及电车道机车、车辆及其零件

除：

ex 86.02：装甲机车，电动
ex 86.03：其他装甲机车
ex 86.05：装甲无蓬货车
ex 86.06：修理用无蓬货车
ex 86.07：无蓬货车

第 87 章： 车辆及其零件、附件，但铁道及电车道车辆除外

除：

87.08：坦克及其他装甲车辆
ex 87.02：军用车辆
ex 87.09：摩托车
ex 87.14：拖车

第 88 章：

除：

ex 88.02：飞机

第 89 章： 船舶及浮动结构体

第 90 章： 光学、照相、电影、计量、检验、医疗或外科用仪器及设备、精密仪器及设备

除：

ex 90.05：望远镜
ex 90.13：未列名仪器，激光器
ex 90.14：测距仪
ex 90.28：电气电子测量仪

第 91 章： 钟表及其零件

2000 年 9 月 29 日 (WT/Let/356)

Chapitre 92:	Instruments de musique; appareils d'enregistrement ou de reproduction du son; appareils d'enregistrement ou de reproduction des images et du son en télévision; parties et accessoires de ces instruments et appareils
Chapitre 93:	Armes et munitions *à l'exception de*: ex 93.01 : Armes blanches ex 93.02 : Pistolets ex 93.03 : Armes de guerre ex 93.04 : Armes à feu ex 93.05 : Autres armes ex 93.07 : Projectiles et munitions
Chapitre 94:	Meubles; mobilier médico-chirurgical; articles de literie et similaires
Chapitre 95:	Matières à tailler et à mouler, à l'état travaillé (y compris les ouvrages)
Chapitre 96:	Ouvrages de brosserie et pinceaux, balais, houppes et articles de tamiserie
Chapitre 98:	Ouvrages divers

29 September 2000 (WT/Let/356)

第 92 章： 乐器及其零件、附件；录音机及放声机、电视图像、声音的录制和重放设备及零件、附件

第 93 章： 武器、弹药及其零件、附件

除：

ex 93.01：刀剑
ex 93.02：手枪
ex 93.03：战争武器
ex 93.04：火器
ex 93.05：其他武器
ex 93.07：炮弹和子弹

第 94 章： 家具；寝具、褥垫、弹簧床垫、软坐垫及类似的填充制品

第 95 章： 雕刻或模塑材料制品

第 96 章： 帚、刷子、粉扑和筛子

第 98 章： 杂项制品

ANNEXE 2

Entités des gouvernements sous-centraux[1] qui passent des marchés conformément aux dispositions du présent accord

Fournitures *Valeur de seuil:* 200 000 DTS

Services (spécifiés à l'Annexe 4) *Valeur de seuil:* 200 000 DTS

Services de construction (spécifiés à l'Annexe 5) *Valeur de seuil:* 5 000 000 DTS

Liste des entités[2]

1. Les autorités publiques cantonales

2. Les organismes de droit public établis au niveau cantonal n'ayant pas un caractère commercial ou industriel

3. Les autorités et organismes publics du niveau des districts et des communes

Liste des cantons suisses:

Appenzell (Rhodes Intérieures/Extérieures)

Argovie

Bâle (Ville/Campagne)

Berne

Fribourg

Glaris

Genève

Grisons

Jura

Neuchâtel

[1] C'est-à-dire les gouvernements cantonaux selon la terminologie suisse

[2] Pour autant que les cantons passent des marchés de produits de défense dans le cadre d'une délégation de compétence du Département militaire fédéral: voir liste des matériels civils de la défense et de la protection civile en annexe

7 February 2003 (WT/Let/437)

附件 2

依照本协定条款进行采购的次中央政府实体[1]

供应品	*门槛金额:*	200 000 特别提款权
服务(附件 4 中列明)	*门槛金额:*	200 000 特别提款权
建筑服务(附件 5 中列明)	*门槛金额:*	5 000 000 特别提款权

实体清单[2]

1. 州一级政府部门
2. 州一级受公法管辖、不具产业或商业性质的机构
3. 市镇一级政府部门和公共机构

瑞士州清单:

阿彭策尔 (外阿彭策尔/内阿彭策尔)

阿尔高

巴塞尔(城市/乡村)

伯尔尼

弗里堡

格拉鲁斯

日内瓦

格里松

汝拉

纳沙泰尔

[1]在瑞士专门术语中即指州政府。
[2]条件是各州根据联邦军事部门授权采购防务产品，请见附件中防务和民防用非军事设备清单。

2003 年 2 月 7 日 (WT/Let/437)

Lucerne

Schaffhouse

Schwyz

Soleure

St Gall

Tessin

Thurgovie

Vaud

Valais

Unterwald (Nidwald/Obwald)

Uri

Zoug

Zurich

Note relative à l'Annexe 2

Le présent accord ne s'applique pas aux marchés passés par des entités mentionnées dans cette annexe et portant sur des activités dans les secteurs de l'eau potable, de l'énergie, des transports ou des télécommunications.

7 February 2003 (WT/Let/437)

卢塞恩

沙夫豪森

施维茨

索洛图恩

圣加仑

提契诺

图尔高

沃

瓦莱

瓦尔登(上瓦尔登/下瓦尔登)

乌里

楚格

苏黎世

附录 2 注释

本协定不适用于本附件所列实体所授予的与在饮用水、能源、运输或电信领域的活动有关的合同。

2003 年 2 月 7 日 (WT/Let/437)

ANNEXE 3

Toutes les autres entités qui passent des marchés conformément aux dispositions du présent accord

Fournitures	*Valeur de seuil:*	400 000 DTS
Services (spécifiés à l'Annexe 4)	*Valeur de seuil:*	400 000 DTS
Services de construction (spécifiés à l'Annexe 5)	*Valeur de seuil:*	5 000 000 DTS

Liste des entités:

Les entités adjudicatrices qui sont des pouvoirs publics[1] ou des entreprises publiques[2] et qui exercent au moins une des activités suivantes:

1. la mise à disposition ou l'exploitation de réseaux fixes destinés à fournir un service au public dans le domaine de la production, du transport ou de la distribution d'eau potable ou l'alimentation de ces réseaux en eau potable (spécifiés sous titre I);

2. la mise à disposition ou l'exploitation de réseaux fixes destinés à fournir un service au public dans le domaine de la production, du transport ou de la distribution d'électricité ou l'alimentation de ces réseaux en électricité (spécifiés sous titre II);

---

[1]Pouvoir public: L'Etat, les collectivités territoriales, les organismes de droit public, les associations formées par une ou plusieurs de ces collectivités ou de ces organismes de droit public. Est considéré comme un organisme de droit public tout organisme:

- créé pour satisfaire spécifiquement des besoins d'intérêt général ayant un caractère autre qu'industriel ou commercial,
- doté d'une personnalité juridique et
- dont soit l'activité est financée majoritairement par l'Etat, les collectivités territoriales ou d'autres organismes de droit public, soit la gestion est soumise à un contrôle par ces derniers, soit l'organe d'administration, de direction ou de surveillance est composé de membres dont plus de la moitié est désignée par l'Etat, les collectivités territoriales ou d'autres organismes de droit public.

[2] Entreprise publique: toute entreprise sur laquelle les pouvoirs publics peuvent exercer directement ou indirectement une influence dominante du fait de la propriété, de la participation financière ou des règles qui la régissent. L'influence dominante est présumée lorsque les pouvoirs publics, directement ou indirectement, à l'égard de l'entreprise:

- détiennent la majorité du capital souscrit de l'entreprise ou
- disposent de la majorité des voix attachées aux parts émises par l'entreprise ou
- peuvent désigner plus de la moité des membres de l'organe d'administration, de direction ou de surveillance de l'entreprise.

附件 3

依照本协定条款进行采购的所有其他实体

供应品	*门槛金额:*	400 000 特别提款权
服务(附件 4 中列明)	*门槛金额:*	400 000 特别提款权
建筑服务 (附件 5 中列明)	*门槛金额:*	5 000 000 特别提款权

实体清单:

属政府机构[1]或公共企业[2]且其至少一项活动属下列任何一项之一的缔约实体:

1. 提供或经营固定网络，旨在向公众提供与饮用水的生产、输送或配送有关的服务或与向此类网络供应饮用水有关的服务(以下标题 I 中列明);

2. 提供或经营固定网络，旨在向公众提供与电力的生产、输送或配送有关的服务或与向此类网络供应电力有关的服务(以下标题 II 中列明);

[1] 政府机构指受公法管辖的国家、地区或地方政府机构，或由一个或更多此类受公法管辖的机构构成的协会。在下列情况下，一机构被视为受公法管辖:

- 为满足符合公共利益的需求这一特定目而设立，不具产业或商业性质;
- 具有法人资格；且
- 主要由国家、地区或地方政府机构或由公法管辖的其他机构提供经费，或者接受上述机构的管理监督，或者设有行政、管理或监督委员会，委员会成员一半以上由国家、地区或地方政府机构或公法管辖的其他机构任命。

[2] 公共企业指任何企业，公共机构可直接或间接通过对其的所有权、对其的资金参与或管辖其的规定而施加主要影响。如政府机构对于一企业直接或间接:

- 持有该企业已认缴资本的大多数；或
- 控制该企业发行股票所附加的投票权的大多数；或
- 可任命该企业行政、管理或监督机构的半数以上成员，则该政府机构应被认定具有主要影响。

2000 年 3 月 1 日(WT/Let/330)

3. l'exploitation de réseaux destinés à fournir un service au public dans le domaine du transport par chemin de fer urbain, systèmes automatiques, tramway, trolleybus, autobus ou câble (spécifiés sous titre III);

4. l'exploitation d'une aire géographique dans le but de mettre à la disposition des transporteurs aériens des aéroports ou d'autres terminaux de transport (spécifiés sous titre IV);

5. l'exploitation d'une aire géographique dans le but de mettre à la disposition des transporteurs fluviaux des ports intérieurs ou d'autre terminaux de transport (spécifiés sous titre V).

I. Production, transport ou distribution d'eau potable

Pouvoirs publics ou entreprises publiques de production, de transport et de distribution d'eau potable. Ces pouvoirs publics et entreprises publiques opèrent conformément à la législation cantonale ou locale, ou encore par le biais d'accords individuels respectant ladite législation.

Par exemple:

- Wasserverbund Regio Bern AG
- Hardwasser AG
- Gruppenwasserversorgung Liechtensteiner Oberland
- Gruppenwasserversorgung Liechtensteiner Unterland

II. Production, transport ou distribution d'électricité

Pouvoirs publics ou entreprises publiques de transport et de distribution d'électricité auxquels le droit d'expropriation peut être accordé conformément à la "loi fédérale du 24 juin 1902 concernant les installations électriques à faible et à fort courant".

Pouvoirs publics ou entreprises publiques de production d'électricité conformément à la "loi fédérale du 22 décembre 1916 sur l'utilisation des forces hydrauliques" et à la "loi fédérale du 23 décembre 1959 sur l'utilisation pacifique de l'énergie atomique et la protection contre les radiations".

Par exemple:

- Bernische Kraftwerke AG
- Nordostschweizerische Kraftwerke AG
- Liechtensteinische Kraftwerke

3. 经营固定网络，旨在在运输领域通过城市铁路、自动化系统、有轨电车、无轨电车、公共汽车或缆车向公众提供服务(以下标题 III 中列明)；

4. 开发一地理区域，旨在向空运承运人提供机场或其他航空站(以下标题 IV 中列明)；

5. 开发一地理区域，以向海运或内河航道承运人提供内陆港口或其他港口设施(以下标题 V 中列明)。

I. 饮用水的生产、输送或配送

生产、输送和配送饮用水的政府机构和公共企业。此类政府机构和公共企业根据当地立法或据此订立的单独协定运营。

例如：

- 瑞士伯尔尼水联合会股份公司
- 硬水股份公司
- 上列支敦士登供水集团公司
- 下列支敦士登供水集团公司

II. 电力生产、输送或配送

根据“1902 年 6 月 24 日《关于电力强弱电流装置的联邦法》”，从事电力生产、输送或配送的政府机构和公共企业。

根据“1916 年 12 月 22 日《关于水力利用的联邦法》”和“1959 年 12 月 23 日《关于和平利用原子能和防辐射的联邦法》”，从事电力生产的政府机构和公共企业。

例如：

- 伯尔尼电力股份公司
- 瑞士东北部电力股份公司
- 列支敦士登电厂

III. Transport par chemin de fer urbain, tramway, systèmes automatiques, trolleybus, autobus ou câble

Pouvoirs publics ou entreprises publiques exploitant des tramways au sens de l'article 2, 1er alinéa, de la "loi fédérale du 20 décembre 1957 sur les chemins de fer".

Pouvoirs publics ou entreprises publiques offrant des services de transport public au sens de l'article 4, 1er alinéa, de la "loi fédérale du 29 mars 1950 sur les entreprises de trolleybus".

Entreprise suisse des postes, téléphones et télégraphes (PTT) au sens de l'article 2 de la "loi fédérale du 18 juin 1993 sur le transport de voyageurs et les entreprises de transport par route".

Pouvoirs publics ou entreprises publiques qui, à titre professionnel, effectuent des courses régulières de transport de personnes selon un horaire, au sens de l'article 4 de la "loi fédérale du 18 juin 1993 sur le transport de voyageurs et les entreprises de transport par route".

Par exemple:

- Transports publics genevois
- Verkehrsbetriebe Zürich

IV. Aéroports

Pouvoirs publics ou entreprises publiques exploitant des aéroports en vertu d'une concession au sens de l'article 37 de la "loi fédérale du 21 décembre 1948 sur la navigation aérienne".

Par exemple:

- Flughafen Zürich-Kloten
- Aéroport de Genève-Cointrin
- Aérodrome civil de Sion

V. Ports intérieurs

Ports fluviaux des deux Bâle: pour le canton de Bâle-Ville, est déterminante la "loi du 13 novembre 1919 concernant l'administration des installations portuaires rhénanes de la ville de Bâle"; pour le canton de Bâle-Campagne est déterminante la "loi du 26 octobre 1936 sur la mise en place d'installations portuaires, de voies ferroviaires et de routes sur le "Sternenfeld" à Birsfelden, et dans l'"Au" à "Muttenz".

III.　城市铁路、自动化系统、有轨电车、无轨电车、公共汽车或缆车服务方面的缔约实体

根据“1957 年 12 月 20 日《关于铁路的联邦法》”第 2 条第 1 处缩进，从事有轨电车经营的政府机构和公共企业。

根据“1950 年 3 月 29 日《关于无轨电车企业经营的联邦法》”第 4 条第 1 处缩进，提供公共运输服务的政府机构和公共企业。

根据“1993 年 6 月 18 日《关于旅客运输和道路运输经营的联邦法》”第 2 条，经营邮政、电话和电报的瑞士企业。

根据“1993 年 6 月 18 日《关于旅客运输和道路运输经营的联邦法》”第 4 条，按照时间表经营客运的政府机构和公共企业。

例如：

- 日内瓦公共交通系统
- 苏黎世公共运输公司

IV.　机场

根据“1948 年 12 月 21 日《关于航运的联邦法》”第 37 条，提供机场的政府机构和公共企业。

例如：

- 苏黎世的科罗登机场
- 日内瓦国际机场
- 锡永民用机场

V.　内陆港口

巴塞尔的 2 个河港：在巴塞尔城市半州的港口由“1919 年 11 月 13 日《关于巴塞尔城市半州莱茵区港口设施管理法》”确定；在巴塞尔乡村半州内的港口由“1936 年 10 月 26 日《关于自斯特恩菲尔德亖比尔斯费尔登及自奥至穆坦兹建立港口设施、铁路和道路法》”确定 。

Notes relatives à l'Annexe 3

Le présent accord ne s'applique pas:

1. Aux marchés que les entités adjudicatrices passent à des fins autres que la poursuite de leurs activités décrites dans cette Annexe ou pour la poursuite de ces activités en dehors de Suisse.

2. Aux marchés passés à des fins de revente ou de location à des tiers, lorsque l'entité adjudicatrice ne bénéficie d'aucun droit spécial ou exclusif pour vendre ou louer l'objet de ces marchés et lorsque d'autres entités peuvent librement le vendre ou le louer dans les mêmes conditions que l'entité adjudicatrice.

3. Aux marchés passés pour l'achat d'eau.

4. Aux marchés passés par une entité adjudicatrice autre que les pouvoirs publics, qui assure l'alimentation en eau potable ou en électricité des réseaux destinés à fournir un service au public, lorsque la production d'eau potable ou d'électricité par l'entité concernée a lieu parce que sa consommation est nécessaire à l'exercice d'une activité autre que celle visée dans cette Annexe sous chiffre I et II et lorsque l'alimentation du réseau public ne dépend que de la consommation propre de l'entité et n'a pas dépassé 30% de la production totale d'eau potable ou d'énergie de l'entité prenant en considération la moyenne des trois dernières années, y compris l'année en cours.

5. Aux marchés passés pour la fourniture d'énergie ou de combustibles destinés à la production d'énergie.

6. Aux marchés passés par les entités adjudicatrices assurant au public un service de transport par autobus, lorsque d'autres entités peuvent librement fournir ce service, soit d'une manière générale, soit dans une aire géographique spécifique, dans les mêmes conditions que les entités adjudicatrices.

附件 3 注释

本协定不适用于：

1. 缔约实体不是为了从事本附件所述其活动而授予的合同。

2. 为再销售或向第三方出租而授予的合同，但条件是缔约实体不享受销售或出租此类合同客体的特殊或专用权，且其他实体有权根据与该缔约实体相同的条件销售或出租此类合同客体。

3. 购买水的合同。

4. 向为公众提供服务的网络供应饮用水和电力、且不属政府机构的缔约实体的合同，如此类实体自己生产这些服务，为从事本附件标题 I 和 II 下所述活动之外的活动而消费这些服务，且向公共网络供应仅取决于该实体自身消费，未超过该实体饮用水或能源总产量的 30%，指以往 3 年的平均值。

5. 供应能源或为生产能源而供应燃料的合同。

6. 提供公共汽车服务的缔约实体所授予的合同，如其他实体有权普遍或在某一特定地理区域以相同条件提供相同服务。

2000 年 3 月 1 日 (WT/Let/330)

ANNEXE 4

Services

Les services suivants qui figurent dans la Classification sectorielle des services reproduite dans le document MTN.GNS/W/120 sont inclus:

Objet	*Numéros de réference CPC* (Classification centrale des produits)
Services d'entretien et de réparation	6112, 6122, 633, 886
Services de transport terrestre, y compris les services de véhicules blindés et les services de courrier, à l'exclusion des transports de courrier	712 (sauf 71235) 7512, 87304
Services de transport aérien: transport de voyageurs et de marchandises, à l'exclusion des transports de courrier	73 (sauf 7321)
Transport de courrier par transport terrestre (à l'exclusion des services de transport ferroviaire) et par air	71235, 7321
Services de télécommunications	752[1] (sauf 7524, 7525, 7526)
Services financiers:	ex 81
a) services d'assurances	812, 814
b) services bancaires et d'investissement[2]	
Services informatiques et services connexes	84
Services comptables, d'audit et de tenue de livres	862
Services d'études de marché et de sondages	864
Services de conseil en gestion et services connexes	865, 866[3]

[1] A l'exclusion des services de téléphonie vocale, de télex, de radiotéléphonie, de radiomessagerie et de télécommunication par satellite

[2] A l'exclusion des marchés des services financiers relatifs à l'émission, à l'achat, à la vente et au transfert de titres ou d'autres instruments financiers, ainsi que des services fournis par des banques centrales

[3] A l'exclusion des services d'arbitrage et de conciliation

附件 4

服务

包括下列取自 MTN.GNS/W/120 号文件所载服务部门分类清单的服务：

事项	*CPC 参考号* *(中央产品分类)*
维护和修理服务	6112、6122、633、886
陆路运输服务、包括装甲车服务和 速递服务、邮件运输除外	712(不含 71235)、 7512、87304
航空客运和货运服务、 邮件运输除外	73(不含 7321)
陆地和航空邮件运输、铁路运输除外	71235、7321
电信服务	752[1] (不含 7524、7525、7526)
金融服务	ex 81
(a) 保险服务 (b) 银行与投资服务[2]	812、814
计算机及相关服务	84
会计、审计和簿记服务	862
市场调研和民意测验服务	864
管理咨询服务及相关服务	865、866[3]

[1]语音通信、电传、无线电话、寻呼及卫星服务除外。
[2]关于证券或其他金融工具的发行、销售、购买或转让的金融服务合同及中央银行服务合同除外。
[3]仲裁和调解服务除外。

2000 年 3 月 1 日 (WT/Let/330)

Services d'architecture; services d'ingénierie et services intégrés d'ingénierie; services d'aménagement urbain et d'architecture paysagère; services connexes de consultations scientifiques et techniques; services d'essais et d'analyses techniques	867
Services de publicité	871
Services de nettoyage de bâtiments et services de gestion de propriétés	874, 82201-82206
Services de publication et d'impression sur la base d'une redevance ou sur une base contractuelle	88442
Services de voirie et d'enlèvement des ordures: services d'assainissement et services analogues	94

Notes relatives à l'Annexe 4

Le présent accord ne s'applique pas:

1. Aux marchés de services attribués à une entité qui est elle-même un pouvoir adjudicateur au sens de l'Annexe 1, 2 ou 3 sur la base d'un droit exclusif dont elle bénéficie en vertu de dispositions législatives, réglementaires ou administratives publiées.

2. Aux marchés de services qu'une entité adjudicatrice passe auprès d'une entreprise liée ou passés par une coentreprise, constituée de plusieurs entités adjudicatrices aux fins de la poursuite des activités au sens de l'Annexe 3, auprès d'une de ces entités adjudicatrices ou d'une entreprise liée à une de ces entités adjudicatrices, pour autant que 80% au moins du chiffre d'affaires moyen que cette entreprise a réalisé au cours des trois dernières années en matière de services provienne de la fourniture de ces services aux entreprises auxquelles elle est liée. Lorsque le même service ou des services similaires sont fournis par plus d'une entreprise liée à l'entité adjudicatrice, il doit être tenu compte du chiffre d'affaires total résultant de la fourniture de services par ces entreprises.

3. Aux marchés de services qui ont pour objet l'acquisition ou la location, quelles qu'en soient les modalités financières, de terrains, de bâtiments existants ou d'autres biens immeubles ou qui concernent des droits sur ces biens.

4. Aux marchés de l'emploi.

5. Aux marchés visant l'achat, le développement, la production ou la coproduction d'éléments de programmes par des organismes de radiodiffusion et aux marchés concernant les temps de diffusion.

建筑设计服务；工程服务与集中工程服务、 城市规划和景观设计服务； 相关科技咨询服务; 技术咨询服务; 技术测试和分析服务	867
广告服务	871
建筑物清洁服务与 物业管理服务	874、82201-82206
收费或合同基础上的出版和印刷服务	88442
排污及废物处理；卫生及类似服务	94

附件 4 注释

本协定不适用于：

1. 授予一列入附件 1 或 2 中、根据一已公布的法律、法规或管理规定享有专用权的采购实体的服务合同。

2. 一缔约实体授予一附属企业的服务合同或由一若干缔约实体组成的、旨在从事附件 3 意义内的活动的合资企业授予的服务合同、或授予一附属于这些缔约实体之一的企业的服务合同。该企业以往 3 年平均营业额的至少 80%应来自于该企业向其所附属的企业提供此类服务。如该缔约实体的附属企业超过一家以上提供相同或服务，则应考虑这些企业从提供服务中所获全部营业额。

3. 购买或租赁土地、现有建筑物或其他不动产或涉及相关权利的合同、无论通过何种方式。

4. 雇佣合同。

5. 广播电台购买、开发、制作或联合制作节目内容的合同和播放时间的合同。

2000 年 3 月 1 日(WT/Let/330)

ANNEXE 5

Services de Construction

Définition:

Un contrat de services de construction est un contrat qui a pour objectif la réalisation, par quelque moyen que ce soit, de travaux de construction d'ouvrages de génie civil ou de bâtiments, au sens de la division 51 de la Classification centrale de produits (CPC).

Liste de services relevant de la division 51 de la CPC

Travaux de préparation des sites et chantiers de construction	511
Travaux de construction de bâtiments	512
Travaux de construction d'ouvrages de génie civil	513
Assemblage et construction d'ouvrages préfabriqués	514
Travaux d'entreprises de construction spécialisées	515
Travaux de pose d'installations	516
Travaux d'achèvement et de finition des bâtiments	517
Autres services	518

Valeur de seuil: 5 000 000 DTS

附件 5

建筑服务

定义：

建筑服务合同是指根据《中央产品分类》第 51 类，以通过任何土木或建筑工程手段实现目的的合同。

CPC 第 51 类清单：

建筑工地的准备工作	511
建筑物的建筑工作	512
土木工程的建筑工作	513
预制构件的组装和装配	514
特种行业建筑工程	515
安装工程	516
建筑物竣工和修整工程	517
与建筑设备有关的租赁服务	518

*门槛金额：*5 000 000 特别提款权

2000 年 3 月 1 日 (WT/Let/330)

NOTES GENERALES ET DEROGATIONS AUX DISPOSITIONS DE L'ARTICLE III

1. La Suisse n'étendra pas le bénéfice des dispositions du présent accord:

- en ce qui concerne les marchés passés par les entités mentionnées à l'Annexe 2 aux fournisseurs de produits et de services du Canada;

- en ce qui concerne les marchés passés par les entités mentionnées au chiffre 3 de l'Annexe 2 aux fournisseurs de produits et de services des Etats-Unis d'Amérique; d'Israël; du Japon; de la Corée; de Hong Kong, Chine; de Singapour; et d'Aruba;

- en ce qui concerne les marchés passés par les entités mentionnées à l'Annexe 3 dans les secteurs suivants;

  - eau: aux fournisseurs de produits et de services du Canada, des Etats-Unis d'Amérique et du Singapour;

  - électricité: aux fournisseurs de produits et de services du Canada, du Japon et du Singapour;

  - aéroports: aux fournisseurs de produits et de services du Canada, de la Corée et des Etats-Unis d'Amérique;

  - ports: aux fournisseurs de produits et de services du Canada;

  - transports urbains: aux fournisseurs de produits et de services du Canada, d'Israël, du Japon, de la Corée et des Etats-Unis d'Amérique;

tant qu'elle n'aura pas constaté que les Parties concernées assurent aux entreprises suisses un accès comparable et effectif aux marchés considérés;

- aux fournisseurs de services des Parties qui n'incluent pas, dans leurs propres listes, les marchés de services passés par les entités mentionnées aux Annexes 1 à 3 et concernant les catégories de services visées aux Annexes 4 et 5.

2. Les dispositions de l'Article XX ne sont pas applicables aux fournisseurs de produits et de services des pays suivants:

- Israël, Japon et Corée en ce qui concerne les recours intentés contre l'adjudication de marchés par les organismes mentionnés à l'Annexe 2, chiffre 2, tant que la Suisse n'a pas constaté que ces pays ont complété la liste des entités des gouvernements sous-centraux;

- Japon, Corée et Etats-Unis d'Amérique en ce qui concerne les recours intentés contre l'adjudication de marchés à un fournisseur de produits ou de services d'autres Parties au présent accord, lorsque ledit fournisseur est une entreprise petite ou moyenne au sens du droit suisse, tant que la Suisse n'aura pas constaté que ces pays n'appliquent plus de

总注释及对第 3 条规定的背离

1. 瑞士在下列方面不将本协定利益给予下列参加方：

- 对于附件 2 中所列实体授予的合同，本协定利益不给予加拿大供应商和服务提供者；

- 对于附件 2 所列除供应品外的合同的授予，本协定利益不给予美国、以色列、日本、韩国、中国香港、新加坡、荷属阿鲁巴供应商和服务提供者；

- 对于附件 3 条款中所列实体授予的合同：

  - 水，本协定利益不给予加拿大、美国和新加坡供应商和服务提供者;

  - 电力，本协定利益不给予加拿大、日本和新加坡供应商和服务提供者;

  - 机场，本协定利益不给予加拿大、韩国和美国供应商和服务提供者;

  - 港口，本协定利益不给予加拿大供应商和服务提供者;

  - 城市交通，本协定利益不给予加拿大、以色列、日本、韩国和美国供应商和服务提供者;

直至瑞士已经认为有关参加方给予瑞士企业对于相关市场的对等和有效的准入机会；

- 本协定利益不给予在其各自承诺范围中未对附件 1 至 3 中相关实体包括相关服务合同和未在附件 4 和 5 中包括相关服务类别的参加方的服务提供者。

2. 第 20 条不适用于下列参加方的供应商和服务提供者：

- 以色列、日本和韩国，在竞争附件 2 第 2 款下所列实体授予的合同时，直到瑞士认为他们的次中央实体的涵盖范围已经完整时止；

- 日本、韩国和美国，在竞争将合同授予已提及的参加方供应商或服务提供者之外的一属瑞士相关规定所定义的小型或中型企业的供应商或服务提供者时，直至瑞士认为他们不再采取有利于某些国内小型和少数族裔企业的歧视性措施时止;

2003 年 2 月 7 日 (WT/Let/437)

mesures discriminatoires pour favoriser certaines petites entreprises nationales ou certaines entreprises nationales détenues par les minorités;

- Israël, Japon et Corée en ce qui concerne les recours intentés contre l'adjudication par des entités suisses de marchés dont la valeur est inférieure au seuil appliqué à la même catégorie de marchés par lesdites Parties.

3. Tant que la Suisse n'aura pas constaté que les Parties concernées assurent l'accès de leurs marchés aux fournisseurs suisses de produits et de services suisses, elle n'étendra pas le bénéfice des dispositions du présent accord aux fournisseurs de produits et de services des pays suivants:

- Canada, en ce qui concerne les marchés portant sur les produits relevant des n° 36, 70 et 74 de la FSC (machines industrielles spéciales; matériel d'informatique général, logiciel, fournitures et matériel auxiliaire (sauf 7010: Configurations d'équipement de traitement automatique des données); machines de bureau, matériel de bureaumatique et d'informatique de bureau;

- Canada, en ce qui concerne les marchés portant sur les produits relevant du n° 58 de la FSC (matériel de communications, matériel de détection des radiations et d'émission de rayonnement cohérent) et Etats-Unis d'Amérique en ce qui concerne les équipements de contrôle du trafic aérien;

- Corée et Israël en ce qui concerne les marchés passés par les entités énumérées à l'Annexe 3, chiffre 2 pour les produits relevant des n° 8504, 8535, 8537 et 8544 du SH (transformateurs électriques, prises de courant, interrupteurs et câbles isolés); Israël, en ce qui concerne les produits relevant des n° 8501, 8536 et 902830 du SH;

- Canada et Etats-Unis d'Amérique en ce qui concerne les marchés de fournitures et de services entrant dans le cadre de marchés qui, tout en étant passés par une entité relevant du champ d'application du présent accord, ne sont pas eux-mêmes soumis à ce dernier.

4. Le présent accord n'est pas applicable aux marchés passés en vertu:

- d'un accord international et portant sur la réalisation ou l'expoitation en commun d'un ouvrage par les Etats signataires;

- de la procédure spécifique d'une organisation internationale.

5. Le présent accord n'est pas applicable aux marchés de produits agricoles passés en application de programmes de soutien à l'agriculture ou de programmes d'aide alimentaire.

6. Les engagements pris par la Suisse dans le domaine des services au titre du présent accord sont limités aux engagements initiaux spécifiés dans l'offre finale suisse présentée dans le cadre de l'Accord général sur le commerce des services.

7 February 2003 (WT/Let/437)

- 以色列、日本和韩国，在竞争瑞士实体授予的合同时，其价值低于这些参加方所授予的相同类别合同所适用的门槛金额。

3. 在瑞士已经认为有关参加方对供应商和服务提供者提供进入其各自市场的机会之前，瑞士不将本协定的收益给予下列参加方的供应商和服务提供者：

- 加拿大，对于 FSC 36、70 和 74 的采购(特殊工业机械；通用自动化处理设备、软件、耗材和配套设备(7010 自动化处理系统结构除外)；办公设备、显露式记录设备和自动化处理设备；

- 加拿大，对于 FSC 58 的采购(通信、探测和相干辐射设备)及美国，对于空中交通管制设备的采购；

- 以色列和韩国，对于附件 3 B 款所列实体关于协调制度编码 HS8504、8535、8537 和 8544(变压器、插头、开关和绝缘电缆)的采购；以色列，关于协调制度编码 HS8501、8536 和 902830 的采购；

- 加拿大和美国，对于虽由本协定所涵盖实体授予、但其货物或服务组成部分本身不受本协定管辖的合同。

4. 本协定不适用于在下列情况下授予的合同：

- 旨在由签署国联合执行或开发一项目的国际协定；

- 国际组织的特定程序。

5. 本协定不适用于为促进农业支持计划和人类供给计划而采购的农产品。

6. 在根据本协定所进行的采购程序中，服务的提供，包括建筑服务的提供，需遵守瑞士依照其 GATS 项下承诺所要求的关于市场准入和国民待遇的条件和资格。

2003 年 2 月 7 日(WT/Let/437)

CHINESE TAIPEI
中国台北

THE SEPARATE CUSTOMS TERRITORY OF TAIWAN, PENGHU, KINMEN AND MATSU*

(Authentic in the English Language)

ANNEX 1

Central Government Entities which Procure in Accordance With the Provisions of this Agreement

Thresholds:	130,000 SDRs	-	***Goods***
	130,000 SDRs	-	***Services*** covered in Annex 4
	5,000,000 SDRs	-	***Construction*** covered in Annex 5

List of entities:

1. Office of the President
2. Executive Yuan
3. Ministry of Interior (including its Central Taiwan Division and Second Division)
4. Ministry of Finance (including its Central Taiwan Division)
5. Ministry of Economic Affairs (including its Central Taiwan Division)
6. Ministry of Education (including its Central Taiwan Division)
7. Ministry of Justice (including its Central Taiwan Division)
8. Ministry of Transportation and Communications (including its Central Taiwan Division)
9. Mongolian & Tibetan Affairs Commission
10. Overseas Compatriot Affairs Commission
11. Directorate-General of Budget, Accounting and Statistics (including its Central Taiwan Division)
12. Department of Health (including its Central Taiwan Division)
13. Environmental Protection Administration (including its Central Taiwan Division)
14. Government Information Office (including its Central Taiwan Division)
15. Central Personnel Administration (including its Central Taiwan Division)
16. Mainland Affairs Council
17. Council of Labor Affairs
18. Research, Development and Evaluation Commission (including its Central Taiwan Division)
19. Council for Economic Planning and Development
20. Council for Cultural Affairs
21. Veterans Affairs Commission
22. Council of Agriculture (including its Central Taiwan Division and Second Division)
23. Atomic Energy Council
24. National Youth Commission
25. National Science Council

15 July 2009 (WT/Let/647/Add.1)

台湾、澎湖、金门、马祖单独关税区*

(以英文为准)

附件 1

依照本协定条款进行采购的中央政府实体

门槛金额：	130,000 特别提款权	-	***货物***
	130,000 特别提款权	-	*附件 4 所涵盖的**服务***
	5,000,000 特别提款权	-	*附件 5 所涵盖的**建筑***

实体清单：

1. 总统府
2. 行政院
3. 内政部(包括中部办公室及第二办公室)
4. 财政部(包括中部办公室)
5. 经济部(包括中部办公室)
6. 教育部(包括中部办公室)
7. 法务部(包括中部办公室)
8. 交通部(包括中部办公室)
9. 蒙藏委员会
10. 侨务委员会
11. 行政院主计处(包括中部办公室)
12. 行政院卫生署(包括中部办公室)
13. 行政院环境保护署(包括中部办公室)
14. 行政院新闻局(包括中部办公室)
15. 行政院人事行政局(包括中部办公室)
16. 行政院大陆委员会
17. 行政院劳工委员会
18. 行政院研究发展考核委员会(包括中部办公室)
19. 行政院经济建设委员会
20. 行政院文化建设委员会
21. 行政院国军退除役官兵辅导委员会
22. 行政院农业委员会(包括中部办公室及第二办公室)
23. 行政院原子能委员会
24. 行政院青年辅导委员会
25. 行政院国家科学委员会

26. Fair Trade Commission
27. Consumer Protection Commission
28. Public Construction Commission
29. Ministry of Foreign Affairs (excluding procurement for the direct purpose of providing foreign assistance)
30. Ministry of National Defense
31. National Palace Museum
32. Central Election Commission

* In English only. With respect to the list of entities, refer to the relevant documents governing the modalities of accession to the Agreement on Government Procurement.

Notes to Annex 1

1. The General Notes shall apply to this Annex.

2. The above central government entities, include all administrative units prescribed by the pertinent organization laws of such entities and entities transferred to the central government pursuant to the 28 October 1998 "Provisional Statute on the Reorganization of the Taiwan Provincial Government", in effect and as amended on 6 December 2000.

3. The Agreement shall not apply to the procurement by the Ministry of Foreign Affairs relating to the construction of the Separate Customs Territory of Taiwan, Penghu, Kinmen and Matsu's overseas representative offices, liaison offices and other missions.

4. This Agreement does not apply to the procurement by the National Space Organization of the National Science Council for five years from its entry into force for the Separate Customs Territory of Taiwan, Penghu, Kinmen and Matsu.

5. This Agreement will generally apply to procurement by the Ministry of National Defense of the following Federal Supply Classification (FSC) categories subject to the decision of the Separate Customs Territory of Taiwan, Penghu, Kinmen and Matsu Government under the provisions of paragraph 1 of Article XXIII.

2510 Vehicular Cab, Body, and Frame Structural Components
2520 Vehicular Power Transmission Components
2540 Vehicular Furniture and Accessories
2590 Miscellaneous Vehicular Components
2610 Tire and Tubes, Pneumatic, Except Aircraft
2910 Engine Fuel System Components, Non-aircraft
2920 Engine Electrical System Components, Non-aircraft
2930 Engine Cooling System Components, Non-aircraft
2940 Engine Air and Oil Filters, Strainers, and Cleaners, Non-aircraft
2990 Miscellaneous Engine Accessories, Non-aircraft
3020 Gears, Pulleys, Sprockets, and Transmission Chain

26. 行政院公平交易委员会
27. 行政院消费者保护委员会
28. 行政院公共工程委员会
29. 外交部(不包括为提供对外援助之直接目的所办理之采购)
30. 国防部
31. 国立故宫博物院
32. 中央选举委员会

* 仅以英文写就。 就实体清单而言，见管辖《政府采购协定》加入模式的相关文件。

附件 1 注释

1. 总注释适用于本附件。

2. 以上中央政府实体包括此类实体相关组织法所规定的所有行政单位及依据 1998 年 10 月 28 日公布并于 2000 年 12 月 6 日修订并生效的《台湾省政府功能业务与组织调整暂行条例》移转至中央政府的实体。

3. 本协定不适用外交部进行的涉及台湾、澎湖、金门、马祖单独关税区驻外代表处、办事处及其他使馆建设的采购。

4. 本协定在其对台湾、澎湖、金门、马祖单独关税区生效起 5 年内不适用于国家实验研究院国家太空中心的采购。

5. 本协定通常适用于国防部对下列《联邦供应分类》(FSC)类别的采购，取决于台湾、澎湖、金门、马祖单独关税区政府根据第 23 条第 1 款规定所做决定。

2510 车辆驾驶舱、车身及车架结构组合件
2520 车辆用动力传动组合件
2540 车用装璜及附件
2590 车辆杂项零件
2610 充气内外胎(非航空器用)
2910 引擎燃料系组合件(非航空器用)
2920 引擎电气系组合件(非航空器用)
2930 引擎冷却系组合件(非航空器用)
2940 引擎空气及滑油滤、滤筛及清洁器(非航空器用)
2990 杂项引擎附件(非航空器用)
3020 齿轮、皮带轮、链齿及传送链条

3416 Lathes
3417 Milling Machines
3510 Laundry and Dry Cleaning Equipment
4110 Refrigeration Equipment
4230 Decontaminating and Impregnating Equipment
4520 Space Heating Equipment and Domestic Water Heaters
4940 Miscellaneous Maintenance and Repair Shop Specialized Equipment
5110 Hand Tools, Edged, Non-powered
5120 Hand Tools, Non-edged, Non-powered
5305 Screws
5306 Bolts
5307 Studs
5310 Nuts and Washers
5315 Nails, Keys, and Pins
5320 Rivets
5325 Fastening Devices
5330 Packing and Gasket Materials
5335 Metal Screening
5340 Miscellaneous Hardware
5345 Disks and Stones, Abrasive
5350 Abrasive Materials
5355 Knobs and Pointers
5360 Coil, Flat and Wire Springs
5365 Rings, Shims and Spacers
5410 Prefabricated and Portable Buildings
5411 Rigid Wall Shelters
5420 Bridges, Fixed and Floating
5430 Storage Tanks
5440 Scaffolding Equipment and Concrete Forms
5445 Prefabricated Tower Structures
5450 Miscellaneous Prefabricated Structures
5520 Millwork
5530 Plywood and Veneer
5610 Mineral Construction Materials, Bulk
5620 Building Glass, Tile, Brick, and Block
5630 Pipe and Conduit, Non-metallic
5640 Wallboard, Building Paper, and Thermal Insulation Materials
5650 Roofing and Siding Materials
5660 Fencing, Fences, and Gates
5670 Building Components, Prefabricated
5680 Miscellaneous Construction Materials
6220 Electric Vehicular Lights and Fixtures
6505 Drugs, Biologicals and Official Reagents
6510 Surgical Dressing Materials
6515 Medical and Surgical Instruments, Equipment and Supplies
7030 Automatic Data Processing Software
7050 ADP Components

3416 车床
3417 铣床
3510 清洗及干洗设备
4110 冷藏设备及附件
4230 去污及浸染装备
4520 空气加温装备及家用热水器
4940 杂项维护及修理工场特种装备
5110 无动力有刃手工具
5120 无动力无刃手工具
5305 螺钉
5306 螺栓
5307 螺杆
5310 螺帽及垫圈
5315 钉、键及销
5320 铆钉
5325 扣系器材
5330 衬垫材料
5335 金属纱网
5340 杂项五金
5345 砂轮及磨石
5350 研磨材料
5355 旋纽及指针
5360 弹簧、卷片、丝
5365 衬圈、衬片、衬柱
5410 预制活动建筑物
5411 硬式护壁
5420 固定与浮动便桥
5430 储藏用池槽
5440 鹰架及水泥模板
5445 预制塔台构架
5450 杂项预制构架
5520 房具
5530 三夹板及美光板
5610 散装建筑用矿料
5620 建筑用玻璃、瓦、砖及成形石块
5630 非金属管料及导管
5640 墙板、建筑用纸料及隔热材料
5650 屋顶及外壁材料
5660 栅篱、围墙及门
5670 建筑及有关金属材料
5680 杂项建筑材料
6220 车辆电灯及装具
6505 药品、培养液及药用试剂
6510 外科包扎材料
6515 医药及外科用仪器、装备及用品
7030 数据处理软件
7050 数据处理零件

7105 Household Furniture
7110 Office Furniture
7125 Cabinets, Lockers, Bins, and Shelving
7195 Miscellaneous Furniture and Fixtures
7210 Household Furnishings
7220 Floor Coverings
7230 Draperies, Awnings, and Shades
7240 Household and Commercial Utility Containers
7290 Miscellaneous Household and Commercial Furnishings and Appliances
7310 Food Cooking, Baking, and Serving Equipment
7320 Kitchen Equipment and Appliances
7330 Kitchen Hand Tools and Utensils
7340 Cutlery and Flatware
7350 Tableware
7360 Sets, Kits, Outfits, and Modules, Food Preparation and Serving
7520 Office Devices and Accessories
7530 Stationery and Record Forms
7910 Floor Polishers and Vacuum Cleaning Equipment
7920 Brooms, Brushes, Mops, and Sponges
7930 Cleaning and Polishing Compounds and Preparations
8105 Bags and Sacks
8110 Drums and Cans
9150 Oils and Greases: Cutting, Lubricating, and Hydraulic
9310 Paper and Paperboard
9320 Rubber Fabricated Materials
9330 Plastics Fabricated Materials
9340 Glass Fabricated Materials
9350 Refractories and Fire Surfacing Materials
9390 Miscellaneous Fabricated Non-metallic Materials
9410 Crude Grades of Plant Materials
9420 Fibres: Vegetable, Animal, and Synthetic
9430 Miscellaneous Crude Animal Products, Inedible
9440 Miscellaneous Crude Agricultural and Forestry Products
9450 Non-metallic Scrap, Except Textile
9610 Ores
9620 Minerals, Natural and Synthetic
9630 Additive Metal Materials and Master Alloys
9640 Iron and Steel Primary and Semifinished Products
9650 Nonferrous Base Metal Refinery and Intermediate Forms
9660 Precious Metals Primary Forms
9670 Iron and Steel Scrap
9680 Nonferrous Metal Scrap
9905 Signs, Advertising Displays, and Identification Plates
9910 Jewelry
9915 Collectors and/or Historical Items
9920 Smokers' Articles and Matches
9925 Ecclesiastical Equipment, Furnishings, and Supplies
9930 Memorials; Cemeterial and Mortuary Equipment and supplies
9999 Miscellaneous Items

7105　家庭家具
7110　办公用家具
7125　箱、橱、柜、架
7195　杂项家具及器具
7210　家月装潢
7220　地毯
7230　窗帘、帷、幕及遮阴装具
7240　家用及商用容器
7290　杂项家用及商用之装潢及用具
7310　食物烹饪、烘烤及温热设备
7320　厨房装备及用具
7330　厨房手工具及炊具
7340　刀叉食用餐具
7350　盛装餐具
7360　成套、成组、烹饪及膳勤装备及用品
7520　办公室用具及附件
7530　文具及纪录表格
7910　地板打蜡及吸尘装备
7920　扫帚、刷、拖把及海绵
7930　清洗及打光剂装备
8105　袋囊
8110　桶罐
9150　切削、润滑、液压用之滑油及油膏
9310　纸张及纸板
9320　橡胶制成材料
9330　塑料制成材料
9340　玻璃制成材料
9350　耐火材料
9390　杂项非金属制成材料
9410　各种植物性原料
9420　动植物性及合成纤维
9430　非食用杂项动物原料
9440　杂项农林原料
9450　除纺织品外之非金属性碎料
9610　矿石
9620　天然及合成矿产品
9630　附加金属之材料及合金
9640　钢铁毛坏及半成品
9650　非铁金属精炼及粗制品
9660　贵重金属原料
9670　钢铁碎料
9680　非铁金属碎料
9905　招牌及广告
9910　珠宝
9915　古物收藏
9920　吸烟用具及火柴
9925　宗教设备、器具及用品
9930　祭祀物品、殡葬设备及用品
9999　其他杂项

ANNEX 2

Sub-Central Government Entities which Procure in Accordance With the Provisions of this Agreement

Thresholds: 200,000 SDRs - ***Goods***
200,000 SDRs - ***Services*** covered in Annex 4
15,000,000 SDRs - ***Construction*** covered in Annex 5
(For the first year from the effective date of the Agreement to the Separate Customs Territory of Tai wan, Penghu, Kinmen and Matsu)
10,000,000 SDRs
(For the second year from the effective date of the Agreement to the Separate Customs Territory of Taiwan, Penghu, Kinmen and Matsu)
5,000,000 SDRs
(From the third year onwards after the effective date of the Agreement to the Separate Customs Territory of Taiwan, Penghu, Kinmen and Matsu)

List of entities:

I. Taiwan Provincial Government

1. Secretariat, Taiwan Provincial Government
2. Petition Screening Committee, Taiwan Provincial Government
3. Regulation Committee, Taiwan Provincial Government

II. Taipei City Government

1. Department of Civil Affairs
2. Department of Finance
3. Department of Education
4. Department of Economic Development
5. Public Works Department
6. Department of Transportation
7. Department of Social Welfare
8. Department of Labor
9. Taipei City Police Department
10. Department of Health
11. Department of Environmental Protection
12. Department of Urban Development
13. Taipei City Fire Department
14. Department of Land Administration
15. Department of Urban Development
16. Department of Information and Tourism

附件 2

依照本协定条款进行采购的次中央政府实本

门槛金额: 200,000 特别提款权 - ***货物***
200,000 特别提款权 - *附件 4 所涵盖的**服务***
15,000,000 特别提款权 - *附件 5 所涵盖的**建筑***
(自本协定对台湾、澎湖、金门、马祖单独关税区生效之日起第 1 年)
10,000,000 特别提款权
(自本协定对台湾、澎湖、金门、马祖单独关税区生效之日起第 2 年)
5,000,000 特别提款权
(自本协定对台湾、澎湖、金门、马祖单独关税区生效之日起第 3 年以后)

实体清单:

I. 台湾省政府

1. 台湾省政府秘书处
2. 台湾省政府诉愿审议委员会
3. 台湾省政府法规委员会

II. 台北市政府

1. 民政局
2. 财政局
3. 教育局
4. 产业发展局
5. 工务局
6. 交通局
7. 社会局
8. 劳工局
9. 警察局
10. 卫生局
11. 环境保护局
12. 都市发展局
13. 消防局
14. 地政处
15. 都市发展局
16. 观光传播局

17. Department of Military Service
18. Secretariat
19. Department of Budget, Accounting and Statistics
20. Department of Personnel
21. Department of Anti-Corruption
22. Commission of Research, Development and Evaluation
23. Commission of Urban Planning
24. Commission for Examining Petitions and Appeals
25. Commission of Laws and Regulations
26. Department of Rapid Transit Systems
27. Department of Civil Servant Development
28. Xinyi District Office
29. Songshan District Office
30. Daan District Office
31. Zhongshan District Office
32. Zhongzheng District Office
33. Datong District Office
34. Wanhua District Office
35. Wenshan District Office
36. Nangang District Office
37. Neihu District Office
38. Shilin District Office
39. Beitou District Office

III. Kaohsiung City Government

1. Bureau of Civil Affairs
2. Bureau of Finance
3. Bureau of Education
4. Department of Economic Development
5. Bureau of Public Works
6. Bureau of Social Affairs
7. Bureau of Labor Affairs
8. Bureau of Police
9. Bureau of Health
10. Bureau of Environmental Sanitation
11. Bureau of Mass Rapid Transit
12. Kaohsiung Fire Department
13. Department of Land Administration
14. Bureau of Urban Development
15. Department of Information
16. Department of Military Service
17. Research and Development Commission
18 Commission of Rules and Regulations
19. Commission for Examining Petitions and Appeals
20. Secretariat

17.　兵役处
18.　秘书处
19.　主计处
20.　人事处
21.　政风处
22.　研究发展考核委员会
23.　都市计划委员会
24.　诉愿审议委员会
25.　法规委员会
26.　捷运工程局
27.　公务人员训练处
28.　信义区公所
29.　松山区公所
30.　大安区公所
31.　中山区公所
32.　中正区公所
33.　大同区公所
34.　万华区公所
35.　文山区公所
36.　南港区公所
37.　内湖区公所
38.　士林区公所
39.　北投区公所)

III.　高雄市政府

1.　民政局
2.　财政局
3.　教育局
4.　经济发展局
5.　工务局
6.　社会局
7.　劳工局
8.　警察局
9.　卫生局
10.　环境保护局
11.　捷运工程局
12.　消防局
13.　地政处
14.　都市发展局
15.　新闻处
16.　兵役处
17.　研究发展考核委员会
18.　法规委员会
19.　诉愿审议委员会
20.　秘书处

21. Department of Budget, Accounting and Statistics
22. Department of Personnel
23. Department of Anti-Corruption
24. Bureau of Human Resource Development
25. Urban Planning Committee
26. Yanchem District Office
27. Kushan District Office
28. Zuoying District Office
29. Nanzih District Office
30. Sanmin District Office
31. Sinsing District Office
32. Cianjin District Office
33. Lingya District Office
34. Cianjhen District Office
35. Cijin District Office
36. Siaogang District Office

Notes to Annex 2

1. The General Notes shall apply to this Annex.

2. The above sub-central government entities include all administrative units prescribed by the pertinent organization laws of such entities.

21.　主计处
22.　人事处
23.　政风处
24.　公教人力发展局
25.　都市计划委员会
26.　盐埕区公所
27.　鼓山区公所
28.　左营区公所
29.　楠梓区公所
30.　三民区公所
31.　新兴区公所
32.　前金区公所
33.　苓雅区公所
34.　前镇区公所
35.　旗津区公所
36.　小港区公所

附件 2 注释

1.　总注释适用于本附件。

2.　以上次中央政府实体包括此类实体相关组织法所规定的所有行政单位。

ANNEX 3

All Other Entities which Procure in Accordance
With the Provisions of this Agreement

Thresholds: 400,000 SDRs - ***Goods***
400,000 SDR - ***Services*** covered in Annex 4
15,000,000 SDRs - ***Construction*** covered in Annex 5
(For the first year from the effective date of the Agreement to the Separate Customs Territory of Taiwan, Penghu, Kinmen and Matsu)
10,000,000 SDRs
(For the second year from the effective date of the Agreement to the Separate Customs Territory of Taiwan, Penghu, Kinmen and Matsu)
5,000,000 SDRs
(From the third year onwards after the effective date of the Agreement to the Separate Customs Territory of Taiwan, Penghu, Kinmen and Matsu)

List of Entities:

1. Taiwan Power Company
2. Chinese Petroleum Corporation, Taiwan
3. Taiwan Sugar Corporation
4. National Taiwan University
5. National Chengchi University
6. National Taiwan Normal University
7. National Tsing Hua University
8. National Chung Hsing University
9. National Cheng Kung University
10. National Chiao Tung University
11. National Central University
12. National Sun Yat-Sen University
13. National Chung Cheng University
14. National Open University
15. National Taiwan Ocean University
16. National Kaohsiung Normal University
17. National Changhwa University of Education
18. National Dong Hwa University
19. National Yang Ming University
20. National Taiwan University of Science & Technology
21. Taipei National University of the Arts
22. National Taiwan Sport University
23. National Yunlin University of Science & Technology
24. National Pingtung University of Science & Technology
25. National Taiwan University of Arts
26. National Taipei College of Nursing
27. National Kaohsiung First University of Science & Technology
28. Taipei University of Education
29. National Hsinchu University of Education

15 July 2009 (WT/Let/647/Add.1)

附件 3

依照本协定条款进行采购的所有其他实体

门槛金额: 400,000 特别提款权 - ***货物***
400,000 特别提款权 - *附件 4 所涵盖的**服务***
15,000,000 特别提款权 - *附件 5 所涵盖的**建筑***
(自本协定对台湾、澎湖、金门、马祖单独关税区生效之日起第 1 年)
10,000,000 特别提款权
(自本协定对台湾、澎湖、金门、马祖单独关税区生效之日起第 2 年)
5,000,000 特别提款权
(自本协定对台湾、澎湖、金门、马祖单独关税区生效之日起第 3 年以后)

实体清单:

1. 台湾电力公司
2. 台湾中油公司
3. 台湾糖业公司
4. 国立台湾大学
5. 国立政治大学
6. 国立台湾师范大学
7. 国立清华大学
8. 国立中兴大学
9. 国立成功大学
10. 国立交通大学
11. 国立中央大学
12. 国立中山大学
13. 国立中正大学
14. 国立空中大学
15. 国立台湾海洋大学
16. 国立高雄师范大学
17. 国立彰化师范大学
18. 国立东华大学
19. 国立阳明大学
20. 国立台湾科技大学
21. 国立台北艺术大学
22. 国立台湾体育大学
23. 国立云林科技大学
24. 国立屏东科技大学
25. 国立台湾艺术大学
26. 国立台北护理学院
27. 国立高雄第一科技大学
28. 国立台北教育大学
29. 国立新竹教育大学

2009 年 7 月 15 日 (WT/Let/647/Add.1)

30. National Taichung University
31. National Chiayi University
32. National University of Tainan
33. National PingTung University of Education
34. National Dong Hwa University (Meilun Campus)
35. National Taitung University
36. National Teipei University of Technology
37. National Kaohsiung University of Applied Sciences
38. National Formosa University
39. National Taipei College of Business
40. National Taichung Institute of Technology
41. National Kaohsiung Marine University
42. National Ilan University
43. National Pingtung Institute of Commerce
44. National Chin-Yi University of Technology
45. Central Trust of China (for procurement on its own account) (has been merged with Bank of Taiwan)
46. China Engraving & Printing Works
47. The Central Mint of China
48. Taiwan Water Supply Corporation
49. Second Office of Ministry of Economic Affairs (for procurement on its own account)
50. National Taiwan University Hospital
51. National Cheng Kung University Hospital
52. Veterans General Hospital-Taipei
53. Veterans General Hospital-Taichung
54. Veterans General Hospital-Kaohsiung
55. Taiwan Railway Administration
56. Keelung Harbour Bureau
57. Taichung Harbour Bureau
58. Kaohsiung Harbour Bureau
59. Hualien Harbour Bureau
60. Bureau of Taipei Feitsui Reservoir Administration
61. Taipei Water Department
62. Central Police University

Notes to Annex 3

1. The General Notes shall apply to this Annex.

2. With regard to the procurement by Central Trust of China and the Second Office of Ministry of Economic Affairs for entities listed in Annexes 1, 2 and 3, the coverages and thresholds for such entities thereunder shall apply.

3. The Agreement shall not apply to the procurement by China Engraving & Printing Works of banknote printing press (intaglio) (HS. No. 8443).

30. 国立台中教育大学
31. 国立嘉义大学
32. 国立台南大学
33. 国立屏东教育大学
34. 国立东华大学(美仑校区)
35. 国立台东大学
36. 国立台北科技大学
37. 国立高雄应用科技大学
38. 国立虎尾科技大学
39. 国立台北商业技术学院
40. 国立台中技术学院
41. 国立高雄海洋科技大学
42. 国立宜兰大学
43. 国立屏东商业技术学院
44. 国立勤益科技大学
45. 中央信托局(适用于以该局自有预算办理之采购)(并入台湾银行)
46. 中央印制厂
47. 中央造币厂
48. 台湾省自来水股份有限公司
49. 经济部第二办公室(适用于以该办公室自有预算办理之采购)
50. 国立台湾大学医学院附设医院
51. 国立成功大学医学院附设医院
52. 台北荣民总医院
53. 台中荣民总医院
54. 高雄荣民总医院
55. 台湾铁路管理局
56. 基隆港务局
57. 台中港务局
58. 高雄港务局
59. 花莲港务局
60. 翡翠水库管理局
61. 台北自来水事业处
62. 中央警察大学

附件 3 注释

1. 总注释适用于本附件。

2. 对于中央信托局及经济部第二办公室为附件 1、2 和 3 中所列实体进行的采购，以上附件中此类实体的涵盖范围和门槛金额应适用。

3. 本协定不适用于中央印制厂有关印钞机(凹版)(HS 8443)的采购。

2009 年 7 月 15 日 (WT/Let/647/Add.1)

ANNEX 4

Services

Of the Universal List of Services, as contained in document MTN.GNS/W/120, the following services are included (others being excluded):

GNS/W/120	*CPC*	*Description*
1.A.a.	861**	Legal services (limited to qualified lawyers under the laws of the Separate Customs Territory of Taiwan, Penghu, Kinmen and Matsu)
1.A.b.	862**	Accounting, Auditing and Bookkeeping services
1.A.c.	863**	Taxation services (excluding income tax certification services)
1.A.d.	8671	Architectural services
1.A.e.	8672	Engineering services
1.A.f.	8673	Integrated engineering services
1.A.g.	8674	Urban planning and landscape architectural services
1.B.a.	841	Consultancy services related to the installation of computer hardware
1.B.b.	842	Software implementation services
1.B.c.	843	Data processing services
1.B.d.	844	Database services
1.B.e.	845	Maintenance and repair of office machinery and equipment including computers
	849	Other computer services
1.D.b.	82203**, 82205**	Services incidental to residential and non-residential buildings and land sales agents
1.E.b.	83104**	Leasing or rental services concerning aircraft without operator (excluding cabotage)
1.E.d.	83106-83109	Leasing or rental services concerning other machinery and equipment without operator

15 July 2009 (WT/Let/647/Add.1)

附件 4

服务

包括载于 MTN.GNS/W/120 号文件的服务通用清单中的下列服务(其他服务排除在外):

GNS/W/120	*CPC*	*描述*
1.A.a.	861**	法律服务(仅限依台、澎、金、马关税领域法律取得律师资格者)
1.A.b	862**	会计、审计及簿计服务
1.A.c.	863**	租税服务(不包括所得税签证服务)
1.A.d.	8671	建筑服务
1.A.e.	8672	工程服务
1.A.f.	8673	综合工程服务
1.A.g.	8674	都市规划及景观建筑服务
1.B.a.	841	与计算机硬件安装有关之咨询服务
1.B.b.	842	软件执行服务
1.B.c.	843	数据处理服务
1.B.d.	844	数据库服务
1.B.e.	845	包括计算机之办公机器设备维修服务
	849	其他计算机服务
1.D.b.	82203**、82205**	附带于居住及非居住建物与土地之销售经纪服务
1.E.b.	83104**	未附操作员之航空器有关之租赁(涉及航空权者除外)
1.E.d.	83106-83109	未附操作员之其他机器和设备有关之租赁

GNS/W/120	*CPC*	*Description*
1.E.e.	8320	Leasing or rental services concerning personal and household goods
1.F.a.	871**	Advertising services (limited to TV or radio advertisements)
1.F.b.	864	Market research and public opinion polling services
1.F.c.	865	Management consulting services
1.F.d.	866**	Services relating to management consulting (excluding arbitration and conciliation services)
1.F.e.	8676	Technical testing and analysis services
1.F.f.	88110**, 88120** 88140**	Consulting services incidental to Agriculture, Animal Husbandry and Forestry
1.F.h.	883, 5115	Services incidental to mining
1.F.i.	884**, 885	Services incidental to manufacturing (excluding CPC 88442 publishing and printing on a fee or contract basis)
1.F.m.	8675	Related scientific and technical consulting services
1.F.n.	633, 8861-8866	Maintenance and repair of equipment (excluding maritime vessel, aircraft or other transport equipment)
1.F.o.	874	Building-cleaning services
1.F.p.	875	Photographic services
1.F.q.	876	Packaging services
1.F.t.	87905	Translation and interpretation services
1.F.s.	87909	Convention services
2.B.	7512**	Land-based international courier services
2.C.a.	7521**	Voice telephone services
2.C.b.	7523**	Packet-switched data transmission services
2.C.c.	7523**	Circuit-switched data transmission services

GNS/W/120	*CPC*	*描述*
1.E.e.	8320	与个人及家用产品有关之租赁
1.F.a.	871**	广告服务(仅限电视或广播广告)
1.F.b.	864	市场研究与公众意见调查服务
1.F.c.	865	管理顾问服务
1.F.d.	866**	与管理顾问相关之服务(仲裁及调解服务除外)
1.F.e.	8676	技术检定与分析服务
1.F.f.	88110**、88120** 88140**	附带于农、牧、林之顾问服务
1.F.h.	883、5115	附带于矿业之服务
1.F.i.	884**、885	附带于制造业之服务(CPC88442 出版及印刷除外)
1.F.m.	8675	与科技工程有关之顾问服务
1.F.n.	633、8861-8866	设备维修服务(海运船只、航空器或其他运输设备除外)
1.F.o.	874	建筑物清理服务
1.F.p.	875	摄影服务
1.F.q.	876	包装服务
1.F.t.	87905	翻译及传译服务
1.F.s.	87909	会议服务
2.B.	7512**	国际快递服务路地运送部分
2.C.a.	7521**	语音电话业务
2.C.b.	7523**	分封交换式数据传输业务
GNS/W/120	*CPC*	*描述*
2.C.c.	7523**	电路交换式数据传输业务

GNS/W/120	*CPC*	*Description*
2.C.d.	7523**	Telex services
2.C.e.	7522	Telegraph services
2.C.f.	7521**, 7529**	Facsimile services
2.C.g.	7522**, 7523**	Private leased circuit services
2.C.h.	7523**	Electronic mail
2.C.i.	7523**	Voice mail
2.C.j.	7523**	On-line information and data-base retrieval
2.C.k.	7523**	Electronic data interchange (EDI)
2.C.l.	7523**	Enhanced/value-added facsimile services including store and forward, store and retrieval
2.C.m.	7523**	Code and protocol conversion services
2.C.n.	843**	On-line information and/or data processing
2.C.o.	75213*	Cellular mobile phone services
2.C.o.	7523**, 75213*	Trunked radio services
2.C.o.	7523**	Mobile data services
2.C.o.	75291*	Radio paging services
2.D.a.	96112	Motion picture or video tape production services
2.D.a.	96113	Motion picture or video tape distribution services
2.D.b.	96121	Motion picture projection
2.D.b.	96122	Video-tape projection services
6.A.	9401	Sewage services
6.B.	9402	Refuse disposal services
6.C.	9403	Sanitation and similar services

GNS/W/120	*CPC*	*描述*
2.C.d.	7523**	电报交换业务
2.C.e.	7522	电报业务
2.C.f.	7521**、7529**	传真业务
2.C.g.	7522**、7523**	出租电路业务
2.C.h.	7523**	电子文件存送服务
2.C.i.	7523**	语音存送服务
2.C.j.	7523**	信息储存、检索服务
2.C.k.	7523**	电子数据交换服务(EDI)
2.C.l.	7523**	加值传真(含存转、存取)服务
2.C.m.	7523**	编码及通信协议转换服务
2.C.n.	843**	信息处理服务
2.C.o.	75213*	行动电话业务
2.C.o.	7523**、75213*	中继式无线电话业务
2.C.o.	7523**	行动数据通信业务
2.C.o.	75291*	无线电叫人业务
2.D.a.	96112	录像带及电影之制作服务业
2.D.a.	96113	录像带及电影之营销服务业
2.D.b.	96121	电影放映服务业
2.D.b.	96122	录像带放映服务业
6.A.	9401	污水处理服务
6.B.	9402	废弃物处理服务
6.C.	9403	卫生及类似服务

GNS/W/120	CPC	Description
6.D.		Others:
	9404	- Cleaning services of exhaust gases
	9405	- Noise abatement services
	9409	- Other environmental protection services not elsewhere classified
7.A.	812**, 814**	Insurance services
7.B	ex 81**	Banking and Investment Services
9.A	64110**	Hotel lodging services
9.A	642	Food serving services
9.B.	7471	Travel agencies and tour operators services
11.C.a.	8868**	Maintenance and repair of civil aircraft
11.E.d.	8868**	Maintenance and repair of rail transport equipment
11.F.d.	6112, 8867	Maintenance and repair of road transport equipment

Notes to Annex 4

1. The General Notes shall apply to this Annex.

2. The symbol of asterisk (*) indicates that the service specified is a component of a more aggregated CPC item. The symbol of double asterisks (**) indicates that the service specified constitutes only a part of the total range of activities covered by the CPC concordance.

3. The offer in telecommunications is limited to enhanced/value-added services for the supply of which the underlying telecommunications facilities are leased from providers of public telecommunications transport networks.

4. This offer does not include:

- research and development;
- coin minting;
- all services, with reference to those goods purchased by the Ministry of National Defense which are not identified as subject to coverage by this Agreement.

15 July 2009 (WT/Let/647/Add.1)

GNS/W/120	*CPC*	*描述*
6.D.		其他：
	9404	- 排气清洁服务
	9405	- 噪音防制服务
	9409	- 其他环境保护服务
7.A.	812**、814**	保险服务
7.B.	Ex81**	银行及投资服务
9.A	64110**	旅馆服务
9.A	642	提供食物服务
9.B	7471	旅行社及旅游服务
11.C.a.	8868**	民用航空器维修
11.E.d.	8868**	铁路运输设备维修
11.F.d.	6112、8867	公路运输设备维修

附件 4 注释

1. 总注释适用于本附件。

2. 星号(*)表示所列服务为更大 CPC 条目的组成部分。双星号(**)表示所列服务仅为该 CPC 索引所涵盖的全部活动的一部分。

3. 电信出价仅限于自公共电信传输网络供应商处租赁基本通信设施而提供的增强型或增值服务。

4. 本出价不含：

- 研究和开发；
- 铸币；
- 与国防部购买的、未确定受本协定涵盖的货物有关的所有服务。

2009 年 7 月 15 日 (WT/Let/647/Add.1)

5. The offer in banking and investment services does not include the following:

(a) procurements for financial services in connection with the issue, sale, purchase or transfer of securities or other financial instruments, and central bank services;

(b) acquisition of fiscal agency or depository services, liquidation and management services for regulated financial institutions, and sale and distribution services for government debt.

5. 关于银行和投资服务的出价不包括下列内容：

(a) 关于证券或其他金融工具的发行、销售、购买或转让的金融服务的采购及中央银行服务的采购；

(b) 财政代理服务或储蓄服务的获得、对受监管金融机构的清算和管理服务以及政府债务的销售和分销服务。

ANNEX 5

Construction Services

Definition:

A construction services contract is a contract which has as its objective the realization by whatever means of civil or building works, in the sense of Division 51 of the Central Product Classification.

List of construction services offered:

All services contained in Division 51 CPC.

Notes to Annex 5

The General Notes shall apply to this Annex.

附件 5

建筑服务

定义：

建筑服务合同是指根据《中央产品分类》第 51 类，以通过任何土木或建筑工程手段实现目的的合同。

CPC 第 51 类清单：

CPC 51 类包含的所有服务。

附件 5 注释

总注释适用于本附件。

2009 年 7 月 15 日 (WT/Let/647/Add.1

GENERAL NOTES

1. For any particular Party whose threshold value listed for a certain coverage is higher than that listed by the Separate Customs Territory of Taiwan, Penghu, Kinmen and Matsu, this Agreement applies only to those procurements above the higher one threshold value for such particular Party for the relevant coverage. (This note does not apply to bidders of the United States and Israel competing on goods, services and construction contracts tendered by entities identified in Annex 2.)

2. Until such time as the Separate Customs Territory of Taiwan, Penghu, Kinmen and Matsu has accepted that the Parties concerned provide access for the Separate Customs Territory of Taiwan, Penghu, Kinmen and Matsu suppliers and service providers to their own markets, the Separate Customs Territory of Taiwan, Penghu, Kinmen and Matsu shall not extend the benefits of this Agreement to suppliers and service providers of the Parties concerned. A service listed in Annex 4 or construction service in Annex 5 is covered with respect to a particular Party only to the extent that such Party has provided reciprocal access to that service.

3. This Agreement shall not apply to any procurement made by a covered entity on behalf of a non-covered entity.

4. Where a contract to be awarded by an entity is not covered by this Agreement, this Agreement shall not be construed to cover any goods or service component of that contract.

5. This Agreement shall not apply to contracts:

- for the acquisition or rental of land, existing buildings, other immovable property or concerning rights thereon;
- for the acquisition, development, production or co-production of programme materials by broadcasters and contracts for broadcasting time;
- contract of employment.

6. This Agreement shall not apply to:

- contracts awarded under an international agreement and intended for the joint implementation or exploitation of a project;
- contracts awarded under the particular procedure of an international organization;
- procurement made with a view to resale or to using in the production of supplies or services for sale;
- procurement of agricultural products made in furtherance of agricultural support programmes and human feeding programmes;
- procurement of the following goods and services (including construction) relating to the electricity and transport projects.

总注释

1.　对于一特定涵盖范围所列门槛金额高于台湾、澎湖、金门、马祖单独关税区所列门槛金额的任一特定参加方，本协定就该特定参加方的相关涵盖范围而言，仅适用于高于该较高门槛金额的采购。(本注释不适用美国和以色列竞标者竞争附件 2 所列实体进行招标的货物、服务和建筑合同。)

2.　台湾、澎湖、金门、马祖单独关税区不将本协定利益给予有关参加方的供应商和服务提供者，直至台湾、澎湖、金门、马祖单独关税区已经认为有关参加方向台湾、澎湖、金门、马祖单独关税区的供应商和服务提供者提供进入其各自市场的准入机会。对于附件 4 中所列一服务或附件 5 所列一建筑服务，仅在一特定参加方已对该服务提供对等准入时，方针对该参加方而涵盖其中。

3.　本出价不适用于涵盖实体代表非涵盖实体所进行的任何采购。

4.　如一合同由本协定未涵盖的实体授予，则本协定不得解释为涵盖该合同的任何货物或服务组成部分。

5.　本协定不适用于下列合同：

- 购买或租赁土地、现有建筑物或其他不动产或涉及相关权利的合同；
- 广播电台购买、开发、制作或联合制作节目内容的合同和播放时间的合同；
- 雇佣合同。

6.　本协定不适用于根据下列内容授予的合同：

- 根据一旨在由签署国联合执行或开发一项目的国际协定授予的合同；
- 根据一国际组织的特定程序授予的合同；
- 旨在转售或用于生产供销售的供应品或服务的采购；
- 为促进农业支持计划和人类供给计划而采购的农产品；
- 下列与电力和运输项目相关的货物和服务(包括建筑服务)的采购。

2009 年 7 月 15 日 (WT/Let/647/Add.1)

Exclusions regarding electricity (goods)

HS 8402	Steam or other vapour generating boilers
HS 8404	Auxiliary plant for use with boilers
HS 8410	Hydraulic turbines, water wheels, and regulators
HS 8501	Electric motors and generators
HS 8502	Electric generating sets
HS 8504	Electrical transformers and converters
HS 8532	Power capacitors
HS 8535	Electrical switches, breakers, switch-gears (for a voltage exceeding 1,000 volts)
HS 8536	Electrical switches, breakers, switch-gears (for a voltage not exceeding 1,000 volts)
HS 8537	switch boards, controller panels
HS 8544	Power cables (including optical fibre cables)
HS 9028	Electricity supply meter

- Notwithstanding the above, this Agreement shall apply to the procurement of HS codes 8402, 8404, 8410, 8501 (electric motors with capacity of 22 megawatts or greater, electric generators with capacity of 50 megawatts or greater)*, 850164, 8502, 8504 (electrical transformers and static converters, with capacity of 1 to 600 megawatts)*, and 8544 (cable related to telecommunications applications) for the goods and suppliers of the United States; the European Communities; Japan; Switzerland; Canada; Norway; Iceland; Hong Kong, China; Singapore; and Israel.

  * Coverage to be effective two years from the date of the Separate Customs Territory of Taiwan, Penghu, Kinmen and Matsu's accession to the WTO.

- Notwithstanding the above, this Agreement shall apply to the procurement of HS codes 8402, 8404, 8410, 850164 and 8502 for the goods and suppliers of Korea.

Exclusions regarding electricity (services and constructions)

CPC 51340	Power transmission line construction work
CPC 51360	Power plant and substation construction work
CPC 51649	Power transmission and distribution automation system construction work
CPC 52262	Power plant construction engineering work
CPC 86724	Power transmission, distribution and substation engineering design services
CPC 86725	Power plant engineering design services)
CPC 86726	Power transmission and distribution automation system engineering design services
CPC 86739	Integrated engineering services for power transmission and distribution turnkey projects

- Notwithstanding the above, this Agreement shall apply to the procurement of CPC codes 51340, 51360 and 51649 for the service providers of Korea; the European Communities; Japan; the United States; Switzerland; Canada; Norway; Iceland; Hong Kong, China; Singapore; and Israel.

15 July 2009 (WT/Let/647/Add.1)

电力排除项目(货物)

HS 8402	水蒸气及其他蒸气锅炉
HS 8404	锅炉之辅助设施
HS 8410	水轮机及其调整器
HS 8501	电动机及发电机
HS 8502	发电机组
HS 8504	变压变流器
HS 8532	电力电容器
HS 8535	断电器及开关设备(逾 1000 伏)
HS 8536	断电器及开关设备(不逾 1000 伏)
HS 8537	开关盘、配电盘
HS 8544	电线电缆(含光纤电缆)
HS 9028	电表

- 尽管有上述规定，但是对于 HS 8402、8404、8410、8501(限 22000 千瓦以上之电动机及 50000 千瓦以上之发电机)*、850164、8502、8504(限 1000 千瓦~600000 千瓦之变压器及变流流器)*及 8544(仅电信电缆部分)的采购，本协定适用于美国、欧共体、日本、瑞士、加拿大、挪威、冰岛、中国香港、新加坡及以色列的货物和供应商。

  * 适用范围自台湾、澎湖、金门、马祖单独关税区加入 WTO 之日起 2 年后生效。

- 尽管有上述规定，但是对于 HS 8402、8404、8410、850164 及 8502 的采购，本协定适用于韩国的货物和供应商。

电力排除项目(服务和建筑)

CPC 51340	输电线路工程施工
CPC 51360	水力发电厂及及变电所工程施工
CPC 51649	输配电线路自动化系统施工
CPC 52262	水力发电厂工程监造
CPC 86724	输配电工程及变电所设计服务
CPC 86725	发电厂工程设计服务
CPC 86726	输配电线路自动化系统工程设计服务
CPC 86739	输配电系统统包服务

- 尽管有上述规定，但是对于 CPC 51340、51360 及 51649 的采购，本协定适用于韩国、欧共体、日本、美国、瑞士、加拿大、挪威、冰岛、中国香港、新加坡及以色列的服务提供者。

- Notwithstanding the above, this Agreement shall apply to the procurement of CPC code 52262 for the service providers of Korea; the European Communities; the United States; Switzerland; Canada; Norway; Iceland; Hong Kong, China; Singapore; and Israel.

- Notwithstanding the above, this Agreement shall apply to the procurement of CPC codes 86724, 86725, 86726 and 86739 for the services providers of the United States; Canada; Korea; the European Communities; Japan; Switzerland; Norway; Iceland; Hong Kong, China; Singapore; and Israel.

Exclusions regarding transport

HS 8601	Rail locomotives, powered from an external source of electricity or by electric accumulators
HS 8603	Self-propelled railway or trainway, coaches, vans and trucks, other than those of heading.
HS 8605	Railway or trainway passenger coaches, not self-propelled, luggage van, post office coaches and other special purpose railway or trainway coaches, not self-propelled
HS 8607	Parts of railway or trainway locomotives or rolling stock
HS 8608	Railway or trainway track fixtures and fittings, mechanical (including electro-mechanical) signalling, safety or traffic control equipment for railways, roads, inland waterways, parking facility, port installations or airfields, parts of the foregoing

- Notwithstanding the above, this Agreement shall apply to the procurement of HS code 8608 for the goods and suppliers of the United States; Canada; the European Communities; Japan; Switzerland; Norway; Iceland; Hong Kong, China; Singapore; and Israel, effective two years from the date of the Separate Customs Territory of Taiwan, Penghu, Kinmen and Matsu's accession to the WTO.

- Notwithstanding the above, this Agreement shall apply to the procurement of HS code 8601, 8603, 8605 and 8607 for the goods and suppliers of Canada; the European Communities; Japan; Norway; Iceland; Hong Kong, China; Singapore; and Israel. For a period of 10 years from the date of the Separate Customs Territory of Taiwan, Penghu, Kinmen and Matsu's accession to the WTO, up to 50 per cent of the procurement amount can be used by the Separate Customs Territory of Taiwan, Penghu, Kinmen and Matsu for offset purposes.

7. Procurement does not include the acquisition of fiscal agency or depository services, liquidation and management services for regulated financial institutions, and sale and distribution services for government debt.

8. Procurement in terms of the Separate Customs Territory of Taiwan, Penghu, Kinmen and Matsu's coverage does not include non-contractual agreements or any form of government assistance, including, but not limited to, cooperative agreements, grants, loans, guarantees, fiscal incentives, and governmental provision of goods and services to persons or governmental authorities not specifically covered under the Separate Customs Territory of Taiwan, Penghu, Kinmen and Matsu's Annexes to this Agreement.

15 July 2009 (WT/Let/647/Add.1)

- 尽管有上述规定，但是对于 CPC52262 的采购，本协定适用于韩国、欧共体、美国、瑞士、加拿大、挪威、冰岛、中国香港、新加坡及以色列的服务提供者。

- 尽管有上述规定，但是对于 CPC86724、86725、86726 及 86739 的采购，本协定适用于美国、加拿大、韩国、欧共体、日本、瑞士、挪威、冰岛、中国香港、新加坡及以色列的服务提供者。

运输排除项目

HS 8601	铁路机车
HS 8603	自力推进之铁路车道用客车、货车
HS 8605	非自力推进之铁路车道用客车、货车
HS 8607	铁路或电车道机车或运输用之零件
HS 8608	铁路或电车轨道固定装置及配件、机械式信号、安全或交通控制设备

- 尽管有上述规定，但是自台湾、澎湖、金门、马祖单独关税区加入 WTO 之日起 2 年后，对于 HS8608 的采购，本协定适用于美国、加拿大、欧共体、日本、瑞士、挪威、冰岛、中国香港、新加坡及以色列的货物和供应商。

- 尽管有上述规定，但是对于 HS8601、8603、8605 及 8607 的采购，本协定适用于加拿大、欧共体、日本、挪威、冰岛、中国香港、新加坡及以色列的货物和供应商。在自台湾、澎湖、金门、马祖单独关税区加入 WTO 之日起 10 年期限内，台湾、澎湖、金门、马祖单独关税区可将最多 50%的采购金额用于补偿目的。

7. 采购不包括财政代理服务或储蓄服务的获得、对受监管金融机构的清算和管理服务以及政府债务的销售和分销服务。

8. 台湾、澎湖、金门、马祖单独关税区涵盖范围内的采购不包括非契约性协议或任何形式的政府援助，包括但不仅限于给予个人或台湾、澎湖、金门、马祖单独关税区在本协定的附件中未具体涵盖的政府机构的合作协议、赠款、贷款、投股、担保、财政激励及政府提供货物和服务。

9. The provision of services, including construction services, in the context of procurement procedures according to this Agreement is subject to the conditions and qualifications for market access and national treatment as will be required by the Separate Customs Territory of Taiwan, Penghu, Kinmen and Matsu in conformity with commitments under GATS.

10. When a specific procurement may impair important national policy objectives, the Government of the Separate Customs Territory of Taiwan, Penghu, Kinmen and Matsu may consider it necessary in particular procurement cases to deviate from the principle of national treatment of the Agreement. A decision to this effect will be made by the Executive Yuan. This Note shall only be applied to Finland, Norway and Sweden under the condition that they maintain the similar note to their Annexes.

11. This Agreement shall not apply to procurements in respect of national security exceptions including procurements made in support of safeguarding nuclear materials, radwaste management, or technology.

12. The Separate Customs Territory of Taiwan, Penghu, Kinmen and Matsu will accede to the Agreement at the time it accedes to the WTO.

15 July 2009 (WT/Let/647/Add.1)

9. 在根据本协定所进行的采购程序中，服务的提供，包括建筑服务的提供，需遵守台湾、澎湖、金门、马祖单独关税区依照其在 GATS 项下的承诺所要求的关于市场准入和国民待遇的条件和资格。

10. 如一特定采购可能损害重要国家政策目标，则台湾、澎湖、金门、马祖单独关税区政府可以认为有必要在一特定采购案中背离本协定的国民待遇原则。有关决定将由行政院做出。本注释仅适用于芬兰、挪威和瑞典，以其在各自附件中保留类似注释为条件。

11. 本协定不适用于有关国家安全例外的采购，包括为支持保护核物质、放射性废物管理或技术而进行的采购。

12. 台湾、澎湖、金门、马祖单独关税区将于加入 WTO 之时加入本协定。

2009 年 7 月 15 日 (WT/Let/647/Add.1)

UNITED STATES
美国

UNITED STATES

(Authentic in the English language only)

ANNEX 1

Central Government Entities which Procure in Accordance With the Provisions of this Agreement

Threshold: 130,000 SDRs for supplies and services
5 million SDRs for construction

List of Entities:

1. Department of Agriculture (not including procurement of agricultural products made in furtherance of agricultural support programmes or human feeding programmes)
2. Department of Commerce (not including shipbuilding activities of NOAA, as excluded in Annex 4)
3. Department of Education
4. Department of Health and Human Services
5. Department of Housing and Urban Development
6. Department of the Interior (including the Bureau of Reclamation)
7. Department of Justice
8. Department of Labor
9. Department of State
10. United States Agency for International Development (not including procurement for the direct purpose of providing foreign assistance)
11. Department of the Treasury
12. Department of Transportation (not including procurement by the Federal Aviation Administration, and pursuant to Article XXIII)
13. Department of Energy (pursuant to Article XXIII, national security exceptions include procurements made in support of safeguarding nuclear materials or technology and entered into under the authority of the Atomic Energy Act, and oil purchases related to the Strategic Petroleum Reserve)
14. General Services Administration (except Federal Supply Groups 51 and 52 and Federal Supply Class 7340)
15. National Aeronautics and Space Administration
16. The Department of Veterans Affairs
17. Environmental Protection Agency
18. National Science Foundation
19. Executive Office of the President
20. Farm Credit Administration
21. National Credit Union Administration

1 October 2004 (WT/Let/482/Rev.1)

美国

(仅以英文为准)

附件 1

依照本协定条款进行采购的中央政府实体

门槛金额: 供应品和服务 130,000 特别提款权
建筑 5,000,000 特别提款权

实体清单:

1. 农业部 (不包括为促进农业支持计划或人类供给计划而采购的农产品)
2. 商务部 (不包括国家海洋和大气管理局的造船活动，已在附件 4 中排除)
3. 教育部
4. 卫生部
5. 住房和城市发展部
6. 内务部 (包括垦务局)
7. 司法部
8. 劳工部
9. 国务院
10. 国际开发署(不包括以提供对外援助为直接目的的采购)
11. 财政部
12. 交通部 (不包括联邦航空局进行的采购，及根据第 23 条)
13. 能源部 (根据第 23 条，国家安全例外包括为支持核物质或技术安全而进行的采购和根据《原子能法》的授权所进行的采购，以及与战略石油储备有关的石油采购)
14. 联邦总务署(联邦供应分组第 51 和 52 组和联邦供应分类 7340 除外)
15. 国家航空航天局
16. 退伍军人事务部
17. 环境保护署
18. 国家科学基金会
19. 总统行政办公室
20. 农场信贷管理局
21. 国家信用合作社管理局

2004 年 10 月 1 日 (WT/Let/482/Rev.1)

22. Merit Systems Protection Board
23. The Corporation for National and Community Service
24. Office of Thrift Supervision
25. Federal Housing Finance Board
26. National Labor Relations Board
27. National Mediation Board
28. Railroad Retirement Board
29. American Battle Monuments Commission
30. Federal Communications Commission
31. Federal Trade Commission
32. Securities and Exchange Commission
33. Office of Personnel Management
34. United States International Trade Commission
35. Export-Import Bank of the United States
36. Federal Mediation and Conciliation Service
37. Selective Service System
38. Smithsonian Institution
39. Federal Deposit Insurance Corporation
40. Consumer Product Safety Commission
41. Equal Employment Opportunity Commission
42. Federal Maritime Commission
43. National Transportation Safety Board
44. Nuclear Regulatory Commission
45. Overseas Private Investment Corporation
46. Broadcasting Board of Governors
47. Commission on Civil Rights
48. Commodity Futures Trading Commission
49. Peace Corps
50. National Archives and Records Administration
51. Advisory Commission on Intergovernmental Relations
52. African Development Foundation
53. Alaska Natural Gas Transportation System
54. Appalachian Regional Commission
55. Commission of Fine Arts
56. Delaware River Basin Commission
57. Federal Election Commission
58. Department of Homeland Security (except procurement by the Transportation Security Administration, and the national security considerations applicable to the Department of Defense are equally applicable to the U.S. Coast Guard)
59. Federal Home Loan Mortgage Corporation
60. Federal Mine Safety and Health Review Commission
61. Federal Reserve System
62. Federal Retirement Thrift Investment Board
63. Holocaust Memorial Council
64. Inter-American Foundation
65. National Capital Planning Commission
66. National Commission on Libraries and Information Science
67. National Council on Disability

22. 功绩制保护委员会
23. 国家和社团服务组织
24. 储蓄机构监理局
25. 住房融资委员会
26. 国家劳资关系委员会
27. 国家仲裁委员会
28. 铁路退休局
29. 美国战争纪念设施委员会
30. 联邦通讯委员会
31. 联邦贸易委员会
32. 证券交易委员会
33. 人事管理办公室
34. 美国国际贸易委员会
35. 美国进出口银行
36. 联邦调解服务机构
37. 选征兵役制度服务局
38. 史密森学会
39. 联邦储蓄保险公司
40. 消费产品安全委员会
41. 平等就业机会委员会
42. 联邦海事委员会
43. 国家运输安全委员会
44. 核管理委员会
45. 海外私人投资公司
46. 广播理事会
47. 民权委员会
48. 商品期货贸易委员会
49. 和平队
50. 国家档案局
51. 政府间关系咨询委员会
52. 非洲发展基金
53. 阿拉斯加州天然气运输系统
54. 阿帕拉契区域委员会
55. 美术委员会
56. 特拉华河流流域委员会
57. 联邦选举委员会
58. 国土安全部(运输安全管理局的采购除外，适用于国防部的国家安全考虑同样适用于美国海岸警卫队)
59. 联邦住房抵押贷款公司
60. 联邦矿业安全和医疗检查委员会
61. 联邦储备委员会
62. 联邦退休储蓄投资委员会
63. 大屠杀纪念委员会
64. 泛美基金会
65. 国家首都计划委员会
66. 国家图书馆和信息科学委员会
67. 国家残疾人委员会

68. National Foundation on the Arts and the Humanities
69. Occupational Safety and Health Review Commission
70. Office of Government Ethics
71. Office of the Nuclear Waste Negotiator
72. Office of Special Counsel
73. Small Business Administration
74. Susquehanna River Basin Commission
75. Federal Crop Insurance Corporation
76. Federal Prison Industries, Inc.
77. Government National Mortgage Association
78. Uranium Enrichment Corporation
79. Department of Defense, including the Corps of Army Engineers

This Agreement will not apply to the following purchases of the Department of Defense:

(a) Federal Supply Classification (FSC) 83 - all elements of this classification other than pins, needles, sewing kits, flagstaffs, flagpoles, and flagstaff trucks;
(b) FSC 84 - all elements other than sub-class 8460 (luggage);
(c) FSC 89 - all elements other than sub-class 8975 (tobacco products);
(d) FSC 2310 - (buses only);
(e) Speciality metals, defined as steels melted in steel manufacturing facilities located in the United States or its possessions, where the maximum alloy content exceeds one or more of the following limits, must be used in products purchased by DOD: (1) manganese, 1.65 per cent; silicon, 0.60 per cent; or copper, 0.06 per cent; or which contains more than 0.25 per cent of any of the following elements: aluminium, chromium, cobalt, columbium, olybdenum, nickel, titanium, tungsten, or vanadium; (2) metal alloys consisting of nickel, iron-nickel and cobalt base alloys containing a total of other alloying metals (except iron) in excess of 10 per cent; (3) titanium and titanium alloys; or (4) zirconium base alloys;
(f) FSC 19 and 20 - that part of these classifications defined as naval vessels or major components of the hull or superstructure thereof;
(g) FSC 5l and 52;
(h) Following FSC categories are not generally covered due to application of Article XXIII, paragraph 1: 10, 12, 13, 14, 15, 16, 17, 19, 20, 28, 31, 58, 59, 95.

68. 国家艺术和人文基金会
69. 职业安全和健康复审委员会
70. 政府纪律办公室
71. 核废物谈判专员办公室
72. 特别检察官办公室
73. 小企业管理局
74. 萨斯奎哈纳河流域管理委员会
75. 联邦作物保险公司
76. 联邦政府监狱
77. 国家抵押贷款协会
78. 浓缩铀公司
79. 国防部, 包括陆军工程军团

本协定不适用于国防部下列采购：

(a) 联邦供应分类(FSC)83—该分类中除别针、针、缝纫工具、旗杆、旗竿及旗杆桅冠外的所有组成部分；
(b) FSC 84—除 8460 子类(行李)外的所有组成部分；
(c) FSC 89—除 8975 子类(烟草制品)外的所有组成部分；
(d) FSC 2310 子类—(仅限公共汽车)；
(e) 国防部采购的产品所必须使用的特殊性能金属，特殊性能金属指在位于美国国内或其领地内的炼钢厂熔炼的钢材，其最高合金含量超过下列一个或多个限额：(1)锰，1.65%；硅，0.6%；或铜，0.06%；或下列金属的任何一种含量超过 0.25%：铝、铬、钴、铌、钼、镍、钛、钨或钒；(2)包含镍、铁镍和钴基合金的金属合金，其他合金金属(铁除外)总含量超过 10%；(3)钛和钛合金；或(4)锆其合金；
(f) FSC 19 和 20—部分定义为海军舰艇或船体主要部件或上部结构；
(g) FSC 51 和 52；
(h) 下列 FSC 类别由于适用第 23 条第 1 款而通常不涵盖：10、12、13、14、15、16、17、19、20、28、31、58、59、95。

2005 年 3 月 22 日 (WT/Let/537)

This Agreement will generally apply to purchases of the following FSC categories subject to United States Government determinations under the provisions of Article XXIII, paragraph 1.

FSC	22	Railway Equipment
	23	Motor Vehicles, Trailers, and Cycles (except buses in 2310)
	24	Tractors
	25	Vehicular Equipment Components
	26	Tyres and Tubes
	29	Engine Accessories
	30	Mechanical Power Transmission Equipment
	32	Woodworking Machinery and Equipment
	34	Metalworking Machinery
	35	Service and Trade Equipment
	36	Special Industry Machinery
	37	Agricultural Machinery and Equipment
	38	Construction, Mining, Excavating, and Highway Maintenance Equipment
	39	Materials Handling Equipment
	40	Rope, Cable, Chain and Fittings
	41	Refrigeration and Air Conditioning Equipment
	42	Fire Fighting, Rescue and Safety Equipment
	43	Pumps and Compressors
	44	Furnace, Steam Plant, Drying Equipment and Nuclear Reactors
	45	Plumbing, Heating and Sanitation Equipment
	46	Water Purification and Sewage Treatment Equipment
	47	Pipe, Tubing, Hose and Fittings
	48	Valves
	49	Maintenance and Repair Shop Equipment
	53	Hardware and Abrasives
	54	Prefabricated Structures and Scaffolding
	55	Lumber, Millwork, Plywood and Veneer
	56	Construction and Building Materials
	61	Electric Wire, and Power and Distribution Equipment
	62	Lighting Fixtures and Lamps
	63	Alarm and Signal Systems
	65	Medical, Dental, and Veterinary Equipment and Supplies
	66	Instruments and Laboratory Equipment
	67	Photographic Equipment
	68	Chemicals and Chemical Products
	69	Training Aids and Devices
	70	General Purpose ADPE, Software, Supplies and Support Equipment
	71	Furniture
	72	Household and Commercial Furnishings and Appliances
	73	Food Preparation and Serving Equipment
	74	Office Machines, Visible Record Equipment and ADP Equipment
	75	Office Supplies and Devices
	76	Books, Maps and Other Publications
	77	Musical Instruments, Phonographs, and Home Type Radios

本协定通常适用于下列 FSC 类别的购买，取决于美国政府根据第 23 条第 1 款所做决定：

FSC	22	铁路设备
	23	地面效应车、机动车辆、拖车和自行车(2310 公共汽车除外)
	24	拖拉机
	25	机动车部件
	26	轮胎和内胎
	29	发动机配件
	30	机械动力传输设备
	32	木工机器和设备
	34	金属加工机器
	35	服务和销售设备
	36	特殊工业机器
	37	农业机器和设备
	38	建筑、采矿、开凿和公路维护设备
	39	材料处理设备
	40	粗绳、电缆、链条和配件
	41	冷却、空调和空气循环装备
	42	消防、援救和安全设备
	43	泵和压缩机
	44	火炉、蒸气设备、烘干设备和核反应堆
	45	管道、加热和卫生设备
	46	水净化和污水处理设备
	47	管和配件
	48	阀
	49	维护和修理商店设备
	53	硬件和研磨剂
	54	预制件和脚手架
	55	木材、木制品、胶合板和饰面板
	56	建筑建材
	61	电线及电力传输设备
	62	照明器材和灯
	63	警报、信号和探测系统
	65	内科、牙科和兽医设备和耗材
	66	仪器和实验室设备
	67	摄影设备
	68	化学药品和化工品
	69	教具和训练器材
	70	自动化处理设备、软件、耗材和配套设备
	71	家具
	72	家用和商用家具和器械
	73	食品加工和供餐设备
	74	办公设备
	75	办公用品和装置
	76	图书、地图和其他出版物
	77	乐器、留声机和家用收音机

78 Recreational and Athletic Equipment
79 Cleaning Equipment and Supplies
80 Brushes, Paints, Sealers and Adhesives
81 Containers, Packaging and Packing Supplies
85 Toiletries
87 Agricultural Supplies
88 Live Animals
91 Fuels, Lubricants, Oils and Waxes
93 Non-metallic Fabricated Materials
94 Non-metallic Crude Materials
96 Ores, Minerals and their Primary Products
99 Miscellaneous

Note to Annex 1

The conditions specified in the General Notes apply to this Annex.

78	娱乐和运动器材
79	清洁设备和耗材
80	刷子、油漆、封条和粘合剂
81	容器、包装材料和包装用品
85	盥洗用品
87	农用品
88	活动物
91	燃料、润滑剂、油和蜡
93	非金属制品
94	非金属原料
96	矿石、矿物及其初级产品
99	杂项制品

附件 1 注释

总注释所列条件适用于本附件。

ANNEX 2

Sub-Central Government Entities which Procure in Accordance With the Provisions of this Agreement

Threshold: 355,000 SDRs for supplies and services
5 million SDRs for construction

List of Entities:

Arizona

Executive branch agencies

Arkansas

Executive branch agencies, including universities but excluding the Office of Fish and Game and construction services

California

Executive branch agencies

Colorado

Executive branch agencies

Connecticut

Department of Administrative Services
Connecticut Department of Transportation
Connecticut Department of Public Works
Constituent Units of Higher Education

Delaware*

Administrative Services (Central Procurement Agency)
State Universities
State Colleges

Florida*

Executive branch agencies

Hawaii

Department of Accounting and General Services (with the exception of procurements of software developed in the state and construction)

16 October 2002 (WT/Let/431)

附件 2

依照本协定条款进行采购的次中央政府实体

门槛金额: 供应品和服务 355,000 特别提款权
建筑 5,000,000 特别提款权

实体清单:

亚利桑那州

各行政机构

阿肯色州

各行政机构，包括大学，但不包括捕鱼和狩猎办公室及建筑服务

加利福尼亚州

各行政机构

科罗拉多州

各行政机构

康涅狄格州

行政服务厅
康涅狄格州运输厅
康涅狄格州公共工程厅
康涅狄格州高等教育机构

特拉华州*

行政管理(集中采购机构)
各州立大学
各州立学院

佛罗里达州*

各行政机构

夏威夷州

会计和总务厅 (关于本州开发软件和建筑服务的采购除外)

2002 年 10 月 16 日 (WT/Let/431)

Idaho

Central Procurement Agency (including all colleges and universities subject to central purchasing oversight)

Illinois*

Department of Central Management Services

Iowa*

Department of General Services
Department of Transportation
Board of Regents' Institutions (universities)

Kansas

Executive branch agencies, excluding construction services, automobiles and aircraft

Kentucky

Division of Purchases, Finance and Administration Cabinet, excluding construction projects

Louisiana

Executive branch agencies

Maine*

Department of Administrative and Financial Services
Bureau of General Services (covering state government agencies
 and school construction)
Maine Department of Transportation

Maryland*

Office of the Treasury
Department of the Environment
Department of General Services
Department of Housing and Community Development
Department of Human Resources
Department of Licensing and Regulation
Department of Natural Resources
Department of Public Safety and Correctional Services
Department of Personnel
Department of Transportation

16 October 2002 (WT/Let/431)

<u>爱达荷州</u>

集中采购机构(包括接受集中采购监督的所有学院和大学)

<u>伊利诺伊州</u>*

集中管理服务厅

<u>爱荷华州</u>*

总务厅
运输厅
校董会(各大学)

<u>堪萨斯州</u>

各行政机构，不包括建筑服务、汽车和航空器

<u>肯塔基州</u>

州财政及总务委员会采购处，不包括建筑项目

<u>路易斯安那州</u>

各行政机构

<u>缅因州</u>*

行政和财政事务厅
总务局 (涵盖州政府机构和学校的建设)
缅因州运输厅

<u>马里兰州</u>*

财政局
环境厅
总务厅
住屋和社区发展厅
人力资源局
许可和规则局
自然资源厅
公共安全和惩教事务厅
人事厅
运输厅

2002 年 10 月 16 日 (WT/Let/431)

Massachusetts

Executive Office for Administration and Finance
Executive Office of Communities and Development
Executive Office of Consumer Affairs
Executive Office of Economic Affairs
Executive Office of Education
Executive Office of Elder Affairs
Executive Office of Environmental Affairs
Executive Office of Health and Human Service
Executive Office of Labor
Executive Office of Public Safety
Executive Office of Transportation and Construction

Michigan*

Department of Management and Budget

Minnesota

Executive branch agencies

Mississippi

Department of Finance and Administration (does not include services)

Missouri

Office of Administration
Division of Purchasing and Materials Management

Montana

Executive branch agencies (only for services and construction)

New York*

State agencies
State university system
Public authorities and public benefit corporations, with the exception of those entities with multi-state mandates

In addition to the exceptions noted at the end of this annex, transit cars, buses and related equipment are not covered.

Nebraska

Central Procurement Agency

16 October 2002 (WT/Let/431)

马萨诸塞州

管理和财务办公室
社区和发展办公室
消费者事务办公室
经济事务办公室
教育办公室
老年人事务办公室
环境事务办公室
健康和公共事务办公室
劳工办公室
公共安全办公室
运输和建设办公室

密歇根州*

管理和预算厅

明尼苏达州

各行政机构

密西西比州

财政和管理厅 (不包括服务)

密苏里州

管理办公室
采购和材料管理处

蒙大拿州

各行政机构 (仅限服务和建筑)

纽约州*

各州立机构
州立大学系统
公共机构和公共福利公司，不包括具有跨州授权的实体

除本附件结尾处所注例外之外，另不涵盖中转车、公共汽车及有关设备。

内布拉斯加州

集中采购机构

2002 年 10 月 16 日 (WT/Let/431)

New Hampshire*

Central Procurement Agency

Oklahoma*

Department of Central Services and all state agencies and departments subject to the Oklahoma Central Purchasing Act, excluding construction services.

Oregon

Department of Administrative Services

Pennsylvania*

Executive branch agencies, including:

Governor's Office
Department of the Auditor General
Treasury Department
Department of Agriculture
Department of Banking
Pennsylvania Securities Commission
Department of Health
Department of Transportation
Insurance Department
Department of Aging
Department of Correction
Department of Labor and Industry
Department of Military Affairs
Office of Attorney General
Department of General Services
Department of Education
Public Utility Commission
Department of Revenue
Department of State
Pennsylvania State Police
Department of Public Welfare
Fish Commission
Game Commission
Department of Commerce
Board of Probation and Parole
Liquor Control Board
Milk Marketing Board
Lieutenant Governor's Office
Department of Community Affairs
Pennsylvania Historical and Museum Commission
Pennsylvania Emergency Management Agency
State Civil Service Commission

6 November 2008 (WT/Let/635)

新罕布什尔州*

集中采购机构

俄克拉何马州*

集中服务办公室及所有受《俄克拉荷马州集中采购法》管辖的州立机构和部门，不包括建筑服务。

俄勒冈州

行政服务厅

宾夕法尼亚州*

各行政机构，包括:

州长办公室
总审计长办公室
财政厅
农业厅
银行厅
宾夕法尼亚州证券委员会
卫生厅
运输厅
保险厅
老年人事务厅
惩教厅
劳工和产业厅
军事事务厅
总检察长办公室
总务厅
教育厅
公用事业委员会
税务厅
州务厅
宾夕法尼亚州警察局
公共福利厅
捕鱼委员会
狩猎委员会
商务厅
缓刑和假释委员会
酒类管制局
牛奶销售局
副州长办公室
社区事务厅
宾夕法尼亚州历史和博物馆委员会
宾夕法尼亚州紧急情况管理局
州立民事服务委员会

2008 年 11 月 6 日 (WT/Let/635)

Pennsylvania Public Television Network
Department of Environmental Resources
State Tax Equalization Board
Department of Public Welfare
State Employees' Retirement System
Pennsylvania Municipal Retirement Board
Public School Employees' Retirement System
Pennsylvania Crime Commission
Executive Offices

Rhode Island

Executive branch agencies, excluding boats, automobiles, buses and related equipment

South Dakota

Central Procuring Agency (including universities and penal institutions)

In addition to the exceptions noted at the end of this annex, procurements of beef are not covered.

Tennessee

Executive branch agencies (excluding services and construction)

Texas

Texas Building and Procurement Commission

Utah

Executive branch agencies

Vermont

Executive branch agencies

Washington

Washington State executive branch agencies, including:

General Administration
Department of Transportation
State Universities

In addition to the exceptions noted at the end of this annex, procurements of fuel, paper products, boats, ships and vessels are not covered.

16 October 2002 (WT/Let/431)

宾夕法尼亚州公共电视网络
环境资源厅
州纳税均等局
公共福利厅
州雇员退休事务委员会
宾夕法尼亚州城市退休局
公立学校雇员退休系统
宾夕法尼亚州打击犯罪委员会
各行政办公室

罗得岛州

各行政机构，不包括船、机动车、公共汽车和相关设备

南达科他州

集中采购机构 (包括各大学和刑罚机构)

除本附件结尾处所注例外之外，另不涵盖牛肉采购。

田纳西州

各行政机构 (不包括服务和建筑服务)

得克萨斯州

得克萨斯州建设和采购委员会

犹他州
所有行政机构

佛蒙特州

各行政机构

华盛顿州

华盛顿州行政机构，包括：

总务署
运输厅
各州立大学

除本附件结尾处所注例外之外，另不涵盖燃料、纸制品、小船、船舶和舰只的采购。

2002 年 10 月 16 日 (WT/Let/431)

Wisconsin

Executive branch agencies, including

Department of Administration
State Correctional Institutions
Department of Development
Educational Communications Board
Department of Employment Relations
State Historical Society
Department of Health and Social Services
Insurance Commissioner
Department of Justice
Lottery Board
Department of Natural Resources
Administration for Public Instruction
Racing Board
Department of Revenue
State Fair Park Board
Department of Transportation
State University System

Wyoming*

Procurement Services Division
Wyoming Department of Transportation
University of Wyoming

Notes to Annex 2

In addition to the conditions specified in the General Notes, the following conditions apply:

1. For those states marked by an asterisk with pre-existing restrictions, the Agreement does not apply to procurement of construction-grade steel (including requirements on subcontracts), motor vehicles and coal.

2. The Agreement shall not apply to preferences or restrictions associated with programs promoting the development of distressed areas and businesses owned by minorities, disabled veterans and women.

3. Nothing in this annex shall be construed to prevent any state entity from applying restrictions that promote the general environmental quality in that state, as long as such restrictions are not disguised barriers to international trade.

4. The Agreement shall not apply to any procurement made by a covered entity on behalf of non-covered entities at a different level of government.

5. The Agreement shall not apply to restrictions attached to Federal funds for mass transit and highway projects.

16 October 2002 (WT/Let/431)

<u>威斯康星州</u>

各行政机构，包括：

总务署
州惩教机构
发展厅
教育交流局
雇佣关系厅
州历史协会
卫生和社会服务厅
保险专员办公室
司法厅
彩票局
自然资源厅
教育管理厅
赛马局
税收厅
州美丽公园董事会
运输厅
州立大学系统

<u>怀俄明州</u>*

采购服务处
怀俄明州运输厅
怀俄明大学

附件 2 注释

除总注释中所规定条件外，另有下列条件适用：

1. 对于用星号标出的先前存在限制条件的州，本协定不适用于建筑用钢(包括关于分包合同的要求)、机动车和煤的采购。

2. 本协定不适用于促进贫困地区发展和少数族裔、残废退伍军人和妇女所拥有商业的项目所附带的优先权或限制条件。

3. 本附件任何规定不得解释为阻止任何州实体实施可提高该州总体环境质量的限制措施，只要此类限制措施不是对国际贸易的变相壁垒。

4. 本协定不适用于一涵盖实体代表一不同政府级别的非涵盖实体所进行的任何采购。

5. 本协定不适用于用于公共交通和公路项目的联邦资金所附带的限制条件。

2002 年 10 月 16 日 (WT/Let/431)

ANNEX 3

All Other Entities which Procure in Accordance With the Provisions of this Agreement

Threshold: 400,000 SDRs for supplies and services (except as specified below)
5 million SDRs for construction

List of Entities:

The following entities at the SDR equivalent of $250,000 for supplies and services:

Tennessee Valley Authority
Power Marketing Administrations of the Department of Energy

- Bonneville Power Administration
- Western Area Power Administration
- Southeastern Power Administration
- Southwestern Power Administration
- St. Lawrence Seaway Development Corporation

The following entities are 400,000 SDRs for supplies and services:

The Port Authority of New York and New Jersey with the following exceptions:

- Maintenance, repair and operating materials and supplies (e.g., hardware, tools, lamps/lighting, plumbing);
- In exceptional cases, individual procurements may require certain regional production of goods if authorized by the Board of Directors;
- Procurements pursuant to multi-jurisdictional agreement (i.e., for contracts which have initially been awarded by other jurisdictions).

The Port of Baltimore (subject to the conditions specified for the state of New York in Annex 2)

The New York Power Authority (subject to the conditions specified for the state of New York in Annex 2)

Rural Utilities Service Financing:

(1) waiver of Buy American restriction on financing for all power generation projects (restrictions on financing for telecommunication projects are excluded from the Agreement);

(2) application of Code-equivalent procurement procedures and national treatment to funded projects exceeding the thresholds specified above.

附件 3

依照本协定条款进行采购的其他实体

门槛金额: 供应品和服务 400,000 特别提款权(下面规定的除外)
建筑 5,000,000 特别提款权

实体清单:

下列实体的供应品和服务为 250,000 美元等值的特别提款权:

田纳西州河谷管理局
能源部下属的电力市场管理局
- 邦纳维尔电力管理局
- 西部地区电力管理局
- 东南电力管理局
- 西南电力管理局
- 圣·劳伦斯航道发展公司

下列实体的供应品和服务为 400,000 特别提款权:

纽约和新泽西港口管理局，下列除外:

- 维护、修理和运行材料和耗材 (如五金器具、工具、灯/照明设备、管道);
- 在例外情况下，如董事会授权，个别采购可以要求某些地区生产的货物;
- 根据跨司法协议进行的采购(即最初由其他司法区授予的合同)。

巴尔的摩港 (受附件 2 中对纽约州规定的条件的管辖)

纽约电力管理局(受附件 2 中对纽约州规定的条件的管辖)

乡村公用事业融资服务:

(1) 豁免所有发电项目融资的购买美国货限制条件(关于电信项目融资的限制条件排除在本协定之外)；

(2) 对于超过以上所列门槛金额的投资项目，适用与商法典同等效力的采购程序和国民待遇。

2004 年 10 月 1 日 (WT/Let/482/Rev.1)

Notes to Annex 3

1. With respect to these entities, the Agreement shall not apply to restrictions attached to Federal funds for airport projects.

2. The conditions specified in the General Notes apply to this Annex.

附件 3 注释

1. 对于这些实体，本协定不适用于用于机场项目的联邦资金所附带的限制条件。

2. 总注释所列条件适用于本附件。

ANNEX 4

Services

Of the Universal List of Services, as contained in document MTN.GNS/W/120, the following services are excluded:

1. All transportation services, including Launching Services (CPC Categories 71, 72, 73, 74, 8859, 8868).

   Note: Transportation services, where incidental to a contract for the procurement of supplies, are not subject to this Agreement.

2. Dredging.

3. All services purchased in support of military forces located overseas.

4. Management and operation contracts of certain government or privately-owned facilities used for government purposes, including federally-funded research and development centers (FFRDCs).

5. Public utilities services, including telecommunications and ADP-related telecommunications services except enhanced (i.e., value-added) telecommunications services.

6. Research and Development.

7. Printing Services (for Annex 2 entities only).

Note to Annex 4

The conditions specified in the General Notes also apply to this Annex.

1 March 2000 (WT/Let/330)

附件 4

服务

不包括载于 MTN.GNS/W/120 号文件的服务通用清单中的下列服务：

1. 所有运输服务，包括发射服务(CPC 第 71、72、73、74 类及 8859、8868)。

   注：供应品采购合同所附带的运输服务不适用于本协定。

2. 疏浚。

3. 为支持海外驻军所采购的所有服务。

4. 某些政府设施或用于政府目的私有设施的管理和运营合同，包括联邦资助的研究和开发。

5. 公用事业服务，包括电信和与自动数据处理相关的电信服务，增强型(即增值)电信除外。

6. 研究和开发

7. 印刷服务(仅针对附件 2 实体)

附件 4 注释

总注释所列条件适用于本附件。

2000 年 3 月 1 日 (WT/Let/330)

ANNEX 5

Construction Services

Definition:

A construction services contract is a contract which has as its objective the realization by whatever means of civil or building works, in the sense of Division 51 of the Central Product Classification.

List of Division 51, CPC:

All services listed in Division 51.

Note to Annex 5

The conditions specified in the General Notes apply to this Annex.

附件 5

建筑服务

定义：

建筑服务合同是指根据《中央产品分类》第 51 类，以通过任何土木或建筑工程手段实现目的的合同。

CPC 第 51 类清单：

CPC 51 类包含的所有服务。

附件 5 注释

总注释所列条件适用于本附件。

2000 年 3 月 1 日 (WT/Let/330)

GENERAL NOTES

1. Notwithstanding the above, this Agreement will not apply to set asides on behalf of small and minority businesses.

2. Except as specified otherwise in this Appendix, procurement in terms of U.S. coverage does not include non-contractual agreements or any form of government assistance, including cooperative agreements, grants, loans, equity infusions, guarantees, fiscal incentives, and governmental provision of goods and services to persons or governmental authorities not specifically covered under U.S. annexes to this agreement.

3. Procurement does not include the acquisition of fiscal agency or depository services, liquidation and management services for regulated financial institutions, and sale and distribution services for government debt.

4. Where a contract to be awarded by an entity is not covered by this Agreement, this Agreement shall not be construed to cover any good or service component of that contract.

5. For goods and services (including construction) of the following countries and suppliers of such goods and services, this Agreement does not apply to procurement by the entities listed in Annexes 2 and 3 or the waiver described in Annex 3:

   Canada

   The United States is prepared to amend this note at such time as coverage with respect to these annexes can be resolved with a Party listed above.

6. For construction services of the Republic of Korea and suppliers of such services, this Agreement applies only to procurement of the entities listed in Annexes 2 and 3 above a threshold of 15 million SDRs.

7. For goods and services (including construction) of Japan and suppliers of such goods and services, this Agreement does not apply to procurement by the National Aeronautics and Space Administration.

8. A service listed in Annex 4 is covered with respect to a particular Party only to the extent that such Party has included that service in its Annex 4.

9. The United States will not extend the benefits of this Agreement to Japan as regards the award of contracts by entities listed in Annex 3 that are responsible for the generation or distribution of electricity.

1 March 2000 (WT/Let/330)

总注释

1. 尽管有上述规定，但是本协定不适用给予小企业和少数族裔企业的合同。

2. 除非本附录另有规定，否则美国的采购范围不包括非契约性协议或任何形式的政府援助，包括合作协议、赠款、贷款、投股、担保、财政激励以及政府向个人或本协定的美国附件未具体涵盖的政府机构提供货物和服务。

3. 采购不包括财政代理服务或储蓄服务的获得、对受监管金融机构的清算和管理服务以及政府债务的销售和分销服务。

4. 如一合同由本协定未涵盖的实体授予，则本协定不得解释为涵盖该合同的任何货物或服务组成部分。

5. 对于下列国家的货物和服务(含建筑服务)及此类货物和服务的供应商，本协定不适用于由附件 2 和 3 中所列实体进行的采购或附件 3 中所述豁免：

   加拿大

   美国准备在能够与以上所列一参加方解决这些附件的涵盖范围之时修改本注释。

6. 对于韩国的建筑服务和此类服务的供应商，本协定仅适用于附件 2 和 3 中所列实体超过 15,000,000 特别提款权门槛金额的采购。

7. 对于日本的货物和服务(包括建筑服务)及此类货物和服务的供应商，本协定不用于国家航空航天局所进行的采购。

8. 对于附件 4 中所列一服务，仅在一特定参加方已将该服务纳入其附件 4 中时，方针对该参加方而涵盖其中。

9. 对于附件 3 所列负责发电或电力配送的实体所授予的合同，美国不将本协定的利益给予日本。

2000 年 3 月 1 日 (WT/Let/330)

APPENDIX II
附录 2

APPENDIX II

PUBLICATIONS UTILIZED BY PARTIES FOR THE PUBLICATION OF NOTICES OF INTENDED PROCUREMENTS - PARAGRAPH 1 OF ARTICLE IX, AND OF POST-AWARD NOTICES - PARAGRAPH 1 OF ARTICLE XVIII

APPENDICE II

PUBLICATIONS UTILISEES PAR LES PARTIES EN VUE DE LA PUBLICATION DES AVIS DE MARCHES ENVISAGES - PARAGRAPHE 1 DE L'ARTICLE IX, ET DES AVIS POSTERIEURS A L'ADJUDICATION DES MARCHES - PARAGRAPHE 1 DE L'ARTICLE XVIII

APÉNDICE II

MEDIOS UTILIZADOS POR LAS PARTES PARA LA PUBLICACIÓN DE LOS ANUNCIOS DE LOS CONTRATOS PREVISTOS - PÁRRAFO 1 DEL ARTÍCULO IX - Y LOS ANUNCIOS DE LAS ADJUDICACIONES - PÁRRAFO 1 DEL ARTÍCULO XVIII.

1 March 2000 (WT/Let/330)

附录 2

各参加方为公布预定招标通知—第 9 条第 1 款
及授标后通知—第 18 条第 1 款所使用的出版物

2000 年 3 月 1 日 (WT/Let/330)

APPENDIX II

PUBLICATIONS UTILIZED BY PARTIES FOR THE PUBLICATION OF NOTICES OF INTENDED PROCUREMENTS - PARAGRAPH 1 OF ARTICLE IX, AND OF POST-AWARD NOTICES - PARAGRAPH 1 OF ARTICLE XVIII

CANADA

Government Business Opportunities (GBO)
MERX, Cebra Inc.

EUROPEAN COMMUNITIES

Belgium	-	Official Journal of the European Union
	-	Le Bulletin des Adjudications
	-	Other publications in the specialized press
Bulgaria	-	Official Journal of the European Union
	-	Държавен вестник (State Gazette) http://dv.parliament.bg
	-	Public Procurement Register (www.aop.bg)
Czech Republic	-	Official Journal of the European Union
Denmark	-	Official Journal of the European Union
Germany	-	Official Journal of the European Union
Estonia	-	Official Journal of the European Union
Greece	-	Official Journal of the European Union
	-	Publication in the daily, financial, regional and specialized press
Spain	-	Official Journal of the European Union
France	-	Official Journal of the European Union
	-	Bulletin officiel des annonces des marchés publics
Ireland	-	Official Journal of the European Union
	-	Daily Press: "Irish Independent", "Irish Times", "Irish Press", "Cork Examiner"
Italy	-	Official Journal of the European Union
Cyprus	-	Official Journal of the European Union
	-	Official Gazette of the Republic
	-	Local Daily Press
Latvia	-	Official Journal of the European Union
		Latvijas vēstnesis (official newspaper)
Lithuania	-	Official Journal of the European Union
	-	Information supplement "Informaciniai pranešimai" to the Official Gazette ("Valstybės žinios") of the Republic of Lithuania

1 January 2007 (WT/Let/556)

附录 2

各参加方为公布预定招标通知—第 9 条第 1 款
及授标后通知—第 18 条第 1 款所使用的出版物

加拿大

《政府商业机遇》
加拿大联邦、省、市公共采购网站

欧洲共同体

比利时	-	《欧洲联盟公报》
	-	比利时招标公告
	-	在其他专业报刊中发布
保加利亚	-	《欧洲联盟公报》
	-	《国家公报》http://dv.parliament.bg
	-	公共采购登记 (www.aop.bg)
捷克	-	《欧洲联盟公报》
丹麦	-	《欧洲联盟公报》
德国	-	《欧洲联盟公报 》
爱沙尼亚	-	《欧洲联盟公报 》
希腊	-	《欧洲联盟公报》
	-	在日报、金融、地区和专业报刊中发布
西班牙	-	《欧洲联盟公报 》
法国	-	《欧洲联盟公报》
	-	《公共采购官方公报》
爱尔兰	-	《欧洲联盟公报》
	-	日报: 《爱尔兰独立报》、《爱尔兰时报》、《爱尔兰报纸》《科克郡观察者》
意大利	-	《欧洲联盟公报》
塞浦路斯	-	《欧洲联盟公报》
	-	《共和国公报 》
	-	当地日报
拉脱维亚	-	《欧洲联盟公报》
		《拉脱维亚先驱报》(官方报纸)
立陶宛	-	《欧洲联盟公报》
	-	《立陶宛共和国公报》信息增刊

Luxembourg	-	Official Journal of the European Union
	-	Daily Press
Hungary	-	Official Journal of the European Union
	-	Közbeszerzési Értesítő - a Közbeszerzések Tanácsa Hivatalos Lapja (Public Procurement Bulletin - Official Journal of the Public Procurement Council)
Malta	-	Official Journal of the European Union
	-	Government Gazette
Netherlands	-	Official Journal of the European Union
Austria	-	Official Journal of the European Union
	-	Amtsblatt zur Wiener Zeitung
Poland	-	Official Journal of the European Union
		Biuletyn Zamówień Publicznych (Public Procurement Bulletin)
Portugal	-	Official Journal of the European Union
Romania	-	Official Journal of the European Union
	-	Monitorul Oficial al României (Official Journal of Romania)
	-	Electronic System for Public Procurement (www.e-licitatie.ro)
Slovenia	-	Official Journal of the European Union
		Official Gazette of the Republic of Slovenia
Slovakia	-	Official Journal of the European Union
		Vestnik verejneho obstaravania (Journal of Public Procurement)
Finland	-	Official Journal of the European Union
	-	Julkiset hankinnat Suomessa ja ETA-alueella, Virallisen lehden liite (Public Procurement in Finland and at the EEA-area, Supplement to the Official Gazette of Finland)
Sweden	-	Official Journal of the European Union
United Kingdom	-	Official Journal of the European Union

HONG KONG, CHINA

Annex 1

The Government of the Hong Kong Special Administrative Region Gazette
Daily Press

Annex 3

Hospital Authority		Any of the following:
	-	Daily Press
	-	Home Page on the Internet (http://www.ha.org.hk)
Housing Authority	-	The Government of the Hong Kong Special Administrative Region Gazette

卢森堡	-	《欧洲联盟公报》
	-	日报
匈牙利	-	《欧洲联盟公报》
	-	公共采购公告--《采购理事会公报》
马耳他	-	《欧洲联盟公报》
	-	《政府公报》
荷兰	-	《欧洲联盟公报》
奥地利	-	《欧洲联盟公报》
	-	《维也纳日报》
波兰	-	《欧洲联盟公报》
		公共采购公告
葡萄牙	-	《欧洲联盟公报》
罗马尼亚	-	《欧洲联盟公报》
	-	《罗马尼亚公报》
	-	公共采购电子系统(www.e-licitatie.ro)
斯洛文尼亚	-	《欧洲联盟公报》
		《斯洛文尼亚共和国公报》
斯洛伐克	-	《欧洲联盟公报》
		公共采购公告
芬兰	-	《欧洲联盟公报》
	-	《芬兰公报》芬兰和《欧洲经济区域协定》地区公共采购增刊
瑞典	-	《欧洲联盟公报》
英国	-	《欧洲联盟公报》

中国香港

附件 1

《香港特别行政区政府公报》
《孖剌西报》

附件 3

医院管理部门		下列任何之一：
	-	《孖剌西报》
	-	因特网主页(http://www.ha.org.hk)
住房管理部门	-	《香港特别行政区公报》

2007 年 1 月 1 日 (WT/Let/556)

Kowloon-Canton Railway Corporation	Any of the following: - The Government of the Hong Kong Special Administrative Region Gazette - Daily Press - Home Page on the Internet (http://www.kcrc.com)
MTR Corporation Limited	Any of the following: - Daily Press - Home Page on the Internet (http://www.mtr.com.hk)
Airport Authority	Any of the following: - Daily Press - Home Page on the Internet (http://www.hkairport.com)

ICELAND

Icelandic newspapers:
Morgunbladid
Dagbladid
Dagur

Other:
Official Journal of the European Communities

ISRAEL

The Jerusalem Post
International Herald Tribune - Ha'aretz

JAPAN

Annex 1

Kanpō

Annex 2

Kenpō
Shihō
or their equivalents

Annex 3

Kanpō

九广铁路公司

下列任何之一：
- 《香港特别行政区政府公报》
- 《孖剌西报》
- 因特网主页 (http://www.kcrc.com)

港铁公司

下列任何之一：
- 《孖剌西报》
- 因特网主页 (http://www.mtr.com.hk)

机场管理部门

下列任何之一：
- 《孖剌西报》
- 因特网主页 (http://www.hkairport.com)

冰岛

<u>冰岛报纸</u>：
《晨报》
《日报》
《日子》周刊

<u>其他</u>：
《欧洲共同体公报》

以色列

《耶路撒冷邮报》
《国际先驱时报 – 国土报》

日本

附件 1

《官报》

附件 2

《宪法》
《司法》
或其等效刊物

附件 3

《官报》

2007 年 1 月 1 日 (WT/Let/556)

THE REPUBLIC OF KOREA

The Korean e-Procurement System: G2B (http://www.g2b.go.kr)
and
Daily Press (if necessary)

For Entities Listed in Annex 2, The Korean e-Procurement System (G2B)
and
Internet Home Page of Each Entity

LIECHTENSTEIN

Daily Press: "Liechtensteiner Volksblatt", "Liechtensteiner Vaterland"

THE KINGDOM OF THE NETHERLANDS WITH RESPECT TO ARUBA

The Aruba Gazette "Landscourant" as well as in local newspapers

NORWAY

Official Journal of the European Communities

SINGAPORE

The Republic of Singapore Government Gazette or
The Government Electronic Business (GeBIZ)

韩国

韩国电子采购系统： http://www.g2b.go.kr
及
《日报》(如需要)

附件 2 中所列实体，韩国电子采购系统
及
各实体因特网主页

列支敦士登

日报：《列支敦士登人民报》、《列支敦士登祖国报》

荷属阿鲁巴

阿鲁巴公报《地政报》及当地报纸

挪威

《欧洲共同体公报》

新加坡

《新加坡共和国政府公报》或《政府电子商务》

SWITZERLAND

Annex 1

Swiss Official Trade Gazette

Annex 2

Official publications of every Swiss Canton (26)

Annex 3

Swiss Official Trade Gazette
Official publications of every Swiss Canton (26)

THE SEPARATE CUSTOMS TERRITORY OF TAIWAN, PENGHU, KINMEN AND MATSU

Government Procurement Gazette
Government Procurement Information System (http://web.pcc.gov.tw)

UNITED STATES

Federal Business Opportunities (http://www.fedbizopps.gov)

For entities listed in Annex 2 and relevant subcentral entities listed in Annex 3, publications utilized by state governments, such as the New York Contract Reporter

-

瑞士

附件 1

《瑞士官方贸易公报》

附件 2

瑞士各州(26 州)官方出版物

附件 3

《瑞士官方贸易公报》
瑞士各州(26 州)官方出版物

台湾、澎湖、金门、马祖单独关税区

《政府采购公报》

政府采购信息公告系统(http://web.pcc.gov.tw/)

美国

《联邦商业机遇》 (http://www.fedbizopps.gov)

附件 2 中所列实体及附件 3 中所列相关次中央实体，
各州政府使用的出版物，如《纽约合同报道者》。

APPENDICE II

PUBLICATIONS UTILISÉES PAR LES PARTIES EN VUE DE LA PUBLICATION DES AVIS DE MARCHÉS ENVISAGÉS - PARAGRAPHE 1 DE L'ARTICLE IX, ET DES AVIS POSTÉRIEURS À L'ADJUDICATION DES MARCHÉS - PARAGRAPHE 1 DE L'ARTICLE XVIII

CANADA

Marchés publics (GBO)
MERX, Cebra Inc.

COMMUNAUTÉS EUROPÉENNES

Belgique	-	Journal officiel de l'Union européenne
	-	Le Bulletin des adjudications
	-	Autres publications de la presse spécialisée
Bulgarie	-	Journal officiel de l'Union européenne
	-	Държавен вестник (Journal officiel) http://dv.parliament.bg
	-	Registre des marchés publics (www.aop.bg)
République tchèque	-	Journal officiel de l'Union européenne
Danemark	-	Journal officiel de l'Union européenne
Allemagne	-	Journal officiel de l'Union européenne
Estonie	-	Journal officiel de l'Union européenne
Grèce	-	Journal officiel de l'Union européenne
	-	Publication dans la presse quotidienne, financière, régionale et spécialisée
Espagne	-	Journal officiel de l'Union européenne
France	-	Journal officiel de l'Union européenne
	-	Bulletin officiel des annonces des marchés publics
Irlande	-	Journal officiel de l'Union européenne
	-	Presse quotidienne: "Irish Independent", "Irish Times", "Irish Press", "Cork Examiner"
Italie	-	Journal officiel de l'Union européenne
Chypre	-	Journal officiel de l'Union européenne
	-	Journal officiel de la République
	-	Presse quotidienne locale
Lettonie	-	Journal officiel de l'Union européenne
		Latvijas vēstnesis (Journal officiel)
Lituanie	-	Journal officiel de l'Union européenne
	-	Supplément d'information "Informaciniai pranešimai" au Journal officiel ("Valstybės žinios") de la République de Lituanie
Luxembourg	-	Journal officiel de l'Union européenne
	-	Presse quotidienne

Hongrie	-	Journal officiel de l'Union européenne
	-	Közbeszerzési Értesítő - a Közbeszerzések Tanácsa Hivatalos Lapja (Bulletin des marchés publics - Journal officiel du Conseil des marchés publics)
Malte	-	Journal officiel de l'Union européenne
	-	Journal officiel
Pays-Bas	-	Journal officiel de l'Union européenne
Autriche	-	Journal officiel de l'Union européenne
	-	Amtsblatt zur Wiener Zeitung
Pologne	-	Journal officiel de l'Union européenne
		Biuletyn Zamówień Publicznych (Bulletin des marchés publics)
Portugal	-	Journal officiel de l'Union européenne
Roumanie	-	Journal officiel de l'Union européenne
	-	Monitorul Oficial al României (Journal officiel de la Roumanie)
	-	Système électronique d'achats publics (www.e-licitatie.ro)
Slovénie	-	Journal officiel de l'Union européenne
		Journal officiel de la République de Slovénie
Slovaquie	-	Journal officiel de l'Union européenne
		Vestnik verejneho obstaravania (Journal des marchés publics)
Finlande	-	Journal officiel de l'Union européenne
	-	Julkiset hankinnat Suomessa ja ETA-alueella, Virallisen lehden liite (Marchés publics en Finlande et dans l'EEE, Supplément au Journal officiel de la Finlande)
Suède	-	Journal officiel de l'Union européenne
Royaume-Uni	-	Journal officiel de l'Union européenne

HONG KONG, CHINE

Annexe 1

The Government of the Hong Kong Special Administrative Region Gazette
Presse quotidienne

Annexe 3

Direction des hôpitaux		L'un ou l'autre des documents suivants:
	-	Presse quotidienne
	-	Page d'accueil sur Internet (http://www.ha.org.hk)
Direction du logement	-	The Government of the Hong Kong Special Administrative Region Gazette
	-	Presse quotidienne
Société du chemin de fer Kowloon-Canton		L'un ou l'autre des documents suivants:
	-	The Government of the Hong Kong Special Administrative Region Gazette
	-	Presse quotidienne

	-	Page d'accueil sur Internet (http://www.kcrc.com)
MTR S.A.		L'un ou l'autre des documents suivants:
	-	Presse quotidienne
	-	Page d'accueil sur Internet (http://www.mtr.com.hk)
Direction de l'aéroport		L'un ou l'autre des documents suivants:
	-	Presse quotidienne
	-	Page d'accueil sur Internet (http://www.hkairport.com)

ISLANDE

Journaux islandais:
Morgunbladid
Dagbladid
Dagur

Autre:
Journal officiel des Communautés européennes

ISRAËL

The Jerusalem Post
International Herald Tribune - Ha'aretz

JAPON

Annexe 1

Kanpō

Annexe 2

Kenpō, Shihō
ou leurs équivalents

Annexe 3

Kanpō

RÉPUBLIQUE DE CORÉE

Système coréen de passation électronique des marchés: G2B (http://www.g2b.go.kr)
et
Presse quotidienne (si nécessaire)

Pour les entités énumérées à l'Annexe 2,
Système coréen de passation électronique des marchés (G2B)
et
Page d'accueil Internet de chaque entité

LIECHTENSTEIN

Presse quotidienne: "Liechtensteiner Volksblatt", "Liechtensteiner Vaterland"

LE ROYAUME DES PAYS-BAS POUR LE COMPTE D'ARUBA

"Landscourant", Journal officiel d'Aruba, ainsi que la presse locale

NORVÈGE

Journal officiel des Communautés européennes

SINGAPOUR

The Republic of Singapore Government Gazette (Journal officiel de Singapour) ou
The Government Electronic Business (GeBIZ)

SUISSE

Annexe 1

Feuille officielle suisse du commerce

Annexe 2

Organe de publications officielles de chaque canton suisse (26)

1 January2007 (WT/Let/556)

Annexe 3

Feuille officielle suisse du commerce
Organe de publications officielles de chaque canton suisse (26)

TERRITOIRE DOUANIER DISTINCT DE TAIWAN, PENGHU, KINMEN ET MATSU

Government Procurement Gazette
Government Procurement Information System (http://web.pcc.gov.tw)

ÉTATS-UNIS

Federal Business Opportunities (http://www.fedbizopps.gov)

Pour les entités énumérées à l'annexe 2 et les entités des gouvernements sous-centraux pertinentes énumérées à l'annexe 3, publications utilisées par les gouvernements des États, comme le New York Contract Reporter

APÉNDICE II

MEDIOS UTILIZADOS POR LAS PARTES PARA LA PUBLICACIÓN DE LOS ANUNCIOS DE LOS CONTRATOS PREVISTOS - PÁRRAFO 1 DEL ARTÍCULO IX - Y LOS ANUNCIOS DE LAS ADJUDICACIONES - PÁRRAFO 1 DEL ARTÍCULO XVIII

CANADÁ

Government Business Opportunities (GBO)
MERX, Cebra Inc.

COMUNIDADES EUROPEAS

Bélgica	- Diario Oficial de la Unión Europea
	- Le Bulletin des Adjudications
	- Otras publicaciones de la prensa especializada
Bulgaria	- Diario Oficial de la Unión Europea
	- Държавен вестник (Gaceta del Estado) http://dv.parliament.bg
	- Registro de Contratación Pública (www.aop.bg)
República Checa	- Diario Oficial de la Unión Europea
Dinamarca	- Diario Oficial de la Unión Europea
Alemania	- Diario Oficial de la Unión Europea
Estonia	- Diario Oficial de la Unión Europea
Grecia	- Diario Oficial de la Unión Europea
	- Publicación en la prensa diaria, financiera, regional y especializada
España	- Diario Oficial de la Unión Europea
Francia	- Diario Oficial de la Unión Europea
	- Bulletin officiel des annonces des marchés publics
Irlanda	- Diario Oficial de la Unión Europea
	- Prensa diaria: "Irish Independent", "Irish Times", "Irish Press", "Cork Examiner"
Italia	- Diario Oficial de la Unión Europea
Chipre	- Diario Oficial de la Unión Europea
	- Gaceta Oficial de la República
	- Prensa diaria local
Letonia	- Diario Oficial de la Unión Europea
	Latvijas vēstnesis (Diario Oficial)
Lituania	- Diario Oficial de la Unión Europea
	- Suplemento informativo "Informaciniai pranešimai" de la Gaceta Oficial ("Valstybės žinios") de la República de Lituania
Luxemburgo	- Diario Oficial de la Unión Europea
	- Prensa diaria

Hungría	-	Diario Oficial de la Unión Europea
	-	Közbeszerzési Értesítő - a Közbeszerzések Tanácsa Hivatalos Lapja (Boletín de Contratación Pública - Diario Oficial del Consejo de Contratación Pública)
Malta	-	Diario Oficial de la Unión Europea
	-	Gaceta Oficial
Países Bajos	-	Diario Oficial de la Unión Europea
Austria	-	Diario Oficial de la Unión Europea
	-	Amtsblatt zur Wiener Zeitung
Polonia	-	Diario Oficial de la Unión Europea
		Biuletyn Zamówień Publicznych (Boletín de Contratación Pública)
Portugal	-	Diario Oficial de la Unión Europea
Rumania	-	Diario Oficial de la Unión Europea
	-	Monitorul Oficial al României (Diario Oficial de Rumania)
	-	Sistema Electrónico de Contratación Pública (www.e-licitatie.ro)
Eslovenia	-	Diario Oficial de la Unión Europea
		Gaceta Oficial de la República de Eslovenia
Eslovaquia	-	Diario Oficial de la Unión Europea
		Vestnik verejneho obstaravania (Boletín de Contratación Pública)
Finlandia	-	Diario Oficial de la Unión Europea
	-	Julkiset hankinnat Suomessa ja ETA-alueella, Virallisen lehden liite (Contratación pública en Finlandia y el EEE, Suplemento de la Gaceta Oficial de Finlandia)
Suecia	-	Diario Oficial de la Unión Europea
Reino Unido	-	Diario Oficial de la Unión Europea

HONG KONG, CHINA

Anexo 1

The Government of the Hong Kong Special Administrative Region Gazette
Prensa diaria

Anexo 3

Administración Hospitalaria		Cualquiera de los documentos siguientes:
	-	Prensa diaria
	-	Página Web en Internet (http://www.ha.org.hk)
Servicio de la Vivienda	-	The Government of the Hong Kong Special Administrative Region Gazette
	-	Prensa diaria
Sociedad del Ferrocarril Kowloon-Canton		Cualquiera de los documentos siguientes:
	-	The Government of the Hong Kong Special Administrative Region Gazette
	-	Prensa diaria

- Página Web en Internet (http://www.kcrc.com)

MTR S.A. Cualquiera de los documentos siguientes:
- Prensa diaria
- Página Web en Internet (http://www.mtr.com.hk)

Administración de Aeropuertos Cualquiera de los documentos siguientes:
- Prensa diaria
- Página Web en Internet (http://www.hkairport.com)

ISLANDIA

Periódicos islandeses:
Morgunbladid
Dagbladid
Dagur

Otras publicaciones:
Diario Oficial de las Comunidades Europeas

ISRAEL

The Jerusalem Post
International Herald Tribune - Ha'aretz

JAPÓN

Anexo 1

Kanpō

Anexo 2

Kenpō, Shihō, o sus equivalentes

Anexo 3

Kanpō

REPÚBLICA DE COREA

Sistema de Contratación Electrónica de Corea: G2B (http://www.g2b.go.kr)
y
Prensa diaria (si fuese necesario)

Con respecto a las entidades enumeradas en el Anexo 2,
el Sistema de Contratación Electrónica de Corea (G2B)
y
la página de cada entidad en Internet

LIECHTENSTEIN

Prensa diaria: "Liechtensteiner Volksblatt", "Liechtensteiner Vaterland"

EL REINO DE LOS PAÍSES BAJOS RESPECTO DE ARUBA

El Boletín de Aruba "Landscourant" y periódicos locales

NORUEGA

Diario Oficial de las Comunidades Europeas

SINGAPUR

Gaceta Oficial de la República de Singapur o
The Government Electronic Business (GeBIZ)

SUIZA

Anexo 1

Feuille officielle suisse du commerce

Anexo 2

Órganos oficiales de publicación de cada cantón suizo (26)

Anexo 3

Feuille officielle suisse du commerce
Órganos oficiales de publicación de cada cantón suizo (26)

TERRITORIO ADUANERO DISTINTO DE TAIWÁN, PENGHU, KINMEN Y MATSU

Government Procurement Gazette
Government Procurement Information System (http://web.pcc.gov.tw)

ESTADOS UNIDOS

Federal Business Opportunities (http://www.fedbizopps.gov)

Con respecto a las entidades indicadas en el Anexo 2 y a las entidades pertinentes a nivel subcentral enumeradas en el Anexo 3, las publicaciones utilizadas por los gobiernos de los Estados, tales como "New York Contract Reporter"

APPENDIX III
附录 3

APPENDIX III

PUBLICATIONS UTILIZED BY PARTIES FOR THE PUBLICATION ANNUALLY OF INFORMATION ON PERMANENT LISTS OF QUALIFIED SUPPLIERS IN THE CASE OF SELECTIVE TENDERING PROCEDURES – PARAGRAPH 9 OF ARTICLE IX

APPENDICE III

PUBLICATIONS UTILISEES PAR LES PARTIES EN VUE DE LA PUBLICATION ANNUELLE DE RENSEIGNEMENTS SUR LES LISTES PERMANENTES DE FOURNISSEURS QUALIFIES DANS LE CAS DES PROCEDURES SELECTIVES - PARAGRAPHE 9 DE L'ARTICLE IX

APÉNDICE III

MEDIOS UTILIZADOS POR LAS PARTES PARA LA PUBLICACIÓN ANUAL DE INFORMACIÓN SOBRE LAS LISTAS PERMANENTES DE PROVEEDORES CALIFICADOS EN CASO DE LICITACIONES SELECTIVAS - PÁRRAFO 9 DEL ARTÍCULO IX.

1 March 2000 (WT/Let/330)

附录 3

各参加方为每年公布关于在选择性招标程序中的合格供应商常设名单信息所使用的出版物--第 9 条第 9 款

2000 年 3 月 1 日 (WT/Let/330)

APPENDIX III

PUBLICATIONS UTILIZED BY PARTIES FOR THE PUBLICATION ANNUALLY OF INFORMATION ON PERMANENT LISTS OF QUALIFIED SUPPLIERS IN THE CASE OF SELECTIVE TENDERING PROCEDURES - PARAGRAPH 9 OF ARTICLE IX

CANADA

Government Business Opportunities (GBO)
MERX, Cebra Inc.

EUROPEAN COMMUNITIES

Member States do not normally operate permanent lists of suppliers and service providers. In the few cases that such lists exist, this will be published in the Official Journal of the European Communities

HONG KONG, CHINA

Annex 1

For the Environment, Transport and Works Bureau of the Government Secretariat:
Home Page on the Internet (http://www.etwb.gov.hk)

For the other Annex 1 entities:
The Government of the Hong Kong Special Administrative Region Gazette

Annex 3

Hospital Authority	-	Home Page on the Internet (http://www.ha.org.hk)
Housing Authority	-	The Government of the Hong Kong Special Administrative Region Gazette
Kowloon-Canton Railway Corporation		Any of the following:
	-	The Government of the Hong Kong Special Administrative Region Gazette
	-	Daily Press
	-	Home Page on the Internet (http://www.kcrc.com)
MTR Corporation Limited	-	Not applicable

15 August 2005 (WT/Let/496)

附录 3

各参加方为每年公布关于在选择性招标程序中的合格供应商常设名单信息所使用的出版物--第 9 条第 9 款

加拿大

《政府商业机遇》
加拿大联邦、省、市公共采购网站

欧洲共同体

成员国通常不设立货物供应商和服务提供者的常设名单。
如在少数情况下存在此类名单，将在《欧洲联盟公报》上公布。

中国香港

附件 1

对政府环境、运输和建筑署：
因特网主页 (http://www.etwb.gov.hk)

对其他附件 1 实体:
《香港特别行政区政府公报》

附件 3

医院管理部门	-	因特网主页 (http://www.ha.org.hk)
住房管理部门	-	《香港特别行政区政府公报》
九广铁路公司		下列任何之一：
	-	香港特别行政区公报
	-	《孖剌西报》
	-	因特网主页 (http://www.kcrc.com)
港铁公司	-	不适用

2005 年 8 月 15 日 (WT/Let/496)

Airport Authority - Daily Press
- Home Page on the Internet (http://www.hkairport.com)

ICELAND

Official Journal of the European Communities:
(Currently no such list exists)

ISRAEL

The Jerusalem Post
International Herald Tribune Ha'aretz

JAPAN

Annex 1

Kanpō

Annex 2

Kenpō
Shihō
or their equivalents

Annex 3

Kanpō

REPUBLIC OF KOREA

The Korean e-Procurement System: G2B (http://www.g2b.go.kr)

机场管理部门 - 《孖剌西报》
- 因特网主页
(http://www.hkairport.com)

冰岛

《欧洲共同体公报》:
(目前不存此类名单)

以色列

《耶路撒冷邮报》
《国际先驱时报 – 国土报》

日本

附件 1

《官报》

附件 2

《宪法》
《司法》
或其等效刊物

附件 3

《官报》

韩国

韩国电子采购系统: http://www.g2b.go.kr

LIECHTENSTEIN

Official Journal of the European Communities (after the entry into force of the EEA Agreement for Liechtenstein)

(Currently no such lists exist)

THE KINGDOM OF THE NETHERLANDS WITH RESPECT TO ARUBA

Non-applicable for Aruba: Aruba does not operate permanent lists of suppliers and service providers

NORWAY

Official Journal of the European Communities

SINGAPORE

The Republic of Singapore Government Gazette or
The Government Electronic Business (GeBIZ)

SWITZERLAND

Annex 1

Swiss Official Trade Gazette

Annex 2

Official publications of every Swiss Canton (26)

Annex 3

Swiss Official Trade Gazette
Official publications of every Swiss Canton (26)

列支敦士登

《欧洲共同体公报》(在《欧洲经济区域协定》对列支敦士登生效后)
(目前不存在此类名单)

荷属阿鲁巴

对阿鲁巴不适用：阿鲁巴无货物供应商和服务提供者常设名单

挪威

《欧洲共同体公报》

新加坡

《新加坡政府公报》 或
《政府电子商务》

瑞士

附件 1

《瑞士官方贸易公报》

附件 2

瑞士各州(26 州)官方出版物

附件 3

《瑞士官方贸易公报》
瑞士各州(26 州)官方出版物

2005 年 8 月 15 日 (WT/Let/496)

THE SEPARATE CUSTOMS TERRITORY OF TAIWAN, PENGHU, KINMEN AND MATSU

Government Procurement Gazette
Government Procurement Information System (http://web.pcc.gov.tw)

UNITED STATES

Federal Business Opportunities (http://www.fedbizopps.gov)

Entities in Annexes 2 and 3 of Appendix I, as an alternative to publication in the Commerce Business Daily, may provide such information directly to interested suppliers through inquiries to contact points listed in notices regarding invitations to participate

台湾、澎湖、金门、马祖单独关税区

《政府采购公报》

政府采购信息公告系统(http:// web.pcc.gov.tw/)

美国

《联邦商业机遇》 (http://www.fedbizopps.gov)

附录 1 的附件 2 和 3 中所列实体，除在《每日商讯》公布外，还可通过向邀请参与的通知中所列联络点咨询的方式向有感兴趣的供应商直接提供此类信息。

2009 年 7 月 15 日 (WT/Let/647/Add.1)

APPENDICE III

PUBLICATIONS UTILISEES PAR LES PARTIES EN VUE DE LA PUBLICATION ANNUELLE DE RENSEIGNEMENTS SUR LES LISTES PERMANENTES DE FOURNISSEURS QUALIFIES DANS LE CAS DES PROCEDURES SELECTIVES - PARAGRAPHE 9 DE L'ARTICLE IX

CANADA

Marchés publics (GBO)
MERX, Cebra Inc.

COMMUNAUTES EUROPEENNES

Les Etats membres ne tiennent pas normalement de listes permanentes de fournisseurs de produits et de services. Dans les rares cas où de telles listes existent, elles sont publiées au Journal officiel des Communautés européennes

HONG KONG, CHINE

Annexe 1

Pour le Bureau de l'environnement, des transports et des travaux publics du secrétariat du gouvernement:
Page d'accueil sur Internet (http://www.etwb.gov.hk)

Pour les autres entités figurant à l'Annexe I:
The Government of the Hong Kong Special Administrative Region Gazette

Annexe 3

Direction des hôpitaux	-	Page d'accueil sur Internet (http://www.ha.org.hk)
Direction du logement	-	The Government of the Hong Kong Special Administrative Region Gazette
Société du chemin de fer Kowloon-Canton		L'un ou l'autre des documents suivants:
	-	The Government of the Hong Kong Special Administrative Region Gazette
	-	Presse quotidienne
	-	Page d'accueil sur Internet (http://www.kcrc.com)
MTR S.A.	-	non applicable

Direction de l'aéroport	-	Presse quotidienne
	-	Home Page on the Internet (http://www.kcrc.com)

ISLANDE

Journal officiel des Communautés européennes:
(Il n'y a pas de liste pour le moment)

ISRAEL

The Jerusalem Post
International Herald Tribune - Ha'aretz

JAPON

Annexe 1

Kanpō

Annexe 2

Kenpō, Shihō
ou leurs équivalents

Annexe 3

Kanpō

REPUBLIQUE DE COREE

Système coréen de passation électronique des marchés: G2B (http://www.g2b.go.kr)

LIECHTENSTEIN

Journal officiel des Communautés européennes (à compter de l'entrée en vigueur de l'Accord sur l'EEE pour le Liechtenstein)

(Il n'existe pas actuellement de listes de cette nature)

LE ROYAUME DES PAYS-BAS POUR LE COMPTE D'ARUBA

Sans objet pour Aruba, qui n'a pas de listes permanentes de fournisseurs de services

NORVEGE

Journal officiel des Communautés européennes

SINGAPOUR

The Republic of Singapore Government Gazette (Journal officiel de Singapour) ou The Government Electronic Business (GeBIZ)

SUISSE

Annexe 1

Feuille officielle suisse du commerce

Annexe 2

Organe de publications officielles de chaque canton suisse (26)

Annexe 3

Feuille officielle suisse du commerce
Organe de publications officielles de chaque canton suisse (26)

TERRITOIRE DOUANIER DISTINCT DE TAIWAN, PENGHU, KINMEN ET MATSU

Government Procurement Gazette
Government Procurement Information System (http://web.pcc.gov.tw)

ETATS-UNIS

Federal Business Opportunities (http://www.fedbizopps.gov)

Au lieu de les faire paraître dans le Commerce Business Daily, les entités énumérées aux Annexes 2 et 3 de l'Appendice I peuvent communiquer directement ces renseignements aux fournisseurs intéressés, sur demande adressée aux services chargés des contacts désignés dans les avis utilisés pour les invitations à soumissionner

APÉNDICE III

MEDIOS UTILIZADOS POR LAS PARTES PARA LA PUBLICACIÓN ANUAL DE INFORMACIÓN SOBRE LAS LISTAS PERMANENTES DE PROVEEDORES CALIFICADOS EN CASO DE LICITACIONES SELECTIVAS - PÁRRAFO 9 DEL ARTÍCULO IX.

CANADÁ

Government Business Opportunities (GBO)
MERX, Cebra Inc.

COMUNIDADES EUROPEAS

Los Estados miembros normalmente no establecen listas permanentes de proveedores de bienes y servicios. En los pocos casos en que existe tal lista, se publicará en el Diario Oficial de las Comunidades Europeas

HONG KONG, CHINA

Anexo 1

Para la Oficina de Medio Ambiente, Transporte y Obras Públicas de la Secretaría del Gobierno:
Página de presentación en Internet (http://www.etwb.gov.hk)

Para las demás entidades del Anexo 1:
The Government of the Hong Kong Special Administrative Region Gazette

Anexo 3

Administración Hospitalaria	-	Página web en Internet (http://www.ha.org.hk)
Servicio de la Vivienda	-	The Government of the Hong Kong Special Administrative Region Gazette
Sociedad del Ferrocarril Kowloon-Canton		Cualquiera de los documentos siguientes: The Government of the Hong Kong Special Administrative Region Gazette
	-	Prensa diaria
	-	Página web en Internet (http://www.kcrc.com)
MTR S.A.	-	no aplicable

Administración de Aeropuertos - Prensa diaria
- Home Page on the Internet (http://www.kcrc.com)

ISLANDIA

Diario Oficial de las Comunidades Europeas
(Actualmente no existe esa lista)

ISRAEL

The Jerusalem Post
International herald Tribune - Ha'aretz

JAPÓN

Anexo 1

Kanpō

Anexo 2

Kenpō, Shihō, o sus equivalentes

Anexo 3

Kanpō

REPÚBLICA DE COREA

Sistema de Contratación Electrónica de Corea: G2B (http://www.g2b.go.kr)

15 August 2005 (WT/Let/496)

LIECHTENSTEIN

Diario Oficial de las Comunidades Europeas (después de la entrada en vigor del Acuerdo de la EEE para Liechtenstein)

(Actualmente no existe tal lista)

EL REINO DE LOS PAÍSES BAJOS RESPECTO DE ARUBA

No se aplica a Aruba: Aruba no mantiene listas permanentes de proveedores calificados

NORUEGA

Diario Oficial de las Comunidades Europeas

SINGAPUR

Gaceta Oficial de la República de Singapur o
The Government Electronic Business (GeBIZ)

SUIZA

Anexo 1

Feuille officielle suisse du commerce

Anexo 2

Órganos oficiales de publicación de cada cantón suizo (26)

Anexo 3

Feuille officielle suisse du commerce
Órganos oficiales de publicación de cada cantón suizo (26)

TERRITORIO ADUANERO DISTINTO DE TAIWÁN, PENGHU, KINMEN Y MATSU

Government Procurement Gazette
Government Procurement Information System (http://web.pcc.gov.tw)

ESTADOS UNIDOS

Federal Business Opportunities (http://www.fedbizopps.gov)

Las entidades incluidas en los Anexos 2 y 3 del Apéndice I, como alternativa a la publicación en el Commerce Business Daily, pueden facilitar esa información directamente a los proveedores interesados, quienes deberán dirigirse a los centros de información que se indican en los anuncios de invitaciones a participar

15 July 2009 (WT/Let/647/Add.1)

APPENDIX IV
附录 4

APPENDIX IV

PUBLICATIONS UTILIZED BY PARTIES FOR THE PUBLICATION OF LAWS, REGULATIONS, JUDICIAL DECISIONS, ADMINISTRATIVE RULINGS OF GENERAL APPLICATION AND ANY PROCEDURE REGARDING GOVERNMENT PROCUREMENT COVERED BY THIS AGREEMENT - PARAGRAPH 1 OF ARTICLE XIX

APPENDICE IV

PUBLICATIONS UTILISEES PAR LES PARTIES EN VUE DE LA PUBLICATION, DANS LES MOINDRES DELAIS, DES LOIS, REGLEMENTS, DECISIONS JUDICIAIRES, DECISIONS ADMINISTRATIVES D'APPLICATION GENERALE ET PROCEDURES, RELATIFS AUX MARCHES PUBLICS VISES PAR LE PRESENT ACCORD - PARAGRAPHE 1 DE L'ARTICLE XIX

APÉNDICE IV

MEDIOS UTILIZADOS POR LAS PARTES PARA LA PUBLICACIÓN DE LEYES, REGLAMENTOS, DECISIONES JUDICIALES Y RESOLUCIONES ADMINISTRATIVAS DE APLICACIÓN GENERAL, ASÍ COMO DE LOS PROCEDIMIENTOS PARA LA ADJUDICACIÓN DE LOS CONTRATOS PÚBLICOS COMPRENDIDOS EN EL ÁMBITO DEL PRESENTE ACUERDO - PÁRRAFO 1 DEL ARTÍCULO XIX.

1 March 2000 (WT/Let/330)

附录 4

各参加方为公布普遍适用的法律、法规、司法判决、行政裁决及本协定涵盖的任何有关政府采购程序所使用的出版物—第 19 条第 1 款

2000 年 3 月 1 日 (WT/Let/330)

APPENDIX IV

PUBLICATIONS UTILIZED BY PARTIES FOR THE PUBLICATION OF LAWS, REGULATIONS, JUDICIAL DECISIONS, ADMINISTRATIVE RULINGS OF GENERAL APPLICATION AND ANY PROCEDURE REGARDING GOVERNMENT PROCUREMENT COVERED BY THIS AGREEMENT - PARAGRAPH 1 OF ARTICLE XIX

CANADA

Laws and Regulations

Statutes of Canada
Canada Gazette

Judicial Decisions

Dominion Law Reports
Supreme Court Reports
Federal Court Reports
National Reporter

Administrative Rulings and Procedures

Government Business Opportunities
Canada Gazette
MERX, Cebra Inc.

EUROPEAN COMMUNITIES

Belgium	-	*Laws, royal regulations, ministerial regulations, ministerial circulars* - le Moniteur Belge
	-	*Jurisprudence* – Pasicrisie
Bulgaria	-	*Laws and Regulations* – Държавен вестник (State Gazette)
	-	*Judicial decisions* - www.sac.government.bg
	-	*Administrative rulings of general application and any procedure* - www.aop.bg and www.cpc.bg
Czech Republic	-	*Laws and Regulations* – Collection of Laws of the Czech Republic
	-	*Rulings of the Office for the Protection of Competition* – Collection of Rulings of the Office for the Protection of Competition
Denmark	-	*Laws and regulations* - Lovtidende
	-	*Judicial decisions* - Ugeskrift for Retsvaesen
	-	*Administrative rulings and procedures* - Ministerialtidende
	-	*Rulings by the Appeal Board for Public Procurement* – Konkurrence raaded Dokumentation

附录 4

各参加方为公布普遍适用的法律、法规、司法判决、行政裁决及本协定涵盖的任何有关政府采购程序所使用的出版物—第 19 条第 1 款

加拿大

法律和法规

加拿大法律
《加拿大公报》

司法判决

自治领法律报告
最高法院报告
联邦法院报告
国家报道者

行政裁决和程序

《政府商业机遇》
《加拿大公报》
加拿大联邦、省、市公共采购网站

欧洲共同体

比利时	-	*法律，皇家法规，部门规章，部门法令*—《比利时公报》
	-	*司法判决*—《比利时法院判决汇编》
保加利亚	-	*法律和规章*—《国家公报》
	-	*司法判决*—www.sac.government.bg
	-	*普遍适用的行政裁决和任何程序*—www.aop.bg 和 www.cpc.bg
捷克	-	*法律和法规*—《捷克共和国法律汇编》
	-	*竞争保护办公室裁决*—《保护竞争办公室裁决汇编》
丹麦	-	*法律和法规*—《公报》
	-	*司法判决*—司法部判决
	-	*行政裁决和程序*—《部长级会议公报》
	-	*公共采购上诉机构裁决*—现有竞争文件

Germany	- *Legislation and regulations* - Bundesanzeiger - *Herausgeber* : der Bundesminister der Justiz Verlag : Bundesanzeiger Bundesanzeiger Postfach 108006 5000 Köln - *Judicial Decisions*: Entscheidungsammlungen des: Bundesverfassungsgerichts; Bundesgerichtshofs; Bundesverwaltungsgerichts Bundesfinanzhofs sowie der Oberlandesgerichte
Estonia	- *Laws, regulations and administrative rulings of general application:* Riigi Teataja - *Judicial decisions of the Supreme Court of Estonia:* Riigi Teataja (part 3)
Greece	- Government Gazette of Greece - epishmh efhmerida eurwpaikwn koinothtwn
Spain	- *Legislation* - Boletin Oficial des Estado - *Judicial rulings* - no official publication
France	- *Legislation* - Journal Officiel de la République française - *Jurisprudence* - Recueil des arrêts du Conseil d'Etat - Revue des marchés publics
Ireland	- *Legislation and regulations* - Iris Oifigiuil (Official Gazette of the Irish Government)
Italy	- *Legislation* - Gazetta Ufficiale - *Jurisprudence* - no official publication
Cyprus	- *Legislation* - Official Gazette of the Republic (Επίσημη Εφημερίδα της Δημοκρατίας) - *Judicial decisions:* Decisions of the Supreme High Court – Printing Office (Αποφάσεις Ανωτάτου *Δικαστηρίου* 1999 – Τυπογραφείο της Δημοκρατίας)
Luxembourg	- *Legislation* – Memorial - *Jurisprudence* – Pasicrisie
Hungary	- *Legislation* - Magyar Közlöny (Official Journal of the Republic of Hungary) - *Jurisprudence* - Közbeszerzési Értesítő - a Közbeszerzések Tanácsa Hivatalos Lapja (Public Procurement Bulletin - Official Journal of the Public Procurement Council)
Latvia	- *Legislation* - Latvijas vēstnesis (Official Newspaper)
Lithuania	- *Laws, regulations and administrative provisions* - Official Gazette ("Valstybės Žinios") of the Republic of Lithuania - *Judicial decisions, jurisprudence* – Bulletin of the Supreme Court of Lithuania "Teismų praktika"; Bulletin of the Supreme Court of Administrative Court of Lithuania "Administracinių teismų praktika"
Malta	- *Legislation* – Government Gazette
Netherlands	- *Legislation* - Nederlandse Staatscourant and/or Staatsblad - *Jurisprudence* - no official publication

德国	-	*法律和法规*—《公告》
	-	*出版者*：联邦司法部长
		出版物：《联邦公报》
		邮箱：108006，5000，科隆
	-	*司法判决*：《联邦宪法法院裁决汇编》、《联邦法院裁决汇编》《联邦行政法院裁决汇编》、《联邦财税法院裁决汇编》
爱沙尼亚	-	*法律、法规和普遍适用的行政裁决*：《政府公报》
	-	爱沙尼亚最高法院司法判决：《政府公报》第 3 部分
希腊	-	《希腊政府公报》
西班牙	-	*法律*—《国家官方通报》
	-	司法判决—无官方出版物
法国	-	*法律*—《法兰西共和国公报》
	-	司法判决—《国务委员会判例报告》
	-	《公共采购审查》
爱尔兰	-	法律和法规—《爱尔兰政府公报》
意大利	-	*法律*—《官方公报》
	-	司法判决 –无官方出版物
塞浦路斯	-	*法律*—《共和国公报》
	-	*司法判决*：《最高法院 1999 年裁决—印刷办公室》
卢森堡	-	*法律*—《备忘录》
	-	*司法判决*—《比利时法院裁决汇编》
匈牙利	-	*法律*—《匈牙利共和国公报》
	-	*司法判决*-《公共采购理事会官方公报—公共采购信息》
拉脱维亚	-	*法律*—《拉脱维亚先驱报》
立陶宛	-	*法律，法规和行政命令*—《立陶宛公报》
	-	*司法判决*—立陶宛最高法院公告《司法实践》以及立陶宛最高行政法院公告《行政判例实践》
马耳他	-	*法律*—《政府公报》
荷兰	-	法律—《官方公报》和/或《公报》
	-	*司法判决*—无官方出版物

Austria	-	Österreichisches Bundesgesetzblatt Amtsblatt zur Wiener Zeitung Sammlung von Entscheidungen des Verfassungsgerichtshofes Sammlung der Entscheidungen des Verwaltungsgerichtshofes – administrativrechtlicher und finanzrechtlicher Teil Amtliche Sammlung der Entscheidungen des OGH in Zivilsachen
Poland	-	*Legislation* Dziennik Ustaw Rzeczypospolitej Polskiej (Journal of Laws – Republic of Poland)
	-	*Judicial decisions, jurisprudence* "Zamówienia publiczne w orzecznictwie. Wybrane orzeczenia zespołu arbitrów i Sądu Okręgowego w Warszawie" (Selection of judgments of arbitration panels and Regional Court in Warsaw)
Portugal	-	*Legislation* - Diário da República Portuguesa 1a Série A e 2a série
	-	*Judicial Publications* : Boletim do Ministério da Justiça
	-	Colectânea de Acordos do SupremoTribunal Administrativo; Colectânea de Jurisprudencia Das Relações
Romania	-	*Laws and Regulations* – Monitorul Oficial al României (Official Journal of Romania)
	-	*Judicial decisions, administrative rulings of general application and any procedure* – www.anrmap.ro
Slovenia	-	*Legislation* Official Gazette of the Republic of Slovenia
	-	*Judicial decisions* – no official publication
Slovakia	-	*Legislation* Zbierka zakonov (Collection of Laws)
	-	*Judicial decisions* – no official publication
Finland	-	Suomen Säädöskokoelma - Finlands Författningssamling (The Collection of the Statutes of Finland)
Sweden	-	Svensk Författningssamling (Swedish Code of Statutes)
United Kingdom	-	*Legislation* - HM Stationery Office
	-	*Jurisprudence* - Law Reports
	-	*"Public Bodies"* - HM Stationery Office

HONG KONG, CHINA

Annex 1

The Government of the Hong Kong Special Administrative Region Gazette

Annex 3

Hospital Authority	-	Home Page on the Internet (http://www.ha.org.hk)
Housing Authority	-	The Government of the Hong Kong Special Administrative Region Gazette
Kowloon-Canton Railway Corporation	-	provided to potential suppliers upon issuance of invitations to participate
MTR Corporation Limited	-	provided to potential suppliers upon issuance of invitations to participate

1 January 2007 (WT/Let/556)

奥地利	-	《奥地利官方公报》、《维也纳日报》 《宪法法院判决汇编》 《行政法庭判决汇编》— 《最高法院民事问题裁决汇编》
波兰	-	*法律*：波兰共和国法律
	-	*司法判决* 《华沙仲裁专家组和地区法庭裁决汇编》
葡萄牙	-	*法律*-《葡萄牙共和国公报》第 1 和第 2 系列
	-	*司法判决*:《司法部公告》
	-	《最高行政法院协定汇编》; 《欧洲法院报告》
罗马尼亚	-	*法律和法规*–《罗马尼亚公报》
	-	*司法判决，普遍适用的行政裁决和任何程序* – www.anrmap.ro
斯洛文尼亚	-	*法律* 斯洛文尼亚政府公报
	-	*司法判决*–无官方出版物
斯洛伐克	-	*法律* 《法律汇编》
	-	*司法判决* – 无官方出版物
芬兰	-	芬兰法律汇编
瑞典	-	瑞典法典
英国	-	*法律* – 皇家文书局
	-	司法判决 – 法律报告
	-	*"公共机构"* – 皇家文书局

中国香港

附件 1

香港特别行政区公报

附件 3

医院管理部门	-	因特网主页 (http://www.ha.org.hk)
住房管理部门	-	《香港特别行政区公报》
九广铁路公司	-	发出参与邀请时向潜在供应商提供
港铁公司	-	发出参与邀请时向潜在供应商提供

2007 年 1 月 1 日 (WT/Let/556)

Airport Authority - provided to potential suppliers upon issuance of invitations to participate

ICELAND

Laws, regulations and rules: Stjórnartíðindi (The Government Gazette)
Judicial decisions and administrative rulings: Hæstaréttardómar (Supreme Court Report)

(District courts do not issue a Court Report, but any interested party can obtain a transcript of a particular case. Administrative rulings are not reported but can be obtained from the relevant authority.)

ISRAEL

The Official Gazette

JAPAN

Annex 1

Kanpō
and/or
Hōreizensho

Annex 2

Kenpō
Shihō
or their equivalents,
or Kanpō
and/or
Hōreizensho

Annex 3

Kanpō
and/or
Hōreizensho

机场管理部门 - 发出参与邀请时向潜在供应商提供

冰岛

法律、法规和规定：《政府公报》
司法判决和行政裁决《最高法院报告》

(区法院不发布法庭报告，但是任何利害关系方均获得某一特定案件的审判记录。行政裁决不报道，但可从相关机构处获得。)

以色列

《官方公报》

日本

附件 1

《官报》
和/或
《法典》

附件 2

《宪法》
《司法》
或其等效刊物
或《官报》
和/或
《法典》

附件 3

《官报》
和/或
《法典》

REPUBLIC OF KOREA

Kwanbo (The Korean Government's Official Gazette)
and/or
The Korean e-Procurement System: G2B (http://www.g2b.go.kr)

LIECHTENSTEIN

Landesgesetzblatt

Liechtensteinische Entscheidsammlung
(Laws, judicial decisions, administrative rulings and procedures regarding government procurement for entities listed in Annexes 2 and 3 of Appendix I are available either through relevant local publications or directly from the listed entities.)

THE KINGDOM OF THE NETHERLANDS WITH RESPECT TO ARUBA

Aruban laws and legislations are published in the Aruban Gazette "Landscourant"

NORWAY

Norsk Lovtidend (Norwegian Law Gazette)

SINGAPORE

The Republic of Singapore Government Gazette or
The Government Electronic Business (GeBIZ)

SWITZERLAND

Compendium of Federal laws
Decisions of the Swiss Federal Court
Jurisprudence of the administrative authorities of the Confederation and every Canton (26)
Compendiums of Cantonal laws (26)

韩国

《韩国政府公报》
及/或
韩国电子采购系统：G2B (http://www.g2b.go.kr)

列支敦士登

《国家公报》

《列支敦士登决议汇编》
(附录 1 附件 2 和 3 中所列实体适用的法律、司法判决、行政裁决和有关政府采购的程序可通过相关地方出版物获得，也可直接从所列实体管理层获得。)

荷属阿鲁巴

阿鲁巴法律和法规在阿鲁巴公报《地政报》中公布

挪威

《挪威法律公报》

新加坡

《新加坡政府公报》或
《政府电子商务》

瑞士

《联邦法律汇编》
瑞士联邦法院裁决
联邦和各州(26 州)行政机构裁决
各州(26 州)法律汇编

2007 年 1 月 1 日 (WT/Let/556)

THE SEPARATE CUSTOMS TERRITORY OF TAIWAN, PENGHU, KINMEN AND MATSU

Government Gazette
Public Construction Commission (http://www.pcc.gov.tw)
Judicial decisions (http://www.judicial.gov.tw)

UNITED STATES

Laws, judicial decisions, administrative rulings and procedures regarding government procurement for entities listed in Annex 1 of Appendix I are published in the Federal Acquisition Regulations (FAR) as part of the US Code of Federal Regulations (CFR), Title 48, Chapter 1

Laws, judicial decisions, administrative rulings and procedures regarding government procurement for entities listed in Annexes 2 and 3 of Appendix I are available either through relevant state and local publications or directly from the listed entities

台湾、澎湖、金门、马祖单独关税区

《政府公报》

公共工程委员会 (http://www.pcc.gov.tw/)

司法判决(http://www.judicial.gov.tw/)

美国

对于附录 1 的附件 1 中所列实体适用的法律、司法判决、行政裁决和有关政府采购的程序在《美国联邦法典》第 48 部分第 1 章中公布。

对于附录 1 附件 2 和 3 中所列实体适用的法律、司法判决、行政裁决和有关政府采购的程序可通过相关地方出版物获得，也可直接从这些实体处获得。

APPENDICE IV

PUBLICATIONS UTILISÉES PAR LES PARTIES EN VUE DE LA PUBLICATION, DANS LES MOINDRES DÉLAIS, DES LOIS, RÈGLEMENTS, DÉCISIONS JUDICIAIRES, DÉCISIONS ADMINISTRATIVES D'APPLICATION GÉNÉRALE ET PROCÉDURES, RELATIFS AUX MARCHÉS PUBLICS VISÉS PAR LE PRÉSENT ACCORD - PARAGRAPHE 1 DE L'ARTICLE XIX

CANADA

Lois et règlements

Lois du Canada
Gazette du Canada

Décisions judiciaires

Dominion Law Reports
Recueil des arrêts de la Cour suprême
Recueil des arrêts de la Cour fédérale
National Reporter

Décisions administratives et procédures

Marchés publics (GBO)
Gazette du Canada
MERX, Cebra Inc.

COMMUNAUTÉS EUROPÉENNES

Belgique	-	*Lois, arrêtés royaux, arrêtés ministériels, circulaires ministérielles* - le Moniteur belge
	-	*Jurisprudence* - Pasicrisie
Bulgarie	-	*Lois et règlements* – Държавен вестник (Journal officiel)
	-	*Décisions judiciaires* - www.sac.government.bg
	-	*Décisions administratives d'application générale et toute procédure* - www.aop.bg and www.cpc.bg
République tchèque	-	*Lois et règlements* - Recueil des lois de la République tchèque
	-	*Décisions de l'Office de la protection de la concurrence* - Recueil des décisions de l'Office de la protection de la concurrence
Danemark	-	*Lois et arrêtés* - Lovtidende
	-	*Décisions judiciaires* - Ugeskrift for Retsvaesen
	-	*Décisions et procédures administratives* - Ministerialtidende
	-	*Décisions de la Commission de recours en matière de marchés publics* - Konkurrence raaded Dokumentation

Allemagne	-	*Législation et règlements* - Bundesanzeiger
	-	*Éditeur*: der Bundesminister der Justiz Verlag: Bundesanzeiger Bundesanzeiger Postfach 108006 5000 Cologne
	-	*Décisions judiciaires*: Entscheidungsammlungen des: Bundesverfassungsgerichts; Bundesgerichtshofs; Bundesverwaltungsgerichts Bundesfinanzhofs sowie der Oberlandesgerichte
Estonie	-	*Lois, règlements et décisions administratives d'application générale* Riigi Teataja
	-	*Décisions judiciaires de la Cour suprême d'Estonie:* Riigi Teataja (partie 3)
Grèce	-	Journal officiel de la Grèce - epishmh efhmerida eurwpaikwn koinothtwn
Espagne	-	*Législation* - Boletín Oficial des Estado
	-	*Décisions judiciaires* - pas de publication officielle
France	-	*Législation* - Journal officiel de la République française
	-	*Jurisprudence* - Recueil des arrêts du Conseil d'État
	-	Revue des marchés publics
Irlande	-	*Législation et règlements* - Iris Oifigiuil (Journal officiel du gouvernement irlandais)
Italie	-	*Législation* - Gazetta Ufficiale
	-	*Jurisprudence* - pas de publication officielle
Chypre	-	*Législation* - Journal officiel de la République (Επίσημη Εφημερίδα της Δημοκρατίας)
	-	*Décisions judiciaires*: Décisions de la Haute Cour suprême - Imprimerie Office (Αποφάσεις Ανωτάτου Δικαστηρίου 1999 - Τυπογραφείο της Δημοκρατίας)
Luxembourg	-	*Législation* - Mémorial
	-	*Jurisprudence* - Pasicrisie
Hongrie	-	*Législation* - Magyar Közlöny (Journal officiel de la République de Hongrie)
	-	*Jurisprudence* - Közbeszerzési Értesítő - a Közbeszerzések Tanácsa Hivatalos Lapja (Bulletin des marchés publics - Journal officiel du Conseil des marchés publics)
Lettonie	-	*Législation* - Latvijas vēstnesis (Journal officiel)
Lituanie	-	*Lois, règlements et dispositions administratives* - Journal officiel ("Valstybės Žinios") de la République de Lituanie
	-	*Décisions judiciaires, jurisprudence* - Bulletin de la Cour suprême de Lituanie "Teismų praktika"; Bulletin de la Cour suprême du Tribunal administratif de Lituanie "Administracinių teismų praktika"
Malte	-	*Législation* - Journal officiel
Pays-Bas	-	*Législation* - Nederlandse Staatscourant et/ou Staatsblad
	-	*Jurisprudence* - pas de publication officielle

Autriche - Österreichisches Bundesgesetzblatt Amtsblatt zur Wiener Zeitung Sammlung von Entscheidungen des Verfassungsgerichtshofes Sammlung der Entscheidungen des Verwaltungsgerichtshofes - administrativrechtlicher und finanzrechtlicher Teil Amtliche Sammlung der Entscheidungen des OGH in Zivilsachen

Pologne - *Législation* Dziennik Ustaw Rzeczypospolitej Polskiej (Journal officiel - République de Pologne)
- *Décisions judiciaires, jurisprudence* "Zamówienia publiczne w orzecznictwie. Wybrane orzeczenia zespołu arbitrów i Sądu Okręgowego w Warszawie" (Recueil des décisions de la cour d'arbitrage et du Tribunal régional de Varsovie)

Portugal - *Législation* - Diário da República Portuguesa 1a série A e 2a série
- *Publications judiciaires*: Boletim do Ministério da Justiça
- Colectânea de Acordos do SupremoTribunal Administrativo; Colectânea de Jurisprudencia Das Relações

Roumanie - *Lois et règlements* – Monitorul Oficial al României (Journal officiel de la Roumanie)
- *Décisions judiciaires, décisions administratives d'application générale et toute procédure* – www.anrmap.ro

Slovénie - *Législation* – Journal officiel de la République de Slovénie
- *Décisions judiciaires* – pas de publication officielle

Slovaquie - *Législation* Zbierka zakonov (Recueil des lois)
- *Décisions judiciaires* - pas de publication officielle

Finlande - Suomen Säädöskokoelma - Finlands Författningssamling (Recueil des lois et règlements de la Finlande)

Suède - Svensk Författningssamling (Bulletin national des lois suédoises)

Royaume-Uni - *Législation* – HM Stationery Office (Office des publications de Sa Majesté)
- *Jurisprudence* – Law Reports
- *Organismes publics ("Public Bodies")* – HM Stationery Office (Office des publications de Sa Majesté)

HONG KONG, CHINE

Annexe 1

The Government of the Hong Kong Special Administrative Region Gazette

Annexe 3

Direction des hôpitaux - Page d'accueil sur Internet (http://www.ha.org.hk)

Direction du logement - The Government of the Hong Kong Special Administrative Region Gazette

Société du chemin de fer Kowloon-Canton - Communiquée aux fournisseurs potentiels dès la parution des invitations à participer

MTR S.A.	-	Communiquée aux fournisseurs potentiels dès la parution des invitations à participer
Direction de l'aéroport	-	Communiquée aux fournisseurs potentiels dès la parution des invitations à participer

ISLANDE

Lois, règlements et règles:	Stjórnartíðindi (Journal officiel)
Décisions judiciaires et administratives:	Hæstaréttardómar (Rapport de la Cour suprême)

(Les tribunaux de district ne publient pas de rapport, mais toute partie intéressée peut obtenir le compte rendu officiel d'une affaire donnée. Les décisions administratives ne font pas l'objet de rapports mais peuvent être obtenues auprès de l'autorité compétente.)

ISRAEL

The Official Gazette

JAPON

Annexe 1

Kanpō et/ou Hōreizensho

Annexe 2

Kenpō, Shihō ou leurs équivalents, ou Kanpō et/ou Hōreizensho

Annexe 3

Kanpō et/ou Hōreizensho

REPUBLIQUE DE CORÉE

Kwanbo (Journal officiel du gouvernement coréen)
et/ou
Système coréen de passation électronique des marchés: G2B (http://www.g2b.go.kr)

LIECHTENSTEIN

Landesgesetzblatt

Liechtensteinische Entscheidsammlung

(Les lois, décisions judiciaires, décisions administratives et procédures relatives aux marchés publics passés par les entités mentionnées aux annexes 2 et 3 de l'Appendice I sont accessibles, soit dans les publications locales y relatives, soit directement auprès desdites entités.)

LE ROYAUME DES PAYS-BAS POUR LE COMPTE D'ARUBA

Les lois et dispositions législatives sont publiées au Journal officiel d'Aruba, "Landscourant"

NORVÈGE

Norsk Lovtidend (Bulletin des lois de la Norvège)

SINGAPOUR

The Republic of Singapore Government Gazette (Journal officiel de Singapour) ou
The Government Electronic Business (GeBIZ)

SUISSE

Recueil des lois fédérales
Arrêts du Tribunal fédéral suisse
Jurisprudence des autorités administratives de la Confédération et de chaque canton (26)
Recueils des lois cantonales (26)

**TERRITOIRE DOUANIER DISTINCT DE TAIWAN,
PENGHU, KINMEN ET MATSU**

Government Gazette
Public Construction Commission (http://www.pcc.gov.tw)
Judicial decisions (http://www.judicial.gov.tw)

ÉTATS-UNIS

Les lois, décisions judiciaires, décisions administratives et procédures relatives aux marchés publics passés par les entités énumérées à l'annexe 1 de l'Appendice I sont publiées dans les règlements relatifs aux achats fédéraux (Federal Acquisition Regulations (FAR)), qui figurent au Titre 48, Chapitre premier, du Code des règlements fédéraux (United States Code of Federal Regulations (CFR))

Les lois, décisions judiciaires, décisions administratives et procédures relatives aux marchés publics passés par les entités mentionnées aux annexes 2 et 3 de l'Appendice I sont accessibles soit dans les publications y relatives des États et des collectivités locales soit directement auprès desdites entités

APÉNDICE IV

MEDIOS UTILIZADOS POR LAS PARTES PARA LA PUBLICACIÓN DE LEYES, REGLAMENTOS, DECISIONES JUDICIALES Y RESOLUCIONES ADMINISTRATIVAS DE APLICACIÓN GENERAL, ASÍ COMO DE LOS PROCEDIMIENTOS PARA LA ADJUDICACIÓN DE LOS CONTRATOS PÚBLICOS COMPRENDIDOS EN EL ÁMBITO DEL PRESENTE ACUERDO - PÁRRAFO 1 DEL ARTÍCULO XIX

CANADÁ

Leyes y reglamentos

Statutes of Canada
Canada Gazette

Decisiones judiciales

Dominion Law Reports
Supreme Court Reports
Federal Court Reports
National Reporter

Resoluciones y procedimientos administrativos

Government Business Opportunities
Canada Gazette
MERX, Cebra Inc.

COMUNIDADES EUROPEAS

Bélgica	-	*Leyes, disposiciones reales, disposiciones ministeriales, circulares administrativas* - le Moniteur Belge
	-	*Jurisprudencia* - Pasicrisie
Bulgaria	-	*Leyes y reglamentos* - Държавен вестник (Gaceta del Estado)
	-	*Decisiones judiciales* - www.sac.government.bg
	-	*Rosoluciones administrativas de aplicación general y procedimientos* - www.aop.bg and www.cpc.bg
República Checa	-	*Leyes y reglamentos* - Colección de leyes de la República Checa
	-	*Reglamentos de la Oficina de Protección de la Competencia* - Colección de resoluciones de la Oficina de Protección de la Competencia

Dinamarca	-	*Leyes y reglamentos* - Lovtidende
	-	*Decisiones judiciales* - Ugeskrift for Retsvaesen
	-	*Resoluciones y procedimientos administrativos* - Ministerialtidende
	-	*Decisiones de la Junta de Apelación de la Contratación Pública* - Konkurrence raaded Dokumentation
Alemania	-	*Leyes y reglamentos* - Bundesanzeiger
	-	*Herausgeber* : der Bundesminister der Justiz Verlag : Bundesanzeiger Bundesanzeiger Postfach 108006 5000 Köln
	-	*Decisiones Judiciales*: Entscheidungsammlungen des: Bundesverfassungsgerichts; Bundesgerichtshofs; Bundesverwaltungsgerichts Bundesfinanzhofs sowie der Oberlandesgerichte
Estonia	-	*Leyes, reglamentos y resoluciones administrativas de aplicación general:* Riigi Teataja
	-	*Decisiones judiciales del Tribunal Supremo de Estonia:* Riigi Teataja (parte 3)
Grecia	-	Diario Oficial de Grecia - epishmh efhmerida eurwpaikwn koinothtwn
España	-	*Legislación* - Boletín Oficial del Estado
	-	*Decisiones judiciales* - no existe publicación oficial
Francia	-	*Legislación* - Journal Officiel de la République française
	-	*Jurisprudencia* - Recueil des arrêts du Conseil d'Etat
	-	Revue des marchés publics
Irlanda	-	*Leyes y reglamentos* - Iris Oifigiuil (Diario Oficial del Gobierno de Irlanda)
Italia	-	*Legislación* - Gazetta Ufficiale
	-	*Jurisprudencia* - no existe publicación oficial
Chipre	-	*Legislación* - Gaceta Oficial de la República (Επίσημη Εφημερίδα της Δημοκρατίας)
	-	*Decisiones judiciales:* Decisiones del Tribunal Supremo - Oficina de publicaciones (Αποφάσεις Ανωτάτου *Δικαστηρίου* 1999 - Τυπογραφείο της Δημοκρατίας)
Luxemburgo	-	*Legislación* - Memorial
	-	*Jurisprudencia* - Pasicrisie
Hungary	-	*Legislación* - Magyar Közlöny (Diario Oficial de la República de Hungría)
	-	*Jurisprudencia* - Közbeszerzési Értesítő - a Közbeszerzések Tanácsa Hivatalos Lapja (Boletín de Contratación Pública - Diario Oficial del Consejo de Contratación Pública)
Letonia	-	*Legislación* - Latvijas vēstnesis (Diario Oficial)
Lituania	-	*Leyes, reglamentos y disposiciones administrativas* - Gaceta Oficial ("Valstybės Žinios") de la República de Lituania
	-	*Decisiones judiciales, jurisprudencia* - Boletín del Tribunal Supremo de Lituania "Teismų praktika"; Boletín del Tribunal Supremo del Tribunal Administrativo de Lituania "Administracinių teismų praktika"

Malta	-	*Legislación* - Gaceta Oficial
Países Bajos	-	*Legislación* - Nederlandse Staatscourant y/o Staatsblad
	-	*Jurisprudencia* - no existe publicación oficial
Austria	-	Österreichisches Bundesgesetzblatt Amtsblatt zur Wiener Zeitung Sammlung von Entscheidungen des Verfassungsgerichtshofes Sammlung der Entscheidungen des Verwaltungsgerichtshofes - administrativrechtlicher und finanzrechtlicher Teil Amtliche Sammlung der Entscheidungen des OGH in Zivilsachen
Polonia	-	*Legislación* - Dziennik Ustaw Rzeczypospolitej Polskiej (Diario Legislativo - República de Polonia)
	-	*Decisiones judiciales, jurisprudencia* "Zamówienia publiczne w orzecznictwie. Wybrane orzeczenia zespołu arbitrów i Sądu Okręgowego w Warszawie" (Selección de decisiones de órganos arbitrales y del Tribunal Regional de Varsovia)
Portugal	-	*Legislación* - Diário da República Portuguesa 1a Série A e 2a série
	-	*Publicaciones judiciales* : Boletim do Ministério da Justiça
	-	Colectânea de Acordos do SupremoTribunal Administrativo; Colectânea de Jurisprudencia Das Relações
Rumania	-	*Leyes y reglamentos* - Monitorul Oficial al României (Diario Oficial de Rumania)
	-	*Decisiones judiciales, resoluciones administrativas de aplicación general y procedimientos* - www.anrmap.ro
Eslovenia	-	*Legislación* - Gaceta Oficial de la República de Eslovenia
	-	*Decisiones judiciales* - no existe publicación oficial
Eslovaquia	-	*Legislación* - Zbierka zakonov (Colección de leyes)
	-	*Decisiones judiciales* - no existe publicación oficial
Finlandia	-	Suomen Säädöskokoelma - Finlands Författningssamling (Colección de leyes de Finlandia)
Suecia	-	Svensk Författningssamling (Colección legislativa de Suecia)
Reino Unido	-	*Legislación* - HM Stationery Office
	-	*Jurisprudencia* - Law Reports
	-	*"Organismos Públicos"* - HM Stationery Office

HONG KONG, CHINA

Anexo 1

The Government of the Hong Kong Special Administrative Region Gazette

Anexo 3

Administración Hospitalaria	-	Página Web en Internet (http://www.ha.org.hk)
Servicio de la Vivienda	-	The Government of the Hong Kong Special Administrative Region Gazette
Sociedad del Ferrocarril Kowloon-Canton	-	se suministra a los proveedores potenciales con las invitaciones a participar

MTR S.A. - se suministra a los proveedores potenciales con las invitaciones a participar

Administración de Aeropuertos - se suministra a los proveedores potenciales con las invitaciones a participar

ISLANDIA

Leyes, reglamentos y normas: Stjórnartíðindi (Gaceta Oficial)

Decisiones judiciales y resoluciones administrativas: Hæstaréttardómar (Informe del Tribunal Supremo)

(Los tribunales de distrito no publican informes, pero toda parte interesada puede obtener una copia del documento original relativo a un determinado caso. Las resoluciones administrativas no se publican, pero pueden obtenerse dirigiéndose a la autoridad competente.)

ISRAEL

The Official Gazette

JAPÓN

Anexo 1

Kanpō y/o Hōreizensho

Anexo 2

Kenpō, Shihō o sus equivalentes, o Kanpō y/o Hōreizensho

Anexo 3

Kanpō y/o Hōreizensho

REPÚBLICA DE COREA

Kwanbo (Diario Oficial del Gobierno de Corea)
y/o
Sistema de Contratación Electrónica de Corea: G2B (http://www.g2b.go.kr)

1 January 2007 (WT/Let/556)

LIECHTENSTEIN

Landesgesetzblatt

Liechtensteinische Entscheidsammlung

(Se pueden obtener las leyes, decisiones judiciales, resoluciones administrativas y procedimientos para la adjudicación de los contratos públicos de las entidades enumeradas en los Anexos 2 y 3 del Apéndice I, mediante la consulta de las publicaciones locales pertinentes o solicitando directamente la información a las entidades incluidas en esos anexos.)

EL REINO DE LOS PAÍSES BAJOS RESPECTO DE ARUBA

La legislación de Aruba se publica en el Boletín de Aruba "Landscourant"

NORUEGA

Norsk Lovtidend (Gaceta Oficial de Noruega)

SINGAPUR

Gaceta Oficial de la República de Singapur o
The Government Electronic Business (GeBIZ)

SUIZA

Recueil des lois fédérales
Arrêts du Tribunal fédéral suisse
Jurisprudencia de las autoridades administrativas de la Confederación y de cada cantón (26)
Colecciones legislativas cantonales (26)

TERRITORIO ADUANERO DISTINTO DE TAIWÁN, PENGHU, KINMEN Y MATSU

Government Gazette
Public Construction Commission (http://www.pcc.gov.tw)
Judicial decisions (http://www.judicial.gov.tw)

ESTADOS UNIDOS

Las leyes, decisiones judiciales, resoluciones administrativas y procedimientos referentes a los contratos públicos de entidades incluidas en el Anexo 1 del Apéndice I se publican en el Federal Acquisition Regulations (FAR), como parte del Code of Federal Regulations (CFR) de los Estados Unidos, título 48, capítulo 1

Las leyes, decisiones judiciales, resoluciones administrativas y procedimientos referentes a los contratos públicos de entidades incluidas en los Anexos 2 y 3 del Apéndice I se pueden obtener o bien consultando las publicaciones estatales y locales pertinentes o bien solicitando la información directamente a las entidades incluidas en dichos Anexos

15 July 2009 (WT/Let/647/Add.1)

REVISION OF THE AGREEMENT ON GOVERNMENT PROCUREMENT

1994年政府采购协定修改本

说明

根据《1994年政府采购协定》的规定，协定参加方于1997年开始进行谈判。谈判的目的有三个：一是参照信息技术和采购方法的进展情况，改善和更新协定文本；二是扩大各协定参加方涵盖范围，即进一步扩大政府采购实体开放清单；三是消除现存的歧视性措施。谈判还旨在便利其他WTO成员加入协定，特别是发展中国家成员。

2006年12月，各参加方就《1994年政府采购协定》修改本达成谅解，形成临时议定文本(Provisionally Agreed Text)。之所以称之为“临时议定文本”是因为：第一，文本需要进行法律核对；第二，生效日期取决于各参加方涵盖范围谈判的结果。

修改本包括对《1994年政府采购协定》的全面修改，目的在于使协定更易于运用。还考虑到了目前政府采购做法方面的发展情况，包括采购过程中电子工具的使用。一些条款包含了更多的灵活性，如缩短了采购商业市场可获得的货物和服务的时限。给予发展中国家特殊和差别待遇的规定更为明确，以便利这些国家未来加入协定。修改本对于供应商质疑的国内审议程序和修改涵盖范围的规则更为关注。对于修改涵盖范围问题，各参加方同意制定仲裁程序以解决分歧。

各参加方原预计全部谈判可于 2007 年结束，因此将修改本称为《2007 年政府采购协定》。但是，这一谈判目前仍在进行之中，修改本的具体生效日期待定。然而各参加方已经同意，修改本应作为正在谈判加入和今后加入协定的 WTO 成员的基础。

World Trade Organization

GPA/W/297
11 December 2006

(06-5935)

Committee on Government Procurement

REVISION OF THE AGREEMENT ON GOVERNMENT PROCUREMENT AS AT 8 DECEMBER 2006

Prepared by the Secretariat

This document contains the text of the revision of the 1994 Agreement on Government Procurement which was referred to by the Chairman of the Committee on Government Procurement in the formal meeting of the Committee on the afternoon of Friday, 8 December 2006.[1]

Table of Contents

[1] See paragraphs 20-21 of the Committee's Report to the General Council (GPA/89 of 11 December 2006).

世界贸易组织

GPA/W/297
2006 年 12 月 11 日

(06-5935)

政府采购委员会

《政府采购协定》修改本

2006 年 12 月 8 日

秘书处起草

本文件包含政府采购委员会主席在 2006 年 12 月 8 日(五)下午委员会正式会议上提及的《1994 年政府采购协定》修改本文本。[1]

目录

[1] 见委员会提交总理事会的报告(2006 年 12 月 11 日 GPA/89 号文件)第 20-21 段。

Preamble

Parties to this Agreement (hereinafter referred to as "Parties"),

Recognizing the need for an effective multilateral framework for government procurement, with a view to achieving greater liberalization and expansion of, and improving the framework for, the conduct of international trade;

Recognizing that measures regarding government procurement should not be prepared, adopted or applied so as to afford protection to domestic suppliers, goods, or services, or to discriminate among foreign suppliers, goods, or services;

Recognizing that the integrity and predictability of government procurement systems are integral to the efficient and effective management of public resources, the performance of the Parties' economies, and the functioning of the multilateral trading system;

Recognizing that the procedural commitments under this Agreement should be sufficiently flexible to accommodate the specific circumstances of each Party;

Recognizing the need to take into account the development, financial, and trade needs of developing countries, in particular the least-developed countries;

Recognizing the importance of transparent measures regarding government procurement, of carrying out procurements in a transparent and impartial manner, and of avoiding conflicts of interest and corrupt practices, in accordance with applicable international instruments, such as the United Nations Convention Against Corruption;

Recognizing the importance of using, and encouraging the use of, electronic means for procurement covered by this Agreement;

Desiring to encourage acceptance of and accession to this Agreement by WTO Members not party to it;

Having undertaken further negotiations in pursuance of these objectives;

Hereby *agree* as follows:

Article I Definitions

For purposes of this Agreement:

(a) **commercial goods and services** means goods and services of a type generally sold or offered for sale in the commercial marketplace to, and customarily purchased by, non-governmental buyers for non-governmental purposes;

(b) **construction services contract** means a contract that has as its objective the realization by whatever means of civil or building works, based on Division 51 of the Provisional U.N. Central Product Classification (CPC);

(c) **country or countries** include any separate customs territory that is a Party to this Agreement. In the case of a separate customs territory that is a Party to this Agreement, where an expression in this Agreement is qualified by the term "national", such expression shall be read as pertaining to that customs territory, unless otherwise specified;

序言

本协定各参加方(以下简称“各参加方”),

*认识到*需要就政府采购建立一个有效的多边框架，以期实现国际贸易更大程度的自由化和扩大、改善进行国际贸易的框架；

*认识到*有关政府采购的措施的制定、采用或适用不应对国内供应商、货物或服务提供保护，也不应在国外供应商、货物或服务之间造成歧视；

*认识到*政府采购制度的完整性和可预见性对公共资源管理的效率和效力、对各参加方经济的运行和多边贸易体制运转的必要性；

*认识到*本协定项下的程序性承诺应充分灵活以适应每一参加方的特殊情况；

*认识到*需要考虑发展中国家、特别是最不发达国家的发展、财政和贸易需要；

*认识到*有关政府采购的透明的措施的重要性，以透明和公正的方式实施采购的重要性，以及依照《联合国反腐败公约》等适用的国际文件避免利益冲突和腐败行为的重要性；

*认识到*对本协定涵盖采购使用和鼓励使用电子方式的重要性；

*期望*鼓励未参加本协定的 WTO 成员接受和加入本协定；

为追求这些目标而*承诺*进行进一步谈判；

特此*协议*如下：

第 1 条　　定义

就本协定而言：

(a) **商业货物和服务**指在商业性市场中普遍销售或标价出售的货物和服务，且通常由非政府购买者为非政府目的而购买；

(b) **建筑服务合同**指根据《联合国临时中央产品分类》(CPC)第 51 类，以通过任何土木或建筑工程手段实现其目的的合同；

(c) **国家**包含为包括属本协定参加方的任何单独关税区。对于本协定的单独关税区参加方，如本协定的措辞被冠以“国家(的)”一词，则此措辞应被理解为与该单独关税区有关，除非另有规定；

(d) **days** means calendar days;

(e) **electronic auction** means an iterative process that involves the use of electronic means for the presentation by suppliers of either new prices, or new values for quantifiable non-price elements of the tender related to the evaluation criteria, or both, resulting in a ranking or re-ranking of tenders;

(f) **in writing** or **written** means any worded or numbered expression that can be read, reproduced, and later communicated. It may include electronically transmitted and stored information;

(g) **limited tendering** means a procurement method where the procuring entity contacts a supplier or suppliers of its choice;

(h) **measure** means any law, regulation, procedure, administrative guidance or practice, or any action of a procuring entity relating to a covered procurement;

(i) **multi-use list** means a list of suppliers that a procuring entity has determined satisfy the conditions for participation in that list, and that the procuring entity intends to use more than once;

(j) **notice of intended procurement** means a notice published by a procuring entity inviting interested suppliers to submit a request for participation, a tender, or both;

(k) **offsets** means any condition or undertaking that encourages local development or improves a Party's balance-of-payments accounts, such as the use of domestic content, the licensing of technology, investment, counter-trade, and similar actions or requirements;

(l) **open tendering** means a procurement method where all interested suppliers may submit a tender;

(m) **person** means a natural person or a juridical person;

(n) **procuring entity** means an entity covered under Annex 1, 2, or 3 of Appendix I of each Party;

(o) **qualified supplier** means a supplier that a procuring entity recognizes as having satisfied the conditions for participation;

(p) **selective tendering** means a procurement method where only suppliers satisfying the conditions for participation are invited by the procuring entity to submit a tender;

(q) **services** includes construction services, unless otherwise specified;

(r) **standard** means a document approved by a recognized body, that provides, for common and repeated use, rules, guidelines, or characteristics for goods or services, or related processes and production methods, with which compliance is not mandatory. It may also include or deal exclusively with terminology, symbols, packaging, marking, or labelling requirements as they apply to a good, service, process, or production method;

(d) 日指日历日；

(e) **电子拍卖**指涉及使用电子方式供供应商展示新价格或与估价标准有关的可量化的投标中非价格因素的新价值或两者兼有，从而产生投标排序或重新排序的迭代过程；

(f) **以书面形式**或**书面的**指以任何可阅读、复制和传达的文字形式措辞或数字形式措辞。可包括以电子方式传输和存储的信息；

(g) **有限招标**指采购实体选择与一个或多个供应商进行接触的采购方法；

(h) **措施**指与涵盖采购有关的任何法律、法规、程序、行政指南或做法，或采购实体的任何行动；

(i) **常用清单**指采购实体已确定符合列入条件，且采购实体有意使用一次以上的供应商清单；

(j) **意向采购通知**指采购实体公布的、邀请感兴趣的供应商提交参加请求、投标或两者兼有的通知；

(k) **补偿**指鼓励当地发展或改善一参加方国际收支账户的任何条件或承诺，如使用当地含量、技术许可、投资、反向贸易及类似行动或要求；

(l) **公开招标**指所有感兴趣的供应商均可提交投标书的采购方法；

(m) **人**指自然人或法人；

(n) **采购实体**指每一参加方附录 1 的附件 1、2 或 3 所涵盖的实体；

(o) **合格供应商**指采购实体承认符合参加条件的供应商；

(p) **选择性招标**指采购实体仅邀请符合条件的供应商进行投标的采购方法；

(q) **服务**包括建筑服务，除非另有规定；

(r) **标准**指经公认机构批准的、规定非强制执行的、供通用或重复使用的货物或相关工艺或生产方法的规则、指南或特性的文件。该文件还可包括或专门关于适用于货物、服务、工艺或生产方法的专门术语、符号、包装、标志或标签要求；

(s) **supplier** means a person or group of persons that provides or could provide goods or services;

(t) **technical specification** means a tendering requirement that:

(i) lays down the characteristics of goods or services to be procured, including quality, performance, safety, and dimensions, or the processes and methods for their production or provision; or

(ii) addresses terminology, symbols, packaging, marking, or labelling requirements, as they apply to a good or service.

Article II Scope and Coverage

Application of Agreement

1. This Agreement applies to any measure regarding covered procurement, whether or not it is conducted exclusively or partially by electronic means.

2. For the purposes of this Agreement, covered procurement means procurement for governmental purposes:

(a) of goods, services, or any combination thereof:

(i) as specified in each Party's Appendix I; and

(ii) not procured with a view to commercial sale or resale, or for use in the production or supply of goods or services for commercial sale or resale;

(b) by any contractual means, including purchase; lease; and rental or hire purchase, with or without an option to buy;

(c) for which the value, as estimated in accordance with paragraphs 6 through 8, equals or exceeds the relevant threshold specified in Appendix I, at the time of publication of a notice in accordance with Article VII;

(d) by a procuring entity; and

(e) that is not otherwise excluded from coverage in paragraph 3 or in a Party's Appendix I.

3. Except where provided otherwise in a Party's Appendix I, this Agreement does not apply to:

(a) the acquisition or rental of land, existing buildings, or other immovable property or the rights thereon;

(b) non-contractual agreements or any form of assistance that a Party provides, including cooperative agreements, grants, loans, equity infusions, guarantees, and fiscal incentives;

(c) the procurement or acquisition of fiscal agency or depository services, liquidation and management services for regulated financial institutions, or services related to the sale, redemption and distribution of public debt, including loans and government bonds, notes and other securities;

(s) **供应商**指提供或能够提供货物或服务的一个人或一组人；

(t) **技术规格**指下列招标要求：

(i) 规定拟购货物或服务的特征，包括质量、性能、安全和体积、符号、术语、包装、标志和标签，或生产或提供的工艺和方法；或

(ii) 关于适用于货物或服务的术语、符号、包装、标志或标签要求。

第 2 条 范围

协定的适用

1. 本协定适用于有关涵盖采购的任何措施，无论该项采购是否全部或部分通过电子方式进行。

2. 就本协定而言，涵盖采购指为政府目的而进行的下列采购：

(a) 货物、服务或货物和服务的任何组合：

(i) 在每一参加方附录 1 中列明；及

(ii) 不以商业销售或转售或用于供商业销售或转售的商品或服务的生产为目的进行的采购；

(b) 通过任何契约方式进行，包括购买、租赁、租购，无论有无购买选择权；

(c) 在依照第 7 条公布通知时，依照第 6 至 8 款估计的价值等于或超过附录 1 中列明的有关最低限额；

(d) 由采购实体进行；及

(e) 未经第 3 款或在一参加方附录 1 中涵盖范围中排除。

3. 除一参加方附录 1 中另有规定外，本协定不适用于：

(a) 土地、现存建筑或其他不动产或其权利的收购或出租；

(b) 非契约性协议或一参加方提供的任何形式的援助，包括合作协议、授予、贷款、股份权益注入、担保及财政激励；

(c) 财务代理或储蓄服务、受控制金融机构的清算和管理服务、或与公债销售、回购和发行有关的服务的采购或收购，包括贷款、政府债券、票据及其他有价证券；

(d) public employment contracts;

(e) procurement conducted:

(i) for the specific purpose of providing international assistance, including development aid;

(ii) under the particular procedure or condition of an international agreement relating to the stationing of troops or relating to the joint implementation by the signatory countries of a project; or

(iii) under the particular procedure or condition of an international organization, or funded by international grants, loans, or other assistance where the applicable procedure or condition would be inconsistent with this Agreement.

4. Each Party shall specify the following information in its Appendix I annexes[2]:

(a) in Annex 1, the central government entities whose procurement is covered by this Agreement;

(b) in Annex 2, the sub-central government entities whose procurement is covered by this Agreement;

(c) in Annex 3, all other entities whose procurement is covered by this Agreement;

(d) in Annex 4, the services covered by this Agreement;

(e) in Annex 5, the construction services covered by this Agreement; and

(f) in Annex 6, any General Notes applicable to the annexes of the Party.

5. Where a procuring entity, in the context of covered procurement, requires persons not listed in Appendix I to procure in accordance with particular requirements, Article V shall apply *mutatis mutandis* to such requirements.

Valuation

6. In estimating the value of a procurement for the purpose of ascertaining whether it is a covered procurement, a procuring entity shall:

(a) neither divide a procurement into separate procurements nor select or use a particular valuation method for estimating the value of a procurement with the intention of totally or partially excluding it from the application of this Agreement; and

(b) include the estimated maximum total value of the procurement over its entire duration, whether awarded to one or more suppliers, taking into account all forms of remuneration, including:

(i) premiums, fees, commissions, and interest; and

---

[2] Negotiators' Note: The Parties are still considering whether to add a specific Annex on goods to Appendix I.

(d) 公共雇佣合同；

(e) 下列采购：

(i) 为提供国际援助的特定目的而进行的采购，包括发展援助；

(ii) 根据与部队驻扎或一项目签署国联合执行有关的国际协定的特别程序或条件进行的采购；

(iii) 根据一国际组织的特别程序或条件进行的采购，或由国际赠款、贷款或其他援助资助进行的采购，其适用程序或条件与本协定不一致。

4. 每一参加方应在其附录 1 的附件中列明以下信息[2]：

(a) 在附件 1 中，采购为本协定所涵盖的中央政府实体；

(b) 在附件 2 中，采购为本协定所涵盖的中央以下政府实体；

(c) 在附件 3 中，采购为本协定所涵盖的所有其他实体；

(d) 在附件 4 中，本协定所涵盖的服务；

(e) 在附件 5 中，本协定所涵盖的建筑服务；及

(f) 在附件 6 中，适用于参加方各附件的任何总注释。

5. 如一采购实体在从事涵盖采购时，要求未列入附录 1 的人依照特殊要求采购，则第 5 条在细节上作必要修改后应适用于此类要求。

估价

6. 在确定一采购是否属涵盖采购而估计采购价值时，采购实体应：

(a) 不得将一项采购分割为几项采购，也不得选择或使用一特殊估价方法对一采购的价值进行估计从而全部或部分将其排除在本协定适用范围之外；及

(b) 包含采购全部期限内其估计最高总价值，无论授予一个或一个以上供应商，并考虑所有形式的报酬，包括：

(i) 奖金、酬金、佣金和利息；及

[2] 谈判者注释：各参加方仍在考虑是否在附录 1 中增加一专门关于货物的附件。

(ii) where the procurement provides for the possibility of option clauses, the estimated maximum total value of the procurement, inclusive of optional purchases.

7. Where an individual requirement for a procurement results in the award of more than one contract, or in the award of contracts in separate parts (hereafter referred to as "recurring procurements"), the calculation of the estimated maximum total value shall be based on:

(a) the value of recurring procurements of the same type of good or service awarded during the preceding 12 months or the procuring entity's preceding fiscal year, adjusted where possible to take into account anticipated changes in the quantity or value of the good or service being procured over the subsequent 12 months; or

(b) the estimated value of recurring procurements of the same type of good or service to be awarded during the 12 months subsequent to the initial contract award or the procuring entity's fiscal year.

8. In the case of procurement by lease, rental, or hire purchase of goods or services, or procurement for which a total price is not specified, the basis for valuation shall be:

(a) in the case of a fixed-term contract:

(i) where the term of the contract is 12 months or less, the total estimated maximum value for its duration, or

(ii) where the term of the contract exceeds 12 months, the total estimated maximum value, including any estimated residual value;

(b) where the contract is for an indefinite period, the estimated monthly instalment multiplied by 48; and

(c) where is it not certain whether the contract is to be a fixed-term contract, subparagraph (b) shall be used.

Article III Exceptions to the Agreement

1. Nothing in this Agreement shall be construed to prevent any Party from taking any action or not disclosing any information that it considers necessary for the protection of its essential security interests relating to the procurement of arms, ammunition, or war materials, or to procurement indispensable for national security or for national defence purposes.

2. Subject to the requirement that such measures are not applied in a manner that would constitute a means of arbitrary or unjustifiable discrimination between Parties where the same conditions prevail or a disguised restriction on international trade, nothing in this Agreement shall be construed to prevent any Party from imposing or enforcing measures:

(a) necessary to protect public morals, order, or safety;

(b) necessary to protect human, animal or plant life or health;

(c) necessary to protect intellectual property; or

(d) relating to goods or services of persons with disabilities, philanthropic institutions, or prison labour.

(ii) 如采购规定选择性条款的可能性，采购的估计最高总价值，包含选择性购买。

7. 如一单项采购要求导致授予一个以上的合同，或使合同分几部分授予(以下简称"续生采购")，则估计最高总价值的计算应依据：

(a) 前 12 个月中或采购实体前一财政年度中授予的相同类型货物或服务的续生采购的价值，如可能，根据在其后 12 个月中采购的货物或服务的数量和金额的预期变化进行调整；或

(b) 在最初合同授予后 12 个月中或采购实体财政年度中授予的相同类型货物或服务的续生采购的估计价值；

8. 对于货物或服务的租赁、租购合同或未列明总价的合同，估价依据应为：

(a) 对于定期合同：

(i) 如其期限等于或少于 12 个月，则为合同有效期内其估计最高总价值，或，

(ii) 如其期限超过 12 个月，则为包括估计的剩余价值在内的估计最高总价值。

(b) 如合同期限不确定，则为月摊付额与 48 的乘积；及

(c) 如不能确定合同是否为定期合同，则使用(b)项的规定。

第 3 条 本协定的例外

1. 本协定的任何规定不得解释为妨碍任何参加方在与武器、弹药或军事物资的采购有关或与国家安全或国防目的所必需的采购有关的基本安全利益方面，采取其认为必需的任何行动或不披露任何信息。

2. 在遵守关于此类措施的实施方式不构成对条件相同的参加方造成任意或不合理歧视的手段或不构成对国际贸易的变相限制要求的前提下，本协定的任何规定不得解释为妨碍任何参加方采取或实施下列措施：

(a) 为保护公共道德、秩序或安全所必需的措施；

(b) 为保护人类和动植物的生命和健康所必需的措施；

(c) 为保护知识产权所必需的措施；或

(d) 与残疾人、慈善机构或监狱囚犯货物或服务有关的措施。

Article IV Developing Countries

1. In negotiations on accession to, and in the implementation and administration of, this Agreement, the Parties shall give special consideration to the development, financial, and trade needs and circumstances of developing countries and least-developed countries (collectively referred to hereafter as "developing countries", unless specifically identified otherwise), recognizing that these may differ significantly from country to country. As provided for in this Article and upon request, the Parties shall accord special and differential treatment to:

(a) least-developed countries; and

(b) any other developing country, where and to the extent that this special and differential treatment meets its development needs.

2. Upon accession by a developing country to this Agreement, each Party shall provide immediately to the goods, services, and suppliers of that country the most favourable coverage that the Party provides under Appendix I to any other Party to this Agreement, subject to any terms negotiated between that Party and the developing country in order to maintain an appropriate balance of opportunities under this Agreement.

3. Based on its development needs, and with the agreement of the Parties, a developing country may adopt or retain one or more of the following transitional measures, during a transition period and in accordance with a schedule, set out in an Annex to its Appendix I, and in a manner that does not discriminate among the Parties:

(a) a price preference programme, provided that the programme:

(i) provides a preference only for the part of the tender incorporating goods or services originating in the developing country applying the preference or goods or services originating in other developing countries in respect of which the developing country applying the preference has an obligation to provide national treatment under a preferential agreement; and

(ii) is transparent, and the preference and its application in the procurement are clearly described in the notice of intended procurement;

(b) an offset, provided that any requirement for, or consideration of, the imposition of the offset is clearly stated in the notice of intended procurement;

(c) the phased-in addition of specific entities or sectors; and

(d) a threshold that is higher than its permanent threshold.

4. In negotiations on accession to this Agreement, the Parties may agree to the delay of the application of any specific obligation in this Agreement, other than Article V:1(b), by an acceding developing country while that country completes its implementation of the obligation. The implementation period shall be for:

(a) a least-developed country, five years after its accession to this Agreement; and

(b) any other developing country, only the period necessary to implement the specific obligation, but not to exceed three years.

第 4 条　　发展中国家

1.　在加入本协定的谈判中及实施和管理本协定的过程中，各参加方应对发展中国家和最不发达国家(以下合称“发展中国家”，除非另有认定)的发展、财政和贸易需要给予特殊考虑，认识到这些需要在各国之间可能存在巨大差别。根据本条规定并应请求，参加方应给予下列成员特殊和差别待遇：

(a)　最不发达国家；及

(b)　任何其他发展中国家，如此种特殊和差别待遇满足其发展需要。

2.　一发展中国家加入本协定时，每一参加方应立即对该国的货物、服务和供应商提供该参加方附录 1 项下向本协定其他参加方提供的最惠国涵盖范围，并遵守该参加方与该发展中国家之间为保持本协定项下机会的适当平衡而谈判达成的任何条款。

3.　根据其发展需要，并经参加方同意，一发展中国家在过渡期内并依照其附录 1 一附件所列减让表且以不在各参加方之间造成歧视的方式，可采取或保留下列过渡性措施中的一项或多项：

(a)　价格优惠计划，但条件是该计划：

(i)　规定优惠仅给予投标中包含源自适用优惠的发展中国家的货物或服务或源自适用优惠的发展中国家根据一优惠协定有义务提供国民待遇的其他发展中国家的货物或服务的部分；及

(ii)　是透明的，且优惠及其在采购中的适用在意向采购通知中明确表述；

(b)　属一项补偿，但条件是实行补偿的要求或考虑在意向采购通知中明确规定；

(c)　特定实体或部门的分阶段增加；及

(d)　最低限额高于其永久最低限额。

4.　在加入本协定的谈判过程中，各参加方可同意一申请加入的发展中国家在完成本协定中任何特定义务的实施过程中，推迟该义务的适用，但第 5 条第 1 款(b)项除外。实施期应为：

(a)　最不发达国家，在其加入本协定后 5 年；及

(b)　任何其他发展中国家，仅在实施特定义务所必需的时间内，但不超过 3 年。

5. Any developing country that has been permitted a period in which to implement an obligation under paragraph 4 shall list in an Annex to its Appendix I the implementation period, the specific obligation subject to the implementation period, and any interim obligation with which it agrees to comply during the implementation period.

6. After this Agreement has entered into force for a developing country, the Committee, on request of the developing country, may:

(a) extend the transition period for a measure permitted under paragraph 3 or the implementation period permitted under paragraph 4; or

(b) approve the application of a new transitional measure permitted under paragraph 3, in special circumstances that were unforeseen during the accession process.

7. A developing country benefiting from a transitional measure provided for in paragraphs 3 or 6, or an implementation period provided for in paragraph 4, or any extension thereof under paragraph 6 shall take such steps during the transition period or implementation period as may be necessary to ensure that it is in compliance with this Agreement at the end of any such period. The developing country shall promptly notify the Committee of such steps.

8. The Parties shall give due consideration to any request by a developing country for technical cooperation and capacity building in relation to that country's accession to, or implementation of, this Agreement.

9. The Committee may develop procedures for the implementation of this Article. Such procedures may include provisions for voting on decisions relating to requests under paragraph 6.

10. The Committee shall review the operation and effectiveness of this Article every five years.

Article V General Principles

National Treatment and Non-Discrimination

1. With respect to any measure regarding covered procurement, each Party, including its procuring entities, shall accord immediately and unconditionally to the goods and services of any other Party and to the suppliers of any other Party offering the goods or services of any Party, treatment no less favourable than the treatment the Party, including its procuring entities, accords to:

(a) domestic goods, services, and suppliers; and

(b) goods, services, and suppliers of any other Party.

2. With respect to any measure regarding covered procurement, a Party, including its procuring entities, shall not:

(a) treat a locally established supplier less favourably than another locally established supplier on the basis of degree of foreign affiliation or ownership; nor

(b) discriminate against a locally established supplier on the basis that the goods or services offered by that supplier for a particular procurement are goods or services of any other Party.

5. 任何根据第4款已经允许使用一期限实施一义务的发展中国家应在其附录1的一附件中列明实施期、需使用实施期的特定义务及其在实施期中同意遵守的临时义务。

6. 本协定对一发展中国家生效后，委员会应该发展中国家请求可：

(a) 延长根据第 3 款允许使用的一措施的过渡期或根据第 4 款可以使用的实施期；或

(b) 在加入过程中未预见的特殊情况下，批准根据第 3 款允许使用的新过渡性措施。

7. 一受益于第 3 或 6 款规定的过渡性措施、或第 4 款规定的过渡期、或根据第 6 款的延长的发展中国家应在过渡期或实施期内采购必要步骤以保证在任何此种期限结束时遵守本协定。发展中国家应及时将此类步骤通知委员会。

8. 参加方应适当考虑一发展中国家与该国加入或实施本协定有关的技术合作和能力建设的任何请求。

9. 委员会可制定实施本条的程序。此类程序可包含就与根据第 6 款提出的请求与关的决定进行投票的规定。

10. 委员会应每 5 年对本条的运用和有效性进行审议。

第 5 条　　总则

国民待遇和非歧视

1. 对于有关涵盖采购的任何措施，每一参加方，包括其采购实体，应立即无条件地给予任何其他参加方的货物和服务及提供货物或服务的任何其他参加方的供应商不低于该参加方，包括其采购实体，给予下列方面的待遇：

(a) 国内货物、服务和供应商；及

(b) 任何其他参加方的货物、服务及供应商。

2. 对于与涵盖采购有关的任何措施，一参加方，包括其采购实体，不得：

(a) 依据外国联营或所有权的程度而给予一当地设立的供应商低于给予另一当地设立的供应商的待遇；

(b) 依据一当地设立的供应商为一特定采购提供的货物或服务属任何其他参加方而歧视该供应商。

Use of Electronic Means

3. When conducting covered procurement by electronic means, a procuring entity shall:

(a) ensure that the procurement is conducted using information technology systems and software, including those related to authentication and encryption of information, that are generally available and interoperable with other generally available information technology systems and software; and

(b) maintain mechanisms that ensure the integrity of requests for participation and tenders, including establishment of the time of receipt and the prevention of inappropriate access.

Conduct of Procurement

4. A procuring entity shall conduct covered procurement in a transparent and impartial manner that:

(a) is consistent with this Agreement, using methods such as open tendering, selective tendering, and limited tendering;

(b) avoids conflicts of interest; and

(c) prevents corrupt practices.

Rules of Origin

5. For purposes of covered procurement, no Party may apply rules of origin to goods or services imported from or supplied by another Party that are different from the rules of origin the Party applies at the same time in the normal course of trade to imports or supplies of the same goods or services from the same Party.

Offsets

6. With regard to covered procurement, a Party, including its procuring entities, shall not seek, take account of, impose, or enforce offsets.

Measures Not Specific to Procurement

7. The provisions of paragraphs 1 and 2 shall not apply to customs duties and charges of any kind imposed on, or in connection with, importation, the method of levying such duties and charges, other import regulations or formalities, and measures affecting trade in services other than measures governing covered procurement.

Article VI Information on the Procurement System

1. Each Party shall:

(a) promptly publish any law, regulation, judicial decision, administrative ruling of general application, standard contract clauses mandated by law or regulation and incorporated by reference in notices and tender documentation, and procedure regarding covered procurement, and any modifications thereof, in an officially designated electronic or paper medium that is widely disseminated and remains readily accessible to the public; and

电子方式的使用

3. 如使用电子方式进行涵盖采购时，一采购实体应：

(a) 保证采购的进行使用可普遍获得且可与其他可普遍获得的信息技术和软件互用的信息技术和软件，包括与信息认证和解码有关的技术和软件；及

(b) 设立保证参与请求和投标人诚实性的机制，包括设立接收时间和防止不当访问。

采购的进行

4. 一采购实体应以透明和公正的且符合下列要求的方式进行涵盖采购：

(a) 与本协定一致，使用公开招标、选择性招标及有限招标等方法；

(b) 避免利益冲突；及

(c) 避免腐败做法。

原产地

5. 就涵盖采购而言，任何参加方对自另一参加方进口或另一参加方提供的货物或服务实行的原产地规则不得区别于在正常贸易过程中对相同参加方的相同货物或服务的进口或供应所实行的原产地规则。

补偿

6. 对于涵盖采购，一参加方，包括其采购实体，不得寻求、考虑、强加或强制执行补偿。

非专门针对采购的措施

7. 第1款和第2款的规定不得适用于对进口征收或与进口有关的关税和任何种类的费用、征收此类税费的方法、其他进口法规或手续以及除管辖涵盖采购外的影响服务贸易的措施。

第 6 条　　采购制度的信息

1. 每一参加方应

(a) 在官方指定的可广泛传播且可使公众容易获得的电子或纸制媒介中，迅速公布任何法律、法规、司法判决、普遍适用的行政裁决、经法律或法规授权并在通知和招标文件中提及的标准合同条款以及关于涵盖采购的程序，及其任何修改；及

(b) provide an explanation thereof to any Party, on request.

2. Each Party shall list:

(a) in Appendix II, the electronic or paper media in which the Party publishes the information regarding the Party's procurement system as required by paragraph 1;

(b) in Appendix III, the electronic or paper media in which the Party publishes the notices required by Articles VII, IX:7, and XVI:2; and

(c) in Appendix IV, the website address or addresses where the Party publishes:

(i) its procurement statistics pursuant to Article XVI:5, as a substitute for the submission of the data required under Article XVI:4;

(ii) its notices concerning awarded contracts pursuant to Article XVI:6, as a substitute for the report required under Article XVI:4.

3. Each Party shall promptly notify the Committee of any modification to the Party's information listed in Appendix II, III, or IV.

Article VII Notices

Notice of Intended Procurement

1. For each covered procurement, except in the circumstances described in Article XIII, a procuring entity shall publish a notice of intended procurement in the appropriate paper or electronic medium listed in Appendix III. Such medium shall be widely disseminated and such notices shall remain readily accessible to the public, at least, until expiration of the time period indicated in the notice. The notices shall:

(a) for procuring entities in Annex 1, be accessible by electronic means free of charge, for at least any minimum period of time specified in Appendix III, through a single point of access; and

(b) for procuring entities in Annexes 2 and 3, where accessible by electronic means, be provided, at least, through links in a gateway electronic site that is accessible free of charge.

Parties, including their procuring entities in Annexes 2 and 3, are encouraged to publish their notices by electronic means free of charge through a single point of access.

2. Except as otherwise provided in this Agreement, each notice of intended procurement shall include:

(a) the name and address of the procuring entity and other information necessary to contact the procuring entity and obtain all relevant documents relating to the procurement, and their cost and terms of payment, if any;

(b) a description of the procurement, including the nature and the quantity of the goods or services to be procured or, where the quantity is not known, the estimated quantity;

(b) 应请求，向任何一参加方提供说明。

2. 每一参加方应在：

(a) 在附录 2 中列明该参加方按第 1 款要求公布有关其采购制度信息的电子或纸制媒介。

(b) 在附录 3 中列明该参加方按第 7 条、第 9 条第 7 款和第 16 条第 2 款公布通知的电子或纸质媒介；及

(c) 在附录 4 中列明该参加方公布下列信息的网址或地址：

(i) 其根据第 16 条第 5 款的采购数字，作为第 16 条第 4 款要求提供数据的替代；

(ii) 根据第 16 条第 6 款授予合同的通知，作为第 16 条第 4 款要求的报告的替代。

3. 每一参加方应迅速将附录 2、3 或 4 中参加方信息的任何修改通知委员会。

第 7 条 通知

预定采购的通知

1. 对于每一涵盖采购，除第 13 条所述情形外，一采购实体应在附录 3 所列适当纸制或电子媒介中公布预定采购通知。此类媒介应可广泛传播且此类通知至少应在通知中所示时间期限结束前可使公众容易我获得。通知应：

(a) 对于附件 1 中采购实体，通知至少在附录 3 中所列任何最短期限内，可通过单一访问点，通过电子方式免费访问；及

(b) 对于附件 2 和 3 中的采购实体，如可通过电子方式访问，则通知至少应通过可免费访问的网关电子站点提供。

鼓励各参加方，包括附件 2 和 3 中采购实体，通过单一访问点以电子方式公布其通知。

2. 除本协定另有规定外，每一预定采购的通知应包含：

(a) 采购实体的名称和地址及其他与采购实体联系并获得所有与采购有关的相关文件所必要的信息，以及其成本和付款条件(如果有)；

(b) 关于采购的描述，包括将予采购的货物或服务的性质和数量，如数量不可知，则为估计数量；

(c) for recurring contracts, if possible, an estimate of the timing of subsequent notices of intended procurement;

(d) a description of any options;

(e) the time-frame for delivery of goods or services or the duration of the contract;

(f) the procurement method that will be used and whether it will involve negotiation or electronic auction;

(g) where applicable, the address and any final date for the submission of requests for participation in the procurement;

(h) the address and the final date for the submission of tenders;

(i) the language or languages in which tenders or requests for participation must be submitted, if other than an official language of the Party of the procuring entity;

(j) a list and brief description of any conditions for participation of suppliers, including any requirements for specific documents or certifications to be provided by suppliers in connection therewith, unless such requirements are included in tender documentation that is made available to all interested suppliers at the same time as the notice of intended procurement;

(k) where, pursuant to Article IX, a procuring entity intends to select a limited number of qualified suppliers to be invited to tender, the criteria that will be used to select them and, where applicable, any limitation on the number of suppliers that will be permitted to tender; and

(l) an indication that the procurement is covered by this Agreement.

Summary Notice

3. For each case of intended procurement, a procuring entity shall publish a summary notice that is readily accessible, at the same time as the publication of the notice of intended procurement, in one of the WTO languages. The notice shall contain at least the following information:

(a) the subject-matter of the procurement;

(b) the final date for the submission of tenders or, where applicable, any final date for the submission of requests for participation in the procurement or for inclusion on a multi-use list; and

(c) the address from which documents relating to the procurement may be requested.

Notice of Planned Procurement

4. Procuring entities are encouraged to publish in the appropriate paper or electronic medium listed in Appendix III as early as possible in each fiscal year a notice regarding their future procurement plans. The notice should include the subject-matter of the procurement and the planned date of the publication of the notice of intended procurement.

(c) 对于续生采购，如可能，公布预定采购随后通知的估计时间；

(d) 任何选择的描述；

(e) 货物或服务交付的时限或合同期限；

(f) 将要使用的采购方式及是否将涉及谈判或电子拍卖；

(g) 如适用，提交参与采购申请的地址和任何最后日期；

(h) 提交投标书的地址和最后日期；

(i) 提交投标书或参加请求所必须使用的一种或多种语文，如不同于采购实体所属参加方的官方语文；

(j) 供应商参加的任何条件的清单和简要描述，包括供应商需提交的具体文件或证书的任何要求，除非此类要求包含在公布预定采购通知的同时使所有感兴趣的供应商均可获得的投标文件中；

(k) 如根据第 9 条，一采购实体有意选择一有限数量的符合条件的供应商邀请招标，则将使用的选择供应商的标准，及如适用，允许参与招标的供应商数量的任何限制；及

(l) 该项采购为本协定所涵盖的说明。

简易通知

3． 对于每一预定采购，一采购实体应以一种 WTO 官方语文，在公布预定采购通知的同时，公布一份可容易获得的简要通知。通知应至少包括下列信息：

(a) 采购标的物；

(b) 递交投标书的最后日期，或如适用，递交参加采购请求或放入常用清单的请求的最后日期；及

(c) 可请求得到与采购相关文件的地址。

计划采购的通知

4． 鼓励采购实体在每一财政年度尽早在列入附录 3 的适当纸制或电子媒介中公布有关其未来采购计划的通知。通知应包括采购标的物和预定采购日期。

5. A procuring entity in Annex 2 or 3 may use a notice of planned procurement as a notice of intended procurement provided that it includes as much of the information in paragraph 2 as is available and a statement that interested suppliers should express their interest in the procurement to the entity.

Article VIII Conditions for Participation

1. A procuring entity shall limit any conditions for participation in a procurement to those that are essential to ensure that a supplier has the legal, commercial, technical, and financial abilities to undertake the relevant procurement.

2. In assessing whether a supplier satisfies the conditions for participation, a procuring entity:

(a) shall evaluate the financial, commercial, and technical abilities of a supplier on the basis of that supplier's business activities both inside and outside the territory of the Party of the procuring entity;

(b) shall base its determination on the conditions that the procuring entity has specified in advance in notices or tender documentation;

(c) may not impose the condition that, in order for a supplier to participate in a procurement, the supplier has previously been awarded one or more contracts by a procuring entity of a given Party; and

(d) may require relevant prior experience where essential to meet the requirements of the procurement.

3. Where there is supporting evidence, a Party, including its procuring entities, may exclude a supplier on grounds such as:

(a) bankruptcy;

(b) false declarations;

(c) significant or persistent deficiencies in performance of any substantive requirement or obligation under a prior contract or contracts;

(d) final judgments in respect of serious crimes or other serious offences;

(e) professional misconduct or acts or omissions that adversely reflect upon the commercial integrity of the supplier; or

(f) failure to pay taxes.

Article IX Qualification of Suppliers

Registration Systems and Qualification Procedures

1. A Party, including its procuring entities, may maintain a supplier registration system where interested suppliers are required to register and provide certain information.

5．　附件 2 或附件 3 中一采购实体可使用计划采购通知作为预定采购通知，条件是该通知应包含尽可能多的第 2 款中的信息和关于感兴趣的供应商应在采购中向实体表明其兴趣的声明。

第 8 条　参加条件

1．　一采购实体应将参加采购的任何条件限于对保证供应商具有履行相关采购的法律、商业、技术和财政能力所必需的条件。

2．　在评价一供应商是否满足参加条件时，一采购实体：

(a)　应根据供应商在采购实体所属参加方领土内外的商业活动评估该供应商的财政、商业和技术能力；

(b)　应根据采购实体在通知或招标文件中提前列明的条件做出决定；

(c)　不得为使一供应商参加一采购而强加该供应商以往被指定参加方一采购实体授予一项或多项合同的条件；及

(d)　可要求对满足采购条件所必需的相关以往经验要求。

3．　如有证据表明，一参加方，包括其采购实体可根据下列条件排除一供应商：

(a)　破产；

(b)　虚报；

(c)　严重或持续未完全履行前一项或多项合同项下任何实质性要求或义务；

(d)　有关严重犯罪或其他严重罪行的终审判决；

(e)　渎职罪或负面影响供应商商业诚实性的行为或不作为；或

(f)　未交税。

第 9 条　供应商资格

登记制度和资格审查程序

1.　一参加方，包括其采购实体，可设立登记制度，供感兴趣的供应商进行登记，并提供某些信息。

2. Each Party shall ensure that:

(a) its procuring entities make efforts to minimize differences in their qualification procedures; and

(b) where its procuring entities maintain registration systems, the entities make efforts to minimize differences in their registration systems.

3. A Party, including its procuring entities, shall not adopt or apply any registration system or qualification procedure with the purpose or the effect of creating unnecessary obstacles to the participation of foreign suppliers in its procurement.

Selective Tendering

4. Where a procuring entity intends to use selective tendering, the entity shall:

(a) in the notice of intended procurement include at least the information in Article VII:2(a), (b), (f), (g), (j), (k), and (l) and invite suppliers to submit a request for participation; and

(b) by the commencement of the time-period for tendering, provide at least the information in Article VII:2 (c), (d), (e), (h), and (i) to the qualified suppliers that it notifies in accordance with Article XI:3(b).

5. A procuring entity shall recognize as a qualified supplier any domestic supplier and any supplier of another Party that meets the conditions for participation in a particular procurement, unless the procuring entity states in the notice of intended procurement any limitation on the number of suppliers that will be permitted to tender and the criteria for selecting the limited number of suppliers.

6. Where the tender documentation is not made publicly available from the date of publication of the notice referred to in paragraph 4, a procuring entity shall ensure that those documents are made available at the same time to all the qualified suppliers selected in accordance with paragraph 5.

Multi-Use Lists

7. A procuring entity may maintain a multi-use list of suppliers, provided that a notice inviting interested suppliers to apply for inclusion on the list is:

(a) published annually; and

(b) where published by electronic means, made available continuously,

in the appropriate medium listed in Appendix III.

8. The notice provided for in paragraph 7 shall include:

(a) a description of the goods or services, or categories thereof, for which the list may be used;

(b) the conditions for participation to be satisfied by suppliers and the methods that the procuring entity will use to verify a supplier's satisfaction of the conditions;

(c) the name and address of the procuring entity and other information necessary to contact the entity and obtain all relevant documents relating to the list;

2. 每一参加方应保证：

(a) 其采购实体努力缩小资格审查程序之间的差异；及

(b) 如其采购实体设立登记制度，则实体应努力缩小登记制度之间的差异。

3. 一参加方，包括其采购实体，不得采用或适用任何具有给外国供应商参与其采购造成不必要障碍的目的或效果的登记制度或资格审查程序。

选择性招标

4. 如一采购实体预定使用选择性招标，则该实体应：

(a) 在预定采购通知中至少包含第 7 条第 2 款(a)、(b)、(f)、(g)、(j)、(k)和(l)项中的信息，并邀请供应商提交参加请求；及

(b) 最迟至招标期限开始时，向依照第 11 条第 3 款(b)项通知的合格供应商至少提供第 7 条第 2 款(c)、(d)、(e)、(h)和(i) 中的信息。

5. 一采购实体应承认满足参加一特定采购的条件的任何国内供应商或另一参加方的任何供应商均为合格供应商，除非采购实体在预定采购通知中规定允许进行投标的供应商数量的任何限制和选择有限数量供应商的标准。

6. 如招标文件自第 4 款所指通知公布之日起未能使公开获得，则一采购实体应保证这些文件可使依照第 5 款选择的所有合格供应商同时获得。

常用清单

7. 一采购实体可设立供应商的常用清单，但邀请感兴趣的供应申请列入清单的通知应：

(a) 每年公布；及

(b) 如以电子方式公布，则应使之可持续获得，

在附录 3 所列适当媒介中。

8. 第 7 款规定的通知应包含：

(a) 对清单可能使用的货物或服务或货物或服务类别的描述；

(b) 供应商参与需要满足的条件和采购实体将用以验证供应商满足条件与否的方法；

(c) 采购实体的名称和地址及其他与实体联系和获得与清单有关的所有相关文件的必要信息；

(d) the period of validity of the list and the means for its renewal or termination, or where the period of validity is not provided, an indication of the method by which notice will be given of the termination of use of the list; and

(e) an indication that the list may be used for procurement covered by this Agreement.

9. Notwithstanding paragraph 7, where a multi-use list will be valid for three years or less, a procuring entity may publish the notice referred to in paragraph 7 only once, at the beginning of the period of validity of the list, provided that the notice:

(a) states the period of validity and that further notices will not be published; and

(b) is published by electronic means and is made available continuously during the period of its validity.

10. A procuring entity shall allow suppliers to apply at any time for inclusion on a multi-use list and shall include on the list all qualified suppliers within a reasonably short time.

11. Where a supplier that is not included on a multi-use list submits a request for participation in a procurement based on a multi-use list and all required documents relating thereto, within the time-period provided for in Article XI:2, a procuring entity shall examine the request. The procuring entity may not exclude the supplier from consideration in respect of the procurement on the grounds that the entity has insufficient time to examine the request, unless, in exceptional cases, due to the complexity of the procurement, the entity is not able to complete the examination of the request within the time-period allowed for the submission of tenders.

Annexes 2 and 3 Entities

12. A procuring entity listed in Annex 2 or 3 may use a notice inviting suppliers to apply for inclusion on a multi-use list as a notice of intended procurement, provided that:

(a) the notice is published in accordance with paragraph 7 and includes the information in paragraph 8, as much of the information in Article VII:2 as is available, and a statement that it constitutes a notice of intended procurement or that only the suppliers on the multi-use list will receive further notices of procurement covered by the multi-use list;

(b) the entity promptly provides to suppliers that have expressed an interest to the entity in a given procurement, sufficient information to permit them to assess their interest in the procurement, including all remaining information required in Article VII:2, to the extent such information is available; and

(c) a supplier having applied for inclusion on a multi-use list in accordance with paragraph 10 may be allowed to tender in a given procurement, where there is sufficient time for the procuring entity to examine whether it satisfies the conditions for participation.

Information on Procuring Entity Decisions

13. A procuring entity shall promptly inform any supplier that submits a request for participation or application for inclusion on a multi-use list of the procuring entity's decision with respect to the request.

(d) 清单的有限期和展期或终止的方法，如未规定有限期，则为关于就清单使用终止作出通知的方法的说明；及

(e) 关于清单可能用于本协定涵盖采购的说明。

9. 尽管有第 7 款的规定，但是如一常用清单在 3 年或 3 年以内有效，则一采购实体可在清单有限期开始时仅公布第 7 款所指的通知一次，但该通知：

(a) 规定有限期，且规定不再公布进一步通知；及

(b) 以电子方式公布且在有限期内可持续获得。

10. 一采购实体应允许供应商随时申请列入常用清单，并应在合理的较短时间内将合格供应商列入清单。

11. 如一未列入常用清单的供应商，在第 11 条第 2 款规定的时限内，提交参加一基于常用清单和所有规定文件与常用清单有关的采购的请求，则一采购实体应审查该项请求。该采购实体不得由于实体没有审查请求的充分的时间而将该供应商排除在考虑范围之外，除非在特殊情况下，由于采购的复杂性，该实体不能在允许提交投标书的时限内完成对请求的审查。

附件 2 和 3 实体

12. 列入附件 2 或 3 的一采购实体可使用邀请供应商申请列入常用清单的通知作为预定采购通知，但条件是：

(a) 该通知依照第 7 款公布，且包含第 8 款中的信息，并尽可能多地包含第 7 条第 2 款中的信息，及包含关于该通知构成预定采购通知的说明或关于只有常用清单上的供应商将收到常用清单涵盖采购的进一步通知的说明；

(b) 该实体迅速向已向该实体表达对一指定采购感兴趣的供应商提供充分的信息，以允许其评估在该项采购中的利益，第 7 条第 2 款要求的所有其他信息，只要此类信息可获得；及

(c) 依照第 10 款已申请列入常用清单的供应商可被允许参与一指定采购的投标，如采购实体有足够时间审查该供应商是否满足参加条件。

关于采购实体决定的信息

13. 一采购实体应迅速将与该采购实体做出的关于请求的决定的通知提交参加请求或申请列入常用清单的任何供应商。

14. Where a procuring entity rejects a supplier's request for participation or application for inclusion on a multi-use list, ceases to recognize a supplier as qualified, or removes a supplier from a multi-use list, the entity shall promptly inform the supplier and, on request of the supplier, promptly provide the supplier with a written explanation of the reasons for its decision.

Article X Technical Specifications and Tender Documentation

Technical Specifications

1. A procuring entity shall not prepare, adopt, or apply any technical specification or prescribe any conformity assessment procedure with the purpose or the effect of creating unnecessary obstacles to international trade.

2. In prescribing the technical specifications for the goods or services being procured, a procuring entity shall, where appropriate:

(a) specify the technical specification in terms of performance and functional requirements, rather than design or descriptive characteristics; and

(b) base the technical specification on international standards, where such exist; otherwise, on national technical regulations, recognized national standards, or building codes.

3. Where design or descriptive characteristics are used in the technical specifications, a procuring entity should indicate, where appropriate, that it will consider tenders of equivalent goods or services that demonstrably fulfil the requirements of the procurement by including words such as "or equivalent" in the tender documentation.

4. A procuring entity shall not prescribe technical specifications that require or refer to a particular trademark or trade name, patent, copyright, design, type, specific origin, producer, or supplier, unless there is no other sufficiently precise or intelligible way of describing the procurement requirements and provided that, in such cases, the entity includes words such as "or equivalent" in the tender documentation.

5. A procuring entity shall not seek or accept, in a manner that would have the effect of precluding competition, advice that may be used in the preparation or adoption of any technical specification for a specific procurement from a person that may have a commercial interest in the procurement.

6. For greater certainty, a Party, including its procuring entities, may, in accordance with this Article, prepare, adopt, or apply technical specifications to promote the conservation of natural resources or protect the environment.

Tender Documentation

7. A procuring entity shall provide to suppliers tender documentation that includes all information necessary to permit suppliers to prepare and submit responsive tenders. Unless already provided in the notice of intended procurement, such documentation shall include a complete description of:

(a) the procurement, including the nature and the quantity of the goods or services to be procured or, where the quantity is not known, the estimated quantity and any requirements to be fulfilled, including any technical specifications, conformity assessment certification, plans, drawings, or instructional materials;

14. 如一采购实体拒绝一供应商的参加请求或列入常用清单的申请、终止承认一供应商为合格供应商、或将一供应商从常用清单中去除，则该实体应迅速通知该供应商，并应该供应商请求，迅速向其提供作出决定的原因的书面说明。

第 10 条　技术规格和招标文件

技术规格

1. 一采购实体不得以对国际贸易造成不必要的障碍为目的或产生此种效果，制定、采用或适用任何技术法规则或规定任何合格评定程序。

2. 在规定将予采购的货物或服务的技术规格时，一采购实体应酌情：

(a) 以性能和功能性要求规定技术规格，而非设计或描述特征；及

(b) 如存在国际标准，则技术法规应依据国际标准；如无国际标准，则应依据国家技术法规、公认的国家标准或建筑规格。

3. 如在技术规格中使用设计或描述特征，则一采购实体应通过将“或相当于”等措辞包含在招标文件中，以酌情说明将考虑确可满足采购要求的相同货物或服务的投标。

4. 一采购实体不得规定要求或指明一特定商标或商号、专利、版权、设计、型号、具体原产地、生产商或供应商的技术规格，除非无足够准确或易懂的方法描述采购要求，且在此类情况下，需在招标文件中包含如“或相当于”等措辞。

5. 一采购实体不得以具有妨碍竞争效果的方式，寻求或接受在制定一具体采购规格时可采用的、与该采购有商业利益的公司提出的建议。

6. 为增加确定性，一参加方，包括其采购实体，可依照本条，制定、采用或适用技术规格，以促进保护自然资源或保护环境。

招标文件

7. 一采购实体应向供应商提供包含允许供应商起草和提交符合要求的投标书的所有信息的招标文件。除非已在特定采购通知中规定，否则该文件应包含下列内容的完整描述：

(a) 该项采购，包括将予购买的货物或服务的特性和数量，如数量不可知，则为估计数量及仨何需要满足的要求，包括任何技术规格、合格评定程序、认证、设计图、图纸或说明材料；

(b) any conditions for participation of suppliers, including a list of information and documents that suppliers are required to submit in connection therewith;

(c) all evaluation criteria to be considered in the awarding of the contract, and, except where price is the sole criterion, the relative importance of such criteria;

(d) where the procuring entity will conduct the procurement by electronic means, any authentication and encryption requirements or other requirements related to the receipt of information by electronic means;

(e) where the procuring entity will hold an electronic auction, the rules, including identification of the elements of the tender related to the evaluation criteria, on which the auction will be conducted;

(f) where there will be a public opening of tenders, the date, time, and place for the opening and, where appropriate, the persons authorized to be present;

(g) any other terms or conditions, including terms of payment and any limitation on the means by which tenders may be submitted, e.g., paper or electronic means; and

(h) any dates for the delivery of goods or the supply of services.

8. In establishing any delivery date for the goods or services being procured, a procuring entity shall take into account such factors as the complexity of the procurement, the extent of subcontracting anticipated and the realistic time required for production, de-stocking and transport of goods from the point of supply or for supply of services.

9. The evaluation criteria set out in the notice or tender documentation may include, among others, price and other cost factors, quality, technical merit, environmental characteristics, and terms of delivery.

10. A procuring entity shall promptly:

(a) make available tender documentation to ensure that interested suppliers have sufficient time to submit responsive tenders;

(b) provide, on request, the tender documentation to any interested supplier; and

(c) reply to any reasonable request for relevant information by any interested or participating supplier, provided that such information does not give that supplier an advantage over other suppliers.

Modifications

11. Where, prior to the award of a contract, a procuring entity modifies the criteria or technical requirements set out in a notice or tender documentation provided to participating suppliers, or amends or reissues a notice or tender documentation, it shall transmit in writing all such modifications or amended or re-issued notice or tender documentation:

(a) to all suppliers that are participating at the time the information is amended, if known, and in all other cases, in the same manner as the original information; and

(b) 供应商参加的任何条件，包括要求供应商提交的与之相关的信息和文件清单；

(c) 授予合同过程中考虑的所有评估标准，及除价格是唯一标准的情况外，此类标准的相对重要性；

(d) 如采购实体将通过电子方式进行采购，则为任何认证和加密要求或与以电子方式接收信息相关的其他要求；

(e) 如采购实体举行电子拍卖，则为规则，包括拍卖据此进行的、与评估标准有关的投标书的要素的确定；

(f) 如举行公开开标，则为开标的日期、时间和地点，如适用，授权参加的人员；

(g) 任何其他条款或条件，包括付款条件，及关于招标书提交方式的任何限制，如纸制或电子方式；及

(h) 货物交付或服务提供的任何日期。

8. 在确定将予采购货物或服务的任何交付日期时，一采购实体应考虑采购的复杂性、预期分包的程度以及生产、缩减储量和自供货点运输货物或提供服务所需的实际时间等因素。

9. 通知中或招标文件中所列评估标准可包括，除其他外，价格和其他成本因素、质量、技术优势、环境特点及交付条件；

10. 采购实体应及时：

(a) 使招标文件可获得，以保证感兴趣的供应商有充分的时间提交符合要求的招标书；

(b) 应请求，向任何感兴趣的供应商提供招标文件；及

(c) 对任何感兴趣或参与的供应商提出的提供相关信息的任何合理请求的答复，但条件是此类信息不使该供应商获得优于其他供应商的有利条件。

修改

11. 如，在授予合同前，一采购实体修改提供给参与采购的供应商的通知或招标文件中的标准或技术规格，或修正或重新发出通知或招标文件，则该实体应以书面形式将所有此类修改或修正或重发通知或招标文件传达：

(a) 至该信息修正时参加采购的所有供应商，如可知，在其他所有情况下，以原信息相同的方式；及

(b) in adequate time to allow such suppliers to modify and re-submit amended tenders, as appropriate.

Article XI Time-Periods

General

1. A procuring entity shall, consistent with its own reasonable needs, provide sufficient time for suppliers to prepare and submit requests for participation and responsive tenders, taking into account such factors as:

(a) the nature and complexity of the procurement;

(b) the extent of subcontracting anticipated; and

(c) the time for transmitting tenders from foreign as well as domestic points where electronic means are not used.

Such time-periods, including any extension of the time-periods, shall be common for all interested or participating suppliers.

Deadlines

2. A procuring entity that uses selective tendering shall establish that the final date for the submission of requests for participation shall not, in principle, be less than 25 days from the date of publication of the notice of intended procurement. Where a state of urgency duly substantiated by the procuring entity renders this time-period impracticable, the time-period may be reduced to not less than 10 days.

3. Except as provided for in paragraphs 4 and 5, a procuring entity shall establish that the final date for the submission of tenders shall not be less than 40 days from the date on which:

(a) in the case of open tendering, the notice of intended procurement is published; or

(b) in the case of selective tendering, the entity notifies suppliers that they will be invited to submit tenders, whether or not it uses a multi-use list.

4. A procuring entity may reduce the time-period for tendering set out in paragraph 3 to not less than 10 days where:

(a) the procuring entity published a notice of planned procurement under Article VII:4 at least 40 days and not more than 12 months in advance of the publication of the notice of intended procurement, and the notice of planned procurement contains:

(i) a description of the procurement;

(ii) the approximate final dates for the submission of tenders or requests for participation;

(iii) a statement that interested suppliers should express their interest in the procurement to the procuring entity;

(iv) the address from which documents relating to the procurement may be obtained; and

(b) 提供充分的时间，使此类供应商酌情修改和重新提交修正后的投标书。

第 11 条 时限

总则

1． 一采购实体，在与其自身合理需要保持一致的情况下，为供应商提供充分的时间准备和提交参加申请和投标书，并考虑下列因素：

(a) 采购的性质和复杂性；

(b) 预期分包的程度；及

(c) 在不使用电子方式的情况下，自国外和国内各地邮寄投标书所需的正常时间。

此类时限，包括该时限的任何展期对所有感兴趣或参加的供应商应相同。

截止期限

2． 一使用选择性招标的采购实体应确定提交参加请求的最后日期自预定采购通知公布之日起原则上不得少于 25 天。如采购实体能够证明的紧急状态表明这一时限不可行，则该时限可缩短至不少于 10 天。

3． 除第 4 款和 5 款中规定外，一采购实体应确定提交投标书的最后日期自下列日期起不得少于 40 天：

(a) 对于公开招标，预定采购公布的日期；或

(b) 对于选择性招标，实体通知供应商其将被邀请提交投标书的日期，无论是否使用常用清单。

4． 在下列情况下，一采购实体可将第 3 款所列时限缩短至不少于 10 天：

(a) 采购实体根据第 7 条第 4 款在预定采购通知公布前 40 天但不超过 12 个月已公布计划采购通知，且计划采购通知包含：

(i) 采购的描述

(ii) 提交投标书或参加请求的大致最后日期；

(iii) 关于感兴趣的供应商应向采购实体表明对此项采购感兴趣的说明；

(iv) 可获得与采购有关的文件的地址；及

(v) as much of the information that is required under Article VII:2 for the notice of intended procurement, as is available;

(b) the procuring entity, for procurements of a recurring nature, indicates in an initial notice of intended procurement that subsequent notices will provide time periods for tendering based on this paragraph; or

(c) a state of urgency duly substantiated by the procuring entity renders such time-period impracticable.

5. A procuring entity may reduce the time-period for tendering set out in paragraph 3 by five days for each one of the following circumstances:

(a) the notice of intended procurement is published by electronic means;

(b) all the tender documentation is made available by electronic means from the date of the publication of the notice of intended procurement; and

(c) the tenders can be received by electronic means by the procuring entity.

6. The use of paragraph 5, in conjunction with paragraph 4, shall in no case result in the reduction of the time-period for tendering set out in paragraph 3 to less than 10 days from the date on which the notice of intended procurement is published.

7. Notwithstanding any other time-period in this Article, where a procuring entity purchases commercial goods or services, it may reduce the time-period for tendering set out in paragraph 3 to not less than 13 days, provided that it publishes by electronic means, at the same time, both the notice of intended procurement and the tender documentation. Where the entity also accepts tenders for commercial goods and services by electronic means, it may reduce the time period set out in paragraph 3 to not less than 10 days.

8. Where a procuring entity in Annex 2 or 3 has selected all or a limited number of qualified suppliers, the time-period for tendering may be fixed by mutual agreement between the procuring entity and the selected suppliers. In the absence of agreement, the period shall not be less than 10 days.

Article XII Negotiation

1. A Party may provide for its procuring entities to conduct negotiations:

(a) in the context of procurements in which they have indicated such intent in the notice of intended procurement required under Article VII:2; or

(b) where it appears from the evaluation that no one tender is obviously the most advantageous in terms of the specific evaluation criteria set out in the notice or tender documentation.

2. A procuring entity shall:

(a) ensure that any elimination of suppliers participating in negotiations is carried out in accordance with the evaluation criteria set out in the notice or tender documentation; and

(v) 根据第 7 条第 2 款要求的有关预定采购通知尽可能多的信息；

(b) 对于重复进行的采购，采购实体在预定采购的最初通知中说明后续通知将提供根据本款规定的投标的时限；或

(c) 采购实体能够证明的紧急状态表明此时限不可行。

5. 一采购实体在下列情形下可将第 3 款所列招标时限缩短 5 天：

(a) 预定采购的通知以电子方式公布；

(b) 所有招标文件自预定采购通知公布之日起以电子方式可获得；及

(c) 采购实体可以电子方式接收投标书。

6. 第 5 款的使用，与第 4 款一起，不得导致第 3 款所列招标时限缩短至自预定采购通知公布之日起少于 10 天。

7. 尽管本条中有任何其他时限，但是如一采购实体购买商业货物或服务，该实体可将第 3 款所列时限缩短至少于 13 天，条件是该实体以电子方式同时公布预定采购通知和招标文件。如该实体也以电子方式接收商业货物和服务的投标书，则该实体可将第 3 款所列时限缩短至少于 10 天。

8. 如附件 2 或 3 中一采购实体已选择所有或有限数量符合条件的供应商，则可通过在该实体与被选供应商之间达成的协议确定投标时限。如未达成协议，则该时限不得少于 10 天。

第 12 条 谈判

1. 一参加方可规定其采购实体在下列情况下进行谈判：

(a) 在各实体在第 7 条第 2 款要求的通知中已表明此种意向的采购中；或

(b) 如评估显示，就通知或招标文件中所列具体评估标准而言，任何投标书均不具明显优势。

2. 一采购实体应：

(a) 保证参加谈判的供应商的任何排除应依照通知或招标文件中所列评估标准进行；及

(b) where negotiations are concluded, provide a common deadline for the remaining participating suppliers to submit any new or revised tenders.

Article XIII Limited Tendering

1. Provided that it does not use this provision for the purpose of avoiding competition among suppliers or in a manner that discriminates against suppliers of the other Parties or protects domestic suppliers, a procuring entity may use limited tendering and may choose not to apply Articles VII through IX, X (paragraphs 7 through 11), XI, XII, XIV, and XV only under the following circumstances:

(a) provided that the requirements of the tender documentation are not substantially modified where:

(i) no tenders were submitted or no suppliers requested participation ;

(ii) no tenders that conform to the essential requirements of the tender documentation were submitted;

(iii) no suppliers satisfied the conditions for participation; or

(iv) the tenders submitted have been collusive;

(b) where the goods or services can be supplied only by a particular supplier and no reasonable alternative or substitute goods or services exist for any of the following reasons:

(i) the requirement is for a work of art;

(ii) the protection of patents, copyrights or other exclusive rights; or

(iii) due to an absence of competition for technical reasons;

(c) for additional deliveries by the original supplier of goods and services that were not included in the initial procurement where:

(i) a change of supplier for such additional goods and services can not be made for economic or technical reasons such as requirements of interchangeability or interoperability with existing equipment, software, services, or installations procured under the initial procurement; and

(ii) such separation would cause significant inconvenience or substantial duplication of costs to the procuring entity;

(d) insofar as is strictly necessary where, for reasons of extreme urgency brought about by events unforeseeable by the procuring entity, the goods or services could not be obtained in time using open tendering or selective tendering;

(e) for goods purchased on a commodity market;

(f) where a procuring entity procures a prototype or a first good or service that is developed at its request in the course of, and for, a particular contract for research, experiment, study or original development. Original development of a first good or service may include limited production or supply in order to incorporate the results of

(b) 如谈判结束，向参加的其他供应商提供一提交任何新的或修改投标书的共同截止期限。

第 13 条　　有限招标

1. 只要一采购实体不将本条用于避免供应商之间的竞争的目的或不以歧视其他参加方供应商或保护国内供应商的方式使用本条，且仅在下列情形下，该实体可使用有限招标，并可选择不适用第 7 条至第 9 条、第 10 条（第 7 款至 11 款）、第 11 条、第 12 条、第 14 条和第 15 条：

(a) 条件是招标文件的要求未做实质性修改，如：

(i) 未提交投标书或无供应商要求参加；

(ii) 未提交符合招标文件基本要求的投标书；

(iii) 无供应商符合参加条件；或

(iv) 提交的投标书属串通性质；

(b) 如货物或服务只能通过一特定供应商提供，且由于下列原因之一不存在合理的选择或替代货物或服务：

(i) 要求针对艺术作品；

(ii) 专利、版权或其他专用权的保护；或

(iii) 由于技术原则而无竞争；

(c) 未包括在最初采购中的货物和服务原供应商的额外交货，如：

(i) 由于经济或技术原因，如与最初采购所购现有设备、软件、服务或安装的互换性或互用性要求，更换此类额外货物和服务的供应商不可行；及

(ii) 此种分离会给采购实体造成严重不便或成本大幅增加；

(d) 在绝对必要的情况下，如由于采购实体未能预见的事件所造成的极为紧急的情况，货物或服务不能通过公开或选择性招标程序迅速获得；

(e) 在商品市场上采购的货物；

(f) 如一采购实体采购应其请求在关于研究、实验、考察或原始开发的特定合同执行过程中开发的原型或第一个货物或服务。第一个货物或服务的原始开发可包括有限的生产或供应，以便包含实地实验的结果，并证明

field testing and to demonstrate that the good or service is suitable for production or supply in quantity to acceptable quality standards, but does not include quantity production, or supply to establish commercial viability, or to recover research and development costs;

(g) for purchases made under exceptionally advantageous conditions that only arise in the very short term in the case of unusual disposals such as those arising from liquidation, receivership, or bankruptcy, but not for routine purchases from regular suppliers; and

(h) where a contract is awarded to a winner of a design contest provided that:

(i) the contest has been organized in a manner that is consistent with the principles of this Agreement, in particular relating to the publication of a notice of intended procurement; and

(ii) the participants are judged by an independent jury with a view to a design contract being awarded to a winner.

2. A procuring entity shall prepare a report in writing on each contract awarded under paragraph 1. Each such report shall include the name of the procuring entity, the value and kind of goods or services procured, and a statement indicating the circumstances and conditions described in paragraph 1 that justified the use of limited tendering.

Article XIV Electronic Auctions

Where a procuring entity intends to conduct a covered procurement using an electronic auction, the entity shall provide each participant, before commencing the electronic auction, with:

(a) the automatic evaluation method, including the mathematical formula, that is based on the evaluation criteria set out in the tender documentation and that will be used in the automatic ranking or re-ranking during the auction;

(b) the results of any initial evaluation of the elements of its tender where the contract is to be awarded on the basis of the most advantageous tender; and

(c) any other relevant information relating to the conduct of the auction.

Article XV Treatment of Tenders and Contract Awards

Treatment of Tenders

1. A procuring entity shall receive, open, and treat all tenders under procedures that guarantee the fairness and impartiality of the procurement process, and the confidentiality of tenders.

2. A procuring entity shall not penalize any supplier whose tender is received after the time specified for receiving tenders if the delay is due solely to mishandling on the part of the procuring entity.

3. When a procuring entity provides suppliers with opportunities to correct unintentional errors of form between the opening of tenders and the awarding of the contract, the procuring entity shall provide the same opportunities to all participating suppliers.

该货物或服务适宜大量生产或供应，达到可接受的质量标准，但并不包括至为形成商业活力或收回科研与开发成本而进行的大量生产或供应；

(g) 对于由于如财产清算、财务清算或破产产生的不寻常的处理等只在非常短的时间内出现的特别有利的条件下进行的采购，但不是自正常供应商处的例行采购；及

(h) 如一合同授予设计比赛获胜者，但条件是：

(i) 比赛是按与本协定一致的原则组织的，特别是与预定采购通知的公布有关；及

(ii) 参加者由独立评判委员会进行评判，以期将设计合同授予比赛获胜者。

2. 一采购实体应就根据本条第 1 款规定授予的每一合同准备书面报告。每一报告均应包含采购实体的名称、所购货物或服务的价值和种类以及表明第 1 款所述情形和条件能够证明有限招标的使用为合理的说明。

第 14 条 电子拍卖

如一采购实体有意使用电子拍卖进行一涵盖采购，则该实体在电子拍卖开始前应向每一参加者提供：

(a) 基于招标文件中所列评估标准并将在拍卖过程中自动排序或重新排序中使用的自动评估方法，包括数学公式；

(b) 在合同依据最具优势的投标书授予的情况下，对投标书中各要素任何最初评估结果；及

(c) 与进行拍卖有关的任何其他相关信息。

第 15 条 投标书的处理和合同授予

投标书的处理

1. 一采购实体应根据可以保证采购程序公正和公平及投标书保密性的程序接收、开启和处理所有投标书。

2. 一采购实体不得惩罚其投标书在接收投标书时间过后收到的任何供应商，如迟延仅由于采购实体处理不当造成。

3. 如一采购实体在开标和授予合同之间向供应商提供更正表格中非故意错误的机会，则该采购实体应向所有参加的供应商提供同样的机会。

Awarding of Contracts

4. To be considered for award, a tender must be in writing and must, at the time of opening, comply with the essential requirements of the notices and tender documentation and be from a supplier that satisfies the conditions for participation.

5. Unless a procuring entity determines that it is not in the public interest to award a contract, it shall award the contract to the supplier that the entity has determined to be fully capable of undertaking the contract and, based solely on the evaluation criteria specified in the notices and tender documentation, has submitted:

(a) the most advantageous tender; or

(b) where price is the sole criterion, the lowest price.

6. Where a procuring entity receives a tender with a price that is abnormally lower than the prices in other tenders submitted, it may verify with the supplier that it can comply with the conditions of participation and is capable of fulfilling the terms of the contract.

7. A procuring entity shall not use option clauses, cancel a procurement, or modify awarded contracts in a manner that circumvents the obligations of this Agreement.

Article XVI Transparency of Procurement Information

Information Provided to Suppliers

1. A procuring entity shall promptly inform participating suppliers of the entity's contract award decisions and, on request, in writing. Subject to Article XVII, a procuring entity shall, on request, provide an unsuccessful supplier with an explanation of the reasons that the entity did not select its tender and the relative advantages of the successful supplier's tender.

Publication of Award Information

2. Not later than 72 days after the award of each contract covered by this Agreement, a procuring entity shall publish a notice in the appropriate paper or electronic medium listed in Appendix III. Where only an electronic medium is used, the information shall remain readily accessible for a reasonable period of time. The notice shall include at least the following information:

(a) a description of the goods or services procured;

(b) the name and address of the procuring entity;

(c) the name and address of the successful supplier;

(d) the value of the successful tender or the highest and lowest offers taken into account in the award of the contract;

(e) the date of award; and

(f) the type of procurement method used, and in cases where limited tendering was used pursuant to Article XIII, a description of the circumstances justifying the use of limited tendering.

合同的授予

4. 投标书必须以书面形式且在开启时符合通知和招标文件中的基本要求，并由符合参加条件的供应商提交，方可被考虑授予合同。

5. 除非一采购实体确定授予一合同不符合公众利益，否则该实体应将合同授予已被该实体确定完全有能力执行合同的供应商，且仅根据通知和招标文件中所列评估标准，其已提交：

(a) 最具优势的投标书；或

(b) 在价格为唯一标准的情况下，最低价格。

6. 如一采购实体收到一项比所提交的其他投标书价格异常低的投标书，则该实体可向该投标人验证其能够遵守参加的条件并能够履行合同条款。

7. 一采购实体不得以规避本协定义务的方式使用选择性条款、取消一采购或修改已授予的合同。

第 16 条 采购信息的透明度

向供应商提供的信息

1. 一采购实体应迅速告知参加投标的供应商该实体有关合同授予的决定，应请求，应以书面形式告知。根据第 17 条，一采购实体应请求，应向未中标供应商提供关于该实体未选择其投标书的理由和中标供应商投标书相对优势的说明。

授予信息的公布

2. 不迟于本协定所涵盖的每一合同授予后 72 天内，一采购实体应在附件 3 所列适当纸制或电子媒介中公布通知。如仅使用一种电子媒介，则信息应在一合理期限内可容易获得。通知应至少包括下列信息：

(a) 所采购货物或服务的描述；

(b) 采购实体的名称和地址；

(c) 中标供应商的名称和地址；

(d) 中标投标书的价值或在授予合同过程中予以考虑的最高和最低报盘；

(e) 授予日期；及

(f) 使用的采购方法，在根据第 13 条使用有限招标的情况下，关于有关情形能够证明有限招标的使用为合理的描述。

Maintenance of Documentation, Reports, and Electronic Traceability

3. Each procuring entity shall, for a period of at least three years from the award of the contract maintain:

(a) documentation and reports of tendering procedures and contract awards relating to covered procurement, including the reports required under Article XIII; and

(b) data that ensure the appropriate traceability of the conduct of covered procurement by electronic means.

Collection and Report of Statistics

4. Each Party shall collect and report to the Committee statistics on its contracts covered by this Agreement. Each report shall cover one year and be submitted within two years of the end of the reporting period, and shall contain:

(a) for Annex 1 procuring entities:

(i) the number and total value, for all such entities, of contracts covered by this Agreement;

(ii) the number and total value of all contracts covered by this Agreement awarded by such entities, broken down by categories of goods and services according to an internationally recognized uniform classification system; and

(iii) the number and total value of contracts covered by this Agreement awarded by each such entity under limited tendering;

(b) for Annex 2 and 3 procuring entities, the number and total value of contracts covered by this Agreement awarded by all such entities, broken down by Annex; and

(c) estimates for the information required under subparagraphs (a) and (b), with an explanation of the methodology used to develop the estimates, where it is not feasible to provide the data.

5. Where a Party publishes its statistics on an official website, the Party may substitute a notification of the website address for the submission of the data under paragraph 4, with any instructions necessary to access and use such statistics, in accordance with the requirements of paragraph 4 .

6. Where a Party requires notices concerning awarded contracts, pursuant to paragraph 2, to be published electronically and where such notices are accessible to the public through a single database in a form permitting analysis of the covered contracts, the Party may substitute a notification of the website address for the submission of the data under paragraph 4, with any instructions necessary to access and use such data.

Article XVII Disclosure of Information

Provision of Information to Parties

1. On request of any other Party, a Party shall provide promptly any information necessary to determine whether a procurement was conducted fairly, impartially and in accordance with this Agreement, including information on the characteristics and relative advantages of the successful

文件、报告的保存及电子可追溯性

3. 每一采购实体，自合同授予起至少 3 年内应保存：

(a) 与涵盖采购相关的招标程序和合同授予的文件和报告，包括第 13 条所要求的报告；及

(b) 可保证通过电子方式进行的涵盖采购的适当可追溯性的数据。

统计数字的收集和报告

4. 每一参加方应收集并向委员会报告关于其本协定所涵盖合同的统计数字。每一报告应涵盖一年，在报告期结束后 2 年内提交，并应包含：

(a) 对于附件 1 采购实体：

(i) 所有此类实体的本协定所涵盖合同的数量和总价值；

(ii) 此类实体授予的所有本协定所涵盖合同的数量和总价值，按一国际认可的统一分类制度的货物或服务类别分解；

(iii) 在有限招标中每一此类实体授予的本协定所涵盖合同的数量和总价值；

(b) 对于附件 2 和 3 采购实体，所有此类实体授予的本协定所涵盖合同的数量和总价值，按附件分解；及

(c) 如提供数据不可行，则为对(a)和(b)项要求信息的估计值，并附对做出估计所使用方法的说明。

5. 如一参加方在一官员网站公布其统计数字，则该参加方可将第 4 款要求提交的数据替换为该网址，并附访问和使用此类统计数字的任何必要使用说明，依照第 4 款的要求。

6. 如一参加方根据第 2 款要求有关授予合同的通知以电子方式公布，且如此类通知通过一单一数据库以可对所涵盖合同进行分析的方式使公众可获得，则该参加方可将第 4 款要求提交的数据替换为该网址，并附访问和使用此类统计数字的任何必要使用说明。

第 17 条 信息披露

向参加方提供信息

1. 应任何其他参加方请求，一参加方应迅速提供确定采购是否公平和公正且依照本协定进行所必需的任何信息，包括中标投标人特点和相对优势的信息。在发布此信息会损害未

tender. In cases where release of the information would prejudice competition in future tenders, the Party that receives that information shall not disclose it to any supplier, except after consultation with, and agreement of, the Party that provided the information.

Non-Disclosure of Information

2. Notwithstanding any other provision of this Agreement, a Party, including its procuring entities, may not provide information to a particular supplier that might prejudice fair competition between suppliers.

3. Nothing in this Agreement shall be construed to require a Party, including its procuring entities, authorities, and review bodies, to release confidential information under this Agreement where release:

(a) would impede law enforcement;

(b) might prejudice fair competition between suppliers;

(c) would prejudice the legitimate commercial interests of particular persons, including the protection of intellectual property; or

(d) would otherwise be contrary to the public interest.

Article XVIII Domestic Review Procedures for Supplier Challenges

1. Each Party shall provide a timely, effective, transparent, and non-discriminatory administrative or judicial review procedure through which a supplier may challenge:

(a) a breach of the Agreement; or

(b) where the supplier does not have a right to challenge directly a breach of the Agreement under the domestic law of a Party, a failure to comply with a Party's measures implementing this Agreement,

arising in the context of a covered procurement, in which it has, or has had, an interest. The procedural rules for all challenges shall be in writing and made generally available.

2. In the event of a complaint by a supplier, arising in the context of covered procurement in which the supplier has, or has had, an interest, that there has been a breach of this Agreement or, where the supplier does not have a right to challenge directly a breach of this Agreement under the domestic law of a Party, a failure to comply with a Party's measures implementing this Agreement, each Party shall encourage the procuring entity and supplier to seek resolution of the complaint through consultations. The procuring entity shall accord impartial and timely consideration to any such complaint in a manner that is not prejudicial to the supplier's participation in ongoing or future procurement or right to seek corrective measures under the administrative or judicial review procedure.

3. Each supplier shall be allowed a sufficient period of time to prepare and submit a challenge, which in no case shall be less than 10 days from the time when the basis of the challenge became known or reasonably should have become known to the supplier.

4. Each Party shall establish or designate at least one impartial administrative or judicial authority that is independent of its procuring entities to receive and review a challenge by a supplier arising in the context of a covered procurement.

来投标中竞争的情况下，除非与提供该信息的参加方进行磋商并达成协议，否则此信息不得向任何供应商披露。

信息的不披露

2．　尽管本协定另有规定，但是一参加方，包括其采购实体，不可向一特定供应商提供可能会损害供应商之间公平竞争的信息。

3．　本协定不得理解为要求一参加方，包括其采购实体、主管机关及审议机构，发布产生下列结果的本协定项下的机密信息：

(a)　妨碍执法；

(b)　损害供应商之间的公平竞争；

(c)　损害特定个人的合法商业利益，包括保护知识产权；或

(d)　违背公共利益。

第 18 条　供应商质疑的国内审议程序

1．　每一参加方应提供及时、有效、透明和非歧视的行政或司法审议程序，一供应商可借此提供下列质疑：

(a)　违反本协定的情况；或

(b)　在供应商根据一参加方国内法无权直接质疑违反本协定的情况下，则为未能遵守一参加方实施本协定的措施的情况；

在供应商对其拥有或曾经拥有利益的一涵盖采购的过程中产生。对所有质疑的程序性规定应为书面形式并可使之普遍获得。

2．　如一供应商就其拥有或曾经拥有利益的一项涵盖采购过程中存在违反本协定的情况，或在一供应商根据一参加方国内法无权直接质疑违反本协定的情况下，存在未能遵守一参加方实施本协定的措施的情况提出申诉，则每一参加方应鼓励采购实体和该供应商通过磋商寻求解决其申诉。采购实体应对任何此类申诉给予公正和及时的考虑，且以不损害供应商参加正在进行的或未来采购或根据行政或司法审查程序寻求纠正措施的权利的方式进行。

3．　每一供应商应被给予充分的时间准备和提交质疑，任何情况下自质疑的依据已知或理应知道时起不得少于 10 天。

4．　每一参加方应制定或指定至少一独立于其采购实体的公正的行政或司法主管机关接收和审查一供应商在一涵盖采购过程中产生的质疑。

5. Where a body other than an authority referred to in paragraph 4 initially reviews a challenge, the Party shall ensure that the supplier may appeal the initial decision to an impartial administrative or judicial authority that is independent of the procuring entity whose procurement is the subject of the challenge.

6. A review body that is not a court shall either be subject to judicial review or have procedures that provide that:

(a) the procuring entity shall respond in writing to the challenge and disclose all relevant documents to the review body;

(b) the participants to the proceedings ("participants") shall have the right to be heard prior to a decision of the review body being made on the challenge;

(c) the participants shall have the right to be represented and accompanied;

(d) the participants shall have access to all proceedings;

(e) the participants shall, have the right to request that the proceedings take place in public and that witnesses may be presented; and

(f) decisions or recommendations relating to supplier challenges shall be provided, in a timely fashion, in writing, with an explanation of the basis for each decision or recommendation.

7. Each Party shall adopt or maintain procedures that provide for:

(a) rapid interim measures to preserve the supplier's opportunity to participate in the procurement. Such interim measures may result in suspension of the procurement process. The procedures may provide that overriding adverse consequences for the interests concerned, including the public interest, may be taken into account when deciding whether such measures should be applied. Just cause for not acting shall be provided in writing; and

(b). where a review body has determined that there has been a breach of this Agreement or, where the supplier does not have a right to challenge directly a breach of this Agreement under the domestic law of a Party, a failure by a procuring entity to comply with a Party's measures implementing this Agreement, corrective action or compensation for the loss or damages suffered, which may be limited to either the costs for the preparation of the tender or the costs relating to the challenge, or both.

Article XIX Modifications and Rectifications to Coverage

Notification of Proposed Modification

1. A Party shall notify the Committee of any proposed rectification, transfer of an entity from one Annex to another, withdrawal of an entity, or other modification (referred to generally in this Article as "modification") of Appendix I. The Party proposing the modification ("modifying Party") shall include in the notification:

(a) for any proposed withdrawal of an entity from Appendix I in exercise of its rights on the grounds that government control or influence over the entity's covered procurement has been effectively eliminated, evidence of such elimination; or

5. 如第 4 款中提及的主管机关之外的一机构最初审查一质疑，则参加方应保证该供应商可向一独立于采购为质疑对象的采购实体的公正的行政或司法主管机关就最初决定提起上诉。

6. 如一审查机构不是法院，则该机构应接受司法审查，或应设立规定下列内容的程序：

(a) 采购实体应书面答复质疑并向审查机构披露所有相关文件；

(b) 申诉程序参加人（“参加人”）有权在审查机构对质疑作出决定前获得听取其意见的机会；

(c) 参加人有权被代表和陪同；

(d) 参加人应可参加所有申诉程序；

(e) 参加人有权请求申诉程序公开进行和请求证人出席；及

(f) 应及时以书面形式提供与供应商质疑有关的决定或建议，并附每一决定或建议的依据。

7. 每一参加方应采用或设立程序规定：

(a) 快速的临时措施，以保持供应商参加采购的机会。此类临时措施可造成采购过程的中止。质疑程序可规定在决定是否应采取此类措施时，可考虑对有关利益包括公众利益所造成的重大不利后果。应以书面形式提供不采取行动的合法理由；及

(b) 如一审查机构确定存在违反本协定的情况，或在供应商根据一参加方国内法无权直接质疑违反本协定的情况下，确定存在一采购实体未能遵守一参加方实施本协定的措施的情况，则为对所受损失或损害的纠正措施或赔偿，此类赔偿可限于为准备投标书的费用或与质疑有关的费用，或两者均包括。

第 19 条 涵盖范围的修改和更正

拟议修改的通知

1. 一参加方应将附录 1 中任何拟议的更正、将一实体自一附件转入另一附件、去除一实体或其他修改（本条中统称为“修改”）通知委员会。提出修改的参加方（“修改方”）应在通知中包括：

(a) 对于以政府对一实体涵盖的控制或影响已有效消除为由，在行使其权利时拟议将一实体自附录 1 中去除，此种消除的证据；或

(b) for any other proposed modification, information as to the likely consequences of the change for the mutually agreed coverage provided in this Agreement.

Objection to Notification

2. Any Party whose rights under this Agreement may be affected by a proposed modification notified under paragraph 1 may notify the Committee of any objection to the proposed modification. Such objections shall be made within 45 days from the date of the circulation to the Parties of the notification, and shall set out reasons for the objection.

Consultations

3. The modifying Party and any Party making an objection ("objecting Party") shall make every attempt to resolve the objection through consultations. In such consultations, the modifying and objecting Parties shall consider the proposed modification:

(a) in the case of a notification under paragraph 1(a), in accordance with any indicative criteria adopted pursuant to paragraph 8 indicating the effective elimination of government control or influence over an entity's covered procurement; and

(b) in the case of a notification under paragraph 1(b), in accordance with any criteria adopted pursuant to paragraph 8 relating to the level of compensatory adjustments to be offered for modifications, with a view to maintaining a balance of rights and obligations and a comparable level of mutually agreed coverage provided in this Agreement.

Revised Modification

4. Where the modifying Party and any objecting Party resolve the objection through consultations, and the modifying Party revises its proposed modification as a result of those consultations, the modifying Party shall notify the Committee in accordance with paragraph 1, and any such revised modification shall only be effective after fulfilling the requirements of this Article.

Implementation of Modifications

5. A proposed modification shall become effective only where:

(a) no Party submits to the Committee a written objection to the proposed modification within 45 days from the date of circulation of the notification of the proposed modification under paragraph 1;

(b) all objecting Parties have notified the Committee that they withdraw their objections to the proposed modification; or

(c) 150 days from the date of circulation of the notification of the proposed modification under paragraph 1 have elapsed, and the modifying Party has informed the Committee of its intention to implement the modification.

Withdrawal of Substantially Equivalent Coverage

6. Where a modification becomes effective pursuant to paragraph 5(c), any objecting Party may withdraw substantially equivalent coverage. Notwithstanding Article V:1(b), a withdrawal pursuant to this paragraph may be implemented solely with respect to the modifying Party. Any objecting

(b) 对于其他任何拟议修改，关于变更对本协定规定的共同议定的适用范围可能产生的结果的信息。

对通知的异议

2. 任何在本协定项下权利可能受到根据第 1 款做出通知的拟议修改影响的参加方可将其对拟议修改的任何异议通知委员会。此类异议应自通知散发各参加方之日起 45 天内做出，且应列出提出异议的理由。

磋商

3． 修改方和提出异议的任何参加方（“异议方”）应尽力通过磋商解决该异议。在此类磋商中，修改方和异议方应按以下方式考虑拟议修改：

(a) 对于根据第 1 款(a)项做出的通知，依照根据第 8 款采用的表明政府对一实体涵盖采购的控制或影响的有效消除证据的任何指示性标准；及

(b) 根据第 1 款(b)项做出的通知，依照根据第 8 款采用的有关对于修改做出补偿性调整的任何标准，以期保持权利与义务的平衡和本协定中共同议定的涵盖范围的可比水平。

修订的修正

4． 如一修改方和任何异议方通过磋商解决异议，且修改方作为磋商结果修订其拟议修改，则修改方应依照第 1 款通知委员会，任何此类修订的修改在满足本条要求后方可生效。

修改的实施

5． 一拟议修改只有在下列情况下方可生效：

(a) 在自根据第 1 款做出的拟议修改通知散发之日起 45 天内无参加方向委员会提交对拟议修改的书面异议；

(b) 所有异议方已通知委员会撤销对拟议修改的异议；或

(c) 根据第 1 款做出的拟议修改的通知散发之日起 150 天已过，且修改方已通知委员会其实施修改的意向。

实质相等的涵盖范围的撤销

6． 如一修改根据第 5 款(c)项生效，则异议方可撤销实质相等的涵盖范围。尽管有第 5 条第 1 款(b)项的规定，但是根据本款的撤销可仅对修改方实施。任何异议方应在该项撤销

Party shall inform the Committee of any such withdrawal at least 30 days before the withdrawal becomes effective. A withdrawal pursuant to this paragraph shall be consistent with any criteria relating to the level of compensatory adjustment adopted by the Committee pursuant to paragraph 8.

Arbitration Procedures to Facilitate Resolution of Objections

7. Where the Committee has adopted arbitration procedures to facilitate the resolution of objections pursuant to paragraph 8, a modifying or any objecting Party may invoke the arbitration procedures within 120 days of circulation of the notification of the proposed modification.

(a) Where no Party has invoked the arbitration procedures within the time-period:

(i) notwithstanding paragraph 5(c), the proposed modification shall become effective where 130 days from the date of circulation of the notification of the proposed modification under paragraph 1 have elapsed, and the modifying Party has informed the Committee of its intention to implement the modification; and

(ii) no objecting Party may withdraw coverage pursuant to paragraph 6.

(b) Where a modifying Party or objecting Party has invoked the arbitration procedures:

(i) notwithstanding paragraph 5(c), the proposed modification shall not become effective before the completion of the arbitration procedures;

(ii) any objecting Party that intends to enforce a right to compensation, or to withdraw substantially equivalent coverage pursuant to paragraph 6, shall participate in the arbitration proceedings;

(iii) a modifying Party should comply with the results of the arbitration procedures in making any modification effective pursuant to paragraph 5(c); and

(iv) where a modifying Party does not comply with the results of the arbitration procedures in making any modification effective pursuant to paragraph 5(c), any objecting Party may withdraw substantially equivalent coverage pursuant to paragraph 6, provided that any such withdrawal is consistent with the result of the arbitration procedures.

Committee Responsibilities

8. The Committee shall adopt:

(a) arbitration procedures to facilitate resolution of objections under paragraph 2:

(b) indicative criteria that demonstrate the effective elimination of government control or influence over an entity's covered procurement; and

(c) criteria that indicate how to determine the level of compensatory adjustment to be offered for modifications made pursuant to paragraph 1(b) and substantially equivalent coverage under paragraph 6.

生效前至少 30 天将此项撤销通知委员会。根据本款的撤销应与委员会根据第 8 款采用的补偿性调整水平有关的任何标准相一致。

便利异议解决的仲裁程序

7. 如委员会根据第 8 款已经采用仲裁程序便利异议的解决,则一修改方或任何异议方可在拟议修改通知散发后 120 天内援引仲裁程序。

(a) 如在时限内无参加方援引仲裁程序:

(i) 尽管有第 5 款(c)项的规定,但是拟议修改应在根据第 1 款所作拟议修改通知散发之日起 130 天过后生效,且修改方已将其实施修改的意图通知委员会;及

(ii) 任何异议方不得根据第 6 款撤销涵盖范围。

(b) 如一修改方或异议方已经援引仲裁程序:

(i) 尽管有第 5 款(c)项的规定,但是仲裁程序完成前,拟议修改不得生效;

(ii) 任何有意行使补偿权利或根据第 6 款撤销实质相等的涵盖范围的异议方,应参加仲裁程序;

(iii) 一修改方在根据第 5 款(c)项使任何修改生效时应遵守仲裁程序的结果;及

(iv) 如一修改方在使任何修改生效时未遵守仲裁程序的结果,则任何异议方可根据第 6 款撤销实质相等的涵盖范围,但条件是任何此种撤销应符合仲裁程序的结果。

委员会的责任

8. 委员会应采用:

(a) 根据第 2 款便利异议解决的仲裁程序;

(b) 表明政府对一实体所涉采购的控制或影响有效消除的指示性标准;及

(c) 表明如何确定对根据第 1 款(b)项所作修改作出的补偿性调整的水平和根据第 6 款实质相等的涵盖范围的标准。

Article XX Consultations and Dispute Settlement

1. Each Party shall accord sympathetic consideration to, and shall afford adequate opportunity for, consultation regarding such representations as may be made by another Party with respect to any matter affecting the operation of this Agreement.

2. Where any Party considers that any benefit accruing to it, directly or indirectly, under this Agreement is being nullified or impaired, or that the attainment of any objective of this Agreement is being impeded as the result of:

(a) the failure of another Party or Parties to carry out its obligations under this Agreement; or

(b) the application by another Party or Parties of any measure, whether or not it conflicts with the provisions of this Agreement,

it may with a view to reaching a mutually satisfactory solution to the matter, have recourse to the provisions of the Understanding on Rules and Procedures Governing the Settlement of Disputes (hereinafter referred to as "the Dispute Settlement Understanding").

3. The Dispute Settlement Understanding applies to consultations and the settlement of disputes under this Agreement, with the exception that, notwithstanding paragraph 3 of Article 22 of the Dispute Settlement Understanding, any dispute arising under any Agreement listed in Appendix 1 to the Dispute Settlement Understanding other than this Agreement shall not result in the suspension of concessions or other obligations under this Agreement, and any dispute arising under this Agreement shall not result in the suspension of concessions or other obligations under any other Agreement listed in Appendix 1 of the Dispute Settlement Understanding.

Article XXI Institutions

Committee on Government Procurement

1. A Committee on Government Procurement composed of representatives from each of the Parties shall be established. This Committee shall elect its own Chairman and shall meet as necessary, but not less than once a year, for the purpose of affording Parties the opportunity to consult on any matters relating to the operation of this Agreement or the furtherance of its objectives, and to carry out such other responsibilities as may be assigned to it by the Parties.

2. The Committee may establish working parties or other subsidiary bodies that shall carry out such functions as may be given to them by the Committee.

3. The Committee shall annually:

(a) review the implementation and operation of this Agreement; and

(b) inform the General Council of the WTO of developments relating to the implementation and operation of this Agreement.

Observers

4. Any WTO Member that is not a Party to this Agreement shall be entitled to participate in the Committee as an observer upon submission of a written notice to the Secretariat. Any WTO observer may submit a written request to the Secretariat to participate in the Committee as an observer, and may be accorded observer status by the Committee.

第 20 条　　碓商和争端解决

1.　　每一参加方应对关于另一参加方针对影响本协定运用的任何事项所提交涉的磋商给予同情考虑，并给予充足的机会。

2.　　如任何参加方认为其在本协定项下直接或间接获得的任何利益丧失或减损，或由于下列原因阻碍本协定任何目标的实现：

(a)　　另一个或多个参加方未能履行其在本协定项下的义务；或

(b)　　另一个或多个参加方实施无论是否违背本协定规定的任何措施；

则该参加方为达成关于该事项的双方满意的解决办法，可援引《关于争端解决规则与程序的谅解》(下称“《争端解决谅解》”)。

3.　　《争端解决谅解》适用于本协定项下的磋商和争端解决，但下列情况除外，即尽管有《争端解决谅解》第 22 条第 3 款的规定，但是在《争端解决谅解》附录 1 所列除本协定外的任何协定项下产生的任何争端，不得导致本协定项下减让或其他义务的中止，且本协定项下产生的任何争端不得导致《争端解决谅解》附录 1 所列任何其他协定项下减让或其他义务的中止。

第 21 条　　机构

政府采购委员会

1.　　应设立由每一参加方代表组成的政府采购委员会。委员会应选举自己的主席和副主席，并在必要时召开会议，但每年不得少于一次，目的在于向各参加方提供机会，就有关本协定运用或促进本协定目标实现的任何事项进行磋商，并履行各参加方可能指定的其他职责。

2.　　委员会可设立工作组或其他附属机构，以执行委员可能给予的职能。

3.　　委员会应每年

(a)　　审议本协定的实施和运用情况；及

(b)　　向 WTO 总理事会报告有关本协定的实施和运用的进展情况。

观察员

4.　　非本协定参加方的任何 WTO 成员在向秘书处提交书面通知后，有权作为观察员参加委员会。任何 WTO 观察员可向秘书处提交书面请求以作为观察员参加委员会，并可由委员会授予观察员地位。

Article XXII Final Provisions

Acceptance and Entry into Force

1. This Agreement shall enter into force on [ ] for those WTO Members whose agreed coverage is set out in Annexes 1 through 6 of Appendix I, and that have, by signature, accepted this Agreement on [ ], or have, by or on that date, signed this Agreement subject to ratification and have subsequently ratified this Agreement before [ ].

Transitional Arrangements

2. Between the Parties to this Agreement that are also Parties to the Agreement on Government Procurement dated 15 April 1994 ("1994 Agreement"), the 1994 Agreement shall cease to apply on the date of entry into force of this Agreement for those Parties. When all Parties to the 1994 Agreement have accepted this Agreement, the 1994 Agreement shall be terminated.[3]

3. The provisions of Articles XVIII and XX of this Agreement shall apply to covered procurement that has commenced after the entry into force of this Agreement.[4]

Provisional Application

4. A Party to the 1994 Agreement may, notwithstanding its commitments in the 1994 Agreement, maintain or adopt any measure that is consistent with the provisions of this Agreement.[5]

Accession

5. Any Member of the WTO may accede to this Agreement on terms to be agreed between that Member and the Parties. Accession shall take place by deposit with the Director-General of the WTO of an instrument of accession that states the terms so agreed. This Agreement shall enter into force for an acceding Member on the 30th day following the deposit of its instrument of accession the date of its accession to this Agreement.[6]

Reservations

6. No Party may enter any reservation in respect of any provisions of this Agreement.

National Legislation

7. Each Party shall ensure, not later than the date of entry into force of this Agreement for it, the conformity of its laws, regulations and administrative procedures, and the rules, procedures, and practices applied by its procuring entities, with the provisions of this Agreement.

8. Each Party shall inform the Committee of any changes in its laws and regulations relevant to this Agreement and in the administration of such laws and regulations.

9. The Parties shall seek to avoid introducing or continuing discriminatory measures and practices that distort open procurement.

---

[3] Negotiators' Note: The Parties are still considering the need for and the content of this paragraph.
[4] Negotiators' Note: The Parties are still considering the need for and the content of this paragraph.
[5] Negotiators' Note: The Parties are still considering the need for and the content of this paragraph.
[6] Negotiators' Note: The Parties are still considering this paragraph.

第 22 条　　最后条款

接受和生效

1.　本协定应于[　]对议定涵盖范围已列入附件 1 至 6、且于[　]通过签字接受本协定，或在该日期或该日期之前虽已签署本协定但尚需核准且随后于[　]之前已核准本协定的 WTO 成员生效。

过渡性安排

2.　对于亦为 1994 年 4 月 15 日《政府采购协定》（“1994 年协定”）参加方的本协定参加方，1994 年协定应在本协定生效之日对这些参加方终止适用。1994 年协定的所有参加方接受本协定后，1994 年协定应终止。[3]

3.　本协定第 18 和 20 条应适用于在本协定生效后已开始的采购。[4]

临时适用

4.　一 1994 年协定参加方，尽管有其在 1994 年协定中的承诺，但是可维持或采用任何与本协定条款相一致的任何措施。[5]

加入

5.　任何WTO成员可根据其与各参加方议定的条件加入本协定。加入在将说明议定加入条件的加入书交存WTO总干事后生效。在交存加入书后，本协定在申请加入成员加入本协定后第 30 天对其生效。[6]

保留

6.　任何参加方不得对本协定的任何条款提出保留。

国内立法

7.　每一参加方应保证，在不迟于本协定对其生效之日，使其法律、法规、管理程序及其采购实体所适用的规则、程序和做法符合本协定的规定。

8.　每一参加方应将其与本协定有关的法律和法规的任何变更及此类法律和法规的管理方面的任何变更通知委员会。

9.　各参加方应寻求避免采用或继续采用扭曲公开采购的歧视性措施和做法。

---

[3] 谈判者注释：各参加方仍在考虑本款内容的必要性。

[4] 谈判者注释：各参加方仍在考虑本款内容的必要性。

[5] 谈判者注释：各参加方仍在考虑本款内容的必要性。

[6] 谈判者注释：各参加方仍在考虑本款。

Future Work

10. Not later than the end of [...] from the date of entry into force of this Agreement, and periodically thereafter, the Parties thereto shall undertake further negotiations, with a view to improving the Agreement and achieving the greatest possible extension of its coverage among all Parties, taking into consideration the needs of developing countries.[7]

11. The Parties shall, in the context of the negotiations referred to in paragraph 10, seek to eliminate discriminatory measures which remain on the date of entry into force of this Agreement.[8]

12. Following the conclusion of the work programme for the harmonization of rules of origin for goods being undertaken under the Agreement on Rules of Origin in Annex 1A of the Agreement Establishing the World Trade Organization and negotiations regarding trade in services, the Parties shall take the results of that work programme and those negotiations into account in amending Article V:5, as appropriate.

13. Not later than the end of the third year from the date of entry into force of this Agreement, the Committee shall undertake further work to consider the advantages and disadvantages of developing common nomenclature for goods and services and standardized notices

14. Beginning two years after entry into force of this Agreement, the Committee shall regularly assess the effective use of Articles XVI:4 and 5.

15. Not later than the end of the fifth year from the date of entry into force of this Agreement, the Committee shall examine the applicability of Article XX:2(b).

Amendments

16. The Parties may amend this Agreement having regard, *inter alia*, to the experience gained in its implementation. Such an amendment, once the Parties have concurred in accordance with the procedures established by the Committee, shall take effect for the Parties that have accepted them upon acceptance by [ ] of the Parties and thereafter for each other Party upon acceptance by it.[9]

17. Amendments to provisions of this Agreement of a nature that would alter the rights and obligations of the Parties, shall take effect for the Parties that have accepted them upon acceptance by [ ] of the Parties and thereafter for each other Party upon acceptance by it. The Committee may decide by a [...] majority of the Parties that any amendment made effective under paragraph 16 is of such a nature that any Party which has not accepted it within a specified period shall be free to withdraw from this Agreement or to remain with the consent of the Committee.[10]

18. Amendments to provisions of this Agreement of a nature that would not alter the rights and obligations of the Parties shall take effect for all Parties upon acceptance by [...] of the Parties.[11]

[7] Negotiators' Note: The Parties shall review the content of this paragraph before the end of the negotiations.

[8] Negotiators' Note: The Parties shall review the content of this paragraph before the end of the negotiations.

[9] Negotiators' Note: The Parties are still considering the need for and the content of this paragraph.

[10] Negotiators' Note: The Parties are still considering the need for and the content of this paragraph.

[11] Negotiators' Note: The Parties are still considering the need for and the content of this paragraph.

未来工作

10. 不迟于本协定生效之日起[ ]及此后定期，参加方应进行进一步谈判，以期改进本协定，并尽最大可能在所有参加方之间实现本协定适用范围的扩大，同时考虑到发展中国家的需要。[7]

11. 参加方在第 10 款所指谈判过程中，应寻求取消在本协定生效之日保留的歧视性措施和做法。[8]

12. 在根据《建立世界贸易组织协定》附件 1A 所列《原产地规则协定》进行的有关协调货物原产地规则的工作计划及关于服务贸易的谈判结束后，各参加方在修正第 5 条第 5 款时应酌情考虑该工作计划和这些谈判的结果。

13. 不迟于本协定生效之日起第 3 年年末，委员会应进一步工作以考虑制定货物和服务目录及标准化通知的优点和缺点。

14. 本协定生效后两年起，委员会应定期评估第 16 条第 4 和 5 款的有效使用。

15. 不迟于本协定生效之日起第 5 年年末，委员会应审查第 20 条第 2 款(b)项的适用性。

修正

16. 各参加方可修正本协定，应特别注意在本协定实施过程中获得的经验。一旦本协定参加方依照委员会制定的程序同意此种修正，应经参加方的[ ]接受后对已接受修正的参加方生效，并在此后对接受修正的每一其他参加方生效。[9]

17. 对于具有改变参加方权利和义务的性质的本协定条款的修正，应经参加方的[ ]接受后对已接受修正的参加方生效，并在此后对接受修正的每一其他参加方生效。委员会可经参加方[ ]多数决定任何根据第 16 款生效的修正是否属如下性质：在指定期限内未接受修正的任何参加方有权退出本协定或经委员会同意仍留在本协定中。[10]

18. 对于具有不改变参加方权利和义务的性质的本协定条款的修正，应经参加方的[ ]接受后对所有参加方生效。[11]

---

[7] 谈判者注释：各参加方应在谈判结束前审议本款的内容。

[8] 谈判者注释：各参加方应在谈判结束前审议本款的内容。

[9] 谈判者注释：各参加方仍在考虑本款内容的必要性。

[10] 谈判者注释：各参加方仍在考虑本款内容的必要性。

[11] 谈判者注释：各参加方仍在考虑本款内容的必要性。

Withdrawal

19. Any Party may withdraw from this Agreement. The withdrawal shall take effect upon the expiration of 60 days from the date the Director-General of the WTO receives written notice of the withdrawal. Any Party may upon such notification request an immediate meeting of the Committee.

20. Where a Party to this Agreement ceases to be a Member of the WTO, it shall cease to be a Party to this Agreement with effect from the same date on which the Party ceases to be a Member of the WTO.

Non-application of this Agreement between Particular Parties

21. This Agreement shall not apply as between any two Parties where either Party, at the time it accepts or accedes to this Agreement, does not consent to such application.

Appendices

22. The Appendices to this Agreement constitute an integral part thereof.

Secretariat

23. This Agreement shall be serviced by the WTO Secretariat.

Deposit

24. This Agreement shall be deposited with the Director-General of the WTO, who shall promptly furnish to each Party a certified true copy of this Agreement, of each rectification or modification thereto pursuant to Article XIX and of each amendment thereto pursuant to paragraph 16, and a notification of each accession thereto pursuant to paragraph 5 and of each withdrawal therefrom pursuant to paragraph 19.

Registration

25. This Agreement shall be registered in accordance with the provisions of Article 102 of the Charter of the United Nations.

Done at [ ] this [ ] day of [ ] in a single copy in the English, French and Spanish languages, each text being authentic, except as otherwise specified with respect to the Appendices hereto.

退出

19. 任何参加方均可退出本协定。该退出应在 WTO 总干事收到书面退出通知之日起 60 天期满后生效。任何参加方在收到此类通知后，可请求立即召开委员会会议。

20. 如本协定一参加方不再为 WTO 成员，则该参加方应自不再为 WTO 成员的同日起不再为本协定的参加方。

本协定在特定参加方之间的不适用

21. 任何参加方，如在自己接受或加入本协定或在另一参加方接受或加入本协定时，不同意在彼此之间适用本协定，则本协定不在该两参加方之间适用。

附录

22. 本协定的附录为本协定的组成部分。

秘书处

23. 本协定由 WTO 秘书处提供服务。

交存

24. 本协定应交存 WTO 总干事。总干事应迅速向每一参加方提供一份本协定经核正的副本、根据第 19 条进行的每一项更正或修改的副本、根据第 16 款进行的每一项修正的副本，以及根据第 5 款所做每一加入和根据第 19 款所做每一退出的通知。

登记

25. 本协定应依照《联合国宪章》第 102 条的规定予以登记。

[ ]年[ ]月[ ]日订于[ ]，正本一份用英文、法文和西班牙文写成，三种文本具有同等效力，除非本协定附录另有规定。

[(DRAFT DECISION)]

Arrangement for the period of co-existence of the 1994 Agreement on Government Procurement and the [2007] Agreement on Government Procurement[12]

The Committee on Government Procurement,

Noting that not all Parties to the Agreement on Government Procurement dated 15 April 1994 (hereinafter referred to as the "1994 Agreement") may become a Party to the Agreement on Government Procurement done on [... 2007] (hereinafter referred to as the "2007 Agreement") as of its date of entry into force,

Considering that, during the period of co-existence of the 1994 Agreement and the 2007 Agreement, a Party to the 1994 Agreement which has become a Party to the 2007 Agreement should have the right to act in accordance with the provisions of the 2007 Agreement notwithstanding any inconsistency with the provisions of the 1994 Agreement, vis-à-vis Parties to the 1994 Agreement that are not Parties to the 2007 Agreement,

Considering moreover that, during that period of co-existence, a Party to the 1994 Agreement which has become a Party to the 2007 Agreement should not be under a legal obligation to extend the benefits accorded solely under the 2007 Agreement to the Parties of the 1994 Agreement which have not yet become Parties to the 2007 Agreement.
Decides as follows:

1. A Party to the 1994 Agreement that is a Party to the 2007 Agreement may maintain or adopt any measure consistent with the provisions of the 2007 Agreement, notwithstanding the provisions of the 1994 Agreement, vis-à-vis a Party to the 1994 Agreement that is not a Party to the 2007 Agreement until the entry into force for that Party to the 2007 Agreement.

2. A Party to the 1994 Agreement that is a Party to the 2007 Agreement is not under any obligation to accord to goods, services and suppliers of any other Party to the 1994 Agreement that has not yet become a Party to the 2007 Agreement the benefits accorded solely as a result of the commitments or other obligations assumed under the 2007 Agreement.

3. The provisions of Articles XX and XXII of the 1994 Agreement shall not apply in respect of measures referred to in paragraph 1.

4. This Decision shall enter into force on the date of entry into force of the 2007 Agreement.

[12] Negotiators' Note: The Parties are still considering the content of this Decision. Some Parties question the need for this Decision.

[(决定草案)]

关于《1994 年政府采购协定》与
《[2007 年]政府采购协定》共存期间安排的决定[12]

政府采购委员会，

*注意到*并非所有 1994 年 4 月 15 日《政府采购协定》(下称“1994 年协定”)的参加方可在[...2007 年]签署的《政府采购协定》(下称“2007 年协定”)生效之日以前成为该协定参加方，

考虑到，在 1994 年协定与 2007 年协定共存期间，一已成为 2007 年协定参加方的 1994 年协定参加方应有权依照 2007 年协定的规定行事，尽管对于不属 2007 年协定参加方的 1994 年协定参加方，存在与 1994 年协定存在不一致之外，

进一步考虑到，在共存期间，一已成为 2007 年协定参加方的 1994 年协定参加方无义务将仅在 2007 年协定项下的义务给予未成为 2007 年协定参加方的 1994 年协定参加方，

*决定*如下：

1. 属 2007 年协定参加方的 1994 年协定参加方可维持或采取与 2007 年协定条款相一致的任何措施，尽管对于不属 2007 年协定参加方的 1994 年协定参加方，存在 1994 年协定的规定，直至 2007 年协定对该参加方生效。

2. 属 2007 年协定参加方的 1994 年协定参加方无义务给予任何未成为 2007 年协定参加方的 1994 年协定参加方的货物、服务和供应商仅由于在 2007 协定项下做出承诺或承担的其他义务而产生的利益。

3. 1994 年协定第 20 条和第 22 条不得适用于第 1 款所指措施。

4. 本决定应在 2007 年协定生效之日生效。

---

[12] 谈判者注释：各参加方仍在考虑本决定内容的必要性。一些参加方质疑本决定的需要。

PROPOSED DECISION OF THE COMMITTEE ON GOVERNMENT PROCUREMENT

Decision of [day/month/year]

The Committee on Government Procurement,

Noting that the Parties to the GPA have completed negotiations on [the non-market-access-related provisions of] a new Government Procurement Agreement (hereinafter referred to as the "2007 Agreement");

Desiring to ensure the effective operation of Article XIX:1(a) of the 2007 Agreement where a Party proposes the withdrawal of an entity from Appendix I in exercise of its rights, and to enhance the predictability of the Agreement;

Noting that Article XIX:8 of the 2007 Agreement requires that the Committee develop arbitration procedures to facilitate resolution of objections, indicative criteria that demonstrate the effective elimination of government control or influence over an entity's covered procurement, and criteria that indicate how to determine the level of compensatory adjustment to be offered for modifications of coverage under Article XIX of the 2007 Agreement;

Recognizing the extensive work already undertaken by the Committee on the development of arbitration procedures to facilitate resolution of objections and indicative criteria, but also that further work is needed,

Decides as follows:

The Committee shall:

(1) complete the development of arbitration procedures and indicative criteria, with the aim of adopting them by the entry into force of the 2007 Agreement; and

(2) develop criteria that indicate how to determine the level of compensatory adjustment to be offered for modifications of coverage under Article XIX of the 2007 Agreement, with the aim of adopting the criteria within 18 months of entry into force of the 2007 Agreement.

The arbitration procedures shall not become effective until the adoption of the indicative criteria.

委员会拟议的关于政府采购的决定

[年/月/日]决定

政府采购委员会，

*注意到*GPA 参加方已结束关于新的《政府采购协定》（下称“2007 年协定”）中[非市场准入性质条款]的谈判；

*希望*保证在一参加方提出在行使其权利时撤销附录 1 中一条目的情况下，2007 年协定第 19 条第 1 款(a)项得到有效运用，并加强本协定的可预见性；

*注意到*2007 年协定第 19 条第 8 款要求委员会起草便利异议解决的仲裁程序、表明政府对一实体所涉采购的控制或影响有效消除的指示性标准及表明如何确定对根据第 19 条所作修改作出的补偿性调整的水平的标准；

*认识到*委员会在起草便利异议解决的仲裁程序和指示性标准方面已经进行的工作，但仍然需要进行进一步的工作；

*决定*如下：

委员会应：

(1) 完成仲裁程序和指示性标准的起草，以期在 2007 年协定生效之时予以采用；并

(2) 起草表明如何确定对根据第 19 条所作修改作出的补偿性调整的水平的标准，以期在 2007 年协定生效 18 个内采用该标准。

仲裁程序在指示性标准采用前不得生效。